Praise for Stuart A. Reid's

THE LUMUMBA PLOT

A *New Yorker*, *Economist*, and *Financial Times*
Best Book of the Year

"[*The Lumumba Plot*] is many things at once: a biography, a history of Congo's chaotic independence, a dissection of the UN's first big peacekeeping mission and a thriller about plots to kill Lumumba. There are villains of every stripe, from rogue Belgian pilots to shamelessly scheming UN officials and racist ambassadors. This is a tragic tale but also a rollicking read.... Lumumba's life might seem of a distant, dramatic era. Yet this story feels timely."
—*The Economist*

"Masterfully stitching together testimonies like these as well as interviews, investigations, diplomatic cables and a thorough assessment of a range of declassified files, the book often reads like a John le Carré novel, partly thanks to Reid's gripping writing style.... Groundbreaking."
—*Financial Times*

"This is one of the best books I have read in years. Stuart Reid writes beautifully, and the story he tells is gripping, full of colorful characters and strange plot twists. There is a powerful lesson here as well. When America gets paranoid about foreign enemies, it can make choices that are politically foolish and morally indefensible."
—Fareed Zakaria, host of *Fareed Zakaria GPS* on CNN,
Washington Post columnist, and *New York Times* bestselling author

Stuart A. Reid

THE LUMUMBA PLOT

Stuart A. Reid is an executive editor of *Foreign Affairs*. He has written for *The Atlantic*, *The New York Times*, *The Washington Post*, *Bloomberg Businessweek*, *Politico Magazine*, *Slate*, and other publications. He lives in New Jersey with his wife and children.

stuartareid.com

THE LUMUMBA PLOT

THE LUMUMBA PLOT

THE SECRET HISTORY OF THE CIA AND A COLD WAR ASSASSINATION

Stuart A. Reid

VINTAGE BOOKS
A Division of Penguin Random House LLC
New York

Published in the United States by Vintage Books, a division of Penguin Random House LLC, New York, and distributed in Canada by Penguin Random House Canada Limited, Toronto. Originally published in hardcover in the United States by Alfred A. Knopf, a division of Penguin Random House LLC, New York, in 2023.

Vintage and colophon are registered trademarks of Penguin Random House LLC.

The Library of Congress has cataloged the Knopf edition as follows:
Names: Reid, Stuart A., author.
Title: The Lumumba plot : the secret history of the CIA
and a Cold War assassination / Stuart A. Reid.
Description: First edition. | New York : Alfred A. Knopf, 2023. |
Includes bibliographical references and index.
Identifiers: LCCN 2023003992 (print) | LCCN 2023003993 (ebook)
Subjects: LCSH: Lumumba, Patrice, 1925–1961—Assassination. | United States.
Central Intelligence Agency. | Congo (Democratic Republic)—History—Civil
War, 1960–1965. | Congo (Democratic Republic)—Politics and government—
1908–1960. | Congo (Democratic Republic)—Politics and government—
1960–1997. | United States—Foreign relations—Congo (Democratic Republic) |
Congo (Democratic Republic)—Foreign relations—United States.
Classification: LCC DT658.22.L85 R45 2023 (print) |
LCC DT658.22.L85 (ebook) | DDC 967.51031—dc23
LC record available at https://lccn.loc.gov/2023003992
LC ebook record available at https://lccn.loc.gov/2023003993

Vintage Books Trade Paperback ISBN: 978-1-9848-9914-9
eBook ISBN: 978-1-5247-4882-1

Map by David Lindroth
Author photograph © Mark Jaworski
Book design by Michael Collica

vintagebooks.com

Printed in the United States of America
10 9 8 7 6 5 4 3 2 1

To my parents

I have never doubted for a single instant that the sacred cause to which my comrades and I have dedicated our entire lives would triumph in the end. But what we wanted for our country—its right to an honorable life, to perfect dignity, to independence with no restrictions—was never wanted by Belgian colonialism and its Western allies.

—Patrice Lumumba, Congolese prime minister

I am relatively certain that he represented something that the United States government didn't like, but I can't remember anymore what it was. Was he a rightist or leftist?... What was wrong with Lumumba? Why didn't we like him?

—Richard Helms, CIA official

Contents

PART III: TARGET

PART IV: CAPTIVE

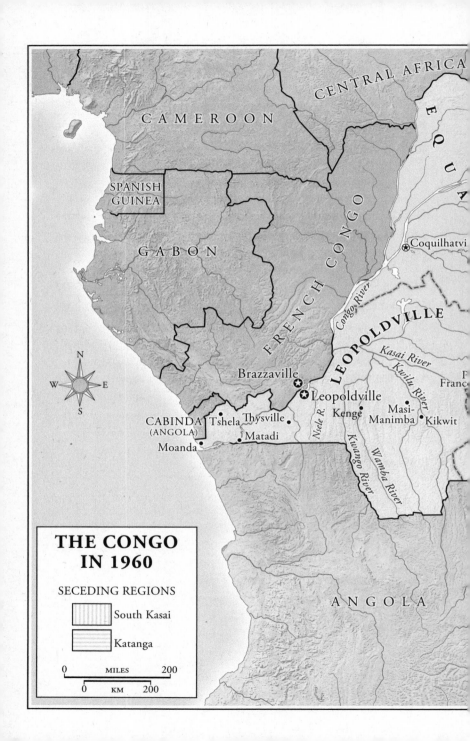

Main Characters

Positions as of the summer of 1960 unless otherwise noted

CONGOLESE

Cyrille Adoula, prime minister (August 1961–June 1964)

Justin Bomboko, foreign minister

Antoine Gizenga, deputy prime minister

Joseph Iléo, president of the senate

Albert Kalonji, president of independent South Kasai

Cléophas Kamitatu, president of Leopoldville province

Thomas Kanza, ambassador to the UN

Joseph Kasavubu, president

Anicet Kashamura, minister of information

Patrice Lumumba, prime minister

Joseph Mobutu, chief of staff of the Congolese National Army

Maurice Mpolo, minister of youth and sports

Pierre Mulele, minister of education

Godefroid Munongo, Katangan minister of the interior

Victor Nendaka, head of the security services (September 1960–October 1965)

Joseph Okito, vice president of the senate

Moise Tshombe, president of independent Katanga

AMERICANS

Richard Bissell, CIA deputy director for plans

William Burden, ambassador to Belgium

Larry Devlin, CIA station chief, Leopoldville

Douglas Dillon, undersecretary of state

Allen Dulles, director of the CIA

Dwight Eisenhower, president

Sidney Gottlieb, assistant for scientific matters to the CIA deputy director for plans

Gordon Gray, national security adviser

Christian Herter, secretary of state

John F. Kennedy, Democratic nominee for president

Henry Cabot Lodge Jr., ambassador to the UN

Richard Nixon, vice president

Justin O'Donnell, CIA senior case officer

Clare Timberlake, ambassador to the Congo

Bronson Tweedy, chief of the CIA's Africa division

UN OFFICIALS

Ralph Bunche, special representative in the Congo (June 30, 1960–August 30, 1960)

Andrew Cordier, special representative in the Congo (August 30, 1960–September 8, 1960)

Rajeshwar Dayal, special representative in the Congo (September 8, 1960–May 27, 1961)

Dag Hammarskjöld, secretary-general

BELGIANS

Baudouin, king of the Belgians

Gaston Eyskens, prime minister of Belgium

Émile Janssens, commander of the Force Publique

Harold d'Aspremont Lynden, head of the Belgian mission to Katanga

Pierre Wigny, foreign minister of Belgium

OTHERS

Andrée Blouin, chief of protocol for Lumumba's government

André Mankel, Luxembourgish CIA agent codenamed QJWIN

Serge Michel, press attaché to Lumumba's government

David Tzitzichvili, French CIA agent codenamed WIROGUE

THE LUMUMBA PLOT

Prologue

The Loose Tooth

NOTHING MUCH HAPPENS in Mélin, a picturesque village of little over a thousand people about an hour's drive from Brussels. If the sleepy town has a claim to fame, it is that many of its buildings—farmhouses, the church and the vicarage, the restaurant—are built from a chalky sandstone unique to the region. The rock, which has been mined from local quarries since the sixteenth century, lends a cream hue to Gothic cathedrals across Belgium. There is no crime to speak of in Mélin. Cows flap their tails between hedgerows. Residents tend to their gardens and ride their bikes to the Saturday farmers' market.

On a cold, drizzly Thursday afternoon in January 2016, two investigators from the federal police force in Brussels arrived in Mélin and pulled up to a redbrick house on the edge of town, across the street from a furrowed field. The "upscale villa in a rural village," as the police later described it in court proceedings, was surrounded by metal fencing. The officers rang the buzzer and were let in through a pointed gate.

A petite, fine-featured woman with a ruby-red pixie cut and expressive eyebrows answered the door. Her name was Godelieve Soete, and though born in Belgium, she had spent much of her life in Africa. Her father had been a colonial police officer in the Belgian Congo, and decades later, after the colony's independence, she herself had worked for Belgium's embassy in the country. Now, at age sixty-six, Soete lived a quiet life in Mélin, caring for her horses and her dogs, but she surrounded herself with reminders of her former home. Masks and spears adorned the walls. Cross-shaped ingots from the Congolese copper belt sat on the mantelpiece.

The police officers introduced themselves, flashed their badges, and presented a search warrant. Soete grumbled. She had been expecting this visit and was tired of the matter. The events under investigation had taken place when she was just eleven, and they were her father's doing, not hers. She knew that someone might show up at her door to punish her for his sins—hence the fencing and the electric gate.

Soete nonetheless gave the police what they were looking for. From a small blue wooden box, she produced a decaying molar capped with a gold crown. In another were a handful of spent bullets. The officers sealed the objects in a plastic bag and left for Brussels.

The tooth and the bullets were evidence in a cold case, an investigation into the murder of a man who had been shot to death in the Congo fifty-five years earlier, almost to the day.

Patrice Lumumba did not last long in the limelight. A former postal clerk and beer pitchman in the Belgian Congo, he took the helm as prime minister when, on June 30, 1960, the Congo celebrated its newfound freedom from Belgium after seventy-five years of colonial rule. Chaos engulfed the new country within days, forcing Lumumba to set aside his governing agenda and focus on survival. He quelled a mutiny in the army, invited in more than ten thousand United Nations peacekeepers, and toured nine world capitals to lobby for help that would save his fledgling nation. But after just two and a half months in office, he was ousted in a military coup. Four months later, he was assassinated. "He passed by like a meteor," his daughter Juliana said.

For decades, Lumumba's murder remained a mystery. Debates raged over who bore the blame. Suspicion fell naturally on the Belgians, who had run their colony with unreserved cruelty before independence and bristled at Lumumba's conception of national autonomy afterward. Others pointed to UN officials, who were drawn into a peacekeeping operation of unprecedented scale and cost in the Congo and seemed to have a hand in his downfall and death. Over the years, evidence came out suggesting that Lumumba's suspected susceptibility to Communist manipulation had made him a target of the Central Intelligence Agency's covert Cold War machinations in newly decolonized countries—and eventually it was revealed that the CIA, acting on the orders of the White House, had dispatched vials of poison to the Congo in an effort to assassinate Lumumba. But what ultimately became of the agency's efforts? What about the man who deposed Lumumba and installed himself as leader, a young army colonel named Joseph Mobutu? And how exactly did Lumumba end up before a firing squad on the night of January 17, 1961, in a remote clearing in the Congolese countryside?

This book tries to at last answer these questions. Drawing on forgotten testimonies, interviews with participants, diaries, private letters, scholarly histories, official investigations, government archives, unearthed diplomatic cables, and recently declassified CIA files, it finds that the conventional narrative about the rise and fall of Lumumba leaves out much of the story. The book pays particular attention to the role played by the United States, laying bare the questionable motivations, unscrupulous methods, and grave damage of the country's policies. It shows how American officials privately displayed racist contempt for the Congolese. And it reveals that their involvement in the Congo was darker and more extensive than commonly thought and started earlier than has previously been known. The CIA and its station chief in the Congo, Larry Devlin, had a hand in nearly every major development leading up to Lumumba's murder, from his fall from power to his forceful transfer into rebel-held territory on the day of his death.

Uncovering the truth about Lumumba's downfall and murder—and assigning blame—matter not just in the name of Lumumba's memory. For the Congo, the episode marked a turning point, the definitive end of a short-lived democratic experiment and the beginning of decades of poverty, dictatorship, and war. But the crisis reverberated far beyond the Congo. It claimed the life of the UN secretary-general Dag Hammarskjöld, killed under mysterious circumstances during a peacemaking trip to the Congo months after Lumumba's murder, and it permanently hobbled the organization Hammarskjöld had led. The mission in the Congo came to be viewed as a dangerous misadventure, and the UN never fully recovered from the resulting damage to its global influence and reputation. No future secretary-general would ever come close to equaling Hammarskjöld's diplomatic heft.

The crisis in the Congo invigorated leaders in the United States, however. Extensive U.S. meddling—carried out by CIA operatives and State Department officials—might not have looked so constructive in the streets of the Congo, but in the halls of power in Washington, D.C., it was seen as a smashing success. As the Cold War intensified, America appeared to have stopped a Communist takeover in its tracks and, in Joseph Mobutu (who later called himself Mobutu Sese Seko), installed a friendly dictator keen on aligning with the Western bloc. While officials fretted about a supposed "missile gap" with the Soviets and the Communists' inroads in Cuba, the Congo was a clear win. There was now a model to copy.

The American intervention in the Congo was an early battle in a decades-long series of covert actions that would showcase the conflict between interests and values in American statecraft. The relatively genteel strategies crafted by the so-called wise men of U.S. foreign policy in the 1940s and 1950s gave way to the darker pursuits of the 1960s, 1970s, and 1980s. Before America launched the disastrous Bay of Pigs invasion in Cuba, before it waded deeply into Vietnam, before it backed the Islamist mujahideen fighters in Afghanistan, before it illegally funded right-wing Nicaraguan militants in the Iran-contra affair, there was the Congo. It was in the Congo that the United States and the Soviet Union first faced off in a theater far from either homeland, transforming the Cold War, until then first and foremost a European affair, into a truly global struggle. And it was in the Congo that the CIA, for the first and only time, could plausibly claim credit—or take the blame—for the assassination of a national leader. The United States still hasn't kicked its habit of intense meddling in the politics of the developing world. That was a habit it picked up in earnest in the Congo.

Stories of armies, governments, agencies, and institutions have a way of obscuring the humans behind them. So it is with the postindependence turmoil in the Congo and Patrice Lumumba. With his murder, the man was lost and the myth replaced him. The French philosopher Jean-Paul Sartre wrote a fulsome introduction to a book collecting his speeches. The Soviet Union named a university after him. Congolese still wear wraps and T-shirts bearing his face. Depending on whom you ask, Lumumba was an agent of chaos who deserved his fate, a hapless fool outmaneuvered by more powerful forces, or a flawless hero cut down by imperial cruelty. Few can acknowledge that he was none of these things yet many other things.

This book seeks to exhume Lumumba, to scrape away the mounds of lies, mythology, and conspiracy that have accumulated around him over the decades. It tries, as much as possible, to present the man in his own words, in the context of his own times, and through the prism of his own experiences. Contrary to a common Western belief at the time, Lumumba was not pro-Communist in any sense of the term, nor was he, as a slightly more sophisticated critique had it, particularly vulnerable to Soviet influence. In fact, all the available evidence suggests he harbored a greater affinity for the United States than he did for the Soviet Union. Nor, however, was Lumumba a naive victim of Western machinations, as left-wing historians sometimes suggest. Yes, he was subject to powerful forces he could not control—and some he could not even see—but he had more agency than many imagine. He made brilliant choices and confounding choices. He was his country's greatest politician and perhaps its worst statesman.

Above all, Lumumba was the author of his own story. It is the story of a striver whose intellect and perseverance lifted him from humble circumstances into his country's highest political office. It is the story of a man who wooed the most powerful nation on earth but ended up accidentally turning it against him. It is the story of a fearful United States, its view clouded by racism and reductive Cold War thinking, lashing out against threats more imagined than real. It is, at base, a story of how a moment of unprecedented hope gave way to unrelenting tragedy.

And it is a story that begins a century ago, in a small hut in the scrubby grasslands of central Africa.

PART I

SUBJECT

Chapter 1

The Boy from Onalua

IT WAS SAID that when Julienne Amatu was pregnant with her second child, the world turned strange, as if it knew that this one would be different. A six-headed palm tree sprouted, an earthquake shook the ground, and a shooting star tore across the night sky. Indeed, when the baby boy was born, he seemed unusual. Placed on the dirt floor of the family's thatched-roof hut, he would crawl away from his mother, not toward her. His darting eyes and fidgeting limbs soon betrayed an inner agitation, and when he began to speak, the words never ceased to flow.

Later, few could say with certainty when the boy was born. His father, François Tolenga, a near-illiterate farmer fond of palm wine, had written down a date on a scrap of paper: July 2, 1925. But that might have simply marked the moment when a white man passed through with forms to fill out. Nor did everyone agree on when exactly the boy had changed his name or why, or even what it had been to begin with. But sometime early in his youth, he gave himself the name Patrice, and eventually he added Lumumba.

He grew up in Onalua, a small settlement surrounded by rolling savanna, right in the center of the Belgian Congo. Patrice was a born leader, and a mischievous one at that. Some days, he persuaded other boys to join him on the branches of a bushy tree that jutted out over a path, to quietly pluck pineapples and ears of corn from the baskets of farmers passing underneath.

Lumumba attended the American Methodist mission school in the nearby village of Wembo Nyama. On March 12, 1937, Dr. Alexander Reid, the Illinois pastor who ran the school, baptized Lumumba, sprinkling water on the boy's head in front of a crowd of youths. The mission was just four miles from Onalua, but culturally it was a continent away. Teachers at the school sought to replace Patrice's village mores with Christian ones. He learned to write and speak in French, the colonizer's language, to recite the Methodist catechism, and to eat with cutlery instead of his fingers. Lumumba was perhaps speaking of himself when, years later, he lamented, "The black pupil finds himself caught between two conflicting forces: the standards of the school and those of the family."

At recess, he would write a new French word on the ground and ask one of his teachers how to say it, but it was a trick: he knew the pronunciation better than some of the adults and would mock them behind their backs afterward. To their faces, he would question the idea that Mary was a virgin, or that God was white. Whether to recognize his gift or hurry him through their charge, the teachers moved him up a grade. When he was a teenager, they kicked him out altogether, citing his taste for "drinking alcohol, seducing others' women, insulting adults, dancing." A similar fate befell him at the Catholic mission school in nearby Tshumbe Sainte-Marie, where he again quibbled with his teachers, causing one to throw a set of keys at him in anger, and soon dropped out.

Yet Patrice knew when to accommodate power, too, once managing to win over a colonial official dissatisfied with the quality of the all-important cotton harvest. Farmers had tried in vain to appease the man with hens and eggs, but Lumumba marched straight to the administrator's house. His three teenage companions backed down at the doorstep, so he went in alone. After a delay so long that his friends figured he must have been arrested, he reemerged with good news: he had been tasked with instructing the farmers on how to better dry their cotton.

That was his style, equal parts charm and pluck. He had a tendency to tell the audience before him whatever it wanted to hear, even if that risked alienating others. He was chameleonic. He improvised rather than planned. Sometimes, Lumumba's approach would pay off, allowing him to rise high and fast. Other times, he flew too close to the sun.

The residents of Onalua had not always bowed to King Cotton. Before cotton, the dominant trade had been rubber, and before rubber it had been elephant tusks and human beings. Patrice's grandfather and the other village elders talked often of how much life had changed—and how quickly. As recently as the 1880s, just half a century earlier, Onalua had been invaded by warriors allied with so-called Arab traders—more accurately, Swahili-speaking Africans, many Muslim, some of Arab descent. The invaders made their money exporting enslaved people and ivory from the east coast of Africa, where a twenty-year-old with good teeth and musculature could fetch 150 gold francs. Men and women were captured, chained, and carted off in caravans, traveling hundreds of miles eastward before being ferried to the island of Zanzibar in the Indian Ocean. From there, ships carried them to Asia or the Middle East. The ivory ended up as false teeth, piano keys, billiard balls, and chess pieces. Soon, though, the Afro-Arab traders and their lieutenants were vanquished by another distant outsider claiming sovereignty over Onalua, and much more beyond: King Leopold II of Belgium.

Created in 1830 as a buffer state among European great powers, Belgium was a compromise of a country, an uneasy and perennially fraught union of Flemish (a dialect of Dutch) speakers in the north and a francophone south. "Small country, small people," Leopold complained. The king went looking for a stage large enough for his ambitions and soon set his sights on Africa.

When Leopold ascended the throne, in 1865, European powers had yet to claim most of the continent. He read with interest the *Daily Telegraph* dispatches of Henry Morton Stanley, a Welsh American explorer and journalist. Stanley—who had become famous for finding the lost Scottish missionary David Livingstone and supposedly greeting him with "Dr. Livingstone, I presume?"—was detailing a grueling journey westward across Africa via the Congo River. In 1878, Leopold hired Stanley to retrace the same route—only this time, going in the other direction, and as a royal emissary rather than as a writer. Steaming upriver, Stanley and his companions collected more than 450 treaties from illiterate chiefs, who, in exchange for cloth, gin, and trinkets, marked an *X* on paper that ceded eternal rights to their land.

Leopold's wish, he confided to a minister, was "to secure for ourselves a slice of this magnificent African cake." The slice he had in mind was the million-plus square miles of land drained by the Congo River. The river's source lay in the southeast of the basin, and the water flowed north, then west, then southwest, tracing a counterclockwise arc in the center of the African continent that crossed the equator twice. The area was spidered with tributaries, which provided a built-in transportation network. Its geography varied on a continental scale: snowcapped mountains and deep lakes in the east, wide open savannas in the north and south, thick tropical rain forests in the middle. Contrary to Stanley's description of an "unpeopled country," it was home to millions of people, organized loosely into hundreds of different societies with their own languages and customs.

By the time Stanley returned from his royal mission in these lands, the "scramble for Africa" was in full swing. Gathering in snowy Berlin in late 1884 for the *Kongokonferenz,* European diplomats, seated in front of a large map of Africa, hashed out rules for colonizing the continent and recognized Leopold's sovereignty over the Congo basin. Soon thereafter, the king issued a royal decree naming the new country the Congo Free State. Legally speaking, it was not a Belgian colony but an independent entity belonging to him personally.

Leopold cloaked his landgrab in the familiar colonial language of altruism, protection, and civilizational tutelage. Decades later, Lumumba himself would praise him, saying that Leopold and Stanley "gave us peace, restored our human dignity, improved our physical well-being, developed our intelligence, elevated our souls." Yet the king's aims were, at base, extractive. His agents, incentivized by commission, gathered up as much ivory as they could, and tusks soon began filling the customhouses of Antwerp. And while he portrayed himself as an antislavery crusader, he created a colonial army—the Force Publique—that relied on the conscription of young African men. For every twenty-five huts, a village owed one soldier. Ruling over these Black conscripts were white officers, mostly Belgians. Occasionally they shot villagers for sport.

One person who saw Leopold's project for what it was was a young Polish mariner named Konrad Korzeniowski, who in 1890 took a job piloting a steamboat on the Congo River. Later, under the pen name Joseph Conrad, he would fictionalize his experience—"a little (and only very little)"—in *Heart of Darkness*. "To tear treasure out of the bowels of the land was their desire," the novel's disillusioned protagonist says, "with no more moral purpose at the back of it than there is in burglars breaking into a safe."

Leopold sought to grow his state, but when he sent the Force Publique on an expedition to annex the upper reaches of the Nile River in Sudan, the rank and file mutinied, kicking off a yearslong rebellion. It was led by the Tetela people, or "Batetela" in the plural, the group Lumumba was born into. As a boy, he doubtless heard stories of his forefathers and their rebellion—in its time, the most threatening revolt that the Belgian colonizers had ever faced.

As an enterprise in imperialist extraction, the Congo Free State wasn't terribly profitable at first. But that changed in the 1890s, after the invention of the pneumatic tire swelled demand for the natural rubber oozing through vines in the Congo's vast forests. As they had done with ivory, colonial officials set high quotas for how many kilograms of rubber each village had to pay as tax, and by the turn of the century their reach extended far enough inland for Onalua to feel the squeeze. To tap enough rubber vines, the men of the village traveled more than one hundred miles and survived weeks in the forest on little food. They knew what would happen if they failed to meet their quota: the Force Publique would arrive, set huts aflame, shoot people at random, and take women as hostages—whose return could be bought only with the requisite amount of rubber. As proof to their superiors that their bullets were well spent, the troops liked to lop off their victims' right hands and pile them in baskets.

Leopold's colonial vanity project would earn a place in the pantheon of human atrocities. Owing partly to outright murder but mostly to social disruption and the mass starvation and disease it caused, the population of the Congo basin is thought to have been cut in half from 1880 to 1920. The exact human toll was incalculable, though estimates of the number of lives claimed would range in the millions. Photos of the atrocities, including infamous shots of severed hands and missing limbs, eventually triggered international outrage, culminating in a campaign to end Leopold's genocidal reign over the colony. In 1908, the king was pressured into selling his state to the Belgian government. He died the next year, having never set foot in the Congo.

Under Belgian government rule, colonialism was gentler, but many of the abuses—conscription, forced labor, whipping—continued, often meted out by the same officials as before (though their paychecks now bore a different signature). For Lumumba's family and other residents of Onalua, the handover in fact heralded a period of greater outside interference. Father Achille de Munster from Flanders set up the Catholic mission in nearby Tshumbe Sainte-Marie that married Lumumba's parents. Bishop Walter Lambuth from Tennessee started the Methodist mission in Wembo Nyama that baptized Lumumba. The greater attention from the outside world wasn't just about saving African souls; colonial officials also issued a decree mandating the collection of cotton, which over the course of Lumumba's early years transformed village life from one of subsistence farming to forced harvesting.

As a teenager in the early 1940s, Lumumba experienced a radical change of his own. When, for reasons that remain obscure, he got kicked out of yet another nearby mission school, this one for aspiring nursing assistants, he hatched a plan B. Lumumba was intelligent, ambitious, charming, and resourceful. Sometime in 1942 or 1943, he returned to Onalua for just a few hours, enough time to scarf down porridge, stuff some clothes into a bindle, and say goodbye to his family. Like hundreds of thousands of other young men across the colony, he would look for work in the city.

Lumumba left Onalua with just 3 francs in his pocket. Walking the long dirt road, he cut a distinctive figure: lithe and more than six feet tall, with intense, wide-set eyes and trousers that were held up by a rope. He traveled mostly by foot, hitching rides on dugout canoes or trucks when he could. Lumumba had none of the documents that colonial officials required of Congolese making such a journey. A scheme to forge a travel pass had gone up in flames, literally, after a friend tried to obscure Lumumba's poor handiwork by singeing the paper. He had no identity card, either. Having never graduated from primary school, he carried a falsified diploma. When a police commissioner questioned him about it, Lumumba, charismatic and eloquent, talked his way out of the situation. Perhaps he flashed his smile, a slightly crooked grin that revealed white teeth.

At last, Lumumba reached Kalima, a tin-mining town one province over from Onalua, and found work in a company canteen. (By now, minerals had replaced rubber as the Belgian Congo's top export.) He encountered running water and electricity. For the first time in his life, he could afford shoes and clothes that fit. But Lumumba soon chose to supplement his wages through an illicit, though common, practice: stealing goods from the company and selling them on the black market. Upon being found out, he fled the city in the night. It was time to remake himself yet again.

Chapter 2

Promising Docility

O N A SUMMER day in 1943, around the time Lumumba was setting out from Onalua, a young U.S. Army officer sat in an orange orchard outside Tunis, on the edge of the Mediterranean. He had landed only recently, part of an Allied push to seize territory from Italian and German forces in North Africa. In climate and topography, the area reminded him of home in California, were it not for the ever-present, sandy dust that hung in the air like a thin haze. As for the people, they looked to him like something out of *National Geographic,* "still living as their ancestors did five hundred years ago." The locals elicited little sympathy in him, striking him as idle, untrustworthy, and just plain odd. "They love to argue over prices," he wrote in a letter home. "But if you show them a bar of G.I. soap they will sell you anything from a wife to a bottle of rotten vino."

The only child of two schoolteachers, Larry Devlin had grown up in San Diego, in a middle-class neighborhood of looping streets and Spanish Revival homes. In 1939, he graduated from high school and enrolled at San Diego State College, just minutes from home. Student life was wholesome and carefree—co-ed trips to Mission Beach, hours spent in the cafeteria knocking back sodas and feeding nickels into the jukebox. Larry was a joiner, racking up one of the longer index entries in the yearbook. Track team, student council, men's group, speaking club, service group, debate club, Sigma Lambda fraternity: page after page featured him, hair parted neatly, thick brows accentuating his eager gaze. He was also fiercely patriotic. Back in high school, he had joined the ROTC; at San Diego State, he clashed with fellow students in the pages of the college newspaper. ("I don't know which you advocate, the Hammer and Sickle land or the Swastika country," he wrote. "But, if you love their ways so much, just remember, 'old fellow,' they still sell boat tickets.") The summer after his sophomore year, Devlin and his friends made a student film, *King Congo*, a feature-length parody of jungle movies recorded in Technicolor in the San Diego hills. Its plot, according to its collegiate producers, was "sort of a Stanley and Livingstone, with a new twist." On the last Tuesday of November 1941, students paid thirty cents a ticket to watch the premiere in an auditorium off campus. A rented spotlight fanned the night sky.

Less than two weeks later, the Japanese attacked Pearl Harbor, and the good life came to an end. Barred from the air force due to poor eyesight, Devlin enlisted in the army in June 1942 and was commissioned as an officer. The next year, he landed in Oran, a port in French Algeria. "I have really been sweating out my French over here, but I picked up enough so that I can get along," he wrote to a former professor. "But if they were to cut off my hands," he joked, "I would be lost."

In short order, his military service brought him to Tunis, then Italy, and then Corsica. The island had recently been liberated by the Free French Forces of General Charles de Gaulle, which continued to fight the Axis powers after the fall of France. While everyone was camped out waiting to land in France, Devlin invited a woman in the Free French Forces on a date. The woman stood him up, so he asked out her tentmate instead, a shy, petite ambulance driver named Colette Porteret who came from an affluent Parisian family. After the liberation of France, in 1945, the couple married in the seaside town of Arcachon.

Devlin returned from war with his hairline a little higher on his forehead and finished up his studies at San Diego State. Colette, who accompanied him back to California, bridled at the early din-nertimes and weak coffee. She worked on improving her husband's French, but he never managed to master the accent, instead forcing out meaning through hard, American consonants. Thanks to the GI Bill, Devlin attended graduate school at Harvard, where he studied international relations. When he and Colette arrived, in the fall of

1947, the campus was stretched past capacity to educate returned troops like himself. To accommodate the overflow, beds had been moved onto a basketball court.

Harvard opened up doors for Devlin. One Sunday afternoon in the winter of 1948–49, he and three other students met with a professor, William Yandell Elliott, who had mentioned a job opportunity. A political theorist known for his staunch anti-Communism, Elliott maintained close ties to the U.S. foreign policy establishment, traveling to Washington, D.C., nearly every week. He was also a consultant to the Central Intelligence Agency. The CIA was little more than a year old, a successor to the Office of Strategic Services, the wartime espionage service. It was charged with procuring secrets and conducting subversive activities abroad, especially in light of the Soviet Union's advances in the rapidly escalating Cold War. The agency needed men with good grades, foreign language skills, and knowledge of the European continent. Academia served as an important conduit for recruiting them. The CIA even came up with a code for recruitment by professor: "the P source."

At his office across from Harvard Yard, Elliott introduced the four students to McGeorge Bundy, a Boston Brahmin and rising foreign policy intellectual, who gave them a pep talk about the CIA. As Bundy pitched it, the agency was the ideal tool for foiling Moscow's geopolitical ambitions without resorting to war. It didn't take long for Devlin to make up his mind: he would join the CIA.

After escaping scandal in Kalima, Patrice Lumumba started over again in Stanleyville, some four hundred miles away. Stanleyville was a step up for Lumumba. It was a provincial capital and the third-largest city in the Belgian Congo. Its location at the farthest navigable point up the Congo River made it a fast-growing trade hub whose population would quadruple over the course of the 1940s. When Lumumba stepped off the train, he must have looked around in wonder at the city's redbrick buildings, broad boulevards, tended gardens, swimming pools, and gurgling fountains. To remind Stanleyville's small community of white settlers of home, some streets bore the names of European composers: Avenue Chopin, Avenue Beethoven, Avenue Mozart.

Lumumba lodged with a man from near Onalua who had come to Stanleyville ten years earlier. Like Lumumba, the man had been in and out of several schools, but he studied to be a medical assistant and took a prestigious job at a hospital laboratory. He spoke French and a bit of English, too. Such were the rewards, Lumumba saw, for those who applied themselves and obediently climbed the colonial ladder.

So he grasped a rung, taking up work as an entry-level clerk at a government administrative office. To improve his French, he enrolled in a correspondence course and took night classes with the Marist Brothers, a Catholic order active in the Belgian Congo. He lost himself in the Larousse dictionary. The boy from Onalua quickly shed his provincial trappings, morphing into the sort of "detribalized" African that European sociologists wrote about with approval. He dressed in pressed trousers and clean white shirts. He wore glasses, even though the Belgians took them as a sign of childish pretension. In his two and a half years as a clerk, his disciplinary file registered not a single infraction. The unruly vagabond had become a model colonial subject.

Lumumba saw a path to an even higher status, perhaps a chance to join the Belgian Congo's growing Black middle class. In the summer of 1947, he boarded a wood-burning steamer downstream to attend a nine-month training program at the government's new postal school in Leopoldville, the colony's faraway capital. Like Stanleyville, Leopoldville was riding a postwar boom. It was a colorful, vibrant city—especially at night, when revelers dressed up and danced to the Congolese rumba, a lively music with roots in Cuba. Lumumba's days were less thrilling, consisting of lessons on calculating postage, filling out money orders, sending telegrams, and performing basic accounting. But the training course was time well spent. He graduated near the top of his class. Most important, he gained a new fluency in French.

Leopoldville also provided a schooling in race relations. Segregation in the Belgian Congo was not enshrined in law, but urban planning and social norms still made it an immutable fact of public life. Cities were neatly divided between "European" and "native" quarters, demarcated by greenbelts. Restaurants, bars, and cafés were theoretically open to everyone, but if a Congolese patron dared enter a white establishment, he could expect to face disparaging remarks intended to shame him into leaving. There were separate hospitals for Black and white patients. In stadiums, white people took the best seats; at shops and offices, they cut in front of Black people waiting in line. Walking through town one day, Lumumba accidently bumped into a white woman. "Monkey!" she yelled.

Things were very different in Brazzaville, the dusty capital of the French Congo, another, much smaller colony that lay on the other side of the Congo River and had been ruled by France since 1882. One Sunday, he took a ferry there and wandered around, peering in shopwindows and eavesdropping on conversations. It was a sleepier, far less impressive capital, but he found French colonial officials kinder than their Belgian counterparts. White and Black residents ate at the same restaurants and stood in the same lines. A mural at a local cathedral depicted a Black Jesus. As the day wore on, Lumumba grew thirsty and prowled around a café, hoping that a waiter might discreetly pass him some water through a hedge. But he caught the eye of the proprietor, a white woman, who insisted he sit at a table among the white customers and served him a glass of mineral water. Mystified and terrified, Lumumba paid his bill and fled without swallowing a drop.

Upon graduation from postal school, Lumumba was made a third-class clerk in the Stanleyville post office. He earned 1,500 francs a month—just enough to pay for his food—plus a housing allowance and a bicycle. He must have felt justly proud as he entered the cavernous brick building each morning, treading its generous stairs to partake in the business of connecting Stanleyville to the metropole and beyond. Pneumatic tubes whooshed messages between floors. From the breezy veranda of the post office, he could glimpse the Hôtel des Chutes, with its porthole windows and curvy facade, and behind it the mighty Congo River. Not far away was the Hôtel Pourquoi Pas?, where Katharine Hepburn and Humphrey Bogart stayed while filming *The African Queen* in 1951. Stanleyville was more than a bend in the river. A rectangle cut out of the equatorial forest, it was a living metaphor for what the Belgians claimed to have accomplished, a patch of civilization in the jungle.

Lumumba got a bank loan and built himself a concrete bungalow with brick pillars and a porch. He started a family, too. There were two brief, failed marriages—the first largely for the purpose of obtaining a supplemental allowance from his employer, the second more sincere but also short-lived—followed by a relationship with a woman named Pauline Kie that produced a son. But in 1951, the twenty-five-year-old Lumumba entered into a marriage arranged by his family back in Onalua, taking the fourteen-year-old Pauline Opango as his bride, sight unseen. Pauline Opango moved to Stanleyville and would eventually bear him four children, whom he insisted attend European schools. As an urbane striver, Lumumba took little satisfaction in being married to a village girl who spoke no French. He resented her lack of interest in having more children and her belief in magical charms. In a letter to a friend, he complained about her "undignified conduct."

Nor was Opango all that pleased to be married to a man so uninterested in domestic life. Her husband spent a great deal of time locked in his room, nose in a book. He awoke at 2:00 a.m. to read, plunged into a cold bath at 5:00 a.m., and left for work at 7:00 a.m. He guzzled black coffee at all hours. In the evenings, he holed up at the public library, devouring Hugo, Molière, Rousseau, and Voltaire. Eventually, he became its librarian and was dismayed to find that he was one of just ten regular readers.

By dint of his fluency in French and "Europeanized" comportment, Lumumba became what in colonial parlance was called an *évolué*. The term—French for "evolved person"—was reserved for subjects who, in their compliance and eagerness to emulate European settlers, were poster children of colonialism's "civilizing mission." The status had an official component. Lumumba was issued a "civic merit card," which the Belgians had introduced to appease a burgeoning urban elite yearning for recognition. When colonial administrators added a more competitive "registration card" for those Congolese men who were "penetrated with European civilization," he was one of the first to apply. At least in theory, this second designation granted *évolués* the same legal status as Europeans. One can only imagine the desperation of anyone willing to go through the invasive application process. In Lumumba's words:

The territorial authority conducts an enquiry into the private and public life of the petitioner. Visits are made to his home:

every room in his house, from the sitting-room, bedroom and kitchen, right down to the W.C., is thoroughly investigated, in order to bring to light anything which is incompatible with the requirements of civilized life. This domestic investigation is intended to enable the investigator to determine his standard of living, his family relationships (the care and education of the children, the care of the house, etc.) and the degree of development of the applicant. Information regarding his private conduct is assembled from all sources.

Lumumba threw himself into Stanleyville's *évolué* circles, taking on leadership positions in a bevy of civic groups. (Overtly political activity, however, remained off-limits.) At one point, he served simultaneously as president, secretary, or treasurer of seven Stanleyville organizations: the Association of Évolués, the Association of Alumni of the Scheut Fathers (despite never having studied under that particular Catholic congregation), the Association of Native Personnel of the Colony, the Association of Native Postmen of Orientale Province, the Tetela Cooperative, the Belgo-Congolese Cultural Group, and, appropriately enough, the Federation of Stanleyville Associations. He also took to writing, often at a frenetic clip. For *The Cross of the Congo,* a Leopoldville weekly, he filed mundane dispatches from Stanleyville: marriage notices, obituaries, an explanation of how mail was sorted. Some of his output took on the moralizing tone of a prefect admonishing fellow students, particularly when touching on the need to abandon local custom in favor of European mores. ("Our women must wear dresses.") Here, he seemed at pains to get across, was a member in good standing of the Congolese elite—an *évolué* worthy of the designation.

When Pierre Clément, a sociologist from Paris, arrived in Stanleyville in 1952 to study African urbanization, he quickly identified Lumumba as a perfect bridge to the city's Congolese residents. He hired Lumumba as a part-time research assistant, using him mostly to arrange interviews. Lumumba's work ethic, enthusiasm, and curiosity made him, in Clément's words, "an incomparable collaborator" and, before long, "a friend in the deepest, truest sense of the word." The two took a monthlong trip together to Onalua—Lumumba's first time home in a decade—and Lumumba paid homage to his new friend by naming his newborn son Patrice Pierre Clément.

Interracial friendships were taboo in any European colony in Africa, but especially so in the Belgian Congo, as the pair would occasionally be reminded. During a boat ride, Lumumba and Clément were told to sit in different sections. When the two sought to distribute a sociological questionnaire, they were denied official permission on the grounds that it would make Black people aware of problems they had never thought of.

Clément learned that Lumumba dreamed of studying at Lovanium University, an interracial institution that was about to open its doors on a plateau near Leopoldville. The mere existence of the school represented an about-face in colonial policy. The Belgians had long opposed higher education for Congolese, emphasizing vocational training instead. "The fascination of becoming a skilled worker handling precision machinery drives out of the Negro's mind the need for politics," Léo Pétillon, the colony's governor-general, had explained. The natives could become carpenters but not architects, veterinary aides but not doctors, laboratory assistants but not scientists, and clerks but not lawyers. The sole avenue for upper-level study was the priesthood. (No wonder so many Congolese, after finishing seminary, suddenly discovered that they weren't fit to be men of the cloth.) Now, with Lovanium University, Belgian officials had relented, although Pétillon forbade the university from having a liberal arts program, which he worried would "turn the heads of the Congolese."

After Clément left Stanleyville, he arranged for Lumumba's admission to the university. But Lumumba was forced to give up his spot, since the school had no housing for married students. He was heartbroken. Even without a degree, though, his stature in Stanleyville was rising, thanks in part to his prolific dispatches in the press. So was his self-regard, as he made clear in a 1954 letter to a friend:

Today, even the Europeans consider me a formidable man. A European friend once said to me, "All the European circles are saying that Lumumba wants to impose his intellectual superiority on both the Congolese and the whites." This idea and this appraisal stem from the fiery arguments I engage in with Europeans in the European press, debates from which I always emerge victorious. Here in Stan, all the Congolese take me for a magician (which is wrong); the Europeans take me for a man who has received higher education.

Lumumba overstated how "fiery" his published work was, but it had moved beyond thanking the Belgians for granting privileges to a select few *évolués* like himself. It was now addressing the main question facing the Belgian Congo: the rights of all Congolese. The Belgians viewed this question through the lens of paternalism, which was the organizing principle of their rule. Each part of the so-called colonial trinity—the colonial administration, the church, the companies—thought of itself as acting in loco parentis. "Negroes have the souls of children," a mining company's official policy read, "souls which mold themselves to the methods of the educator; they watch, listen, feel, and imitate." The government prohibited Black people from buying liquor and banned them from viewing the same movies deemed unsuitable for white children.

Cannily, Lumumba chose not to openly reject this view. What he contended was that the Congolese had come of age. Thanks to the noble efforts of the Belgians, he argued, colonialism had succeeded in its civilizing mission, and it was time to give the civilized their due. Black people, he contended, should receive full and equal access to education. ("While thanking the Government and our dedicated Missionaries...we now wish to receive a little more in the intellectual domain.") He also proposed raising the borrowing limit for Congolese at banks and took to task those hotels, restaurants, and bars that denied entry to Black patrons.

All this was couched in delicate terms. Lumumba professed to assume good faith on the part of the Belgians, lavished them with credit, and extended the hand of friendship. "We promise docility," he wrote, "loyal and sincere collaboration to all those who want to help us achieve, in union with them, the element that is beyond us: civilization." Any flaws in the colonial system were mere failures of execution—the mistakes of a handful of Belgians out of sync with official policy. Lumumba's rhetorical restraint won him the confidence of certain colonial officials, including the provincial governor of Stanleyville. After meeting Lumumba in 1954, the governor called him "undoubtedly the most striking personality among Stanleyville's *évolués*." That same year, Lumumba was granted an audience with Belgium's minister for the colonies, Auguste Buisseret, and handed him a letter on behalf of the city's *évolués* complaining about the racism of "low-level staff" in the administration. If only he could get his message to the top, all would be fixed.

Chapter 3

The Most Impossible
Job on Earth

THEY THOUGHT THEY had found a harmless bureaucrat. In the spring of 1953, the United Nations was in search of a new secretary-general. The incumbent, Trygve Lie, a large and overbearing Norwegian, had lost the confidence of the Soviet Union after leading the UN into the Korean War on behalf of the Americans. The Soviets refused to deal with Lie any longer, rendering him incapable of doing his job, and he agreed to resign. Just seven years after its postwar founding in the name of global cooperation, the UN was falling victim to a new struggle, this one between East and West.

The task of finding a new man for the job fell on the UN Security Council, the eleven-member body charged with ensuring global peace. The only thing that its members could agree on when they met on March 31, in an oak-paneled conference room at UN headquarters in New York, was that Lie's successor must be politically inert—someone who came from a country aligned with neither superpower and who would approach the job not as an independent political actor but as a mere clerk. No one objected when the British representative, unsure of the man's exact title, put forth the name of a little-known Swedish official: Dag Hammarskjöld.

Outside the conference room, members of the press stood vigil, waiting for the UN equivalent of the Vatican's white smoke. When an official emerged to announce the suggested candidate, the assembled reporters were left puzzled. Who was this man Hammarskjöld? And how did you spell that tongue twister of a name?

Even the candidate himself was confounded by the announcement. Answering a phone call from the Associated Press correspondent in Stockholm, who was calling to verify a tip, Hammarskjöld said that it was a day early for an April Fools' Day joke. Hours later, a cable from the UN confirmed the news. Hammarskjöld felt he had little choice but to accept. "What has just happened to me," he said, "is like being lifted by the scruff of the neck, as if I were a little dog."

Although he was a high-ranking official in the Swedish Foreign Ministry, Hammarskjöld was not a household name in international diplomatic circles. Those who knew him, however, agreed that he was brilliant. He spoke extemporaneously in neat, print-ready paragraphs, recalling statistics, dates, and legal clauses with ease—not just in his native Swedish, but also in impeccable English, French, and German. A colleague who dined with Hammarskjöld just after his nomination found that he showed little interest in the UN—until the next day, when he expertly fielded questions about the organization at a press conference. The dinner guest figured Hammarskjöld had spent the night speed-reading a stack of books about the UN.

"You are going to take over the most impossible job on earth," Trygve Lie told Hammarskjöld upon his arrival at New York's Idlewild Airport the following week. Hammarskjöld's blue eyes stared out nervously as he approached a bouquet of news microphones. Reporters noted a steep forehead and round, full jowls—"as if he had hidden a couple of chestnuts in his cheeks," in the words of one professional caricaturist. Addressing continued curiosity regarding his name, he explained, with a smile, "Well, I pronounce it myself in Swedish 'Hamma-shold,' but if you say 'Hammer-shield,' that's all right with me."

There were limits to how much they would know of him, he signaled. Like everyone, he had his personal views. Yet, he added, "in my new official capacity, the private man should disappear, and the international public servant take his place."

Who was the private man? As Hammarskjöld himself explained, he descended from "generations of soldiers and government officials on my father's side" and "scholars and clergymen on my mother's."

His was a noble family richer in tradition than in property, the ancestral estate having been lost in the 1880s to a series of unsuccessful timber and railway ventures. Nonetheless, because his father, Hjalmar Hammarskjöld, was governor of the Swedish province Uppsala, Dag grew up in Uppsala Castle, an austere, salmon-colored mansion whose broad, flat face had supervised the university city below since the sixteenth century. As a boy, he surveyed its secret passages, turrets, and dungeons.

During World War I, Hjalmar served for three years as Sweden's prime minister; the public considered him authoritarian and pro-German, and he spent the rest of his life detested. That might have been one reason young Dag kept to himself, collecting bugs and butterflies in lieu of playing soccer. As he would later write in a poem,

> A box on the ear taught the boy
> That Father's name
> Was odious to them.

Mother left warmer memories. Of her four boys, Agnes Hammarskjöld preferred him, the youngest. "Dag is the only one I really own on earth, the only one who cares about me," she wrote to him while, at age seventeen, he toured Central Europe with one of his less-loved brothers. "There you hear, my little larva, how much you mean to mother."

Before his twenty-sixth birthday, Hammarskjöld added three degrees from Uppsala University to his CV. First he studied the humanities—French literature, philosophy, history—and then he turned to economics and the law. He continued to socialize little, confessing to a friend that he led "an awfully dry life," though he did find time between home and the library to attend meetings of a French club. He spent a term at Cambridge, where his supervisor, the economist John Maynard Keynes, considered him smart but unoriginal. "I don't think we can expect much from *him*," he told a colleague.

In 1930, Hammarskjöld followed in the footsteps of his father and brothers by becoming a public servant. He moved to Stockholm and joined the civil service. It was the Depression, so he worked on an unemployment commission, picking up a doctorate in economics along the way. At the dinner after his thesis defense, one of his examiners asked him, "Do you speak at home, too, in these long, eloquent, carefully constructed cycles?"

Hammarskjöld soon climbed the peaks of Swedish bureaucracy. At age thirty, he was tapped as undersecretary of the Ministry of Finance, the highest nonpolitical position in the department, raising some colleagues' eyebrows. All the while, he sought to balance public service with filial duty, as if torn between careerism and boyhood. He liked to take long bicycle rides outside Stockholm, yet when he neared the city, he would pause to pull on a pair of pants, mindful of the indignity of an undersecretary caught in shorts. His parents had moved with him to Stockholm, where the three of them shared an apartment overlooking a park, a home he would stay in until age forty. On workdays, he returned there to eat lunch and dinner, often picking up flowers for his mother on the way. Afterward, he would head back to the office. Those who walked past the Ministry of Finance late at night could see a single window illuminated and know who was at work.

During World War II, Hammarskjöld became chair of Sweden's central bank, a position in which he ostensibly reported to the bank's governor but exercised so much authority that he became known as its "real governor." Still, Hammarskjöld viewed himself as an apolitical civil servant. Even once he moved to the Foreign Ministry and, in 1951, was made a member of the cabinet, he remained a member of no party. Impartiality was his default mode. As the Swedish delegate to the series of postwar conferences in Paris organized to administer U.S. aid to competing European countries, he spent his days playing peacemaker. At night, he dragged his colleagues to highbrow plays. It was in Paris that he would impress the diplomats who, in time, would put forth his name for UN secretary-general.

Nineteen fifty-three was an auspicious year to take charge of the UN. In January, Dwight Eisenhower, who had campaigned on a promise to end the Korean War, was inaugurated as U.S. president. In March, Joseph Stalin, whose hard-line policies toward Washington had raised tensions, died from a stroke, and there were signs that a softer approach would emerge from the ensuing power struggle. Maybe the Cold War would dissipate, after all.

Hammarskjöld kept a journal, into which he poured his constitutional loneliness. He called it, in terms that perfectly captured his devotion to both spirituality and bureaucracy, "a sort of white paper concerning my negotiations with myself—and with God." Yet even the brooding diarist found reason for hope in 1953. Sometime that year, he opened its pages and wrote these lines:

> For all that has been—Thanks!
> To all that shall be—Yes!

Chapter 4

To Brussels and Back

B Y 1955, NEARLY half a century had passed since King Leopold II had relinquished ownership of the Congo Free State, formally ceding to the Belgian state what had until then been his private property. Even so, the reigning monarch—King Baudouin, Leopold's great-great-nephew—was still, at least nominally, the highest authority in Belgium's prized African colony. A childhood marked by tragedy had earned Baudouin the moniker "the sad king." When he was three years old, his grandfather King Albert I tumbled down a mountain to his death. The following year, his mother was killed when her car went off the road in Switzerland. When Baudouin was nine, the Germans tore through Belgium—abetted, some believed, by the premature surrender of his father, King Leopold III—and the royal family spent most of the war in their Brussels palace under Nazi guard. News of King Leopold III's second marriage—held behind closed doors in 1941, at a time when the captive, widowed monarch was ostensibly sharing in the wartime hardship of the Belgian people—further tarnished his reputation. It never recovered, and he abdicated in 1951 amid public protest. That was how Baudouin, shy, awkward, and just twenty years old, ascended the throne.

At home, Baudouin shrank from the pageantry inherent in his job, but that evaporated in the African sun. On a visit to the Congo in 1955, he reveled in the elaborate show put up in his honor: Force Publique troops standing at attention, bare-breasted dancers in face paint and raffia skirts twirling the Belgian flag, a canoe regatta, women in commemorative dresses emblazoned with the king's face. The display, captured in Technicolor by a pith-helmeted film crew, suggested happy colonial subjects celebrating their benevolent leader.

In Stanleyville, Baudouin held a reception for local notables in the garden of the provincial governor's mansion. Despite not making the original guest list, Lumumba somehow wrangled an invitation. When this model subject was presented to the king, he was expected to behave like everyone else: speak a few words and let His Majesty move on to the next man. But Lumumba buttonholed the king for several minutes, using the opportunity to speak about a "Belgo-Congolese community" and list various grievances of the city's *évolués*. Baudouin found the conversation memorable enough that later, touring an African neighborhood, he recognized Lumumba in the crowd and spoke to him again. Upon his return to Belgium, Baudouin cited race relations as the chief problem facing the Congo and obliquely addressed its political future, promising unspecified changes to the colony's status to ensure "the continuing existence of a true Belgo-Congolese community." Lumumba was pleased. King and subject were on the same page.

Lumumba's brush with royalty burnished his local reputation. In a six-page feature on the king's visit, *The Postal Echo,* a new quarterly, proudly reported that the president of the Association of Native Postmen of Orientale Province "had a long interview" with Baudouin and that "His Majesty took a keen interest in it"—a degree of press coverage explicable only by the fact that Lumumba had founded the magazine, was its editorial board, and wrote the article himself.

To veer off script and dare talk colonial politics with the Belgian king required exceptional gumption and courage. Just as striking, however, was how modest Lumumba's hopes for the future of his people were at a time when calls for full-fledged independence were already ringing out across the continent. Some of these independence movements were peaceful: in the Gold Coast, nationalist leaders had persuaded the British to share power and were busy transitioning the colony into an independent state called Ghana, and in much of French Africa, politicians were peacefully demanding self-determination. Others spilled blood: Mau Mau rebels were terrorizing the white population in Kenya, and the National Liberation

Front was waging war against the French in Algeria. The Congo had experienced anticolonial revolts earlier, but nothing widespread or with nationalist aspirations. Belgium had so successfully kept the Congolese politically illiterate—and so successfully co-opted the small class of *évolués*—that anyone looking for evidence of a Congolese independence movement in 1955 would have come up empty-handed. A popular colonial adage—"no elites, no problems"—had proved true. In the Congo, the word "independence" was not on anyone's lips.

Nor could it be heard in Belgium. There was no Belgian equivalent to Britain's Movement for Colonial Freedom, an advocacy group that included several members of Parliament. Unlike France's left-wing parties, which tended to oppose colonialism, the Belgian Communist Party waffled on the issue and had no influence anyway. The prevailing view held that, the colonial project being incomplete, independence was an absurd and foolhardy proposition. Leaving the Congo now would have grave consequences, predicted Léo Pétillon, its governor-general: "The jungle will close in. It will take over what we have wrested from it."

Even the meekest dissent to colonial orthodoxy could land one in hot water. Late in 1955, A. A. J. Van Bilsen, a professor at the University Institute of Overseas Territories in Antwerp, published a critique of Belgian colonial policy, taking aim at the utter failure to open up new professional pathways to the Congolese. "It is our fault, not theirs," he wrote, "that there are among the Blacks no doctors, veterinarians, engineers, functionaries, or officers." The Belgian government needed to accept that "emancipation is inevitable" and start planning for it, or else risk being overtaken by events. Van Bilsen's proposed timeline for independence: thirty years. That was how long he thought it would take to raise up a corps of administrators and other high-level employees to run the Congo autonomously. Only by the distant decade of the 1980s, Van Bilsen reasoned, would it be ready for self-rule.

Belgium's political class unanimously rejected the proposal as dangerously premature. Critics worried about the ramifications for the colonizers, not for the colonized. "How can you encourage a young man to come work in the Congo," one politician asked, "if you tell him at the same time that he hasn't even before him the time to make a full career?" Van Bilsen's circumspect intervention nearly cost him his job.

In such a cramped context, even Lumumba's measured interventions attested to his boldness. At least in part, they were the result of deliberate restraint rather than a failure of political imagination. In private, he seethed at the daily indignities of the colonial system. Pierre Clément, the visiting sociologist, found him "highly sensitive to any word, any gesture, however innocent it may be, which seems to stem from an attitude of racial prejudice." Lumumba felt acutely stung when a white man failed to shake his hand or offer him a chair. His white bosses at the post office addressed him by his first name and with the familiar second-person *tu*. Even teenage Belgian typists working in an office, barely out of school, thought nothing of talking down to Congolese colleagues decades their senior.

Outwardly, though, Lumumba evinced more confidence than caution. One Monday afternoon in April 1956, he wrapped up his work and headed to Pilipili, a bar near his house. There, he complained to a fellow patron about three local administrators in Stanleyville, who he claimed were embezzling money. Perhaps fortified by a beer or two, he pledged to expose their dishonesty to the minister for the colonies and the king himself. "We'll see if one of the three finishes the year in Stan," he said of the corrupt administrators. Although tattling might seem risky, Lumumba added, "No one dares do anything to me."

As he had done before, Lumumba was distinguishing between high-level officials in Brussels and the petty functionaries in Stanleyville. He knew he would soon have the chance to speak to the former. He had been invited to join a group of notable Congolese on a government-sponsored tour of Belgium—a departure from Brussels's "no elites, no problems" policy. He would leave in four days.

As Lumumba exited the bar, he probably did not notice that a stranger had been eavesdropping. Within twenty-four hours, the informant's report would land on the desk of a local administrator. In fact, unbeknownst to Lumumba, local colonial authorities had grown suspicious of his growing public profile and attempts at political networking. They had enlisted several informants to watch his moves. They were even rifling through his mail.

As Lumumba prepared to leave for Brussels, Larry Devlin was getting ready for his own trip to the Belgian capital. It was a turning point in his nascent intelligence career. Having left Harvard and joined the CIA in 1949, he had undergone six months of training in spycraft in New York—how to shake a surveillance tail, how to use invisible ink, how to photograph documents, and so on. Devlin was then sent to Paris, to the delight of his wife, Colette. Soon the couple had a daughter, Maureen. As a toddler, she tagged along while her father plied sources in the city's cafés.

As far as most people knew, Devlin was a writer for Fodor's, a popular series of travel guides. The guides' eponymous creator, Eugene Fodor, was a Hungarian native distressed to watch Eastern Europe fall into the Soviet orbit, and as a naturalized U.S. citizen, he considered it his patriotic duty to let the CIA use his company as a front. (The funding he received in exchange didn't hurt, either.) The profession of travel writer was an ideal cover for a spy like Devlin, since it offered a ready excuse for ranging widely across Europe while taking extensive photographs and notes. The problem was that Fodor insisted on getting actual work out of his charges, telling the CIA to send "real writers, not civil engineers." Devlin was credited as an editor in the early 1950s editions of Fodor's guides to Austria, Britain, France, Switzerland, Italy, Scandinavia, and the Benelux countries. How did he manage to submit travel reports for Fodor's while spying for the United States? He plagiarized.

There was another snag: as Fodor's employee, Devlin was, in CIA parlance, under "non-official cover," meaning that unlike spies pretending to be State Department employees, he had less access to important sources and no diplomatic immunity. To get ahead, he realized, he had to be on the inside. That opportunity came when Devlin landed a posting at the CIA station in Brussels, where he would pose as a political officer at the U.S. embassy. His main responsibility was surveilling Soviet intelligence personnel in Europe. It was top Cold War spycraft, an impressive job for a thirty-four-year-old.

—

When Lumumba stepped off the DC-6 outside Brussels shortly before noon on April 25, 1956, he was met by drizzling rain and a shock of cold air. Joining him were fifteen other shivering members of the Congolese elite—clerks, chiefs, businessmen, journalists—each handpicked by the governor-general for a one-month tour of Belgium.

The trip was wasted on most of them, in Lumumba's estimation. Overwhelmed by the back-to-back visits to factories, hospitals, government offices, newsrooms, and museums, the travelers showed little curiosity and sometimes nodded off during meetings. Not Lumumba, who scribbled away furiously in his notebook. His sole complaint, other than the conduct of his fellow voyagers, was that he didn't have enough time at the end of the day to both record his impressions and unwind at the bar.

It was Lumumba's first time outside the Congo—he had received his first passport for the trip—and never had he seen anything like Belgium, with its towering Gothic spires, plush offices, shiny department stores, and curving highways. Lumumba didn't encounter the king on this trip, but he did meet, for the second time, with Auguste Buisseret, the minister for the colonies. They posed for a picture together in front of a giant map of the Belgian Congo. Within the confines of a government junket, Lumumba also took the measure of Belgian society. He descended more than half a mile down a coal shaft, where he saw white people doing jobs that, in the Congo, were reserved for Black workers. In a Brussels slum, an eighty-one-year-old woman invited him into her small apartment. "It is shabby, but clean," she said proudly. Lumumba was also taken aback by the respect accorded to him. "The colonial who today maintains the distance between himself and the Congolese would, if met tomorrow in Belgium, receive you with open arms as a brother and a sincere friend," he soon wrote.

All this kindled in Lumumba's heart a sort of vicarious patriotism. He noted with solemnity his visit to "the rock where King Albert tragically died." He spoke about "the great humanitarian work of Leopold II, of whom we are the beneficiaries." At a grave site near the Royal Museum of the Belgian Congo, he paid his respects to seven Congolese who, in his telling, "were invited by King Leopold II in

1897 to spend a summer in Belgium." By all appearances, he was not told that they had been among 267 compatriots forced to live in a human zoo in the park for the World's Fair in Brussels. The deceased had caught pneumonia and influenza during that year's unseasonably cold summer, and their bodies were dumped into an unmarked pit.

Lumumba finished the tour with his idealized conception of Belgium intact. "Certainly, mistakes were made at the beginning of colonization, and perhaps some are still being made," he told a news agency before leaving, but such mistakes were inevitable and did not undo Belgium's colonial achievements. A perplexed left-wing Belgian journalist concluded that the interview must have been "instigated—if not fabricated"—by conservative pro-colonial forces.

Democracy had not been a foreign concept to Lumumba, but perhaps seeing it in the flesh convinced him that it was something worth bringing home. Upon his return from Brussels, he bemoaned with new candor the Congolese people's inability to select their own leaders. "Since we are in a country with a democratic regime, it should be left to the inhabitants to choose their representatives themselves," he told a crowd at a packed hall in Stanleyville where people had gathered to hear about his trip.

Lumumba's prestige had reached an apogee. It had been twelve years since he alighted in Stanleyville, unemployed, uneducated, and unknown. Now he was addressing a rapt audience that included both fellow *évolués* and Belgian colonial administrators—even some of those he had denounced at the bar. He had made personal contact with every link in the colonial chain of command running from Stanleyville to Leopoldville to Brussels: the governor of Orientale province, the governor-general of the Congo, the Belgian minister for the colonies, and King Baudouin himself. A rumor even circulated among some of the more gullible Congolese that the king had personally put Lumumba in charge of repairing race relations.

It was all too good to be true.

Chapter 5

Not a Slave

A MONTH LATER, LUMUMBA was arrested. He submitted to an interrogation on the afternoon of July 6, 1956.

"As I told my bosses, I committed irregularities," Lumumba said. "I admit that, and I sincerely regret it."

"Why did you commit these irregularities?" asked the interrogator.

"Because I was having financial difficulties. What I received in pay did not allow me to raise my three children, two of whom attend the European Athenaeum."

"How much were you making?"

"Net, 4,955 francs."

"Did you feel that this salary was not enough?"

"I have a boy in my service," Lumumba pleaded. "I have a house with running water and electricity. I have to feed my wife and children."

For at least three years, Lumumba had been abusing his position as a postal clerk by secretly intercepting deposits made into the bank accounts that businesses kept at the post office. A customer might send a payment slip to a local pharmacy. Lumumba would record the debit in the customer's account as usual. But the credit would end up on the ledger for his own personal account. If the pharmacy inquired about the missing payment, Lumumba simply corrected his "error" and repeated the scheme with a different business. For a while, this shell game evaded detection. In eighty-five separate transactions, Lumumba embezzled a total of more than 125,000 francs—the equivalent of two years' salary for him. It was a delicious scandal. News of the high-flying *évolué*'s arrest even made the papers in Brussels.

The motive was simple: Lumumba had run out of money to fund the lifestyle of a "Europeanized" African. The books, the newspaper and magazine subscriptions, the school fees, the house payments, the Western food—it all added up to more than even the most industrious colonial subject could realistically afford. He was the most celebrated *évolué* in Stanleyville, a first-class postal clerk who had given eleven years of service to the colonial administration, and yet he was making a fifth of what a white colleague earned for the same work.

"How can a man improve his standard of living, secure decent conditions for his family, pay for his children's education and, in general, enter the ranks of the civilized, with such an inadequate income?" Lumumba asked. If his sons' white classmates at the European school in Stanleyville had bread and jam for breakfast, then that's what François and Patrice Jr. would have, too—not chewy cassava sticks.

The Stanleyville Central Prison, where Lumumba languished for months as he awaited trial, dated to the turn of the century, but with its rampart, battlements, arrow slits, and pair of towers flanking the gate, it brought to mind a medieval fort. Filled well past capacity, the prison reeked of urine and the unwashed fish fed to inmates— food, Lumumba said, that "a European would never serve to his dog." He also recoiled at what he perceived as the depravity of his fellow inmates:

> To console themselves in their misery they devise all kinds of immoral diversions: men change themselves into women and the majority of the influential prisoners each have their "special" woman. Many prisoners follow this path, either willingly or under skillful compulsion. This is common currency in prisons. How scandalous this is! Those who did not smoke hemp outside prison smoke it inside. In spite of the most careful searches, hemp circulates in prisons in large quantities. The morale of the prisoners is undermined by it day and night.

It was an adjustment, walking the courtyard barefoot and sleeping on a wooden board. Even behind bars, however, his status as a card-carrying *évolué* bestowed certain privileges. He wore khaki shorts and a shirt in lieu of the standard indigo prisoner's uniform. Like his children, he ate bread with butter and jam instead of cassava. He had the right to keep the lights on in his cell three hours later than his unaccredited counterparts and used this prerogative to the fullest, spending his evenings reading periodicals and books lent by friends.

He was also permitted a typewriter. As ever, he wrote—to his lawyers, to the judge, to the prosecutor, to the governor of the province, to the minister for the colonies, and even to King Baudouin, reminding him of their brief interaction the previous year. Much of his epistolary lobbying concerned the well-being of his three children. He had left his sons, François and Patrice Jr., and his baby daughter, Juliana, in the care of his brother and could no longer afford the boys' school fees. When one official suggested that he simply ship them back to Onalua, Lumumba was indignant. "To send them into a traditional environment where there is no school," he wrote to the provincial governor, "where they will be in daily contact with other children who have received no education, where uncles and aunts will instill in them ideas and principles of traditional life contrary to the European civilization in which I want to raise them, where they would immediately lose the use of the French language . . . would do them a disservice and turn them into failed children."

Lumumba wrote for the public, too. Prohibited from appearing in the press, he had his articles smuggled out and published in Stanleyville and Brussels under another writer's byline. Most of his writing time, however, was devoted to a book manuscript. He titled it *The Congo, Land of the Future: Is It Threatened?* In its introduction, he promised to reveal "the mysteries of the African soul: what the Congolese think of the hard facts of life, of their future and their union with the Belgians." Addressed to the Belgian public, the book offered Lumumba a chance to establish himself as a leading voice on the questions of the day and curry favor with the Belgian political class.

At the time Lumumba typed up his thoughts in Stanleyville Central Prison—the summer of 1956—the first glimmers of Congolese nationalism were appearing in the capital, Leopoldville. Inspired by

A. A. J. Van Bilsen's thirty-year plan, a group of *évolués* published a manifesto calling on Belgium to put forward a plan for "total emancipation." Within weeks, a counter-manifesto from a rival group of intellectuals appeared. It went further and demanded that "emancipation should be granted us this very day."

Following the debate from his cell, Lumumba considered these appeals premature. "It is easy enough to shout slogans, to sign manifestos," he wrote in his book, "but it is quite a different matter to build, manage, command, spend days and nights seeking the solution to problems." Like the Leopoldville elites, he envisioned an independent Congo, but his would be united in a loose federation with Belgium and still nominally ruled by its king. And he did not foresee that end state arriving anytime soon. Universal suffrage, he said, should wait until the population was sufficiently educated. Political rights could not be granted "to people who were unfit to use them, to dull-witted illiterates; that would be to put dangerous weapons in the hands of children." Only the elites should be allowed to govern. Lumumba was not calling for the swift end of colonial rule; he was asking permission for *évolués* like him to have a say in it.

For now, Lumumba argued, the colonial administration should focus on addressing the grievances of the Congolese, particularly those in the elite. He passionately condemned racial inequality, laying bare the pain of discriminatory pay and segregation. Complaining about urban curfews that applied only to Black people, he wrote, "We are not chickens to be shut up in our houses when we have no desire to sleep." Yet he framed such indignities less as violating natural law than as tactically misguided. If the Belgians failed to attend to the needs of the nascent university-trained elite, they might inspire the sort of radicalism cropping up in other colonies such as Kenya. They might "make Jomo Kenyattas—leaders of revolt—out of Congolese university students." The Congo needed none of that. After all, it was "amongst the best administered and happiest colonies in the African continent."

Lumumba mailed his manuscript off to Brussels under a cover letter bursting with ambition. He spoke of future studies and novels he hoped to write. He elided his current imprisonment, writing, "I have always been in Government service, but at present I have no commitments, for personal reasons." In a follow-up letter, he expressed a willingness to let the publisher design his book's cover, as if this would help his submissions's chances.

Lumumba never heard back. In an internal memo at the publisher's office, an anonymous reviewer described the work as "a mix of cunning and naivete, verbiage and pertinent ideas, crazy claims and justified remarks," written in the style of "petit nègre"—literally, "little Negro," but more charitably translated as "pidgin French." Lumumba's grand statement of his political philosophy, the project that kept him busy during the long, stuffy days in his cell, would languish unpublished.

After eight months, Lumumba's criminal case was finally heard. "Hounded by almost insurmountable financial difficulties and having no other way of getting out of trouble, I, after much patience, succumbed to temptation," he wrote to the court. He swore he had intended to pay back the stolen sums as soon as possible, pointing to the records he kept of every transaction. Unimpressed, the court found him guilty of embezzlement and sentenced him to two years in prison.

Lumumba had been caught with his hand in the till, yes, but there was reason to believe he was also being punished for the sin of picking sides in metropolitan politics. Debates were raging in Belgium over the role of religion in schooling, with a coalition government of liberal and socialist parties working to reduce the traditionally firm grip of Catholic institutions on the country's education system. That effort spilled over into the Congo, with Auguste Buisseret, the minister for the colonies, proposing to cut Belgian state subsidies to Catholic missions there. Lumumba had joined the Liberal Party's Stanleyville branch, perhaps less out of political affinity than out of a desire to sign up for every possible club open to Congolese évolués in the city. It was through that group that he first met Buisseret and came to align himself with the anticlerical stance of the prominent Liberal politician. In doing so, he irritated both conservative local colonial officials, who already despised the upstart postal employee, and Catholic missionaries.

That political context likely figured into his prosecution and sentencing. Other Congolese caught doing similar misdeeds received a reprimand, or perhaps a fine and a few months in prison—to say nothing of the leniency habitually accorded to whites, who were sometimes permitted to serve their sentences in Europe. The prosecution seemed to single out Lumumba. Even after he confessed, the prosecutor's office tried to dig up dirt, interviewing neighbors to determine if he kept a concubine.

The vindictive nature of the prosecution became even clearer when it appealed the Stanleyville court's two-year sentence, asking for ten years. "We are dealing with a cunning, wily, mean, fundamentally dishonest, and completely unscrupulous individual," the prosecutor argued. The judges in Stanleyville, in handing down their original sentence, had noted a mitigating factor: that Lumumba, despite his status as an *évolué*, "is still not that far away from the most primitive natives." His crime, the judges claimed, was "a product of an evolution in progress." (One can imagine how that must have stung a defendant who took such pride in his education.) The prosecutor contended that the court had it backward: "This is not about one of those natives, still naive and close to nature, who cannot resist a fleeting temptation," he wrote. "Lumumba skillfully organized his embezzlement." In a final twist of the knife, the prosecutor noted that Lumumba hailed from a region where, half a century earlier, the Belgians had fought the Afro-Arab slave traders. "Without our presence in Congo, what would Lumumba be?" he asked. Lumumba, he answered, "owes it to the state that he is not a slave."

As it happened, the prosecution's request for a longer sentence was denied, and the king issued a royal pardon to Lumumba. His debt to the post office was repaid, and new employment was arranged. His hidden savior, it turned out, was Buisseret, the minister for the colonies. Proximity to the minister had gotten Lumumba into trouble in the first place, but now Buisseret, out of apparent loyalty to his pen pal, pulled some strings, and on September 7, 1957—fourteen months after his arrest—Lumumba became a free man. Just as he had a decade and a half earlier, after the scandal at the mining canteen in Kalima, he needed another city to reinvent himself, out of sight and earshot of hostile local officials.

Whereas Stanleyville marked the farthest navigable point upriver, Leopoldville was the farthest one could go in the other direction before running into the unpassable Livingstone Falls. At that point, cargo destined for the Atlantic Ocean had to be unloaded onto a rail line, the construction of which, under King Leopold, was said to have cost the lives of ten laborers per mile. In the decade after World War II, Leopoldville's population more than tripled as the capital of the Belgian Congo grew from a riverine trading post into one of the most modern cities in Africa. (It was then and there, in the bordellos servicing the city's migrant workers, that a deadly virus began its spread outward, eventually becoming known as HIV.)

There were two Leopoldvilles, really. The whites took the best parts for themselves: the downtown, close to the riverbank and the train station, along with the hilly suburbs, where a gentle breeze whisked away the muggy air. In these neighborhoods, the Belgians sought to import all that was European and repress all that was African, taking over with the fervor of an invasive species. They built blocky office buildings in the International Style popular in the West, shading the windows and slitting the walls to keep the tropical heat at bay. Fourteen-story buildings sprang up, elevated on piers to promote air circulation, as if raising a trouser hem to keep it from the rainy-season mud. "Europe in Leo weighs down on the African soil in the form of skyscrapers," the novelist Graham Greene wrote when he visited the city. At Lovanium University, a nuclear reactor, Africa's first, was installed as part of Eisenhower's Atoms for Peace program.

This Leopoldville was an orderly colonial capital. By virtue of its proximity to the equator, the sun rose and set at nearly the same time all year—6:00 a.m. and 6:00 p.m. To combat malaria, a helicopter regularly circled above and emitted from its stinger a plume of DDT, infusing the city with the chemical whiff of progress. Below, specially designed trucks did the same, engulfing the cars behind them in a disorienting fog. White passengers were chauffeured gently through streets named for Belgians: former kings, princes, colonial governors-general, vice-governors-general, and other notables unknown to the Congolese drivers. Servants, nannies, gardeners, cooks, and other domestics commuted to the European quarters on gyrobuses, state-of-the-art vehicles made in Switzerland and powered by electrically charged flywheels. Inside their employers' houses, the yen for Europe extended to the smallest of creature comforts. Instead of filling their vases with tropical flowers, some Belgians paid for wilting carnations flown in from Brussels. It helped them feel at home. Here, one could forget that there were just 100,000 Europeans in the Belgian Congo, compared with 12 million Congolese.

The main European quarter was bounded on the south by a thick greenbelt—a cemetery, a golf club, a zoo, botanical gardens, a market—a cordon sanitaire designed to keep African diseases from jumping races. To cross this border, as a handful of white tourists did in the morning and thousands of Congolese workers did every night, was to enter the other Leopoldville. The *cité*, as the African quarters were known, was a maze of unpaved streets pulsing with life. Children splashed about in the ditches, and the smell of roasting chestnuts, tended to by crouching women, wafted freely.

Black residents weren't allowed into the white neighborhoods past 9:00 p.m. unless they had a special pass, but in the *cité* they could laugh and dance late into the night. A bar was never far away; one Belgian publication counted 330 of them in the African neighborhoods. The humbler ones consisted of nothing more than an open yard hung with Chinese lanterns, a few folding tables and chairs in the middle and a record player in the corner. Others, like O.K. Bar, Air France, and Quist, were established hot spots known for live music. A double bass, an electric guitar or two, a drum set, and perhaps some congas would crowd a makeshift stage of overturned beer crates, keeping time as sweaty patrons in sandals jitterbugged and twisted. Off the dance floor, the kitchen served heaps of chicken, rice, and cassava paste wrapped in leaves.

Coursing through everything, naturally, was beer. When Heineken sent a representative to the Congo in 1953 to evaluate prospects for expansion in the colony, he estimated that Congolese men spent a quarter of their income on beer. "Breweries consider this the promised land," he reported. It wasn't until 1955 that the ban on selling liquor to Africans was lifted, and even then what the *cité* bought was beer, tipped lukewarm into small glasses.

When Lumumba left prison, in the fall of 1957, 90 percent of the Leopoldville beer market belonged to Primus, a pale lager advertised as "happiness in a bottle." The remaining share went to Polar, introduced three years earlier by a new brewery that promised drinkers "the freshness of the Pole under the tropics." The head of the brewery's Leopoldville operations, Gilbert Roland, was a Liberal and, overlooking the misappropriation at the Stanleyville Post Office, hired Lumumba into the accounting department. Lumumba repaid the favor by naming his newborn son Roland-Gilbert.

Restless and extroverted, Lumumba was never meant to push paper, and his talents were quickly redirected toward salesmanship. Promoting beer might have been an unlikely profession for a man who had denounced the "cancer of alcoholism" in his book manuscript, but he took to his new vocation with zeal. Night after night, he toured the cafés, dance halls, and bars of the *cité*, homing in on customers drinking Primus and offering them free Polar, sometimes cracking open the bottle himself with his teeth. He quickly learned Lingala—the lingua franca in Leopoldville and the rest of the Congo's west, in contrast to the Swahili of the east that he knew well. He gave increasingly polished speeches and mastered the art of capturing a crowd. He hired a dozen "propagandists" to spread a new slogan: "Polar is health, Polar is friendship." He launched fan clubs for market segments, such as Polar Papa for men and Polar Mama for women. At least once, he chartered an airplane to leaflet the *cité* with advertisements. Sip by sip, Polar cut into Primus's market share.

So began Leopoldville's "beer war," waged in the theater of innuendo and identity. When a woman who miscarried was found to have attended a party where Primus was flowing, a rumor circulated that the brand of beer was to blame, a notion that Lumumba and his associates did little to dispel. Primus's sales plummeted, only to recover with the outbreak of a new rumor, which had it that Polar made men impotent. Over time, affinities hardened, and opposing supporters tumbled into fistfights. The rivalry had a political and ethnic dimension: Primus was brewed by Catholics and drunk by the Kongo people, an ethnic group from the lower Congo; Polar was brewed by Liberals and the beer of choice for upriver newcomers like Lumumba.

The most prominent of the Bakongo was Joseph Kasavubu, a onetime seminarian and, like Lumumba, a former colonial clerk. These days, Kasavubu was the leader of Abako, a cultural association for the Bakongo that, over time, had strayed into politics. It was Abako that had issued the 1956 manifesto calling for immediate independence, and Kasavubu who had dared to read it aloud at a public meeting. Short, fat, and inscrutable, Kasavubu seemed to float through life with a Zen-like detachment that earned him the moniker "the Bakongo Buddha." Perhaps that, plus his supposedly Asian facial features, explained why he was said to be the grandson of one of the Chinese railway workers hired by King Leopold. Because Primus came in a squat bottle and Polar in a taller and thinner one, the temptation to anthropomorphize the two rival figures—Kasavubu for the Bakongo, Lumumba for the Batetela and other outsiders—proved irresistible. "Pesa ngai Lumumba!" customers ordering a Polar would bark in Lingala. "Give me a Lumumba!"

In this sudsy environment, Lumumba endeared himself to the drinkers of Leopoldville and developed his talent for oratory. Within months of his arrival, the ex-convict who barely spoke the local language was one of the best-known figures in the capital. He handed out business cards with his impressive new title: "Patrice Lumumba, Commercial Director." Now earning five times his old post office salary, he traded his bicycle for a Fiat 1100, a stubby sedan. For the first time in his career, moreover, he realized that his ambitions did not require pleasing colonial authorities—a freedom his politics would come to reflect.

As he had in Stanleyville, Lumumba threw himself into the city's évolué scene, becoming president of a group for fellow Batetela and vice president of one for Congolese supporters of Belgium's Liberal Party. But the milieu had become much more contentious; the stakes, higher. The Leopoldville of 1958 in which Lumumba now lived was on a different planet, politically speaking, from the Stanleyville of 1956 that he had left behind. Debates over the future of the Congo no longer concerned bromides about a Belgo-Congolese community and "emancipation" in the distant future. Independence was on the lips of the beer drinkers. A group of angry students even threatened, in a nod to the insurgency ravaging France's settler colony in North Africa, to "make the Congo a second Algeria." As the Congo experienced its first nationalist stirrings, Lumumba risked being left behind.

Chapter 6

Awakenings

THE CENTERPIECE OF the 1958 World's Fair in Brussels was the Atomium, a 334-foot-tall model of an iron crystal enlarged by a factor of 165 billion, with nine spherical atoms clad in polished aluminum. An elevator whisked visitors upward to the top atom, where they could look out from an observation deck, dine at a restaurant, or take an escalator encased in a tube to travel to another module—all while marveling at the promise of the atomic age.

Just a short walk past the Atomium, visitors were awoken from their futuristic reveries and "thrust into a corner of faraway bush," as one contemporary account put it. Here, in Expo 58's section on the Belgian Congo, workers had planted tropical greenery in artificially heated soil and erected replicas of thatched-roof huts. Sitting on the dirt floor, a dozen or so Congolese men and women wove cloth, pounded grain, and sculpted wood as white fairgoers tossed candy and bananas over the bamboo fence. Little had changed since Brussels's first World Exposition sixty-one years earlier, which had also showcased a human zoo.

The villagers plucked from the interior of the colony were not the only Congolese specimens on display for the exposition's forty-one million visitors. As proof of their successful civilizing mission, the Belgians had also flown in several hundred members of the Congo's emerging urban elite. Among them was a young journalist named Joseph Mobutu, a columnist for the Leopoldville daily *L'Avenir*. During the exposition, Mobutu spoke to an auditorium of fellow writers for colonial newspapers, making the case for an institute to train

Congolese journalists. He also gave news interviews, his lanky frame wrapped in a trim suit, his serious eyes darting through wire-rim glasses. Asked about his journalistic work, he reflected on the fickle moods of his readers, who might praise one of his columns, only to condemn the next one as treasonous. "The public fluctuates," he said softly, rocking the palm of his hand back and forth.

It was the twenty-seven-year-old's first trip to Belgium, as it was for nearly all the other Congolese attendees. In fact, about a hundred times as many Congolese visited Expo 58 as had visited Belgium in the preceding seventy-plus years of colonialism. In trying to show-case men like Mobutu, the Belgians had unwittingly offered them a chance to mingle and network against the inspiring backdrop of the World Exhibition, not all of whose pavilions were as retrograde in outlook as the Belgians' human zoo. For the first time, civically active Congolese from different corners of the colony had a chance to meet one another and exchange ideas. They could wander into the United Nations' pavilion, where a poster displayed the Universal Declaration of Human Rights and an exhibit touted the organiza-tion's concern for the plight of nonautonomous peoples. They could freely patronize bars and cafés, which were filled with workers and tourists from the world over. They could learn, as one Congolese observer put it, "that man is the same everywhere, that human quali-ties as well as virtues and flaws are not the monopoly of a people or a race."

Mobutu's eyes were opened; his horizons broadened. He had learned of this world in the mission schools of his youth but had never been able to reach out and touch it. He would come back, he told himself.

Joseph-Désiré Mobutu had spent his whole life moving from place to place. He was born in 1930 in Lisala, a small town on the right bank of the Congo River, to a mother who had escaped the harem of a prominent chief and a father who worked as a cook for a Belgian couple. The wife in that couple, Madame Delcourt, had no children of her own and took little Joseph under her wing. She let him sit at the table and brought him along as she shopped, turning the heads of those unaccustomed to seeing a white woman holding the hand of a Black boy. "In a way she adopted me," Mobutu would say fondly. Crucially for his future, she taught him proper French.

When Monsieur Delcourt was assigned to Leopoldville, the cook and his family followed. But when Mobutu was just seven, his father died, and so began a sort of reverse migration back into the interior—"to-ing and fro-ing with my mother," as he would put it. He was in and out of four different mission schools in four different towns before finally landing with an uncle in Coquilhatville, the capital of Équateur province, in the Congo's north. In Coquilhatville, he studied under Christian missionaries and sang solos at Mass. But much like Lumumba in his mission school days, he had a penchant for mischief. After one too many infractions—depending on who told the story, the last straw was either stealing from the mission library or going AWOL for a three-week trip to Leopoldville—he was expelled and sent off to the Force Publique.

He initially kept up his rebellious streak, scoring a dismal five out of twenty for discipline at the end of his second year as a soldier. But the officers eventually tamed the unruly young man, who came to find purpose and mentorship in his seven years of military service. He also found a wife, the fourteen-year-old Marie-Antoinette. For their wedding, Mobutu contributed a humble crate of beer.

When a day of soldiering was over, Mobutu would curl up with a flashlight to read whatever he could get his hands on: mostly scraps of newspapers left behind by the officers but also a little Winston Churchill and Niccolò Machiavelli. Soon, he began writing himself, as a contributor to the weekly "African News" section of L'Avenir, using a pseudonym so as not to put his army job at risk. Eventually, he left the Force Publique to join the newspaper full-time. It was at work, in the offices of L'Avenir, that Mobutu first met the politically active beer promoter he knew by reputation. "Oh, Mr. Lumumba," Mobutu said. "I have heard of you for a long time, but now I get to see you in the flesh." Lumumba, in turn, knew Mobutu's byline from articles he had read behind bars.

Mobutu and hundreds others like him returned from Expo 58 with a new sense of confidence and strength in numbers, and demands for the independence of the Congo soon grew louder and bolder. For the time being, however, the Belgians weren't all that interested in what the Congolese thought. The government had set up a working group to chart a new course for the Congo but had not thought to include a single Congolese member.

On August 24, General Charles de Gaulle, France's prime minister, visited Brazzaville, in the French Congo. Speaking before thousands of cheering Black residents, whom his country had already granted the right to become French citizens and to vote for politicians to represent them in Paris, de Gaulle promised, "Whoever wants independence can take it right away." Across the river in Leopoldville, the Congolese wondered, *Why don't the Belgians speak this way to us?* Two days after de Gaulle's speech, Lumumba and fifteen other *évolués* signed a petition presented to the new minister of colonies, Léo Pétillon. (Auguste Buisseret had left when the Liberals lost power.) The petition decried the Congo's "anachronistic political regime" and demanded an eventual date for "total independence." It was, one legal scholar said, "the Belgian Congo's Declaration of Independence."

One Friday in October 1958, Lumumba went to the offices of *L'Avenir* and found Mobutu. The two men had already struck up a close friendship, undergirded by their shared politics, including their sense that Congolese nationalism had to overcome not just Belgian domination but also the centrifugal forces of ethnic divisions—not a minor concern in a massive, resource-rich land populated by hundreds of groups, not all of whom were on good terms with one another. By now the two friends were on a first-name basis, but Mobutu, younger and less well known, was the junior partner in the relationship.

"You have to come to a meeting tonight," Lumumba told him. Most of those who had signed the recent petition would be there.

"I'll do a write-up," Mobutu proposed.

That wasn't what Lumumba had in mind. He was trying to get his friend to make the leap from journalism to politics. But Mobutu held fast and stayed home.

Hours later, Lumumba joined twenty or so other notables in a building on a side street in Dendale, a neatly gridded African neighborhood built to accommodate overflow from the main *cité.* The plan was to organize into a political party, and the first order of business was to choose a president. Lumumba coveted the post, but he was not on anyone's short list. For all his success as a beer promoter, he was still a newcomer to Leopoldville, an ethnic Tetela in Kongo territory, and an ex-convict to boot. But one after another, the more prominent members of the group declined to vie for the presidency, pleading overcommitment and suggesting that the decision be postponed. As a stopgap measure, they agreed that each member would vote for himself, creating a tie and leaving the position vacant for the time being. When the ballots were read aloud, everyone garnered one vote— except Lumumba, who received two. Perhaps out of distraction or shyness, no one had asked why he had brought along an uninvited newcomer. It was this man, Lumumba's replacement for Mobutu, who had cast the decisive extra vote.

The room was dumbfounded. The newborn political movement was now burdened with a president who had been convicted of embezzlement. As the members distributed the remaining leadership roles, they consoled themselves with one thought: at least we didn't make him treasurer.

In a press communiqué, the group announced its name: the Congolese National Movement, known by its French initials, MNC. In contrast to Joseph Kasavubu and his more radical organization, Abako, the MNC positioned itself as reformist rather than revolutionary. Still holding out hope for cooperation with Belgium, the party called not for immediate independence but for independence "within a reasonable time." It distinguished itself in another way: whereas other nascent parties were vehicles for ethnic nationalism, it pledged to "forcefully fight any form of regional separatism."

In aligning itself with a single, united Congo, the MNC was swimming upstream. After all, the very idea of the Congo was a fiction, the product of lines on a map drawn in Europe that arbitrarily grouped together hundreds of different ethnic groups while dividing others. Why, if given the chance to become independent, would one choose to continue the pretense of a single nation—especially in the largest colony in sub-Saharan Africa, with arguably the most diverse population on the continent?

Moreover, wasn't a powerful unitary government part of the problem? Compared with the British and the French, the Belgians ruled their colony in a particularly centralized fashion, devolving little authority to local colonials (and none at all to the native population).

The Congolese had been ruled for too long by distant, out-of-touch officials. If there was going to be self-rule, many thought, it was only natural that the artificial colony fracture into smaller units whose inhabitants could govern themselves.

Other political groups saw this logic. Kasavubu's Abako considered itself the protector of the Bakongo people, the proud heirs to the Kingdom of Kongo, which had reigned over the area around the lower Congo River for nearly five hundred years. They had little interest in answering to authorities who came from Stanleyville or elsewhere.

Nor did people in Katanga, the province in the Congo's southeast. Katanga was special. A prospector sent there in 1892 was awed by its mineral riches, reporting that he had uncovered a "veritable geological scandal." In King Leopold's era, the running of Katanga was outsourced to a private company; for decades afterward, it retained its separate status and even fielded its own military. Now Belgian settlers in the province, accepting that independence was inevitable, proposed a federal structure for the future state, with a view toward safeguarding Katanga's considerable revenues from greedy hands in Leopoldville. Some Congolese in Katanga were moving in the same direction, but for a different reason. Those who called themselves "authentic Katangese" resented the influx of workers from outside the province. They sought to reclaim a territory and a society they considered theirs. Soon, such separatist thinking in the Congo would acquire a slogan: "chacun chez soi" or, roughly, "stay home."

But Lumumba was a nomad. "Stay home" was an impossible order. He had moved from Onalua to Kalima to Stanleyville to Leopoldville. A Congo divided into separate sovereign states would have precluded the life of mobility he had lived. On a more spiritual level, in wandering, Lumumba had transcended an identity tied to his birthplace or his ethnicity. He had become Congolese.

"At 11:30 o'clock on Saturday morning, December 6, three well-dressed Africans, carrying top-coats and briefcases, dashed into the lobby of the Consulate General, disregarded the receptionist's request to stop, and started up the stairs." That was how, in the waning weeks of 1958, James Frederick Green, the U.S. consul general in

Leopoldville, reported the United States' first official contact with Lumumba. A clerk caught up with the trio on the second floor and reluctantly ushered them into Green's office.

Like everything in the city, the consulate was built under the impression that the Belgian Congo would remain a placid colony for a long time. The new three-story building had broad glass windows that exposed an inner stairwell, and the front was shaded with concrete latticework. Lumumba and two fellow MNC members had come to talk about the All-African People's Conference, a meeting of nationalist leaders from across the continent that was about to take place in Accra, the capital of newly independent Ghana. Belgian authorities had denied Joseph Kasavubu permission to travel to Accra, but Lumumba's more moderate group had been issued passports and was free to leave. What the three MNC members didn't have was money for their airfare. Might the United States, rich world power that it was, spare them some francs?

The consul general turned them down, and the three hurried out of the consulate. They managed to secure funding elsewhere—likely from Lumumba's brewery—and arrived in Accra in time for the conference. Although the Belgians had stipulated that Lumumba could attend only "in a personal capacity and as a mere observer," once in Accra he ignored the order and presented himself as president of the MNC. The conference brought together an intoxicating mix of some three hundred budding politicians, labor organizers, and rebel leaders from independent and colonized Africa, along with American civil rights activists, Soviet diplomats, and other international observers. Frantz Fanon, a Martinique intellectual and member of Algeria's National Liberation Front, was there. So was Shirley Graham Du Bois, filling in for her husband, the scholar and activist W. E. B. Du Bois, who was sick. The CIA was also represented in the person of Irving Brown, an American labor leader who worked for the agency, as well as indirectly, through the delegates from the Congress for Cultural Freedom and the American Society of African Culture—U.S. organizations that were secretly receiving agency funding. (Lumumba's allies suspected that the CIA's presence was even deeper, claiming that an American enlisted to serve as his English interpreter was also spying for the agency.) But the most lasting contact Lumumba made was the conference's organizer, Kwame

Nkrumah, the father of Ghanaian independence and now the country's prime minister, a man whose philosophy he would adopt and counsel he would seek time and again.

Accra marked a turning point in Lumumba's thinking. For one thing, it gave him his first real exposure to pan-Africanism, the idea that indigenous people from across the continent were engaged in the same collective struggle. For another, the conference gave him a chance to compare notes with other African nationalists. As he did so, he could only have come to the disappointing conclusion that the Congo lagged far behind its peers. Lumumba's months-old political party and its tepid demands looked quaint in comparison to the well-organized, militant movements pushing for immediate independence in other colonies. The MNC was still a long way away from the language and views of activists like Tom Mboya, a Kenyan trade unionist, who told the conference crowd that the Europeans should reverse the "scramble for Africa" and "scram from Africa."

Lumumba returned to Leopoldville brimming with new ideas. The MNC planned a public meeting to present its report on the conference, and he insisted on delivering it himself. The other members, still smarting from the ploy that had made him president, relented on the condition that he do so merely as a spokesperson on behalf of the group. Lumumba had other plans. He fed the speech into a typewriter and inserted a title at the top: "Address of Mr. Lumumba."

"No way, young man!" a more senior member said when he saw the text. With a flourish of correction fluid, he whited out Lumumba's name.

The gesture had little effect. When several thousand Congolese gathered in a public square in Kalamu, one of the new Black neighborhoods, Lumumba was the center of attention. At the first political rally in the history of the Belgian Congo, Leopoldville witnessed the debut of an altogether new Lumumba. Where he had once embraced the Belgians' infantilizing attitude toward their African subjects, he now called for the Congo to "free itself from the chains of paternalism." Where he had once sought to reform the colonial system rather than overthrow it, he now decried Belgium's halfhearted moves toward autonomy as tokenism and vowed to "wipe out the colonialist regime." Where he had once left indefinite the date of the Congo's eventual independence, he now demanded it by the end of 1960. And where he had once shown little interest in other colonies, he now spoke in the pan-African language of the Accra conference. "Africa," he said, "is irrevocably engaged in a merciless struggle against the colonizer for its liberation."

Everyone who watched Lumumba speak was dazzled by his fluid mixing of rational argumentation and emotional appeal. He had the rare ability to speak three of the Congo's four main languages: Swahili, Lingala, and Tshiluba. Of all those listening in the crowd that day, Lumumba was perhaps most pleased that he had gotten through to Mobutu, who now made up his mind: he would take the plunge into politics. Mobutu formally joined the MNC that same day, receiving membership card No. 201.

On January 4, 1959, Lumumba went to Mobutu's for an early lunch. Having quit the brewery three days earlier, he was newly unshackled from what constraints remained of his job—though by the end, much of the Polar marketing budget had been funding his political activities. Lumumba came often to the modest house that Mobutu had built in Bandalungwa, a new neighborhood designed for white-collar Congolese, in the hills overlooking downtown Leopoldville.

While Mobutu's wife, Marie-Antoinette, cooked, the two friends talked about the rally that Joseph Kasavubu was scheduled to hold that day. The event was Abako's bid to reclaim the vanguard of the Congolese independence movement. Perhaps owing to the unexpected popularity of the MNC rally the week before, Abako had been denied permission to meet. Mobutu said he was going anyway. "It'll probably make good copy for 'African News,'" he reasoned.

While the journalist smelled a story, the politician saw a chance to skim voters from his rival. Lumumba could distribute MNC literature and sell membership cards.

"Let's go together," he said.

Mobutu kick-started his motor scooter, with Lumumba riding on the back. It was a sweltering afternoon in the middle of the rainy season, and as the pair blew down Avenue Baudouin, the rush of air cooled their sticky skin. By the time they arrived, thousands of Congolese, mostly young men, had gathered despite the missing permit. They spilled out of a YMCA basketball court into the street and onto the roof, dangling their feet from its ledge. The crowd was twice the size of the one at the MNC's rally, and rowdier. At 3:00 p.m., Kasavubu appeared at half-court to tell the crowd that although the rally was postponed, the fight for independence was not over. But in the cacophony, few could hear his soft-spoken message. Kasavubu's quiet, squeaky voice, at odds with his imposing body, had long been one of his greatest liabilities. And that day especially, it was not enough to satiate the restive audience.

"Things could turn ugly," Mobutu said to Lumumba.

Soon they did. The demonstrators formed a mob, which grew even bigger once it merged with twenty thousand or so soccer fans leaving King Baudouin Stadium. Victoria Club had just lost 3–1 to Mikado, a mostly Black team with a handful of white players, and fans accused the referee of racial bias. The mass rolled outward from the African quarter and toward the European neighborhoods like "a human tide," one witness recalled.

Lumumba and Mobutu followed on motor scooter. They saw a city convulsing. Rioters were vandalizing every symbol of white privilege and power they could find: police stations, churches, schools, hospitals, restaurants, shops. They hurled fence posts, metal chairs, and chunks of concrete. They knifed Belgian flags, smashed storefronts, torched houses, and flipped cars. It was a paroxysm not just of anger but of exuberance, too. One man was seen attempting a backflip, only to land headfirst on the pavement.

Outnumbered, the police first fired on the rioters and then pulled back. Some white civilians took matters into their own hands. Shopkeepers reached for their rifles. An enterprising member of the local aviation club nose-dived his plane twice over a crowd. Whites who showed up at armories were handed guns and ammunition.

After dropping off Lumumba, Mobutu roamed the city on his own, wanting to witness for himself and for his readers what it looked like when decades of repressed frustration were let loose. By now, the troops of the Force Publique had taken over from the police. Black neighborhoods had been abandoned to the mob; all the soldiers could do was attempt to seal off the white ones. As night fell and flames billowed from ransacked buildings, the streets glowed an otherworldly orange.

Mobutu knew he had to get to the offices of *L'Avenir*. The riot was the biggest news story in the Belgian Congo since—well, there didn't seem to be any precedent. After navigating the checkpoints lining the avenue that separated the main African quarter from downtown Leopoldville, Mobutu managed to reach the newspaper's headquarters. He sat down at his typewriter, pecking its keys late into the night.

Belgian news outlets took pains to paint the riots not as a spontaneous outpouring of pent-up rage at the colonial system but as deliberate instigation on the part of a handful of rabble-rousing politicians. Mobutu's reporting, splashed across the front page of "African News," corrected the Belgian line. He exonerated Kasavubu, crediting him for making "a solemn appeal for calm." But he also took care not to aggravate the authorities, making a point of praising a police commander who received a rock to his face yet "kept his cool and asked his troops not to fire."

After filing his copy, Mobutu spent the night at the office. He fell asleep to the scent of burning gasoline and the echoes of gunfire. The roll of thunder could be heard in the distance. The masses had awoken.

The next morning, a rain shower washed the blood from the streets and extinguished the burning cars, but it did little to interrupt the riots. It took four days to restore order. Soldiers of the Force Publique, joined by paratroopers requisitioned from the Belgian military, rumbled through the streets in jeeps, firing their submachine guns at residents, whether they were part of a mob or not. When the ashes cooled, it turned out that not a single white person had died in what were the worst riots the colony had ever experienced. But forty-nine Congolese had been killed, by the administration's count, along with more than two hundred wounded. Most agreed that the true toll was far higher. One tract circulating estimated that at least six hundred people had perished.

Colonial authorities wasted no time reacting. One of their first steps was to crack down on political leaders. Force Publique officers showed up at Lumumba's doorstep while he was away and searched every room, ostensibly for valuables looted in the pillage. All they found were endless shelves of books.

"Who are these for?" one of them asked.

"They're for Daddy," Lumumba's seven-year-old son, François, responded.

"He's read all that?"

Despite the attention he had paid to colonial sensitivities, Mobutu was interrogated three times by the police, who tried in vain to make him retract his article. Some Belgian officials proposed shutting down his newspaper.

Abako, for its part, was formally dissolved and its leaders rounded up. Kasavubu was arrested for "exciting Africans to violence," jailed for two months, and spirited away to forced exile in Belgium. Thousands of jobless men who supported Abako were expelled from the city and sent back to the countryside, but rustication backfired because the returnees brought their pro-independence politics to the villages.

A parliamentary investigation into the riots was ordered, as if it were a mystery why so many people—poor, maltreated, and denied the simple right to hold a peaceful political rally—had risen up against their unelected rulers. In truth, the message of the protesters was not hard to divine. In one vandalized biology classroom, strewn with loose papers and the bones of a skeletal model, someone had written on the chalkboard, "The Congolese demand independence."

The forceful crackdown notwithstanding, Brussels knew it would have to give in. The specter of more violence, perhaps even a costly and bloody colonial war, was too much to countenance. On January 13, 1959—less than two weeks after the riots had erupted—King Baudouin's voice beamed out from the radio in Belgium and the Congo:

> The object of our presence in the Dark Continent was thus defined by Leopold II: to open these backward countries to European civilization, to call their peoples to emancipation, liberty, and progress, after having saved them from slavery, disease, and poverty. In continuance of these noble aims, our firm resolve today is to lead, without fatal evasions but without imprudent haste, the Congolese peoples to independence in prosperity and peace.

There, at long last, hidden among the ceaseless paternalism and usual qualifications, was the magic word, one never before seen in an official statement about the Belgian Congo: "independence."

Important questions remained: When would independence be granted, and what would it actually mean? But two things were clear. One, as an American reporter wrote, "The picture that had been built up by Belgian authorities—and accepted widely in the rest of the world—of the Belgian Congo as an Eden in Africa was little more than an illusion." And two, Belgium would have to part with its treasured possession not in a matter of decades but in a matter of years.

Chapter 7

The Year of Africa

N O ONE KNEW a damn thing about the Congo." Such was Larry Devlin's impression of the first ever briefing he was given on what would become a career-defining posting. It was 1959, and Devlin, briefly on leave from Brussels to visit his ailing father back home in Washington, had just been told he would be the next CIA station chief in Leopoldville. It was a testament to how insignificant the agency considered the Belgian Congo that it tapped an untested thirty-seven-year-old with zero experience in Africa as its top spy in the colony.

The posting wasn't a prestigious one, but it was cushy. The incumbent station chief in Leopoldville, a genial Yale graduate named Paul Springer, had felt comfortable bringing his five children along with him and having two more after he arrived. Security was lax enough that he left open the window to his ground-floor office at the consulate to catch the breeze. "You'll be on the golf course by two o'clock every afternoon," he told Devlin. He recommended packing two tropical dinner jackets so there was always one to wear when the other was at the cleaners. Berlin this was not.

The State Department was only barely more on top of Africa than the CIA was. When the department set up its Africa Bureau, in 1958, there were more Foreign Service officers in West Germany than in all of Africa, and the continent served as a dumping ground for the mediocre among them. At the State Department's headquarters in the Foggy Bottom neighborhood of Washington, just one analyst in the department's research division covered all of French-speaking Africa south of the Sahara.

The Belgian Congo was a backwater within a backwater. The U.S. consulate in Elisabethville, the capital of Katanga province, was staffed not with State Department diplomats but with personnel from the U.S. Bureau of Mines. At any given time, the U.S. consulate in Leopoldville had only around seven employees, and their French was of uneven quality. None were Black. The State Department worried that sending African Americans might give the Congolese ideas about independence.

"All in all, it is just a little bit sleepy and relaxed," a freshly arrived Foreign Service officer wrote to his family from Leopoldville in 1958. "In my shop—the Consular office—some reports are four months late, some of the record keeping (visa book, for instance) is two years in arrears, the filing has been done by the whim of the individual, and things are done the way they always have been rather than by the book—the Foreign Service handbook."

Bureaucratically, the consulate in Leopoldville was an appendage to the U.S. embassy in Brussels. Cables from the consulate had to be painstakingly encrypted by hand, rather than by means of a cipher machine, a convenience enjoyed by more prominent posts. When the political officers in Leopoldville bothered to comment on the political scene, Brussels made sure to add its own, much longer commentary.

In truth, Leopoldville didn't have much to say. The officers there knew little more about Congolese leaders than what could be gleaned from the newspaper, largely because Belgium forbade contact with them. U.S. embassy officials had to meet with Abako's leader, Kasavubu, clandestinely, sneaking him through the cook's entrance in the kitchen of the consul general's residence. One political officer met with Lumumba at an out-of-the-way restaurant near the Leopoldville zoo; for this and other outreach efforts, he was declared persona non grata in the colony.

America felt it had to tread carefully in Africa. President Dwight D. Eisenhower told the National Security Council, the White House–based group advising him on foreign policy, that he "would like to be on the side of the natives for once." But even the feeblest attempts to win over Congolese sympathies were met with intense Belgian pushback. The U.S. consulate housed a small library run by the U.S. Information Service—Lumumba was a patron—but Belgium lodged a complaint when the consulate offered English classes and started a jazz club. Clarence Randall, a top economic adviser to Eisenhower, summarized the American dilemma in Africa after touring the continent in 1958:

> We must make up our minds whether we stand with the metropole powers in endeavoring to maintain their centralized control over the economies and political freedoms of the developing areas in Africa, or whether we shall throw our influence on the side of those who seek political and economic autonomy. On the one hand, we risk damaging our relationship with some of our NATO partners, but, on the other, we risk for all time losing the friendship of large areas of Africa which inevitably, sooner or later, will be independent. It is a serious dilemma, but we must not take refuge in equivocation.

But the United States could, in fact, equivocate. For now, it stood back and watched events play out, threatening neither European sensitivities nor African aspirations.

The Leopoldville riots might not have roused the United States, but they did perk the Soviets' ears. Moscow's anti-Western worldview seemed to align naturally with the anticolonial movements taking shape across what was now called the Third World (the First World being the capitalist West and the Second World being the Communist East). Under Nikita Khrushchev, the Soviet Union had begun actively courting African nationalists, seeking to bring them into its fold and thereby turning them against the West. It was not long before this strategy brought Moscow into contact with Lumumba.

In April 1959, Lumumba flew to Conakry, the capital of Guinea, for another pan-African conference. The country was still reeling from its traumatic transition into nationhood. In a referendum held the year before, Guinea had been the only one of twenty French territories in the world to vote for immediate independence. The French, hoping to make an example of Guinea, adopted a scorched-earth policy as they left. Thousands of administrators, teachers, and engineers were withdrawn, but not before they had a chance to destroy medicines and burn files. They even unscrewed lightbulbs from office ceilings. The vindictiveness of the French had driven the new country into the arms of the Soviets, and it was thanks only to aid and technicians from Moscow that Guinea was still functioning.

Guinea's president, Ahmed Sékou Touré, surely made that clear to Lumumba when the two met several times at the 1959 conference. So Lumumba's interest must have been piqued when, on the evening of April 17, while eating dinner at a restaurant in Conakry, a Guinean official introduced him to Peter Gerasimov, the recently arrived Soviet ambassador. Lumumba accepted the diplomat's invitation to come by the embassy the next day.

When they met, Lumumba laid the flattery on thick. He wished to visit the Soviet Union, he said, in order to best counter the anti-Communist propaganda circulating in the Congo. Establishing diplomatic ties with Moscow, he promised, would be among the first acts of an independent Congolese government. Then Lumumba got down to business, requesting financial assistance for his political party. Gerasimov promised nothing, noting only that Moscow was following the Congo's struggle closely and that "the African people have a true friend in the Soviet people."

In fact, to the extent that Lumumba was even on Moscow's radar screen, he was seen as an obstacle in the way of Joseph Kasavubu, whom the Soviets accurately identified as the less compromising, more radical leader of the two. After the January riots, the Soviet embassy in Brussels had written a report trying to make sense of the Congo's emerging domestic politics and its key players. Cobbled together from newspaper reports, it concluded that because Lumumba opposed Kasavubu, he must have "succumbed to the provocation of the Belgian colonizers."

Undeterred, Lumumba traveled from Conakry to Brussels, where he again tried to solicit Soviet support, this time through the Belgian Communist Party. Over the course of a five-hour meeting with one of the party's leaders, he praised the Belgian Communists for having finally condemned their country's colonial policy, and he inquired about the possibility of sending Congolese to study in the Soviet Union. When the Soviet embassy in Brussels informed Moscow about the meeting, it allowed that "Lumumba holds a progressive position" and noted that the Congo's large urban population offered promising prospects for Marxism. But once again, no help was forthcoming. Lumumba seemed interested in the Soviets only insofar as they could provide funds. He did not look to them for ideological inspiration. And the Soviets didn't see him as a horse worth backing.

Over the rest of 1959, Lumumba traveled the length and breadth of the Congo, spreading his message of nationalism and unity and signing up MNC members wherever he went. His energy knew no bounds. He could write a press release, find a printer, and get it in the hands of factory workers coming off the line—all in the course of a single day. Taking a page from his beer-marketing playbook, he created affinity groups within the MNC, including a youth wing and a women's section. "He does . . . have the ability to arouse the crowd," reported the U.S. consulate, struggling to assess the strength of this upstart. Lumumba held rallies in provincial capitals and small villages, allowing the party to flourish beyond its Leopoldville origins. Some older Congolese he met on his travels initially viewed him with skepticism. "The whites will never give us independence," they said. Yet after hearing Lumumba, they believed him.

In fact, the whites were losing control. In Kasavubu's stronghold, the area downstream of Leopoldville, the population was boycotting the colonial regime, refusing to pay taxes or appear in court. Whereas ordinary Congolese felt cheated, sensing that Brussels was dragging its feet in implementing the king's promise of independence, white residents felt abandoned in a hasty retreat. When the new minister for the colonies, Maurice Van Hemelrijck, toured the Congo in the spring of 1959, the native population greeted him with placards reading, "No more Colonial Ministers, no more Governor Generals." White settlers splattered him with rotten tomatoes.

Lumumba, having finally given up hope of a cooperative solution to the Congo's future, broke definitively with the Belgian administration. "Down with colonialism!" he cried at an MNC meeting. "Down with the Belgo-Congolese community! Long live immediate independence!"

By March, according to Lumumba, the MNC boasted fifty-eight

thousand members. Yet there was discord within its ranks. Lumumba's co-founders bristled at his tendency to make unilateral commitments on behalf of the party. They resented his contacts with foreign leftists, which grew as he made trips in 1959 not only to Guinea and Belgium but also to Nigeria and Ghana. And they were disturbed by what they viewed as his increasing radicalism. The party was turning into a one-man show, and others wanted some stage time. In July, the MNC formally split in two, leaving Lumumba with a group of loyal supporters but shrinking the party's territorial reach.

Although Lumumba's party had gotten a head start, it was soon but one of many political groups competing for attention. "New political parties have been springing up here like weeds in a vacant lot," a foreign correspondent reported. By November, their number exceeded fifty. "Not a week goes by without a few clerks getting together and deciding to found a party," one member of Belgium's parliament complained. Indeed, the competition was approaching absurdity: a new group called itself the Opposition Party and announced that its purpose would be "not to compete with other parties but to monitor the work of the future government very closely."

In this crowded field, politicians had an incentive to distinguish themselves by issuing ever more aggressive demands. In a matter of weeks, Lumumba advanced his preferred date of independence by a full year, from the beginning of 1961 to the beginning of 1960. Belgian officials grew alarmed. When Lumumba toured his home region, administrators warned him not to undermine colonial authority. Police took notes on his speeches. The Force Publique was called in to put on a show of strength, its soldiers told that "a madman will soon be passing through."

Lumumba was undaunted. "More than sixty chieftains have rallied to the MNC," he wrote to a friend in September. "I am foiling the administration's maneuvers. I have had dazzling success everywhere."

Lumumba was at his most optimistic. That same month, he published a poem in the MNC's newspaper, *Independence*. Its final stanzas overflowed with hope:

The shores of the great river, full of promises,
Henceforth belong to you.

This earth and all its riches
Henceforth belong to you.
And the fiery sun, high in a colorless sky,
Will burn away your pain
Its searing rays will forever dry
The tears your forefathers shed
Tormented by their tyrannical masters
On this soil that you still cherish.
And you will make the Congo a free and happy nation
In the heart of this giant Black Africa.

In late October 1959, Lumumba flew to Stanleyville for a convening of parties that all opposed federalism in favor of a unitary state postindependence. He was welcomed as a favorite son. At the airport, a crowd insisted on carrying him across the tarmac. "Long live the king of kings!" they cried. This sort of reception was not unusual. "Lumumba's mission is to convert," his secretary put it. "He's our Christ."

At 7:00 p.m. on Thursday, October 29, Lumumba stood before an excited crowd of three thousand in the Stanleyville neighborhood where he'd once lived. By now, the Belgians had offered more details about their plan for independence. It was, Lumumba said, "a simulacrum of democracy." In elections in December, voters would choose local councils, which would then select some members of provincial legislatures, with the Belgian government filling some of the seats itself in what it spun as "training for democracy." The executive branch would remain largely in Belgian hands; only in five years would complete sovereignty be granted. To Lumumba, this was just another stalling tactic, and if the Congolese didn't push back, they would never obtain their freedom. "Independence has never been given," he liked to say. "It must be wrested."

Lumumba enjoined his audience to boycott the coming local elections and partake in a campaign of civil disobedience. He asked people to parade peaceably through the streets of Stanleyville to demand real independence.

"We will walk with dignity and show that we are determined," he said. "That, being unarmed, we fear nothing."

"Yes!" the crowd cried out.

"We don't care!"

"Yes!"

"We will die for the country."

"Yes!"

"Today, Belgian colonization has ended," he said. "It's over! Today, there's another program. There's another way. We have always walked forward and forward. That's over. There's a danger in that. Let's not continue. We are going to turn our backs on Belgium."

The crowd broke out in glee. What they didn't know, however, was that somewhere in the room a portable tape recorder was capturing Lumumba's every word. Soon the audio would be transcribed and used as evidence.

The governor of the province had been following Lumumba's activities in Stanleyville with concern. Late at night, after Lumumba had delivered his fiery speech, the governor worried aloud to his diary, writing that "Lumumba has declared war on Belgium." He feared things might turn violent: "Tonight at the meeting, listeners waved machetes and spears. That hasn't been seen before. I think it is time for me to intervene."

The next morning, the city erupted in riot. Congolese protesters with painted faces launched stones and spears at the police, who responded with tear gas and gunfire. At the local prison, inmates tore bricks from the walls and whipped them at white prisoners. What had happened in Leopoldville in January was now happening in Stanleyville. Again, the Force Publique was sent in, with extra companies arriving from outside the city, including a tank division that patrolled the streets. As before, the dead, who numbered in the dozens, were all Black.

Lumumba was charged with inciting the riot, with officials claiming he had drawn on "lessons in revolutionary technique" imparted during his travels abroad. He evaded arrest for two days, shuttling between friends in the *cité*, before the police caught up with him at his brother's house, sitting at the kitchen table. A high-ranking officer made the arrest. Lumumba was so hated among whites that the administration feared a junior officer might prove trigger-happy.

One white Stanleyville notable, a doctor, approached the provincial governor to express disbelief that the arresting officers couldn't simply have shot Lumumba on sight and claimed self-defense. The governor countered with his own suggestive proposal: "If I send you to his prison, will you give him an 'effective injection'?" The notion of assassinating Lumumba, joke or not, was now in the air.

Once again, Lumumba found himself imprisoned in Stanleyville, this time for explicitly political reasons. "I have committed no crime, no misdeed, other than having demanded our independence," he wrote to a friend. He spent a month confined to a prison bathroom, trying to catch up on sleep yet lacking a blanket to keep him warm at night.

While Lumumba was awaiting trial, two VIPs passed through Stanleyville. The first was King Baudouin, who faced a far frostier reception this time than he had four years earlier. When he stepped off the plane, a crowd of angry MNC supporters rushed toward him, forcing his guards to form a protective huddle around him, bayonets fixed. During his previous visit, crowds had chanted, "Long live the King." Now they were yelling, "Free Lumumba!" and "Independence now!"

The king's first priority was to visit a monument of King Leopold II to pay his respects on the fiftieth anniversary of his death, but here, too, a massive crowd of protesters blocked his path. Only after it was cleared with smoke grenades could Baudouin lay a wreath. Dispirited, he turned to the governor and predicted, "We will abandon the Congo in shame."

The second prominent visitor to pass through town was Dag Hammarskjöld, the UN secretary-general. His stopover in Stanleyville was just one of twenty-five he was making in Africa, for the purpose of forming contacts in what he called "the great new continent coming to the United Nations." Hammarskjöld shared British Prime Minister Harold Macmillan's sense that "the wind of change is blowing through this continent" and had declared 1960 the "Year of Africa." French Cameroon had just become independent, and Nigeria, French Togoland, and Somalia were scheduled to follow suit. Yet on New Year's Day, it wasn't evident that the Congo would join them in the ranks of independent nations.

Accordingly, Hammarskjöld's stop in Stanleyville lasted less than twenty-four hours, more refueling break than substantive visit, and he made no effort to meet with the political prisoner whose name he likely had never heard. The Belgians had discouraged the secretary-general from visiting Congolese political leaders and instead took him sightseeing in a dugout canoe near the rapids of Stanley Falls. There, he watched fishermen at work straddling wooden poles as they raised cornucopia-shaped nets from the froth below. Hammarskjöld snapped away with his Hasselblad.

It was the odd moment of leisure on an exhausting five-week trip. The secretary-general and several staffers flew from city to city, greeted each time by red carpets and military bands, and rarely spent more than two nights in any given place. The group rode a plane chartered from Scandinavian Airlines that was furnished with beds and tables, which offered a respite from the sweltering African cities and endless glad-handing below. "Nice to be home again," the travelers would say after boarding. In Liberia, a Christmas tree appeared in the cabin, and en route to Guinea, a holiday feast was held: herring, sardines, and pig's trotters, served with mulled wine. Hammarskjöld sipped a Norwegian aquavit. The sense of home aboard the plane was shattered briefly in Addis Ababa, where, upon landing, a flooded carburetor caused the left engine to burst into flames. A fast-thinking crew member, armed with a fire extinguisher, warded off catastrophe.

Those who worked for Hammarskjöld considered him aloof. Colleagues who made the mistake of trying to be chummy found themselves coldly rebuffed. But he was loyal and could come through with touching, thoughtful gestures. Near the end of his whirlwind tour of the continent, he placed an order with a Stockholm jeweler. The staffers accompanying him each received a pair of solid-gold cuff links, stamped with the United Nations emblem, a projection of the globe wreathed by olive branches.

As an organization devoted to world peace, what was the UN's proper role in newly independent Africa? Hammarskjöld's main worry was not that self-rule would lead to armed conflict but that the new states were unprepared for the economic and administrative disruption that lay ahead. "The image I take back with me is a refreshing one of youth and vigor," Hammarskjöld told the press near the end of his trip, but "independence still represents a kind of shock impact."

—

After a short trial, the court in Stanleyville sentenced Lumumba to six months in prison for his role in the riots. The next day, he was tossed into a van—"like a chimpanzee," he said—and shoved into the rear compartment of a plane bound for Elisabethville, the capital of Katanga. "Thrown on plane barefoot, shirtless, handcuffed and physically assaulted till arrived," read a frantic cable to his lawyers. A police commissioner escorted him onto the tarmac, slick with rain, where a group of whites jeered and photographed him. "Dirty monkey!" they yelled, reaching for the all-purpose insult. Then he was driven to a prison in an isolated mining town hours away—a place where the authorities hoped he would be forgotten.

While Lumumba was behind bars once more, however, Belgium caved to a key demand of Congolese activists. It grudgingly announced that instead of dictating the terms of the Congo's eventual independence, it would negotiate with leading Congolese politicians at a "roundtable." "I accept this expression, no matter how romantic it may be, even if it evokes King Arthur," August De Schryver, the new minister of colonies, said. Yet with Lumumba in prison, the roundtable would be missing its most celebrated knight.

Chapter 8

The Rounded Table

NINETEEN FIFTY-NINE WAS poised to be a turning point in the history of the modern Congo, yet for Joseph Mobutu the bulk of it went by in a cramped flat in Brussels. He had moved to the capital, wife and children in tow, for an internship with Inforcongo, a media operation responsible for churning out cheery propaganda about Belgium's prized African possession. It was far from an obvious move for a pro-independence journalist-cum-political operative, but the posting was prestigious enough that Mobutu had put great effort into obtaining it. The family lived in a small apartment at 44 Rue Georges Garnir, a redbrick row house near the train tracks in the working-class neighborhood of Schaerbeek. To get around, he drove a compact *voiturette*, the only car he could afford.

Outside his internship, he enrolled in journalism classes and ran errands for Lumumba. When Lumumba visited Brussels, Mobutu helped sort through the stacks of mail addressed to him. After Lumumba was arrested, Mobutu arranged for the shipment of books—a biography of Gandhi, among others—to his prison cell. Yet the renewed imprisonment of his patron left Mobutu in an awkward position in January 1960. As scores of Congolese delegates dressed in three-piece suits and porkpie hats arrived in Brussels for the Belgo-Congolese Roundtable, he found himself offstage, with no part to play.

He sought to change that one afternoon, as various influential Congolese delegates met discreetly in the basement of the stately Plaza Hotel. In a bid to wring serious concessions from the Belgian government, they had formed a common front and come together to talk strategy. Half an hour into the meeting, Mobutu walked in. He pulled up a chair and sat down as the room fell silent.

"Are you a student or an intern here in Belgium?" asked Cléophas Kamitatu, the politician presiding over the meeting.

"Yes," Mobutu said.

The common front had a rule about this: compatriots who had spent too much time in Brussels were deemed a liability, potentially corrupted by Belgian interests. Only delegates who had come straight from the Congo were allowed to participate.

"Well, please excuse me," Kamitatu said, "but you don't belong here."

Mobutu didn't budge. "I am part of the MNC delegation, and I must attend this meeting."

Kamitatu threatened to adjourn the meeting if Mobutu stayed. Finally, a fellow MNC delegate intervened. "Joseph," he said gently, "you have to leave."

Mobutu relented and got up, slamming the door on his way out.

The encounter didn't sit right with Kamitatu. How had Mobutu come to know the exact time and location of a secret meeting? Mobutu's colleagues from the MNC denied having let anything slip. The only outsiders who had been in the know were the hotel's managers. Yet the Belgian government was no doubt interested in these internal deliberations, and Congolese students living in Brussels were known to earn extra cash by feeding information to the State Security Service, Belgium's intelligence agency. All this led Kamitatu to an uncomfortable conclusion: Mobutu had to be an informant for Belgian intelligence.

In fact, Mobutu had probably been in the pay of Belgian intelligence as early as 1956, the year he had left the army. According to the head of Belgium's intelligence operations in the Congo, Mobutu furnished the Belgians with detailed information about Congolese political leaders, much of which was passed along to the CIA station in Brussels, where Larry Devlin worked. There was also the curious fact that the man who had arranged for Mobutu's internship at Inforcongo, William Ugeux, had served as the head of intelligence for the Belgian resistance during World War II, further suggesting links between the ambitious young Congolese journalist and the Belgian spy establishment.

Lumumba claimed he knew about his protégé's extracurricular activities but excused the spying as an innocent way of making ends meet. In Mobutu's defense, he was hardly alone. By one estimate, more than half of the Congolese political class at the time had, at one point or another, collaborated with Belgian intelligence. At any rate, Lumumba had made up his mind: Mobutu could be trusted.

On the morning of January 20, the delegates stepped onto the plush carpet of the Congress Palace, a convention center in downtown Brussels, for the official opening session of the roundtable. Upon entering the conference room, they discovered that the eponymous table was not round but merely had rounded corners—an omen, perhaps, of the Belgian government's penchant for partially fulfilled promises. For what it was worth, the Belgians were at least deigning to negotiate with them. Congolese leaders took their seats next to Belgian ministers and parliamentarians. Potted palm trees lined the wooden walls, as if to bring a hint of the tropics to Europe.

Soon, the room was bursting with activity. More than a hundred journalists pushed against one another and against some eighty Congolese delegates representing twenty-odd parties. Many of the delegates were meeting one another for the first time, and many held opposing views on what independence would mean in practice. Some, such as representatives of Abako and the MNC, envisioned an immediate and definitive break from Belgium. Others, among them the traditional chiefs and members of the National Progress Party, preferred to maintain strong ties. Critics suspected this moderate faction of being in the pocket of Belgian interests. Riffing on the National Progress Party's French initials, PNP, they called it *le Parti des Nègres Payés*—"the Party of Paid Negroes."

At 10:40 a.m., a bell rang, and the doors closed. The Belgian prime minister, Gaston Eyskens, approached the rostrum. "From the bottom of our hearts, we beg you to speak without fear," he told the Congolese delegates. There was no need for such encouragement. Any hopes the Belgian negotiators had of peeling off the moderates from the hard-liners evaporated when the common front announced two ultimatums: First, for negotiations to proceed, any agreement reached would need to be binding. This was a departure from the conference's framework, but the Belgians gave in. Second, Lumumba had to be released from prison in Katanga so he could attend the roundtable. Lumumba's allies naturally wanted their leader present; his enemies worried that if he were kept away, he would denounce the conference as a sellout and refuse to abide by its conclusions. Everyone would have to leap into the unknown together, arms linked.

On this second issue, the Belgians also relented, as they, too, considered Lumumba a bigger threat outside the meeting room than inside. On the morning of the fourth day of negotiations, they announced Lumumba's immediate release. The room broke out in applause. The only one evidently not pleased with this development was Joseph Kasavubu, who walked out in a huff and was soon seen speeding away from his hotel in a taxi. Kasavubu's long-standing rivalry with Lumumba was no secret, but not even his fellow Abako members had expected him to quit the conference. At 8:00 the next morning, they were spotted at the Plaza Hotel clutching their heads and commiserating over glasses of neat whiskey.

Lumumba landed in Brussels that same day. Mobutu drove his *voi-turette* to the airport to meet him. He had sacrificed his bedsheets to serve as a canvas: "LONG LIVE LUMUMBA! LONG LIVE THE MNC! LONG LIVE THE CONGO!" Lumumba posed in front of the makeshift banner, arms raised, displaying bandages on his wrists that covered cuts where handcuffs had dug into his skin, stigmata from his recent captivity.

Lumumba's new home was room 53 of the Cosmopolitan Hotel, modest quarters with a bed too short to accommodate his rangy frame. On a table were scraps of paper bearing hand-drawn designs for a new Congolese flag. After three months in prison, the leader of the MNC had a lot of catching up to do. The telephone rang constantly; visitors interrupted him at all hours. Soon, Lumumba was back to his old schedule, rarely sleeping more than four hours per night. He enlisted Mobutu to serve as his personal secretary, a job that included monitoring the voluminous coverage Lumumba was receiving in the Brussels press. Belgian newspaper readers, used to skipping the articles about the Congo, now engrossed themselves in blow-by-blow reports from the roundtable. Glancing up from their papers, they couldn't help but notice the unusual sight of hundreds of Black men in downtown Brussels, boarding specially chartered streetcars that ferried them to and from the conference. One day, Lumumba was speaking with a journalist when a woman approached and asked him who he was. "There," she said to her companions, "I told you it was that man Lumumba."

From the moment Lumumba joined the roundtable, he dominated the proceedings. As Mobutu put it, "In less than twenty-four hours, the prisoner was promoted to a statesman." Lumumba's opening shot was to demand independence by June 1—just four months away. The Congolese were stunned when the Belgians agreed to a compromise, settling on June 30. No one had expected it would be this easy, but as it happened, they were pushing against an open door. More and more Belgian politicians worried about getting dragged into a lengthy colonial war, the type of conflict that had humiliated the Dutch in Indonesia and that the French had fought in Indochina and were now fighting in Algeria. Those who opposed holding on to the colony came up with a slogan: "Not a centime, not a soldier for the Congo." It was time to let go.

The story of Congolese independence was less that of a long struggle undertaken by the oppressed Africans than that of a colonial state suddenly off-loading its prized possession, much to the surprise of a people who had only recently come to view freedom as an attainable goal. "We are all feeling like someone who has been given a present which he has wanted for a long time but did not dare believe that he would get," a Congolese journalist wrote of the prevailing mood among delegates.

That night, Lumumba and the others celebrated at the Plaza Hotel to the sound of the Congo's biggest band, African Jazz. The Belgians in the room, used to thinking of their colonial subjects as primitive drum beaters, couldn't believe their ears. Suspecting that these tuxedoed Black men were miming to a hidden record player, they lifted the instruments to see if they were real. The band debuted a catchy number it had just composed for the occasion, "Indépendance Cha-Cha":

Independence, cha-cha, we got it
Oh! Independence, cha-cha, we reached it

Oh! The roundtable, cha-cha, they won it
Oh! Independence, cha-cha, we got it.

The subsequent verses listed a string of politicians and parties, championing the spirit of unity that had made victory possible:

Assoreco and Abako
Are acting as one
Conakat and the Cartel
Joined forces in the common front
Bolikango, Kasavubu
Lumumba and Kalonji
Bolya, Tshombe, Kamitatu
Oh Essandja, Honorable Kanza

The MNC and Ugeco
Abazi and the PDC
The PSA and African Jazz
At the roundtable, they won

The unity crumbled the next morning, not long after the delegates filed into the conference room, hungover and late. Congolese independence now had a set date, but everything else remained to be decided and fought over. From the future state's system of government to its national anthem, opinions diverged on almost every issue.

The thorniest among them was whether to set up a unitary state with authority concentrated in the capital, a federal one with power devolved to the provinces, or something in between. The Belgians had governed the Congo as a single centralized entity. Lumumba wanted to keep things that way, arguing that the new state would need a strong central government to manage the strains of fledgling nationhood. "If federalism were to triumph," he warned, "the Congo would split apart before five years—Belgium and the world be my witness."

Not everybody agreed. One of the more vocal dissenters was a delegate named Moise Tshombe, a politician from the province of Katanga. Tshombe's party, Conakat, was built on the notion that

Katanga's vast mineral revenues should stay within the province and rightfully belonged to the ethnic groups who had lived there the longest. In almost every way, Tshombe and Lumumba were a study in contrasts. Unlike the lithe, bookish, and refined MNC leader, Tshombe was thick, blunt, and flashy. He was not a self-made man born to unknown parents but the scion of one of the Congo's few wealthy Black families, the owners of plantations, hotels, and stores. His father had reportedly been the first Congolese to buy his own car. Tshombe was ready to make common cause with the white elites and their conservative politics if it suited his interests. And whereas Lumumba fancied himself a leader of all Congolese and pan-African in outlook, Tshombe couldn't see past his people and his province.

The conflict between the two came to a head when negotiations at the roundtable turned to the question of mining rights. The stakes were massive: Union Minière du Haut Katanga, the powerful and highly profitable Belgian mining monopoly operating in Katanga, generated half of all tax revenue in the Congo. Lumumba considered these riches as belonging to the nation at large, not just to a single province. Tshombe vehemently disagreed, leading Lumumba to accuse him of doing the bidding of Belgian financial interests—not an altogether outlandish claim, considering that Tshombe's adviser for the roundtable discussions was the leader of a white settler group in Katanga. The dispute turned physical during a recess, forcing other delegates to step in and keep the two men from lunging at each other. Cries and slaps echoed through the lobby.

The Belgians, it soon became clear, had their own conception of what Congolese self-determination would look like. "Independence will not mean much if the date of June 30 coincides with an economic decline in your country," one of their representatives, Raymond Scheyven, warned one morning. Scheyven recalled a trip he had taken to Indonesia two years prior, not long after the country had gained independence from the Netherlands. The economy was in tatters, exports had cratered, and bandits roamed the countryside—the consequence of the Indonesians having scared away Dutch technicians and money. It was an odd choice of example, for if anyone was to learn a lesson from Indonesia's four-year war of independence, it was a small European state trying desperately to hold on to its faraway colony. Scheyven then launched into a two-hour lecture on the Congolese economy. He threw statistic after statistic at the room—population projections, export shares, copper prices, budget estimates, revenue growth rates—all of which pointed to the conclusion that the Congolese economy was a finicky machine in need of expert Belgian maintenance.

If the presentation seemed designed to confuse the Congolese—who had for years been barred from studying economics—that was because it was. Right before the roundtable opened, William Ugeux, not only Mobutu's boss at Inforcongo but also a longtime Belgian source for the U.S. embassy, met with American officials to preview his country's negotiating strategy. The Belgians were reportedly operating on "the thesis that words were not of great importance—that concepts like independence, sovereignty and the right to give out ministerial and other titles were something which should be taken at a rather cheap value, and therefore granted in exchange for concessions on important things." The U.S. embassy's memorandum continued:

> The Belgian play would therefore be to give up without too much difficulty the things of no consequence, or of consequence only in semantic terms, and to try on the other hand to maintain Belgian control over essential central services—the army, economic policy, foreign policy—at least for a certain period. The tactic would be, as soon as the week or so's wrangling over procedure is over with, to begin to throw at the Congolese the concrete problems that they would have to deal with once power is transferred, and thus to demonstrate to them their own inability to carry out these tasks by themselves at least for a first period. The hope is that the Congolese would then themselves turn around and ask the Belgians to continue to handle these questions.

Scheyven's scare tactics worked beautifully. After his lecture, all economic questions were postponed to a separate conference in the spring.

The Belgian government was defining "independence" narrowly in other areas, too. It envisioned a Congolese government in which Belgians still occupied key posts, including those of ambassadors and ministers. The Ministry of Defense was to be headed by General Émile Janssens, the conservative, unbending commander of the Force Publique. Just days before giving his economics lecture, Scheyven told the U.S. embassy that Janssens would act on behalf of Belgium, not the Congo. "He would presumably take his orders from the President of the new Congolese republic," the embassy notes summarized, "but if these orders were of a destructive nature, the Belgian government would hope that he would use his common sense and not follow them."

Throughout the negotiations, Belgium pushed for the new state to be made in its image. When a Congolese delegate proposed creating a body for resolving disputes between the two chambers of parliament—a feature of many democracies—the chief Belgian negotiator dismissed the idea, saying, "Belgium does not know of institutions of this kind." At one point, a Belgian member of parliament even begged the Congolese delegates to let Belgian expatriates vote in Congolese elections, or else be guilty of "racial segregation." (When the Congolese asked whether this would mean that they would be able to vote in Belgian elections, the matter was dropped.)

The Belgians also envisioned a continued role for King Baudouin as head of state. In designing the new state, the Congolese had good reasons to choose the stability and strength of a presidential system of government, with a powerful executive staying in office for fixed terms, rather than a parliamentary system with the risk of frequent cabinet reshuffles and snap elections. But without debate, everyone agreed to transpose Belgium's system of government to the Congo. Real decision-making authority would lie with a prime minister, but floating above him would be a head of state. In Belgium, that was the king—endowed with certain constitutional powers but reduced over the years to a figurehead—and the Belgians made it clear that Baudouin should remain the head of state of an independent Congo, too. So, in fact, did many of the Congolese present. The queen of England was still the head of state of independent Ghana, was she not? Lumumba would have none of it. "On July 1, the sovereign of the Congolese state must be a Congolese, just as the sovereign of Belgium is a Belgian," he said.

Ultimately, the question was deferred, with some imagining that

the Congo would choose its own head of state and others thinking Baudouin would remain. With or without Baudouin, the new
country would have its executive leadership split between a head of
state and a prime minister, but without the decades of parliamentary
tradition that had made the former largely impotent. It was a recipe
for conflict.

The outcome of the debate on federalism also built instability into
the new state's structure. In the end, Lumumba and Tshombe split
the difference between a federal and a unitary design. The Congo
would remain a single state with a central government, but to fend off
the threat of secessionism, voters would also elect their own provincial legislatures, which would in turn pick provincial leaders—fertile
ground for rivalries between national and regional players.

In just four weeks, the delegates had drafted a system of government from scratch, a process that usually took years. Sections of the
constitution were copied and pasted straight from the Belgian one.
The conference had occasionally degenerated into what *Time* called
"a mad mélange of inflammatory speeches, door-slamming walkouts,
rival press conferences and angry communiqués." Still, after weeks
of haggling, the Congolese had accomplished something that until
recently had seemed unthinkable: they had reached an agreement
with the Belgian government on the contours of an autonomous
Congo. "We are now going home with independence in our pockets,"
Lumumba said at the closing session of the roundtable. He added,
"We will now forget all the errors of the past, all the causes of dis-
sension between us, and look only to this marvelous, smiling future
that awaits us."

For all the weighty decisions made inside the conference hall during
the day, much of the action took place outside it in the evening, in
the homes, hotel rooms, and embassies of Brussels. Delegates met to
talk strategy. Plainclothes policemen stalked hotel lobbies, trying to
pick up rumors of Congolese plans. And diplomats from both sides of
the Cold War were feeling out the Congolese political class. For both
the Americans and the Soviets, the former colonies now entering
global life offered a chance to spread their foundational ideologies—

freedom, in Washington's case, and justice, in Moscow's. At a more strategic level, the Third World promised each power an opportunity to rack up allies and contain the influence of the other.

On February 19, Lumumba entered the apartment of Jean Terfve, a lawyer and a leading figure in the Belgian Communist Party, and took a seat in an armchair. He had struck up a friendship with Terfve and his wife—it was she who had changed his wrist bandages when he first arrived—but his visit was more than a social call. Terfve had invited him to meet with Boris Savinov, first secretary at the Soviet embassy. Savinov praised Lumumba as an "ardent fighter for freedom" and pledged Moscow's support for an independent Congo. Yet when Lumumba asked for Soviet money—elections for the Congo's new, independent parliament were less than five months away, and he had a campaign to run—the ambassador was noncommittal, just as his colleague in Guinea had been. Savinov promised only to convey the request to Moscow.

In truth, Lumumba remained an unappealing candidate for Soviet support. Reporting back to Moscow, Savinov cautioned that Lumumba wanted "aid without any strings attached." Lumumba might be popular enough to become president or prime minister, but there was little reason to think he would be a natural friend to the Soviets. "The ideological and political views of Lumumba are still not fully developed," Savinov wrote.

Worse, Lumumba bridled at the Soviet Union's attempts to influence Congolese affairs. At the roundtable, he denounced "certain delegates to the conference who have flown off to other countries that I do not care to mention," a reference to trips that the Belgian Communist Party had organized to East Germany, the Soviet Union, and Czechoslovakia.

Other Congolese delegates seemed to think more like Moscow. Promising Marxists, they spoke in the language of class warfare and called for the nationalization of Belgian companies. For them, Lumumba was too cozy with the imperialists, a charge they whispered into Soviet ears. Just three days before meeting Lumumba, Savinov heard from one skeptic, Alphonse Nguvulu, a founding member of the MNC who had defected from the party, that Lumumba was a pro-American demagogue.

Lumumba did not hide his interest in the United States even as he solicited aid from the Soviets. On February 25, after canceling once, he met with Savinov's American counterpart, William Burden, a Vanderbilt heir who had donated his way into becoming Eisenhower's ambassador to Belgium. Lumumba "made it very clear that he wanted an invitation to the U.S.," noted a memorandum of the meeting. On Communism, "Lumumba talked a very good game indeed," claiming that Eastern influence harmed the Congo.

Yet Burden harbored some of the same concerns as the Soviets, suspecting that Lumumba was merely telling the Americans what they wanted to hear: "He gives the impression of a man who would probably go far in spite of the fact that almost nobody trusts him; who is certainly for sale, but only on his own terms; and who would probably not meet the famous definition which was given a century ago of the honest politician as one who, when bought, stayed bought."

Lumumba had made two faux pas in particular. First, he kept a taxi waiting for the entirety of his meeting with Burden, which the Americans took as a sign of profligacy or, worse yet, of secret third-party funding for the young politician. Second, he arrived in the company of Jean Van Lierde, a Belgian pacifist who had made his name as a conscientious objector and had come to know Lumumba through anticolonial circles. Van Lierde did not sit in on the conversation with Burden, but his ties to Lumumba disconcerted the buttoned-down embassy staff, who wrote with evident disdain of his "shifty" eyes and his "beatnik-type scraggly beard."

American officials assumed the worst about Lumumba. Ever since he landed in Brussels, cables from the U.S. embassy there and from the consulate in Leopoldville had portrayed him as unprincipled, interpreting as sinister behavior typical of any shrewd politician. January 28: "He has again demonstrated his quick-footed opportunism by taking a position more moderate than the 'moderate' parties." February 3: "He is a rank opportunist, but nonetheless a practical politician." February 10: "Lumumba is presumably looking for support in whatever quarter he can find it, with typical opportunism." February 13: "He will likely pick up most followers in tribal areas through demagogy and usual brilliant weathervane tactics." February 15: "Lumumba's glibness and oratorical qualities attract the mob."

More often than not, these opinions were shaped by meetings with Lumumba's political rivals, who were jockeying for American support, and Belgian officials, who had a particular distaste for the anticolonial rabble-rouser. Their views were passed on credulously to Washington, as were allegations of Communist support for Lumumba. An employee of Inforcongo told the U.S. embassy that Lumumba was receiving 30,000 francs a month from Guinea, presumably of Soviet origin. Another contact told the CIA that Lumumba was getting campaign advice from the Belgian Communist Party. Such hearsay was relayed with no mention of potential bias. Backbiting became biographical fact.

Larry Devlin was good at getting people to talk. He knew when to lay on the flattery, when to crack a disarming joke, when to offer an inviting drink or cigarette. With generous eye contact and attentive questioning, he made whomever he spoke with feel like the most important person in the room. And he had a remarkable ability to get any meeting.

Devlin had been tapped to serve as CIA station chief in Leopoldville, but for now, he remained in Brussels, meeting Belgians and Congolese on the sidelines of the roundtable. One night, he dined with a Belgian journalist and complained that he had been denied an appointment with Joseph Kasavubu. "Well, I see him tomorrow," the reporter said. "You can go as my secretary." That was how Devlin met the reclusive Kasavubu—pretending to be an assistant, holding the journalist's briefcase, and keeping his mouth shut for fear that his rough accent would betray him.

Like others in the U.S. embassy, Devlin became a receptacle for negative assessments of Lumumba. When he met with a group of traditional chiefs, conservatives who resented the urban politicians dominating the roundtable, they suggested that Lumumba was receiving foreign money to fund his frequent trips abroad, suspicions that Devlin dutifully passed on to Washington. (One of the leaders, whom he described as "a small bird-like Congolese with a small moustache that seems to go with his stature," could not speak French but expressed himself in his native language with "the dramatic gestures and movements of a tribal dancer.") Devlin heard similar allegations from Victor Nendaka, a Leopoldville bar owner and former high-ranking member of the MNC, but noted the "extremely vague and often contradictory" bent of Nendaka's accusations.

Among a series of less than credible sources, one man stood out. In an effort to get to know the Congolese delegates, the U.S. embassy threw a cocktail party. Afterward, the staff gathered to share their impressions. "One name kept coming up," Devlin said: Joseph Mobutu. "Everyone agreed that this was an extremely intelligent man, very young, perhaps immature, but a man with great potential."

Chapter 9

Uhuru!

"WHAT IS INDEPENDENCE?"
"Will it come in a package?"
"When will it come?"
"May I unwrap it right away?"

According to a tale making the rounds in 1960, those were the questions many Congolese were asking as they learned of the coming change. Outside elite circles, independence often remained an abstract, alien concept. On street corners, swindlers were said to be selling mysterious shoeboxes wrapped in brown paper scrawled with the word "independence." Buyers paid 50 francs and were told not to open the package until June 30. (When they did, they would find it filled with dirt.) Those with deeper pockets could spend 2,000 francs on a dubious certificate entitling them to take over the house of a departing Belgian—and his car for another 1,000 francs. Nervous settlers swapped stories about answering a knock on their door to find a stranger asking for a tour of the house he would soon own.

As June 30 neared, fantasies spread. Taxes would cease to be levied; salaries would multiply; prisoners would walk free. "Everyone will have plenty to eat, lots of clothes, cars to drive," a rural villager told an American anthropologist. Families scrubbed the gravestones of their ancestors, hoping they would rise from the dead.

In the months after the roundtable, the Belgians did little to clear up the confusion surrounding independence. Although the new administration would nominally be in the hands of Congolese ministers, its top ranks were to remain filled with Belgian bureaucrats.

Meanwhile, some three hundred Congolese were rushed through a bare-bones, monthlong training program for aspiring functionaries in Brussels.

Economic arrangements were similarly rash. A new group of Congolese delegates gathered in Brussels for a follow-up roundtable to address all the economic questions that had been conveniently postponed—namely, what would happen to the colony's considerable shares in mines, factories, railroads, and other companies? Again, Congolese representatives and Belgian officials sat in the lavish conference room of the Congress Palace, only this time the Congolese politicians sent mostly lower-level delegates in their stead. Lumumba stayed in the Congo, thinking his time was better spent campaigning for the colony's upcoming, first-ever legislative elections. He sent Mobutu. "I need you," Lumumba told his friend.

It was a decidedly uncomfortable experience. Mobutu felt outmatched by the Belgian bigwigs on the other side of the negotiating table. In many cases, university students found themselves facing off against their professors. "I felt like the cowboy in the western who is systematically ripped off by city slickers," he said. The outcome of the negotiations reflected this imbalance. Most of the companies operating in the Congo would move their registration to Belgium, thus depriving the new state of tax revenue. The lion's share of the colony's ownership in companies would also stay in Belgian hands, while the new state would be left holding most of the public debt. "We got rolled," Mobutu admitted.

Meanwhile, the facade of a peaceful and united Congo—as envisioned by the roundtable delegates—was beginning to show cracks. For decades, the colonial regime had stifled tensions among the Congo's many different ethnic groups, disputes motivated by perceived inequities or historical wrongs. (In some cases, the Belgians had exacerbated those tensions by playing favorites.) But with independence looming, many groups—especially ethnic minorities—worried about their place in the new state. In Kasai province, long-simmering ethnic grievances boiled over between the Luba people, relative newcomers in that region who called themselves "the Jews of the Congo," and the more numerous but less politically powerful Lulua. In May, militants from each side raided areas occupied by the other. Men armed with homemade guns, spears, and knives set thatched-roof huts aflame and hacked up the residents. Body parts littered the streets.

One Belgian administrator dealt with the collapse of state authority by simply giving up. As he formally transferred responsibility for his territory to Congolese leaders months before independence, he said, "I have nothing left to say but to appeal to all, young and old, men and women, to reestablish yourselves an authority and save your country from anarchy." *Good luck,* he seemed to be saying as he tossed over the keys. *You'll need it.*

The impending arrival of self-rule struck fear in the hearts of the 113,000 whites living in the Congo. Although the Belgian government was ready to part with its colony, the Belgians living in it were not. Many had spent decades here, where a strict racial hierarchy and cheap Black labor afforded them status and luxuries they could scarcely access back home. Few were ready to trade the spacious villas of Leopoldville or Elisabethville, along with their gardeners, maids, cooks, and drivers, for ordinary apartments on the outskirts of Bruges or Ghent.

Yet staying past independence would bring its own ignominy. To many, the idea of addressing a Black man as "Monsieur," of waiting behind him in line, of advising rather than commanding him—all that was simply unthinkable, a nightmare saturnalia that upended the natural positions of master and servant. The mere prospect of independence had already filled the Congolese with new swagger. They signed chits at cafés with no intention of paying. They circulated blacklists of "anti-African" Belgian administrators who were to be expelled as soon as possible. Boards spiked with nails appeared in the roads, and when white motorists stopped to remove them, they were pelted with stones. Break-ins and purse snatchings multiplied. A young police officer reported that villagers used to wave at him with their children. Now, he complained, "you see pantomimes of throat-cutting."

In a colony where white men had for a century had their way with Black women, the notion that the tables might be turned spread hysteria unlike anything else. "Until now, it was African mothers who had to look after their mulatto offspring," a Congolese newspaper editorialized. "Now the white woman will have to take care of mulattoes born from African men." Such predictions were taken as unequivocal threats of rape. Rumors told of white women picking up the telephone to hear a stranger telling them he had "chosen" them for the time after independence. A group of Belgian civil servants appealed for protection to King Baudouin from the looming "massacre of the Belgians, and rape of our wives and daughters." Anxious white families fired their houseboys and hired white babysitters to care for their children. They flooded their gardens with bright lights and bought Doberman pinschers to stand guard at their doors. Some hid grenades under their beds. When leaving their houses, many whites carried nine-millimeter revolvers.

Others simply left. Belgians in the Congo usually took a long summer vacation every year, but in 1960 thousands flew out early on one-way tickets. Schools moved up final exams. Sabena, Belgium's national airline, was booked solid through June; it had to lease planes from other airlines in order to add an extra seventy flights a month from Leopoldville. Ships steaming to Antwerp were packed to the gunwales with preemptive refugees. They took with them what they could, emptying their houses of every valuable that wasn't nailed down and transferring their funds to European banks. So much money was leaving the colony—$182 million in the first quarter of 1960—that Belgium capped remittances at 10,000 francs per family per month.

An official at Union Minière in Katanga province downplayed the exodus of his Belgian workers as a minor adjustment in vacation schedules, made to avoid the celebrations surrounding independence. "They are afraid some drunken Congolese will make trouble," he told the press. "But very few are leaving for good." But far more than excessive drinking, many of the departing Belgians feared Black rule itself. Rather than cede power, some settlers considered carving out their own state in Katanga, an independent territory where white rule would endure. They explored the possibility of merging the province with the neighboring Federation of Rhodesia and Nyasaland, a British colony to the southeast. Roy Welensky, the federation's prime minister, met secretly with a Belgian delegation from Katanga and let it slip to a reporter that he might "hold out the hand of friend-ship" to the province when the Congo became independent, raising the possibility of a white-ruled, mineral-rich superstate.

To the extent that Americans were paying attention, most sided with the whites. An editorial in the *Honolulu Star-Bulletin* lamented that the Belgians had administered their colony "efficiently and sympathetically," only to face a descent into "riot and rapine"—the inevitable consequence of African self-rule. A twenty-five-year-old Kenyan student at the University of Hawaii pushed back with pal-pable anger in a letter to the editor. "Speaking as one who has been in the Congo and who has seen with my own eyes how the Africans there were whipped and put to jail for as petty offenses as walking on the wrong side of the street," wrote Barack H. Obama, a year before he would have his famous American-born son, "it struck me that maybe you needed more first-hand information before you spoke about their efficiency and sympathy."

Amid the fear and uncertainty gripping the colony, Lumumba still had an election to win. As the date of the Congo's first elections neared, he and other candidates for parliament raced around their regional strongholds, enrolling voters and making their pitches. Colonialism had stunted the Congolese political class, and now poli-ticians were competing for voters who just months earlier had never imagined they would be allowed to vote. By definition, there was no incumbent to align with or oppose, nor did anyone have a record to run on. The result was that many politicians lacked coherent plat-forms, resorting instead to "politics-on-credit," as one observer put it. Their limitless promises inflated voters' already unrealistic expec-tations about what independence would bring. Candidates pledged that tractors would relieve farmers and that troublesome Belgians would disappear. A tract handed out by Lumumba's MNC told vot-ers what race relations would look like in the new Congo:

> If you must travel by foot to go somewhere and happen to meet a European who drives a car, he must stop and pick you up if you think there is room for you. Otherwise, do not hesitate to

take down the license plate number and report it to the national president.... [The European] will be brought to trial in Leopoldville and will be forced to go back to Europe, for he is an enemy of the Congolese.

Most politicians had little national reach and spoke mainly to their regional or ethnic brethren, who received their leaders with royal pomp. Joseph Kasavubu toured his realm in a blue-and-white Cadillac convertible as supporters hailed "King Kasa." He also continued to espouse federalism. In Katanga, Moise Tshombe likewise continued to stir separatist sentiment. Such ethnic identity politics had a natural appeal. What many Congolese sought—and so what many parties promised—was a place of one's own after independence. Lumumba was nearly alone among the candidates in his devotion to a strong central government, and though he was not above positioning himself as this or that group's biggest defender, he denounced the divisive force of ethnic particularism. "Congo United," went one of his rallying cries.

Perhaps more powerful than the message, however, was the messenger. People were drawn to Lumumba's confident, calm voice, and they stayed through rain and darkness to hear it. Although more lecturer than firebrand, the MNC leader electrified his audiences. "Lumumba, slender, with horn-rimmed spectacles and a wispy little goatee, looks and talks like a provincial schoolmaster," one reporter noted. "He has been described in the world press as a demagogue, yet he never hollers or jumps about, and usually sounds no more inflammatory than a board chairman at the annual stockholders' luncheon. Nevertheless, the crowds hang on his every word."

When he passed through rural roads, villagers lined the shoulder to load his convertible with gifts. In the lakeside town of Bukavu, in the Congo's east, he was greeted with a chorus of workers and youths who chanted in Swahili: "Our country is beautiful; everyone, look at it. Lumumba is a handsome man; everyone, love him." Touring the dirt streets of Stanleyville's left-bank slums, Lumumba, wearing a feathered chieftain's headdress, was mobbed by thousands of supporters waving boughs and yelling, "Freedom!" They followed him to the banks of the Congo River, where they nearly swamped the ferry carrying him back to the other side. Some of the more zealous leaped into the river, swimming after their hero.

Lumumba's charisma was matched by his organizational prowess. During his imprisonment leading up to the roundtable, the MNC had fallen into disarray, showing just how dependent on his leadership the party had become. It only grew more so after his release. Upon returning from Brussels, he established near-dictatorial control over every aspect of the party's operations. Almost every decision passed through him, including the hiring of employees and the selection of parliamentary candidates.

In addition to holding the MNC presidency, Lumumba was serving as one of six members of the interim governing council established to ease the transition to independence. With so many obligations, he was more than ever running on fumes. A typical twenty-four hours went like this: In the early morning, he met visitors in his house before heading to his office to attend to his day job on the governing council. In the evening, he returned home to be greeted by as many as sixty petitioners at his door. Dealing with them took until eleven or twelve o'clock, after which he got to work on campaign matters. After two or three hours of sleep, the cycle began anew.

Lumumba kept up the frenetic pace in part to overcome a disadvantage vis-à-vis his rivals: unlike politicians with a built-in base of ethnic support and ambitions confined to a particular district or province, he had to earn every vote and campaign everywhere. To spread his message, his party dispatched vans with loudspeakers blaring propaganda and distributed buttons, pamphlets, and posters. Its powerful youth wing came in handy, providing free labor and bodies for rallies. Still, all this campaigning cost money, and every political party in the Congo seemed to be spending more than it could possibly have raised on its own. The MNC funded itself in part by selling membership cards, which many voters bought in the mistaken belief that the cards would serve as proof of identity after independence. But at 60 francs apiece—about the cost of a dozen eggs—the revenue from membership card sales did not come close to covering the party's spending on cars and other equipment.

—

The funding gap was clearly being filled by foreign money—but how much and whose was the subject of much speculation. One Belgian journalist claimed that Lumumba had received 140 million Belgian francs, $2.8 million at the time, in outside campaign donations from Belgian capitalists and sympathetic foreign governments. Albert Kalonji, a onetime Lumumba ally who had split from the MNC a year before, alleged that the Belgian Communist Party had sent Lumumba 10 million francs to spend on a fleet of Czech cars. As evidence, Kalonji produced a photocopy of the supposed check, which he said had been stolen from Lumumba's luggage on his way out of Brussels.

The claim quickly took hold. Some rivals joked that MNC stood for *Moscou nous conseille* (Moscow guides us). Moise Tshombe's party in Katanga printed a caricature in which a sullen Lumumba held on to a briefcase labeled "Moscow" while a giant boot kicked him out of the province. In Brussels, a high-ranking Belgian official swore to Ambassador William Burden that Lumumba was in contact with Communist agents and taking their money.

Given its interest in Lumumba, the Belgian Communist Party likely did give him money, and it, in turn, did receive subsidies from Moscow. Every Congolese party was receiving some sort of outside financing, whether from foreign governments or interested corporations. Lumumba's was hardly the only one to receive Communist money, nor was that its sole source of support. Nor, moreover, did such funding necessarily indicate Communist sympathies or fealty to Moscow. When a journalist considered publishing a story about the 10 million francs Lumumba had allegedly received from the Belgian Communist Party, Mobutu defended his friend. "Believe me, Lumumba is not Communist," he insisted. "The Communists are trying to use him, to act through him. That's clear. But Lumumba is no fool."

For a man supposedly in Moscow's pocket, Lumumba certainly displayed little loyalty to his paymasters or affinity for their ideology. He explicitly rejected the nationalization of private industry. His vision of national success, pitched at campaign rallies, included sending promising Congolese youth to be educated at British and American schools. Never tiring of denying his supposed Communist sympathies, he described his preferred national outlook as "positive neutralism," by which he meant that the independent Congo should reject the East-West schism and seek "economic and scientific cooperation with any friendly country."

The Soviets, for their part, remained passive observers to developments in the Congo. Belgium had allowed the Communists, in the words of a colonial administrator, just "one eye" in the Congo: a Czechoslovakian consulate, which doubled as a dealership for Škoda, a Czech manufacturer of cheap compact cars. With such limited visibility, the Soviets formed most of their impressions from meetings with Congolese politicians passing through Brussels.

What they heard was that Moscow was on the back foot. In May, when Thomas and Philippe Kanza, brothers and budding Congolese politicos, met with two Soviet diplomats, they "expressed regret that the USSR, in their opinion, is insufficiently active in aiding the national liberation movement in the Congo," as the diplomats recounted. To boot, the Soviet Union had "badly conducted its propaganda in the Congo." When Philippe asked whether the Congo could count on Soviet aid, the diplomats once again demurred. For Moscow, the Congo was a place worth watching, but not yet investing in.

On a steamy Monday morning in May, Lumumba readied himself for a full day of campaigning that would take him eighty miles north of Stanleyville, where he would rally voters and berate Belgian administrators. He placed a wad of newspapers in his cream convertible as reading material and ducked into a candy shop to stock up on sweets. As he emerged, he was greeted by several hundred cheering supporters. But just as he began to address them, a Belgian officer and a squad of Congolese soldiers pulled up in a Force Publique truck. The men were there to enforce a recent ban on gatherings of five or more people, imposed by colonial authorities as a riot-control measure. The officer raised a megaphone to his lips and ordered the crowd to disperse.

Lumumba picked up his own megaphone. "This is a provocation," he protested. "These people came here only to see me. They are not attacking Europeans. They are perfectly peaceful."

"Uhuru!" the crowd shouted in Swahili. "Freedom!"

The officer doubled down. "I must disperse them," he repeated.

As the soldiers dismounted from the truck with their rifles, Lumumba climbed out of his car and moved toward them, megaphone raised. "These people, your brothers, are friendly and happy," he said. "You get back in your truck."

Caught between two orders, the soldiers hesitated for a moment before obeying Lumumba's. Their officer shrugged his shoulders, and the group sped away.

Months earlier, such a scene would have been unthinkable. In March, Lumumba had told a reporter that he was "delighted with the Belgian spirit" and pledged his full cooperation with the administration. But things had changed. Lumumba had hardened his attitude toward the Belgians. Sensing that order was slipping out of its hands, the Belgian military had reinforced its bases in the Congo with three infantry companies, a move that Lumumba denounced as a ploy to "establish a puppet government" postindependence. He threatened to resign from the interim governing council and laced his speeches with rhetorical attacks against Belgian maneuvering.

The day after defying the Force Publique officer in Stanleyville, Lumumba met with its top commander, General Émile Janssens. Janssens wanted the officer corps to remain all Belgian for the foreseeable future. Only by 1966 were all members of the first Congolese class sent to the Royal Military School in Brussels scheduled to have graduated under Janssens's plan. For now, the Force Publique would remain segregated, a thin white strip atop a thick black band.

On this, Lumumba was of two minds. Although he recognized that the swift "Africanization" of the Force Publique had been a key demand during the struggle for independence, he worried that an untutored Congolese officer corps would not be up to the job of keeping the country together the way that the experienced Belgians would be. Military training took time. As he had reassured a group of Belgian officers, "We are not, just because the Congo is independent, going to turn a private into a general."

When the rank and file heard this comment, they were irate. A group of them took to the pages of *Emancipation,* a Leopoldville newspaper, to warn that while the Congo's political class seemed set to benefit from independence, its soldiers risked being left behind, subject to the same low pay and discrimination they had endured for years. Lumumba had no military experience and therefore no right to decide what made a competent officer. The letter ended with a warning to the offending politician: "The time to push us around like sheep has passed.... We guarantee you the hellish ruination of your powers and of your Congo so long as you insult us as ignorant and incapable of taking the place of your white brothers."

Thus, by the time of his May meeting with Janssens, Lumumba had fully antagonized the Force Publique: its privates considered him unresponsive to their demands, and its officers viewed him as a troublemaker. Now its commander was finding him petulant. Lumumba towered over Janssens, whose five-foot-four stature had led the U.S. embassy to call him a "Napoleonic-style fighting cock." During the course of their fifty-minute conversation, Janssens complained that Lumumba was encouraging lawlessness. Lumumba responded by accusing the soldiers of provoking the population. He said he could take charge.

"Let me do it," he said. "Withdraw your troops and everything will be fine!"

Janssens declined the offer. *If this man ever becomes my boss,* he said to himself, *things will get very difficult.*

Chapter 10

The King's Sword

T HE STATE DEPARTMENT'S handout for employees newly assigned to the Belgian Congo warned of the privations—both real and imagined—that awaited. "The climate in Leopoldville is hot, humid and generally unpleasant," it said, noting "the warm sticky dampness which encourages mildew and rust." Traffic was dangerous; so were unpasteurized milk and germ-infested swimming pools. Employees should leave delicate tableware stateside, since "houseboys are clumsy and careless." Their laundry methods were "primitive." "Forget about good nursemaids locally," one staffer at the consulate added in a letter to an incoming colleague. "They're warm black bodies *period*."

But many of the young Americans taking up posts in Leopoldville found it glamorous. Clean, sunny, and spacious, it reminded them of Miami. There was a yacht club, whose sloops were rigged with outboard motors to help becalmed sailors avoid the rapids, and an equestrian society, which boasted well-groomed horses and floodlights for night rides. The U.S. consulate was modern and inviting, "like a Hollywood conception of a Foreign Service post," wrote Alison Palmer, a twenty-eight-year-old Foreign Service officer.

Like nearly all diplomatic posts, the consulate also hosted CIA officers under diplomatic cover, who in this case were working overtime to make sense of the local scene. In the rush toward independence, the Belgian intelligence services, perhaps feeling overwhelmed, had turned over reams and reams of disorganized files on Congolese leaders to Paul Springer, the CIA station chief in Leopoldville. Nearly everything the U.S. government knew about the Congo's political class could be gleaned from the newspaper, so when the documents showed up at the U.S. consulate, the CIA reassigned extra staff from other stations to go through the hulking filing cabinets that stored the papers. But the new material turned out to be "junk," in one secretary's words. Even the Belgians had gotten a late start trying to know the men who would lead the independent Congo.

As the date of the power transfer neared, the U.S. government ramped up its efforts to track developments in the colony. In cables to Washington, State Department officials on the ground worried that the hasty transition to independence offered "fertile ground open to Commies in Congo": the relatively uneducated population, they feared, was susceptible to Communist agitation, while its political class was strapped for cash and deeply hostile to Western imperialism. Given the Congo's abundant natural resources and massive geographical expanse, the Soviets would no doubt be tempted to establish a foothold there. America had seen this movie before and didn't like how it ended: after Guinea's independence from France two years earlier, the Soviets had flooded the country with aid, and it now seemed firmly in their orbit.

In the spring, William Burden, the U.S. ambassador to Belgium, took a three-week tour of the Congo with Larry Devlin, hoping to get a firsthand impression of the colony's postindependence prospects. The duo returned to Brussels alarmed. "The general economic situation in the Congo is very much worse than we had had any reason to believe," Burden reported to Washington. "There is a very real possibility that the Congo will start its life as an independent nation with a completely empty till and heavy debts." Burden argued for a $5 million package of American aid, in part to keep up with the Soviets, who he believed were making inroads.

Washington would also need to send a "top-notch Ambassador" to the new African nation, Burden said. The State Department's answer was Clare Timberlake, a twenty-nine-year veteran of the Foreign Service who was then at the U.S. embassy in Bonn, West Germany. Timberlake was a mustachioed, bow-tied speaker of passable Arabic, French, German, Italian, Portuguese, and Spanish, equal parts fastidious and dogmatic—perhaps the type of career diplomat President Harry Truman had had in mind when he complained about the State

Department's fussy "striped-pants boys." And indeed, Timberlake would prove to be as inflexible as they came.

Timberlake soon busied himself with the long-distance logistics of furnishing his home-to-be in Leopoldville, where he would live without air-conditioning with his wife, his three daughters, their German governess, and his eighty-three-year-old father-in-law. (There was no space for his teenage sons, who would remain in the care of the Jesuits at Georgetown Prep.) Timberlake arranged for his Plymouth station wagon to be shipped to the Congo, along with two cases of cigarettes, and requested fine china, silverware, and lamps, so as to bring the consul general's residence up to ambassadorial standards. He also spent two days in Brussels, where embassy officials, including Devlin, gave him a crash course on the rapidly changing politics of his new posting.

Perceptions of Lumumba within the U.S. government, meanwhile, were hardening, informed by uncharitable reports from Devlin and others at the U.S. embassy in Brussels. If the man wasn't a Communist, he certainly seemed Communist-friendly. But Washington was in a bind. On the one hand, it wanted as pro-American a government in Leopoldville as possible, which in its view meant doing what it could to weaken Lumumba's electoral prospects. On the other hand, with Lumumba's campaign picking up momentum, it seemed increasingly likely he would lead the new government anyway. So trying and failing to sideline him would ensure that the United States would be "left on the outside looking in," as one CIA message worried. Was this a risk worth taking?

American officials did not agree on the right strategy. For Bronson Tweedy, the head of the Africa division at the CIA and Larry Devlin's boss, the best choice was to flood the Congolese elections with as much CIA money as possible, given that "there is so much at stake in preventing the placing of Lumumba in a prominent role," as he wrote in a memo to his superiors. He urged that American "money and influence get in there quick!" Officials in the field were not so sure. In a joint message, CIA and State Department representatives in Brussels opposed a "Stop Lumumba" campaign. Since the thirty-four-year-old was "one of the few, if not only, Congolese leaders with a Congo-wide appeal and standing," such a campaign could backfire. In fact, far from working to undermine Lumumba, they suggested the CIA give him "limited funding" to keep him in America's fold.

In the end, the agency decided against a full-fledged influence campaign, settling instead for a lighter touch. Although it is not clear whether Lumumba ever received any CIA money, the agency did issue small payments to various politicians it deemed promising and pro-Western. The goal was less to influence the elections per se than to develop sources; the bribery was, in the agency's words, "in the realm of intelligence acquisition, not political action." It was too soon to pick winners. "In most cases the political leaders of the Congo today have not matured ideologically," an internal CIA paper argued. Why permanently alienate some of the Congo's most important politicians just because they might have taken some francs from Moscow?

Lumumba's electoral campaign continued to gain steam, and the CIA eventually resigned itself to his victory. At a meeting of the National Security Council in May 1960, the agency's director, Allen Dulles, told President Dwight Eisenhower that Lumumba was likely to lead the free Congo. Dulles did not hide his dislike of the candidate, describing him as an "irresponsible" embezzler, susceptible to bribery and Communist influence.

Eisenhower already had little faith in the Congo's prospects. A footdragger on civil rights at home, the president was a skeptic of independence in Africa, too. When Dulles pointed out that some eighty political parties were vying for power in the Congo, Eisenhower quipped that he didn't realize so many people in the colony could read. (In fact, the Congo's literacy rate, at more than 40 percent, was among the highest on the continent; for all the deficiencies in secondary and higher education, access to primary school was widespread.) It was not the first time the U.S. president expressed his low regard for Africans. At a National Security Council meeting earlier that year, a White House official fresh from a trip to the Congo had told him that "many Africans still belonged in the trees," and were thus easily manipulated. To that, the president replied in apparent agreement that "man's emotions still have control over his intelligence."

—

By the spring of 1960, the UN's General Assembly building in New York was bursting at the seams. When ground broke on UN headquarters, in 1948, the organization had fifty-eight member states, only four of which were African. The architects of the saddle-shaped building on the East River had been told to plan for an eventual seventy nations. But now the UN had eighty-two member states, and—this being the Year of Africa, with more than a dozen former colonies scheduled to gain independence—more were on the way. Committees were meeting on alternate days to avoid overcrowding. In the General Assembly auditorium, a plan to decorate the wall behind the rostrum with saucerlike seals of every member country had been shelved for lack of space. As a stopgap measure, the organization began a $100,000 renovation to make room for ten additional members. Crews ripped up the forest-green carpet to install extra tables and seats in the rear. Along First Avenue, new flagpoles were erected to accommodate the extra countries.

From the thirty-eighth floor of the Secretariat Building, Dag Hammarskjöld was pondering what else African independence meant for his organization. Since his tour of the African continent months earlier, he had grown worried. Once British, French, and Belgian colonial administrators left their desks and returned home, their local replacements would need a great deal of foreign assistance, both technical and financial, to make it through the early stages of independence. But if that aid were channeled bilaterally—through individual countries in the Eastern or Western blocs—the superpower rivalries already cleaving the rest of the world could divide Africa, too. "I have a feeling that Africa is a part of the world which at present is outside the conflict, the competition, the Cold War...under which we are all suffering at present," Hammarskjöld told a group of businessmen. "And I would like to see that part of the world remain outside." Hence a role for the UN: a neutral organization through which aid could pass, no political strings attached. Hammarskjöld estimated that the UN would need to increase its annual aid budget by a modest $2.5 million to meet the needs of new African countries.

No one in the UN understood those needs better than Ralph Bunche, a high-ranking official in the organization and one of the most prominent African Americans in public life. A barber's son from Detroit, Bunche had overcome boyhood tragedy—when he was thirteen, his father abandoned the family and his mother died—to embark on an astonishing career. He graduated at the very top of his class at the Southern Branch of the University of California, in Los Angeles, and earned a PhD in government from Harvard, where he wrote his dissertation on French colonial policy in Africa. At the London School of Economics, he did postdoctoral work in anthropology and took Swahili lessons from a student from British Kenya named Jomo Kenyatta, who would go on to become that colony's leading independence activist. During World War II, Bunche joined the Office of Strategic Services, the CIA's predecessor, as an Africa specialist. "Dr. Bunche has an almost unique knowledge of Africa," wrote a supervisor. "It would be practically impossible to replace him."

Bunche served as a State Department adviser to the U.S. delegation at the 1945 San Francisco conference, where the UN was born, and the following year joined the organization itself, back when it was still occupying temporary headquarters at Hunter College in the Bronx. In 1949, he spent eighty-one days negotiating an Arab-Israeli armistice—an experience that won him the Nobel Peace Prize. After Hammarskjöld became secretary-general, Bunche became his most trusted deputy.

So it was natural when, in May 1960, Hammarskjöld called Bunche into his office to talk about the Congo. Hammarskjöld told his deputy that he would send him to Leopoldville the next month, initially to represent the UN at the upcoming independence ceremonies. Afterward, however, Bunche was to stay on to offer UN assistance to a government that would surely need it. "I foresee great trouble there," he told one of Bunche's colleagues, adding, "It's more of a hunch than anything else."

Voting, restricted to Congolese men twenty-one and older, took place over the course of two weeks in late May. Some 2.8 million Congolese made their way to the polls, where they joined long lines to proudly slip ballots into wooden boxes that bore candidates' photographs. There were hitches: ransacked polling stations, stolen ballot boxes, a sunken riverboat carrying uncounted votes, and party workers voting repeatedly for their own side. Kasavubu's party alleged that witch doctors had seeded voters' dreams with images of a snake—the symbol of a rival party. But at the end of the day, the election was an achievement. In the countryside, men had walked or bicycled as far as thirty-five miles for the privilege of choosing their own leaders.

When the votes were tallied, moreover, most agreed that the results were representative. In Orientale province, it was a blowout for Lumumba's MNC, which won twenty-one of the province's twenty-five allotted seats in the Chamber of Representatives. Elsewhere, the party put in a creditable performance, picking up twelve seats, which, after adding in allied politicians, brought its effective total in the chamber to forty-one seats—more than any other group. The Belgians, who had been expecting a win for their preferred party, the PNP, were shocked.

Yet the result was hardly an unambiguous mandate for Lumumba. He led the biggest group in the chamber, but there were 137 total seats, putting the MNC far below the threshold for an absolute majority. Meanwhile, in the Senate, whose members were chosen indirectly by provincial legislatures, Lumumba's party won just nineteen of eighty-four seats. And in Katanga, the MNC did not garner a single representative in the provincial legislature. Lumumba's party had emerged as the sole one that could claim something resembling a national following, but what the vote revealed above all was just how fragmented the Congo was.

This was hardly a surprising outcome. As with many other European colonies, the borders of the Belgian Congo had been drawn with no consideration of ethnic boundaries, and so its fourteen million people were not a natural grouping but a jumble of hundreds of different ethnicities with little shared sense of national belonging. Along the way, the Belgians had heightened ethnic distinctions, demanding that subjects fill in the blank for "tribe" on official forms and developing stereotypes about which groups were supposedly lazy and which were hardworking. Ethnicity formed the basis of government in rural areas and operated as a source of solidarity in the cities. Most voters still identified first as Kongo, Mongo, Luba, and so on—not, as Lumumba did, as Congolese. Accordingly, the election was, in one observer's words, "largely an ethnic census."

As the leader of the party with the most seats in parliament,

Lumumba was the natural pick when it came to forming a government. But the Belgians, as wary as ever of him, opted to stall. To manage the handover, King Baudouin sent Walter Ganshof van der Meersch, a distinguished jurist who was hostile to the prospect of an MNC-led government. He played for time, hoping that a coalition of anti-Lumumba parliamentarians would coalesce. He also tried, without success, to pave the way for a government led by Kasavubu, whose party had won just twelve seats in the Chamber of Representatives.

Yet Ganshof van der Meersch's stalling tactics backfired, radicalizing parliamentarians who had initially hesitated to support Lumumba. The U.S. consulate also weighed in, arguing that a government without the MNC leader would lack authority. After several weeks of maneuvering, Lumumba managed to amass the necessary support. The cabinet list was telegraphed to Brussels and signed by King Baudouin. After more than seven decades of Belgian rule, Lumumba would be the first prime minister of the independent Congo. It promised to be the pinnacle of his political career and an uphill battle: against mayhem at home and interference from abroad, against his rivals and at times against his own worst impulses.

That left only the question of who would fill the post of president. By now, the idea that King Baudouin would act as head of state had been set aside. In his place, Lumumba settled on none other than his longtime rival, Kasavubu. When he instructed his coalition to vote accordingly, some of his allies were horrified. Kasavubu remained, first and foremost, a voice for his own ethnic group, the Bakongo, and some suspected he might try to lead the group's stronghold in the lower Congo into secession.

On the day of the vote, several of Lumumba's colleagues cornered him in a corridor and tried to talk him out of the endorsement. The most senior among them was Daniel Kanza, patriarch of the politically active Kanza family. Kanza was a former ally of the Abako leader but had chafed at his dictatorial style.

"I know Joseph Kasavubu well—far better than you do," he told Lumumba. "For a time he will appear to collaborate with you, and later he will betray you."

Kanza's son Thomas echoed his father's warning with tears in his eyes and begged to at least delay the vote. But Lumumba refused to budge. Better to include Kasavubu than to keep him on the sidelines, from where he might decide to put his separatist leanings into action, he countered. It was also important to have the support of the population in Leopoldville, which Kasavubu did, in spades.

Finally, it was the turn of Maurice Mpolo, a stalwart MNC leader and a minister in the new government. One of the few politicians to address Lumumba with the familiar *tu*, he implored the prime minister not to ignore his closest allies.

"You'll regret it one day," he said, "always thinking you know the best."

Despite the many weeks of postelection haggling over who would get to run the country, and despite the objections of Lumumba's colleagues, the final result had a certain logic, almost an air of inevitability. Lumumba—lively, political, elected—would serve as head of government. Kasavubu—senior, distant, regal—would become head of state. The Congo's two most prominent politicians, the two biggest rivals, would enter an uneasy alliance.

Lumumba's government was itself a model of compromise. It had twenty-three ministers, plus, at a lower rank, ten secretaries of state and four ministers of state—so many members that some existing colonial-era administrative departments had to be split into multiple ministries to accommodate everyone. The goal, however, was not efficiency but inclusion. And as members of the government gathered for a group photo on a freshly mowed lawn overlooking the Congo River, they presented a picture of remarkable unity.

There was Lumumba, standing as straight and tall as the palm trees behind him. He was flanked by men with backgrounds and beliefs as diverse as the country they would lead. The government included men from all six provinces, twelve different political parties, and an even greater number of ethnic groups. They had worked as clerks, medical assistants, teachers, planters, and journalists. Many had paid a steep price for their activism; at least ten had served time in a colonial prison. Behind everyone lurked Mobutu, now a secretary of state, his eyes shaded by dark glasses.

There were two notable absences from the photo. The first was

Albert Kalonji, who had split off from the MNC the year before and, during the campaign, had alleged that Lumumba was in the pay of Belgian Communists. Mobutu, who thought of himself as a moderating influence on Lumumba, had tried and failed to engineer a last-minute reconciliation between the two. The second was Moise Tshombe of Katanga. His political ambitions never extended past the borders of his province. Although his party had won just a handful of seats in the national parliament, it had dominated in Katanga. Thanks to a last-minute legal change engineered by Brussels, Tshombe had managed to ram through a provincial government composed almost entirely of loyalists, all of whom were, at best, skeptical of Lumumba and the new central government.

There was another problem the photo obscured. Some of the men in it, perhaps intent on demonstrating their readiness to get down to business, had posed clutching leather portfolios. In truth, the group was singularly unprepared for what lay ahead. The Belgians had banned Congolese men from studying anything other than the priesthood until the 1940s, resulting in a cabinet of the unschooled. There were fewer than twenty Congolese university graduates in the entire world, and only two of them—Justin Bomboko, the foreign minister, and Thomas Kanza, the ambassador to the UN—were part of the new government. Among the rest of the cabinet, only a handful had finished high school.

In this respect, the Congo lagged far behind the colonies of other European powers. In part to appease nascent nationalist movements, Britain and France had established proto-legislatures in their colonial territories in the decades leading up to independence. Populating these institutions were European-educated lawyers—a pool of highly trained local elites who upon independence stood ready to take over the country's political and administrative apparatus. The Congo's new parliament included just one lawyer—a senator who, as the son of a Congolese mother and an Italian father, had slipped through the cracks and studied law in Belgium. It also counted seventeen traditional chiefs, most of whom were illiterate.

African politicians elsewhere were far better prepared. The man who was set to lead Senegal into independence later in the year, Léopold Senghor, was a noted poet, a graduate of the University of Paris, and a former deputy in France's National Assembly. Julius Nyerere, who was about to take the reins of independent Tanganyika, had a master's degree from the University of Edinburgh and would soon translate *Julius Caesar* into Swahili. Ghana's first president, Kwame Nkrumah, held two master's degrees from the University of Pennsylvania and had studied philosophy at University College London. Lumumba, though an autodidact and an organizational whiz, had advanced no further than the Leopoldville Postal School.

He and the men by his side looked serious but also weary, resigned. In less than a week, they would be in charge of twenty-five thousand soldiers and nearly as many administrators. They would have to sign international treaties, resolve domestic disputes, and oversee the country's infrastructure and education.

Yet in their first meetings, days before independence, they concerned themselves with frivolities. They reveled in their new titles, making a show of calling one another "Your Excellency" or "Comrade," depending on their respective politics. They argued over the allocation of ministerial cars and residences. They haggled over their order in motorcades and, after appealing to the Belgian Foreign Ministry for help in deciding who would go in front of whom, ended up largely copying Belgium's order of precedence.

Behind the scenes, the administration was in chaos. Given the subdividing that had occurred to make room for such a large cabinet, many ministers were clueless about their jobs. Who worked for them? Where was their office? Meanwhile, resentful Belgian officials were bent on making their jobs harder. In some offices, departing administrators burned papers or took the keys with them. This was a liquidation, not a transition. An anonymous diplomat confessed to *Time*, "I have an uneasy feeling this place is tottering on the brink of disaster."

On the morning of June 25, Ralph Bunche stood outside Leopoldville's main airport, Ndjili, looking lost. Accompanying the UN envoy was his forty-year-old assistant, F. T. Liu. The son of a distinguished Chinese painter, Liu had been sent to a Parisian boarding school as a boy and thus spoke perfect French, unlike Bunche, who spoke none. No one had come to greet Bunche and Liu, and they didn't know where to go. All they had been told in New York was that the Congolese government had reserved a villa for them, but after several phone calls it became clear that no one knew anything about any villa. A U.S. embassy employee drove the two men downtown. As she tried to show them the city, a helicopter spewed a cloud of DDT, obscuring the view.

Bunche and Liu were dead tired after their eight-hour flight from Brussels, and still a bit perplexed by their meeting with Belgian officials there. The UN seemed to grasp the challenges that might await an independent Congo, but Raymond Scheyven, the Belgian minister who had scared the Congolese with his economic presentation at the roundtable, did not. One of the biggest problems facing the country, he had told Bunche and Liu, was deciding what role the Flemish language would play.

Bunche and Liu ended up at the Stanley Hotel, a modern, no-frills establishment across the street from the fancier Memling Hotel. They bathed and caught some sleep before heading to a lunch in honor of Kasavubu, Lumumba, and the rest of the new government. Just a week earlier, the situation had seemed hopeless as politicians quarreled over the formation of a government. At lunch, however, "everybody was smiling and optimistic," Liu wrote to his wife, "and Belgian officials were confident that everything would work out well—at least for two weeks."

This was the first in a nonstop series of meals and receptions that introduced the UN representatives to the Congolese leadership. In a letter to Hammarskjöld, Bunche withheld judgment on Lumumba, but his words hinted at a nascent skepticism:

> Everyone agrees that Lumumba is quick and politically agile, but he is obviously young and untried and many consider him lacking in integrity, this being based mainly on his conviction for embezzlement when he was in the post office. He is tall and sharp-eyed and rather raffish looking in his mustache and beard—and long hair. Whether the latter is an affectation or due to lack of time for a haircut, I do not yet know.

Lumumba woke up on June 29 determined to offer something special to his people the next day—a grand gesture to match the gravity and high hopes of independence. He could not raise the dead or end work, but he could, he decided, free some prisoners. Having just been released from a cell five months earlier, he certainly knew the feeling the act would instill. Although Lumumba originally wanted to reduce all sentences by ten years, he had been persuaded to drop the number to three. That act of clemency would still liberate two-thirds of the prison population. The text of the decree was finalized in the morning. He could take to the radio that night to announce the good news.

The plan seemed to be on track until the outgoing governor-general got wind of it. He reached Lumumba in his office by telephone and asked him to consider watering down the amnesty so that it would apply to just a sliver of prisoners. Lumumba had no interest in that, so the governor-general appeared to relent but proposed a different modification. What if King Baudouin issued the decree? Lumumba thought about it and agreed. He seemed pleased by the notion of extracting such a pledge from King Baudouin. "Thus the last act of the king will be an act of generosity," he mused. "That will make an excellent impression."

The king landed that afternoon. He stepped out of his military airplane in tropical regalia: a cream jacket with gold buttons and braided epaulets, cinched high on the waist by a black belt, and matching cream trousers. His head was covered with a peaked cap, around his neck hung crown jewels, and in his gloved hand he held a sword. Lumumba and the other Congolese officials greeted him with evident esteem. They had in fact competed to get to the airport first, ignoring the order of precedence that had been established and commanding their chauffeurs to overtake the cars carrying officials they deemed less important. Mobutu bowed generously toward the king.

Others were less reverent. As Baudouin entered the city, saluting the soldiers of the Force Publique from the back of his black Lincoln Continental convertible, an onlooker emerged from the crowd. The man, dressed neatly in a blazer and tie, leaped toward the car and snatched the king's sword. He took off running, sabering the air triumphantly until he was tackled by police.

The Western press would describe Ambroise Boimbo variously as an "eccentric souvenir-hunter," "a mentally unbalanced African," and "a half-crazed African nationalist." In some Congolese neighbor-hoods, people worried about what would befall a man who had dared steal the sacred totem of a chief. Radio announcers downplayed the incident, insisting that it carried no political significance. But its symbolism seemed obvious: the Congolese had taken the nation's fate into their own hands. This was their country now.

Or was it? At dinner that evening, the king bestowed on Lumumba Belgium's Order of the Crown, but there was no word of the expected royal decree that would free so many prisoners. Lumumba inquired with August De Schryver, Belgium's minister for the colonies, who now proposed an amnesty that would apply only to those prisoners with sentences of six months or less—a far cry from the promised three years. Furious, Lumumba demanded that the decree be issued unchanged. De Schryver did not relent, and it was too late to do anything about it. Lumumba canceled the speech he had planned to give on the radio.

The young prime minister was worn out. The past months had exhausted him, and it showed in his haggard appearance. The work had just begun—and already, friends wondered how long he could last.

PART II

PREMIER

Chapter 11

The Newest Country

O N J UNE 30, Leopoldville awoke to a brisk, clear morning, its last as a colonial capital. The city was in fine form. The Belgian tricolor fluttered on flagpoles. Gardens had been immaculately tended; the air, freshly perfumed with DDT. The Belgian government had allocated 62 million francs for celebrations across the Congo, more than three times the amount it spent on education in the colony every year. The city was full, too: with some sixty countries having sent representatives to mark the occasion, many visitors could not find hotel rooms and had to sleep in cars and riverboats. While the world watched, Belgium was determined to paper over the difficulties and injustices that had defined its rule right up to the very last weeks and days.

Lumumba spent the morning at his house, an impressive block of red bricks and deep verandas across from the golf course on Boulevard Albert I, a home that had once belonged to the mayor of Leopoldville. The Congo's new prime minister padded around his living room in slippers, his shirt unbuttoned. He was stressed. Personal matters weighed on him—a row with his wife, Pauline, who continued to bemoan his increasing "Europeanization," had intensified—but he had more important business to attend to. His closest advisers, summoned urgently by telephone, gathered around him excitedly.

"Sit down and read this," Lumumba barked at one of them, Thomas Kanza, handing him a sheaf of papers. "Quickly."

It was a speech Lumumba was not supposed to deliver. As the

official program had it, the ceremonies that day would begin with an address by King Baudouin, to be followed by one by his ostensible equal as a head of state, President Kasavubu—and that was it. But Lumumba had gotten ahold of the text of Kasavubu's speech, a dull and obsequious homage to Western development, written by Belgian advisers, and could only imagine the sort of colonial paean it was responding to. So he decided to write his own.

Lumumba's speech would serve as a corrective, and it was born out of fresh anger toward the Belgians. A week earlier, they had tried to prevent him from forming a government. The previous day, they had foiled his amnesty announcement. Now, considering how high expectations about independence had soared, Lumumba had to give the people something. Why not a parting shot at the Belgians, a chance for the Congolese to articulate some of the collective anger they held? It didn't hurt, of course, that stealing the show would be good politics. On a day of solemnity and pomp, Lumumba would tell the Belgians what the Congolese really thought of them, and while they were still technically colonial subjects.

When Kanza read the draft, he was shocked. Lumumba had written a diatribe against Belgian colonialism—all true, Kanza thought, but not at all appropriate for the stately ceremony marking the end of that era. And at any rate, a speech of such importance had no business being written hours before delivery.

Kanza looked around and sensed that he might be outnumbered. "I quite understand your point of view," he told Lumumba, "but I don't see what I can do."

Lumumba said that he had made up his mind to give the speech, but he asked Kanza to give it a once-over. "Tidy up the text, and make it acceptable—a bit less explosive."

The prime minister headed upstairs to slip on his shoes, don his jacket, tie his bow tie, and tuck a handkerchief into his breast pocket. Kanza followed, begging him to skip over the more incendiary paragraphs in the speech. But it was time to go, and as Pauline threw his belongings off the balcony in anger, Lumumba was whisked away, leaving his aides with the speech. Kanza followed in another car, editing as he rolled west along the boulevard. Marginalia cramped the pages.

—

Lumumba arrived at the Palace of the Nation shortly before eleven o'clock. A squat building fronted by slender rectangular columns and a bursting white facade, the palace seemed a stripped-down version of the kinds of Beaux Arts châteaus one might find in the Belgian countryside. Its cupola, clad in Katangan copper, was the only perceptible trace of the building's true whereabouts. The lawn, embroidered with a zigzag of trimmed hedges and triangular reflective pools, stretched out gloriously toward the river. When construction on the palace began, in 1956, it was intended to serve as the governor-general's mansion for decades to come. Events, of course, intervened, and it had been hastily repurposed as the new country's parliament. Inside, velvet drapes concealed gaps in the plastering of the large rotunda where the ceremonies would take place. "Looked at closely," noted one reporter, "the noble palace is uncomfortably reminiscent of an insubstantial film set."

Lumumba strode in. His hair was neatly parted and short—he had seen a barber in time—and he wore the maroon sash of the order that had been bestowed on him the night before. His ministers filed in, as did representatives, senators, and other dignitaries from across the Congo. Chiefs in traditional raiment—feathered headdresses, carved wooden crowns, leopard-skin sashes, jangly necklaces, beaded armbands—sat shoulder to shoulder with parliamentarians in dapper suits.

With them were hundreds of dignitaries from around the world. The Belgians had sent a delegation more than a hundred strong, but countries with hardly any connection to the Congo were also represented, eager to align themselves with newly decolonized Africa. The Ethiopian empire and the Moroccan kingdom each dispatched a prince; the U.K., a Scottish nobleman. West Germany, South Korea, and Israel all sent ambassadors. Portuguese Angola, South Africa, and the Central African Federation, each still ruled by a white minority, had pointedly not been invited. The twelve members of the Soviet delegation passed along well wishes from Nikita Khrushchev, who commended the Congolese on having "dealt another telling blow at the moribund colonial system." The Soviets were joined by fellow

Communists from Bulgaria, Romania, and Czechoslovakia. No one from Communist China had come, but its government had organized a rally in Peking to celebrate Congo's independence.

Bunche represented the UN, handing Lumumba a congratulatory letter from Hammarskjöld pledging the organization's full support. "There will be in the coming days one of the most demanding ordeals for the Congo and its leaders," Hammarskjöld wrote. "I am confident that they will be able to face up to this test wisely."

The United States' five-man delegation, led by the State Department official Robert Murphy, settled in, too. Ambassador Timberlake was in attendance, as were several other U.S. diplomats and William Paley, the chairman of CBS and a friend of Eisenhower's. (Larry Devlin remained in Europe and was not scheduled to take up his post until later.) With them, the Americans brought an offer of three hundred scholarships for Congolese students and a bust of Abraham Lincoln, "who himself had some doings with the independence of Negroes," a State Department spokesman noted. Yet it wasn't exactly a progressive group. Murphy confessed that he considered the Congolese "primitive people." Timberlake viewed them the same way. Paley, for his part, was the executive who had brought the minstrelsy of *Amos 'n' Andy* to American television. Eisenhower's letter of congratulations, moreover, had been watered down for fear of offending Belgian sensitivities. Originally, Ike was on record celebrating "the freedom of 13.5 million Congolese" and calling it "encouraging." But presumably because "freedom" implied a preceding lack thereof, the White House opted to note merely the Congo's "attainment of independence" and omit any mention of encouragement.

Finally, all rose, and King Baudouin and President Kasavubu, one a technical royal, the other an aspirational one, ambled up to their place of honor on the carpeted dais. The king, baby-faced at just twenty-nine years old and resplendent in his ornate uniform, stood before the crowd to deliver his speech. Sun streamed in through the concrete filigree behind him, and klieg lights illuminated the stage for the global press corps packed into the hall.

The king began by praising his great-grandfather's brother. "The independence of the Congo," he said in a voice that hid no shame, "represents the culmination of the work conceived by the genius of King Leopold II, undertaken by him with tenacious courage and continued with perseverance by Belgium." He went on: "For eighty years, Belgium sent to your soil the best of its sons—first to deliver the Congo Basin from the odious slave trade that was decimating its population, and then to bring together the various ethnic groups that were once enemies."

Baudouin eulogized the "pioneers" of Belgian colonialism as selfless do-gooders, singling out Leopold II for having ruled "not as a conqueror but as a civilizer." He reminded the audience of the cities, railroads, highways, shipping routes, airports, factories, farms, hospitals, and schools that the Belgians had built, along with the "remarkable progress" they had achieved with respect to "living conditions and hygiene."

With Belgium having agreed to place all this in jeopardy, he continued, "it is now up to you, gentlemen, to show that we were right to trust you." Independence, he explained, "is not achieved through the immediate satisfaction of simple pleasures but through work." Even though the keys were being handed over, he warned the Congolese, "do not jeopardize the future with hasty reforms, and do not replace the structures that Belgium has given you until you are sure you can do better." As the king formally declared the Congo independent, an artillery battery boomed outside—a celebratory grace note, perhaps, but also an acoustic reminder of Belgian power.

Kasavubu spoke next. In his high voice, he mumbled polite words echoing the king's call for unity and caution. Lumumba, seated off to the side, was not impressed: his knees pressed together to form an impromptu desk, he scribbled furiously as he listened to Kasavubu's speech, rewriting his own.

When Kasavubu stopped talking, the audience assumed the proceedings were coming to an end, since no other speaker was listed on the program. Some turned to their neighbors to note their satisfaction. But then, to everyone's surprise, Lumumba, papers in hand, sprang up to the podium—"like a jack-in-the-box," as one attendee put it.

In a calm yet strong voice, Lumumba spoke:

Men and women of the Congo, victorious independence fighters, in the name of the Congolese government, I salute you.

To all of you, my friends who have battled tirelessly by our side, I ask you to make this day, June 30, 1960, an illustrious date that you keep indelibly engraved in your hearts, a date whose meaning you will proudly teach your children so that they, in turn, can tell their sons and their grandsons the glorious history of our struggle for freedom.

Although the independence of the Congo is being proclaimed today in agreement with Belgium, a friendly country we treat as an equal, no Congolese worthy of the name can ever forget that it was obtained through a fight—a daily fight, an intense and idealistic fight, a fight in which we spared no force, hardship, suffering, or blood. It was a fight made of tears, fire, and blood. We are deeply proud of it, because it was a just and noble fight, indispensable for putting an end to the humiliating slavery that had been forced upon us.

That was our lot for eighty years of colonial rule, and our wounds are still too fresh and painful to erase from our memories. We have known backbreaking work, demanded in exchange for wages that allowed us neither to feed, nor dress, nor house ourselves decently, nor to raise our children as loved ones.

We have suffered contempt, insults, and blows morning, noon, and evening, because we were Negroes. Who can forget that a Black was addressed by the familiar *tu,* certainly not as a friend, but because the formal *vous* was reserved for whites alone?

We have known that our lands were seized in the name of supposedly legal texts that recognized only the rights of the strongest.

We have known that the law was never the same for whites and Blacks: accommodating for one, cruel and inhumane for the other.

We have known the atrocious suffering of those who were marginalized for their political or religious beliefs. Exiled in their own homeland, they experienced a fate truly worse than death itself.

We have known that in the cities, there were magnificent houses for whites and decrepit huts for Blacks, that Blacks could not enter so-called European movie theaters, restaurants, and stores, and that Blacks would travel in the hold of a riverboat, underneath the whites in their luxury cabins.

Who can forget, finally, the shootings in which so many of our brothers perished, or the dungeons where those who did not want to submit to the oppressive and exploitative regime were brutally thrown?

The audience interjected with thunderous applause. Cries of "Uhuru!" echoed through the hall. Lumumba's words were being broadcast over loudspeakers to a crowd assembled outside the palace. Farther out, in villages and cities across the Congo—from the salty marshes of the Atlantic coast to the green hills of the east—people sat transfixed before battery-operated radios, listening to the prime minister's words, which were translated into Kikongo and Lingala. Those who missed it live could soon get their hands on a copy, twenty thousand of which were being distributed in the provinces. Lumumba continued:

All that, my brothers, has brought us deep suffering. But we who have been voted by your elected representatives to lead our beloved country, we who suffered in our bodies and hearts from colonialist oppression, we say to you out loud: from now on, all that is over.

The Africans in the room were enraptured; the Americans and Europeans alarmed. Baudouin, witnesses noticed, "sat shocked and pale," veins bulging from his forehead. Some saw the king half rise, as if about to leave right then and there.

As Lumumba laid out his program for the new Congo—peace, prosperity, social justice, free thought, fair pay, ethnic harmony, and adherence to the Universal Declaration of Human Rights—the audience cut him off with applause again and again. Improvising, he expanded his imagined audience, declaring that the Congo's independence marked "a decisive step toward the liberation of the entire African continent," earning him yet more cheers. He concluded: "Glory to our freedom fighters! Long live independence and African unity. Long live the independent and sovereign Congo!"

The applause went on and on. Outside, a delirious crowd broke through a police barricade and rushed the building.

Lumumba could have mimicked Kasavubu and played the role of grateful subject, but he chose boldness over easiness—and, predictably, he soon paid for it. His words immediately set off a diplomatic incident. Mobutu took it upon himself to circulate among the Belgians and gauge their reactions; the mood was not good, he reported back to Lumumba. Some Belgians had tears in their eyes, devastated that the coda to their eighty-year project had been so off-key. "Lumumba might have spared us this indignity," one official told a reporter. "Surely we did not deserve such gross insults."

Lunch was delayed for more than an hour as the Belgian delegation threatened to leave Leopoldville immediately. Thomas Kanza did damage control, reinterpreting the speech as a moderate little thing to anyone who would listen. Lumumba himself was taken aback by the reaction. After all, he told a member of the Belgian delegation, he had been saying the same words for years. After much wrangling, a compromise was found: at lunch, Lumumba would make a corrective speech, written by the Belgian prime minister.

And so, as hundreds of guests sat before their now-cold fish under tents on the vast lawn behind the palace, Lumumba rose to toast Baudouin. "The entire government wishes to pay a solemn tribute to the King of the Belgians, and to the noble people he represents, for the feat accomplished here in three quarters of a century," Lumumba said in tones less strident than before, his head tilted toward the paper he held in his hands. "I do not want my thoughts to be misinterpreted," he added. Lumumba expressed hope for "a lasting and fruitful collaboration" with Belgium, and raised a glass to the king's health.

Lumumba's backpedaling rescued the afternoon, but it was too late to undo the broader damage that his truth telling had caused. The dispatches had already gone out; minds had already been made up. Belgians across the political spectrum were apoplectic. *Le Soir*, a progressive Brussels daily, wrote that Lumumba "seemed to think he was not in the Palace of the Nation but on the tables of a public square." All his opponents took his lunchtime toast as proof that he was untrustworthy. "We certainly knew that Mr. Lumumba was a master at expressing fanatic states," huffed one Belgian columnist. "But we didn't know that he was as fickle, as slippery, as those cats whose gait he mimics." Timberlake reported to Washington that Lumumba "once again showed his unreliability and shiftiness." Bunche put the effect this way: "Lumumba seems to have more than one face. At times, he impresses as God's angry young man, but he can also laugh heartily and be excitable or otherworldly."

After lunch, the festivities continued with a parade of soldiers, police, and youths. Lining the route were thousands of enthusiastic, well-dressed Congolese standing twelve deep. Teenagers climbed treetops to improve their view. The well-wishers waved miniature Congolese flags, whose design was a near replica of the flag adopted in 1877, a yellow star on a royal blue background. Six smaller stars, one for each province, had been added to the hoist.

Indeed, the pageantry seemed to mark less a clean break with the past than a subtle shift in arrangements. With no national anthem having yet been selected, a brass band played American standards such as "Marching Through Georgia," a liberation song from the Civil War. Troops still under the command of Belgian officers goose-stepped along an avenue named for a colonial governor. "This is not going to last," an American diplomat in the stands remarked to his wife.

That night, the dignitaries gathered on the lawn of the Palace of the Nation for yet another celebration. Dressed in white tie, they endured additional speeches and an unexpected chill as a chef wheeled in a five-tier cake. When midnight approached—it was then that the Congo would legally become independent—they turned their gazes upward as brilliant fireworks lit up the sky. King Baudouin headed to the airport, taking off before the clock struck twelve. He thus never had to set foot on soil that was no longer his kingdom.

The first few days of Congolese independence proceeded with restrained celebration. At King Baudouin Stadium, people watched folk dancing, gymnastic displays, and a soccer match. In honor of a popular Belgian pastime, a bicycle race was held. Residents of the African quarter, flush with cash thanks to the "independence bonus" that most companies had paid out, feasted on goat meat and guzzled beer. The white population breathed a sigh of relief; the expected looting had not arrived. Belgian flags remained in the streets for days.

Not everything went perfectly. Transport workers, denied an independence bonus, went on strike. In some of the outlying communes of Leopoldville, beer-fueled street brawls broke out between rival political and ethnic groups, as did similar disputes in Luluabourg, the capital of the Kasai province. But the rifle butts and nightsticks of the Force Publique put them down, and with less inhibition than the army displayed in colonial times. "There will be no Belgian paternalism in our suppression of these tribal scraps," a Congolese official promised. Lumumba broadcast an appeal for calm over the radio, and the government imposed a curfew; bars closed at six o'clock, and people had to leave the streets by eight.

Nonetheless, Lumumba—who turned thirty-five on July 2— allowed himself some late-night celebration. He swung through a suburban nightclub, accompanied by a team of bodyguards and fellow politicians, and picked up the check. Mobutu came along, but he sensed that the relationship with his patron had changed. Lumumba now occupied what used to be the governor-general's residence, a two-story specimen of colonial architecture built in the 1920s that had housed Hammarskjöld during his visit at the beginning of the year. Lumumba's office was an oblong rotunda on the ground floor. As the prime minister settled into his new official quarters, Mobutu found himself suddenly unable to see him alone, surrounded as he was by other politicians, relatives, petitioners, and foreign advisers with strange titles. Mobutu was no longer asked to answer the mail or arrange press interviews. A distance grew.

With the transition so hastily arranged, Lumumba's government had no shortage of work to do. But in the early days of independence, ministers seemed more interested in being driven around town in plush cars by uniformed chauffeurs. Questions about official motorcades, residences, travel, and titles continued to dominate their discussions. Bunche reported to Hammarskjöld, "Kasavubu and Lumumba studiously ignore each other, exchange no words beyond those absolutely necessary and, through their cohorts, at times openly squabble about protocol precedence."

Another trivial issue attracted a great deal of ministerial attention: sorting out the official name of their new country. Hammarskjöld telegrammed members of the government asking how to distinguish their Congo from the smaller Congo across the river, set to become independent from France and join the UN later that summer. The government in Leopoldville negotiated with its neighbors to call the former Belgian colony "the Republic of Congo" and the former French one "the Congolese Republic." Such were the weighty issues occupying the government.

Lumumba himself seemed tired and tense. At least that was the opinion of Murphy, the head of the U.S. delegation, who met with him before leaving Leopoldville. Murphy also found him naive. Although the prime minister asserted his opposition to Communism, which he said was anathema to a Christian, freedom-loving people, he seemed confused about the details of that ideology—which, far from evidence of his imperviousness to Communist ideas, Murphy thought made him "useful for the Soviet Government's purposes as an outright agent."

Lumumba also told Murphy that even though he wanted to chart a neutral course for his country, he hoped President Eisenhower would be the first foreign leader to visit the Congo after independence. Instead of interpreting this as evidence of genuine affection for the United States, the report about the meeting sent back to Washington saw it as further proof of wiliness: "Lumumba's quick switch from neutrality to expression of seemingly pro-US, pro-Western sentiments is typical of his character in suiting his words to his audience."

Despite the confusion that marked these early days, it all seemed manageable. The amateur ways of Lumumba and his new government—that could be expected of an unschooled political class. The occasional clashes in the streets—it was only natural that after the colonial cap on ethnic tensions had been lifted, some ruffians would take advantage. Considering what could have happened, the transition was a success. "Independence has come and gone; it was very quiet," the U.S. embassy employee Alison Palmer wrote to her parents. "About five people are getting killed in the city every night but there are so many soldiers about we feel quite safe."

On July 4, when the U.S. embassy celebrated America's more distant and far messier independence, the mood was jubilant and relaxed. Three hundred guests crowded the embassy's riverside garden, sipping on cocktails as the sun set behind the Congo River. Embassy officers and secretaries mingled with Congolese politicians whose names they were just beginning to learn.

Journalists at the party prowled for scoops in a city that wasn't producing much news. One of them approached General Janssens, the commander of the Force Publique, who was in full dress and a jolly mood. How were Congolese soldiers greeting independence?

"The Force Publique? It is my creation," Janssens assured him. "It is absolutely loyal."

Chapter 12

A Nonexistent Army

THE FORCE PUBLIQUE mutinied the next day. Morale had long been slipping. Soldiers were exhausted from all the overtime they had pulled in recent months to monitor voting, to quell riots, and to supervise the festivities during the handover. They were fed up with the foul food they were served, the shabby bunks they slept in, the low pay that hadn't gone up, and the unrelenting discipline imposed by their superiors. Although they now raised the Congolese flag every morning, they still stood guard and saluted white Belgian officers. In essence, an army chaplain reported, the rank and file felt that "independence was eluding them."

That was the dry tinder that had been piling up. General Janssens provided the spark. At 8:00 a.m. on July 5, he gathered everyone on duty at the Force Publique's headquarters in Leopoldville to clear up a misconception. Soldiers had been spilling loose talk, suggesting that independence meant that they no longer had to obey their officers; just as in politics, the Congolese would now take charge. Janssens gathered the troops to set the record straight. "The soldier has a special nature that compels him to obey his superiors in all circumstances," he told them. Just because the Belgian Congo had become the Republic of the Congo didn't mean that the Force Publique would operate any differently. Approaching a blackboard and gripping a stick of chalk, he summed up his view in large letters: "before independence = after independence."

The message was received. At Camp Leopold II, a massive Force Publique base at the edge of the capital, murmurs were growing. By

5:00 p.m., several hundred angry soldiers filled the mess hall, demanding Janssens's firing and the "Africanization" of the officer corps. They roughed up white officers, liberated soldiers who had been jailed for disobedience, and battered the doors of the camp's weapons depot. The seventy-five-year-old Force Publique was widely considered, as a Belgian newspaper put it that very day, "the miracle of the Congo" and "the only solid institution of this country." Now it was in revolt.

When news of the disturbance reached Janssens by telephone, he was back home in the government district, a small collection of offices and houses beside the Palace of the Nation on the Congo River. The prime minister's residence was close, and Janssens immediately walked over to it.

"I knew something was wrong with the Force Publique," Lumumba told him bitterly. He listened as the general laid out his plan to shock the mutinous troops into submission. Janssens would arrive at Camp Leopold flanked by a company of burly Belgian paratroopers and announce the "ruthless repression of all disobedience." (This show of force could not be Congolese, Janssens maintained. As he would explain, "In the Force Publique, the prestige of the officer was reinforced by the prestige of the white man.") But Lumumba opted for accommodation. "No way are we punishing the mutineers," he told Janssens. Instead, the prime minister would go to Camp Leopold himself and announce a mass promotion.

By this point, however, the mutiny was spreading beyond Leopoldville. Eighty miles south, in the railroad town of Thysville, troops at Camp Hardy had been called up to calm the revolt at Camp Leopold—but promptly mutinied themselves. Soldiers made officers strip down to their underwear and locked them in the camp's prison cells. Drunk and frenzied, some fanned out from the camp to loot stores and arrest white civilians. Some detainees had their sunglasses—a colonial status symbol—taken away and smashed. One group of soldiers cornered three Belgian women and made them repeatedly dress and undress. Another forced three civilians to flatten barbed wire with their bare feet.

Undeterred, Lumumba followed through on his plan to placate the mutineers with a promotion. "I have a piece of good news for you," he told a crowd of soldiers at the army camp's parade ground the following day. "All privates and noncommissioned officers are to be promoted, as of July 1, 1960, to the next highest rank." Privates would become corporals, corporals would become sergeants, and so on. *Time* magazine called it "the most sweeping army promotion in history"; when President Eisenhower heard about the scheme, he quipped that Congolese soldiers were being promoted even faster than he had been. The idea, Lumumba explained, was to "remove all traces of racial discrimination in the military." Janssens seethed as he stood on the podium beside Lumumba. He thought the response "crazy and demagogic." The soldiers themselves found it inadequate. Until that point, the highest-ranking Congolese military man had been a first sergeant major—a rank the Force Publique had waited until two weeks before independence to bestow—and although he would now be a warrant officer, he would still be outranked by most Belgian officers. The troops booed and hissed at Lumumba. "Lies!" they yelled as he hurried to a waiting car.

Seeking to extract more sweeping reforms, a group of a hundred or so newly promoted soldiers flooded out of the camp and made their way toward the government district. Though unarmed, they yanked off their leather belts—thick, with big brass buckles—and brandished them at whites. Others hurled stones at passing cars. When the soldiers reached the government district, they cracked the windows of Kasavubu's office, mistaking it for that of Lumumba. (After seeing the broken glass, Kasavubu stayed inside and requested that his family be evacuated to Brazzaville. As far as he was concerned, this was a dispute between the prime minister and the army.) Soon the soldiers realized their mistake and caught up with Lumumba at his official residence. They extracted from him a promise bigger than the promotions he had announced that morning: he would fire General Janssens.

Janssens and Lumumba had been at odds in the months leading up to independence, but each had accepted an uneasy coexistence with the other: Janssens begrudgingly admitted that Lumumba was a politician he could not afford to ignore, and Lumumba figured that Janssens was the only authority figure who could hold the Force Publique together. But now it dawned on Lumumba that Janssens was part of the problem.

This belief only strengthened in the hours that followed. While huddling in his residence with a group of his ministers, Lumumba learned that Janssens had approached the commander of Belgian forces in the Congo for help. The last remaining Belgian troops were split between a base near the mouth of the Congo River on the Atlantic and another in Katanga, facilities the Congolese had agreed to leave in place after independence. These forces answered to Brussels alone, and to act in the Congo, they needed the permission of the Congolese government—permission that was in no way Janssens's to grant. What the general had in mind was a squadron of snub-nosed Belgian fighter planes opening fire on the camp in Thysville, a show of aerial force that would send the mutineers scurrying back to their barracks.

Janssens's request to Belgian forces was a remarkable contravening of the chain of command: the ostensible commander of the Congolese military was in effect asking a foreign country to intervene behind the backs of his civilian overseers. It was only when the Belgian ambassador sought Lumumba's approval for the intervention that the prime minister was clued in. Upon learning of Belgium's plans, Lumumba burst out in anger. He decided to dismiss Janssens immediately. And no, he told the ambassador, he would not consent to the use of Belgian troops on Congolese soil.

Janssens learned of his firing later that day—from his subordinate officers, embarrassingly enough. After briefly considering flying to another province to start an anti-Lumumba rebellion with loyal Force Publique troops, he changed out of uniform, fled via helicopter over the border to Brazzaville, and from there returned to Belgium. At a square in Brussels, Janssens wore a rumpled suit and approached a bronze statue of King Leopold II, mounted on horseback. Standing at attention, he saluted the founder of the Congo. "Your Majesty," he said, "they fouled it up for you."

If Lumumba thought that firing Janssens would mollify the soldiers, he was mistaken: Janssens was more his grievance than theirs. In fact, the situation on the ground kept getting worse. From Thysville, trucks of soldiers were spreading chaos to other towns across the lower Congo. Some rounded up whites and held a "trial" at the military camp to separate the good from the bad. When a tank squadron was sent to Thysville to scare the mutineers into submission, its members instead disarmed their own officers and joined the revolt. And now roving bands of mutineers were on their way north to Leopoldville, to take their protests directly to the government.

Mobutu was in Lumumba's office as reports came in from Thysville. "There's only one thing to do," Mobutu told the prime minister. "Talk with them to persuade them to not raid Leo." He volunteered to go himself.

As a native of Équateur province, Mobutu had no ties to the lower Congo region, but he had spent seven years in the army. He made the journey to Thysville by helicopter, which cut the three-hour journey to forty-five minutes. The scrubby forests and baked earth rushed past below, and soon the neat grid of Thysville came into view. But upon approaching the army camp, the helicopter drew fire, likely because of its white pilot. Mobutu diverted to a nearby village, left his pilot behind, and headed toward the camp by car.

En route, Mobutu encountered a column of soldiers destined for Leopoldville. "Let's talk calmly," he beseeched them. "Arriving in Leo won't solve anything. We're here to understand what exactly your demands are. Go back to your camp. We'll come with you."

The soldiers agreed, and when they got to the camp, Mobutu somehow persuaded them to free the whites they had imprisoned. So confident was he in his standing among the mutinous troops that he slept in the military camp that night, surrounded by armed men angry at the government he served. Lumumba arrived later, but he left once he saw that the situation was under control. Mobutu had proved that he knew how to reason with military men. He had confirmed his reputation as a troubleshooter.

Mobutu succeeded in preventing the soldiers from reaching Leopoldville, but not news of their acts. At 8:15 p.m. on July 7, two days after the start of the revolt, a trainful of white women and children fleeing the lower Congo pulled in to the Leopoldville station, a blocky new building near the port in the city's east. The bedraggled refugees shared horror stories—some witnessed, others heard secondhand—of the Force Publique running wild in the lower Congo. Civilians were being forced to parade nude in the street, it was said. Soldiers were alleged to have raped thirty women sheltering in a convent, sparing only three obviously pregnant women. Typical of the reports was this one, summarized by the Belgian government, with the victim's name redacted:

> On the 6th of July, 1960, at Inkisi, Miss—— was at home around 8:30 p.m. with three friends, when five or six soldiers entered the house. Two or three of them dragged one of the young women in a room. When she cried for help, Miss—— burst into the room where her friend was fighting the assaulters, but the soldiers grasped her and dragged her from one side to another of the room. They tried to rape her, tearing her clothes and hitting her. But they did not succeed. A black policeman put an end to the scene. A few minutes later, a Congolese sergeant broke into the room and tried several times to rape one of the ladies in the presence of her four children. The lady fainted two or three times. The soldier thereupon attacked another young lady and dragged her into an adjoining room from which cries for help could be heard. The soldier remained about fifteen minutes with his victim.

These were horrific acts. They were also less widespread than the rumor mill suggested. One estimate put the number of rapes at that point at no more than fifty—terrifying, to be sure, but in the press and on the grapevine the numbers multiplied. This was to be expected. For months, whites had swapped unverified "independence stories," like the one about a blond stewardess who was shocked to discover that she had been "sold" by a Congolese merchant for delivery after June 30. The hallmark of these tales was the idea that Congolese men couldn't wait to get their hands on European women. Now that fear seemed to be coming true. And so in the white neighborhoods, phones rang and windows lit up as Belgians shared what they had heard, with the atrocities growing in the telling.

By midnight, the white population was in a panic. "The word rape was all over the European section of Leopoldville," one newsman reported. "A sound, a car backfiring, was enough to cause a fresh wave of panic." Families fled their houses in nightgowns and pajamas for the safety of Brazzaville. They sped toward the ferry terminal, abandoning their Volkswagens and Citroëns on the riverbank, engines still

running. Passengers lay down on the ferry decks to protect themselves from gunfire, even though no one was shooting at them. Others
went to the Yacht Club to cross the river on skiffs and motorboats.

Then it was the soldiers' turn to panic. At Camp Leopold, a rumor
broke out that a Soviet or Czech plane had landed at the airport,
full of commandos ready to take over the Congo. Soldiers rushed
the weapons store and armed themselves. An officer asked Mobutu
for help in quelling the hysteria; three ministers were sent to the
camp to stop the disturbance, but to no avail. Soldiers mounted their
jeeps and tore toward the airport to repel the supposed invaders. Of
course, there were none to be found.

At midnight, the Belgian ambassador went to the prime minister's
house to meet with Lumumba. Once again, he sought to persuade
Lumumba to accept a military intervention. Belgium had the troops
necessary to end the unrest, the ambassador said, but the Congo had
to ask for them. "I didn't come to the Congo to stand idly by and witness the massacre or rape of my compatriots," he added.

Lumumba exploded. It was the Belgians who had stirred up this
chaos, beginning with General Janssens. Even the rumor of a Soviet
invasion was started by a Belgian officer, he alleged. Lumumba had
been told to flee for Brazzaville like the whites, but he wouldn't leave.
If the Belgians wanted to get rid of him, he said, they would have to
murder him at this very desk. Lumumba's eyes seemed to be throwing flames, the ambassador thought. "Tall and goateed, with his long
arms beating the air, in the silence of this African night he embodied
rather well a new Lucifer."

The argument dragged on until Lumumba abruptly excused
himself. The ambassador waited, noticing the seven volumes of the
Larousse encyclopedia behind Lumumba's desk and studying the
mediocre paintings of African landscapes on the wall while a servant
stood watch. The prime minister came back twenty minutes later. It
was now 2:00 a.m.

Lumumba led the ambassador outside to a guardhouse. "A European wanted to assassinate me," he announced. "He has just been
arrested on my property." He held up a leather belt with a revolver
holster, plus a box of ammunition.

Lumumba's growing anxiety had gotten the best of him. There
was no plot; a Belgian police officer had simply driven to his office

across the street to retrieve his service revolver when jumpy soldiers had arrested him. Mobutu, who had a knack for smoothing over these sorts of misunderstandings, would release him the next day. No one was trying to assassinate Lumumba. Not yet, at least.

By the morning, when mutinous soldiers closed down the ferry and patrolled the river in motorboats, as many as six thousand white residents had fled across the river. "Leopoldville has become a desert," one journalist reported. The city's white neighborhoods were dead, emitting their own peculiar last gasps through open windows: the howling of abandoned dogs and the dulcet music of unattended radios.

Against this eerie soundscape, disheveled soldiers marauded the city, many with a bottle of Polar beer in one hand and a Mauser rifle or tommy gun in the other. Their helmets were laureled with leafy branches for camouflage, a reminder that the Force Publique had been designed to put down ethnic violence in the bush, not restore order to a city. Fearing a repeat of the 1959 riots, when armed white vigilantes had threatened Congolese protesters, the troops searched the cars and homes of any remaining Belgians for weapons. They set up roadblocks, collecting watches and wallets as a toll. This was not an army or even a militia; it was a mob.

To contain the panic spreading among white residents, soldiers closed the airport and cut off all communications in the city. Telephone and telegraph lines went dead. The U.S. embassy now had one sole link with the outside world: a walkie-talkie connection across the river to the U.S. consul in Brazzaville. The consul stood on his office's balcony, a hundred yards from the river, antenna extended, straining to hear the latest from Leopoldville. Then he dashed inside to relay the news by telephone to the U.S. embassy in Paris, which cabled it to Washington. Through that circuitous route, the embassy in the Congo was able to send a simple message to the State Department: "All recognized authority in Leopoldville has broken down."

Inside the embassy, staff were dumping classified documents and official seals into special "burn barrels" loaded with magnesium, ready to be set aflame if the building were overrun. American citizens—

dowdy missionaries, mostly—were streaming into the embassy for protection, carrying babies, blankets, and food. Some were collected by an embassy Volkswagen, which led convoys that snaked their way through roadblocks toward the embassy. An American flag was draped over the hood to signal to the men at the checkpoints that these whites weren't Belgian. But even so, soldiers occasionally forced everyone out and made them line up before letting them go. The message: we are in charge now.

The refugees were directed to the second floor, where 130 of them crowded into the library. Everyone felt vulnerable. The embassy was encased in glass—"not eminently suited for repelling mobs," as Ambassador Timberlake put it. From the window, the refugees watched the silent pantomime of soldiers stopping cars and searching their drivers. One of the Americans, a missionary man, found the scene too interesting to resist photographing. When the soldiers saw his camera pointed at them through the glass, they banged on the embassy door with their rifle butts. Like their frantic search for weapons, their fixation with the camera grew out of the 1959 riots: the Belgians had convicted some of the participants based on photographic evidence.

Timberlake opened the door a crack. "You cannot come in here," he said through an office boy who spoke Lingala. Timberlake pulled out his cigarette case. "Here," he said. With a few smokes and a promise that the curious missionary would put away his camera, the soldiers were persuaded to leave.

Across the Boulevard Albert, the UN was dealing with its own group of rogue soldiers. At 11:30 a.m., Ralph Bunche was in his room on the fourth floor of the Stanley Hotel when he heard a commotion. Bunche looked down from his balcony at a chaotic scene. Several soldiers were holding two British photographers and three Israeli diplomats at gunpoint against the back of a truck. One of the soldiers spotted Bunche, shouldered his rifle, and took aim. Bunche ducked inside, just as a shot rang out.

Moments later, the door of the hotel room burst open. In rushed two rough-looking soldiers. "Over there!" they yelled, gesturing toward the door and poking their muzzles into his ribs. This was dicier than anything he had faced in Palestine, Bunche thought. After discreetly hiding confidential documents behind the toilet, he was ushered downstairs into the lobby, which was full of other guests deemed mischievous Belgians. Then, as suddenly as they had come, the troops jumped into their jeeps and screeched away.

Bunche sent a short cable to Hammarskjöld, transmitted via the U.S. embassy. "Powder keg here," he wrote.

At 2:00 p.m., Lumumba's cabinet met at Camp Leopold, straining to resolve the crisis. The ministers gathered in a hall guarded by mutinous soldiers who wouldn't let them leave until a solution had been found. As the politicians debated how to react, they were periodically interrupted by the arrival of Belgian Force Publique officers, dragged in barefoot by their Congolese subordinates. The officers were forced to kneel in a corner with their arms in the air, holding aloft their shoes in another act of humiliation. In this undignified atmosphere, Lumumba made two important decisions. First, he eliminated the entire officer corps, instantly removing all whites from the military. A few Belgians deemed sympathetic would stay on, but only as foreign advisers. Second, Lumumba picked a man to oversee this process: Mobutu.

Mobutu was made a colonel—the first Congolese to ever hold that rank—and named army chief of staff. "Go outside and try to find a uniform of a colonel," Lumumba said to him. "We're going to introduce you to the soldiers."

With his quiet charisma and history of military service, Mobutu had proved adept at calming mutinous soldiers, persuading them to let this or that group of white hostages free. Lumumba valued his protégé's calm confidence, his grace under fire. And even though they were not as close as they had been in the early days of the MNC, Lumumba trusted him.

Mobutu felt little gratitude for the "really dirty job" the prime minister had pushed his way. "He put me in charge of this nonexistent army without really believing in it himself," he said. "It was a dreadful time." But the role would prove to be the turning point in Mobutu's career—and the Congo's history.

—

As the sun set over Leopoldville on July 8, Ralph Bunche sat down at his desk in the Stanley Hotel and composed a letter to his sixteen-year-old son back in the United States, describing his harrowing run-in with soldiers earlier in the day. Bunche, the descendant of free Blacks in Virginia who married British colonists, was Black enough to face discrimination in the United States, but his skin was too light for the average Congolese soldier to consider him African. "Wouldn't it be ironic," he wrote to Ralph Jr., "if I should now get knocked around here in the very heart of Africa because of anti-white feeling—the reason being that I am not dark enough and might be mistaken for a 'blanc'!"

Not far away, the American embassy heaved with the weight of scores of American refugees. With the city run by soldiers—inebriated young men armed with rifles and plenty of pent-up rage—the building's glass facade, once inviting, suddenly seemed vulnerable. Still, the staffers did what they could to make the new arrivals feel at home, serving coffee and ham sandwiches. Timberlake's office was commandeered by young mothers and turned into a nursery. A kitchenette downstairs had an electric stove and oven, which the secretaries and employees' wives used to heat up canned vegetables, cook beef stew, and fry steaks. People slept where they could: on bedrolls on the floor, or suspended between two office chairs.

In the morning, Moise Tshombe, the governor of Katanga, prepared to leave Leopoldville. He had been in town to work out details of the relationship between his province and the central government, but the unrest of the past few days strengthened his belief that Katanga would be better off with as much autonomy as possible. The governor met with Bunche and expressed dissatisfaction that the independent Congo had opted for centralized government. According to Bunche, Tshombe favored "a loose (and weak) federation" along the lines of the U.S. Articles of Confederation. When Bunche told him that the Articles of Confederation had failed—the feckless national government couldn't collect taxes or enforce any of the laws it passed, and it struggled to put down a rebellion in Massachusetts—Tshombe "seemed only to be encouraged." Tshombe had tried to meet with Lumumba, too, but could not get an appointment.

At the Memling, across the street from Bunche's hotel and a dash from the U.S. embassy, Tshombe ran into Thomas Kanza, the young university graduate who served as the Congo's ambassador to the UN. "I came specially to see Patrice Lumumba," Tshombe told him, "but I have not been able to see him." He bent his ample body into a car headed for the airport. "I am going back to Katanga now, but Lumumba will regret having ignored me."

Chapter 13

A Body Without a Head

S INCE THE INCEPTION of the Force Publique, Belgium had made
sure that the military's most important functions were controlled
by Belgians. Weapons were locked away in armories to which only
officers had a key. No Congolese were trained as pilots. But one asset
was carelessly put into Congolese hands: the military radio network.
On the frequencies that connected the Force Publique's sixty-odd
nationwide garrisons, Congolese operators communicated in Lingala,
hindering supervision by their francophone officers. It was through
these unmonitored airwaves that the mutiny, initially contained to
Leopoldville and points downriver, spread across the entire country.

General Janssens was no more, white officers were on the way
out, mass promotions for the Congolese were promised, and the
Force Publique would henceforth be known as the Armée Nationale
Congolaise, or ANC. But news of these developments was slow to
propagate even over the radio. Instead, rumors—of impending foreign interventions, of Belgian atrocities, of the politicians' nefarious
plans for the army—crackled into the headsets of nervous soldiers,
sending garrisons hundreds of miles apart into a frenzy.

In Kongolo, an outpost in northern Katanga, suspicions between
twenty white officers and more than a thousand Black soldiers fed off
each other. When the camp commander placed gasoline drums in the
weapons stores so that the depots could be set on fire in the event of
a mutiny, the rank and file suspected a plot to incinerate not just the
weapons but also the men who bore them. They punched and kicked
two officers, one of whom fired a warning shot from his pistol, and

broke down the doors of the weapons stores and armed themselves. In the ensuing clashes, two men—one Belgian and one Congolese—were killed, the first fatalities of the mutiny. "The Congo is falling apart," a British diplomat told a reporter. "This has become a country which is a body without a head. Everything is crippled. All is chaos."

Hoping to quell the unrest and spread the word of Africanization, the government sent delegations to military bases across the country. Lumumba and Kasavubu headed downriver into the lower Congo. They stopped at the port of Matadi, where paranoid troops had taken control of the Metropole, an upscale neo-Gothic hotel known for its tranquil inner courtyard. "We're the masters now," the soldiers announced as they held the hotel's 250 European guests hostage. "Serve us some beer."

Lumumba and Kasavubu freed the hostages, apologized for their treatment, and promised a swift investigation into the misbehaving soldiers. In a brief speech at the hotel, Lumumba begged the Belgian guests to stay. "We will help those who wish to leave, but we say to you: do not leave us!" he implored. "There has been a change of regime. There are some difficulties. We find ourselves facing a psychological problem. You must help us build our new country." But the plea fell on deaf ears. The next day, fewer than ten white people were left in the whole city.

Mobutu, meanwhile, had been sent to his native province of Équateur, in the country's northwest. Named for the line of latitude running through its capital city, the region stretched over an area bigger than Japan. Mobutu crisscrossed it by plane, helicopter, and jeep, and at times by bicycle and by foot. At base after base, he calmed soldiers and negotiated the release of imprisoned whites. Troops who had greeted Mobutu with hostility in the morning were dining with him by the evening. "Because I was one of them and knew how to talk to them and was not trying to disarm them, they listened to me and understood me," he said.

When he saw young men pillaging stores while crying, "Long live the MNC!" he confronted the looters and flashed his own MNC card, imploring them to stop bringing shame upon the party. In Coquilhatville, the provincial capital, he organized a military parade and managed to get Black and white residents alike to applaud the troops.

At the garrison in Ikela, a tiny trading post on a tributary of the Congo River, the rank and file had chased all the white officers into the bush. When Mobutu and his entourage touched down on the dirt airstrip, their plane was swarmed by wary soldiers, fingers on triggers. Shouting from the plane, Mobutu did his best to explain who he was. The soldiers looked at him askance. This stranger in civilian clothes—despite Lumumba's urging, he hadn't been able to find a uniform that fit—this was supposed to be the army chief of staff? And since when were there Black colonels in the Congo?

Mobutu once again managed to talk the men down. When informed of the decisions being made in Leopoldville to Africanize the army, the leader of these mutineers had his men line up and welcome the passengers off the plane. Mobutu listened patiently as the soldiers complained about delayed wages and low rations, promising to look into the problems. And in a move that was fast becoming second nature, he took from his pocket 3,000 francs, all he had.

"With this you can go and buy your own food," he said as he passed the wad of bills to the soldiers. "But now I'm counting on you."

When news of the mutiny reached Belgium's prime minister, Gaston Eyskens, he dismissed the rumblings as "slight twinges"—nothing out of the ordinary for a fledgling state. Within days, however, these twinges became harder to ignore. Reports of humiliation and rape were flowing in, as were the first refugees from the Congo. In Brussels, protesters—many of whom had relatives living in the former colony—demanded that Belgium take charge of the deteriorating situation. "How far will the government's cowardice go?" asked one protester's sign.

In preparation for a possible intervention, Eyskens sent troop reinforcements to Belgium's two remaining military bases in the Congo. But for the moment, the government thought it best to wait for calm to return on its own. Barring that outcome, leaders in Brussels hoped the Congolese government would issue a formal request for help from the Belgian army—a step that might improve the poor optics of sending troops back onto the streets of the ex-colony so soon after independence. The Belgian public had supported the decision to let go of the Congo, but it did not share its government's reservations about intervening. Hearing news of their fellow citizens being harassed and raped, Belgians wanted the troops to leave their bases, put down the mutiny, and protect Belgian lives and property—with or without Congolese permission. "It would be madness to worry now about legal scruples," urged the *Libre Belgique*. The newspaper continued: "Belgium has recognized the independence of the Congo—yes. But not any kind of independence. Not independence in anarchy or disorder." There it was again, the notion that had so irked Lumumba in his days as a political agitator in Stanleyville: the idea that independence was a gift to be given, not a right to be claimed—and, it turned out, a gift that could be taken back if maltreated.

In Leopoldville, the Belgian ambassador continued, to no avail, to try to get the Congolese government to approve Belgian troop deployments. But with domestic pressure in Belgium mounting, a unilateral military intervention looked more and more likely. By the afternoon of July 9, less than a week after the start of the mutiny and not even a fortnight after independence, Prime Minister Eyskens had made up his mind: if the Congolese government did not give the green light, Belgian troops would intervene regardless.

Before sunrise the next day, they did just that. Early in the morning, ten planes carrying two companies of soldiers took off from the Kamina air base in Katanga and flew to Elisabethville. The copper province's capital was in jeopardy: an army camp in the city had revolted, and a group of Congolese soldiers had set up a machine gun beside a road and fired into passing cars, killing five white civilians. Welcomed by Tshombe, who saw the mutiny as a Leopoldville plot, the three hundred Belgian troops took Elisabethville's airport and army camp without firing a shot.

At 1:00 p.m. on July 10, the U.S. ambassador Clare Timberlake hopped into a bakery truck—the only available method of transportation, in the circumstances, that would allow him to part the sea of crowds in Leopoldville—and drove to the airport. He was there to meet with Lumumba and Kasavubu upon their return from their hostage-negotiation mission at the hotel in Matadi. The ambassador caught up with the two leaders on the runway and ushered them into a maintenance shed. There, out of earshot from their entourage, Timberlake complained that the breakdown in the army was driving white women and children out of the country; even U.S. embassy staff were being manhandled by out-of-control Congolese soldiers. If women and children left, he pointed out, white men would follow. Their departure, Timberlake feared, would throw the country back into a "primitive way of life"; it would, as he put it in a cable to Washington, "convert modern Congo to jungle."

Timberlake's suggestion was to turn to the UN for help in reorganizing the military. The UN could put one of its own in charge of the Congolese army, or it could even form its own separate force, drawing first on Belgian troops already stationed in the Congo and eventually on soldiers from other countries. Whatever the design, Timberlake explained, the UN would be able to intervene quickly if needed. All the Congolese government had to do was make a formal request to Bunche, who would then tell Hammarskjöld, who would convene the Security Council within hours. UN troops could deploy in the Congo in just days.

Lumumba replied that he was not interested in handing over his newly Africanized army to the UN, nor was he interested in legitimizing the presence of Belgian troops by placing them under the aegis of that organization. But he expressed some interest in a potential UN mission comprising soldiers from other countries and promised to discuss the idea in a cabinet meeting. He asked Timberlake to have Bunche join it.

For most of the hour that Timberlake and Lumumba talked in the airport shed, Kasavubu stood by in characteristic silence. What little he did say betrayed his naivete. Just before independence, Kasavubu had asked Bunche how far away New York was and how long it took to get there. Now he asked Timberlake whether UN troops could leave behind their valuable military equipment when they eventually withdrew from the Congo.

In a cable to Washington, Timberlake explained why he had advised Lumumba to call in the UN—a daring recommendation offered without permission from the State Department. As a mediator composed mostly of troops from neutral countries, a UN force could stabilize the situation without drawing in either the United States or the Soviet Union. "This should keep the bears out of the Congo caviar," he wrote.

After the airport meeting, Timberlake shared with Bunche his vision of a UN mission. Close collaboration between the United States and the UN wasn't unusual in 1960. The two were largely aligned. The West had four of the five permanent members of the Security Council—China's seat was still held by the Nationalist government in Taiwan, not the Communist one in Peking—and most of Hammarskjöld's advisers, like Bunche, were American. Indeed, Bunche was sending his cables through the U.S. embassy (which read them, naturally), and he planned to take refuge there in the event of an emergency. He was even given an office in the embassy.

Nonetheless, when he heard of Timberlake's proposal for a UN mission, Bunche was skeptical. He found the idea lacked precision: the possibilities ranged from dispatching a UN adviser to assembling a massive international force to occupy the country. And he reminded Timberlake that although the UN had in the past sent monitors to keep the peace between warring armies, it had never done what was being suggested now: put down a mutiny inside a country.

Indeed, the very idea that the UN could field its own forces was still novel. Small groups of unarmed UN observers had monitored cease-fires in Palestine in 1948 and along the Indo-Pakistani border in 1949. The first armed peacekeeping mission had come only in 1956, with UN forces monitoring the withdrawal of British, French, and Israeli troops from the Suez Canal in Egypt. Hammarskjöld, then three years into his tenure as UN secretary-general, had invented the legal framework for the world's first nonviolent military operation over the course of a day. To distinguish UN troops from the aggressor armies, the plastic inner liners of surplus U.S. Army helmets were spray-painted UN blue. Thus the "blue helmets" were born.

From this meager precedent, Timberlake was trying to extract something much more ambitious. Though innovative in their own right, previous missions had taken on merely a monitoring role. Never before had the UN been tasked with restoring order to an entire country, much less one as big and complex as the Congo. Bunche nonetheless agreed to sit in on the cabinet meeting at which Lumumba would raise the issue with his government.

At 5:00 p.m. that same day, Bunche accompanied Lumumba to Kasavubu's hillside house, a modernist stack of rectangles originally built as a home for the Belgian governor of the Leopoldville province. They were joined by fifteen cabinet members. The meeting turned into a seminar of sorts, with Bunche trying to explain the workings of UN peacekeeping. Midway through, Lumumba and Kasavubu excused themselves to broadcast radio statements on the evolving security situation. Kasavubu's was an appeal for Belgian civilians to return to the independent Congo, while Lumumba's was a diatribe against the former colonial power and its ongoing troop deployments to the Congo. "Belgium bears a grave responsibility," Lumumba said. "We call upon all Congolese to defend our republic against those who seek to threaten it."

Not long after the president and the prime minister returned to Bunche's presentation, it was interrupted again—this time by a telegram. In Luluabourg, the capital of Kasai province, Congolese soldiers had laid siege to an office building sheltering half the city's white residents, and the two sides had traded potshots for hours. Just before dusk, Belgian forces, alerted by an SOS message scrawled in large letters on the roof, had parachuted onto the scene from above and taken the building—a further escalation of the Belgian intervention.

The news eradicated any remaining doubts that the country was facing a deep crisis. The Congo's leaders had lost control of not only their country's army but now its sovereignty, too. Even so, Bunche steered them toward a modest UN mission, one in which the organization would merely send military advisers to reform the army. The Congolese leaders were especially enthused about the prospect of French-speaking experts from neutral countries like Lebanon, Switzerland, and Tunisia. After four hours, the meeting ended with Bunche promising to pass on a request for such a mission to Hammarskjöld.

The secretary-general was in Geneva, but he had been keeping a close eye on the Congo ever since the mutiny had broken out. A deft UN switchboard operator managed to connect him with Andrew Cordier (his deputy) in New York and Ralph Bunche in Leopoldville, setting up a halting and fuzzy three-way phone call spanning three continents. Using the tortured language he had worked out with the

Congolese, Bunche conveyed the government's request for "techni-cal assistance in the military field"—words designed to thread the needle between innocuous technical assistance and full-scale mili-tary aid. Hammarskjöld decided to return at once to New York to organize a response. Bunche explained to him that Lumumba and the others grasped the problem better than the solution. They rec-ognized that the Congolese military was in shambles and in need of outside help to put it back together (provided that outside help came from somewhere other than Belgium). But they had only a vague conception of what the UN could do about this. "Thus, they appeal to the UN, without any clear notion as to what they want or might reasonably expect," Bunche wrote in a follow-up cable. "But they wish and they need quick action and I greatly hope we can at least partially meet this challenge. They will gladly take any type of military assistance we can propose."

Yet there was one type of UN mission that was off the table. "I made it perfectly clear that the UN could not—repeat not—participate in actual policing internally or in providing fighting men," Bunche told Hammarskjöld. The promise would not last long.

Larry Devlin was on vacation with his family in the Loire Valley when he heard a radio in the back room of a bistro announce some-thing about a mutiny. Probably in Latin America, he thought. Then he heard it was in the Congo—the independent Congo, not the one that was still part of France. As the CIA's incoming station chief, Devlin had to get to Leopoldville right away. He dropped his wife and daughter off in Arcachon, the seaside town of his wedding, where Colette's family had a summerhouse. "Daddy, don't go," Maureen said as he prepared to leave. "They are killing people down there."

Devlin tried to fly on Sabena, Belgium's national airline, but all flights to the Congo were canceled. The airline's entire fleet had been commandeered to bring Belgian troops into the Congo and airlift refugees out of it, with armrests pulled out and babies placed onto hat racks. He flew Air France to Brazzaville instead, arriving too late in the day to catch a ferry to Leopoldville. He spent the night on the concrete floor of the U.S. consulate in Brazzaville, falling asleep under a borrowed blanket to the sound of bullfrogs in the garden and to anxious thoughts of what awaited him across the river.

The next day, Devlin boarded a ferry that had just emptied its load of terrified refugees; he was one of few to board in the other direction. From the deck, he watched the sepia water rush by, carrying with it chunks of water hyacinth. A year earlier, Graham Greene had noticed them, too. "From as far as one could see the little islands of grass flowed down towards the sea they would never reach—some as small as a bucket-top, some as large as a dining table," Greene had written. "In the distance, coming out of Africa, they looked like families of ducks."

Devlin gazed at Leopoldville, coming into view. It looked calm, he thought.

Chapter 14

Magic Men from the Sky

O N THE MORNING of July 11, the Belgian minesweeper *Lecointe* docked in Matadi. The Congo's link to the Atlantic, Matadi was a mountain-lined choke point through which 60 percent of the country's imports and exports passed. The port had ceased functioning amid the turmoil of the rebellion, and the Belgian military planned a peaceful mission to open it. But in the hours before the *Lecointe* arrived, the plan inexplicably morphed into a forceful operation to seize the city, even though no Belgians had been in any danger since Lumumba and Kasavubu had defused the hostage situation at the city's hotel two days earlier. Since then, nearly all the city's whites had fled to ships anchored offshore.

As soon as soldiers bounded off the *Lecointe,* they took fire from a nearby artillery cannon manned by Congolese soldiers. The Belgians returned fire and summoned four fighter planes to strafe the town, setting off an hours-long battle that shattered windows and littered the street with spent cartridges. Belgian troops gunned down a quartet of Congolese policemen who had sought refuge in a small office, staining the walls with blood. By the end of the day, eighteen Congolese had been killed.

As news of the attack spread over the army radio network, the clash, as lethal as it was, grew in the telling into a full-fledged massacre, an aerial bombardment that had left hundreds dead. More uprisings at still more bases followed, with soldiers demanding retribution against the Belgian attackers. At the Thysville garrison, a Congolese staff sergeant vowed revenge: "There will be as many European coffins in Thysville as there were Black coffins in Matadi!"

The mutiny was a fire that would not go out. No sooner did the government bring one restive garrison under its control than a new conflagration would flare up at another. By the time that latest outbreak had been contained, smoldering resentment at the first site would reignite, with Belgian acts of brutality—some real, others exaggerated or imagined—providing ample fuel. Racing from one town to the next, Lumumba and Kasavubu did their best to smother the flames.

As fighting was under way in Matadi, the two leaders—unaware of the escalating violence on the Atlantic coast—made their way to Kasai province, a few hundred miles east of Leopoldville. In Luluabourg, the provincial capital, Belgian paratroopers had just freed a thousand-plus Europeans held hostage, and Lumumba and Kasavubu arrived to find the airport packed with whites trying to escape. Rows of abandoned cars stretched out behind them. Toddlers wandered between suitcases as their parents waited for news of a flight out.

Similar scenes were playing out across the country. In Stanleyville, white residents organized convoys and drove through the bush to reach Sudan or Uganda. In Katanga, some 250 whites spilled over the border into Northern Rhodesia every hour.

The exodus hit the Congo fast, and it hit hard. The white elite that had stayed on after independence—doctors, pharmacists, teachers, accountants, mechanics, engineers, telegraph operators, air traffic controllers—was now leaving en masse, draining the young country of badly needed expertise. Of the Congo's 175 Belgian postal officials, only one resolved to stay. Of its 542 university-educated agricultural engineers, none did. The national radio fell silent as inexperienced Congolese operators blew through the fuses. At the Ministry of the Interior, two lonely clerks manned an office usually run by dozens of employees. This was white flight on an unprecedented scale: within two weeks of independence, some 60,000 of the 80,000 Europeans remaining in the Congo had left.

At the airport in Luluabourg, Lumumba clasped a loudspeaker to address the departing whites. "Foreigners who wish to work faithfully in the interest of our country, we ask you to stay with us," he said. But words were not enough. The Belgian consul general in the city told Lumumba that white residents needed assurance of their security. Lumumba agreed, and the two negotiated a deal that would allow Belgian troops to stay in Kasai for two months.

It was the first time Lumumba authorized the presence of Belgian soldiers—and the last. For that evening, just as Lumumba could feel that he had succeeded in calming Luluabourg, came an unsettling announcement that eliminated any of his remaining goodwill toward the Belgians. It was not entirely unexpected.

A few minutes before 8:00 p.m., Moise Tshombe strode into Elisabethville's radio station, arms swinging with confidence, sat down in front of a microphone in the recording studio, and declared Katanga's independence from the Congo. As gunfire between Congolese and Belgian soldiers echoed in the distance, Tshombe tore into the central government. This, he explained, was Lumumba's Congo: a nation drowning in chaos, likely in keeping with a Communist plot masterminded by the prime minister. Katanga, he went on, could no longer submit to "the arbitrary will and Communistic intentions of the central government," and so it would have to go its own way. "May God protect independent Katanga," Tshombe said, signing off.

Yet more than divine intervention, he would need assistance from Western powers that might take his side in a face-off with Lumumba and the central government, chief among them Belgium and the United States. Tshombe had been seeking such help for some time. A week before the Congo's independence, the U.S. consul in Elisabethville, William Canup, learned that Tshombe's party, Conakat, intended to declare Katanga's secession through a formal statement in the provincial legislature. Members of Conakat would then call Canup down from the visitors' gallery to receive an official request for American military help. When Tshombe's followers approached Canup about the plan, he did not push back. That earned him a reprimand from his superiors in Foggy Bottom, who worried that his presence might "be interpreted as evidence of U.S. connivance with the plans of Conakat to declare independence." Canup was told to make the U.S. position clear—namely, that secession "might very well result in disorder and bloodshed." Canup complied, and the plan was shelved.

The day he read his declaration of independence over the radio, Tshombe tried again to solicit U.S. support. He informed Canup of his plans in the morning and asked whether he could count on the United States. Instead of firmly rebuking the idea, or even just asking Tshombe to reconsider, Canup meekly replied that he had no new instructions but didn't think it was likely that the United States would recognize independent Katanga. He was hedging, and now so were his superiors in Washington. For the moment, the State Department told Canup, "there is absolutely no possibility the U.S. would recognize." But given where things appeared to be headed, who, in the long run, could say for certain? "In general, we wish Tshombe to be discouraged," the department's instructions went on, "but do not wish to close the door completely, since the detachment of Katanga could conceivably be in the interest of the West if the rest of the Congo continues in its present status."

Belgium was less interested in hedging. Before the ongoing crisis, it had resolutely opposed Katangan independence. In the waning days of colonial rule, the province's Belgian vice-governor had threatened to arrest Tshombe just for flirting with the idea. Now, though, Brussels saw Katanga as the one part of the Congo it could hold on to—the richest part—and decided to offer Tshombe everything short of formal recognition. From the first days of the mutiny, white Force Publique officers in Katanga refused to step aside and follow Lumumba's orders to Africanize the national army, the ANC. The Belgian troops there, meanwhile, acted well beyond their supposed mandate of protecting the European population. Instead, they got to work expelling Congolese soldiers whose ethnicity was thought to mark them as hostile to Tshombe, setting up a new army of Katangan loyalists.

When Lumumba got the news of Tshombe's declaration, he recognized that his strategy for dealing with Katanga had failed. The prime minister had hoped that his own government, through the legal strictures created at the roundtable, would be able to force the province to accept rule from Leopoldville. But the mutiny and general atmosphere of lawlessness had given Tshombe an unexpected opening. If Tshombe's gambit succeeded, the consequences would be dire: just eleven days after independence, the Congo was now at risk of losing a fifth of its territory and, with it, many of its most valuable natural resources. How Lumumba would withstand such a devastating blow to his leadership was hard to imagine. An intelligence briefing given to Eisenhower grimly predicted, "The secession of Katanga may presage the overthrow of Lumumba within the next two months."

For now, however, Lumumba's government remained in power, and it needed to figure out fast how to contend with the Congolese army mutiny, Belgian intervention, and Katangan secession. On July 12, with Lumumba and Kasavubu still in Luluabourg, the rest of the cabinet held an emergency meeting in the capital. In a sign of the ministers' naivete and desperation, they gathered in the presence of the Belgian and American ambassadors. What the Congo needed now, they agreed, was outside military help—boots on the ground from a neutral foreign country. A minister suggested Israeli forces, but the idea was quickly dismissed as impractical. Then someone suggested inviting American troops. Timberlake agreed to pass on the request. "We kindly ask you to intervene immediately with the U.S. government to have a contingent of 3,000 troops directed urgently to Leopoldville," it read.

Timberlake liked the idea, telling the State Department that "even a token force of two companies of American forces might serve to stabilize the situation long enough." But the reply was not encouraging. Washington doubted the "advisability of sending in U.S. troops for many reasons, principally among them being the question of language and color." White troops who could not communicate with any of the involved parties were not what the Congo needed at the moment. The secretary of state, Christian Herter, called President Eisenhower, who was vacationing in Newport, Rhode Island. Both agreed that a U.S. intervention was out of the question. Not only was there little appetite for a far-flung operation among the American public; there also seemed to be no surer way of encouraging Soviet meddling in central Africa than sending in American GIs. Eisenhower had been a skeptic of African nationalism from the beginning, and he now viewed the Congo's difficulties as vindication. "Maybe after this situation some of these people won't want now to be independent," he said.

From Newport, the president's press secretary quickly announced that U.S. troops would not be forthcoming. But the United States did flex its military muscle in response to the crisis. Two companies of a U.S. infantry division stationed in West Germany were put on alert. The USS *Wasp*, a 33,000-ton aircraft carrier loaded with fifteen planes and helicopters and a contingent of marines, was sent from the Caribbean toward Africa, ready to invade the Congo if the Soviets did first.

On the morning of July 12, Lumumba and Kasavubu went to the military camp in Luluabourg and approached a Belgian paratrooper commander with a question.

"If I ordered you to leave town, would you?" Kasavubu asked.

"No," the officer replied. "That could only be done by order of my superiors."

It was a clear distillation of the political realities facing independent Congo: the prime minister and the president, the highest authorities in the land, had no power over the troops on their soil. Even Kasavubu, who only weeks prior had extolled the legacy of Belgium's rule at the independence ceremony, understood as much. "Belgium isn't changing its ways," he told the paratrooper commander. "It got into the habit of deciding without us before independence, and it has continued to do so since."

Belgium's intervention was a stunning imposition on another sovereign country. In the days immediately after independence but before the mutiny, if the Force Publique wanted to use Belgian military planes to transport troops from one garrison to another, Lumumba himself had to submit a formal request to Belgium. And yet now across the Congo, Belgian paratroopers were streaming down onto remote airstrips and open fields without his permission. Thomas Kanza, Lumumba's ambassador to the UN, laid out the situation in plain terms: "Since June 30, Belgium has been a foreign country, and we cannot tolerate continued foreign occupation."

To be sure, that occupation did not always turn violent. Sometimes the "magic men from the sky," as some Congolese described the Belgian paratroopers, rescued civilians or took a military base without firing a shot. But at other times, they came in guns blazing. In a sense, Belgium was at war with its former colony, and its trigger-happy soldiers seemed to care little about their targets. *Time* magazine's correspondent reported that a Belgian soldier shot at him and then apologized upon realizing that he was a white journalist. "In the dark," the Belgian said, "I thought you were an African." What had begun as an ostensible rescue mission meant to recover Belgian civilians was looking more and more like an attempt at de facto recolonization.

Nikita Khrushchev, the Soviet premier, was quick to seize on this development. Cold War tensions were already running high: The Soviets had shot down a CIA U-2 spy plane over their territory in May, walked out of a disarmament conference in late June, and shot down another U.S. spy plane in Arctic waters on July 1. Events in the Congo, Khrushchev now argued, were part of a larger struggle against Western imperialism. "The Congolese people have stood up against colonial oppression and won," he said at a press conference. "Now, the colonialists are trying to turn the tables. That is why the imperialists are now sending their troops to the Congo."

To those wondering what right Belgium had to wage this campaign, the country's foreign minister, Pierre Wigny, had a defiant retort: "Do we really have to prove with legal phrasing and quoting of legal textbooks the rightness of our intervention, when the arrivals of our refugees prove beyond doubt its necessity?"

In Luluabourg, Lumumba and Kasavubu, still seething after their conversation with the paratrooper but even more concerned about the secession of Katanga, left the military camp and made their way to a hotel by the city's airport. There, more bad news awaited them. Over lunch, the men learned that a military delegation they had sent to Katanga as part of their nationwide push to Africanize the armed forces had been turned away at the airport in Elisabethville and threatened with imprisonment. Lumumba now recognized that apart from offending the Congo's national dignity, the Belgian troop presence was threatening the power of his government. As he ate with Kasavubu, Lumumba called over a Belgian police official to take down a statement about the incident "so that the truth of it could not be questioned later."

From lunch, Lumumba and Kasavubu decided to continue their national tour to Katanga, despite what had happened to the last delegation that tried to land in the city. "It might mean our death," Lumumba thought, "but if so, we would die."

They touched down at Kamina, a Belgian military base northwest of Elisabethville, at 5:45 p.m., just as the sun was dipping below the horizon. Getting off the plane, the two leaders were greeted by Belgian soldiers and refugees, who made their feelings known. "Apes!" the crowd shouted. "Apes!"

The Belgian commander of the base escorted them into a small office near the entrance to the airfield and told them not to continue on to Elisabethville. When Lumumba and Kasavubu protested, the commander said he needed the permission of his superiors. Lumumba scolded him. "When the head of state asks your help, don't waste time waiting for the approval of your government," he said.

Then the two Congolese leaders fired off a pair of messages. The first was a communiqué, signed at 6:26 p.m., ordering all Belgian troops back to their two bases within two hours. The second was a cable to Elisabethville, announcing the politicians' impending arrival. The response—a telegram addressed "to Lumumba personally" from the "Government of Katanga"—was decidedly inhospitable:

> In the interest of the country and in the interests of Lumumba himself, he must not risk showing up in Katanga. First let him bring order to lower Congo, the Orientale province, and Kasai. Then, if necessary, Katanga will call on him.

The president and the prime minister carried on regardless. Lumumba was surprised to find that they were given not a comfortable passenger plane, but a World War II–era cargo plane with no seats. Their aircraft reached Elisabethville around 10:00 p.m. and made radio contact with the airport. At the control tower that night was Godefroid Munongo, one of Tshombe's top deputies. Munongo radioed the plane, which was circling helplessly around the city, and asked for Lumumba, who folded his frame into the cockpit and took the receiver. "Go away," Munongo told him. Munongo then asked for Kasavubu. He apologized to the president, saying that he would be happy to receive him without Lumumba.

For the past three days, Lumumba and Kasavubu had put aside their differences while touring the country. It was an admirable display of unity for bitter rivals, yet now, as they huddled in an uncomfortable plane in the skies over Katanga, someone was trying to divide them. Belgian military personnel at the airport ordered the pilot to turn around. Then the lights on the runway flicked off, preventing a landing. The duo retreated in humiliation back to Luluabourg.

Their only hope now, it seemed, lay in getting a response to a telegram they had sent hours earlier from Luluabourg by commercial cable to New York—a message in a bottle, tossed desperately from a provincial capital with iffy communications: "We strongly stress the extremely urgent need for the dispatch of United Nations troops to the Congo."

Chapter 15

A Political Miracle

Dᴵᴅ'ꜱᴛ Tʜᴏᴜ ɢɪᴠᴇ me this inescapable loneliness so that it would be easier for me to give Thee all?" Hammarskjöld once asked in his journal. From its earliest pages, written when he was still a student in his twenties, Hammarskjöld confessed an inability to connect with others, writing across decades about "the anguish of loneliness." Solitude appeared to him the price of a life devoted to God and a career devoted to public service. "For him who has responded to the call of the Way of Possibility," he wrote in the journal, "loneliness may be obligatory."

Hammarskjöld never married or even dated, and from the moment he was nominated as secretary-general, his opponents used this fact against him, whispering that he was "a fairy." Those close to him insisted he wasn't gay, preferring to describe him as a "born bachelor" or "asexual." "He was not afraid of women, and could speak expertly on feminine beauty," one of his Swedish friends said, "yet I sometimes felt that for all his polite talk at parties he never visually discriminated between a shapely woman and, say, a sofa or a chair."

In an era when homosexuality was a crime, it was of course possible that Hammarskjöld repressed his urges, denying them perhaps even to himself. The photographs he took of his personal aide, Bill Ranallo, on a vacation the two of them took to the Bahamas in 1959—here, shirtless with legs spread on a boat; there, lying crotch upward on a beach—suggest at least the eye of a man interested in male beauty. That same year, Hammarskjöld wrote a poem about the rumors surrounding his private life:

Because it never found a mate
Men called
The unicorn perverted.

On one of his desks, Hammarskjöld kept a silver figurine of a unicorn, a gift from Ranallo, and he jokingly referred to his apartment as "the unicorn stable."

The unicorn stable was at the corner of East Seventy-Third Street and Park Avenue, a "maisonette" in real estate parlance, which meant that it had two stories and its own private entrance. Hammarskjöld staffed the apartment with "the world's sweetest and most competent Swedish butler-cook couple" and filled it with select artifacts and mementos from around the world, giving it the feel of an airy museum wing. Long-haired Scandinavian rugs and a leopard skin covered the wooden floors. In an alcove, a pair of antlers framed a Chinese vase. A menorah sat on one mantelpiece; a Nepalese Sherpa's ice ax hung below another. But most of the walls remained bare. "Is it monastic enough for you?" Hammarskjöld once asked a visiting UN photographer.

Most evenings, the apartment really did feel like an abbey. Hammarskjöld rejected nearly all dinner invitations and spent his evenings reading—Joseph Conrad was a favorite—often as Bach or Vivaldi played. Then he would lie down in a spartan twin bed, a phone beside him, ready to ring in the event of some international crisis, and fall asleep alone.

Occaionally, however, an eclectic assemblage of guests turned the place into a lively salon. Hammarskjöld counted among his friends the composer Leonard Bernstein, the poet W. H. Auden, the columnist Walter Lippmann, and the novelist John Steinbeck. Even Greta Garbo, a notorious recluse and the person who confined Hammarskjöld to the slot of second-most famous Swede in New York, sometimes surfaced in his apartment. Amid the worldly curios and guests romped a vervet monkey, a gift Hammarskjöld had been given on his African tour in January, during a stopover in Somalia. He named him Greenback, for the slight tint of his coat, and let him swing on a vine hanging from the banister. Never housebroken, the animal soiled Hammarskjöld's shoe and wet his collar, but this did nothing to spoil the secretary-general's affection. "Dag is crazy about the little monkey," Ralph Bunche, one of the few colleagues to earn an invitation to Hammarskjöld's, wrote after one dinner just before he left for the Congo.

On the evening of July 13, however, the apartment on Seventy-Third Street lay still and dark. Hammarskjöld held court not in his dining room but at the horseshoe table of the UN Security Council. The mood was grave. At 8:30 p.m., as New York fell dim, the eleven delegates took their seats. Across from an intricate mural depicting a phoenix rising from the ashes of war, they considered how to rescue the Congo from its own inferno.

"I must do this," Hammarskjöld had said when he first learned that the Congolese were asking for UN help. "God knows where it will lead this organization and where it will lead me." The desperate cable from Lumumba and Kasavubu, which came as a complete surprise, led him to conclude that the Congo needed an infusion of armed international troops to restore order. His view was reinforced the morning of July 13, when he arrived at work to find another cable from Lumumba and Kasavubu on his desk, this one clarifying that they wanted "a United Nations force consisting of military personnel from neutral countries." Bunche, who had earlier thought that only civilian aid was needed, also cabled Hammarskjöld, saying that deteriorating conditions had caused him to change his mind. As Hammarskjöld concluded, "Nothing short of a major military intervention sailing under the proper flag would do the trick."

Among the UN Charter's 111 articles is exactly one that gives the secretary-general substantive powers: Article 99. The provision allows him to "bring to the attention of the Security Council any matter which in his opinion may threaten the maintenance of international peace and security." Hammarskjöld thought it authorized the secretary-general "to try all he can to smooth out conflicts," and it was the crisis in the Congo that caused him to drop what he called this "political H-bomb," the first time he had ever invoked Article 99. He called an emergency meeting for that evening to consider a UN response in the Congo. Hammarskjöld was running toward the crisis. "I had a tough decision on my hands in the morning of the thirteenth," he told a friend, "when, without sufficient information and without any possibility of consultation, I had to decide whether to throw the UN into this major adventure or not."

Hammarskjöld had spent the day laying the groundwork for the meeting, lining up support for a potential UN intervention among members of the Security Council and beyond. He knew he was walking a fine line: On the one hand, he would need to put forward a mission with enough punch to satisfy the Eastern bloc and post-colonial governments across Africa and Asia, both of which agreed with Lumumba that the Congo's main problem was the Belgian troop presence. On the other hand, he would need the West on his side, especially the U.K. and France. As fellow colonial powers, they remained somewhat sympathetic to the Belgian intervention and might wield their Security Council vetoes to block any UN response they deemed too extreme. Consequently, a potential UN mandate could not appear to be directed against Belgium, and a formal condemnation of Belgian aggression, as favored by the Soviets, was out of the question.

The U.S. government shared the Europeans' view. In between rounds of golf, President Eisenhower, still on vacation in Newport, received periodic updates from Secretary of State Christian Herter about the unfolding Congo drama at the UN. Herter sympathized with Belgium, and he wanted the Security Council resolution to not even mention the country. "The Belgians obviously have not committed aggression and the U.S. could not support any UN force on this basis," went Herter's instructions to the U.S. mission in New York. "Given the inability of the Congolese Government to maintain law and order, Belgian actions to protect lives and property and to assist and evacuate its own citizens are clearly justified."

Eisenhower had no edits. He told Herter that he was handling this exactly right.

At the Security Council that evening, Hammarskjöld, undeterred by a series of petty procedural fights and accusatory exchanges between the U.S. and Soviet representatives, put forward his vision for a UN mission. Whether the Belgian intervention in the Congo had been justified or not, it was clear that the Congolese government considered it unacceptable. "In these circumstances," he said, "the presence of the Belgian troops cannot be accepted as a satisfactory stopgap arrangement." Instead, he went on, the urgent task of restoring order to the country should fall to a United Nations force composed mostly of troops from African nations, authorized to act only in self-defense and barred from intervening in the Congo's internal affairs. If UN troops succeeded in that mission, "the Belgian Government would see its way to a withdrawal."

The ensuing debate lasted until three in the morning as bleary-eyed, chain-smoking delegates scrutinized the text before them. But when the final vote was taken by a show of weary hands, neither the United States nor the Soviet Union objected. It was hard for the two superpowers to agree on anything, but neither wanted its own troops to get involved in the Congo, and a UN intervention seemed like the surest way to avoid a Cold War fight in a distant territory of little immediate importance to either side. What's more, the intervention had the support of the African and Asian states, and neither Washington nor Moscow wished to alienate this group of largely nonaligned countries. The resolution passed 8–0. Britain and France abstained—the final text's implicit criticism of Belgium was simply too much for them to bear—but made it clear that they welcomed the UN's efforts to resolve the crisis in the Congo.

It took an especially vague resolution to earn support from such disparate quarters. The text, just 144 words long, left much to the imagination, merely calling for a Belgian withdrawal and assigning Hammarskjöld responsibility for supplying the Congo with military assistance. As the Tunisian representative, who had introduced the resolution, admitted, "The text is intentionally imprecise about certain points in order to avoid arguments in the Council."

Imprecision had been the UN's modus operandi of late. Delegates would agree on a loose resolution and then let Hammarskjöld sort out the details. "Leave it to Dag" became a catchphrase; one joke had it that his motto was *Per Ambigua ad Astra*—"through ambiguity to the stars." But that ambiguity often papered over crucial questions, and this time was no different. Henry Cabot Lodge Jr., the U.S. representative, explained that, in his view, the resolution allowed Belgian troops to stay until the UN mission established control; Arkady Sobolev, the Soviet ambassador, interpreted it as requiring "immediate and unconditional" Belgian withdrawal. Views also differed on whether "withdrawal" meant a return to Belgium or merely to the Belgian bases in the Congo. The secession of Katanga went unmentioned.

Yet by 3:25 a.m., as the delegates rose from their chairs, they had achieved something historic. For the first time, the UN was intervening not to supervise a truce but to restore security to an entire country still in the throes of disorder and conflict. Hammarskjöld was putting into action his vision of the UN as a friend to newly independent states. The African countries would be playing a prominent and constructive role in aiding one of their own. The great powers had set aside their bitter differences. The Security Council's decision was, in Hammarskjöld's estimation, a "political miracle."

Across America, in the late-edition newspapers flying through printing presses, headlines about the Security Council's decision competed for space with the evening's other big story: in Los Angeles, at the Democratic National Convention, the Democratic Party had just nominated John F. Kennedy as its candidate for president. He would face Vice President Richard Nixon, the presumptive Republican nominee, in November.

With the resolution passed, the gears of the UN's multinational machinery began to turn. From the chamber of the Security Council, Hammarskjöld and a handful of aides headed straight to his thirty-eighth-floor office overlooking the East River. It was already daytime in Africa and Europe, so the secretary-general's staff worked the phones, calling up leaders and asking for troops, air transport, food, staging sites, and equipment. The United States, the U.S.S.R., and the U.K. agreed to operate an airlift. Britain also offered a Royal Air Force base in northern Nigeria as a staging area. Ghana pledged to send nearly its entire army to the Congo. Tunisian troops would be waiting on the runway in Tunis in an hour, ready to be picked up.

From time to time, Hammarskjöld would walk into another room, where aides were drawing up an organizational chart and a financing plan and making arrangements for a headquarters and a staff in Leopoldville. Military equipment and UN insignia were rustled up from around the globe. A name was chosen: Organisation des Nations Unies au Congo, or ONUC.

Hammarskjöld and his staff continued working as the sun rose. By the time they left for breakfast at 6:30, stubble sprouting from their cheeks, the largest, most expensive, and most ambitious UN operation in history was in motion.

Even though the Security Council had responded to his call with alacrity, Lumumba had little reason or time to celebrate. The prime minister was worn out; he and Kasavubu had barely slept or eaten in the course of their frantic tour across the Congo, and the setbacks would not let up. The two leaders had just learned that Belgian troops had moved into Leopoldville, rattling off machine-gun fire inside the airport and driving down the abandoned Boulevard Albert to the cheers of the city's remaining white residents. But beyond this bit of information, Lumumba struggled to parse which news to take seriously and which to discount. Communications were still sporadic, and Lumumba suspected that Belgian saboteurs were sending fake cables to stir up confusion. Radio reports were no more reliable: news broadcasts claimed that Belgian soldiers had killed thousands while seizing the capital's airport, though in fact the death toll was in the single digits.

Amid this confusion, Lumumba and Kasavubu dashed off an angry cable to the Belgian ambassador in Leopoldville. They announced that they were "breaking off all diplomatic relations with Belgium." In Brussels, the message served only to persuade the Belgian government to give up on working with Lumumba and throw its weight behind what was now being called "the Katanga experiment." The Belgian foreign minister confided in the Americans that he now considered Lumumba "a source of trouble and an instrument for a Soviet take-over." He also made the case that it was time to "undermine Lumumba's position and pave the way for other, better people to take his place." What that entailed, and who those people were, was left unsaid.

Unaware of the reaction to their cable, Lumumba and Kasavubu boarded an army plane to reach the next stop on their tour: Stanleyville, the prime minister's erstwhile home in the country's northeast. Local officials and residents were waiting for them at the city's airport, expecting the duo to land at 1:30 p.m. But at 2:00, the plane was still in the air. Lumumba entered the cockpit. When pressed, the pilot, a Belgian, admitted that he had received orders to take the leaders to Leopoldville.

Lumumba upbraided him and ordered him to turn around for Stanleyville at once. "We are independent now, and Belgium is a separate country now, just as France and America and other countries are," he said. "What you are doing is an act of high treason."

The pilot pretended to comply with his new orders, cutting a wide arc in the sky that Lumumba assumed would put them back on course to Stanleyville. But as the plane finally began its descent, he looked outside and saw not the dense forests of Stanleyville but the patchy grass of the capital. Lumumba and Kasavubu had been tricked.

Their bewilderment only intensified when they were greeted on the tarmac by two Belgian generals, their hands raised in salute, and a Belgian honor guard. Lumumba and Kasavubu recoiled, suspecting some sort of ambush.

"We have no intention of taking you prisoner," one general said. "We only wanted to welcome you with the honors due to your rank."

"We don't need your honors," Lumumba snapped back.

He and Kasavubu tried to sidestep the generals, but the Belgians would not be ignored.

"Look at our women a few hundred yards from here who are headed for Belgium," one of them said. "They have been raped by your people. Our men have been ridiculed and mistreated." He went on: "I beg you, blood must no longer be spilled. The situation is dramatic. Help us maintain order."

Lumumba could hardly contain himself. "If blood is spilled this evening," he said, "it will be you Belgians who will bear the responsibility."

Declining a Belgian escort, Lumumba and Kasavubu sped off toward Leopoldville, whizzing past shattered shopwindows and hulking frames of burned-out cars. In an hour, they were back at Ndjili airport, determined to try once again to reach Stanleyville. The mood had grown rowdier. A throng of departing whites now accosted the two leaders.

"Apes!" they cried.

"Murderers!"

"Hoodlums!"

"Break their necks!"

Lumumba was jostled, his glasses were snatched, his goatee tugged. He was spit upon. "Why don't you go see the women who have been raped?" demanded a man, before lunging from the crowd and punching the prime minister in the face. Lumumba, dazed, walked on and climbed into the waiting plane.

The plane took off, but soon it was back on the runway in Leopoldville. The pilot, implausibly, claimed radio trouble. Lumumba and Kasavubu had wasted an entire day—one marking two weeks of supposed independence, as it happened—trying in vain to fly to one of the country's most important cities, only to be stymied, in their own airspace and on their own soil, by their former colonial masters. They were livid.

Then the plane door opened. In walked Larry Devlin.

Chapter 16

An Experiment in Peace

IN THE SEVERAL days since he had stepped off the ferry in Leopoldville, Devlin had had little time to assume the main duties of a CIA station chief—developing sources and collecting intelligence. Instead, he had mostly been busy taking precautions for his own safety in a city fast descending into lawlessness, a descent Devlin had witnessed personally during his first encounter with the Congolese military in the city. Not long after his arrival, he had been picked up by a group of soldiers and carted off to their base. In a room clouded with marijuana smoke, a tall soldier straddled a chair and removed his boot. "Kiss my foot," he demanded.

When Devlin protested, the soldier presented a revolver. "Ever played Russian roulette?" he asked.

Devlin, sweating, shook his head. "Then I will do it for you," the soldier said, pressing the barrel into Devlin's head. "Shit," Devlin said. *Click.* Nothing. Again, *click.* Again, nothing. Devlin, under official cover as a U.S. consul, reminded the soldier of diplomatic immunity. The only answer he got was three more clicks, as the hammer hit more empty chambers.

"Last chance, boss," the soldier said. "Kiss this foot." *Click.*

The room broke out in laughter. The gun was empty. "Congolese roulette," the soldiers explained, offering him a swig of wine and a ride downtown.

Shaken by the experience, Devlin decided he would be better off armed. He bought a tommy gun from an opportunistic Congolese soldier and picked up two Browning semiautomatic pistols from a departing Belgian officer. But in keeping with the unpredictable nature of the disorder roiling the city, the soldiers seemed to lose interest in him, and the next days went by without incident.

Ambassador Timberlake soon took to using Devlin as a fixer of sorts, which was why Devlin now found himself climbing aboard Lumumba and Kasavubu's plane as it sat on the tarmac. Timberlake, alarmed by their decision to break off relations with Belgium, had sent him to get the prime minister to reverse course. But Lumumba wasn't in the mood for a debate.

"I cannot discuss such matters while I am being held prisoner," he said.

"But you aren't a prisoner," Devlin protested.

Lumumba gestured toward the crowd of angry Belgians outside the plane window. *Point taken,* Devlin thought. "The reception was polite but frigid—both men being under great strain and obviously very angry with Belgians," a cable informed the State Department.

Hoping to get Lumumba away from the mob, Devlin left the plane and arranged for a van. Lumumba and Kasavubu ducked into it against a renewed chorus of obscenities and racist epithets. Two Belgian paratroopers grabbed the bumper and rocked the van as hard as they could. "Turn it over!" one yelled. Lumumba and Kasavubu sat petrified inside. Devlin fought off one man attempting to pour a can of gasoline on the car, and the trio finally made their escape. The Congolese leaders had Devlin to thank for ending the ordeal. Yet Lumumba, evidently still angry about the whole affair, would not talk to him.

Instead, Lumumba summoned a little-known adviser whom the press would take to calling "Africa's woman of mystery": Andrée Blouin.

So epic was Blouin's life that, in one scholar's view, it "reads like a chapter out of Balzac." Blouin was born in a small village in the colony of Ubangi-Shari, part of French Equatorial Africa, to a fourteen-year-old girl and a forty-one-year-old Frenchman. At the age of three, she was deposited in a Catholic orphanage for mixed-race children in Brazzaville. After the nuns tried to pressure her into an arranged marriage at fifteen, she escaped the orphanage, only to become, in her words, an "African concubine" to a Belgian aristocrat who directed a company in the Congo. They lived in Dima, a company town on the Kasai River. She had to hide in the kitchen when guests came over.

Blouin's political awakening came during World War II. By then, she had married a French businessman and was living in Bangui, the capital of Ubangi-Shari. Their two-year-old son, René, was hospitalized with malaria, but because he was one-quarter African, he was ineligible for the quinine shot that could have saved him, and he succumbed to the disease. "The death of my son politicized me as nothing else could," Blouin would write. Colonialism, she realized, "was no longer a matter of my own maligned fate but a system of evil whose tentacles reached into every phase of African life."

Eventually, she remarried, to a French engineer who worked for a diamond-mining company. He was posted to Guinea, and she threw herself into the colony's independence movement, organizing rallies and delivering speeches. Blouin's familiarity with the Congo from her childhood in Brazzaville and time in Dima made her a natural adviser to Congolese politicians. She landed a role with Antoine Gizenga, Lumumba's deputy prime minister.

That was how Blouin found herself meeting with Lumumba and a dozen or so friends and aides when he came back from Ndjili. He served the group martinis as he relayed the events of the past week, including the latest humiliation at the airport. He was surprisingly relaxed, given the gravity of the moment. Perhaps that was because he thought he had a trump card to play with the Belgians.

"We will have them yet," Lumumba said, "with this!" He reached into the breast pocket of his crisp white shirt and produced a copy of a telegram that he and Kasavubu had sent that morning. "It's for Moscow," he said. "If people want to say that because of it I am a Communist, then the president is too!"

The message, addressed to Nikita Khrushchev, warned the Soviet premier that they might be obliged to demand his country's intervention—"the Congolese national territory being militarily occupied by Belgian troops and the lives of the president of the republic and the prime minister being in danger." (When Hammarskjöld read that cable, he figured they were detained.)

But if Lumumba thought the appeal would solve his problems, he was deeply mistaken. Even though the cable went straight to the top of the Soviet system, with every member of the Presidium receiving a copy, Khrushchev's response was noncommittal. He condemned the "imperialist aggression," but endorsed the Security Council's resolution as "useful" and pledged no concrete Soviet support to the Congolese government.

To the Americans, the cable only confirmed growing suspicions that, as Devlin put it, Lumumba was "playing into Soviet hands." In a meeting with Secretary of State Herter, the Belgian ambassador in Washington raised the specter of a World War III instigated by Lumumba's flirtation with the Soviets. He pressed the United States to go easy on the Katanga secession. That movement "should not be suppressed at too early a stage as it might be the last stronghold we have," the Belgian ambassador said, according to a memo of the meeting. (Privately, Herter admitted, "Should other states recognize Katanga, it is possible that the U.S. might reconsider its position, but under no circumstances will we take the lead.") At a National Security Council meeting, Allen Dulles, the CIA director, called Lumumba "anti-Western"—although Herter said he thought that went too far. The State Department warned the embassies in Brussels and Leopoldville that "the attitude of Lumumba vis-à-vis the U.S.S.R. and the West appears to be a matter for serious concern."

Within forty-eight hours of Hammarskjöld's triumph at the Security Council, UN troops were streaming out the backs of cargo planes onto the tarmac at Ndjili. The airlift was primarily the work of a handful of countries with the logistical resources to get the job done quickly: Britain, the Soviet Union, and, above all, the United States. Canadian units—their French skills a useful asset in the francophone Congo—provided signals support. By contrast, Hammarskjöld thought it best that any ground troops involved in the operation be African, not white: after all, he explained, "the whole trouble started by a revolt of colored soldiers against white officers." Bunche, however, cautioned that white troops were needed to reassure the Congo's European population. Thus, in addition to troops from Ethiopia, Ghana, Guinea, Liberia, Mali, Morocco, and Tunisia, the UN arranged for a Swedish battalion and 650 Irish soldiers to join the mission.

For most of the African troops, the flight to the Congo marked their first time in the air, and cleaning crews had to sop up the gallons of vomit and disinfect the hold after each trip. Navigators, relying on old, imprecise charts, occasionally found themselves one hundred miles off course and had to fix their position by peering through sextants at the stars. Despite these difficulties, the airlift was a logistical masterstroke. In its first three days, the U.S. military landed one hundred flights in the Congo. It flew in Jeeps, Land Rovers, and helicopters. When Leopoldville seemed poised to run out of food, the United States sent four hundred tons of flour. In little over a week, more than six thousand UN troops had landed. The Guineans walked off with live chickens poking out of their rucksacks. The Ghanaians brought goats. In hours and tonnage, Operation Safari, as the mission was named, would eventually surpass even the Berlin Airlift of 1948–49, when the U.S. Air Force had foiled the Soviets' ground blockade of the divided German city.

Many of the arriving troops were poorly equipped and poorly informed about their exact mission, with some disembarking soldiers asking whose side they would be fighting for. But their mere presence, Hammarskjöld and Bunche hoped, would help contain the chaos engulfing the Congo, provided the patchwork of troops and matériel descending on Leopoldville could be made into a coherent and capable force.

Most Congolese, it soon became apparent, were also in the dark about the mission's exact purpose. A local official asked Bunche, "The UN—which tribe is that?" The few among them who had heard of the UN considered it some sort of benevolent world government that had arrived to punish the Belgians. Others met the peacekeepers with open suspicion and hostility: one morning, Bunche visited Camp Leopold with two Congolese ministers, only to beat a hasty retreat when the soldiers nearly rioted. "The men understood nothing about the UN," he cabled Hammarskjöld. "UN identifications were generally meaningless. We hope to give them meaning."

To that end, Bunche had a simple statement read on Congolese radio, explaining that the UN troops were mostly from fellow independent African countries and came in peace. He ended with a plea:

I would like to ask you all not to expect miracles.... It will take some time to put everything to rights, and to close the wounds so recently inflicted. There has been enough violence. Too many people have been hurt; too many killed. There now exist tension, fear, and bitterness that are dangerous indeed. I hope that everyone—both government and people—will give evidence of patience and moderation in the next few days. This alone can save your marvelous country from disaster.

To command the troops, Hammarskjöld pulled a Swedish general, Carl von Horn, from the UN's mission in Jerusalem. But his plane was waylaid by engine trouble, so Bunche was made temporary commander. Donning a blue military cap, his belly poking through his suit jacket, he took over a small, stuffy office in the control tower to welcome incoming troops and give them their marching orders. Within hours, they fanned out to protect the city's radio station, power supply, and other key infrastructure. Tunisian and Moroccan blue helmets patrolled Leopoldville's African quarters, while the Swedes were sent to guard the European quarters—to achieve the "desired psychological effect" among the white population, Hammarskjöld explained to von Horn. The Irish were sent to the other side of the country, to Kivu province, an area whose temperate climate had attracted a large white settler population now demanding protection. They arrived to great fanfare wearing woolen, World War I–era service dress, with puttees, green and saffron kilts, and bagpipes.

Bunche ordered a Moroccan regiment to reopen the rail line to the lower Congo and restore order to the area's main cities. The peacekeepers made their way westward aboard a white diesel train, a UN flag draped across its locomotive. At each whistle-stop, the Moroccans disembarked, and their leader, Colonel Driss Ben Omar, announced that the UN was taking over. The townspeople welcomed the foreign soldiers with large bunches of bananas. The mutineers, for their part, put up next to no resistance. Sparked by accumulated frustration, their rebellion had been a spontaneous, decentralized, and haphazard project, lacking any clear leadership structure or action plan. And whereas the soldiers had viewed Belgian paratroopers as the enemy, they were less sure what to make of the mostly African peacekeepers now marching into their garrisons. When the Moroccans reached Camp Hardy in Thysville, a hotspot of the mutiny, Colonel Driss Ben Omar encountered a slovenly Congolese man and asked him whether he was a soldier. The man replied in the affirmative. "Then go get dressed like one!" the colonel bellowed. Someone, at last, seemed to be in charge.

In parallel to the UN soldiers' efforts to instill a sense of security, a massive civilian assistance program was set in motion, designed to fill the enormous governance gaps left by the fleeing Belgian administrators. Never allowed to advance before independence, the new Congolese bureaucrats were utterly unprepared to run the country. One minister came to a UN adviser's office and asked to sit there for three days, saying that he had never used a desk before. When another official who suddenly found himself in charge of an entire province's communications system was asked for its plans, he presented a phone book. The UN rushed in not only telephone operators but also electricians, air traffic controllers, teachers, finance experts, agronomists, geologists, and meteorologists. To prevent a humanitarian crisis, doctors from the World Health Organization and the Red Cross were dispatched, while UNICEF organized emergency food distribution.

The chaos and ensuing international response were big news, and journalists rushed in to cover what newspapers abroad were now calling "the Congo crisis." "Every other person appeared to have a shorthand notebook and pencil," an American missionary observed. At one point, the number of foreign correspondents in the country reached 142. The Americans among them—credulous and jingoistic to a degree that later, post–Vietnam War generations of reporters might have winced at—thought nothing of working hand in hand with the U.S. government. At the end of a long day, they would hash out their stories with officers at the U.S. embassy before meeting their filing deadlines in New York. Journalists and diplomats traded tips in an informal atmosphere in which classification rules were set aside. Sometimes, the officers asked to censor the news; at other times, the newsmen helped draft diplomatic reports to Washington.

The press coverage often reflected, and embedded, racist stereotypes of Africa—images, as one African American writer put it, of "half-naked black savages dancing around a boiling pot of missionary soup." Reports, published under headlines such as "New Congo Mumbo-Jumbo," emphasized drums and cannibalism and painted the Congolese, even the political elite, as knuckle draggers. "With a primeval howl, a nation of 14 million people reverted to near savagery, plunged backward into the long night of chaos"—that was *Time* announcing the mutiny. There was a distinct emphasis on sexual violence. Early in the crisis, as Belgian civilians waited for evacuation at the airport, a British TV reporter, cameraman in tow, plowed through the crowd. Every so often, he stopped to ask, "Anyone here been raped and speaks English?"

In the United States, Walter Lippmann used his influential column to extol the virtues of the mission to his readers, in terms that surely flattered his friend the secretary-general: "This U.N. enterprise is the most advanced and the most sophisticated experiment in international cooperation ever attempted. Among all that is so sad and so mean and so sour in world politics, it is heartening to think that something so good and so pure in its purpose is possible."

Chapter 17

Powerless

Lumumba was at his best on a podium. He lectured and he preached. Cerebral yet passionate, he interspersed chapter-and-verse legal arguments with raw emotion to great persuasive effect. "He was a fluent and felicitous speaker and could wield great influence with his oratory," Bunche thought. Timberlake liked to say that Lumumba was such a spellbinder that even if he had walked into a gathering of Congolese politicians as a waiter with a tray on his head, he would have walked out as prime minister.

Lumumba's rhetorical powers were on full display at the rostrum of the Palace of the Nation, where the Congolese parliament met on July 15. After touring the country alongside Kasavubu to calm the army, Lumumba had come to report on the fruits of his efforts, and to warn of the depths of Belgium's malice. Brandishing telegrams and quoting official documents, he interrupted his narrative to announce reports of fresh clashes between Congolese and Belgian troops. Above all, as he addressed parliamentarians who represented so many different ethnic groups and regions, he made an appeal for unity in a time of crisis. "My dear honorable deputies," he said, "it is with deep emotion and tears in my eyes that I have given you this report on the grave and dramatic situation confronting our homeland, this country that we all love and that we proudly hope to make a beautiful and great one."

Diplomats, journalists, and members of the public stood silent in the gallery; the politicians in their seats interrupted him only with applause. Despite the chaos that had engulfed the fledgling country from its very first day, Thomas Kanza, the Congolese ambassador to the UN, looked at Lumumba and saw a leader in control. "Lumumba's mastery of his audience," he concluded, "his power of persuasion, his elegance, his gestures, the force of his argument, all these produced a total impact which he was alone among the hundred deputies in the chamber in possessing."

Yet for all that Lumumba could entrance parliament, running a cabinet meeting proved more of a struggle. While the Congo burned, he and his ministers debated such matters as whether they could use official cars in the evening and whether the new country's passport would risk looking too similar to Belgium's if it featured a lion on its cover. At least one meeting broke up due to a supposed sighting of a Belgian paratroop drop, which prompted Lumumba and his ministers to join a truckful of soldiers in a search. Bunche and other UN officials were shocked by the disorderly way in which the Congo's politicians did business. Their conversations were constantly interrupted by all manner of petitioners. At a long meeting with Bunche, Lumumba excused himself to answer a ringing telephone, rising from a table to head toward his desk, yards away. "Who's there?" he said into the receiver. It was someone looking for Lumumba's wife. Lumumba, in Andrée Blouin's view, "had the annoying habit of trying to see everyone who asked for him," with the consequence that visitors were constantly "streaming through his office as if it were a train station."

Lumumba enjoyed the trappings of power but could not exercise it. Not when the situation was changing by the hour, when communications were still on the fritz, and when the Belgians were constraining his travel. "We were ministers," Kanza thought. "We, the colonized, now had titles and dignity; but we had no power at all over any of the instruments we needed to carry out the functions expected of us." It was like cycling in the mud: no matter how hard you tried, you couldn't gain traction. A Belgian diplomat was exaggerating only slightly when he complained that there was no Congolese government, "merely two men running around, out of touch with the situation."

Those close to Lumumba found him distrustful. Just as he had when running the MNC before independence, he delegated precious little authority as prime minister. Such suspicion was understandable, given the rivalry within his cobbled-together coalition government. Ministers had their own constituencies to worry about, their own ethnic clientele to reward, their own axes to grind. Their transformation from, as Kanza put it, "being vote-catching demagogues to being responsible and thoughtful statesmen" never quite took. When a minister wanted to vent his spleen on a given rival, he would simply walk into the radio station and let the invective flow. Confronting Lumumba was a more daunting endeavor. "It was the king in his council," as one adviser described the cabinet's dynamics. "Most ministers lived in fear of Lumumba's frown." The minister of public health, a short-statured former medical assistant who had something of a Napoleon complex, was so terrified of the tall Lumumba that he waited two weeks after taking office to speak directly to him.

Mobutu had known Lumumba longer than nearly everyone else in the cabinet, yet he increasingly found himself on the outside. After a week calming troops in his native province, Équateur, the freshly minted colonel returned to Leopoldville to learn that he had been replaced. Lumumba had named another MNC loyalist, Maurice Mpolo, as the acting chief of staff of the Congolese army. Mpolo, the thirty-one-year-old minister of youth and sports, was now walking around in a colonel's uniform, a kepi on his head and a baton in his hand. Mobutu was furious. This was the thanks he got for his courageous work in Équateur? He confronted Lumumba at a cabinet meeting in the prime minister's residence.

"It's a question of honor," Mobutu said. "I was on a mission. Either I was unworthy, and you have to dismiss me, or I faithfully accomplished my mission and so I keep my rank and functions."

Someone proposed that both men—Mobutu and Mpolo—be promoted to general. Mobutu dismissed the idea out of hand. "Make Mpolo a general if you want to, but I'm not going to take part in this madness." He slammed the door behind him. The dysfunction of Lumumba's cabinet offended his sense of professionalism.

Perhaps Mobutu took some consolation from the fact that Lumumba, worn out by weeks of political turmoil, was growing more suspicious of everyone. The latest object of his mistrust was the UN and its forces in the Congo. Lumumba had originally imagined that the blue helmets' express aim would be to expel the Belgian military as quickly as possible, a task he thought would take a little more than a week. But the Security Council had failed to set a clear timeline for Belgian troop withdrawal, and the mission's primary purpose was to restore order, not to wage war against Belgian troops, so a prompt expulsion was not in the offing. When that became clear, Lumumba worried that the blue helmets might in fact be collaborating with the Belgians. Shouldn't the UN take orders from the Congolese government, which had invited the organization into the country to begin with? Meeting with Lumumba on July 16, Bunche tried to disabuse him of this notion, explaining that the troops answered to the UN, not to Leopoldville. But he had a hard time getting through.

Further tension between the two men arose over Lumumba's travel plans. During his tour of the country alongside Kasavubu, Lumumba had twice tried to reach Stanleyville and twice failed owing to Belgian interference. Determined to try a third time, he now asked Bunche to arrange a UN plane for the trip. Bunche, however, could not understand why the prime minister wanted to leave the capital during a deep political crisis for a frivolous junket in his political stronghold. What he missed was that Lumumba viewed a trip to Stanleyville as critical to restoring political stability: his radio messages from Leopoldville appealing for calm and announcing the Africanization of the army had turned out to have little reach outside the capital. Everywhere else he and Kasavubu had visited on their tour of the country, their physical presence, much more than their radio broadcasts, had reassured civilians and soldiers alike. Replicating that success in Stanleyville, one of the country's most important cities, might make all the difference.

The prime minister and the diplomat were talking past each other. Bunche failed to see Lumumba's perspective—that of an embattled leader, thwarted at every turn by Belgian meddling. Lumumba couldn't see Bunche's—that of the representative of a global organization, constrained by the great powers of the Security Council. Their relationship never recovered from this misunderstanding. Lumumba professed to be baffled as to why the UN had sent "this American Negro" to the Congo. Bunche, for his part, seethed at a leader he had come to view as a "fluent but utterly maniacal child."

Lumumba had more success with his request with Timberlake, the U.S. ambassador, who allowed him and Kasavubu to hitch a ride on a U.S. Air Force C-130 headed to Stanleyville. Intent on preventing any further subterfuge, Lumumba and Kasavubu stood in the cockpit the whole trip, keeping a watchful eye on the pilot. This time, they reached their intended destination, but bad news followed them there.

A day after reaching Stanleyville, the two leaders learned that five planeloads of Belgian paratroopers had just landed in the city of Kindu to disarm the Congolese soldiers there. Evidently, the Belgians were not heeding Lumumba's demand to withdraw to their bases; they were doubling down and continuing to intervene across the country. Lumumba decided to once more turn to the UN, this time in the form of an ultimatum. In a letter addressed to Bunche, written mostly in the first-person singular but also signed—perhaps reluctantly—by Kasavubu, Lumumba cited the Belgian action in Kindu and demanded that the blue helmets expel all Belgian troops from the Congo within two days. Failing that, the letter went on, "we may be obliged to call upon the Soviet Union to intervene."

Why the repeated interest in Soviet help? Lumumba did not appear to have any fondness for the Soviet Union's political system or Communist ideology. But he did appreciate its stance on the Belgian military intervention, which both Khrushchev and Moscow's representative at the Security Council had condemned as an imperialist attack. The Belgian military presence had stopped Lumumba from reaching Elisabethville and Stanleyville, preventing him from exercising his authority as the Congo's leader. The hope of removing that presence was the idea behind inviting the UN into the country in the first place, and the UN's failure to do so was the reason he now threatened to supplant the organization. Lumumba was dismayed to find that neither Bunche nor Timberlake—and, by extension, neither the UN nor the United States—shared his sense of urgency. Anyone who did was a friend, a lifeline. "We need the fastest and most efficacious help," Lumumba told reporters. "We are willing to accept anybody ready to bring that help, the United States or Russia or anybody. There are no politics or ideologies involved in this. We just need help." He put it in starker terms to parliament: "We will call on the devil if need be."

But in spite of their rhetorical support, the Soviets showed little interest in offering anything more. The Belgian intervention was beautiful propaganda—a former colonial power and NATO member was strangling a new African state in the cradle!—but no reason for Moscow to step in. If the Soviets tried to send in troops by sea, they would be beaten to the punch by the USS *Wasp*, which now lay just off the coast of the Congo. The Soviets' airlift capabilities, as their paltry contribution to the transportation of UN troops had shown, amounted to a fraction of the United States'. Even if Soviet troops attempted to fly in, Washington could easily pressure African countries to deny them overflight rights. And in any case, in the summer of 1960, Moscow was not in the habit of intervening militarily outside Eastern Europe. It was happy to leave the job of cleaning up a mess in Africa to the UN.

For the moment, therefore, the Congo crisis was useful to the Soviets only insofar as it gave them fodder for their efforts to tar the United States with the brush of imperialism. When the Associated Press reported that twenty U.S. airmen were stationed at Ndjili to help with the UN airlift, the Soviet foreign minister, claiming to see these forces as part of an effort to dominate the operation, lodged a formal protest with the U.S. government and broadcast it over Moscow radio. Arkady Sobolev, the Soviet UN representative, met with Hammarskjöld to deliver the same complaint, but did so halfheartedly. "The meeting ended in a general laugh," Hammarskjöld noted, "indicating that the whole story was only for the record."

Chapter 18

A Humiliating Defeat

WHEN BUNCHE RECEIVED Lumumba's ultimatum to the UN, he was furious. Meeting with the Congolese cabinet—without Lumumba, who remained in Stanleyville—he tore into the prime minister's "silly threat." Lumumba was demanding a withdrawal that defied physics. Thousands of Belgian troops were not going to disappear from the country in forty-eight hours. And by threatening to call once again on Moscow, Lumumba was injecting toxic Cold War politics into a crisis that—posturing and bluster aside—had remained relatively free from open U.S.-Soviet conflict. The ministers agreed, worrying that a Russian military intervention would provoke a nuclear war.

At 7:00 p.m. the next day, Bunche headed to the prime minister's residence to communicate his displeasure to Lumumba, who by now was back in the capital. His anger notwithstanding, Bunche had good news to report: at his urging, Belgian forces had agreed to withdraw from Stanleyville within a few days—not fast enough to satisfy Lumumba's ultimatum, nor applicable to the rest of the country, but a start nonetheless. There were now more UN troops in the Congo than Belgian troops.

Lumumba was unimpressed. He pulled out a local newspaper and pointed to a headline that he considered a personal affront: "Ultimatum Rejected by Mr. Bunche." Midnight—the deadline for the ultimatum—was fast approaching, Lumumba added. There was no way the Belgian troops would be gone by then. Bunche threw his hands up in the air. "Well, then," he said. With that, he thought the matter was over.

But in the morning, Lumumba still wouldn't drop the subject. He summoned Bunche to his home again and invited him into an elegant drawing room. Inside, an unsuspecting Bunche found himself surrounded by a gaggle of reporters and photographers, pens out, bulbs flashing. Once again brandishing the newspaper with the offending headline, Lumumba asked Bunche to deny having ever criticized the ultimatum. Microphones bent toward Bunche. "I have made no public statement about the letter by him, which has been characterized by the press as an ultimatum," Bunche offered, choosing his words carefully. A few feet away, Mobutu stood by looking sullen, watching the gauche spectacle.

Lumumba alternately praised and chastised the UN. Bunche's efforts to achieve a Belgian withdrawal were "impressive," the prime minister explained to the assembled reporters, but unless the UN delivered soon, it would reveal itself as a mere "tool of imperialism— a plot by capitalists to grab the Congo." At the same time, he asked for the UN to protect him from political opponents in the Senate, who he said were plotting to assassinate him. "The request," Bunche wrote to Hammarskjöld afterward, "had an ironic touch since he had just been threatening to run us out of the country." Bunche had spent much of his Detroit boyhood at the Second Baptist Church, and he thought of the biblical figure known for extraordinary patience in the face of diabolical troubles. "Sitting through such sessions without erupting convinces me that Job had nothing on me," he wrote. "Really."

For all his frustration with Lumumba, Bunche, too, was exasperated with the Belgians. He was particularly perturbed by their insistence that their troops withdraw not back to Belgium, as the Congolese were demanding, but merely to the Belgian bases in the Congo, which leaders in Brussels still imagined they could somehow hold on to. A Belgian general told Bunche, "If the U.N. forces Belgium to leave the bases, they will have to cope with a revolution in Belgium." The Belgians were in denial, Bunche thought, unable to accept that they had lost out. "They simply could not be worse," he wrote to Hammarskjöld. "One can really understand a Lumumba only by knowing the Belgians of the Congo."

In Belgium's intransigence, the Soviets saw an opportunity. On July 18, Moscow called another Security Council meeting on the Congo. Anticipating Soviet remonstrations about the Belgian intervention, Washington pressed Brussels to announce a token withdrawal of troops until the UN could take full control, but to no avail. Belgium would thus be walking into the Security Council chamber with a target on its back.

From his hotel on Park Avenue, Thomas Kanza stepped into a boat of a black Cadillac and was driven the few blocks east to UN headquarters. It was July 20. Only two years earlier, while attending a summer program at Harvard, he had visited the complex as a tourist. Now, on this hot and hazy New York day, he was back to take up his post as the Congo's permanent representative to the UN, all of twenty-six years old, flown specially to New York by the U.S. Air Force and waved through customs despite his lack of a passport. Three weeks after independence, the Congo would have its first opportunity to tell its side of the story.

Ahead of the Security Council session, Hammarskjöld welcomed Kanza into his office to talk about Lumumba. From Bunche's cables and the press, Hammarskjöld had formed a negative opinion of the Congolese prime minister: weak, unlikely to last long in power, and "crazy," as he wrote down privately. Kanza shared much of this assessment. Although he could not admit it to the secretary-general in so many words, he found his prime minister impulsive and overly mistrustful. The two agreed to do what they could to "save" Lumumba from his worst instincts. In the immediate term, that meant getting him to settle for a realistic timeline for Belgian withdrawal.

Diplomats in New York were quick to warm to the self-effacing and university-polished Kanza. He struck Hammarskjöld as "very reasonable." The patrician U.S. ambassador to the UN, Henry Cabot Lodge Jr., found the young delegate "soft-spoken, mild-mannered and poised." He proved to be a quick study of Cold War politics. With Vasily Kuznetsov, a high-ranking Soviet official who was now representing Moscow at the UN, Kanza sensed that "fundamentally the Soviet Union had no definite plan for coming to the aid of the Congo with any troops." Its bluster, he realized, was just that.

That night, Kanza made the Congo's case before the Security Council. There was an air of theater as visitors in the gallery peered through binoculars at the delegates. "The Congo behaved like a good child and trusted Belgium," Kanza said, and Belgium's decision to intervene without permission had been a breach of that trust. Lumumba's ultimatum to the UN, which Kanza realized had gone down poorly, had been an overreaction, the product of a "young Congolese government facing heavy responsibilities." Still, Kanza insisted, it was now incumbent upon the UN to force a prompt Belgian withdrawal.

Belgium, for its part, had sent a heavy hitter to New York. Pierre Wigny, the country's foreign minister, was more than twice Kanza's age, a seasoned lawyer and politician who had once held the Congo portfolio in the Belgian government. His hair slicked back confidently as he sat across the horseshoe table from Kanza, Wigny launched into a fiery attack on Lumumba, whose ineptitude, he said, had forced Belgium to intervene to restore order. Stabbing the air with his glasses and speaking so fast a subordinate had to interrupt and tell him to slow down for the interpreters, Wigny rattled off a long list of alleged atrocities committed against Belgian civilians in the Congo—a missionary whose beard was burned, a baby struck in its mother's arms, a woman whose pubic hair was ripped off and stuffed in her mouth, and woman after woman raped. "What do you wish, gentlemen?" Wigny said. "Should I continue?"

At a follow-on session, Wigny contested the notion that Belgium was breaking up the Congo. "Where Congolese unity is concerned, may I recall that this unity is Belgium's doing," he said. "Before we came to Africa, there was no Congo." (There were echoes of what the colonial prosecutor had said of Lumumba three years earlier: "He owes it to the state that he is not a slave.") As impassioned as Wigny's rhetoric was, he was fighting a losing battle. By refusing to grant any concessions, Brussels had made it hard for even its closest allies to take its side without alienating the African and Asian countries whose friendship they sought. It had, in effect, already resigned itself to a rebuke by the Security Council, and that was what it got. In a unanimous decision, the council called on Belgium to "speedily" withdraw its troops. In an allusion to Katanga, it also asked all countries to "refrain from any action which might undermine the territorial integrity and the political independence of the Republic of the Congo."

The session ended at 1:00 a.m. Shortly thereafter, Kanza called Lumumba. The prime minister was still skeptical about the potential of the UN to solve his country's woes, but he knew when to accept a victory. "Go and have a good sleep," he told Kanza. "You certainly deserve it."

Later that day in Leopoldville, Lumumba's voice crackled through radio sets. "This morning, I received a telephone call from New York informing us of a great victory. The Security Council, which represents every nation throughout the world, has just now passed an important resolution, under the terms of which the Belgian troops must leave the territory of our republic tomorrow, or day after tomorrow at the very latest."

This was a generous interpretation of both the Security Council and its resolution, which once again had set no timeline for withdrawal. But Lumumba was not wrong when he encouraged Congolese to celebrate with a glass of beer that "Belgium has, in fact, suffered a humiliating defeat."

Chapter 19

Hail Lumumba!

Larry Devlin was at the U.S. embassy one evening when a young Congolese clerk stopped by to ask for twenty-four visas. The clerk didn't seem to know what visas were, only that they involved travel, nor did he come with any passports to affix them to. Devlin asked the man the purpose of his request. He replied that Lumumba wanted to meet Eisenhower and Hammarskjöld. This came as a surprise, since state visits were usually organized months in advance. But Washington told the embassy to approve the travel, and a resourceful Foreign Service officer issued last-minute visas on blank pieces of paper.

Lumumba knew the United States only by reputation. His first sustained contact with outsiders had been with Americans, the Methodists who had taught him at the mission school in the village of Wembo Nyama. In an ironic twist, the same people who had once expelled Lumumba were now the ones to float the idea of a visit to America. Through their connections with the Tetela people—the ethnic group to which Lumumba belonged—Methodist missionaries had been urging the prime minister to travel to the United States in the hope of showcasing a "Christian democracy" for the Congo to emulate. Their White House liaison in this endeavor was none other than Dr. Alexander Reid, the midwestern missionary who had baptized Lumumba twenty-three years earlier.

Lumumba was eager to make the trip. He had tried to go in April, but the busy election campaign had kept him in the Congo. Now seemed like an even worse time to go, as some of his advisers pointed out. But to Lumumba, the benefits outweighed the risk: He could defend his actions, report on the reality on the ground in the Congo, and tell the world that his government was not composed of "bandits and criminals." In Washington, he could woo President Eisenhower and ask for American money and help, not to mention burnish his government's prestige by visiting the White House. In New York, he could make his case before Hammarskjöld and the Security Council, pushing the UN to follow through on the latest resolution and evict Belgian troops.

UN headquarters was not pleased to have a visit sprung on it. When Bunche called Hammarskjöld at 4:15 in the morning with news that the prime minister was insisting on going to New York, Hammarskjöld noted, "I reacted violently and said that Lumumba's stand made him ridiculous." The secretary-general was planning to check in on the UN operation in the Congo, and it would be awkward, to say the least, if Lumumba were in New York while Hammarskjöld was in Leopoldville. Bunche tried to talk Lumumba out of his rash decision, but, as he reported back to New York, it "was wasted breath." Hammarskjöld reluctantly agreed to delay his trip. He scrawled "Lumumba" in his appointment book.

"Having been informed of your excellency's departure for New York and your desire to meet me there for conversations, I have done my best to accommodate your desire and have postponed my departure until Tuesday evening," Hammarskjöld cabled Lumumba, with a hint of irritation. "That will leave us only three days for conversations." He feared that might not be enough. Mongi Slim, a confidant of Hammarskjöld's and Tunisia's representative to the UN, estimated that it would take "one week's education" in New York to get Lumumba to "the emotional level where he could make a contribution" to solving the crisis. Other UN representatives felt the same way. After speaking with Alex Quaison-Sackey, Ghana's Oxford-trained ambassador, Hammarskjöld recorded, "Q.S. transmitted the feeling that he and his colleagues in New York regarded Lumumba as just as crazy as I do and looked forward to his arrival with apprehension."

For Bunche, on the other hand, Lumumba's departure from Leopoldville had a silver lining. With the prime minister out of town, he could hold serious discussions with the rest of the Congolese cabinet.

It would also be good for diplomats in New York to meet the man himself and see what the UN was up against in the Congo. Besides, Bunche predicted bitterly, "he would be insufferable if turned down."

The United States in July 1960 didn't think much of Lumumba. William Burden, the U.S. ambassador in Brussels, concluded after Lumumba's troubling appeal to Khrushchev that the Congolese prime minister had allied himself with the Soviet bloc and was beyond redemption. The primary objective of U.S. policy in the Congo, Burden wrote in a cable on July 19, should therefore be to "destroy the Lumumba government as now constituted." To accomplish that goal, he went on, American propaganda should cast Lumumba as a Soviet puppet. Meanwhile, Washington should lean on neutral African countries to distance themselves from Lumumba and take "internal action" to empower his domestic enemies. As a potential successor to replace Lumumba, Burden identified President Joseph Kasavubu, who "might well prove to be a rallying point for more moderate and constructive elements."

That summer, foreign policy debates in Washington routinely centered on the advance of Communism in postcolonial countries. Marxist guerrillas were on the march in Laos and Vietnam, and Cambodia was threatening to accept military aid from Communist China. Frighteningly closer to home was the emergence of a Communist state in Cuba. A year and a half earlier, Fidel Castro's ragtag mountain-dwelling revolutionaries had overthrown the country's American-backed military dictator. When Vice President Richard Nixon met Castro in Washington, in April 1959, he judged the bearded, fatigue-wearing leader as clueless when it came to how to run a country and likely "incredibly naive about Communism"—yet not inherently anti-American. A little more than a year later, however, Castro had firmly aligned himself with the Soviet Union. He was staffing his government with avowed Communists, seizing U.S. oil refineries, and receiving deliveries of Soviet arms.

This was the paradigm in which Dulles saw Lumumba: a young revolutionary of questionable character and facial hair who, no matter what he said, was likely to bring his country into Moscow's orbit. At a meeting of the National Security Council on July 21, Dulles told the room that he found Lumumba's background "harrowing." He mentioned the 1956 embezzlement conviction and claimed that Lumumba had attended a Communist youth meeting in 1959—likely a confused reference to his visit that year to Guinea for the steering committee of the All-African People's Conference, an anticolonial group. The CIA also believed that Lumumba was receiving Soviet money, either directly or through Egypt. "It is safe to go on the assumption that Lumumba has been bought by the Communists," Dulles said. "This also, however, fits with his own orientation." Dulles concluded that the Congo's leader was "a Castro or worse."

Talk then turned to how the Soviets might occupy the Congo if Lumumba invited them in. The chairman of the Joint Chiefs of Staff drew an imaginary air route from Odessa to Khartoum to Stanleyville. The secretary of defense piped up to say that the chaos in the Congo appeared to be Communist inspired. Citing the suspicions of missionaries, he suggested that the army mutiny had seemed strangely synchronized, as if planned in advance and directed by Lumumba—a wildly implausible conspiracy theory, considering how much the prime minister's own authority had suffered from the revolt.

The State Department's own intelligence analysts took a more measured view. "We have no evidence, beyond rumors, that would link the mutiny to a Communist plot," a memo noted. Because Communists had been prevented from operating in the Congo during colonial times, their influence had been, and remained, largely limited to long-distance moral support from the Belgian Communist Party and the Soviet bloc. Lumumba himself could hardly be counted on to implement their will, the memo went on:

> Despite charges by the Belgians and his Congolese opponents that Lumumba is a Communist or Communist sympathizer, we have nothing to substantiate this allegation. The most accurate summary of his views is probably his own declaration of July 5, 1960, "We are not Communists, Catholics, or Socialists. We are African nationalists. We reserve the right to be friendly with anybody we like according to the principles of positive neutrality."

But the State Department memo would not reach Secretary Herter's desk for four days. Just hours after listening to Dulles call Lumumba "a Castro or worse," Herter received a phone call informing him that the two highest-ranking Americans in Leopoldville—Timberlake of the U.S. embassy and Bunche of the UN—thought it important that Lumumba arrive in New York on an American plane. If the prime minister were seen as being aided and welcomed by the United States, the country could score a point in its public-relations competition with the Soviet Union. Might the U.S. government give Lumumba a ride?

Herter saw no reason. In fact, his department now thought, better if Lumumba came by Soviet plane, to show the world his true colors. Herter rejected Timberlake and Bunche's request. Lumumba would have to find his own way to America.

So he did. On July 22, Lumumba and an entourage of fifteen—ministers, advisers, secretaries, journalists—turned up at Ndjili airport. With no aircraft having been designated for their trip, Lumumba commandeered a British jet being used to ferry Ghanaian UN troops to the Congo. But as the plane prepared to taxi, Lumumba realized that he had forgotten a press attaché. The door opened, and the prime minister eyed a gaggle of aides waving goodbye. "You!" he shouted, pointing to a twenty-five-year-old assistant. Stairs were rolled back to the plane, and the man climbed aboard. He had no visa, passport, or luggage, and would fly to the United States with only a pen, a notebook, and the clothes on his back. This would set the tone for the trip: organized by the seat of Lumumba's pants.

Just before takeoff, Lumumba spoke briefly to the press. At Herter's direction, the U.S. embassy in Leopoldville had urged the prime minister to publicly walk back his call for Soviet help, arguing that the latest Security Council resolution rendered it moot. At the airport, Lumumba did just that. Backtracking from previous statements, he pronounced himself "extremely gratified" by the UN's endorsement of a Belgian troop withdrawal and announced that the Congo no longer needed Moscow's help. "There is no further need for Soviet intervention," he said. The American press viewed the about-face as the result not of changing circumstances but of Lumumba's capriciousness. "His temperament is like the New England weather," *Time* wrote. "If you don't like it, wait a minute."

Reporters also explained Lumumba's new, pro-Western mood as the result of a curious deal he had just struck: a fifty-year, $2 billion contract handing over all the Congo's mineral and hydroelectric resources to Edgar Detwiler, a dazzling American entrepreneur who was joining him on the plane to New York.

Detwiler had a grand vision for the Congo. A fast-talking financier with a Wharton degree and a fondness for three-piece suits, he kept an apartment on Park Avenue and a country house outside London. At the height of the mutiny, Detwiler, sixty-two, flew into Leopoldville, accompanied by a blond secretary-cum-girlfriend, to pitch Lumumba. He introduced himself as the president of the Congo International Management Corporation, or CIMCO, which had been incorporated weeks earlier in Delaware, and claimed to have the backing of the titans of New York finance, as well as that of the U.S. government. He presented Lumumba with two letters signed by State Department officials endorsing CIMCO's endeavors.

One reporter described Detwiler as "a quick-moving bundle of nervous energy who acts as a sort of catalyst on others to get projects under way." In exchange for a share of profits and an exemption from taxes, he would turn the Congo into the modern economic powerhouse it deserved to be. But Detwiler had a reputation for never finishing what he started. Behind him lay a trail of abandoned projects, including a plan to build underground parking garages that doubled as nuclear fallout shelters in downtown Edmonton, Canada, and a $25 million dream of turning England's Canterbury Cathedral into a "Protestant Vatican," replete with a massive auditorium for pilgrims. Recently, he had turned his eye to Africa. He had tried to develop mineral resources in Ghana and Liberia but quickly aggravated his hosts in both countries before setting his sights on the Congo.

Lumumba knew none of this. But some around him, including Thomas Kanza, counseled caution. American officials worried that the Congo's inexperienced leaders were "ripe to be taken to the cleaners by the first carpetbagger" and judged Detwiler to be just such a con man. A young MIT field researcher in Leopoldville who had heard about Detwiler's reputation from a contact in the U.S. embassy took it upon himself to track down an aide to the prime minister and send a warning. Lumumba ignored all this advice. So confident was he in his own judgment, in fact, that he never consulted his own economic minister about the deal.

At the airport before leaving, Lumumba announced the agreement and claimed that it would create jobs and stabilize the new currency. It would also demonstrate his affinity for the United States. "This shows we are not lacking friends," he said.

To Lumumba, the contract with Detwiler was a talisman. As a French journalist watching put it, the deal was intended to prove "that Patrice was a good little boy who had no connection to those naughty gentlemen from Moscow." Who could criticize him for meeting with Soviet diplomats or sending cables to Khrushchev when he was entrusting his country's entire economic future to an American?

The sun had just risen when Lumumba's plane descended toward Idlewild Airport in Queens, early in the morning of Sunday, July 24. The journey to New York had been long and tiring. At a refueling stop in Accra, Ghana, where the runway had been so clogged with the prime minister's admirers that the pilot considered aborting his landing, Lumumba had met for two hours with Kwame Nkrumah, his Ghanaian counterpart. During a second stopover in London, he had met with a mid-level minister from the British Foreign Office. For most of the twelve-hour flight across the Atlantic, Lumumba slept—a moment of airborne peace before the mental combat of one-on-one meetings, press conferences, and working meals that awaited him.

"From speaking to various members of the party, we believe Lumumba does not have much idea of what he wants to do during this trip nor when he wants to do it," the U.S. mission to the UN reported to Washington. "His party was pulled together at the last minute and came with no advance preparation (and no money)." The main task, however, was clear: to negotiate with Hammarskjöld. Most of Lumumba's first days in New York were spent in the secretary-general's wood-paneled suite at the top of the UN building, discussing the fate of the Congo as clouds slid by through the glass. The contrast between the two men could hardly have been starker. The secretary-general was diplomatic and cautious; the prime minister, blunt and impatient. At one point, Lumumba's advisers switched from French to Lingala to implore their boss to act more tactfully, but as usual he ignored them. To Hammarskjöld, the meeting confirmed what the cables from Leopoldville had related: in his words, the man sitting across from him was "ignorant, very suspicious, shrewd but immature in his ideas—the smallest in scope of any of the African leaders."

Yet it wasn't just a clash of styles; Lumumba and Hammarskjöld were miles apart on substance as well. The nub of the matter was the presence of Belgian troops in the Congo. By now, UN forces were in the process of replacing Belgian forces in every Congolese province but one: Katanga. There, Moise Tshombe and white settlers made common cause to oppose Lumumba and advance secession. Tshombe and his local supporters wanted to break free from Leopoldville, retain the region's mining revenues, and run the province to the benefit of the ethnic groups they considered indigenous, as opposed to the "strangers" who had migrated from elsewhere in the country. The whites wanted their lives and businesses to continue as if independence had never occurred. These secessionist claims had a common refrain: unlike the rest of the Congo, Katanga was orderly and therefore in need not of UN liberation but of continued Belgian help. King Baudouin agreed, sympathizing with secession in a radio broadcast: "Whole tribes led by sober and honest men have asked us to stay and help them build a real independence in the midst of the chaos."

Hammarskjöld did not buy the argument that with Katanga calm there was no need for Belgian troops to leave. But Tshombe was resisting the plan to introduce UN forces, suggesting that they might be met with violence. Hammarskjöld didn't want a battle; as always, he preferred to achieve his aims through negotiation, which would take some time. Lumumba, however, was demanding a timetable for the Belgian troops' complete withdrawal that Hammarskjöld considered "impossible."

Lumumba also failed to grasp the role of the UN, at least in Hammarskjöld's view. Having invited the organization in, he thought he could command it, too. Hammarskjöld often identified himself as an "international civil servant," and Lumumba latched onto the "servant" part of that job description, giving off the impression that he considered the secretary-general a mere functionary in contrast to himself, the leader of a great nation. Kanza found Lumumba "extremely demanding and impatient" while Hammarskjöld remained calm, quietly taking down notes.

There were glimmers of understanding. On Lumumba's second day in New York, Hammarskjöld held a lunch in his honor. Thirty-eight men—mostly ambassadors from African countries and Security Council member states—sat and listened as Lumumba deployed his gift for oratory to great effect. Even Hammarskjöld was rapt, saying to a colleague, "Now no one can tell me that man is irrational!" But it might have been the booze talking: Hammarskjöld and his lunch mates consumed ten bottles of Chardonnay, ten bottles of Bordeaux, nine bottles of champagne, two bottles of vermouth, plus a bottle each of rye, scotch, gin, brandy, and liqueur.

Despite this tab, Lumumba somehow managed to hold a successful press conference immediately after the lunch. Seated behind a microphone and taking down notes, the man eloquently holding forth to a roomful of three hundred journalists did not seem like the rabble-rouser the press had expected. "There was nothing in the restrained remarks of the slightly more than 6-foot Congolese to suggest the impassioned leader who had been jailed by Belgium for inflammatory speechmaking," reported *The New York Times*. Lumumba backpedaled on the Detwiler deal, which he now seemed to recognize as a mistake, describing it as merely "an agreement in principle" that his government needed to study further.

Going into great detail about the mutiny and his travels across the Congo to quell it, Lumumba made a convincing case that the chaos in his country was Belgium's fault. It had failed to prepare the Congolese state for independence, backed Katanga's secession, and now insisted on keeping troops in the Congo even though they were no longer welcome. "If the Belgian troops leave the Congo today," Lumumba declared, "order will be completely restored five minutes after they have gone." How long would he be prepared to wait? "It would be fine if they left tomorrow. But if they left today, it would be even better."

As for his now-revoked appeals to Khrushchev, Lumumba clarified that his government considered the Soviet Union "a nation like any other," since "questions of ideology do not interest us." But that indifference should not be taken as signifying acquiescence or subordination. "We have no desire to get out from under one colonial regime only to fall under another dictatorship," Lumumba said. "We want democracy, the sort of genuine democracy we see here in the United States, for instance, where every sort of philosophy is respected, where the dignity and the rights of each and all are respected."

This was a generous description of American democracy in 1960. Lumumba never linked the global fight against colonialism to the U.S. civil rights struggle. Leaving unmentioned the United States' mass killings of Native Americans and its imperialist adventures abroad, he spoke of America as a bastion of freedom and emphasized its own origins as a former colony. Even in the smallest Congolese villages, he said, people knew that the United States had fought for its independence. Still, he saw African Americans, in particular, as natural allies—brothers in the anticolonial cause and potential recruits to help rebuild the Congo.

On a drive through Harlem, Lumumba found that he was beloved by the neighborhood's Black residents. ("They're all Africans here!" one of his aides said with glee.) Pedestrians persuaded the prime minister to step out, and soon he was delivering a speech on the corner of 125th Street and Seventh Avenue. The crowd broke through a ring of police and carried Lumumba on its shoulders. One speaker, invoking a Black nationalist from another era, praised him as "a second Marcus Garvey." *The Black Challenge,* a journal headquartered a block away, soon celebrated the visitor in poetic verse:

Hail Lumumba! Man of Africa
Who stands like a mighty dam
Against the floods of oppression
A granite wall of reality before
The white man's dream of madness
To keep the African his slave and Africa
His feasting ground of exploitation.

Others were unimpressed. Alex Quaison-Sackey, the Ghanaian ambassador to the UN, held a lunch in honor of Lumumba at his house in New Rochelle, just north of the city. When an American diamond merchant in attendance complained that one of his men was having trouble getting a visa to the Congo, Lumumba took the subordinate's passport, wrote in it, "This is a visa," and scribbled his signature underneath. More disturbing than this informal approach to immigration law was the prime minister's flighty and unstable comportment. The businessman had the impression he was on drugs. Some diplomats were irked by Lumumba's tendency to show up late to appointments. One UN staffer thought he evinced "adolescent pathos." "If I were Lloyd's of London," he wrote at the time, "I would not insure his political future."

In another misstep, Lumumba spent two hours with Vasily Kuznetsov, a top Soviet diplomat. Kanza would claim that "nothing the least sensational was discussed." *Pravda* gave the meeting a few column inches at the bottom of page 5, noting dryly that Lumumba and Kuznetsov "discussed issues related to recent events in the Congo." Radio Moscow announced that Lumumba had accepted an invitation to visit the Soviet Union. Once news of the meeting got out, Lumumba told a sympathetic journalist not to make much of it. "If I should some day go to Moscow," he said, "this voyage should be taken to have no more significance than that of Western heads of state when they visit the Soviet capital."

In a political climate in which Cold War anxiety at times verged on paranoia, however, the meeting with Kuznetsov was a greater faux pas than Lumumba grasped. To meet with a high-ranking Soviet diplomat and accept an invitation to Moscow would in itself have set off alarm bells in Washington; doing so while visiting the United States was all the more explosive. But as far as Lumumba was concerned, he was the leader of a sovereign nation, free to decide whom he would or would not talk to, and where. "Let us not overestimate the ability of Congolese politicians at that time to understand the Cold War," Kanza would point out. "In Congo, you were pro-Belgium or nationalist.... Only the outside world brought to us the idea of being pro-communist or pro-capitalist." Without realizing it, Lumumba had crossed a line.

Lumumba also rubbed his State Department escort the wrong way. The prime minister stayed at the Barclay Hotel on Forty-Eighth Street, where he and the other Congolese delegates overwhelmed the staff with orders of beer, whiskey, and fruit but seemed to have no intention of picking up the tab. On a shopping spree in Manhattan, Lumumba came up $150 short when buying leather luggage and, rather than put the item back on the shelf, asked the young Foreign Service officer to make up the difference. In the limousine on the way back to the Barclay, the officer was dismayed to see Lumumba pull out his handkerchief and send three $100 bills tumbling to the floor. "He nonchalantly scooped them up and never looked at me," the officer noted. "Cute guy."

Of all the people Lumumba had to impress in New York, the most important was Hammarskjöld. It was he who could decide where UN troops would go and whether to marshal international pressure to force Belgium to withdraw. But the prime minister and the secretary-general simply could not connect. Instead of engaging in a constructive dialogue, the two leaders traded monologues. Lumumba failed to get any commitment from the UN on forcing an immediate withdrawal; Hammarskjöld failed to persuade Lumumba to wait. "The meetings ended without love or animosity," one UN staff member wrote. "In truth the two had never really met."

They would never meet again.

Chapter 20

The Lamp and the Statue

I f Lumumba's visit to New York had been less than a success, perhaps he could make up for it in Washington. As a politician who had risen by virtue of his powers of persuasion, Lumumba must have thought that in talking to Dwight Eisenhower, he might well win the trust of the most powerful world leader—despite any misconceptions the president or his administration might have about him or the Congo. Lumumba brought with him a carved ivory lamp and a wooden statue, gifts he planned to present to Eisenhower at the White House. He had announced that he wished to "thank him for the American people's continued efforts to bring about progress in Africa."

Henry Cabot Lodge Jr., the U.S. ambassador to the UN, recommended that Lumumba be received at the "highest levels in Washington." Unlike Hammarskjöld, Lodge found the Congolese leader "on the whole encouraging." Lumumba might be "a little flighty and erratic in some respects, but he knows exactly what he is doing." His appeal to the Soviets, for instance, had likely been just an attempt to pressure the UN into moving faster. Treating the Congolese leader with due respect, Lodge concluded, could pay "big dividends."

But the Congolese delegates were told that Eisenhower would be unable to welcome Lumumba, a decision they interpreted as a deliberate snub. In fact, it was not. For the days when Lumumba was to visit Washington, Eisenhower had been scheduled to interrupt his working vacation in Newport with trips to Chicago, for the Republican National Convention, and Denver, to visit his dying mother-in-law.

These plans had been made well before Lumumba announced his voyage to the United States.

Although the president had not deliberately absented himself from Washington, the U.S. government was pointedly declining to accord Lumumba high honors. Before the visit, Secretary of State Christian Herter decided that a meeting with him and Lumumba "with no social functions offered should be the most we should do." For the sake of Cold War appearances and relations with Belgium, U.S. officials found ample reason to keep Lumumba at arm's length.

And so the U.S. government reduced its honors to the bare minimum required by diplomatic protocol. When Lumumba stepped out of the airplane at Washington National Airport, in brown loafers and a blue suit with a pocket square, he was welcomed with a hastily sewn Congolese flag, rush ordered for the occasion, and a Marine Corps band with no Congolese anthem to play (since none yet existed). Artillery rang out nineteen times—two fewer than when King Baudouin, a head of state as opposed to a head of government, had visited the year before. Lumumba nonetheless judged the reception "a dignified welcome of the sort granted a head of state." Since this was an official visit, Lumumba and his party stayed at Blair House, the presidential guest quarters across the street from the White House. These lodgings were "a magnificent house," in his view.

But even this bare-bones reception, designed in part to accommodate Belgian colonial sensitivities, prompted immediate protest from Brussels. "A cordial handshake for the Negro who is responsible for an unknown number of rapes of Belgian women, Belgian nuns, wives of American missionaries," raged a columnist for the conservative newspaper *Libre Belgique*. "Nineteen cannon shots and military honors for a Negro prime minister of a so-called state whose army, after deciding to rebel against its prime minister, turned around and focused its fire on women of white skin." With evident disgust, the columnist conjured up the image of "smelly Patrice" interloping at Blair House, a "savage swindler" in a four-poster bed "wallowing in the sheets of the King of the Belgians, Charles de Gaulle, and Khrushchev." Noting that the residence was managed by an elderly white woman, the author added, "Let's hope nothing happens to her."

Before Lumumba had even laid his head down at Blair House, Ambassador William Burden called Herter from Brussels to relay

Belgian officials' displeasure with the "catastrophic" optics. Soon, Belgium's foreign minister, Pierre Wigny, was also on the phone complaining to Herter, hinting that this, along with U.S. policies he deemed too favorable to Lumumba, would endanger Belgian support for NATO. At a meeting of the military alliance in Paris, two Belgian diplomats—one of them the secretary-general of NATO—made the same threat. To Brussels, Lumumba's treatment was evidently a question of national honor, something worth risking relations with the United States over.

In the past, the United States never had to choose between European colonial powers and newly independent states. But over Belgium and the Congo, that tension was now coming to a head. Herter was still trying to keep both parties happy, apologizing to the Belgian ambassador while pointing out that the United States hadn't selected Lumumba as prime minister of the Congo but "inherited him along with independence." The U.S. embassy in Brussels, however, took the side of the touchy Belgians, urging Washington that "the balance of the visit be played in the lowest possible key in order to hold the damage to a minimum."

Lumumba would rightly say that the episode demonstrated Belgian pettiness, but he avoided blaming the United States. On the contrary: at a press conference held in Blair House's stuffy basement, he called for American troops to intervene in the Congo and help hasten the Belgian withdrawal. These didn't seem like the words of a man in Moscow's pay.

With no White House visit on the agenda, Lumumba's delegation filled its schedule with sightseeing and shopping. At the Lincoln Memorial, the Congolese learned about the Civil War, a secessionist conflict Lumumba could not avoid comparing to his own, likening Jefferson Davis to Moise Tshombe. "All those who want secession are bound to be beaten in the end," he declared. From there, his fixation on pomp unabated, he visited a Cadillac dealership near the Capitol to look at official cars for his government. A reporter noted, "He tested doors, poked seat cushions, asked prices—but in the end, bought nothing."

Lumumba and his party also toured Mount Vernon, George Washington's riverside plantation. A guide emphasized the first American president's legacy as an anticolonial fighter.

"What was the attitude of the English towards him?" Lumumba asked when they reached Washington's bedroom.

"Oh, they treated him with respect."

"Modern-day colonists are not so gallant," Lumumba replied with a smile.

Part of Lumumba's goal in visiting the United States was to recruit skilled Americans who could fill the posts left vacant by Belgian workers—people who could serve as engineers, lawyers, doctors, dentists, and nurses in the Congo. On the campus of Howard University, the United States' premier historically Black college, he met with a small group of professors and students. (He already knew well the former head of the school's political science department: Ralph Bunche.) Most of Howard's six thousand students were American, but eighty-three hailed from Africa, and Lumumba jumped at the chance to chat with some of them in their native tongues. None came from the Congo, but he pledged that would change soon and urged Howard's American students to cross the ocean to "work on the land of their ancestors."

At the Mayflower Hotel, just north of Blair House, he met with a Methodist missionary couple who had known him in Wembo Nyama and encouraged them to send more teachers and medical workers to the Congo. In the ballroom below, diplomats, journalists, and various friends of Africa mingled at a reception held in his honor. Lumumba and his aides took the opportunity to redouble their recruitment efforts.

Yvonne Reed, just twenty-two years old and fresh out of college, attended the reception in the stead of her mother, who was active in the civil rights movement. Like her mother, Reed had often felt the sting of racism—Washington was still largely segregated at the time—and although she felt out of place at the reception, she was eager to meet the Congolese prime minister. By the time she arrived, the receiving line had broken and Lumumba was enmeshed in a circle of reporters. But she buttonholed one of his aides, who told her that the Congo was looking for American talent. Might she come work there?

The next morning, Reed dressed herself in a suit and took a taxi to Blair House. A man from the Soviet embassy pushed past her to ring the bell but was told Lumumba was busy. Reed, however, was ushered into a waiting room. Lumumba walked down the staircase.

"So you're interested in going to the Congo?" he asked.

She was. No discussion ensued about what, exactly, this young, inexperienced woman would do, but Lumumba instructed his aides to see to it that her paperwork was taken care of. He would be leaving for the Congo from New York in a matter of days. "That's it," he said, with a decisiveness that impressed Reed. "I'll see you on the plane."

It was a sign of just how bad the Belgian brain drain from the Congo was that Lumumba was willing to accept all comers, no matter how short their résumés. And as it turned out, Reed did not get on the plane in New York, because her parents thought better of the idea. Still, she would always look back fondly on her fleeting encounter with Lumumba. "He was a strong leader," she said. "He knew what he was doing."

While Lumumba was in Washington, so was Devlin, who had been flown back on a C-130 alongside Ambassador Timberlake to brief policy makers about the Congo crisis. Timberlake had warned Washington that "the Congo may be in its death throes as a modern nation." Soon, he would be helicoptered to Newport to fill in President Eisenhower.

Devlin stayed with his parents at their apartment in Arlington, Virginia. His first morning there, the CIA called to say that its director, Allen Dulles, had already asked for him twice. Devlin rushed to the agency's headquarters, across the street from the State Department in Foggy Bottom, to find Dulles waiting for him. The director wanted to know more about Lumumba, and Devlin laid out his theory of the case. The Soviets, Devlin contended, wanted to control Lumumba and "use the Congo as a base to infiltrate and extend their influence over the nine countries or colonies" that bordered it. The Soviets' play, if successful, would give them "an extraordinary power base in Africa," including control over the continent's resources, public affections, and UN votes. With this African empire in hand, Devlin said, Moscow could "outflank NATO in Western Europe" by dominating the southern Mediterranean coast. And by cornering the global market on cobalt—mined primarily in the Soviet Union and the Congo—it could deprive the American defense industry of an essential material, thus giving the Soviet Union technological supremacy over the United States. Far from being a backwater or a basket case, the Congo was a key prize in the Cold War.

Given that Soviet interest in the Congo thus far appeared tepid at most, the tale Devlin was spinning could only be called an elaborate conspiracy theory. Sympathetic statements from Khrushchev and regular floggings of Belgium on the floor of the UN Security Council—none of this came close to a concerted plan to dominate the Congo. Although Devlin believed Dulles was on the same page as him, the CIA director viewed the situation with more nuance. As Dulles had explained at a recent National Security Council meeting, the Soviet Union, after hearing Lumumba's threat to request Soviet troops, probably "felt it was getting too involved in the Congo" and thus "induced Lumumba to abandon his idea of calling for Soviet forces." Yet Dulles shared Devlin's overall assessment of Lumumba as a source of danger.

Across the street from the White House, some of Lumumba's American interlocutors, already primed to view Black leaders as rubes, nitpicked about his lack of familiarity with Western manners. Between courses of lunch at Blair House, a State Department officer suppressed a smirk when the prime minister, upon being delivered a finger bowl—for washing one's hands—drank out of it. State Department escorts found fault, too, in Lumumba's improvisational approach to scheduling. They were constantly trying to hustle along the Congolese delegation, usually in vain. Lumumba stood up an Indiana politician who had flown from out of town to talk about foreign aid. "You just don't do that to a U.S. Senator when you are asking for money," an aide vented to *Time*.

One incident would become legendary in diplomatic circles. According to the young State Department officer assigned to Lumumba in D.C., the prime minister discreetly requested a "blonde" for the evening. The officer, Thomas Cassilly, called a contact in the CIA, who promptly arranged a hotel room and a suitable woman. Lumumba had railed against philandering in his book manuscript— "the wife is not like a shirt which one can change at will: marriage is 'a life contract'"—but expressed satisfaction with the choice that night.

Coming on the heels of stories about Black men raping white women in the Congo, Lumumba's assignation, which became known to the White House yet was never exploited, played especially poorly within the Washington establishment (never mind that it gave a free pass to serial adulterers such as Allen Dulles). Officials were already giving Lumumba mixed reviews. One anonymous official characterized him to a reporter this way: "Erratic, but a tough, clever guy." But there was one chance for Lumumba to speak directly to the highest levels of the American government and make his own impression. The centerpiece of Lumumba's trip to the nation's capital was a meeting at the State Department. Washington had heretofore known him only telescopically, judging him from a distance through cables and news clippings. Now it could examine him up close.

The meeting began at 3:00 p.m. in the secretary of state's grand fifth-floor office, the afternoon light piercing venetian blinds. Herter presided, joined by three other State Department officials and an interpreter. Lumumba, who brought three Congolese officials, began with praise. "The people of the Congo, even in their most remote villages, have faith in the United States," he said. "We know that the United States is anticolonial." He went on to correct Brussels's version of events, explaining how Belgium had emptied the treasury, intervened illegally across the country, and engineered the secession of Katanga. He knew the United States and Belgium were allies, but couldn't Washington talk some sense into its transatlantic partner? In fact, he said, the United States might serve as a good mediator, a role in which the UN seemed to be failing. Lumumba also reiterated his request for U.S. aid. His government was unable to make payroll. Could the United States lend it money? What about equipment? He had twice been thwarted from flying where he needed to go in the Congo. "Would it be possible for us, through official channels, to obtain a plane, which could be used by the head of state and me for the trips we have to make into the interior of the country?"

Herter was sixty-five years old, a grandfather several times over. He had begun his diplomatic career during World War I and spoke in the soothing, mid-Atlantic accent one would expect of a Massachusetts Republican and husband of a Pratt heiress. He had broad shoulders and bushy eyebrows and, the day he met Lumumba, sported a polka-dot bow tie. He was the very picture of American diplomacy.

Thus he had little problem deflecting Lumumba's many requests. Pressuring Belgium to withdraw its troops? That was a matter for Hammarskjöld now. Direct bilateral economic aid? All funds had to be channeled through the UN. A plane? Also a question for the UN.

"I wonder if it would not be proper for me to present my respects to the president," Lumumba said.

"Unfortunately I do not know his schedule," Herter replied.

When Lumumba asked whether he might be able to merely meet one of the presidential candidates, Vice President Richard Nixon or Senator John F. Kennedy, Herter again demurred.

Officials had steeled themselves for an erratic child, but over the hour-and-a-half meeting, according to contemporaneous accounts, Lumumba convinced them that he was fundamentally reasonable. *Time* reported that "Washington officials, who had expected a ranting fanatic, found instead a poised, almost impassive, man." *The Christian Science Monitor* announced that Lumumba had "made a favorable impression"—"favorable by contrast to the advance stories out of the Congo that had pictured the youthful Congolese Premier as wielder of threats and ultimatums, as the Congo's Castro, as an anti-West, pro-Soviet revolutionary-turned-statesman."

A career Foreign Service officer in attendance echoed this assessment, finding "no evidence" that Lumumba was crazy, as critics had suggested. Other officials registered his "brilliance" and "articulateness." Lumumba also reassured them by seeming to change tack vis-à-vis Edgar Detwiler, who was desperately following around the prime minister to salvage his deal and had tried in vain to get a State Department meeting that very morning. When told that Detwiler had no connection to the U.S. government, Lumumba said the whole affair was a big misunderstanding and that Detwiler was no longer welcome in the Congo. Even Lumumba's solicitation of a plane was viewed somewhat sympathetically, with Herter passing on the request to the UN.

Years later, however, one official present would offer a very different account of the meeting. Douglas Dillon, the number two at the State Department, would claim that he found Lumumba "psychotic" and "impossible to deal with":

When he was in the State Department meeting, either with me or with the Secretary in my presence, he spoke in a manner that seemed almost messianic in quality. And he would never look you in the eye. He looked up at the sky. And a tremendous flow of words came out. He spoke in French, and he spoke it very fluently. And his words didn't ever have any relation to the particular things that we wanted to discuss. And it was just like ships passing in the night. You had a feeling that he was a person that was gripped by this fervor that I can only characterize as messianic. And he was just not a rational being.

Whether Dillon's assessment reflected the private consensus of July 1960 or was an ex post facto exaggeration, colored by knowledge of what Lumumba became, one cannot know for sure. Regardless of what stylistic impression the Congolese leader made, the meeting was a failure on a substantive level. Back in Leopoldville, one of Lumumba's political rivals warned the U.S. embassy of the dangers of allowing the prime minister to leave the United States empty-handed. If Lumumba said that Washington had turned him down, then he would have justification for asking the Soviet bloc for help. Yet the things he wanted most from America—the prestige of a meeting with the president, a commitment to pressure Belgium on the troop withdrawal, a promise of bilateral aid, and legitimate private investment—he didn't get. His visit to Washington had failed.

"Our talks with the United States government were completely successful," Lumumba nevertheless declared upon landing in Montreal. In Canada, which he noted was "not a colonial nation," he hoped to have better luck securing bilateral aid and recruiting French-speaking experts. Over the course of five hours in Montreal, he found time to dash off a telegram to Herter. Thanking the secretary of state for the "warm welcome" in Washington, Lumumba saw the beginnings of "excellent relations between our two countries, which have both fought, though at different times, for their freedom and dignity." But he also sensed that a misunderstanding had to be cleared up. Colonial powers, Lumumba wrote, "are presenting any African leader fighting for the independence of his country as a communist agent or an enemy of the white man." "Africa is not communist," he added. "It is only struggling to free itself."

From Montreal, Lumumba made the short flight to Ottawa. His hosts in the capital had been primed to view him with hostility ever since Belgium's representative to Canada, determined to forestall another welcome reception with the wrong optics, told the Canadian foreign minister that Lumumba was a Communist trained in Moscow and Prague (cities he in fact had never visited). The Congolese prime minister's Communist sympathies seemed to be confirmed when he received the Soviet ambassador for half an hour at his hotel, the imposing Château Laurier.

Lumumba did himself no favors by showing up late to a meeting with Canada's prime minister, John Diefenbaker, a conservative from the prairies. As Diefenbaker tried to draw out Lumumba about the needs of the Congo's civil service, the Congolese prime minister grew suspicious, refusing to discuss what he considered details to be handled by subordinates. "Mr. Lumumba was behaving like a hostile witness," a Canadian record of the encounter noted. Like his American counterparts, Diefenbaker disappointed Lumumba by telling him that all assistance would have to go through the UN.

Lumumba had hoped to find a receptive audience in North America, a land of former colonies. But he failed to recognize that the United States and Canada were white-dominated, European-descended societies that were inclined to identify with the colonizer over the colonized, to trust the Belgian version of events in the Congo over his own. Lumumba had come to Montreal and Ottawa with high hopes, only to discover that "although honest, Canada was just another imperialist country." The official Canadian record of his trip was devastating: "Mr. Lumumba left us with the impression that he is vain, petty, boorish, suspicious and perhaps unscrupulous."

Back in Manhattan briefly, Lumumba shopped at Macy's and bought some records. He signed an agreement with a philanthropy wishing to send Black Americans to volunteer in the Congo. He met again with Kuznetsov, the Soviet diplomat, raising U.S. suspicions that he was seeking bilateral aid from Moscow. And he had a quick conversation at the UN with Andrew Cordier, Hammarskjöld's deputy, who found Lumumba "hostile and frustrated."

"I am rather pressed for time," Lumumba said, noting that he still hadn't packed for his flight. He got straight to the point. "Before I left the Congo, we repeatedly asked that United Nations forces should be sent to Katanga Province," he said. "To this day, not one United Nations soldier has set foot in Katanga." The secretary-general, he continued, "instead of doing his work with impartiality, decided to hearken to the Belgian authorities only." Lumumba was exasperated. "While you may be satisfied with the progress achieved," he told Cordier, "our people, our government, and our parliament are disappointed."

The conversation ended abruptly, with no headway made. Cordier pleaded for "patience from all quarters," but Lumumba was in a hurry. Even more he felt the sense of urgency he had shown at a press conference in the same building the week before. As he put it then, "I must go back to Leopoldville immediately, for many problems await me there."

...leyville Central Prison, where ...ice Lumumba was sent after ...g caught embezzling from the ... office. Filled well past capacity, ... prison reeked of urine and the ...ashed fish fed to inmates—food, ...numba said, that "a European ...ld never serve to his dog."

Lumumba in the late 1950s. At one point, he served simultaneously as president, secretary, or treasurer of seven organizations in Stanleyville.

...e Leopoldville riots, ...uary 1959. Congolese ...nonstrators knifed Belgian ...s, smashed storefronts, ...ched houses, and flipped ...s.

Lumumba in Elisabethville after being sentenced for inciting a riot, January 1960. He was escorted by Frans Verscheure, a po[li]ce commissioner. They would meet again one year later.

Below: Lumumba displaying fresh wounds f[rom] handcuffs as he arrives in Brussels, January 1960. He had just been freed from prison to attend a roundtable to negotiate independe[nce] with the Belgian government. "In less than twenty-four hours, the prisoner was promo[ted] to a statesman," Mobutu would recall.

Left: Congolese delegat[es] at the roundtable, February 1960. Many of the delegates were meeting one another fo[r] the first time.

The first Congolese government, June 1960. Lumumba is in the center; Mobutu is in the second row on the right.

Above: Ambroise Boimbo taking King Baudouin's sword the day before the independence celebrations, June 29, 1960

Right: Lumumba, President Joseph Kasavubu, and Baudouin the same

Left: Larry Devlin, CIA station chief i
Leopoldville, by the ferry, late 1960 o
early 1961

Below: Congolese troops, July 1960.
Their camouflage served as a remind
that the army had been designed to p
down ethnic violence in the bush, not
restore order to a city.

osite, top: Belgians
ing the mutiny, July
0. Within two weeks
ndependence, some
000 of the 80,000 whites
he Congo had left.

bt: Lumumba speaking
oldiers in Stanleyville,
1960. Lumumba had
e tried to reach the
and twice failed owing
Belgian interference.

w: Lumumba and
avubu touring the
ngo to quell the
tiny. Their trip was an
irable display of unity
bitter rivals.

w right: Joseph Mobutu
ching as Lumumba
aks to the press, July
0. The dysfunction
Lumumba's cabinet
nded his sense of
fessionalism.

Above: Lumumba and Dag Hammarskjöld at UN headquarters in New York, July 1960. "The meetings ended without love or animosity," one UN staff member wrote.

Left: At the State Department with Douglas Dillon and Christian Herter, July 1960

Below left: With Thomas Kanza at the UN, July 1960

Below right: Andrew Cordier

Opposite, bottom left: Moise Tshombe, the leader of secessionist Katanga

ve: Antoine Gizenga, the
~~ngo's~~ deputy prime minister,
~~h~~ the UN's Ralph Bunche
~~d~~ Hammarskjöld at a banquet,
~~g~~ust 1960

~~ht:~~ The Royal, the apartment
~~l~~ding in Leopoldville that
~~v~~ed as the headquarters of the
~~N~~ operation

Above left: Andrée Blouin, "Africa's woman of mystery"

Above: Lumumba posing for his official portrait, August 1960

Left: Mobutu in his office, 1960. Mobutu felt little gratitude for the "really dirty job" the prime minister had pushed his way. "He put me in charge of this nonexistent army without really believing in it himself," he said.

Right: Protests marred Lumumba's pan-African conference. They were organized by Larry Devlin.

Left: Eisenhower in Newport, Rhode Island, July 1960. By then, Eisenhower had largely lost interest in the duties of his job and played golf almost daily.

Above: Allen Dulles, CIA director; Clare Timberlake, U.S. ambassador to the Congo

BAS LES MAINS
DEVANT LE CONGO!

Above: Mobutu announcing his coup, September 1960

Below: Kasavubu swearing in the College of Commissioners, October 1960. The new body consisted of university students and graduates, most in their twenties.

Opposite, top left: Rajeshwar Dayal, the UN's representative in the Congo

Right: Lumumba speaking at a rally. "A political personality cannot be eliminated overnight," a supporter pointed out.

Opposite, middle: Lumumba showing the agreement he had signed with Kasavubu, September 1960. Kasavubu immediately denied having signed it.

Below: Louis Armstrong in Leopoldville, October 1960

Above: Lumumba under house arrest, October 1960. Larry Devlin requested that the CIA send a "high-powered, foreign-make rifle with a telescopic sight and a silencer," adding, "the hunting is good here when the light's right."

Right: Lumumba with his two-year-old son, Roland

Lumumba after being captured, with help from the CIA and the UN, December 2, 1960. That night, Lumumba was tortured by Mobutu's men. He was killed the next month.

Right: Katanga's interior minister, Godefroid Munongo, announcing the death of Lumumba. "I'd be lying if I said that the death of Lumumba makes me sad," he said.

Below: A cable to Devlin from the CIA officer in Elisabethville reporting Lumumba's arrival in the city

```
PRITY LEOP INFO DIR CITE ELIZ 0283          19 JAN 61
   1.  THANKS FOR PATRICE.  IF WE HAD KNOWN HE WAS COMING WE WOULD
HAVE BAKED A SNAKE.
   2.  PER    Source    GOK HAD NO ADVANCE WORD WHAT SO EVER.
LUMUMBA SEVERLY BEATEN AT AIRPORT BY GENDARMERIE, THEN TAKEN JADOTVILLE
PRISON WHERE GUARDED BY ALL WHITE GUARDS.  GOK DOES NOT PLAN LIQUIDATE
LUMUMBA.  Source  FEARS CHANCES OF BALUBAKAT UPRISING IN EVILLE
CONSIDERABLY INCREASED.
```

Above: Lumumba's widow,
~~line~~ Opango, after her
~~band's~~ transfer to Katanga,
~~uary~~ 1961

Above: Patrice Jr., Juliana, and François
Lumumba at a soccer game in Cairo, February
1961. The children had escaped the Congo
using Egyptian passports with intentionally
blurry photographs and aliases.

Left: Hammarskjöld in the Security Council
after the announcement of Lumumba's death,
February 1961. Hammarskjöld's aides worried
about his safety and arranged for extra
security guards.

Opposite, bottom: Julien Gat of the Katangese
Gendarmerie showing reporters a staged
scene of Lumumba's supposed escape,
February 1961. Gat was present the night of
the murder.

John F. Kennedy and Mobutu, May 1963. "General, if it hadn't been for you," the president said "the whole thing would have collapsed and the Communists would have taken over."

Lwimba Movati Ndjibu, an antelope hunter who witnessed Lumumba's murder, standing by the execution site in 2010

PART III

TARGET

Chapter 21

The Katanga Question

O NE OF THEM was Hammarskjöld. The meetings with Lumumba in Manhattan had left the secretary-general with little respect for the Congolese leader, whose intermittent denunciations of the UN he considered ungrateful and petulant. Lumumba appeared to Hammarskjöld to be tilting toward the Soviets. "In the West, Lumumba has been disappointed," he recorded. "He has decided to play with the East against...the UN." En route to the Congo, Hammarskjöld darkly predicted where the prime minister's antics would lead him: "Let him play with fire if he wants to—but he'll certainly get burnt."

Nonetheless, Lumumba had succeeded in convincing Hammarskjöld of one thing: rightly or wrongly, the Congolese government was obsessed with the continued presence of Belgian troops on Katangan soil. Only their prompt expulsion from the province, he now recognized, could resolve the Congo crisis. To that end, Hammarskjöld made a rush trip to Brussels for six hours of back-to-back meetings with Foreign Minister Pierre Wigny, Prime Minister Gaston Eyskens, and King Baudouin. The secretary-general was running on little more than a glass of orange juice, but the Belgian message came through loud and clear: don't invade Katanga. A UN intervention there, the Belgians argued, would convince the white population that Lumumba was taking over the province, triggering a mass exodus followed by ethnic warfare. "I hope that your stay in Belgium will have convinced you of one thing," the king wrote to Hammarskjöld afterward, "which is that a present withdrawal of Belgian troops in

Katanga would create insecurity among the Belgian population and risk spreading chaos to this province."

Determined to avoid the appearance of a pro-Belgian bias, Hammarskjöld chose not to fly direct to Leopoldville on Sabena and instead flew KLM to Brazzaville, in the French Congo, planning to boat over to Leopoldville from there. In a fitting introduction, even the simple matter of crossing the Congo River turned out to be fraught with political one-upmanship and comic disorganization. The UN staff in Leopoldville had booked a lumbering ferry to take Hammarskjöld across, but before he could board it, he was taken aside by Fulbert Youlou, the mystical Catholic priest set to lead the French Congo into independence as president in a matter of weeks. Youlou, whose white Dior cassock fluttered in the wind, ushered Hammarskjöld onto a speedboat, which deposited him on the Leopoldville beach twenty minutes ahead of schedule. The UN secretary-general was left to stand awkwardly on the riverbank, the sun beating down on his dark suit as he waited to be picked up.

Hammarskjöld saw before him a city far different from the one he had visited during his African tour seven months earlier. It was July 28. Gone was the relative calm of colonial rule, even though the mutiny was over, Belgian troops had left, and the international UN force patrolled the streets. Hammarskjöld was met at the landing by some two thousand protesters carrying signs saying, "Total retreat of Belgians" and "Down with Tshombe." Congolese women clutching babies crowded around, looking for a ferry to flee across the river. Mosquitoes buzzed about; for weeks, no one had sprayed the streets with DDT.

Finally, Hammarskjöld was driven to the Royal, a new eight-story apartment block that UN staff had recently commandeered in their search for air-conditioned living and working quarters. But beyond offering an escape from the heat, the Royal was ill-suited to serve as the headquarters of a complex operation. Its telephone system was inadequate. Some of the original occupants, resisting eviction, remained. The only source of fresh food was a Greek restaurant on the ground floor, but so unpalatable was its fare that staffers preferred to warm military field rations on electric grills in their rooms. The cramped elevators routinely broke down, forcing inhabitants to brave a narrow emergency staircase.

The salon of the top-floor suite was converted into the nerve center of the UN operation, a room staffers affectionately called "the Snake Pit." A long dining table sagged under the weight of cables, reports, maps, and empty Coke and Evian bottles. Disorderly though it was, at a time of unreliable telephone communication, the Snake Pit served as a practical channel through which a diverse cast of supplicants—politicians, diplomats, and journalists—could register their advice or complaints. There were few secrets in these close quarters; one favorite pastime was listening in on the phone calls that F. T. Liu, Bunche's assistant and translator, would have with Lumumba.

Hammarskjöld, pale and exhausted, set himself up in the Snake Pit and dove into a marathon briefing. As he caught up on the latest twists in the Congolese drama, he gained an appreciation for the complexity of the problem before him, and for the disarray of the UN mission. "My God!" Hammarskjöld said. "This is the craziest operation in history. God only knows where it is going to end."

The next day, July 29, Hammarskjöld turned fifty-five. From the thirty-eighth floor in New York came a cable expressing the hope that the occasion "be marked by the continuing advancement of the UN cause in the Congo."

Alas, that would not be the case. Aside from a hastily thrown party in the Snake Pit, for which his resourceful staff had procured a case of champagne, a couple of balloons, and a Flemish birthday card, Hammarskjöld spent the day in exasperating negotiations with the Congolese cabinet. Lumumba was still in North America, so the cabinet meeting was presided over by Antoine Gizenga, the deputy prime minister, who had shown more open sympathy toward Moscow and whom Hammarskjöld considered stupid and malevolent.

Katanga was the main topic of discussion. Moise Tshombe had sent telegrams to eighty-three countries requesting diplomatic recognition and received no favorable replies. This lack of international recognition notwithstanding, Tshombe's government had been hard at work acquiring other trappings of sovereignty, with enough success that independence was increasingly becoming an irreversible fact. Most important, Tshombe was setting up an indigenous military, which would become known as the Katangese Gendarmerie. Its organizational chart was taken wholesale from the Force Publique, whose equipment and matériel in Katanga it inherited. The force was commanded and officered by Belgians whose salaries were paid by Brussels; its rank and file was composed of native-born Katangans. Meanwhile, the region had been printing its own banknotes and postage stamps. Outside government offices flew a new Katangan flag: red, white, and green, with three crosses representing the copper ingots once exchanged as a form of payment in the area. At the Elisabethville airport, passengers arriving from Leopoldville were treated as foreign travelers. "This is not the Congo," a Belgian immigration official told a reporter upon landing. "This is the independent Republic of Katanga. Passport, please."

Hammarskjöld agreed with the ministers in Leopoldville that, legally speaking, the Security Council's call for a Belgian withdrawal clearly applied to all of the Congo, including Katanga. But he pleaded practical reasons for delaying the entry of UN forces: namely, to avoid a war in Katanga. "We must act with wisdom and avoid violence," he told members of the Congolese government. Yet they were unanimous in their determination that UN troops must immediately enter Katanga, using force if necessary. Any hopes Hammarskjöld had that Lumumba's absence would allow cooler heads to prevail were dashed. Of the assembled men, he thought that only two or three were moderates, "men of real integrity, intelligence and sense of national responsibility." The rest, by contrast, "have a highly emotional and intransigent attitude on Katanga," so much so that the moderates had to side with them in order to preserve any influence. Writing to the Belgian foreign minister, Pierre Wigny, twenty-four hours after arriving in Leopoldville, Hammarskjöld admitted that the Congolese government's preoccupation with Katanga was even firmer than he had expected. "I must confess that I had not fully realized the continuing deep seriousness of the situation," he said. "It may still easily trigger a major conflict."

The unceasing pressure from Lumumba's ministers to invade Katanga punctuated the ceremonial atmosphere of the visit. At a dinner of river fish and gazelle hosted by Kasavubu at the presidential residence overlooking Livingstone Falls, Hammarskjöld was harangued by ministers. Soviet and Guinean diplomats weaved through the crowd berating the UN. "The Secretary General is pulling the wool over your eyes," one whispered to a Congolese guest.

Another evening, it was Gizenga's turn to host a dinner for Hammarskjöld. The banquet was held at La Devinière, a white-tablecloth restaurant in a wealthy white neighborhood. The secretary-general was relieved to learn that no formal speeches would be given, and the occasion seemed to offer a respite from the strenuous negotiations with the Congolese government. "In this delightful place tonight, I feel very far from the Security Council," Hammarskjöld remarked. UN employees mingled with tuxedoed Congolese bigwigs and foreign reporters under strings of lights. The food was extravagant, to the point that some guests felt uncomfortable, given that the head of UNICEF had warned that very day of the risk of famine in the Congo. The wine flowed freely.

As the kitchen readied dessert, men from the radio station erected microphones and strung wires across the floor. Andrée Blouin, the Gizenga adviser who had recently been promoted to the position of chief of protocol for Lumumba, clasped a bundle of mimeographs. Hammarskjöld looked at Kanza in puzzlement. Then Gizenga rose and asked for silence.

His speech was, depending on one's perspective, an ungrateful tirade against the UN or an earnest plea for the organization to live up to its promise. "Excellency, must I hide from you the following two facts that are troubling the Congolese people?" he asked. The first was that the UN was forcing Congolese soldiers to lay down their arms. "The people of the Congo do not understand why we, the assaulted, we who are in our land, we who made an appeal to international armed forces, are systematically and methodically disarmed while the aggressors, the Belgians, who are here in a conquered country, still retain their arms and their power of death." The second fact, he said, was that the UN was "allowing secession to consolidate in Katanga," where "the Belgians are behaving as if they are in a conquered country under the fallacious cover of a pseudo-government."

Blouin, who had written the speech, distributed copies as guests eyed one another nervously. Hammarskjöld, white-faced, listened to the scolding in silence with glass in hand. He held his applause when it ended.

The secretary-general chose to respond indirectly, rising to tell the crowd that this was neither the time nor the place to answer Gizenga's complaints. Rather, he made a general appeal for the Congolese to abandon their resentment of the Belgians and focus on a productive vision for the new Congo:

> History can enchain us. What is important is to work for the future of peoples. Men are happiest when they have the strength and the courage to rid themselves not of their great national memories but of their resentments and of their unhappy memories. That gives them new strength, makes them more productive, makes them better workers, not only for the progress of their country, but for world peace.
>
> It is for that reason that, as secretary-general, I have a certain tendency to be anti-historic, to be as much as possible—I and my associates—creators. Creation, that is to succeed in building something new, something built on human values, which exist everywhere and which can always be saved if we have the courage to do so.

If Congolese leaders lacked the courage Hammarskjöld expected, he found that quality scarce among the Belgians, too. Brussels wanted to wriggle out of the Security Council resolution, which envisioned a UN presence in Katanga. The Belgians knew, however, that they couldn't say as much, so instead they stoked fears that a UN intervention would lead to calamity, hoping that Hammarskjöld himself would decide it wasn't worth going in. "Belgium considers itself obliged to place before me all risks they see so that if things go wrong the responsibility would be entirely ours," he reported to New York. "Thus, without saying anything which can be construed as refusal to comply with [the Security Council] they present a maximum of de facto resistance."

If the Katanga problem could not be solved, Hammarskjöld saw a frightening path ahead for the Congo—and the world. The Belgians would continue to slow-roll withdrawal from the province, and Katanga would entrench its independence. As Brussels proved its own malfeasance, the moderates in Leopoldville—those, like Mobutu and Justin Bomboko (the foreign minister), who were more forgiving and patient than Lumumba—would get sidelined. Not only would Lumumba lose confidence in the UN's ability to enforce its own resolution but so would his ministers and fellow African leaders, while the West would close ranks behind Belgium. The Security Council would be split; Hammarskjöld, discredited. The Congolese government would likely band together with other African states, perhaps with Soviet help, to bring Katanga to heel outside the auspices of the UN. Following orders from home, African soldiers who were part of the UN mission might cast aside their blue berets, join forces with the Congolese army, and invade Katanga. The result could be a bloody territorial conflict in which the UN and the West fought for one side and the Communists and their allies for the other—in other words, another Korean War.

That outcome had to be avoided at all costs. But using UN troops to take control of Katanga by force was out of the question. The UN had neither the military capability nor the political support to carry out such a mission. So Hammarskjöld would have to undo the secession peaceably.

He sent his top Africa adviser, the German-born American Heinz Wieschhoff, to Brussels with a proposition. The Belgian government would face a domestic backlash if it openly endorsed the entry of UN forces into Katanga. But might it instead be willing to live with a statement from Hammarskjöld, saying he had received assurances from Belgium that it accepted his interpretation of the Security Council resolution? Such a statement would imply that UN forces could enter the separatist province. The Belgians took the offer. It gave them domestic political cover while sparing them more international opprobrium.

Hammarskjöld gave another emissary a harder task: flying to Katanga to hammer out the practical details with Belgian representatives and Tshombe. Provided that Katangan and Belgian forces put up no resistance, the first planeloads of UN troops would land in Elisabethville on August 6, in an operation Hammarskjöld codenamed Simba, Swahili for "lion." Belgian troops would then withdraw to their military base in Katanga and, eventually, to Belgium. Such, at least, was the plan.

Hammarskjöld evinced confidence. "Only about two weeks after the final decision of the Security Council entrusting me with the task of carrying out its will," he said over Congolese radio, "United Nations troops will thus be in control of the security of the whole territory of a united Congo." Reassuringly, he pointed out, the plan did "not meet with the opposition of any government."

Hammarskjöld had spoken too soon. In fact, all three relevant governments—the Congolese, the Katangan, and the Belgian—hated the plan and complained about it to him. Lumumba, on his way back from North America, was "delighted" with the decision to send UN troops to Katanga but argued that it was completely inappropriate for the UN to be talking directly to Tshombe, a rogue provincial governor deserving of subjugation, not negotiation. Tshombe, for his part, promised that the arrival of UN troops would precipitate a "general uprising in Katanga" and told the press, "They will have to fight their way in." The Belgians, despite having given the green light, thought the timeline was too tight and warned that the provincial government's autonomy should remain intact.

But Hammarskjöld was running out of time and needed to act boldly. Lumumba would be returning to Leopoldville the following week, and if the UN had still not set foot in Katanga by then, the prime minister and his government might band together with the Soviet Union and set the Congo on a path to Communist dictatorship. "The bad appendix had to be operated," he wrote. "The operation was bound to be difficult and even quite dangerous. But one thing is increasingly certain: that without operation the appendicitis would have been lethal."

The only man with the requisite skills for such an operation, Hammarskjöld decided, was Ralph Bunche.

Chapter 22

Simba

"So much, and most of it awful, happens here each day," Bunche wrote to his wife, Ruth, before he left Leopoldville for Katanga. "The work is the toughest, roughest, and most intensive I have ever experienced—far more so even than Palestine."

Bunche was days away from turning fifty-seven but looked and felt at least a decade older. His sojourn in the Congo was supposed to have ended by now, and nagging health problems hastened his desire to leave. A blood clot in his left calf—the result of a football injury from his college days—required him to wrap a tight rubber bandage around his leg, and in the heat and humidity of the Congo, it chafed his skin raw. More troubling was his recent diagnosis of diabetes. Bunche found that fresh milk lessened the symptoms and arranged for this commodity, unavailable in Leopoldville, to be flown in daily with the UN airlift, but still he suffered from poor vision, low appetite, and constant fatigue. "There has been no time for writing—and very little for sleeping or eating," he continued in his letter to Ruth. "I am indescribably tired—so much so that I scarcely feel it any more—a sort of paralysis."

Officially, Bunche was in Katanga to discuss "modalities for the withdrawal of Belgian troops and their replacement by troops of the UN Force," but in reality his quest was less about how the soldiers would leave than about whether they were willing to leave at all. There was a good chance Bunche would discover that Simba, the introduction of UN forces in Katanga, was too risky to try, since the province's coalescing military units and its civilian population would resist it by force. Realizing that in Elisabethville he would be dependent on Belgian channels to communicate, Bunche formulated a code by which he could inform Hammarskjöld of his findings. "Will report soonest" would mean proceed; "Reporting fully" would mean abort.

Bunche and eight other UN employees left Ndjili airport at 8:00 a.m. Thursday, August 4. During the bumpy ride, he composed a letter to Ruth:

> This is being written as we are about an hour from Elisabethville (Katanga) in a UN plane.... What awaits us we do not know. There may be hostility, of course.
>
> I've been working all morning on the plane—preparing papers in French and English, and I'm dreadfully tired now and sleepy too, as I got less than 3 hours sleep last night and even that was more than the night before.
>
> I cannot begin to tell you how complicated and maddeningly frustrating our operation out here is. Dag says he couldn't believe my cables until he came out here. Now he knows. It is like trying to give first aid to a wounded rattlesnake. How much longer we can hang on here is anybody's guess. How much longer I can stand this physically is still another question.... Must stop now!

"Thank heaven, *no* Tshombe," Bunche wrote in a note to Hammarskjöld describing the airport reception in Elisabethville. Already worried that his visit would be seen as legitimating Tshombe, Bunche was relieved to be met only by two Belgian representatives and a large crowd of Black and white residents.

His relief was short-lived. Bunche and his assistants were immediately ushered into a limousine flying a Katangan flag and driven to a three-star hotel, where, for an hour and a half in the dining room, they listened to the performative remonstrations of the two Belgian diplomats, noblemen both. The men, Baron Robert Rothschild and Count Harold d'Aspremont Lynden, tried to strike fear in Bunche's heart. Should the UN forces arrive Saturday, as planned, the result would be "great violence," the diplomats said. Young men of Katanga would mobilize into militias; warriors with face paint and poison-tipped spears would emerge from the bush and unleash chaos on the cities.

The macabre scenario sketched by the two diplomats was conjured up again later that afternoon during a negotiating session at Tshombe's residence. Tshombe, who preferred bold suits, jaunty hats, and a pearl tiepin, put on a show for Bunche, reading a long prepared statement (written, it seemed, by Belgian aides) in which he professed his love for democracy and self-determination and his disappointment in the UN, pausing intermittently to sip orange soda. "An instrument of peace," he said dramatically, "the UN in Katanga is preparing to become an instrument of war." Tshombe mimed the act of mowing down innocent Katangans with a machine gun.

Even less subtle was Godefroid Munongo, Tshombe's interior minister, a frog-necked former seminarian known as "the strong man of Katanga" whom Bunche considered the most hostile of his interlocutors. The UN, Munongo complained, "protects a criminal like Lumumba, who is responsible for the murders of many Europeans and the violations of many women, while refusing to recognize an honest government like that in Katanga, where calm exists and everyone is safe." Even if the multinational force somehow managed to parachute in and defeat the Katangan army, he said, tribal warriors would "riddle your soldiers with arrows." To that end, he had already sent planes to drop leaflets over the Katangan countryside, telling the population to prepare for invasion.

Bunche was struck by the intensity of the men's hatred toward the UN and the shallowness of their knowledge about it. (Munongo, for one thing, had evidently mixed up Hammarskjöld and Bunche and was shocked to discover that the envoy sitting across from him wasn't Swedish.) "There were egotism, arrogance and ignorance galore," Bunche reported. He asked Tshombe what he would do if UN forces landed in Elisabethville that Saturday, as Hammarskjöld had planned. Would he really order the local population to oppose their entry by force?

"Absolutely," replied Tshombe.

The meeting ended with no common ground reached and no decisions made. Tshombe falsely announced to reporters that the UN had "suspended" its planned operation. To counteract this ploy,

Bunche's assistant issued a clarification: "Bunche has said only that he will report fully to the Secretary-General on the day's discussions." But this caused only more confusion, because Hammarskjöld now wondered whether Bunche was trying to transmit his "reporting fully" code.

"I am still not firm in my evaluation of the Katanga situation as regards UN troop movements," Bunche cabled Hammarskjöld that night. "I sense a generous portion of bluff."

The next morning, a plane of twenty-one UN military advisers, unarmed and in civilian clothing, neared the Elisabethville airport. They were coming from Leopoldville to discuss logistics and a timetable for the withdrawal of Belgian troops from Katanga. These were the advance men for the Swedish, Moroccan, and Tunisian soldiers packing their gear in Leopoldville in preparation for their mission to Katanga, should an agreement be reached. But unbeknownst to the men on the plane, trouble was brewing at the airport below.

Around the control tower, a barricade of oil drums and barbed wire had sprung up. Five trucks positioned themselves close to the runway, and another pulled a trailer with sixty empty oil drums. Katangan soldiers and Belgian officers milled about in far greater numbers than normal. Grenades dangled from their belts; some had their guns trained toward the tarmac. Inside, the airport chief was on the phone with Godefroid Munongo, who was issuing orders: Roll empty barrels onto the runway to prevent the UN plane from landing. Fire upon it if it did land.

Bunche was back at Tshombe's residence for a new round of negotiations. Just as he seemed to be making progress, he was interrupted by a panicked d'Aspremont and Rothschild, who burst into the room to announce that the UN invasion they so dreaded had already begun. Evidently, Belgian and Katangan authorities were under the mistaken impression that the plane approaching Elisabethville was carrying UN troops, part of an armed operation to retake the province—hence also the preparations under way at the airport.

Bunche tried to calm the diplomats, explaining that they were misinformed, then sped to the airport. He was met by Munongo—"wild with excitement and rage," in his estimation—who, despite

Bunche's denials, held on to his belief that the plane was part of a UN-led assault. "We're going to shoot!" Munongo shouted. Only through an elaborate show of reassurance—climbing the stairs of the control tower with Munongo, grabbing the radio microphone, and personally communicating with the pilot to confirm that the men were unarmed—was Bunche able to persuade him to let the plane land. But Munongo insisted on inspecting the cabin himself and refused to let its passengers disembark, leaving them to bake in the noontime sun. He then demanded that the plane leave immediately and take Bunche with it. Soldiers pointed their weapons at Hammarskjöld's envoy as he climbed the ladder. "Tell your boss that this is no joke here," Munongo yelled before the hatch closed.

Bunche had already done so. Before leaving Elisabethville, he had sent Hammarskjöld a cable containing the prearranged signal: "Reporting fully."

Simba was off.

Did Bunche make the right call? He himself suspected that he had been fooled into thinking Simba would start a war. "I think it... not unlikely that what happened at the airport this morning was a scene in the play and was staged for our benefit," he wrote to Hammarskjöld. "If so, it was well enacted, well cast and effective."

There was good reason to conclude that Tshombe could not have followed through on his threat to resist the UN. "Katanga had no military force of consequence at that time," Bunche would admit. The Katangan army probably comprised only 350 soldiers, the remnants of the mostly disbanded Force Publique in the province. Tshombe's sway over the locals, moreover, was hardly as total as he portrayed it; in provincial elections earlier that year, he and his allies had received only half the votes. A Western diplomat speaking to *Newsweek* before the planned UN operation was probably correct when he predicted, "One little breath from the U.N. will blow Katanga over like a house of cards."

As would become painfully clear later, in canceling Simba, the UN had let a valuable opportunity slip by. Never would it be easier to move into Katanga than in early August 1960; the Katangese Gendarmerie was embryonic and weak. Taking over would have transferred responsibility for order in the province from the Belgian and Katangan troops to the UN. In the process, the question of whether Katanga could achieve independence would likely have been downgraded to a lesser, constitutional problem: how exactly to structure the province's relationship to the central government. But Hammarskjöld felt he could not call Tshombe's bluff. Doing so would have risked a fight, and the UN mission was not authorized to fight. Nor had the governments supporting it signed up for that, even if some of them now wished they had.

Hammarskjöld returned immediately to New York. He had predicted that calling off Simba would put him "in very deep waters," and it did. One of his chief fears had been that the African countries contributing troops to the UN mission would reassign their soldiers to the Congolese government, and now it seemed to be coming true. Ahmed Sékou Touré, the president of Guinea, sent a telegram urging Hammarskjöld to use Guinean UN troops to invade Katanga, threatening that if he did not do so, Guinea would order them to answer to the Congolese government. From Ghana, Kwame Nkrumah pledged to do the same. The Soviets also pounced, with Khrushchev now raising the possibility of direct military assistance. "The difficulties of your struggle are clear and known to us," he assured Lumumba in a letter.

In reaction to the failure in Katanga and the ensuing backlash, Hammarskjöld convened the Security Council to once again discuss the situation in the Congo. In a sign of how urgent the crisis had become, the meeting was to be held on a Sunday; only Korea and Suez had merited that treatment before.

"The Congo problem is a question of peace or war," Hammarskjöld told the delegates, his voice strained. "And when saying peace or war, I do not limit my perspective to the Congo." He expressed his dismay with nearly everyone who could be blamed for the current impasse: the bellicose Katangans, the impatient Congolese, the two-faced Belgians, the unhelpful Guineans and Ghanaians.

By the end of the debate, which lasted until nearly 4:30 in the morning, Hammarskjöld got what he had come for: in a new resolution, the council insisted once more that the Belgian troops withdraw and, crucially, gave express permission for UN troops to enter Katanga. The Belgians, naturally, were disappointed. At one point,

Pierre Wigny, representing Belgium, took aside Lodge, the U.S. representative, and begged him to veto the resolution. Lodge refused and told him that a misstep could "make the present state of affairs in the Congo look like a tea party." Everyone besides the Belgians—the Western powers, the Soviet bloc, the Africans, the Asians—endorsed Hammarskjöld's compromise approach to the Congo crisis. It would be the last time they mustered such unity for him.

Chapter 23

The Long Way Home

THERE WAS GOOD reason for Lumumba to attend to matters at home immediately, but he took the long way back from New York, wending his way toward Leopoldville through several world capitals. He hobnobbed with pro-Western leaders who encouraged him to mend fences with the UN and networked with leftists who nurtured his newfound grievances, although it was only the latter who would catch the attention of his growing number of critics. In London, he was received by a mid-level British diplomat and by a visiting member of the Belgian Communist Party, who reportedly recommended he expel all Belgian diplomats from the Congo and "try a bit of 'dictatorship,' that is, proclaim a state of emergency and establish military courts."

From London, it was on to Tunisia, where Lumumba talked colonialism over dinner with two exiled leaders of Algeria's National Liberation Front, then nearly six years into its violent war against the French. He also paid a visit to the seaside villa of Habib Bourguiba, Tunisia's moderate, pro-Western president, and the two paraded through town in a convertible. Bourguiba's influence was evident in remarks Lumumba gave to the press afterward: "Africa is not opposed to the West. Africa is not Communist. Africa will remain African." Following a meeting with King Mohammed V of Morocco in Rabat, Lumumba continued on to Conakry, the capital of Guinea. At a champagne reception in the presidential palace, the country's left-leaning president, Ahmed Sékou Touré, urged him not to compromise with Belgium, in a meeting that left Lumumba "completely hypnotized," in Thomas Kanza's estimation. Then it was off to Liberia, whose pro-American president, William Tubman, counseled patience instead of further escalation vis-à-vis the West. In Togo, Sylvanus Olympio—whom Eisenhower considered his favorite African leader—did the same.

But the highlight of the trip was Accra. Just as he had been during his first visit to the city in 1958, Lumumba was taken with the pan-Africanism of Ghana's president, Kwame Nkrumah. The two leaders approved a pair of agreements. The first, which they read out at a press conference, threatened to work outside the UN if the organization couldn't effect a Belgian troop withdrawal. The second, signed in secret in Nkrumah's private quarters, endorsed a union between their two countries, with a common currency and foreign policy. It was a thoughtlessly grandiose gesture, given the crises brewing back in Leopoldville.

Near the end of his weeklong roundabout journey home, Lumumba sent a cable to Médard Olongo, his trusted cabinet secretary (and fellow Tetela), who had been keeping him updated on events in Leopoldville during his extended absence:

> My voyage across Africa is very fruitful and profitable for Congo. The King of Morocco invited me and gave me a very warm welcome. As in Tunis, I was the object of a high distinction. The little intrigues hatched during my absence will end as soon as I arrive. I have experience with this. Be vigilant and keep a close watch on the cabinet. All the other questions will be settled as soon as I arrive.... Kiss the whole family for me.

Lumumba's family life, alas, was getting complicated. His wife, Pauline Opango, was pregnant with his child—their fourth—but so was his secretary, Alphonsine Masuba. Lumumba seemed to view Pauline as an inconvenient holdover from his earlier life, and it must have frustrated both members of the couple that their interests overlapped little. Pauline had been right to worry that her husband would be tempted by a more sophisticated, "Europeanized" woman. Unlike Pauline, Alphonsine—Miss Stanleyville 1956—could read and write. She knew how to type his letters and organize his library. According to the son they would eventually have, Lumumba planned on leaving Pauline for Alphonsine. The two were scheduled to wed in a few months—at least if things were calm by then.

As a little girl, Juliana Lumumba used to react the same way whenever her father was gone: she fell ill. When he returned, she was cured. This psychosomatic pattern had occurred while he was on the campaign trail in the spring, and so it was during his international travels that summer. When Lumumba returned to Leopoldville late at night on August 8 and scooped up four-year-old Juliana in his arms, she grinned with relief and delight.

Juliana was not the only one who keenly felt her father's absence. Lumumba had been prime minister for thirty-nine days. Between his trips with Kasavubu to the interior and his foreign tour, he had spent only nine full days in the capital. Even so, Lumumba preferred to lead his government with meticulous—many would say excessive—supervision. So dependent was his rule on personal attention that when he was abroad, nothing seemed to get done. "Premier Patrice Lumumba, in the Belgian view, has run away from the job of directing his country and has turned into an international gadabout and headline chaser," opined *The New York Times*. Rebuking Lumumba's absenteeism, a wry critic wrote on the lost and found blackboard in the lobby of the Palace of the Nation something big that had gone missing: "a republic."

The economic situation, in particular, was worsening by the day. In Leopoldville, shops and factories remained shuttered, and jobless men roamed the streets. The city was a ghost town. Upriver, once-humming rubber, banana, and coffee plantations were abandoned. The mining royalties from Katanga were now being paid to Tshombe's separatist government in Elisabethville, not the national treasury in Leopoldville. Union Minière, the copper giant and enthusiastic backer of the secession, had recently advanced the Katangan provincial government $25 million in tax payments. The central government in Leopoldville had no idea what to do about any of this. When the finance minister was asked about his plans for balancing the budget, he replied, "Well, there is no problem: we have the machine to print the money now." As *Time* magazine put it, "Lumumba's Congo was flat broke."

In the government, the "little intrigues" Lumumba had dismissed in his cable turned out to be not so little after all. Members of his own cabinet were distancing themselves from him publicly and tearing into him privately. Lumumba had put Antoine Gizenga, the deputy prime minister, in charge during his time abroad, but now he was hearing rumors that Gizenga was plotting a coup to oust him. President Kasavubu, likewise, was irritated with Lumumba, who he felt had kept him out of the loop. Gone was the bonhomie, or at least civic-minded détente, that had prevailed during the two leaders' national tour to quell the mutiny. "I'm not kept informed of anything," Kasavubu complained bitterly to a confidant.

Meanwhile, Kasavubu's supporters were openly calling for the downfall of Lumumba's government. It had always been particularly unfortunate for Lumumba that Leopoldville, of all places, was the Congo's capital. Despite his years as a beer salesman in the city, he remained an ethnic outsider and lacked large numbers of local devotees, putting him at a distinct disadvantage vis-à-vis Kasavubu. When the Lumumba Youth Party held a demonstration to protest the UN's failure to enter Katanga, fewer than fifty people turned up. The listless rally quickly dissipated. (Bunche, who was watching, counted more photographers than participants.) Kasavubu, by contrast, owned the *cité*, the area that had been the capital's African neighborhoods under Belgian rule. Hundreds of Kasavubu's young partisans welcomed Lumumba home with a mass demonstration and cries of "Down with Lumumba!" When the prime minister was driven through the *cité* one night, residents stoned his car. One rock beaned him in the face, causing blood to run down his cheeks. (Hammarskjöld said he was glad Lumumba wasn't killed in the melee, not wanting him to "become a martyr.") Worried about the deteriorating security situation, Bunche discreetly requested that five thousand nightsticks be flown in as soon as possible.

In Katanga, Tshombe was flush with pride from standing up to the UN. The phone was ringing off the hook with congratulatory calls. He joyfully shouted into the receiver: "We are victorious!" Secessionism was in the air in other parts of the country, too. In Leopoldville province, a high-ranking member of Kasavubu's political party endorsed a federal system of government for the Congo, by which all provinces would operate more or less autonomously. To the east, Albert Kalonji, the former MNC member who had split with Lumumba's party in 1959 and who had been excluded from his cabinet, once again went his own way. Citing the prime minister's "incompetence in the face of the country's problems after independence," he announced that the southeastern chunk of Kasai province, which bordered Katanga, was now independent as well. The region exported three-quarters of the non-Communist world's industrial diamonds, and Kalonji christened the new entity "the Mining State."

All this meant that after two weeks' absence, Lumumba came back to a country very different from the one he had left. He now confronted an even deeper economic crisis, mass protests, a renewed rivalry with the president, rumors of a coup d'état, and proliferating secessionism. It was time to act.

The night of his return, Lumumba called an emergency cabinet meeting. By the time it ended the next morning, two major decisions had been made. The first was to declare a nationwide state of emergency. "The army will arrest anyone, be he white or African, who tries to stir up trouble in the Congo," Lumumba promised at a press conference. "It will show no mercy."

Under the state of emergency, the government introduced new rules for political associations: henceforth, all such groups had to apply for government authorization. Attending the meeting of an unlicensed group would be punishable by two months in prison. Not long after the announcement, MNC partisans sacked the headquarters of Abako, Kasavubu's party. Police raided the offices of the Belga News Agency and ordered its staff to stop transmitting reports to Brussels. The editor of the conservative newspaper *Le Courrier d'Afrique* was thrown in jail. Lumumba, who had built his national profile with large public addresses and once spent three months in jail for holding a political rally, was now himself curtailing freedoms of speech, assembly, and the press.

It was a remarkable authoritarian turn for a man who had once written about Belgian colonial rule, "You do not win the confidence, respect or obedience of a subject people by wickedness, cruelty or harshness, but by good administration, respect for the rights of citizens, and just and humane treatment." Unable to offer good administration, however, Lumumba opted for harshness. Squelching the free press, in his view, was a matter of survival. His opponents were attacking him mercilessly in the Leopoldville papers, and from across the river, Radio Brazzaville was doing the same. Unknown critics were handing out tracts that warned, "Lumumba is going to sell your women to Russia."

The second late-night cabinet move was to give concrete meaning to the decision, made weeks earlier, to break off diplomatic relations with Belgium: the government was immediately expelling the Belgian ambassador and closing Belgium's embassy. "In the entire history of colonization in Africa," Lumumba explained, "no nation has ever behaved so scandalously toward a people that has always lived in peace with it. Belgium is what it is today because of the Congo."

Perhaps for reasons of personal satisfaction, or perhaps because he feared that the decision, like so many others, would remain lodged in the planning stage, Lumumba carried out the expulsion order himself. A little before 4:00 in the afternoon, he marched over to the Belgian embassy, a stilted building across from an open-air ivory market, and rode the elevator to the fifth floor. Jean van den Bosch, the ambassador, had already left.

"I see that the ambassador is gone," Lumumba said to an embassy employee busy packing boxes. "But did everyone here go with him, the advisers, the secretaries? I am notifying you, as minister of national defense, that if all the staff of the embassy do not leave the Congo this very evening, I will have those who remain arrested." With that, he handed over a letter formalizing the expulsion, turned around, and left.

The embassy employees needed no encouragement. Earlier that day, teary-eyed Belgians had watched as van den Bosch lowered his country's black, yellow, and red flag from the roof of the building. He sped away in a limousine through a crowd of hundreds of dancing and cheering Congolese. Seventy-five years after King Leopold II had claimed the Congo, Belgium's ambassador was rushing toward the river to meet a motorboat that would hurry him to Brazzaville. Rocks and chunks of wood pelted his car.

"Drive on," he told his chauffeur.

Chapter 24

Operation L. Suggestions

T HE PRIME MINISTER'S office was the picture of disorder. Weeks of letters piled up in unopened mailbags. The tables were littered with bottles of beer and champagne. Clouds of cigarette smoke thickened the air, stirred lazily by a ceiling fan. Plastic flowers poked out of crystal vases. On the walls hung reproductions of Renoir, Braque, and Modigliani. On the floor stood a pair of elephant tusks and a piano, both inherited from the office's previous occupant, the Belgian governor-general.

Gatekeeping was haphazard. An ambassador seeking an audience would be left waiting on the lawn outside, arms crossed, feet toying with a pebble, whereas other visitors came and went as they pleased, attracted not only by the chance to present any minor complaint or harebrained scheme to the prime minister but also by the butlers serving free alcohol and sandwiches. Daily press conferences, held in the garden, were scheduled for 11:00 but usually didn't start until 1:00, leaving ample time for reporters to roam the grounds and help themselves to foie gras, cake, whiskey, beer, and champagne. The prime minister's wife, Pauline Opango, would regularly wander around, children in tow. Seven-year-old Patrice Jr. had a knack for finding which of the many telephones was ringing at any given moment. Eight-year-old François was less enthused about the crowds, annoyed that his home could be filled with as many as one hundred grown-ups at a time.

At the center of this chaos, amid the multiplying advisers, the accreting mounds of correspondence, the onslaught of telegrams, the reams of loose files, the stacks of newspapers, the clinking champagne flutes and beer glasses, the jangling telephones, the placard men shouting through the window, the questing journalists, the special envoys from nations far and wide, the jostling petitioners, the senators, governors, and party officials from this or that province or ethnic group, each with his own special plea or conspiracy theory, was Lumumba, still just thirty-five years old, overworked, overtired, and overwhelmed. He trusted no one. He typed most letters himself. He saw personally to the management of his residence's garage. At one point that summer, he spent several hours posing for his official portrait, waiting as photographers had legal books carted in from the Ministry of Justice and procured a flag from the army to form a suitable background. Propelled by a messianic belief in his historical destiny—"The Congo made me; I shall make the Congo," he liked to say—he worked at all hours.

He might have been propelled by more than conviction alone. Some who met him claimed he was pushing through exhaustion thanks to the types of performance-enhancing amphetamines favored by professional cyclists. Others, noting his glazed eyes and short attention span, thought he smoked marijuana, an allegation that fit neatly with the mid-century stereotype of a Black jazz-loving reefer addict. Both Bunche and Hammarskjöld believed Lumumba was taking some sorts of drugs. The rumor even reached Eisenhower, who could not have reacted favorably: the president so opposed drug use that he had signed a law making the sale of narcotics to minors punishable by death. No one had any real proof of Lumumba's habit, and one aide would claim that the only drug the prime minister and his entourage used was champagne. But it became an accepted truth among his enemies.

Lumumba was desperately collecting foreign advisers, at one point even suggesting that a friendly Spanish journalist take Congolese citizenship in order to serve as an ambassador in Latin America. (He accepted the offer.) The prime minister seemed to be surrounding himself with all the wrong types of outsiders. Ambassador Timberlake warned Washington of the "Communist advisers who now surround Lumumba." *Time* wrote about "a growing coterie of Red-lining advisers."

No aide raised eyebrows higher than Andrée Blouin, who was still serving as the prime minister's chief of protocol. Because she had come to the Congo by way of Guinea, where she had worked for Ahmed Sékou Touré, Blouin was seen as exerting a powerful leftward pull on the Congolese government. "Most Western diplomats here regard her as the Congo's strongest link with the Communist world," declared an article in *U.S. News & World Report,* alongside a photo of Blouin glowering at the camera. When an official in Brussels was asked about her, he sighed with a mixture of exasperation and admiration. "Madame Blouin!" he said to a reporter. "A beautiful woman—but also a dangerous woman, perhaps the most dangerous in all Africa."

Unsurprisingly, given the times, Blouin's critics ignored her skills as a political tactician and speculated that she must have slept her way to influence. A cable from the U.S. embassy claimed that she was making the rounds of "various high-placed bedrooms" and described her as a "Madame de Pompadour," in reference to a mistress of King Louis XV's. Hammarskjöld, evoking another famed French courtesan, called her the "Madame du Barry of the Congo." Blouin denied these rumors, as well as the allegation that she was a Communist. And for all the fears about her seducing and subverting Lumumba's inner circle, she herself admitted she had relatively little influence. Despite being chief of protocol, for instance, she found it impossible to control the flow of the prime minister's visitors. One reporter seeking an interview with the prime minister managed to talk her way past his guards and crash a cabinet meeting. "Would you walk in on President Eisenhower like that?" Lumumba barked.

But Lumumba's European advisers aroused suspicion, too. "Who are all these white men?" a *Newsweek* reporter asked one Congolese aide, adding, "the ones who do your thinking for you." The reporter had in mind first and foremost a thirty-eight-year-old Frenchman named Serge Michel. Born Lucien Douchet to a socialist family on the outskirts of Paris, Michel moved to Algiers in the 1950s to work as a speechwriter, editor, and caricaturist for the Algerian independence movement. He was said to be under a French death sentence for his support for the Algerian nationalist cause. Lumumba had picked him up in Tunisia, where the anti-French Algerian government in exile had offered his services as a press attaché. Michel was fiercely anticolonial—"You have a Black heart," Lumumba once complimented him—and a Marxist. But he was not, as commonly alleged, Polish, nor was he, as Devlin believed, a Soviet agent. In fact, he was an open critic of the Soviet Union and had protested its crushing of the Hungarian Revolution in 1956. And like Blouin, he could not claim a great hold over Lumumba, likening himself to a tourist, a "wanderer through the tragic and burlesque era of decolonization."

The only other European adviser of any prominence was Jozef Grootaert, a Belgian who had worked as a judge in Katanga before independence and now advised Lumumba on legal questions. Grootaert had won the prime minister's confidence by virtue of his fierce anticlericalism. Yet the respect was not mutual. Too punctilious for Lumumba's chaotic entourage, Grootaert clashed with Michel and griped to the U.S. embassy about the left-wing advisers Lumumba had chosen.

Within his cabinet, Lumumba favored ministers who were suspicious of outside interference, whether from the UN or Belgium. One bugbear in Western eyes was Anicet Kashamura, the minister of information. A firebrand with Coke-bottle glasses, Kashamura controlled the national radio and took to the airwaves regularly to berate the Belgians—to the point that Lumumba himself had to tell him to tone it down. Although Timberlake thought Kashamura had turned the station into "a virtual communist mouthpiece," that characterization once more confused anti-imperialism for Marxism; in fact, Kashamura was eager to visit the United States.

Then there was the deputy prime minister, Antoine Gizenga. During the roundtable in January, he had visited East Berlin, Leningrad, and Moscow (where he paid his respects to Lenin and Stalin at the mausoleum they shared). He advocated an ambitious plan to redistribute land in the Congo, and his broadcasts on Leopoldville radio seemed to mimic the Communists' anti-imperial rhetoric. It was Gizenga who had publicly dressed down Hammarskjöld during the secretary-general's recent visit to the Congo, an incident that Bunche might have been thinking of when he told his wife that compared with Lumumba, Gizenga was "just as bad, only more stupid." Yet even Gizenga was more open to the West than some of his polemics might have suggested: at the height of the mutiny, he had asked Timberlake for U.S. troops and even expressed impatience when Washington did not respond immediately.

More moderate members of the government wished Lumumba and others would stop with the UN bashing but found themselves increasingly sidelined. At one point, Lumumba contemplated firing Thomas Kanza, the UN representative, who had long harbored doubts about Lumumba's leadership. As Kanza saw it, the prime minister was besieged by loose-lipped hangers-on who made it "the easiest thing in the world for anyone with connections in high places to get information about Lumumba's plans and intentions."

Relations between Lumumba and his erstwhile friend and ally Mobutu, still serving as the army's chief of staff, remained equally chilly. Within the prime minister's inner circle, complaints about Mobutu were piling up, most of which centered on the impression that he was not a team player. Although this flaw irritated Lumumba, he knew that Mobutu had something he did not: the respect of the ANC, the national army. Mobutu was now living in an officer's house in Camp Leopold. Since having helped quell the mutiny, he was spending much of his time thwarting the UN's halfhearted campaign to disarm the army. "Hold on to your arms," he would tell Congolese troops as he traveled from garrison to garrison. "Whatever you do, don't hand them over." When UN officers seized a stock of weapons from one garrison, Mobutu burst into the UN mission's headquarters at the Royal to demand they be returned; the UN relented. The army, fractured and disobedient though it was, was the key to exerting control in the Congo, and Mobutu's lobbying was winning him the loyalty of its ranks. As far as Lumumba was concerned, Mobutu was untouchable.

Still, Mobutu and the army were just one concern among many. Lumumba saw saboteurs everywhere. He alleged the existence of a sophisticated Belgian spy network operating to undermine him. "Belgium and the Belgians are acting like submarines now," he told reporters. "Since they can no longer operate on the surface, they are operating below it."

Lumumba's allegations struck many as overwrought, but behind the scenes Belgium was working assiduously to undermine him. As early as July 13, two weeks after Congolese independence, the Belgian cabinet had considered toppling Lumumba and installing a more pliant government. But envoys dispatched to Leopoldville to investigate this possibility concluded that Lumumba was too powerful to be removed in a coup d'état. A more plausible strategy was to replicate the Katanga model and promote secessionist movements in other provinces. "Any rallying of other Congolese provinces to Katanga is to be encouraged," Pierre Wigny, the Belgian foreign minister, instructed Harold d'Aspremont Lynden, one of Belgium's diplomats in Katanga. D'Aspremont quietly got to work rallying Tshombe and other provincial leaders behind a federal system for the Congo, which he viewed as the surest way to erode the central government's power.

In addition to undercutting Lumumba's hold on the provinces, the Belgian government secretly financed anti-Lumumba groups in the capital. In early August, it was approached by a network of Congolese labor and student leaders in Leopoldville whose stated goal was to turn Congolese public opinion against Lumumba, with a view to the "overthrow and liquidation" of his government. Eyskens personally authorized Belgian funding for the group.

Around the same time, even more aggressive plans were making the rounds in Brussels. As laid out in a memo titled "Operation L. Suggestions," one Belgian intelligence officer worked to obtain blueprints of the prime minister's residence and recommended mining Lumumba's political opponents and European advisers for intelligence. He also suggested exploiting a known weakness of Lumumba's. "The taste of the person concerned for women is well known," he wrote. A honey trap might lead the man to let his guard down and "abandon his usual personal security measures." Then the author got more specific about what to do with the access gained:

> It is likely that Mr. L. manages to maintain his lifestyle, his energy, and his dynamism only with the help of drugs, either traditional or pharmaceutical. In either case, he must have suppliers or "medical advisers"—at any rate, people who have great influence over the person concerned. Perhaps a substitution of drugs could be considered.

Although Lumumba could not have known the extent of the Belgian subterfuge, he smelled a plot. "As you can see, Belgium is destroying us, Belgium is sabotaging us, Belgium is stealing our money," he told reporters. "But we will get help elsewhere."

Hiding any lingering disappointment with his visit to the United States, he assured his audience that American assistance would be forthcoming. The United States, after all, had been born in "the very same sort of fight for freedom that we have been waging, today and yesterday, against the imperialists."

Chapter 25

Changing the Scenery

B ACK IN LEOPOLDVILLE from Washington, Larry Devlin was relieved to find that his small station had been reinforced with another CIA officer—his new deputy and temporary roommate. He was less relieved to see the direction the Congolese government was heading. On August 11, he cabled his concern to CIA headquarters: "The embassy and station believe that Lumumba is moving left and Commie influence is increasing. Unless he is stopped in the near future, we believe he will become a strongman, eliminating moderate opposition and establishing a regime under the influence of, if not fully controlled by, the Commies."

Ambassador Timberlake's judgment was even harsher. Although he acknowledged his political acumen, he considered Lumumba "unscrupulous and untrustworthy" and believed he was "moving steadily toward a very strong dictatorship." He also saw Lumumba as an unreformed product of the jungle and freely joked that he was a cannibal. "Have you heard the one about Lumumba at lunch on a PanAm clipper?" he asked in a letter to an old State Department friend. "After looking long and hard at the menu, he cast it aside and asked the stewardess for the passenger list."

It was a perspective shared by the editorial writers at the conservative *National Review*, who deemed Lumumba "a cheap embezzler, a schizoid agitator (half witch-doctor, half Marxist), an opportunist ready to sell out to the highest bidder, ex-officio Big Chief Number One of a gang of jungle primitives strutting about in the masks of

Cabinet Ministers." Among American conservatives, at least, there was now a consensus about Lumumba.

All this led Washington, much like Brussels, to consider anew whether to replace Lumumba with someone more suited to U.S. interests, just as it had during his rise in the lead-up to independence. "We wondered whether there was any way of changing the scenery in the Congo," Undersecretary of State Douglas Dillon said. As before, identifying a credible replacement proved tricky. But the State Department pledged to continue the search, calling it "a program of reinsurance against Lumumba."

The subject came up at an interagency conference Dillon attended at the Pentagon. Someone raised the prospect of assassinating Lumumba, but a CIA representative shut down the discussion, perhaps because the group was too large for such a sensitive topic, or perhaps because the idea was deemed impractical. Nonetheless, a new idea had been floated, a moral boundary probed.

In the meantime, the CIA station in Leopoldville thought up a subtler way of changing the scenery. Its plan began with Joseph Kasavubu. On the morning of August 8, Paul Springer, the former station chief, met with Kasavubu to take leave after three years in the Congo. It was a routine formality, but Springer, acting in concert with Timberlake and likely Devlin, delivered a special message, in an unofficial capacity to preserve plausible deniability: Lumumba was to blame for the dismal state of the country, and Kasavubu had the legal authority to orchestrate his removal. Under the Congo's provisional constitution, Springer explained, the president had the power to call a special session of parliament, which could then hold a vote of no confidence and bring down the government. The initiative could also come from parliament itself, which could censure a minister, a move that would in turn give Kasavubu the right to demand a new government. Either way, assuming that enough members of parliament were on board, Lumumba would be out.

Kasavubu perked up. To Springer's surprise, he appeared unaware of his constitutional powers. Springer recommended he look into the matter with his legal advisers. It was not clear, however, whether the president had fully gotten the message: Kasavubu quickly moved on to other topics, including his ambition to visit the United States, and the meeting ended with Kasavubu's plans unclear.

What was clear, however, was that the tide was turning against Lumumba. Rumors of an impending coup d'état (allegedly set to take place between August 15 and 20) persisted, as did talk of a supposed plot to assassinate him. But like Springer, Devlin urged his contacts to stick to the parliamentary scheme. Devlin would help them, of course. He proposed to headquarters that he inject CIA cash into local political groups that opposed Lumumba, just as the Belgians were doing, and that he help organize the vote of no confidence in the Senate. Since these efforts might come to naught, however, Devlin wanted to hedge by recruiting members of Lumumba's government as CIA assets. "Although we believe it would be better to oust him, we do not want to become tied irrevocably to the opposition if it is not able to achieve its goals," he wrote on August 11.

The response from headquarters was ambivalent. Bronson Tweedy, Devlin's superior in Washington, thought Lumumba's removal "might breed more problems than it would solve." In this, he echoed the State Department, which recommended a "more or less neutral" approach toward Lumumba. Devlin could support anti-Communist politicians, but he was to downplay American opposition to Lumumba. "I realize the above is not a clear-cut reply," Tweedy concluded his cable, "but HQ...believes the above still leaves you considerable operational latitude."

The cables were obsolete nearly the minute they were sent. Around the same time, further up the hierarchy of the U.S. government, as Devlin and Tweedy would soon learn, the White House authorized a secret CIA program to "replace the Lumumba Government by constitutional means." It might not have seemed so at that point, but the decision was a watershed moment for the agency. For the very first time, its pursuits in the Congo would go beyond intelligence collection to include covert action—activities designed to transform Congolese politics, but in a way that hid the American hand.

It was a summer of beginnings not just at the CIA. In 1960, Americans were tentatively leaving behind the prudish propriety of the 1950s and loosening up ever so slightly for the new decade. The Food and Drug Administration approved the first contraceptive pill. Sam Cooke's "Wonderful World," Roy Orbison's "Only the Lonely," and Chubby Checker's "The Twist" topped the charts. In Greensboro, North Carolina, after months of sit-in protests against segregation, the Woolworth's lunch counter served its first meal to a Black patron.

Americans were also choosing who would lead them through this new era. John F. Kennedy and Richard Nixon presented voters with a stark choice. The Massachusetts senator was youthful and charming; the outgoing vice president was neither, despite being just four years older. Kennedy's campaign pamphlets promised "a new leader for the 60's," while Nixon's highlighted his experience under Eisenhower.

As it happened, both candidates had been styling themselves as Africa experts of sorts. Kennedy argued that the United States, wary of angering its allies in Europe, was too neutral and tentative in its attitude toward the decolonizing world. He had developed this view early, during a 1951 tour of Indochina, and in 1957 he stuck his neck out, condemning the Eisenhower administration for siding with France in the colonial war in Algeria. His endorsement of Algerian independence earned him the ire of not just the Eisenhower administration, which suggested he focus on Communist imperialism in Eastern Europe, and the French, which accused him of encouraging violence, but also fellow Democrats. The former secretary of state Dean Acheson said Kennedy's intervention had accomplished nothing but "harm in our foreign relations."

Yet Kennedy's position forever endeared him to African leaders. When visiting Washington, D.C., many made a point of meeting the Massachusetts senator who had taken an early stance against colonialism. In 1958, Kennedy met with Thomas Kanza, then at Harvard for a summer program for international students organized by Professor Henry Kissinger. (Eleanor Roosevelt introduced them, telling Kanza, "Here is the future president of the United States of America.") The next year, Kennedy headed the newly established Africa subcommittee of the Senate Foreign Relations Committee. Over the course of 1959 and 1960, Kennedy delivered thirteen speeches about Africa, needling the Eisenhower administration on its slow-footed approach to the continent: "The word is out—and spreading like wildfire in nearly one thousand languages and dialects—that it is no longer necessary to remain forever poor or forever in bondage."

Nixon, for his part, had gone on a three-week, eight-nation vice presidential tour of Africa in 1957. In Accra, he represented the United States at Ghana's independence celebrations and quizzed Nkrumah on what the new country's nonaligned foreign policy would mean in practice. Nixon returned alarmed about the declining European influence in Africa and recommended that Eisenhower lavish newly independent African states with aid. He did not reach this conclusion out of respect for Africans, toward whom he was racist in private, once saying that they had an "animal-like charm." Rather, he viewed Africa as an emerging battleground between "the forces of freedom and international communism." The goal was to put as many African states as possible into the Western column. Kennedy criticized Nixon's Cold War conception of Africa, arguing that its people were "more interested in development than they are in doctrine."

Kennedy's support for Algerian independence had helped him win the favor of Michigan's staunchly progressive governor, G. Mennen Williams, and thus most of Michigan's fifty-one votes at the Democratic National Convention. But after clinching the nomination in July, Kennedy was in trouble. An August poll put him six percentage points behind Nixon. White southern Democrats were learning from their Baptist preachers that a Catholic president would answer to Rome. Meanwhile, Kennedy's centrist voting record, including on civil rights, turned off Black voters and the Democratic Party's liberal wing. He needed to find an issue on which he, often regarded as a cautious, finger-in-the-wind politician, could inspire those voters but without alienating the Dixiecrats he needed to win southern states.

At some point that summer, an idea arose among his advisers: What if Kennedy made Africa a campaign issue?

Chapter 26

Sound and Fury

A T UN HEADQUARTERS, the summertime crisis in the Congo was sucking up the time and attention of Hammarskjöld and his closest advisers. Most days, the secretary-general gathered with a small group to discuss the cables from Leopoldville and coordinate decisions over lunch. Eventually known as "the Congo Club," it featured a rotating cast of staffers. After going their separate ways for the afternoon, the group's members would reconvene. Dinner would be served—the main courses often prepared by Hammarskjöld's Swedish cook—along with soda, beer, and cigars. One participant set the scene:

> Late every evening, when the debating halls were silent and the last of the delegates had folded his papers and departed, after the lights had gone out in the vast glass edifice, Hammarskjöld's suite would come to renewed life. Battered after an exhausting day's work, tired but unruffled, the faithful would reassemble, this time around a conference table. There would again be a review of the day's trials and activities, more telegrams would have come in from the Congo posing new and yet more unexpected problems. Decisions would be taken and replies drafted, some dictated by Hammarskjöld himself, others by his colleagues, and all would once again be discussed and sometimes revised before dispatch. By eight or nine o'clock in the evening, those with families would excuse themselves, but others would remain with the chief to share with him a well-earned dinner.

On occasions of special crisis, the full team would remain and continue its discussions till well after midnight.

Backstopped from New York, the UN operation in the Congo trudged onward. On the civilian side, its technicians now constituted a sort of parallel administration, a "shadow government" that did the actual work of running the country while Congolese politicians remained nominally in charge of their ministries. (A Ghanaian expert sent to help Africanize the administration was disheartened to find the Congolese uninterested in the work of running a country: "The so-called ministers spent most of their time in bars.") On the military side, there were now nearly twelve thousand UN troops in the Congo. The speed with which Hammarskjöld had stood up such a large and complicated mission was both impressive and expensive. The UN operation was on track to hit a yearly cost of $150 million—more than double the UN's entire annual budget. To finance the mission, Hammarskjöld raided the UN's emergency fund and went country to country, hat in hand, asking for voluntary contributions. The United States chipped in $30 million.

Joining the initial cohort of mostly African soldiers in the Congo were reinforcements from across the continent and beyond: Sudan, the United Arab Republic (a new union between Egypt and Syria), India, Pakistan, Indonesia, Malaya, Italy, Norway, Denmark, Yugoslavia—all in all, twenty-seven nations were now taking part in some way in the UN operation. To forge a coherent force from so many disparate parts was not easy. Mechanics eventually had to service forty types of vehicles, and armorers had to manage a welter of ammunition of varying calibers.

Divisions of language, culture, and race added further complications. Salaries varied widely. Each contingent was paid in its own currency by its own government, plus a bonus of eighty-six cents per day, courtesy of the UN—an arrangement that allowed a soldier from northern Europe to earn more than ten times his Third World counterpart. When military commanders in Leopoldville dispatched orders to soldiers in the field, their messages had to be translated into half a dozen languages. The Canadians insisted on living and eating separately from African soldiers. Muslim troops refused to eat Israeli jam and demanded halal meat.

Insulating this multihued coalition from Cold War politics also proved a near-impossible task. In his capacity as the UN mission's top official, Bunche in no way took orders from the U.S. government—he disagreed strongly with Timberlake about the wisdom of disarming Congolese troops, for instance—but he did coordinate with the Americans to a degree that belied the notion of the UN as a neutral force. He was regularly fed top-secret memos by U.S. officials and shared those officials' revulsion toward Communism. His core staff was made up almost entirely of Western nationals, many of them American. To compensate for this asymmetry, Mikhail Potrubach, a Soviet diplomat and an assistant to Hammarskjöld in New York, was flown out to Leopoldville to serve as a Russian fig leaf on Bunche's staff. But Potrubach soon returned to headquarters in shame, having been caught copying Bunche's cables and taking orders from the Soviet embassy.

Communication caused endless headaches as well. Eventually, the staff managed to set up their own links to New York and were no longer relying on the U.S. embassy, but the new channels were hardly dependable. In the best of circumstances, Leopoldville could expect urgent cables to be answered within two or three hours; more often, it could take twice as long. Some messages, sent in encrypted code to prevent interception, would cut off midway and turn into incomprehensible garble. The Canadian-supplied radio transmitters used to convey orders to UN troops spread out across the Congo were designed to bridge distances of 250 miles, but the shortest circuit in the country measured 500 miles, so operators had to set the units to maximum power to extend their range. That caused its own problems: even with three air conditioners running, the temperature of the transmitter room at the Royal building averaged ninety-five degrees Fahrenheit.

Bunche clashed constantly with the military commander of the UN operation, Carl von Horn, a graying Swedish general with most of his career behind him. Von Horn complained that Bunche was preventing him from communicating directly with New York and threatened to resign; Bunche felt he needed to micromanage a subordinate who suffered from a problematic mix of vanity, jumpiness, and lack of combat experience. Hammarskjöld's military adviser came to a dispiriting conclusion: "He was a lost man."

Katanga remained the UN mission's greatest challenge. After Bunche's failed attempt to win UN troops access to the province, it was time to try again. This time, Hammarskjöld was armed with a new UN Security Council mandate that singled out Katanga as a special problem, and he believed that he could finally usher the Belgian troops out of the province. Do that, and he would rob Lumumba of his primary cudgel against the UN and thereby weaken the prime minister's position. Moreover, provided Hammarskjöld assured Katanga that it could retain some degree of autonomy, he might be able to reverse its secession. Thus the two problems that he thought lay at the heart of the Congo crisis—an out-of-control Lumumba and a breakaway Katanga—would be solved in a stroke. Here was an opportunity, he told Secretary of State Christian Herter, to "break the logjam."

Instead of sending another emissary to Katanga, Hammarskjöld would go himself. Ahead of his visit, Tshombe sent him a list of ten conditions for the entry of UN troops—"Moises's ten commandments," the press dubbed them—which the secretary-general dismissed out of hand. Lumumba had his own demand: that some of his people join Hammarskjöld on the trip. But in order to allay Tshombe's fears of a Lumumba takeover of Katanga, Hammarskjöld needed this to be a UN initiative, not a central government one. Feeling that his hands were tied, he made a fateful choice: he would head straight to Katanga, without first meeting with Lumumba in the capital as diplomatic custom prescribed. Bypassing Lumumba would no doubt be perceived as a deliberate snub, but it would prevent the prime minister from hijacking the mission and at the same time send the right signal to Tshombe.

Following Hammarskjöld into Katanga would be two companies of Swedish UN troops, "in uniform but with the understanding that they will be under my exclusive personal authority," as he told Tshombe. This token contingent would replace the Belgian troops guarding the Elisabethville airport, and if Hammarskjöld's negotiations with Tshombe succeeded, more UN troops would follow and eventually replace the Belgian forces across the province. Given Bunche's runway humiliation in Elisabethville a week earlier, however, success was hardly guaranteed. Tshombe had made it clear that the arrival of the Swedish contingent would "not prejudge a definitive deployment" of any other UN troops. "And so," Hammarskjöld wrote to Bunche, "cross fingers."

Hammarskjöld left New York on August 10 with much of world opinion at his back. Editorial pages praised him as a "supranational figure" (the Netherlands), a "world-famed arbitrator" (Italy), and "the bridge between the reality of the world situation and the ideal of world peace" (Japan). "This remarkable man is proving to be one of the great natural resources in the world today, and it is difficult to think of another in the field of world diplomacy who could do the job as well," marveled the *New York Times* columnist James Reston. "He is tireless. He is infinitely patient." Hammarskjöld's deft touch "is one reason why the U.N. is now a refuge for common sense in a satanic world."

On his flight to the Congo, the secretary-general took pen to paper and expounded on the Security Council resolution, which referred vaguely to the UN's noninterference in "any internal conflict." In practice, he explained in a legalistic memo, this would mean that UN troops could in no way be used by the Congo's central government to subdue Katanga. One might think that because the UN was tasked with restoring order to the country, it might also help extend Leopoldville's writ to all the Congo. But that was not to be.

A demanding boss under normal circumstances, Hammarskjöld could become particularly peeved when he thought shoddy process was impeding his work. Upon arriving at the Royal late at night, he grew irritated when staff there had trouble translating his English memo into French. The Snake Pit contained no professional translators, so anyone within earshot who spoke French was encouraged to have a go. The process took hours, and the secretary-general made it clear that he would be leaving for a historic mission exhausted thanks to their incompetence.

In the morning, Hammarskjöld left for Elisabethville tired but in somewhat better spirits. Staying behind in Leopoldville, Ralph Bunche, also running on no sleep, had the thankless task of delivering a signed copy of Hammarskjöld's memo to Lumumba.

Lumumba's reaction, Bunche recorded, "verged on rage." The

notion that UN troops could not use force to help him bring Katanga back under control was incorrect, the prime minister insisted after skimming the text. Out of his mouth flew a series of contradictory threats and demands. He might get Ghana and Guinea to pull their troops from the UN operation and invade Katanga on their own. He might even kick out the UN altogether. No, he added, Congolese troops should be placed under UN command, and a UN plane should be provided to fly his ministers to Katanga at once. As always, telephones were ringing incessantly in the background, and Lumumba occasionally interrupted his outburst to answer, not always picking up the right receiver. At another point, he mellowed, declaring himself a "man of peace" and offering friendly reassurances. Bunche had come to expect such volatility. "We'd have a real chance to work some miracles in this country were it not for that schizophrenic," he had written days earlier.

What vexed Lumumba most was that Hammarskjöld had transited through Leopoldville without making contact with him. He sensed that Hammarskjöld was according more respect to Tshombe, the rogue leader of a secessionist province, than to him, the country's democratically elected leader. He was right.

As Bunche dealt with Lumumba, Hammarskjöld made his way to Elisabethville. Trailing his white UN plane were four more, which carried the two hundred Swedish troops he was personally escorting into Katanga. As his plane descended to two thousand feet, Hammarskjöld peered through a porthole at the runway below. There, in an apparent repeat of the incident a week earlier, a blockade seemed to be forming. A fire engine, a steam shovel, and five trucks lined the runway, ready to close in. They were joined by two hundred troops from Katanga's new army—matching the Swedish contingent, man for man.

Outside the terminal, Moise Tshombe fidgeted with a tourist pamphlet titled "Elisabethville Welcomes You," evidently unsure whether such hospitality should extend to Hammarskjöld and the soldiers with him. For nearly half an hour, the planes circled the airport as their crews negotiated with Tshombe via the control tower.

"It seemed entirely possible," one of Hammarskjöld's aides thought, "that he might be descending into a violent and potentially fatal situation."

After some hesitation, Tshombe allowed all five planes to land. Soon he was energetically shaking Hammarskjöld's hand, flashing his jack-o'-lantern smile as if nothing were amiss. So began a reception that another UN aide considered "an act out of a comic opera." To jeers from a crowd of mostly Belgian onlookers chanting anti-UN slogans, Tshombe steered Hammarskjöld past a Katangan honor guard—Black soldiers and white officers, as if Belgian rule had never ended—and stationed him directly in front of the province's new flag. A scrappy military band played "La Katangaise," its equally newfangled, and decidedly martial, anthem:

Children of Katanga,
Defend it to the death
Make it proud and make it strong
With your arms and your blood
With your teeth.

Standing stiff in his double-breasted suit, Hammarskjöld stared blankly at the flag. But he paused and bowed forward just enough for some to feel they had witnessed an endorsement. ("There it is," a woman was heard saying, "he's recognized the independence of Katanga.") So he could only have been pleased when the first of the remaining planes landed. Its Swedish passengers marched down the tarmac, blond hair flowing out from blue helmets.

In negotiations held behind the iron gates and wide lawns of the governor's residence in Elisabethville, Hammarskjöld conceded much and extracted little. The secretary-general reiterated his position that the UN could not and would not assist Lumumba in taking Katanga back by force. And even though Hammarskjöld had officially rejected Tshombe's "ten commandments" ahead of his trip, he wound up implicitly agreeing to eight of them. Among other assurances, this meant that any UN forces landing in Katanga would exclude troops from Ghana or Guinea, countries Tshombe considered hopelessly biased in favor of Lumumba.

Appeasement seemed to bear fruit. By the next day, Tshombe had agreed on a plan for the withdrawal of Belgian troops from the province. The Belgian government was on board, too, and was now pushing him to accept UN troops in return for a guarantee that the UN wouldn't interfere in his power struggle with Lumumba. At a somber ceremony that afternoon, General Roger Gheysen, the commander of Belgian troops in the Congo, formally bade farewell to his country's military presence in Katanga and thus the entire former colony. As the Belgians in the crowd wept, the general pumped Tshombe's hand for an awkwardly long time—as if by delaying the release, Belgium could hold on to its last shred of authority in the Congo. Then he let go. Soon, four thousand UN troops streamed into Katanga by road and rail from across the Congo. Irishmen came from Kivu province, Malians and more Swedes from Leopoldville, Moroccans from the lower Congo, and Ethiopians from Orientale province. By August 13, a month to the day after the UN had authorized its mission in the Congo, UN troops were at last standing guard on Katangan soil.

Triumph for Hammarskjöld though this was, it was hardly a concession on Tshombe's part. The departing Belgian troops had been crucial weeks earlier, when the Congolese army was in revolt, but since then, the Belgians had mostly been staying in their barracks. Tshombe had purged the Congolese army in the province of its disloyal elements, retained two hundred Belgian officers, and rebuilt the force as the Katangese Gendarmerie. In fact, without the visible presence of a foreign military propping him up, he looked more powerful and independent than ever.

Hammarskjöld had no illusions about Tshombe, but he ultimately privileged the breakaway leader's concerns over those of the central government. The Belgian diplomatic representatives in Katanga, Harold d'Aspremont Lynden and Robert Rothschild, privately bragged that the secretary-general was "preserving the de facto territorial integrity of Katanga," which would henceforth be "protected by UN troops." Hammarskjöld had also dealt Tshombe a propaganda victory. "The president of the Republic of Katanga no longer looks like the head of a rebellious puppet state in the pay of the Belgians," a journalist opined, "but like a genuine, powerful African leader who is fiercely opposed to the destructive fury of the Communist Lumumba."

Lumumba, predictably, was livid. Bunche warned Hammarskjöld,

"He is recklessly attacking us now, with deliberate concentration on you." The prime minister remained furious at Hammarskjöld for not having met with him, and he objected to the use of white UN troops in Katanga, who he alleged were nothing but "Belgians in disguise." He seemed to be speaking both figuratively and literally, claiming not only that European troops would be inherently unsympathetic to the Congolese cause but also that Belgian troops had been spotted wearing UN uniforms. An aide captured his thinking: "How can you imagine that, just like that, a helmet painted blue is enough to eliminate the complexes of conservative officers from Sweden, Canada, or Great Britain?... How can you assume that a blue armband inoculates someone against racism and paternalism?"

In Hammarskjöld's mind, however, the trip was a "breakthrough." With the Belgians on their way out and the UN on its way in, he hoped that Katangan secession had been downgraded from a near fait accompli to a political clash between the prime minister and a provincial leader.

Next on Hammarskjöld's agenda was Leopoldville, where he would have to deal with the backlash to his concessions to Tshombe, as well as the shambolic state of the central government overall. "Returned from Elisabethville and Kamina to meet Leo situation in all its mad splendor," he wrote to UN headquarters. *Macbeth* came to mind. "The sound and fury in Leopoldville rhymes with the Shakespeare quotation I have in mind, as it truly is a story told by an idiot." Lumumba's fulminations signified nothing, and one way or another his opponents would deal with him. "Idiots break like the famous Shakespearean prototype if reason is consistently maintained." Still, Hammarskjöld held out hope that he might manage to talk some sense into Lumumba, so he invited him for a drink at the Royal on August 15. "We shall see what some good Scotch achieves with a proper background in hard realities."

Though still smarting from Hammarskjöld's earlier snub, Lumumba accepted the invitation. (He would have preferred to be across the river in Brazzaville, where the other Congo was celebrating its independence that day, but the new country's conservative president, Fulbert Youlou, had pointedly disinvited him.) A second meeting between Hammarskjöld and Lumumba offered the chance of a fresh start. But a few hours before the planned cocktail, Lumumba informed an aide that the rendezvous was off. Instead, the prime minister was gathering with other advisers to draft a note to Hammarskjöld. A messenger rushed the letter out of the prime minister's residence, down Boulevard Albert, and to the Royal.

Whatever hope Hammarskjöld might have had of reaching an accommodation with Lumumba was dashed as he leafed through the four-page letter. It was a personal broadside against him. By bypassing Leopoldville on the way to Katanga, Lumumba wrote, "you are acting as though my Government...did not exist." In sending Swedes and Irishmen to Elisabethville, "you have acted in connivance with the rebel Government of Katanga and at the instigation of the Belgian government." The letter ended with a list of demands for the UN: donate aircraft to his government, turn over the airports to Congolese soldiers, seize all weapons from the Katangan forces, and withdraw all white UN troops from Katanga. The UN force, in this view, would be little more than a division of the Congolese army.

Lumumba's letter also advanced a sophisticated legal critique of Hammarskjöld's interpretation of the most recent Security Council resolution, which he considered "unilateral and erroneous." Hammarskjöld fired back a terse reply: "There is no reason for me to enter into a discussion here either about those unfounded and unjustified allegations or about the interpretation of the Security Council's resolutions."

Another letter zipped across town. Lumumba now asked Hammarskjöld to tell him "in clear terms" whether he was rejecting his demands. Most observers assumed a ghostwriter. "For an ex–post office clerk with a limited education," remarked Time, "Lumumba was sending off some fairly polished and legalistic notes." Some thought they were written by Serge Michel, the new press attaché, or one of Lumumba's other advisers, such as Andrée Blouin or Jozef Grootaert. Another theory had it that Andrei Fomin, the Soviet chargé d'affaires in Leopoldville, was drafting the notes. "Western sources said Mr. Lumumba's acid letters to Mr. Hammarskjöld demonstrated the Soviet technique of interpreting the ambiguous, and frequently self-contradictory language of United Nations resolutions to fit the Soviet Union's position," The New York Times reported.

Lumumba signed his second missive "in expectation of an immediate reply," and he promptly got one: "I have nothing to add to my reply to your first communication." Hammarskjöld told Lumumba that he would be returning to New York at once to convene the Security Council, whose members he would furnish with copies of the exchange.

The epistolary duel was becoming absurd. "I have just this moment received your letter of today's date in reply to the one I sent you an hour ago," began Lumumba's rejoinder. He once again imputed a sinister cause to the arrival of Swedish troops in Katanga, alluding to the fact that King Baudouin's mother, Astrid, had been a Swedish princess. (Hammarskjöld considered this particular allegation an "illustration of political life in a world of stupidity abused by evil.") Hammarskjöld, Lumumba went on, had caved to Tshombe and, by extension, to the Belgians behind him.

"In view of all the foregoing," he continued, "the Government and people of the Congo have lost their confidence in the Secretary-General of the United Nations." But he had one last request: Might Hammarskjöld delay his departure by twenty-four hours so that the Congolese delegation could travel to New York for the Security Council meeting?

That letter went unanswered. For the world's most celebrated diplomat, Hammarskjöld evinced little desire in his correspondence to engage in a real back-and-forth with Lumumba. The letters, an aide admitted, "brought out the cold, unbending side of Hammarskjöld's nature." Alex Quaison-Sackey, Ghana's UN ambassador, thought they also revealed Hammarskjöld's prejudice, proving that he "failed to comprehend how an African could possibly aspire to cross swords with him."

It was now evening. Strictly speaking, the invitation for a drink still stood, so Hammarskjöld waited for Lumumba at the Royal until 10:00 p.m. It was the last chance for the two men to mend relations—to come to a modus vivendi, if not a true understanding, over a scotch or perhaps a local Polar beer. But the prime minister never showed.

Resigned, Hammarskjöld headed to the airport. On "that famous Monday," as his staff called August 15, his opinion of Lumumba reached a nadir. Hammarskjöld's judgments of people, an aide admitted, "could be harsh and irrevocable, often being based on a single mistake or misunderstanding." So they were in this case. Hammarsk-jöld thought the Congolese leader was being used by leftist Africans and the Soviet Union. "In this game," he wrote, "I hold Lumumba to be an ignorant pawn." Compared with Lumumba, the Middle Eastern fanatics he had dealt with in the Suez and Lebanon crises now seemed to him like gentlemen. Speaking to U.S. diplomats, he said that the prime minister's fiery letters challenging the UN showed how "stupid" he was. Even the Soviets could see that: "Moscow realizes that it cannot build on anyone as erratic and inept as Lumumba." The UN mission couldn't continue with Lumumba in power. "One or the other would have to go."

Chapter 27

Desperate Measures

H<small>E HAD BEEN</small> thinking about it for weeks. He had threatened it in his ultimatum to the UN. He had perhaps discussed it in hushed tones in the Château Laurier in Ottawa and in the private office of an African ambassador in New York. It was a scheme born of desperation, rather than confidence, the last resort for a man nearing defeat, the only way he could take back Katanga and thus restore the country he was meant to rule. Lumumba was ready to make a choice that would alter the history of the Congo and of Africa: to formally request military aid from the Soviet Union.

The Americans had declined to send him direct assistance. The UN was refusing to help him in Katanga and was even putting its thumb on the scale in favor of Tshombe. Help from the Soviet Union seemed like the only way to retake the breakaway province.

So far, however, Moscow had extended only token support. Soviet leaders had denounced Western imperialism at the UN, in the pages of *Pravda,* and in their communications with the Congolese, each statement long on Western castigation but short on concrete promises. What tangible help the Soviets did provide—food aid, twenty doctors, planes for the airlift, among other things—was being channeled through the UN mission rather than directly to the government. Yet Moscow had hinted that it might be willing to do more. On August 1, the Kremlin released a statement warning that if the "aggression against the Congo" continued, it would "take resolute measures to rebuff the aggressors." Four days later, the Soviet premier, Nikita Khrushchev, sent Lumumba a letter promising his "friendly and unselfish aid" and assuring him that the Soviet Union would not stand by if the Congo remained under imperialist attack. In the meantime, he gifted Lumumba a twin-engine plane for his personal use.

Lumumba saw an opening. If the Soviets made good on their offer, he might obtain enough trucks and planes to transport his troops to South Kasai and Katanga and bring those breakaway provinces back into the fold. On August 15, he sent Khrushchev a wish list:

> The Government of the Republic of the Congo would be very grateful if you would indicate the immediate assistance that your government could provide *directly* in the following areas:
> 1. Troop transport planes, plus crew.
> 2. Troop transport trucks.
> 3. Various high-quality armaments.
> 4. State-of-the-art military communications equipment.
> 5. Food rations for troops in the field.

Until now, the Soviets had avoided committing significant resources to the Congo. It was a heavily Catholic country with no Communist party, and five thousand miles away to boot. It was not evident, a Canadian diplomat conceded, that "many Congolese have the foggiest idea what communism is." Even the Kremlin thought it more natural for the Congo to side with the United States. When Khrushchev learned that the U.S. government had brushed off Lumumba's request for aid, he was mystified. "Why? Explain to me why," Khrushchev said at a meeting, banging his fist on the table in disbelief. "Really, are the Americans that stupid?"

Lumumba himself saw the Soviets as his third choice, behind both the United States and the UN. "I approached the U.S. State Department to see if they had even just one plane that we could buy, and I made sure to pledge that this plane would be used for the movement of members of the government and troops across the country," he said. "We were told that such aid could not be given to us directly, only through the United Nations." Bunche, Lumumba reported, had said the same thing: "As ever, not a single plane was available to us."

So lukewarm were the Soviets that for the first several weeks after independence they didn't even have an embassy in Leopoldville. Their delegation there had been locked in an endless back-and-forth with Moscow, which had insisted that it would be more fiscally prudent to buy, rather than rent, space for an embassy; only after Ambassador Mikhail Yakovlev sent a fiery cable directly to Khrushchev was he permitted to lease a two-story villa in downtown Leopoldville.

The Soviets also felt downright outmatched. Alexander Shelepin, the head of the KGB, warned that the Congo was crawling with Western advisers and that the United States was winning the battle for hearts and minds there. Soviet attempts at influence, by contrast, were ham-fisted. When the merchant ship *Leninogorsk* called at Matadi, the nine thousand tons of wheat it carried were never unloaded; the Congo had no mills to grind it into flour. The ship also brought bananas—one of the Congo's main exports.

Despite the threats, however vague, to take action in the Congo, actual military options were limited. The Soviet Union had no foreign military bases outside Eastern Europe. Its naval forces rarely strayed beyond neighboring waters, and any attempt to send forces into the Congo by sea would be easily thwarted by the superior U.S. Navy, whose USS *Wasp*—one of twenty-seven aircraft carriers under U.S. command, compared with zero on the Soviet side—remained stationed in the Atlantic near the mouth of the Congo River. The Soviet Union's meager air force was in no position to fly troops in either, as its largely symbolic part in the UN airlift had made clear: the country had provided five transport planes, compared with the United States' eighty.

In warning that he might intervene, Khrushchev was bluffing. This approach had worked during the 1956 Suez Crisis, when he had complained loudly enough about the French-British invasion of Egypt that the Eisenhower administration pressured its allies to withdraw. The hope was that this time, too, the mere threat of Soviet intervention would persuade the United States and its European ally to cease their neocolonial meddling. But by asking for military aid—a request reiterated at a meeting with Ambassador Yakovlev—Lumumba had unwittingly called Khrushchev's bluff.

—

As he waited for a response from the Kremlin, Lumumba tried to tighten his control of Leopoldville. On August 16, a week after imposing a state of emergency, he went a step further and declared martial law for a period of six months. "We have decided to take immediate steps to get rid of the trouble-makers once and for all," he told the press.

That same day, Congolese security forces, ostensibly looking for undercover Belgian soldiers, stormed hotels and harassed anyone with a UN armband. At the Royal, Congolese soldiers arrested a dozen UN staff for the crime of lacking official passes, mocking them as they ushered them into a paddy wagon. Other targets managed to improvise their way out of trouble. A journalist stopped by soldiers at a restaurant folded his menu into the size of an identity card and presented it to his illiterate interrogators, pointing to his name: *Escargots de Bourgogne.*

Bunche was disgusted with the harassment, which he suspected had taken place by order of Lumumba. Yet he and the rest of the UN staff were not letting the pressure get to them. "The spirit and morale of the staff are high," he told Hammarskjöld. "If the idea behind the morning of the 16th molestations was to intimidate us, it was a dismal failure. But our respect for our 'hosts' is at an all-time low."

It could go lower. Late the next evening, Bunche sent two UN messengers to Lumumba's house to deliver a letter. The soldiers on guard inspected the pair of UN staffers' pink passes and, unimpressed, declared the duo spies. The men were dragged into a shed where, for half an hour, they were forced to hold their hands above their heads while six soldiers relieved them of their revolvers and their wallets. When the messengers appealed to the guards' commander, he drunkenly threatened to shoot them. Only upon the arrival of a top-ranking UN military official were the men freed. The letter, in which Bunche denied the prime minister's request for the use of UN planes, was not delivered.

Clare Timberlake also ran into trouble with Lumumba's guards. On August 18, the U.S. ambassador had an appointment to see the prime minister to complain about another incident in which Congolese troops had harassed and briefly detained six American airmen. Evidently unaware of the appointment, Lumumba's guards escorted Timberlake across the street from the prime minister's house and left him waiting on a curb. He returned in a huff to the U.S. embassy, where he had two calls from an apologetic aide inviting him back. When the meeting finally took place, Lumumba bent over backward to declare his admiration for the United States. He told Timberlake that it was obvious he was not a Communist, since he had first asked an American—Edgar Detwiler—to exploit the Congo's riches. The United States, he said, would have the honor of receiving the first Congolese ambassador to any country. In a short radio broadcast later that day, Lumumba once again praised the friendship of the American people. "We know that the U.S. understands us," he said.

Even as this charm offensive was under way, however, UN troops once again came under sudden attack. At Ndjili airport, fourteen Canadian signalmen bound for the interior of the Congo were ready-ing for takeoff when a band of Congolese soldiers rushed the plane, raised their guns, and ordered everyone off. The Canadians were forced to lie down on the tarmac, arms splayed, as their blue berets were plucked off their heads. One Canadian was kicked repeatedly in the cheeks. Another was knocked unconscious by a rifle butt. The problem, it turned out, was that several of the Canadians wore para-trooper badges—wings, a maple leaf, and a parachute—and were therefore mistaken for Belgians. The incident underscored not only the problem of Congolese hostility toward the UN but also the uncer-tain allegiance of the African soldiers serving in the UN force. Gha-naian troops had stood idly by as the Canadians were manhandled, intervening belatedly and only at the urging of their British officers.

Following events closely from Accra, the Ghanaian president, Kwame Nkrumah, worried about his protégé. Writing to "Dear Patrice," he recommended that Lumumba "keep the Force Publique under restraint." Ominously, he added, "If the present activities of your army are not checked, this very army will eventually turn on you."

For Hammarskjöld, the situation in the Congo was becoming untenable. If the attacks against UN personnel didn't stop, he wrote in a formal letter of protest to the Congolese government, "further activities may be rendered impossible." Privately, he confessed that he was considering withdrawing the entire force. The UN would have to admit defeat in the Congo. The organization's first experi-ment in nation building would end in failure.

—

For Larry Devlin, on the other hand, the growing tensions came as a gift. A week earlier, the station chief had pleaded for permission from CIA headquarters to help oust the prime minister but received only a lukewarm response. Lumumba's sharp break with the UN changed things. The prospect that the Soviet Union would take over as the most influential outside power in the Congo now seemed more real than ever.

On August 18, before most of Washington had woken up, Devlin dashed off another urgent cable to headquarters: "The embassy and station believe the Congo is experiencing a classic Communist effort to take over the government." The Soviets, the Czechs, the Ghanaians, the Guineans, and the Belgian Communist Party—all were tugging Lumumba in that direction, he said. "Whether or not Lumumba is actually Commie or just playing the Commie game to assist his solidifying of power, anti-West forces are rapidly increasing their power in the Congo, and there may be little time left in which to take action to avoid another Cuba or Guinea." Devlin went on to explain that the prime minister's opponents were moving forward with a plan to overthrow him. He recommended that the United States give them money and advice to ensure its success.

By the summer of 1960, President Eisenhower was sixty-nine years old, nearing the end of his second term, and running out of steam. He had survived Cold War crises in Cuba, Korea, Hungary, and the Suez, not to mention a heart attack, a stroke, and intestinal surgery. After the shootdown of a U-2 spy plane over Russia in May scotched an East-West peace summit in Paris, the president largely lost interest in the duties of his job and played golf almost daily. "I wish someone would take me out and shoot me in the head so I wouldn't have to go through this stuff," he huffed one day in July, after a National Security Council meeting brought him bad news from Cuba and the Congo.

Eisenhower was cranky to begin with. Dubbed "the terrible-tempered Mr. Bang" by the press, he once launched a golf club at his doctor so forcefully it nearly broke the man's leg. But the disorder in the Congo made him even more crotchety than usual. In Eisenhower's view, the "winds of change" in Africa were turning into a "destructive hurricane." His impression of the Year of Africa was not favorable: "The determination of the peoples for self-rule, their own flag, and their own vote in the United Nations resembled a torrent overrunning everything in its path."

This distinct lack of enthusiasm for the African nationalist cause was hardly surprising. Given his time leading the invasions of France and Germany in World War II and his service as NATO's top commander afterward, it was only natural that Eisenhower looked at a postcolonial crisis through a European lens. And just as he dragged his feet on civil rights domestically, he thought the Black population of Africa should move cautiously and under the tutelage of their white former rulers. The raffish Lumumba particularly offended his sense of decorum.

At 9:00 a.m. on Thursday, August 18, the president walked into the Cabinet Room of the White House, a high-ceilinged chamber off the Oval Office with a fireplace, a portrait of George Washington, and views of the Rose Garden through arched windows. He sat down in the leather chair designated for him, slightly taller than everyone else's, and called to order the weekly meeting of the National Security Council. Joining him around the massive mahogany table were twenty other men, including the director of the CIA and the secretaries of defense, the treasury, and commerce.

The agenda that day was Africa. Each participant was given a map of the continent, and the bulk of the meeting was devoted to the Congo. The undersecretary of state, Douglas Dillon, the only man in the room who had met Lumumba, led the discussion. He said that Lumumba's break with Hammarskjöld portended disaster. The UN was the vehicle for U.S. policy in the Congo, and if the organization were forced out of the country, the Soviets might swoop in. Dillon considered that prospect "altogether too ghastly to contemplate." Maurice Stans, the director of the Bureau of the Budget, weighed in next. By virtue of his big-game hunting habit and his Belgian-born father, Stans was what passed for a Congo expert at the White House. After declaring that independence had come to Africa fifty years too soon, he argued that Lumumba's true goal was to drive out the whites and seize their property. Allen Dulles, the director of the

CIA, jumped in to repeat his allegation that Lumumba was in the Soviets' pay.

The notes from the meeting would barely conceal Eisenhower's anger. It was "simply inconceivable" that the UN would be forced out. The United States therefore had no choice but to keep the UN in the country, even if this meant that all the African troops left the force, even if the Soviets used this as a basis for picking a fight with the United States, and even if the Congolese government itself objected. When Dillon meekly suggested that it would be hard to keep UN troops in the Congo without the permission of the Congolese, Eisenhower shot him down. What the world was contending with was "one man forcing us out of the Congo"—"Lumumba supported by the Soviets."

It was likely at this point in the discussion that the president made a fateful utterance. Robert Johnson, the official note taker for the meeting, noticed the president turn toward Dulles. Then, he recalled, "President Eisenhower said something—I can no longer remember his words—that came across to me as an order for the assassination of Lumumba." Fifteen seconds of stunned silence followed Eisenhower's remark, as the room digested the apparent directive. It was just one sentence, and a somewhat euphemistically phrased one at that, but Johnson would forever remember the shock he felt in that moment.

When Johnson returned to his desk to type up his notes, he asked his boss what to do with the comment and was told not to mention it. The only written record of the order that appears to survive comes from the notes of Gerard Smith, the State Department's director of policy planning. It is an admittedly inconclusive piece of evidence: in the margins of his legal pad, he wrote "Lumumba" and, beside that, a bold X.

Eisenhower's words would become the subject of debate for decades to come. Douglas Dillon would claim to remember no "clearcut order" at the meeting but would admit that the "general feeling" of the U.S. government at the time was that Lumumba had to be gotten rid of. Eisenhower's more ardent defenders would swear that the president had never suggested that Lumumba be killed and that he could never have even conceived of committing such a sin. His son, John Eisenhower, attended the August 18 National Security

Council meeting in his capacity as an aide. According to John, "If Ike had something as nasty as this to plot, he wouldn't do it in front of twenty-one people." John also claimed to recall one of his father's aides once joking about killing Lumumba. The president, he said, turned red and replied with anger, "That is beyond the pale." Three other people at the August 18 meeting also averred that Eisenhower had never issued anything that could be interpreted as an assassination order.

Subsequent events would belie these defenses. Whatever the exact phrasing, Ike's message that day came through clear enough: Will no one rid me of this turbulent prime minister?

Eisenhower's directive did not appear to weigh heavily on his conscience. Having just become the first-ever U.S. president to order the assassination of a foreign leader, he headed to the whites-only Burning Tree Club in Bethesda, Maryland, to play eighteen holes of golf with his son and grandson.

Chapter 28

Jungle Demagogue

IT WAS TO be a "showdown" with Lumumba. That was how Hammarskjöld advertised the UN Security Council meeting he convened on the afternoon of August 21. More than one thousand New Yorkers lined up for passes to watch the proceedings that Sunday, the hottest ticket since the Suez Crisis. Only two hundred spectators were able to get in and see Hammarskjöld lay out the facts before the members of the Security Council and let them decide who was being unreasonable, he or Lumumba.

With all Belgian soldiers set to depart Katanga within eight days, Hammarskjöld declared the problem of their presence "definitively resolved." (In fact, it would take three more weeks for the last Belgian troops to leave.) That accomplishment put the focus back on the central government in Leopoldville. Although he refused to utter Lumumba's name in the chamber, Hammarskjöld made his feelings clear and gleefully entered his recent "somewhat lively correspondence" with the prime minister into the record. Speaking next was Antoine Gizenga, the Congo's deputy prime minister, whom Lumumba had removed from the Leopoldville scene and sent to New York on account of the rumors that he was planning a coup d'état. It was a poor choice of proxy: the unsophisticated, conspiracy-obsessed Gizenga made a far worse impression than had the urbane, reasonable Kanza. At one point, Gizenga even repeated Lumumba's accusation that Hammarskjöld had chosen white Swedes to accompany him to Elisabethville so that Belgian troops would be able to disguise themselves as members of the UN force.

The Soviet representative, Vasily Kuznetsov, took the floor to echo Lumumba's complaints about the UN's deference to Tshombe. Not incorrectly, he pointed out that the UN's supposedly neutral position on Katanga was having one-sided consequences by effectively strengthening the separatists' position. Less reasonably, he also demanded the withdrawal of the Canadian UN contingent on account of Canada's and Belgium's shared membership in NATO, going so far as to suggest that the beating of the Canadian soldiers at Ndjili had been justified.

Hammarskjöld's rebuttal was a letter from a Congolese military official apologizing for the attack and promising accountability for the Congolese soldiers involved. It was signed at the bottom: Colonel Mobutu, Chief of Staff of the Congolese National Army.

Mobutu had stayed mostly in the background during the chaos of the past few weeks. But whereas Lumumba had excused the soldiers at Ndjili and initially tried to shift blame for the attack on the Canadians, Mobutu was apologizing for his troops' behavior. Hints of a split between the government and the military were showing: on one side, Lumumba and his steadfast insistence on Congolese infallibility, and on the other, Mobutu and his recognition that the country could not alienate the world powers key to its survival. Still, the young army chief of staff remained a blurry figure. Newspapers around the world referred to the contrite words of one "Colonel Mobuto."

The Security Council meeting ended with no resolution being passed, which counted as a victory for Hammarskjöld and a defeat for Lumumba. The outcome amounted to a tacit agreement on the part of the Soviets and the African states that for now their support for the prime minister would not advance beyond the rhetorical. Andrew Cordier, Hammarskjöld's deputy, judged his boss's Security Council performance "the best of his whole career as Secretary-General."

Bunche no doubt reveled in the Security Council victory, too, but he was about to be out of the game. He had been in the Congo for nearly two months, regularly working twenty-hour days since the crisis began. His appetite had abandoned him, and he was shedding weight. His leg was in constant pain. Reluctant to complain himself,

Bunche had his wife, Ruth, drop in to Cordier's office and express worry about her husband's illness and fatigue in the hopes that Hammarskjöld would recall him. He also wanted to return to the United States in time to take his high-school-age son on a tour of Brown, Harvard, and Colby. "This means so much to his future and he has his heart set on the trip," Bunche pleaded in a letter to Cordier.

There was another reason Bunche was eager to leave: he was no longer on speaking terms with Lumumba. He found himself unable to get an appointment with the prime minister, who considered him in the pocket of white men and accused him of failing to think "like an African." Bunche, for his part, could no longer conceal his disdain for Lumumba. In some ways, the prime minister struck him as "like Hitler"; in any case, he was the "lowest man I have ever encountered." "I despise Gizenga but I hate Lumumba," he wrote to his wife. "It would be unkind to the animal kingdom to describe him as having the morals and conduct of an ape," read another letter. In his diary, he referred to Lumumba as a "jungle demagogue" and "Congolese ogre."

Hammarskjöld agreed to relieve Bunche. He'd be stateside by Labor Day. Before leaving Leopoldville, Bunche let slip an uncharacteristically candid comment to the press. "I don't think I have ever been anywhere where misunderstanding was so deep," he said. He added, "I'm a patient man, but my patience has worn thin."

A week after the Security Council meeting, Bunche boarded a plane in Leopoldville. As it took off, the Congo River gleaming below, Bunche told a fellow passenger that he at last felt relaxed. He slumped into his seat cushion, closed his eyes, and fell asleep.

Lumumba's "one great dream," Thomas Kanza maintained, had been to hold a conference of high-ranking African politicians in Leopoldville. He hoped to recapture the pan-African spirit of the conference in Accra in 1958, to establish the Congo as the heart of a continent-wide independence movement. As plans for the meeting solidified, he hyped it as "a major summit conference that will bring all the African states together."

Reality fell short of his dream. The conference had been envisioned as a gathering of heads of state, but Lumumba's attacks on the

UN were alienating his African counterparts. The Liberian president, William Tubman, declared himself "perplexed and frustrated"
by the prime minister's hostility toward the organization. The Tunisian president, Habib Bourguiba, announced, "There is a limit to how
far Tunisia will go along with the Congo." After Kwame Nkrumah
of Ghana and Gamal Abdel Nasser of Egypt canceled their attendance, the conference was downgraded to a foreign-minister summit.
It ended up even less than that, since only half of Africa's twenty-
six independent countries sent delegates, and only two among that
group sent foreign ministers. The Congolese organizers couldn't
keep track of who was coming, and Ndjili airport was in such disarray
that attendees had to fly into Brazzaville. Some then made the last leg
of the journey to Leopoldville by ferry, only to be met by Congolese
soldiers who refused them permission to disembark.

Even Lumumba had difficulty arriving at his summit. It was
held at the recently built modernist Palace of Culture, deep in the
cité—hostile Abako territory. His advisers thought he'd get killed if
he tried to go, but Lumumba waved them away. He arrived at the
conference on the afternoon of August 25, standing up in the back
of an open-topped limousine, gliding past the flags of various African nations as he waved to a crowd of thousands. A thin cordon of
troops, led by Mobutu, saluted the prime minister. At first, the crowd
appeared to be all supporters. Their homemade banners read, "Long
live united Congo." But then out came other signs: "Dictator," "Fascist." Lumumba ignored them, entered the hall, and took the stage.

"This is our year," he said in his opening speech to the delegates.
"The world knows that Algeria is not French, that Angola is not Portuguese, that Kenya is not English," he said. "We know that Africa
is not French or British or American or Russian; it is African." He
called for African solidarity and neutrality at a time when the world
was forcing newly decolonized countries to pick sides:

> We know what the goal of the West is. Yesterday, it divided us at
> the tribal level, at the level of clans and rural districts. Because
> Africa is freeing itself, the West is trying today to divide us at
> the state level. It is trying to create antagonistic blocs and sat-
> ellites, and to exploit this cold war status by accentuating our
> differences, thereby perpetuating its eternal guardianship. I do

not believe I am mistaken when I maintain that a united Africa wants nothing to do with such conniving.... We refuse to be the battleground of international intrigues, the focus and the prize of cold wars.

Loudspeakers outside the hall broadcast his speech to the crowd outside, but soon his words were drowned out. Around the time Lumumba told delegates that they were finally "coming into personal contact with the reality of the African Congo," anti-Lumumba demonstrators began throwing stones at the pro-Lumumba crowd. After a rock hit a policeman in the face, Mobutu's men intervened. They clubbed the protesters to the ground and beat them with their rifle butts. Then the soldiers knelt down and fired their guns, aiming above the protesters' heads.

The sound of gunfire outside alarmed the delegates. "Those people out there are not true Congolese; they are representatives of white imperialism," Lumumba said, interrupting his address. "When you leave here, you may be assaulted in the streets; you may even be assassinated tonight in your homes or hotels. I too may be assassinated. But if we die, it will be for Africa." Accra 1958 this was not.

Having battered and hauled off many of the protesters, the soldiers turned their focus to members of the press. Mobutu instructed his men to rough them up and seize their property. *The Washington Post*'s correspondent was slapped in the face when he refused to surrender his camera. Mobutu looked on calmly. "What do you expect?" he said to reporters. "They have orders."

Lumumba had hoped to project the image of a man who, in his battle against nefarious foreign forces, at least enjoyed the support of his own people. The clashes outside the Palace of Culture painted a different picture. But something about these protesters seemed amiss. One of the men in the crowd carried a sign saying, in French, "Down with the xenophobic government," but when an observer approached, it turned out that the man spoke no French. At a press conference, Lumumba surprised few by alleging that the protests were "organized by some fascist groups instigated by Belgians."

In fact, they were organized by Larry Devlin. As part of the CIA's program to remove Lumumba, Devlin had worked with one of his agents—a Belgian plantation owner—to pay the protesters. The idea, as a CIA memo explained, was to lay the groundwork for a vote of no confidence in the Senate. The "preplanned demonstration" was just one of the "preparations... in the making to support this by radio, propaganda and various types of demonstrations."

But at the very hour Lumumba's voice was competing with the cries of paid protesters in Leopoldville, a small, secretive group at the White House was setting in motion a far more sinister plot against him.

Chapter 29

The Special Group

WITHIN THE U.S. intelligence community, the more innocuous and bureaucratic a committee's name, the greater its
importance, the more scandalous its activities. The CIA's predecessor,
the Office of Strategic Services, had the Morale Operations Branch,
which during World War II spread rumors behind enemy lines—
including that German soldiers' lonely wives were cheating on them
en masse. From 1948 to 1952, all of the agency's covert operations,
including kidnappings behind the Iron Curtain, were the work of the
Office of Policy Coordination. The group that met weekly at lunchtime in the White House—known either as the 5412 Group, after the
National Security Council directive that created it, or simply as the
Special Group—was no exception to this Washington rule.

Eisenhower established the Special Group in 1955 as a way to
reassure Congress that he was keeping the CIA in line. The body
was charged with scrutinizing the agency's covert actions and ensuring that none of them blew up in the president's face. It consisted of
the CIA director, Allen Dulles, the number-two officials at the State
and Defense Departments, and Gordon Gray, Eisenhower's national
security adviser. Quickly, however, the group strayed from its original remit as a check on the CIA's excesses. It became a forum for discussing matters too sensitive to be brought before the full National
Security Council and, in effect, an influential cabal carrying out the
president's dirty work and offering him plausible deniability. Dulles
wouldn't have let it be anything else: he was a master of bureau-

cratic politics, practiced at the art of snowing busy officials to avoid interference.

No organizational chart truly captured the Special Group's power. Gray referred to it as "a group which considered unattributed activities in the government." Richard Bissell, Dulles's deputy at the CIA and a frequent attendee of the meetings, was more explicit. "The Special Group... was, I suppose, in a legal sense an instrumentality of the National Security Council," he elaborated. "In fact, however, it functioned as an autonomous cabinet committee."

The Special Group usually met Thursdays at 12:15 p.m. For months, Cuba had dominated the agenda as it mulled over various plans to embarrass Fidel Castro—spraying his broadcast studio with an LSD-like chemical, lacing his cigars with a disorienting drug, and dusting his shoes with a poison that would cause his beard to fall out. But on this Thursday, August 25, the group turned its attention to the Congo.

Dulles's assistant began by outlining the influence campaign that Devlin was mounting against Lumumba. In Leopoldville, the CIA was working with friendly trade union leaders and politicians to organize a no-confidence vote in the Senate. Gray interjected. He made it clear that he was unimpressed with the CIA's progress, and everyone present knew he spoke for the president. According to the notes of the meeting, Gray commented "that his associates had expressed extremely strong feelings on the necessity for very straightforward action in this situation, and he wondered whether the plans as outlined were sufficient to accomplish this." He was speaking in euphemism. "Associates" meant "the president" and served to preserve plausible deniability.

Dulles had chosen to ignore the president's apparent order to assassinate Lumumba. (Such lack of follow-through was hardly unusual: by this point in his presidency, Eisenhower had lost confidence in the sixty-seven-year-old Dulles and was actively excluding him from meetings.) But now Eisenhower's national security adviser seemed to be reminding him of the order and making it clear that nonviolent means were not enough. The CIA director understood. "Mr. Dulles replied that he had taken the comments referred to seriously"—meaning that he had not forgotten Eisenhower's directive—"and had every intention of proceeding as vigorously as the situation permits or requires." Despite the indirect language, everyone at the meeting knew what had been decided: the CIA would try to kill Lumumba.

Richard Bissell, the CIA's deputy director of plans, had not attended the meeting but soon learned of it. "There isn't any doubt in my mind," he admitted, "that the president did want a man whom he regarded (as did lots of others, myself included) as a thorough scoundrel and a very dangerous one, got rid of. He would have preferred if it could be done in the nicest possible way, but he wanted it done and wasn't prepared to be too fussy about how."

The next day, Dulles wrote a cable to Devlin. Usually, instructions to station chiefs went out under the name of a lower-ranking official, but Dulles signed his own name to this message. Devlin would know to treat it with importance and discretion.

"In high quarters here it is the clear-cut conclusion that if LLL"—L stood for Lumumba, and the letter was triplicated to make sure that at least one came through in transmission—"continues to hold high office, the inevitable result will at best be chaos and at worst pave the way to Communist takeover of the Congo," Dulles wrote. "Consequently, we conclude that his removal must be an urgent and prime objective."

Devlin could not have failed to understand that when the director of the CIA was referring to "high quarters," he could only mean one man: the president. And he must have understood further that when the CIA director ordered an enemy's urgent "removal," he probably did not have in mind merely a parliamentary vote of no confidence.

The director authorized Devlin to spend up to $100,000 to carry out the order, to be used at Devlin's discretion. Station chiefs usually had to ask permission to spend anything above $50. Devlin was being handed a gigantic mission budget, equivalent to about ten times his own annual salary.

He must have been pleased: his weeks-long crusade to get Washington to understand just how dangerous Lumumba was had succeeded. He now had the U.S. president on his side, enormous financial resources to draw on, and carte blanche to dispose of Lumumba as he saw fit.

—

Back in the Congo, Lumumba's floundering conference continued. He sought refuge from it by leaving hostile Leopoldville for the one city where he was guaranteed a friendly audience: Stanleyville. Flying in his Soviet-gifted plane to his home base with a handful of journalists and advisers, he promised to show "how peaceful everything there is." Lumumba hadn't been to Stanleyville for more than a month, since he had toured the country with Kasavubu during the mutiny. Now waiting for him at the airport was a massive crowd of supporters, as many as ten thousand people, by one estimate. It was a festive group, with workers in overalls, young people in the shirts of Lumumba's MNC party, and older men wearing leopard-skin loincloths and feathered caps.

As so often in the Congo, however, a visit designed to underscore calm revealed more chaos. While Lumumba's plane was still in the air, a U.S. Air Force Globemaster, crewed by Americans and carrying Canadian telecommunications experts, landed at the airport. As the Americans and Canadians got out, a rumor ripped through the crowd: these were Belgian paratroopers sent to assassinate Lumumba. Suspicious Congolese soldiers swarmed the unarmed white men. When one of the Canadians tried a few words of French, their suspicions were confirmed. The soldiers knocked over the men, pistol-whipping them until scalps split, ribs fractured, and lungs collapsed. Blood pooled on the tarmac. Only the intervention of an Ethiopian nurse saved the men from death.

When Lumumba arrived forty-five minutes later, one of the injured Americans was sitting on the pavement bleeding, less than twenty feet away from the prime minister. Lumumba took no notice of him. Instead, he gave a brief speech in which he told the soldiers, "I am very happy to see you in combat uniform, ready to descend on Katanga."

Even though the beating had happened before Lumumba's plane landed, Timberlake blamed the prime minister for the renewed eruption of violence. "Hope Stanleyville incident has removed any lingering trace of the fiction that we are dealing with a civilized people or a responsible government in the Congo," he cabled to the State Department. Lumumba's days were numbered, Timberlake added.

"He may just be on his last spectacular lap, and it could not end too soon for me," he wrote. "His only demonstrated skill is in attack and incitement." Once again, it was Mobutu who took it upon himself to repair the damage. He apologized to the UN and visited the victims in the hospital.

The day after the attack, Lumumba relived his campaign days by driving through Stanleyville's African communes in a convertible. Wiping sweat from his brow with a handkerchief, he waved to the supporters lined up along the red-dirt roads yelling, "Uhuru!" Children sprinted behind his car, trying to catch the bumper. At 10:00 p.m., he held a rally at Stanleyville's stadium in front of some forty thousand people. In the dark arena, lit weakly by the headlights of cars, he made no mention of the airport attack but appealed for friendly relations with whites. Pointing to a Belgian woman standing nearby, he announced that she was married to a Congolese man. "That's true friendship!" he said.

"Are you against the whites?" he asked the crowd.

"No!" the people cried.

"Have you tried to make Europeans leave?"

"No!"

Whites must be protected, Lumumba said. "If they have no beer, give them yours. If they have no bread, give them your manioc."

Lumumba's speech succeeded in improving race relations in Stanleyville, at least in the short term. Members of the crowd shook the hands of whites as they left. Now the city's European residents were greeted with a smile. But instead of convincing Westerners of Lumumba's good intentions, the speech was seen as something more sinister. As one D.C. reporter noted, "The call for fraternization between Congolese and Europeans launched by Mr. Lumumba on Sunday is generally interpreted in Washington as intended to prepare the Congolese population for the arrival of white Communist technicians sent by the U.S.S.R."

Lumumba knew none of this. After the rally, he unwound with his aides at a restaurant. Waiters served Coca-Cola, champagne, wine, whiskey, and gin. A saxophone wailed in the background. The prime minister was at ease. The troubles of Leopoldville, of the UN, of the Belgians, of the Cold War, seemed very far away. When the going got tough in the capital, he could always return to Stanleyville.

Lumumba turned to one of his advisers. "Tomorrow, it's back to the jungle," he said. "Leopoldville."

Lumumba's pan-African conference, *Newsweek* declared, "was a fizzle." Observers from Communist China and North Vietnam arrived only on the last day. Frantz Fanon, the Martinican psychiatrist and political philosopher who served as a diplomat for Algeria's nationalist government in exile, was delayed in transit and missed the event altogether. So did the entire Libyan delegation.

Lumumba likely sensed that he had lost the West and the UN. He probably had not expected to lose most African countries, too. His agenda for the conference had limited the discussion to grand projects furthering pan-Africanism: cultural exchanges, free-trade agreements, a center for scientific research in Leopoldville. But the only thing the delegates wanted to talk about was the Congo crisis. The disorder of Leopoldville and the evident flightiness of Lumumba gave them an appreciation for the difficulties the UN faced. The head of the Sudanese delegation was baffled by the prime minister's insistence, in the middle of one meeting, that he rush to the airport to pull down the UN flag. "Lumumba's childish behavior is damaging all Africans," one North African attendee complained to a reporter. The goal of the conference, another delegate confided anonymously to the press, had shifted and was now to "calm down Lumumba." Rather than rallying behind the prime minister, the African diplomats privately demanded that he take measures to prevent further violent incidents with UN troops.

On the last day of the conference, delegates called on the Congolese government to cooperate closely with the UN. They also read a letter paying homage to Ralph Bunche's work. Listening to the tributes to the UN at the final session, Lumumba fidgeted uncomfortably in his seat. Then he rose to give a closing speech in which he threaded the needle. One moment, he blamed the UN for lacking "a spirit of cooperation." The next, he praised "the magnificent work the United Nations is doing in the Congo."

In truth, Lumumba had given up on trying to use the UN as an instrument for enacting his own policy, having finally accepted that it did not answer to him. In fact, he now concluded, it was just as paternalistic as the Belgians. Because the UN could not be relied upon to crack down on secessionism, the Congo's own army, the ANC, would have to do the job itself. Congolese soldiers "are obsessed with the idea of entering Katanga without delay and liberating their brothers," he announced to the hall. "They burn with impatience."

Chapter 30

Bakwanga

EARLY IN THE morning of August 27, trucks carrying one thousand Congolese troops rolled into Bakwanga. Before independence, Bakwanga had been a sleepy company town, home to just three hundred Europeans and some fifteen thousand Congolese. It was the center of the Congo's diamond industry, but life there was uneventful. Much of the indigenous population worked at the mines, sifting through tons of gravel for low-quality stones, most smaller than a carat, for use in drill bits and abrasives. But in recent weeks, Bakwanga had been making headlines as the capital of the secessionist state of South Kasai, led by the erstwhile Lumumba ally Albert Kalonji. Kalonji styled his state a home for his fellow Baluba, the minority ethnic group that had long been scattered across the country, and he called on them to return to their ancestral homeland. The ensuing arrival of tens of thousands of Baluba quickly overwhelmed the new capital, exhausting its supply of food and shelter.

Like Moise Tshombe in neighboring Katanga, Kalonji had been busy equipping South Kasai with the trappings of independence. The province would soon have its own flag and postage stamps, both bearing a *V* for "victory." And just like Tshombe, Kalonji had set up his own army. But his was a small force of local police officers, dressed in tattered World War I–era uniforms and commanded by a "general" all of twenty-two years old. Some of the men were armed with rifles they did not know how to use; others carried spears or improvised guns made from steel pipes. Many of the ANC troops who arrived in Bakwanga, by contrast, were commandos; they had been sent by

Mobutu from Leopoldville on planes requisitioned from Sabena, the Belgian national airline. Armed with mortars, machine guns, and grenades, and supplied with four truckloads of ammunition, the central government's soldiers took the town with barely a shot fired. Kalonji was nowhere to be found, having fled to Katanga, where he had formed an alliance with Tshombe.

The expedition to Bakwanga was Mobutu's idea. Officially, it was intended to quell ethnic fighting—"national emergency," he told the press curtly—but its true purpose was different. The invasion of South Kasai was the first step in the central government's plan to retake Katanga. After snuffing out Kalonji's secessionist state, Mobutu hoped, ANC troops would make the one-hundred-mile trek to the Katangan border. As they invaded Katanga from the west, another detachment of ANC troops would set out from Stanleyville and attack from the north. Caught in this pincer movement, Tshombe's nascent army would collapse, and Lumumba would replace Katanga's secessionist leaders with his own men.

But after a smooth start, the invasion of Bakwanga turned bloody. Unpaid and unfed ANC soldiers looted the town of the dried fish, tinned meat, rice, and sugar that the Red Cross had flown in for the 200,000 starving refugees, Baluba who were looking for safety from ethnic conflict elsewhere. The soldiers tortured and executed a minister in Kalonji's secessionist government and killed men merely suspected of working for it. Many of the ANC troops were ethnic Lulua, and they sought revenge against the Baluba, with whom their people had been clashing for a year. What had begun as a reconquest quickly turned into an orgy of ethnic violence. When Kalonji's fighters ambushed an ANC patrol near a Catholic mission, the central government soldiers entered the grounds of the stone church to find at least seventy unarmed Baluba, mostly women and children, hiding under desks in classrooms. The soldiers opened fire, killing nearly everyone. A girl who tried to flee was shot at point-blank range, still clutching her textbooks.

A foreign reporter was caught up in the violence as well. Harry Taylor, a thirty-one-year-old Scripps-Howard correspondent, had been in the country for just five days when he and two other journalists set off from Bakwanga with a hundred ANC troops. During a standoff with a group of Luba warriors, Taylor, whom they believed to be a Communist commander, was shot to death. He was the first American to die in the Congo crisis.

As Lumumba's soldiers moved out from Bakwanga into the surrounding villages, they targeted more civilians. The troops dragged residents from their houses, raped, bayoneted, or shot them, and then torched their huts. They left behind empty towns and a grisly quiet interrupted only by the bleats of goats wandering through the charred ruins and rotting corpses. The death toll numbered in the thousands. One soldier interviewed by a Red Cross representative admitted killing so many Baluba that he lost count. "They are bad, bad people," he explained. "We had to teach them a lesson."

When reports from Bakwanga reached Hammarskjöld, he concluded that the massacres amounted to the greatest crime imaginable. The ANC's deliberate and specific targeting of ethnic Baluba, he told the Security Council, had "all the characteristics of the crime of genocide." Although Lumumba denied that he had anything to do with the massacres, the involvement of high-ranking state officials dispatched to the region by the prime minister suggested otherwise. Jacques Omonombe, a top official in the National Police and the prime minister's first cousin, helped round up civilians, including a local bishop. Jacques Lumbala, a junior minister in Lumumba's government and a close friend of Mobutu's, egged on the rapacious soldiers. Accompanying them on their patrols, he yelled at the population from the back of a truck, "The lions are here! The owners of the country are here! Get out!"

The UN was not blameless either. As the massacre unfolded, the contingent of Tunisian troops deployed to the area did little other than guard Bakwanga's white population, which barricaded itself in its club, drinking beer, eating corned beef, and playing Ping-Pong. G. C. Senn, the Red Cross's representative in the Congo, attributed the UN force's passivity to what he viewed as its excessive worry about interfering in the Congo's internal matters. He wrote bluntly in a report, "If the U.N. would have in mind the well-being of the rank and file of the native population, instead of trying to please and to satisfy political leaders and their ambitions, greed, and lust for power, no human lives would have been lost in the Bakwanga area."

Lumumba's campaign lost him the support not only of the UN but also of potential political allies in Leopoldville. Bakwanga was the last straw. "There was a feeling late in August 1960 that Patrice Lumumba must die," one British journalist wrote. "It was in the grass and in the wind. Nobody said so aloud, though Congolese politicians in Leopoldville muttered it to each other as the story of the death and destruction in the South Kasai became more widely known."

In addition to the moral opprobrium, Lumumba's operation in Kasai was now facing a military challenge. Taking Bakwanga was one thing, but getting into Katanga was another. From Elisabethville, Tshombe announced that he had blown up the main road and rail bridges into his province and would be providing weapons and men to help "chase Lumumba from Kasai." Indeed, six hundred supporters of Kalonji in Elisabethville had volunteered to go to the front. Joined by fifty women to do their cooking and washing, the irregulars affixed *V*s to their helmets and boarded a train for the border.

Facing logistical difficulties, including supply shortages, and fearing that his troops would falter in the face of determined Katangan resistance, Mobutu ordered the ANC to retreat—without consulting Lumumba. When the prime minister learned of the decision, he summoned Mobutu to his office.

"You're just a simple colonel, and you ordered a cease-fire," Lumumba said, exasperated. He told Mobutu that he was forbidding him to direct the military mission in Kasai and would reverse his order to retreat.

"You don't know what you're talking about," Mobutu shot back. "You can't imagine the difficulties of such an operation." He went on: "We need trucks, food, equipment."

The acrimony between the former friends had reached an apogee. "You're sabotaging me!" Lumumba yelled. "I need to fire you."

"Gladly," replied Mobutu. And with that, he slammed shut the doors to the prime minister's office.

Mobutu was right. The logistical obstacles to continuing the fight in Kasai were formidable. The military balance of power, once promising for the central government, now looked precarious. But Lumumba had an ace up his sleeve. The Soviet Union had granted his request for military aid.

First there were the trucks. Back in July, the Soviet Union had pledged one hundred four-wheel-drive troop carriers to the UN mission, part of the outpouring of global support in response to Hammar-skjöld's appeal for military contributions. In Odessa in early August, the trucks, along with spare parts, fuel, a mobile repair shop, and a team of mechanics, were loaded onto the cargo ship the *Arkhangelsk*. But the Soviets had soured on the UN mission and announced that they would lend the one hundred trucks directly to the Congolese government. After the *Arkhangelsk* docked at Matadi, the hammer and sickle on its funnel looming incongruously over the colonial river port, the vehicles never made it into UN hands.

More significantly, in response to Lumumba's call for military aid, the Soviet Union lent the Congolese government ten Ilyushin Il-14s, twin-engine planes that could carry twenty troops apiece. The Russian-crewed planes left Moscow with interpreters, mechanics, and boxes of food and landed in Stanleyville around the end of August. There, they were repainted in the blue and yellow of the Congolese flag and emblazoned with "Republic of the Congo," dispelling any hopes that these were for the UN's use. Meanwhile, the Soviet Union packed five Antonov An-12 cargo planes with arms and ammunition and dispatched them to Cairo, for eventual transport to the Congo.

Disturbed by the planes and arms shipments, Larry Devlin was watching closely for other signs of Communist penetration. He learned that two members of the Belgian Communist Party were on their way to the Congo—Albert de Coninck and Jean Terfve, both of whom Lumumba had been in contact with. A cable warned Devlin, "If they and other BCP members can gradually take over the function of advising Congolese leaders from the present col-lection of fly-by-nights, carpetbaggers, embittered ex–civil servants and African Communists, the result could be a substantial increase in the effectiveness and coordination of Communist influence in the Congo Government." Devlin bugged an office occupied by Czech representatives, installing a listening post in a nearby house. To track further infiltration, he paid a contact at Ndjili airport to tell him how many Soviet personnel were flying in and was alarmed to learn that they numbered in the hundreds.

Eisenhower, who had never thought much of Lumumba to begin with, was now convinced that the man was "a Soviet tool" and "a Communist sympathizer if not a member of the Party" and that Moscow's military assistance amounted to a "Soviet invasion." These concerns were now a matter of bipartisan consensus. Senator John F. Kennedy, now tied with Richard Nixon in the polls, sent a telegram to Secretary of State Christian Herter from the campaign trail, stating that he was "extremely concerned... about expanding Communist influence in the Congo," which he viewed as "a Russian test for the United Nations." Well-sourced journalists echoed the official U.S. line. The Congo was "sliding slowly but surely into the Communist bloc," *The Washington Post* declared. "Premier Lumumba's startling changes of position, his open challenge to the United Nations and Secretary-General Dag Hammarskjöld, his constant agitation of the largely illiterate Congolese can be explained in no other way, veteran observers say." In Washington, the debate about Lumumba's orientation was settled.

The Soviet planes, trucks, weapons, and personnel—all the elements of the "classic Communist effort to take over the government" that Devlin had warned about—seemed in place. Yet his assessments were more hyperventilation than fact. For one thing, Devlin's methods of intelligence gathering were decidedly crude: his airport source, "a newly recruited and untried Congolese agent," simply counted the number of white people disembarking from the Soviet planes supporting the UN airlift, all of which he thought could safely be considered Soviet citizens. Devlin made a further leap by assuming that "many, if not most" of these arrivals were intelligence officers.

In truth, the total number of KGB personnel in the Congo in the summer of 1960 appears to have been just three: two officers who worked under diplomatic cover, and one who was a correspondent for TASS, the Soviet state-owned news agency. A CIA estimate put the total number of "bloc personnel" in the country—people from the Soviet Union, its satellite states, and its allies—at somewhere between 232 and 364. But the vast majority of these were flight and ground crew; an estimated 55 to 75 were medical workers from the Soviet Union, Czechoslovakia, and East Germany.

Lumumba's overtures to the Soviets lent themselves to all sorts of Communist apparitions. It became an article of faith among

Lumumba's critics, for example, that the ANC's assault on Bakwanga was led by a trio of shadowy Czech military advisers, when the three men in question were in fact Western journalists embedded with Congolese troops. Then again, Soviet military aid, although meager, was real and desired. At a time when Lumumba's troops were bogged down in South Kasai and about to face a much more powerful enemy across the border in Katanga, Soviet-provided planes, guns, and trucks were likely to provide a badly needed fillip. The State Department concluded as much, estimating that Soviet aircraft "clearly enhanced" Lumumba's military capability, easing the way for him to take over Katanga. And Lumumba saw no reason not to accept a helping hand. As he asked legisators, "Why would our government, our parliament, deal with the British, the Americans, the French and not the Russians?"

But in a bitter twist, much if not all of the Soviet matériel never reached its final destination. The fate of the one hundred trucks delivered to Matadi is a matter of dispute, with some alleging that they were loaded onto a barge and sent upriver to meet up with Lumumba's campaign in South Kasai. UN officials wondered whether the trucks the ANC troops used in their roving campaign of terror against the Baluba were Soviet in make. But observers in the field concluded that the soldiers relied on old Force Publique trucks, plus vehicles looted from the population. As for the airplanes, the ten Il-14s that landed in Stanleyville got their new paint job, but there is some question as to whether they made it to South Kasai. And although Hammarskjöld suspected that these planes carried small arms, while refueling in Athens, they were inspected by Greek authorities, who found nothing amiss. The five An-12s, which were indeed carrying weapons, sat on the runway in Cairo, only to turn back to Moscow. As the CIA concluded at the time, "There is no conclusive evidence that bloc arms have yet been brought into the Congo."

The truth was, Soviet leaders had waited too long to respond to Lumumba's call for help. Events in Leopoldville would overtake them.

PART IV

CAPTIVE

Chapter 31

The Sleeping Crocodile

How do you make a coup d'état?" Kasavubu asked sometime in the summer of 1960. He was speaking to the man in charge of administering all the UN's nonmilitary aid to the Congo. The official was taken aback. He wondered if the president was joking.

"Why do you ask?" he replied.

"Oh, just as a matter of interest."

After the CIA approached him in early August about getting rid of Lumumba, Kasavubu had expressed little enthusiasm for using his constitutional prerogatives to do so. Although any Congolese president had the power to instigate a vote of no confidence in the prime minister, this Congolese president was by nature cautious—"like a water buffalo," Hammarskjöld said.

The presidential residence was an elegant structure designed in the International Style and made of concrete and glass, with a wide balcony offering a full view of Livingstone Falls. It was a comfortable place from which to watch Congolese politics play out at a distance. And so as August wore on and Lumumba alienated the UN, the West, and much of Africa, Kasavubu mostly kept to himself in his riverside mansion. He told confidants that he planned on lying low until Lumumba was thrown out by others, at which point he would intervene.

Ambassador Timberlake considered Kasavubu "a political zero." His cables to Washington described the president as "naive, not very bright, lazy, enjoying his newfound plush living, and content to appear occasionally in his new general's uniform." Whenever Timberlake met with Kasavubu to persuade him to take action against Lumumba, the president listened silently, eyes half-closed. Efforts to have him call a special session of parliament went nowhere.

Devlin wasn't having much success, either. For now, he had chosen not to act on headquarters' insinuation that he could move beyond nonviolent means for ousting Lumumba. Instead, he busied himself bribing members of the Senate, lining up votes against the prime minister. As part of what came to be known as "Project WIZARD"—in the CIA's deliberately impenetrable cryptonomic system, the prefix "WI" meant the Congo—the CIA was subsidizing at least two opposition senators. When Devlin learned from a source that Kasavubu was considering firing Lumumba, he readied a three-page "how-to" paper that outlined the series of steps he should take before, during, and after the dismissal. The White House did what it could to help, with the Special Group authorizing the provision of funds to Kasavubu as part of an anti-Lumumba program. But Kasavubu, Devlin learned, had only glanced at his proposal.

Belgian diplomats were equally frustrated with Kasavubu's passivity. Expelled by Lumumba from Leopoldville, they regrouped in Brazzaville, continuing to undermine the prime minister from across the river. Their goal, as a cable to Brussels put it, was "the overthrow of the government in accordance with our wishes." Belgian diplomats financed his political opponents, printed anti-Lumumba leaflets for distribution in Leopoldville, and set up a secret radio station to broadcast propaganda. "There is a veritable climate of conspiracy here in Brazzaville at the moment," one Belgian intelligence officer boasted in a cable to headquarters. Kasavubu's party, Abako, had announced that it would get rid of Lumumba "by legal or illegal means," but the party leader and president himself remained tight-lipped. To prod him, Brussels began flooding Kasavubu with legal advice. Whereas Devlin and others had been pushing their vote-of-no-confidence plan, Belgium had seized on Article 22 of the Congo's provisional constitution. It stated simply, "The Head of State appoints and dismisses the Prime Minister and ministers." All Kasavubu had to do was announce that he was dismissing Lumumba. Unlike in the Senate plan being pressed by Devlin, under this one no parliamentary approval was required.

Yet this was a more legally dubious maneuver. Article 22, like the rest of the Congo's provisional constitution, was lifted straight from the Belgian one, which gave the power of ministerial dismissal to the king. But in Belgium, as in other constitutional monarchies, a tradition had developed whereby the legislature was dominant and the king exercised only ceremonial powers. It had been nearly fifty years since a Belgian monarch had dismissed a minister without involving parliament. Employing Article 22 would mean experimenting with a technicality, rather than exercising a tried-and-true procedure.

Kasavubu understood that on paper he possessed the power to fire Lumumba. Back in July, when the mutiny broke out, he had reminded the Belgian ambassador that he could do so whenever he wanted to. (When Kasavubu gave Paul Springer, Devlin's predecessor as station chief, the impression he was unaware of his presidential powers, he was likely feigning ignorance.) But the president was hesitant to invoke such a nakedly antidemocratic loophole. Brussels redoubled its lobbying push, with Foreign Minister Pierre Wigny and other high-ranking officials personally developing arguments about the legitimacy of the proposed move. Even Belgium's prime minister, Gaston Eyskens, entered the fray, instructing one of Kasavubu's Belgian advisers to remind the Congolese president about his constitutional power to dismiss Lumumba. When Kasavubu heard the Belgian prime minister's advice, he seemed receptive. After all, Kasavubu said, Lumumba was momentarily weakened, like "a wounded animal that will meet his death." But there was still no indication as to when the president would pounce.

The wounded animal, for his part, refused to see Kasavubu as a potential predator. "Impossible," Lumumba replied when told that the president had his sights set on him. "We're working together every day." Everyone in Leopoldville seemed to know that Lumumba's days in office were numbered except for the prime minister himself. Thomas Kanza lamented that lack of awareness. "Lumumba gave little thought to Kasavubu, whom he considered a lazy man, physically weak, and politically a robot," he wrote. "This was a fatal error, for Kasavubu was in fact the crocodile sleeping open-eyed beside the river—in his sumptuous residence."

Like Belgium and the United States, the leadership of the UN had turned definitively against Lumumba. Hammarskjöld admitted in a cable that since their epistolary row, "I keep him in the doghouse." Elsewhere, he called Lumumba "a stooge." The secretary-general had come to a simple conclusion: Lumumba must be "broken."

To replace the departing Bunche in Leopoldville, Hammarskjöld had picked Rajeshwar Dayal, a respected Indian diplomat whose appointment would help deflect charges that the UN operation in the Congo was American run. But there would be nearly a weeklong gap between Bunche's departure and Dayal's assumption of the role, so Hammarskjöld sent a temporary representative to fill the interregnum: Andrew Cordier, his executive assistant.

It was a curious choice, since Cordier had never run a UN field operation. A creature of the air-conditioned corridors of the UN building, "Uncle Andy," as he was known to his intimates, seemed ill-suited for the chaos of the Snake Pit or the guns and jeeps of Leopoldville. But what Cordier lacked in experience he made up for in loyalty. He prided himself in sharing a mind with his boss. He even picked up his habits: Hammarskjöld smoked cigarillos, and soon so did Cordier. A magazine profile of Hammarskjöld described Cordier as "a chunky, blue-eyed former Hoosier schoolmaster who is invariably cheerful and relaxed, with a phenomenal memory and an enormous capacity for work," and noted that "anything of concern to Hammarskjöld is in Cordier's domain too." Since the Congo crisis began, the two men had been spending eighteen-hour days together—from the time Hammarskjöld arrived in his office to late at night, Cordier liked to point out. "The only time I did not lunch with him was when he had a luncheon to which I was not invited, but that was very rare," he once said.

Cordier seemed to feel what Hammarskjöld felt, only more intensely. To him, Lumumba was a "little Hitler"—"an irresponsible and even mad type of personality." Cordier, who had developed a distaste for Lumumba after meeting him in person in New York, thought the embezzlement conviction said all one needed to know about his character, not to mention Lumumba's rumored drug use. "The only real solution" to the Congo's problems, Cordier agreed, "is a change in leadership."

When Cordier arrived in the Congo, he quickly grew alarmed.

Russian military planes with unknown cargo were landing in Stan-leyville, the ANC was on a murderous rampage in South Kasai, and tensions between Kasavubu and Lumumba were rising. On the morning of September 3, he met with Kasavubu, who announced that he had "decided to take measures, definite measures." Kasavubu handed Cordier a letter.

> Dear Mr. Cordier,
>   I have taken action at eight A.M. this morning,
> September 3, to dismiss Mr. Patrice Lumumba as Prime
> Minister of the Republic of the Congo for grave misuse
> of power.

Cordier glanced up from the document. "Mr. President, it is now ten o'clock," he said. "I haven't heard anything about it. Have you really dismissed him?"

"No," replied Kasavubu. "I wanted to show you the letter first."

The letter went on to demand that the UN help the president with his takeover. Kasavubu envisioned the organization disarming the ANC in order to neutralize a force he did not control, guarding his residence to prevent arrest (or worse) at the hands of a rival, and securing access to the radio station. To prevent foreign intervention, the country's borders would be sealed. The airports would be closed, too, to stop Lumumba from flying in loyal troops from elsewhere in the Congo or fleeing to Stanleyville to set up a rival government. Kasavubu then asked Cordier if the UN could arrest twenty-five or so people. Cordier refused. How about just one arrest? Kasavubu asked. It went without saying that the target was Lumumba. Again, Cordier demurred.

The two officials were engaged in a delicate dance. Because he did not control the army, Kasavubu clearly wanted the UN's help in establishing order after a takeover, but he wasn't sure just how the organization would react. Cordier, though eager to see Lumumba gone, knew that in the eyes of most of the world the slightest hint of UN involvement would be a scandalous betrayal of its professed neutrality. Cordier promised nothing except to meet again.

That night, he consulted Hammarskjöld by cable and telex. Ham-marskjöld insisted that the UN could not be seen to be a party to an internal conflict in the run-up to a coup. But if, hypothetically speaking, Kasavubu took over and formed a government, at that point the organization could "regard it as constitutional." Despite the risk of a conflict breaking out, Hammarskjöld expressed confidence in his deputy, giving him wide latitude: "At any time, you may face the situation of complete disintegration of authority that would put you in a situation of emergency, which in my view would entitle you to greater freedom of action in protection of law and order." Never did he counsel him to urge Kasavubu to stand down.

Hammarskjöld and the rest of the Congo Club were squeezed into a small room. He signed off with excitement. "Good luck," he wrote to Cordier. "We cross our fingers.... The whole team is in the cable office and joins me in good wishes." In Hammarskjöld's and Cordier's eyes, the prospect of dismissing the Congo's democratically elected prime minister on murky legal grounds was not cause for concern; it was reason for celebration. But the UN's hand would have to remain invisible. Hammarskjöld instructed Cordier to "burn immediately all texts on your side pertaining to this matter."

The next day, a Sunday, Cordier again met with Kasavubu. The president wanted the UN force to act as his personal army in the event that he dismissed Lumumba, but above all he was still searching for reassurance. Cordier provided it, explaining in detail what the UN could do in the event of an emergency. Working with his military staff, he mapped out a response. As part of a "dry run," five thousand UN troops, without knowing why, practiced exerting instant control over Leopoldville. Upon receipt of the code word "top," they were to strengthen the guard at the president's house. Another code word—"lob"—would have them shut down the city's two airports.

By now, a replacement for Lumumba had emerged: Joseph Iléo, the president of the Senate and an avowed Lumumba opponent, whom the American embassy had identified weeks earlier as the "most likely successor" as prime minister. For the Americans, Iléo was a welcome choice, because he was in the CIA's pocket: in the spring, the agency had funded his campaign for the presidency of the Senate and felt it could claim some credit for his narrow victory, 41 votes to 39. On the night of September 4, Cordier met with Iléo and impressed upon him the urgency of the situation, emphasizing the risk of Soviet intervention in the Congo.

The next morning, Kasavubu once again summoned Cordier to his house. Whatever was said, it was enough to reassure the president to move forward with his plan, and at yet another meeting that afternoon—Cordier's fifth with the president in three days—Kasavubu revealed he would announce the dismissal of Lumumba over the radio that evening.

What role would the UN play? Hammarskjöld thought that should be up to the men in the field, but he tipped his hand in a cable to Cordier, offering what he called "an irresponsible observation": "that responsible people on the spot may permit themselves, within the framework of principles which are imperative, to do what I could not justify doing myself—taking the risk of being disowned when it no longer matters." In other words, the secretary-general had to remain officially neutral, but if one of his subordinates just so happened to help Kasavubu seize power, then what could one do?

At 7:00 p.m. on September 5, Kasavubu called for one of his Belgian advisers, who met the president at his residence. When Kasavubu asked him to hand the UN mission a formal written request for the organization to close the radio station and the airport and guard the president's house, the adviser naively suggested that it might be hard to find a top UN official at such a late hour. Kasavubu picked up a telephone, dialed a number, and immediately had someone on the line. "Cordier here," came the voice. The veil had been lifted: Kasavubu's plan was not a spur-of-the-moment decision but, as Devlin noted in a cable that day, "coordinated with [the UN operation] at the highest levels here."

Shortly after 8:00 p.m., Kasavubu arrived at the radio station, a small cube of a building with stone siding. He positioned himself in front of a microphone, laid one hand on a table for support, and clutched his script in the other. A UN-sponsored English-language instruction program that was playing came to an abrupt stop. Then, in his halting, squeaky voice, Kasavubu said, "I have some extremely important news to announce."

He told the Congolese people that Lumumba—whom in his excited state he mistakenly called "the prime mayor"—had "ruled arbitrarily," had "deprived many citizens of basic freedoms," and was "throwing the country into an atrocious civil war." That was why, Kasavubu explained, he had "found it necessary to immediately dismiss the government." He named Iléo as the new prime minister, called on the ANC to temporarily lay down its arms, and asked the UN to take charge of maintaining peace and order.

Lumumba's opponents were ecstatic. "It's about time," a nameless U.S. official told *The New York Times*. One Leopoldville hotel offered drinks on the house when the news broke. Cordier and other UN staffers were gathered around a radio in the Snake Pit. One of them observed that "it was impossible not to detect an atmosphere of relief, almost of satisfaction." Mercifully, Lumumba's sixty-seven-day tenure as prime minister of the Congo had come to an end.

Chapter 32

A Bungled Firing

O R H A D I T ? After issuing his proclamation, Kasavubu made the puzzling decision to return home and go to bed. Lumumba, however, sprang into action, racing to the radio station in his black limousine, flanked by a pair of soldiers. As per the plan worked out between Kasavubu and Cordier, a jeep-load of Ghanaian troops was guarding the building. They were led by a British officer under orders to stop the prime minister at all costs, but he felt he couldn't do so without shooting him. Lumumba burst past the UN soldiers into the studio. The text of Kasavubu's speech still lay on the table.

Less than an hour after Kasavubu's broadcast, Lumumba took the same microphone in rebuttal: "No one, not even the president of the republic, has the right to dismiss a government elected by the people." From 9:00 p.m. to 10:30 p.m., Lumumba issued three separate statements, two in French and one in Lingala. "At the very moment that the Congo was moving ahead, at the very moment that the Congo was enjoying the entire world's admiration," he told the people, "Mr. Kasavubu dealt it a severe blow." Because the president had "publicly betrayed the nation," Lumumba announced that he was dismissing him. "There is no longer a head of state in our republic," he declared. The Congo's two top leaders had fired each other.

The UN forces quickly sought to neutralize the ANC, whose reaction to the coup could not be predicted. To prevent Congolese troops from moving about the country, Cordier ordered all airports closed to non-UN flights, grounding the ten Soviet Il-14s in Stanleyville. In Leopoldville, UN cars cruised down eerily calm streets.

A Moroccan detachment replaced the Congolese troops guarding Kasavubu's house, preventing any trouble there. A Moroccan general, Ben Hammou Kettani, instructed Mobutu—who had not, in the end, been fired by Lumumba—to stop the four thousand troops garrisoned at Camp Leopold from making any rash moves. Mobutu did as he was told, assembling the soldiers and urging them to remain calm. He also turned over the camp's arms and communications equipment to the UN and promised not to distribute them in the morning. Cordier cabled Hammarskjöld to ask for $1 million to pay Congolese troops—money that was quickly provided courtesy of the U.S. government.

Mobutu hardly had the rank and file in the palm of his hand, however. As a precaution, he arranged for himself and his family to spend the night at Kettani's house. In fact, he himself had not fully decided whose side he should take. After midnight, he went twice to UN headquarters at the Royal to talk to Cordier, who tried to broker a rendezvous between the colonel and the president, but word came back that Kasavubu was still in bed and would not be meeting Mobutu. "Strange country," Cordier remarked.

Mobutu was, however, able to see Lumumba. Sacrificing sleep for action, the prime minister gathered thirteen of his ministers at his residence for an emergency session that stretched into the wee hours of the morning. Congolese troops stood guard in front of the house, bayonets fixed. When Mobutu was let in, he found the prime minister drafting another radio speech. Lumumba read the statement on the radio half an hour before sunrise on September 6, declaring Kasavubu's action "null and void" and finding the president guilty of "high treason." Lumumba had now spoken to the nation four times to Kasavubu's one.

Devlin was following events closely. He had not expected Kasavubu to act on September 5; so far as he knew, the plan had been for the president to coordinate with his collaborators in the Senate and dismiss Lumumba on September 7. "Unfortunately, and for reasons which are not yet fully clear to us, Kasavubu jumped the gun on this operation two days too early and (illegally) declared Lumumba out of office and failed further to implement his action," a CIA memo noted, laying bare the agency's disappointment, as well as its initial opinion on the constitutionality of the move. The document went on: "Kasavubu's precipitate action has at least seriously jeopardized the plan for ousting Lumumba."

To Devlin's further astonishment, Kasavubu had ignored the CIA's advice and failed to secure the radio station to prevent his more charismatic rival from addressing the Congolese people. It was Coup Plotting 101: if the deposed leader was allowed to rule the airwaves, the takeover could lose momentum. Now playing catch-up, Devlin considered cutting off the power to the station, but he didn't know how. American officials on the ground were dismayed. Clare Timberlake called Cordier every half hour, urging the UN to arrest Lumumba. Watching the drama from across the river, the top U.S. diplomat in Brazzaville concluded that Lumumba still firmly controlled Leopoldville. "Kasavubu's coup has failed," he reported bluntly to Washington.

Like Devlin, Cordier desperately sought to compensate for Kasa-vubu's inaction. Shortly after noon, he ordered UN troops to take over the radio station and sent a UN technician to remove a key piece of equipment, the crystal oscillator, rendering it mute. Recalling Hammarskjöld's "irresponsible observation" that it might be better to keep New York out of the loop and risk being disowned, Cordier did not consult the secretary-general.

The shutdown favored the president at the expense of the prime minister. Pro-Kasavubu propaganda remained on the airwaves, now broadcast from an allied radio station over in Brazzaville, while Lumumba was cut off from the masses. "The man whose magic touch with audiences had been his greatest asset was suddenly deprived of an outlet for his oratory," noted *The New York Times*. Lumumba tried in vain to regain that outlet, returning to the station with a bevy of aides and a truckload of soldiers, only to be blocked by UN guards.

The grounding of all airplanes likewise hurt Lumumba more; Kasavubu's supporters were concentrated in and around Leo-poldville, whereas his were not, and now they could not fly into the capital. Moreover, the ban was unequally enforced: in Katanga, where Tshombe had just announced his support for Kasavubu, Bel-gian planes managed to take off freely from the Elisabethville airport.

Lumumba, predictably, was irate that the UN was putting its thumb on the scale. He had Mobutu visit the Royal to convey his displeasure. (The besieged army chief of staff was "in a rather distraught state," Cordier noted.) When Lumumba tried to arrange a meeting, Cordier refused to see him.

"We have not chosen sides," Cordier cabled to Hammarskjöld, but the fiction of neutrality was becoming hard to maintain. In effect, Hammarskjöld was trying to get rid of Lumumba without being seen to do so and thus harming the UN's reputation or his own. It was all about "gamesmanship," he confided to an American diplomat: "how to win without actually cheating."

The radio shutdown, however, struck Hammarskjöld as excessive. He wrote privately that the move was "basically regrettable" and made a point of noting that Cordier had never consulted him about it. He was relieved when Cordier's replacement, Rajeshwar Dayal, was ready to take over. Cordier slipped across the river into Brazzaville and flew back to New York.

"During the few days that he was in the Congo at the head of the UN, Cordier could be described as having been in effect the Congolese head of state," Thomas Kanza wrote. It was not a position Cordier enjoyed having on his résumé, and soon, as Hammarskjöld assigned more and more of his duties to others, Cordier felt that his actions in Leopoldville had cost him the secretary-general's confidence. More than a decade later, dying of cirrhosis, he would read and reread surviving copies of the cables that Hammarskjöld had sent him in Leopoldville, wondering if he had made the right call.

When Kasavubu finally awoke, his halfhearted attempt to depose Lumumba was falling apart before his eyes. He made a last-ditch effort to formalize the dismissal, and he managed to get two disloyal members of the government to cosign his order, adding a veneer of constitutionality. He also had an arrest warrant for Lumumba drawn up that cited his "violent public speeches."

But it was too little, too late. Lumumba's designated successor, Joseph Iléo, was lying low, nowhere to be found. ("A phantom," Hammarskjöld quipped.) Lumumba's followers detained and handcuffed Albert Delvaux, one of the ministers who had signed the dismissal order; the other, Justin Bomboko, sought refuge in the U.S. embassy. The plan to arrest Lumumba also went nowhere. The closest anyone came was when a group of soldiers forcibly brought him to Camp

Leopold, where other troops promptly freed him again. As Kasavubu cloistered himself in his residence, Lumumba rode around town in a car fitted with a loudspeaker. "Fear not, your prime minister is free!"

Lumumba also made his case to parliament. Armed, as always, with documents to brandish and detailed recollections to recite, he spoke to the Chamber of Representatives for two hours, defending himself against charges that he was pro-Soviet and attacking his detractors as imperialist stooges. "We must follow neither American policy nor Russian," he declared, but "remain in our rightful place: the middle." No doubt concealing his true feelings, he extended an olive branch to the man who had fired him. "In all frankness, I personally admire Mr. Kasavubu a great deal," he told the chamber. "He has always been my close friend; at no time whatsoever has there been the slightest quarrel between us, either before or after independence." He ended with a call for unity. "We are all part of the same country."

It was an act of "rhetorical wizardry," British diplomats reported, a master class in the art of political persuasion. "To watch Premier Lumumba perform in Parliament, in a press conference, or a public meeting is a fascinating and also frightening experience," wrote *The New York Times*'s correspondent in the Congo. "Here is a man who combines the skills of the late Senator McCarthy and the brashness of a ward-heeler with the mystic touch of the African witch doctor." And what a touch it was: after Lumumba's speech, legislators voted 60–19 to restore the status quo ante, nullifying the two leaders' mutual dismissals. Lumumba had even more success in the Senate, where all but two members voted against Kasavubu's dismissal of Lumumba. The clear-cut outcome came as a surprise to Devlin and most other observers. Even Timberlake could not deny that Lumumba had "devastated" his opponents' points and "made Kasavubu look ridiculous."

Lumumba also benefited from a more sympathetic leader of the UN operation in the person of Cordier's successor, the Indian diplomat Rajeshwar Dayal. An avid equestrian with an Oxford degree, a matching English accent, and a taste for pocket squares, Dayal was a coolheaded diplomat respected for his extreme patience. After India's independence, he had represented his country in Moscow, Belgrade, Karachi, and New York, and he had last been lent to the UN for a mission in Lebanon. Although Hammarskjöld had no doubts about the new envoy's loyalty to the UN, Dayal in some ways embodied his own country's nonaligned stance in the Cold War and was less susceptible to hysteria about Communist penetration of the Congo than his American predecessors had been. Having begun his career as a magistrate under the British Raj, he also stuck to the letter of the law. He considered Kasavubu's dismissal of Lumumba unconstitutional, arguing that in acting without legislative approval, the president had chosen to "substitute the broadcasting station for parliament."

When Dayal and Lumumba met, even as the two tangled over specifics, they quickly developed a rapport. By now, it was no secret that Kasavubu had acted with at least the tacit approval of UN officials in Leopoldville. Disturbed by this apparent anti-Lumumba bias, African leaders pressed the UN to reopen the airports and the radio station. A day after his first meeting with Lumumba, Dayal yielded to the pressure and lifted the bans, allowing civilian flights in the Congo to resume and freeing Lumumba to retake the airwaves. (In an amateurish oversight, a member of Lumumba's team briefly misplaced the key to the station, delaying the transmission of a taped speech.) Parliament held yet another meeting about the crisis, and again Lumumba emerged victorious, with a joint session of both houses voting to grant him "full powers," 88–1. After being carried triumphantly from the Palace of the Nation on the shoulders of his supporters, a grinning Lumumba returned to his house and hugged his wife, Pauline Opango, now visibly pregnant.

One week had now passed since Kasavubu's announcement, and even the president's Belgian supporters grumbled that their man had lost the initiative. Word circulated that a compromise was in the offing, whereby Lumumba would remain prime minister but reshuffle his cabinet to include more moderates. "Lumumba in opposition is almost as dangerous as in office," Larry Devlin concluded. And many had underestimated the prime minister. "Lumumba's talents and dynamism appear to be the overriding factor in reestablishing his position each time it seems half lost," wrote Bronson Tweedy, Devlin's boss in Washington. Kasavubu, by contrast, had moved with "the speed of a snail" and was "acting more like a vegetable every day," another official lamented. The CIA director, Allen Dulles, agreed, telling Eisenhower that no matter the struggle Lumumba always seemed to come out on top. It was "not easy to run a coup in the Congo," he added.

On September 8, the White House Special Group sat down for its weekly Thursday meeting. In characteristically euphemistic tones, Gordon Gray, Eisenhower's national security adviser, expressed his hope that CIA officers in the Congo understood "the top-level feeling in Washington that vigorous action would not be amiss." It was yet another prod to have Devlin do something about Lumumba.

The U.S. government recognized that the key to breaking through the current impasse was the army. Soldiers held the real power in the Congo—the ability to protect or not protect a politician, to invade or not invade a province, to calm the streets or raise hell. "Power at this point was a highly relative concept; a little could go a long way," one observer wrote. "The ability to move a few armed men about Leopoldville was of decisive importance."

That meant there was one man the CIA had to win over.

Chapter 33

Hamlet of the Congo

T wo days after Kasavubu's radio announcement, Larry Devlin drove to the president's house, easing the way through army roadblocks with cigarettes. As he waited in a small anteroom, he thought about what he would tell Kasavubu. But when the door opened, he saw not the president's familiar, rotund figure but a young, rail-thin man in full military dress.

Devlin knew Joseph Mobutu only dimly. He had met him just twice before—once in Brussels during the roundtable conference, and a second time in the streets a few weeks earlier, briefly, when Mobutu was sorting out a misunderstanding with the army. But now they were suddenly discussing the most sensitive matters of Congolese politics. To Dayal, Mobutu had come off as genuinely torn between Lumumba and Kasavubu. But as Devlin now learned, the colonel was perfectly willing to turn against his onetime patron. Mobutu had recalled the ANC's top commanders to Leopoldville, as well as a company of troops whose loyalty was certain. But arresting Lumumba was too risky. Instead, he explained, he would arrange his murder through mob violence. Somehow, Lumumba would be enticed to show up at a massive street rally of his opponents, and police and troops would arrive too late to prevent his lynching. Devlin told Mobutu he thought the plot impractical, since UN troops would surely intervene. He decided to offer his support anyway. This was a man with long-term potential, he thought.

Mobutu also proposed a more traditional method for eliminating Lumumba: a military coup. The colonel explained that he wanted to eliminate the country's elected government and replace it with a panel of handpicked technocrats, with him supervising from behind the scenes. But before taking action, he wanted the United States' blessing.

Devlin said that as a thirty-eight-year-old officer, he had no authority to set U.S. policy. But Mobutu said he could not afford to wait.

Devlin paused. Then, he extended his hand. "I guarantee you American support," he said.

"The coup will take place within a week," Mobutu replied curtly, before asking for $5,000 to secure the support of fellow officers. Devlin delivered a briefcase stuffed with cash the next day.

In the week following their first meeting, the conviction Mobutu had shown Devlin dissipated, or perhaps Devlin had been wrong to detect it. In frequent meetings at the Royal, the army chief of staff unburdened himself to Dayal over generous pours of whiskey. He said he owed his career to Lumumba, and he wished the prime minister and the president could reconcile. UN officials found the colonel nervous, hesitant, weak. "Mobutu has no influence," Hammarskjöld concluded. So terrified for his life was Mobutu that he now moved around only with a UN guard. Dressed in khaki shirts and shorts, he looked like a "frightened boy," one witness recorded, and at times it almost seemed as if tears could be detected behind the tinted glasses he never removed. Everyone at the Royal felt sorry for a man who, in Dayal's estimation, "was so troubled by his unfamiliar and onerous responsibilities and overwhelmed by the problems of his country."

Indeed, the pressure was getting to Mobutu. "I can't go on like this," he confessed to a journalist. One day, Mobutu turned up at the Royal in civilian clothes and announced that he was going to resign. Lumumba, unaware of Mobutu's designs against him, had begged him to stay, but he had refused. He would retire from the military and from politics and return to his home in Équateur. Dayal knew nothing about the coup plan and saw Mobutu as a force of stability. Over the course of their meeting, he appealed to Mobutu's patriotism and persuaded him to stay on, although for how long was left unsaid.

Mobutu kept on wavering. Kasavubu had ordered him to arrest Lumumba, and he briefly did. Lumumba was marched out of his house at gunpoint, hands raised in the air, and driven to Camp Leopold. But there, he reminded Mobutu of their once-strong friendship, and the colonel relented and set him free. Mobutu could not make up his mind. He was "the Hamlet of the Congo," one journalist wrote.

The choice before him was not obvious. On the one side was Lumumba: dynamic, popular, and authentic, but also erratic and uncompromising, a lost cause to foreign diplomats and the UN. On the other was Kasavubu: sluggish, parochial, and detached, but at least predictable, tractable, and supported by the West. "Mobutu's heart was swinging between the two," Thomas Kanza wrote. "But his heart could not go on swinging indefinitely, for the Americans had no time to lose."

Chapter 34

This Is Not a Military Coup

T HIS IS NOT a military coup," came the voice through the radio, interrupting a broadcast of the "Indépendance Cha-Cha." "It is, rather, a simple peaceful revolution. No soldier is going to take power."

"That's me!" Mobutu said, pointing excitedly at the small receiver. It was 8:30 p.m. on September 14, and the young colonel was once more sipping whiskey at the Royal, this time in the bedroom of two UN staffers. His message had been recorded a short while earlier and broadcast by the reopened radio station. In it, he filled in details of the plan he had sketched for Devlin: to get the Congo out of its current impasse, the army had "neutralized" not just Lumumba but Kasavubu, too—as if Mobutu were a stern parent collectively punishing two children who were unwilling to share. Mobutu explained that he was now commander in chief and that a group of apolitical experts, Congolese and foreign, would rule until the end of the year, giving the politicians enough time to sort out their differences. After this short transition period, the army would return power to a democratic government. "Long live the Congo!" Mobutu concluded his speech. "Long live the Congolese National Army!" Most listeners had no idea who the man they had just heard speaking was.

Alarmed by the presence of a coup plotter in the UN mission's headquarters, and no doubt wishing to avoid yet another round of recriminations about their organization's involvement in an illegal change in government, the two UN aides escorted a disappointed Mobutu out of the Royal.

He turned up later that night on the sidewalk bar of the Regina, a dated three-star hotel at the other end of the Boulevard Albert. Ringed by soldiers, he addressed reporters from atop a beer-stained table. "The army's task is to save the country from chaos," he shouted awkwardly into the microphones shoved his way.

Though shielded by his trademark shades, Mobutu was sweating under the lights of the cameramen. Waving a pamphlet of Communist propaganda in his hands—a collection of Khrushchev's recent speeches titled *Hands Off the Congo!*—he declared that the Soviet and Czech embassies had forty-eight hours to shut down. He announced a cease-fire with Katangan separatists and called on Congolese students in Europe to return home to manage the country. But other than that, the new leader had precious little to say about his expert-led interim regime.

"What will its foreign policy be until January 1?" one reporter asked.

"Everything will depend on the university students in power," he replied. "It will be a college."

"And the UN?"

"The government has called on the UN to help the army," he said.

"How many are there in your college?"

"This is none of my business."

The press might have found the Congo's new leader awfully vague, but that did not bother the hotel's Belgian guests. "Bravo Mobutu!" they cried, raising their glasses. Larry Devlin, watching quietly from the crowd, was pleased to see his new contact seize power. "I see you pulled a coup," a U.S. embassy staffer who knew nothing of the CIA's involvement joked to Devlin.

"What can we do?" Devlin replied innocently.

Mobutu drove off in the official limousine he had swapped for his military jeep. And just like that, sub-Saharan Africa's very first military coup d'état had become a reality.

Lumumba's first reaction was a statement claiming that Mobutu had been "corrupted by the imperialists to stage a coup." Then he confronted him at Camp Leopold. Mobutu was taken aback. For his own safety, Lumumba had spent the night at a friend's house, and he had not had time to change into fresh clothes. He wore wrinkled pants and a casual shirt. His hair was disheveled.

"What are you doing here?" Mobutu asked.

"I want to speak to the soldiers," Lumumba said.

"Out of the question," Mobutu said. "First, I neutralized you and, second, a minister doesn't address the troops in a Lacoste polo."

"Watch your tone," Lumumba replied. "I am your prime minister."

"No," Mobutu said, "you are not."

Lumumba turned and headed to the officers' mess hall. If he wasn't allowed to speak to the rank and file, perhaps he might win over their superiors. But before he could do so, he was mobbed by a hundred-odd angry soldiers. Most were Baluba, members of the Luba ethnic group whose kin Lumumba's troops had massacred in South Kasai two weeks earlier. Some spat at him; others struck him.

Lumumba took refuge upstairs in the laundry room, protected by a contingent of Ghanaian UN troops and by Mobutu, who now seemed to only want him neutralized, not dead. Outside, the ring of Congolese soldiers was thickening, heavily armed and threatening to cut off Lumumba's hands, feet, and testicles. It was growing dark now, and the soldiers lit torches as they dug trenches and set up mortars around the building. Inside, no one knew how much longer the mob could be fended off.

Upon hearing the news and realizing that Lumumba's life was in danger, Rajeshwar Dayal rushed to the site of the standoff. The laundry room was a sad sight. Lumumba, in shirtsleeves, sat in a chair in a corner while a deranged soldier shouted in front of him, stamping his feet. Dayal had the soldier dragged away, and Lumumba stood up in thanks, clasping the diplomat's hand in both of his. With Dayal's help, he slipped out the back door and sped away in a UN jeep. The siege had lasted seven hours. Lumumba was unharmed aside from a torn shirt. But the episode revealed that whatever control he once exerted over the ANC in Leopoldville had vanished.

Mobutu was once asked in an interview why he took power. "What power?" he retorted. "There no longer was any."

It was true. The central government's writ barely extended across Leopoldville, let alone the rest of the country. The treasury was empty. The administrative offices were nearly vacant. Mobutu's own control over the troops, albeit far greater than Lumumba's, remained tenuous. The men's allegiances were based largely on ethnic group, political affinity, and cash. Their discipline, questionable to begin with, had further eroded when their rebellion in the days after independence earned them not punishment but promotions. No one was in charge of anything.

Rather than merely taking power, Mobutu had to build it. He got to work showing that he, unlike those bickering politicians, could take decisive action. In keeping with his announcement at the Regina, he expelled diplomats from the Communist bloc. The ten Soviet Il-14s in Stanleyville scrambled back to Moscow, their new paint job not yet dry. Two Soviet cargo ships just days away from Matadi stilled their engines as they waited for instructions. Left-wing advisers to the prime minister, including Serge Michel and Andrée Blouin, were ordered to leave the Congo. (The CIA took credit for the latter's expulsion, with Allen Dulles claiming at a White House meeting that his agency "had succeeded...in neutralizing Mme. Blouin.") In downtown Leopoldville, plumes of smoke billowed from the chimney of the Soviet embassy as its staff frantically burned documents. Mikhail Yakovlev, the ambassador, glumly watched the hammer and sickle slide down the embassy's flagpole.

For the United States, the sight of Soviet and Czech personnel retreating from the Congo marked a clear win at a moment of seeming Communist advances around the world. "This new and troubled African country has given the boot to the bloc," an exuberant Timberlake wrote. "Local clerks who worked for Lumumbavitch are being methodically arrested," he added, Russifying the prime minister's name. In Mobutu, the ambassador assured Washington, the United States had finally found a "completely honest" and "dedicated" Congolese leader. White House officials could hardly believe their luck. Dulles declared that "aside from Lumumba, Mobutu appears to be the only man in the Congo able to act with firmness."

In another decisive move, Mobutu swiftly put an end to the ANC's attempted invasion of Katanga and Kasai and flew the soldiers on the front back to their bases. He also filled in the details about the mysterious team of experts that would be replacing the elected politicians. "The College of Commissioners" consisted of thirty-three university students and graduates, most in their twenties. The CIA advised Mobutu on its composition, and its nominal head was Justin Bomboko, who still held the foreign affairs portfolio and was the only of Lumumba's ministers to join the group. But ultimately, the military was in charge. Mobutu's soldiers swarmed parliament and expelled all the legislators. They also cleared out the remaining ministers and staff from their offices and escorted the commissioners in. The old government was no more.

On one key issue, however, Mobutu was proving to be a man of inaction: Lumumba. Rather than arresting and silencing the ex-premier, Mobutu was content to assert that he had neutralized both him and Kasavubu. Having detained and promptly released Lumumba, he seemed reluctant to take further action. This indecision offered hope—and soon set off rumors—that Lumumba and Kasavubu might unite to reverse the coup, since neither seemed to have anything to gain from a Mobutu-run regime.

The possibility that Lumumba might return to power was too much for the United States to countenance. At one National Security Council meeting, Dulles declared that Lumumba's "actions indicate that he is insane"; at another, he said that Lumumba "remained a grave danger as long as he was not disposed of." President Eisenhower, for his part, told the British foreign secretary that he wished "Lumumba would fall into a river full of crocodiles." Devlin might have put it the same way. If Lumumba were allowed even a minor role in government, Devlin feared, he would inevitably "come out on top." Thus, he concluded, "the only solution is to remove him from the scene soonest." But that would require getting through to Mobutu.

Mobutu, his wife, Marie-Antoinette, and their three children were now living on the grounds of Camp Leopold, where they occupied a dingy split-level ranch with yellow plaster walls, rubber plants, and banged-up furniture. Now that he was the most important man in the Congo, politicians, diplomats, and spies lined up at his door. His office was a madhouse, with officials of all stripes conducting business while children and dogs wandered about.

On September 18, four days after the coup, an old friend of

Mobutu's showed up at the house and drew a revolver from his pocket. In an instant, Mobutu leaped forward and threw himself on him. The two men grappled with each other until Mobutu pried the gun from the would-be assassin's hand. Word had it that he had been sent by Lumumba's followers. The next day, someone fired a bullet into Mobutu's house, cracking a window. Afterward, Devlin met with Mobutu and alerted him to even more plots against him. Paired with this warning was a recommendation: the "arrest or other more permanent disposal of Lumumba." What Mobutu thought of this idea wasn't clear. Devlin found him oddly unresponsive, as if in a trance.

Even so, Mobutu made it clear he wanted something, too: he needed money to pay his troops and officers. Devlin readily provided the requested cash, as did the Belgian government, which paid Mobutu some $400,000 through a back channel. Soon, UN military officers in Mobutu's orbit could not help but notice the bulging briefcases filled with thick brown envelopes. The colonel suddenly stopped asking the UN for money to pay the troops. When asked, he claimed new funds were coming "from company sources." Dayal protested to Timberlake, but the U.S. ambassador feigned ignorance.

Mobutu finally summoned the energy to follow through on Devlin's advice and tried once more to have Lumumba arrested. The former prime minister, his pregnant wife, and his four children had been in hiding, moving from place to place—the house of his Italian doctor, the Ghanaian and Guinean embassies, the Regina Hotel—before returning to the prime ministerial residence under the protection of a platoon of Ghanaian UN troops. On September 20, Mobutu sent a group of twenty ANC soldiers, but finding the house heavily guarded, his men drove off in frustration.

After this second halfhearted attempt, Mobutu again wobbled. Devlin was not the only one whispering in his ear, and the cacophony of competing advice from Congolese politicians, UN officials, and Western diplomats proved paralyzing. "I have no time to eat or sleep, and everyone calls on me—soldiers, politicians, journalists," Mobutu complained to a reporter. Asked whether he would draw up an arrest warrant for Lumumba, the colonel grew testy. "You ask if I am going to arrest Lumumba!" he said, throwing up his hands. "Why do you continue to ask? Why does everyone ask me everything? You will see what will happen when it happens."

Dayal worried that Mobutu was succumbing to American flattery and developing "illusions of grandeur," but the Americans felt that whatever flattery they were laying on wasn't working. To Devlin's disappointment, it seemed that Mobutu had once again dropped the idea of arresting Lumumba—at least in part at the urging of Dayal.

Lumumba, for his part, was pinning his hopes on a reconciliation with Kasavubu. Since they were both victims of Mobutu's coup, perhaps they could mend their rift and join forces against him. A group of parliamentarians, working with African diplomats, drew up a proposal by which the two would be restored to their pre-coup positions and govern cooperatively. Both men expressed their interest, and Lumumba announced that they had signed a "joint declaration that puts an end to the Congo crisis." He proudly displayed the document to photographers.

Remarkably, Mobutu revealed that he was not opposed to such a deal, even though it would end his brush with power. On September 22, he showed up tired and stubbly to see Dayal and proposed a similar plan of his own, under which Lumumba and Kasavubu would come together under UN auspices and hold a new roundtable conference to decide the future of the Congo. He also met directly with both men, leading Lumumba to tell the press that negotiations were on the "right track." It was as if Mobutu wanted to undo his coup altogether, to wake up from a brief dream in which he had ruled the Congo.

Lumumba had stubbornly refused to fade from the picture and now seemed poised for a comeback. After a week spent shacked up inside his home, he began venturing outside again. He cruised through the *cité* in his black limousine, still flanked by his Ghanaian escort, but with his confidence restored. Afterward, he chatted with journalists, debuting a new tone: He now said he wanted the UN to stay in the Congo and supported a rapprochement with Moise Tshombe. Whether the expelled Soviet diplomats could return was a question for parliament. The same went for the issue of federalism. On the biggest questions facing the Congo, Lumumba suggested that he was open to compromise and ready for a do-over. On September 25, *The New York Times,* citing "high-ranking African diplomats," made a bold prediction: "Patrice Lumumba will make a spectacular comeback within two or three days."

Chapter 35

Spitting on the UN

Hammarskjöld was a reader. (In that, if nothing else, he had something in common with Lumumba.) In the corridors of the UN building, even late at night with the Congo Club, the secretary-general routinely turned the conversation to the arts and letters, not always to the delight of his colleagues, who would much rather listen to him gossip about Jackie Kennedy than endure a lecture on contemporary poetry. For Hammarskjöld, however, the melding was essential, and he made it a priority. Before the Congo crisis, he had been able to set aside two or three hours a day for what he called "serious matters"—namely, literary translation.

As he explained to a French journalist, "I don't believe that the taste for literature can be reduced to what Americans call a 'hobby,' that is to say, to entertainment and relaxation, to a pastime." He elaborated: "It is an important complement and, for a diplomat, an indispensable one." Poetry and diplomacy both required a keen sense of the *mot juste*. More practically, he needed something to pass the time during Security Council sessions while he waited for delegates' remarks to be translated from languages he already knew.

Although the Congo crisis had reduced his time for such work, he had still managed to translate the work of his friend Saint-John Perse, a French poet and ex-diplomat. He had produced a Swedish version of Perse's *Chronique,* a long, dense meditation on man and earth, and as Hammarskjöld prepared for the UN General Assembly's annual meeting in September, he wrote a letter to his friend:

You must have wondered about my life during these troubled times, when I had to be a protagonist for reason and decency in a world disrupted by the revolution of those Africans who up to now have been suppressed and prevented from developing normally and who now will demand everything. I don't have to tell you how many times I would have liked to think aloud with a friend like you, whose experiences are as rich in the political and diplomatic fields as in the purely human field, which in this case is the most important.... Your poem has expressed with a divinatory clarity my profound reactions as one of the actors in the great ongoing crisis.

Chief among "those Africans" who in Hammarskjöld's mind liked to "demand everything" was, of course, Lumumba. Although the secretary-general retained his enmity for the man, he recognized that he had perhaps shown it too openly. Increasingly, Hammarskjöld was chastened.

In certain New York consulates, the UN's slow progress on Katanga had raised eyebrows. Its closure of the Congo's airports and the Leopoldville radio station after Kasavubu's power grab had already stirred considerable controversy, and Mobutu's subsequent coup made its management of the crisis look either incompetent or malevolent. African and Asian nations, many of which were contributing troops to the peacekeeping operation and some of which were threatening to pull them at any moment, demanded a new approach—one that would see the UN drop its bias against Lumumba and pledge never to work with Mobutu's illegal government. "The key melody here was pro-Lumumba," Hammarskjöld told Dayal after a stormy Security Council meeting.

To settle the debate, diplomats held an emergency meeting of the General Assembly on September 17, just before the long-scheduled annual session was to begin. Representatives from more than eighty countries padded across the green carpets of the cavernous hall to take their seats. Divisions ran deep, and along familiar fault lines: the U.S. ambassador, James Wadsworth, sought to defend Hammarskjöld's record in the Congo, and declared with a straight face that his government had "not taken one single step in the Congo independent of the United Nations." (As a deputy recently promoted to fill his superior's position, he certainly did not know about the advice and money the CIA was lavishing on Mobutu.) To the Soviet ambassador, Valerian Zorin, UN officials' behind-the-scenes maneuvering against Lumumba had once more showed them to be neo-imperialist puppets. "Their pretense of 'neutrality' has disappeared, and the unseemly nature of their actions has been fully revealed," Zorin fumed.

It was unfair to call Hammarskjöld the lapdog of imperialists. He believed passionately in equality and self-determination. His private correspondence on the Congo was rife with frustration with the Belgians' colonialist attitudes. Yet at heart, he was an opponent of Communism and a man of the West, and his unforgiving judgment of Lumumba put him at odds with most of the new African member states. Although he retained their support—they had no alternative—he was on thinner ice with them now. At the end of the emergency session, delegates unanimously endorsed a "conciliation" between the Congo's two rival leaders.

Khrushchev was en route to New York on a Soviet ocean liner, the *Baltika,* having chosen to travel by ship instead of plane to avoid the humiliation of refueling midway, since no Soviet aircraft available could make the trip from Moscow nonstop. In between games of shuffleboard, the Soviet leader followed with concern events in the Congo. "I spit on the UN," he said after hearing the latest piece of bad news from the country, which he felt was slipping through his hands thanks to Hammarskjöld's interference. "That good-for-nothing Ham is sticking his nose in important affairs which are none of his business."

After docking in New York, Khrushchev laid into the secretary-general from the rostrum of the General Assembly. "Mr. Hammarskjöld used the armed forces of the United Nations not to support the legitimate Parliament and Government of the Congo, at whose request the troops had been sent," he said, "but to support the colonialists who were, as they still are, fighting...to fasten a new yoke upon the Congo." Hammarskjöld should resign, Khrushchev said, and his post should be abolished and replaced with a three-man committee representing the Western, Eastern, and nonaligned blocs. If implemented, the proposal would paralyze the organization, ending the UN as everyone knew it.

Hammarskjöld, not usually known for fiery oratory, was so incensed that he delivered what was perhaps the most impassioned riposte in his career:

> It is not the Soviet Union or indeed any other big powers who need the United Nations for their protection. It is all the others. In this sense, the organization is first of all *their* organization, and I deeply believe in the wisdom with which they will be able to use it and guide it. I shall remain in my post during the term of office as a servant of the organization, in the interest of all those other nations as long as they wish me to do so.
>
> In this context, the representative of the Soviet Union spoke of courage. It is very easy to resign. It is not so easy to stay on. It is very easy to bow to the wish of a big power. It is another matter to resist. As is well known to all members of this assembly, I have done so before on many occasions and in many directions. If it is the wish of those nations who see in the organization their best protection in the present world, I shall do so again.

Most of the room rewarded him with a standing ovation; Khrushchev and his allies hammered their desks with their fists in protest. (The much-mythologized shoe-banging incident would occur the following week.) Hammarskjöld passed a note to Ralph Bunche, rested from his exhausting two months in the Congo and recently returned from his college tours with his son. "Did I read it all right?" Hammarskjöld asked. "Perfectly," Bunche scrawled back. "The greatest and most spontaneous demonstration in UN annals."

Eisenhower agreed. In his own speech at the General Assembly, the U.S. president praised the "outstanding secretary-general" and urged countries not to sow further disorder in the Congo by sending in troops or arms, "or by inciting its leaders and peoples to violence against each other."

It was a curious statement, for at that very moment, the U.S. government was planning a murder in Leopoldville.

Chapter 36

Sid from Paris

THE TWO SPIES found each other easily. Devlin had just received a phone call in his embassy office from a man with a Bronx-accented voice who announced himself as "Sid from Paris." They arranged to meet in front of the Stanley Hotel, the six-story building where the UN had set up shop before moving to the Royal. They agreed on a time, but in a minor deception in case the line was being tapped, both knew to show up an hour earlier.

News of the mysterious visitor had first landed on Devlin's desk a week before, on September 19. The cable bore a special designation—"YQPROP"—indicating that its dissemination was to be highly restricted. In Leopoldville, only Devlin and the code room operator ever saw it. The message from headquarters explained that at the hotel, Devlin should look for a man carrying in his left hand a copy of *Paris Match*, a photography-heavy French weekly.

There he was, in front of the Stanley. The man had traveled to the Congo under an alias, Sidney Braun, but he turned out to be a familiar face: Sidney Gottlieb, a trim forty-two-year-old scientist with piercing blue eyes and a stutter. He was well known within the agency for his intellect and ability to translate complicated technical concepts to the lay officers in the field—and for his familiarity with poison and biological weapons.

Devlin and Gottlieb ducked into a car and drove to the station chief's new apartment in a high-rise on the Boulevard Albert. Looking out over Leopoldville, they caught up on agency gossip—who was up, who was down—before getting down to business. Devlin was to undertake an assassination. The intended target went without saying. The order had come from Eisenhower.

Devlin squirmed. He looked grim, Gottlieb thought. As the station chief nervously smoked a cigarette, Gottlieb produced a small carry-on bag he had brought with him from the United States. Inside were a gauze surgical mask, a pair of rubber gloves, a syringe, and several glass vials. Devlin's graduate degree was in international relations, not chemistry, and he confessed that he knew nothing about how to handle such materials. Gottlieb carefully explained how it would work: put on the gloves and mask for protection, fill the syringe, and inject the liquid into someone's food, drink, or toothpaste—anything the target would ingest. It would not take long. And unlike with a poison such as cyanide, these substances were biological in nature. If an autopsy was conducted, a pathologist would find nothing to suggest foul play.

Gottlieb handed over the kit, and Devlin stashed it in the bottom drawer of a combination safe in his office. "Eyes only," he scribbled on top.

The next day, Devlin sent a cable through the YQPROP channel reporting that he had met with Gottlieb. "We are on the same wavelength," he wrote.

For Socrates, it was hemlock, the alkaloid-filled herb the Greek philosopher was forced to drink as a death sentence for impiety. For the empress Xu Pingjun of the Han dynasty, it was aconite, a deadly buttercup given to her by a suborned physician. For the Roman emperor Claudius, it was an intoxicating compound infused into mushrooms that were served to him by his eunuch waiter. For Dmitry Shemyaka, the Grand Duke of Moscow, it was arsenic with which a rival had adulterated his chicken dinner. As long as powerful people have walked the earth, their enemies have had occasion to kill them with poison.

The CIA's poisoning plots were the logical extension of the covert action programs it had been developing since its postwar founding. With American power at a new high, the temptation to quietly tip events in foreign countries to the United States' advantage—sometimes by helping overthrow democratically elected leaders it deemed bothersome—proved irresistible. Eisenhower had already presided over two such plots. In 1953 in Iran, the CIA launched Operation Ajax, bribing politicians, military officers, and street gangs in service of a coup that removed the country's prime minister, Mohammad Mosaddegh. During Operation Success the following year, the agency armed Guatemalan rebels and bombed the country's capital to remove the president, Jacobo Árbenz. In both cases, the ousted leader survived: Mosaddegh was imprisoned and Árbenz exiled.

Assassination offered the alluring possibility of removing enemy leaders permanently, and in one stroke. Over the course of the 1950s, the CIA considered sabotaging Stalin's limousine, blowing up the Chinese premier Zhou Enlai's plane, and passing a deadly infection to the Indonesian president, Sukarno, via an airline stewardess, but it never brought any of these plots to fruition. Only in the final year of Eisenhower's presidency, as the promise of détente with the Soviet Union faded, did the CIA get into the assassination game in earnest.

The agency's initial focus was on Fidel Castro, and in the first half of 1960 schemes to drug the Cuban leader escalated into plans to outright kill him. In May, Eisenhower had told State Department officials that he would like to see Castro "sawed off." Two months later, an opportunity to strike Castro's inner circle arose when a Cuban pilot and CIA asset informed his agency handler that he was scheduled to fly Raúl Castro—Fidel's brother and Cuba's defense minister—from Prague to Havana. When the pilot suggested arranging an "accident" that would kill Raúl, CIA headquarters green-lighted the proposal, granting the pilot's request that the U.S. government pay for his sons' college education should he die during the operation. As it happened, the pilot lost his nerve, and Raúl Castro returned to Cuba unharmed. But the episode marked a first: never before had the CIA authorized the assassination of a high-ranking foreign official.

Increasingly, the CIA was developing its own capacities for what it called "executive action." Its efforts quickly homed in on poisoning as the method of choice. A small vial was much easier to smuggle behind enemy lines than a gun or a bomb. The relative inconspicuousness of the act and the usual delay between ingestion and death enhanced plausible deniability and offered the perpetrator a better chance of avoiding identification and slipping away. In fact, if everything went as planned, the world might never know that the victim had been assassinated, since with many poisons the deceased would appear to have died of natural causes. This was the ne plus ultra of assassination: leave-no-trace killing.

As the CIA's master chemist, Sidney Gottlieb had been a key architect of this strategy. Among the Waspy Ivy League–educated World War II veterans who dominated the CIA in its early days, Gottlieb—the son of Orthodox Hungarian Jews and a University of Wisconsin and Caltech graduate—stood apart. Eager to serve his country but disqualified from military service because of a limp, he joined the CIA's Technical Services Staff, whose members worked on the agency's hidden cameras, listening devices, hollow coins, and other spy gadgets. Gottlieb's interest, however, lay in medicine, chemistry, and biology—in learning how to enhance, or lay waste to, the human mind and body. For a decade, he ran MKULTRA, the CIA's human experiments in mind control for use in interrogation. Gottlieb and his men gave LSD to unwitting subjects—prisoners, college students, drug addicts, johns, and psychiatric patients, many of them Black. At an addiction treatment center in Lexington, Kentucky, seven human guinea pigs were kept on LSD for seventy-seven days straight. Gottlieb even ran his LSD tests on colleagues, once spiking the triple sec of an army scientist named Frank Olson; nine days later, Olson died after falling from the tenth floor of a New York City hotel.

Gottlieb's pharmacological expertise and ethical flexibility made him the obvious man to turn to for killing Lumumba by covert means. Earlier in 1960, he had provided the poisons for at least two brewing plots, one to "incapacitate" an Iraqi colonel with a poison-soaked handkerchief (a plot overseen by a group of officers bearing the macabre moniker of the "Health Alteration Committee"), the other to lace Castro's beloved cigars with a lethal dose of botulinum toxin, a potent paralyzing agent. Neither scheme went anywhere.

As Gottlieb had told Devlin, his involvement in the Lumumba plot was the result of Eisenhower's assassination order, by way of several intermediaries. Not long after the August 25 Special Group meeting—in which National Security Adviser Gordon Gray reminded Allen Dulles of the president's interest in "very straightforward action" in the Congo—Dulles relayed the instruction to his right-hand man and deputy, Richard Bissell. Bissell, in turn, approached Gottlieb and asked him to prepare a substance for assassinating an unnamed African leader, although newspaper headlines that summer left little doubt about who that might be.

Gottlieb turned to the U.S. Army Chemical Corps at Fort Detrick, Maryland, about an hour's drive from CIA headquarters. The Chemical Corps ran the country's biological weapons program and had a number of lethal agents on hand. He scanned a list of biological materials that would, in his words, "either kill the individual or incapacitate him so severely that he would be out of action." He was looking for something that would make it appear as if Lumumba had died of a disease endemic to sub-Saharan Africa.

Bacteria seemed a promising option. Tularemia, also known as rabbit fever, would produce fever, chills, skin lesions, and vomiting. Brucellosis, or undulant fever, usually spread through unpasteurized milk, would cause many of the same symptoms. Both might prove fatal if left untreated. Tuberculosis, the scourge of the urban poor, would eat away at Lumumba's lungs and make it impossible to breathe. So would anthrax, which, if inhaled, would cause his chest cavity to fill with liquid and probably kill him within days. Gottlieb also considered viruses. The Venezuelan equine encephalitis virus would inflame Lumumba's brain, bringing about seizures and partial paralysis, and eventually put him in a coma. Smallpox would cover him with lesions, overwhelm his immune system, and kill him within two weeks.

And then there was botulinum toxin, the bacterial protein, better known by the disease it caused—botulism. In crystallized form, just one gram was enough to kill more than a million people, making it one of the most potent toxins known to man. It infiltrated a victim's nerve cells and interrupted the release of neurotransmitters, causing paralysis. In a matter of days, it might reach the nerves that controlled the lungs or heart, killing its target through respiratory failure or cardiac arrest. There was no antidote. Botulinum toxin had been applied to the box of cigars destined for Castro, and Gottlieb decided it was the right pick for Lumumba, too.

Chapter 37

Homebound

L UMUMBA'S ANTICIPATED COMEBACK had yet to materialize. The former prime minister's deal with Kasavubu had caused a stir, as had Mobutu's seeming willingness to consider stepping down and returning power to the two leaders he had sidelined. But the deal fell apart almost as soon as it was announced.

For Devlin, Timberlake, and other U.S. officials, this was not an entirely unexpected outcome. They were now playing a more heavy-handed role in Congolese politics than ever and had likely done their fair share to sabotage the Kasavubu-Lumumba reconciliation. Kasavubu and Lumumba had been prepared to read an agreement on the radio—cars were idling outside both men's houses, ready to drive each leader to the broadcasting station—but then the president received a phone call from a Western diplomat in Leopoldville. The caller's identity and message are lost to history, but within twenty-four hours Kasavubu announced that the deal was off.

A concerted propaganda campaign further dashed hopes for a reconciliation. A series of documents, purportedly taken from Lumumba's briefcase, were released by Mobutu and published in the anti-Lumumba *Courrier d'Afrique*. Mixed in with some genuine letters from Kwame Nkrumah were obvious forgeries. In one, clumsily titled "Measures to Be Applied During the First Stage of the Dictatorship," Lumumba supposedly recommended rounding up critics and "leading all the republic's inhabitants by the tip of their nose like sheep" before signing off, "Long live the Soviet Union, long live

Khrushchev." Another had Lumumba threatening to invite Soviet troops "to brutally drive out the UN from our republic."

In the paranoid atmosphere of Leopoldville, where all too many were prepared to believe the worst about Lumumba, these crude fakes managed to convince UN officials, Western diplomats, and even fellow MNC members. They became fodder for Joe Alsop, the fervently anti-Communist dean of Washington's foreign policy columnists, who told readers that they proved the extent of "the Soviet design to establish a communist base in the rich heart of Africa," where Lumumba was already acting as a "Soviet front man." The documents suggested that Lumumba was more than a nationalist willing to accept Soviet aid out of opportunism; he was a die-hard Communist and a committed ally of Moscow. Dayal, himself initially fooled, consulted UN experts, who determined categorically that at least one of the letters was a forgery. Since the Congolese didn't have the know-how to produce such a document, it was clear to him that "some foreign hand was behind the conspiracy."

That foreign hand was most likely Belgian: Brussels and its diplomats had been working tirelessly to prevent Lumumba from returning to power in any form as part of a plan called Operation Barracuda. One of those Belgian officials, Harold d'Aspremont Lynden, newly promoted from his position in Katanga to minister of African affairs, sent a barrage of orders to Brazzaville, where the Belgian consul general was coordinating his country's campaign against Lumumba. D'Aspremont's cables ranged from an order to freeze Lumumba's bank account in the Congo to his wishing for "Lumumba's definitive elimination."

With a potential deal between Lumumba and Kasavubu averted thanks to American and Belgian interference, U.S. officials now pushed for Kasavubu to strike a bargain with Mobutu instead. In this scheme, Mobutu would retain power, but Kasavubu would endorse the College of Commissioners, thus providing Mobutu's government a fig leaf of legitimacy. After Clare Timberlake met with Kasavubu to lay out the plan, Kasavubu, as if on cue, had a sudden change of heart about Mobutu. He now praised the colonel's coup, which he had condemned only a week prior, and on September 29 he swore in the colonel's College of Commissioners in a ceremony at his residence. "In the best interest of the nation," Kasavubu told the assembled guests, including much of Leopoldville's foreign diplomatic corps, "we ratify Colonel Mobutu's decision, and today we officially install this college." The president was whitewashing Mobutu's illegal government and, in so doing, accepting a reduced, ignominious role for himself. But hitching his wagon to Mobutu's star evidently seemed like the best option for him—better to have the military on his side—and it was the one that U.S. diplomats and his Belgian advisers were pushing.

The United States had gotten through to Kasavubu, but Mobutu was a tougher nut to crack. One imagines that he must have felt some sense of personal loyalty to Lumumba, his onetime friend and patron, the man who had brought him into politics, employed him in Brussels, invited him into government, and promoted him to army chief of staff. Mobutu owed him his career. That was certainly how Lumumba saw it. "I never thought that Joseph, after all the help I gave him, and my appointing him to the Army just because he was so loyal, could treat me as he has," he confided to Thomas Kanza.

Whatever Mobutu's feelings about Lumumba, he appeared to be second-guessing his own coup more than ever. Overwhelmed by the burden of managing a chaotic state and unable to handle the barrage of advice, entreaties, and questions coming his way, he confessed that he sometimes wondered why he had made that radio announcement at all. He had survived at least one assassination attempt but feared that he might not be so lucky the next time. Too anxious to eat, he lost some thirty pounds. He guzzled whiskey to ease his troubled mind. Devlin reported that Mobutu "was so fed up that he was ready to throw in the sponge, reopen parliament, and let the politicians fight it out themselves." By early October, a Belgian confidant considered the colonel on the edge of a nervous breakdown. The Hamlet of the Congo was living up to his name.

While Mobutu unraveled, it seemed that in some ways home confinement allowed Lumumba to catch his breath. Out of power and stuck inside the prime minister's residence, an elegant two-story building with a cream facade and surrounded by palm trees, he caught up on sleep, notching ten-hour nights. He played with his children for the first time in a year.

But the respite did little to soothe his outrage—over Kasavubu's betrayal and the UN's support of it, over Mobutu's brazen coup and repeated attempts to have him arrested, and over the untimely death of a reconciliation deal that would have restored him to power. But he was not one to give up and watch events pass him by. Clinging to the idea that he remained prime minister, he simply acted like one. He announced a new cabinet, although Mobutu swiftly had many of its members arrested and announced that no such government existed. He released communiqués, although the Western press dismissed them as "invented." He refused to vacate his official residence, although Timberlake pushed for his eviction, arguing that the living arrangement gave Lumumba a "psychological advantage."

He also seemed to free himself from earthly fears and began to act carelessly. He acquired a pistol and fired a shot in his house to test it. A British diplomat was struck by his "Messianic" beliefs and his declaration that he would rather die than resign. He traveled freely about Leopoldville, protected from arrest by an escort of Ghanaian and Moroccan UN troops. He accepted dinner invitations at allied embassies, went shopping, stopped at restaurants, danced, and visited friends. Sometimes he cruised through the streets with a megaphone and yelled, "I am still prime minister—all the countries recognize me!"

On October 9, Lumumba put on shiny black shoes and a light suit and embarked on a pub crawl, swanning from bar to bar as if he were still marketing Polar beer or campaigning for votes. In the noisy, sweaty beer halls of the *cité*, he danced the cha-cha, ordered a round of drinks for the crowd, and delivered fiery political speeches that earned loud applause—remarkable, since this was Kasavubu territory. As during his campaigning days, supporters crowded around him, vying to touch the hem of his garment and shouting, "Savior!" At the Regina, where Mobutu had announced his coup just a few weeks earlier, he sat down at a table in front of onlookers stunned to see the former prime minister out on the town. Joined by a group of attractive women, he ended the night at the house of a dismissed minister conducting an impromptu press conference in between sips from a frosty glass of beer.

By this point in the night, according to a report from the U.S.

embassy, Lumumba was "not very sober." Staggering back to his car, he told reporters he was retaking power, no matter the consequences:

> If I die, it will be because whites have paid black men to kill me. You can tell the United States and the United Nations we don't need them anymore. One can only be respectable with the West if one is a fascist.... I created Mobutu with my own hands. I gave him money. Mobutu exploits the military because they have discipline. I've tried to make Dayal and the Security Council understand this, but they won't. Mobutu was given five million francs from the UN.... Mobutu couldn't go into bars because he would be killed like a dog. The whole Western world is dishonest. The United States is dishonest. Mobutu and Kasavubu were paid by the United States.

The next day, nine-year-old François Lumumba was waiting to be chauffeured from school with Patrice Jr., his younger brother. François realized something was off when no car came. The brothers waited one hour, then two hours, then three, before deciding to walk home. There, in addition to the usual blue-helmeted UN guards, they happened upon Mobutu and two hundred Congolese soldiers. Lumumba's defiant bar tour had been the last straw. The pressure to crack down on him had been ceaseless, and it was a miracle Mobutu had wavered this long. But Kasavubu was now on his side, and American cash was exerting its effect. What was more, his Belgian military adviser had offered an explicit quid pro quo: Belgium would train cadets and radio operators in return for Lumumba's arrest.

This time, Mobutu would personally oversee the arrest. He had called in the two hundred soldiers from the military camp in Thysville. One of the men fired a warning shot into the air. A group of reporters arrived to inspect the hubbub. Lumumba strode onto the balcony in his shirtsleeves, hands on his hips. "I challenge Mobutu to a duel," he shouted to the crowd. "Let him choose his weapons and we will see who is the strongest."

The UN guards were under strict orders to let no harm come to Lumumba. After exchanging sharp words with one of their officers,

Mobutu backed down once again, accepting that he wouldn't be able to penetrate the compound for the time being. He could, however, surround the house with his own men. From now on, the deposed prime minister would be doubly encircled: an inner ring of UN soldiers preventing anyone from coming in, and an outer ring of ANC soldiers preventing anyone from coming out.

"If he wants a trial of strength, I will give it to him," Mobutu said. "Nobody enters or leaves this house from now on."

"Is this how you betray your country?" Lumumba yelled back. Furious to be insulted in front of his troops, Mobutu peeled off in a jeep.

Little François watched helplessly as the ANC troops took up their posts. One of them caught his eye.

"Tell your dad not to be afraid," he said.

Chapter 38

Backup Plans

JOHN F. KENNEDY talked about Africa on the campaign trail more than any U.S. presidential candidate before or since. By one count, he referenced the continent 479 times in his campaign speeches. As he saw it, the Eisenhower administration's lack of interest in Africa had allowed the Soviets to gain ground. "I have seen us ignore Africa," he said in his last televised debate against Richard Nixon. In a campaign booklet, he railed against "policies which refuse to accept the inevitable triumph of nationalism in Africa—the inevitable end of colonialism."

Kennedy's focus on Africa was unusual but not accidental. It was part of a careful political triangulation: For white southern voters jumpy about racial politics at home, talk of Africa was comparatively harmless—a matter of foreign policy that meant little to their lives. Kennedy's choice of the Texan Lyndon Johnson as his running mate was just one of several signals that he would not upset their racial hierarchy. Meanwhile, Kennedy's focus on Africa, it was hoped, would score points with African American voters and liberal politicos. It would show to the former that he cared about the plight of oppressed Black people, and it would remind the latter of his progressive views on Third World nationalism.

Kennedy also sent an éminence grise of the Democratic Party, Averell Harriman, on a three-week fact-finding tour of Africa. A wealthy railroad heir, onetime ambassador to London and Moscow, and former New York governor, Harriman was expected to play an influential role in foreign policy if Kennedy won. As it happened, he arrived in Leopoldville on September 8, just after Kasavubu's coup but before Mobutu's. Harriman met with Lumumba for an hour and a half. The prime minister said all the right things, telling Kennedy's emissary that a Communist dictatorship would be as bad as colonialism and that his preferred foreign policy was not pro-Soviet but nonaligned.

Yet if the Kennedy camp held more sympathy for Lumumba, there was no sign of it from Harriman. On his way home, he told the press Lumumba was unleashing a "reign of terror" and wrote Kennedy a message that could have come from Timberlake's desk:

> Whether Lumumba is in control of the government or in jail or out, he will continue to cause difficulties in the Congo. He is a rabble-rousing speaker. He is a shrewd maneuverer who has clever left-wing advisers, with the aid and encouragement of Czech and Soviet ambassadors.... He of course counts on full support from the USSR.

There were glimmers of a new approach, however, in an October speech that Kennedy delivered in Bowling Green, Kentucky. Outside the county courthouse, a crowd of some five thousand people listened as Kennedy explained that no matter the "long way from the troubled streets of the Congo to this peaceful lawn in Kentucky," security at home depended on American influence abroad. And in the Congo, the United States was paying for its past failures. "Assembled here on this lawn is enough talent and skill, knowledge and education to have saved the Congo from chaos and confusion—permitting an orderly transition to independence—and halting the threat of Communist subversion without intervention," Kennedy said. "But the Congo did not have the skills of the people assembled here." Instead, he pointed out, the Belgians left behind a woefully unprepared population.

There is no evidence that the Bowling Green speech ever reached Lumumba. He certainly would not have appreciated Kennedy's view that the UN had "accomplished wonders" in the Congo, nor his contention that Lumumba was "pro-Russian and anti-American." Yet he would no doubt have agreed that Belgium bore considerable blame for the Congo crisis—public criticism of a U.S. ally that would have been unthinkable under Eisenhower. He would likely also have welcomed the notion that self-determination was "the most powerful force of the modern world" and Kennedy's call to support "the rising tide of nationalism in Africa."

Though he might not have realized it yet, for Lumumba—dismayed by the lack of direct U.S. aid, unable to win over an unyielding American ambassador, and rightly suspicious that covert American cash was warping Congolese politics—the Kennedy campaign offered a straw to grasp at. Maybe America would change.

When the passenger jet opened its hatches at Ndjili at dawn, Maureen Devlin was hit with a wall of hot damp air. Holding her mother's hand as she got off the plane, she looked around and counted more soldiers than she had ever seen in her eight years of life. It was late September, and the rainy season had arrived. Leopoldville's sidewalks teemed with umbrellas, and a pleasant petrichor wafted up from the puddly streets. The city's sounds and smells were so different from those of Brussels. Maureen loved them.

The reunited Devlin family moved to a villa on the banks of the Congo River that had once housed the top Sabena representative in Leopoldville. Shaded by palm trees, the house was a short drive from the U.S. embassy and had entrances on two parallel streets, making it easier for Devlin's intelligence contacts to come and go discreetly. Devlin's wife, Colette, had never shown much interest in housework and enjoyed the luxury of Congolese domestic workers, especially after the relative privation of apartment life in Brussels. For the gardener who cut the vast lawn by hand, stooping over with a machete, she bought a push mower. For the houseboy caught stealing towels, she drove to the *cité* to confront him at his home. Maureen was enrolled in the Sacré Coeur girls' school, where she befriended Joseph Kasavubu's daughter Justine.

Larry Devlin was once again weighing the best means of completing YQPROP—his mission to assassinate Lumumba, named after the encrypted cable channel dedicated to the operation. The kit Sidney Gottlieb had handed him still sat inside a safe in his office, but poisoning was just one option among several. In all, Devlin was exploring seven possibilities, although some were more viable than others. He knew of one man who, in turn, knew of a four-man hit squad that might be contracted. Another contact was in touch with five Baluba who were eager to murder Lumumba but needed weapons. There was also an army captain who claimed to be raising a force of fifteen hundred soldiers to storm Leopoldville. More promising, however, was Devlin's recruitment of a man in Lumumba's orbit, a European adviser to one of Lumumba's lesser ministers. The man, referred to in cables as "Schotroffe," was thought to have access to the prime minister's house. In a message to Washington, Devlin proposed that Schotroffe "act as inside man to brush up details to razor edge"— perhaps a reference to getting the poison into Lumumba's tooth-brush or shaving kit. Schotroffe would also "provide info on the food and agricultural problem"—which likely meant figuring out how to adulterate Lumumba's meals. (Although he was communicating through an encrypted cable whose circulation was severely limited, Devlin worded his messages in what he called "a double-talk way" so that even the code room employees wouldn't understand them.)

But when Devlin, without revealing his intentions, probed whether Schotroffe had access to Lumumba's kitchen and bathroom, he was disappointed: Schotroffe no longer thought he could gain entry to the prime ministerial residence. Plus, he had spent time in the United States, which raised the risk that the YQPROP operation might be tied back to the U.S. government. The only route to poison-ing Lumumba, Devlin figured, was to have headquarters send a true "third-country national"—someone who was neither American nor Congolese—who could penetrate Lumumba's sanctum. For now, the poisoning plot stalled.

Devlin's bosses in Washington suggested a number of alterna-tives. What about forming a "praetorian guard" within the Congolese army, with the CIA providing ten thousand rounds of ammunition and a 25 to 50 percent pay raise? Maybe the CIA could hire a *féticheur*, or witch doctor, to cast a spell to undermine Lumumba's "spiritual support"? And might he consider using a commando team to abduct Lumumba, attacking his house from the Congo River or ambushing him on one of his tours of the city?

None of these ideas went anywhere. Even the most promis-ing suggestion, the abduction plan, was highly impractical. Devlin argued that the commandos would have to be led by a third-country national, which the Leopoldville station lacked. And with Lumumba now under house arrest, there was no longer any chance of capturing him outside. (Ironically, Lumumba was staying inside not just because Mobutu's men were camped out front but also because Washington had pressured UN troops to stop accompanying and protecting him during his outings.) Devlin's superiors were growing impatient. "It seems to us your other commitments are too heavy to give the necessary concentration to YQPROP," Bronson Tweedy wrote on October 15.

Devlin would later claim that he deliberately slow-walked execution of the plan, but the record of the cable traffic is mixed. In a series of what he termed "progress reports," he did pour cold water on headquarters' proposals for killing Lumumba, but after Tweedy's nudge he also took some initiative. He talked to a Congolese security officer who implied he was trying to kill Lumumba; what encouragement Devlin offered the man is not known. He also proposed a more traditional method of assassination: a week after Lumumba had yelled at Mobutu from his balcony, the station chief requested that the CIA send him by diplomatic pouch a "high-powered, foreign-make rifle with a telescopic sight and a silencer," adding, "The hunting is good here when the light's right."

House arrest was exacting a steep toll on Lumumba. He was not, as rumor had it, under a psychiatrist's care, but his situation still amounted to "great mental torture," as he reported to the UN. Neither his secretary nor his houseboy could come to work, and the few staff trapped in the residence missed their families. For a while, there was barely any food left in the kitchen, since no one had been allowed to deliver groceries. A plan to cut off his water and electricity was afoot. A doctor sent to see his pregnant wife could not get past the ANC troops outside. Lumumba had been preparing to leave her, but that was no longer a physical possibility, and the planned wedding to his secretary, Alphonsine Masuba, was off. His eldest sons, François and Patrice Jr., could not attend school. His five-year-old daughter, Juliana, played on the balcony, looking out at the trees flowering brilliant red and the mighty Congo River coursing by. She tried not to think about the menacing rings of troops below.

The UN soldiers outside the residence were now under strict

orders to never again escort Lumumba; their job was to protect him in his house but not beyond. Even so, Lumumba managed to stay abreast of political developments, aided by a group of teenage girl supporters who managed to gather intelligence for him from members of the College of Commissioners. Sympathetic UN guards smuggled messages in and out. The wife of his cook also carried letters, including mutual notes of encouragement between Lumumba and Andrée Blouin, until the latter's expulsion from the country under orders from Mobutu. "Our difficulties are certainly many, but I have the firm hope that we shall win!" Lumumba wrote to Blouin. "Know that you can always count on me, through thick and thin. For my part, I am used to adversity." Yet his own advisers were also leaking intelligence to Mobutu, and the calls he placed using the UN guards' phone line—his own line had been cut—were being monitored by the CIA.

As the number of Congolese troops surrounding his house grew—at one point swelling to nearly a thousand—Lumumba decided that his three eldest children, François, Patrice Jr., and Juliana, should be sent abroad. No longer could he stand to see them languish in a home prison with no access to schooling. (Two-year-old Roland would stay behind.) Egypt's president, Gamal Abdel Nasser, agreed to welcome the three Lumumbas to Cairo, and an Egyptian diplomat in Leopoldville, Abdelaziz Ishak, arranged an escape plan.

After dusk on October 28, Lumumba gathered François, Patrice Jr., and Juliana and told them that they would be leaving. He tried to reassure them about their new home. "You're going to learn Arabic," he said, "and you're going to study." He kissed them goodbye. A UN jeep, violating the official policy of neutrality, pulled up to the house. The three children were ushered into the back, bundled in blankets, hidden under empty bottle crates, and told to play dead. The jeep passed through the outer ring of Mobutu's troops without arousing suspicion and drove to the Egyptian embassy. There, the children were handed Egyptian passports with intentionally blurry photographs and aliases. They would be traveling as Mustapha, Omar, and Fatima.

They arrived at the airport close to midnight. To make it through customs, the diplomat accompanying them, Ishak, pretended to be their father. Ishak, who had blond hair and blue eyes, dispelled the suspicions of an airport official by claiming that his wife was Black. The ruse worked. The group boarded a Sabena plane and flew away.

The day Lumumba's children departed, an American celebrity arrived. Louis Armstrong was playing Africa on a goodwill tour sponsored by the State Department and Pepsi-Cola. At King Baudouin Stadium, ten thousand people—UN soldiers, foreign diplomats, and government officials but mostly everyday Congolese—paid twenty cents for admission. Carried into the venue on a red sedan chair, an honor usually reserved for chiefs, "the King of Jazz" was introduced by Ambassador Timberlake, who had memorized some lines of Lingala for the occasion. The crowd tapped along tentatively to the sounds of "Mack the Knife" and "When the Saints Go Marching In"; this music was new to most. "Give those cats time," Armstrong remarked to a reporter. "They'll learn." Armstrong and his wife, Lucille, had no dinner plans that evening, so the Devlin family hosted a meal. Maureen, who had never heard of the jazz great, reluctantly emerged to say hello.

But the feel-good interlude did not change the fact that the Congo was coming apart. Western diplomats had assumed that Lumumba was the source of the country's woes; sideline him, and calm would return. In fact, the chaos had only deepened. Leopoldville was the epicenter of the disorder. "Many murders, assaults, rapes, burglaries are taking place without any action by police," Dayal told Hammarskjöld. It was not unusual in the city to see soldiers pinning families up against a wall and strip-searching them. Gangs of youths, allied with one politician or another, prowled the streets. Lumumba's supporters beat and stabbed Albert Ndele, a member of Mobutu's College of Commissioners, outside a hotel. An unknown assassin shot and killed a pro-Lumumba provincial minister visiting from Kasai while he was in a taxi; his body was tossed out the car's window.

The situation was not much better in the provinces. What little government control prevailed in the provincial capitals extended no farther than the city limits. In Kasai, the site of Lumumba's failed bloody campaign to crush the secession of the Mining State, armed bands roved the scorched countryside. Starving Luba refugees numbered in the hundreds of thousands.

The dismissal of Lumumba was supposed to bring Katanga back into the fold—a make-or-break issue for the central government, given the massive profits and tax revenues from the region's mining sector—but Mobutu was hardly having more success. A week after he had sealed off Lumumba's house, he flew to Elisabethville to negotiate with Tshombe, trading his khaki military uniform for a suit and a bow tie. He came out of the meeting announcing he had won the Katangan leader's "full moral, economic, and financial backing." As Tshombe's Belgian military adviser revealed to King Baudouin, Mobutu had earned this support by pledging to "neutralize Lumumba completely (and if possible physically . . .)."

And yet despite this blood pact, Tshombe showed no intention of reversing the Katangan secession. Emboldened by the political dysfunction in Leopoldville, he pressed further for independence or, depending on the day, at least for a very loose confederation that achieved the same aims. He sent a lobbyist named Michel Struelens to set up an office on Fifth Avenue in New York City, which printed a newsletter called *Katanga Calling* and boasted a direct telex connection to the secessionist leader's house in Elisabethville. Brussels, although it had withdrawn its troops and refused to formally recognize Katanga as independent, continued supporting it. Nearly three hundred Belgians now served in the Katangese Gendarmerie and police.

Even with all this outside help, new challenges to Tshombe's rule had arisen, spoiling Katanga's image as the last bastion of stability in the Congo. Local leadership in the north of the province—dominated by Baluba, whose leaders were not represented in Elisabethville— had decided it would be better off under central government rule and began putting up armed resistance to Tshombe. In the town of Kabalo, the Katangese Gendarmerie battled three thousand warriors who sought to replace the Katangan flag with Lumumba's MNC flag. At a bridge near the small village of Niemba, an Irish peacekeeping patrol was ambushed by a group of Luba fighters who mistook them for Belgian members of Tshombe's force. Eight soldiers died in a welter of arrows, spears, and clubs, and one who escaped was found and killed days later. The attack marked what was then the deadliest day in the history of UN peacekeeping—although the Congo mission would soon break that grim record again—as well as Ireland's first wartime casualties since its own struggle for independence. In Irish slang, "Balubas" would come to mean "savages."

Despite Mobutu's promises, his College of Commissioners was failing to bring effective governance to the Congo. According to notes from one meeting, its plan for fixing the country consisted of sending ambassadors abroad, arresting fifty pro-Lumumba politicians, providing a thousand jobs to combat unemployment, and negotiating a financial aid package from the Belgian government. Equally inexperienced as the ministers they had replaced, the commissioners compensated by leaning on Belgian experts—in many cases, their own former professors—who clashed with the UN experts who had been brought in to revive the administration. (The arrival of these Belgian specialists was just one part of a broader influx of Belgians, who, attracted by the newly Belgian-friendly climate, were returning to the Congo at a rate of three hundred per week.) Adding insult to injury, Mobutu could not control the governing body he himself had installed. Pointing to his failure to arrest Lumumba, the commissioners openly criticized him as soft.

Relations with the army were even worse. The briefcases of American and Belgian cash notwithstanding, Mobutu's control of officers and enlisted men alike was slipping. Rumors swirled that another colonel was about to remove him in another coup. The three thousand ANC troops in Stanleyville were a lost cause, having thrown their lot in with Lumumba. Those in Leopoldville were unruly. As an intelligence briefing for Eisenhower noted, "Mobutu is encountering serious difficulties in maintaining discipline among his army supporters." So worried was the White House about his weak grip over the ANC—and the resulting possibility that he might be overthrown by Lumumba or his supporters—that the Special Group approved a contingency plan to pre-position stockpiles of arms and ammunition in friendly neighboring countries. To prepare for "the possibility of a pro-Soviet Lumumba government," the CIA would arm and train any anti-Lumumba elements within the ANC. Realizing that sleeping next to a thousand-plus soldiers was too risky, Mobutu himself traded his bungalow at Camp Leopold for a palatial villa in the suburb of Binza, protected by a smaller group of loyal troops and near the British and U.S. military attachés.

Much of the ANC's time was spent arresting, and sometimes

torturing, Lumumba's political allies, although it often wasn't clear whether it did so at Mobutu's orders, since he often freed the detainees under pressure from the UN. Over the course of one night alone, fifteen Lumumba supporters—members of parliament, party officials, and youth leaders—were rounded up. Thomas Kanza moved to the Royal to avoid arrest. The Americans had complained vociferously about Lumumba's brief authoritarian turn, which was focused mainly on curtailing the freedom of the press. They were conspicuously silent on the detention and torture under Mobutu.

They were hardly pleased with their client's behavior, however. Mobutu still appeared to be a bundle of nerves. He was said to be popping tranquilizer pills and eating little other than bouillabaisse. Worried for his own safety, he at one point quietly asked the UN for an apartment at the Royal and considered sending his family to Brussels. His political positions changed by the day. At a White House meeting, Secretary of State Christian Herter complained that Mobutu was "a childish individual." Like others, Herter feared that Mobutu "might suffer a nervous breakdown."

Mobutu had just turned thirty, but the United States treated him with an almost parental protectiveness, shielding and guiding him at the same time as it sought to kill Lumumba. When Devlin heard rumors that Kasavubu wanted to rein in the colonel, he persuaded the president not to do so. When he got wind that five soldiers intended to assassinate Mobutu, he warned him of the plot, saving his life. When Mobutu wanted to fly to New York to meet with Hammarskjöld, U.S. officials talked him out of the plan, worrying that any absence from the Congo would further jeopardize his hold over the army. If a stern talking-to didn't work, there was always the option of bribery. When Devlin learned that Mobutu was considering a second coup in which he would assume Kasavubu's position as head of state, he sought to dissuade him. The Special Group approved a plan by which Devlin would offer Mobutu funds for his troops, as well as a "personal subsidy," in order to "convince him of the advantages of remaining in the position of a 'strong man' behind the government avoiding an overt role." The budget for this operation: $250,000, a massive sum at the time.

In just a few short weeks, Devlin had effectively become an unofficial adviser to Mobutu, privy to the most sensitive matters of political life and death in the Congo. He began working closely with what would soon be known as the Binza Group. Named after the Leopoldville suburb where most of its members lived, this informal caucus centered on Mobutu, with Justin Bomboko, the head of the commissioners and the foreign minister, and Victor Nendaka, the head of the security services, serving as the other core members. At restaurants and one another's homes, the Binza Group would reach a consensus in the evening and run it by their Western advisers the next day.

Devlin was also getting to know Mobutu at a personal level. The colonel would regularly swing by the station chief's house and dump his peaked cap on "la petite Maureen," as he called Devlin's daughter. Unlike others, Devlin did not seem to worry about Mobutu's mental state. He found him intelligent, serious, and eloquent, a man who had great ambitions for the Congo. He liked him.

Chapter 39

Cold Storage

T HE SAME COULD not be said for Rajeshwar Dayal. As Dayal saw it, Mobutu was "basically a weak person with good intentions," hopelessly misled by the military and other noxious influences. Like U.S. observers, he felt that Mobutu's erstwhile control over the army was by now "practically nonexistent" and predicted that the colonel would fall out of favor with his supporters, who were "beginning to realize that they have been backing a losing horse." He reminded the press that Mobutu was only a chief of staff—"a lousy one at that"—called his army "a disorderly rabble," and openly mocked the commissioners as "schoolboys." Mobutu returned the compliment by complaining that Dayal was treating him "like a child."

Whereas Western embassies, led by the U.S. one, had come to see Mobutu and the College of Commissioners as the key to stability in the Congo, Dayal was convinced that Mobutu was its main obstacle. In this, he had Hammarskjöld's full support. Hemmed in by the reality of African and Asian opinion at the UN—which had made itself known during the recent General Assembly session—the secretary-general had concluded that the best path forward for the Congo was not rule by an extralegal council but a return to constitutionality.

At the core of Hammarskjöld's unexpected change of tack was the begrudging recognition that any political settlement to the crisis in the Congo would need to include Lumumba. For one thing, the African and Asian countries whose troops made up much of the UN force in the Congo demanded it. For another, as frustrating as the man was as a partner, he was too politically popular to ignore, too effective even on the outside to exclude. "A political personality cannot be eliminated overnight," Cléophas Kamitatu, a pro-Lumumba politician, pointed out in a press conference, "nor are the ranks of Mr. Lumumba's followers so negligible that this can be done without consequences." Even Kasavubu had intimated as much, once admitting that there was "no other leader of sufficient stature to replace Lumumba." Accordingly, the UN continued to protect Lumumba's residence. In preparation for an eventual political settlement, he would be kept "in cold storage," as Dayal put it.

In pursuit of that settlement, the UN needed to broker a reconciliation between Kasavubu and Lumumba, reopen parliament so that legislators could form a new government, and, all the while, prevent Mobutu's illegal government from entrenching itself. None of these tasks would be easy. Others had tried and failed to persuade the two leaders to set aside their differences, and Kasavubu's European advisers were hardly going to encourage him to engineer Lumumba's return to power. ANC soldiers had blocked off access to parliament, and many of its members had fled Leopoldville for the relative safety of their home provinces. Katanga had no interest in sending delegates to what it effectively considered a foreign capital. Refusing to deal with Mobutu, meanwhile, raised practical problems for UN officials—he was the de facto authority, after all—and risked greater friction with his Western backers. But as hazardous as this path was, Dayal viewed it as the "way out of the constitutional jungle."

The main fault line in the Congo was becoming clear. On one side were Mobutu and Kasavubu, backed by the Americans and the Belgians. On the other was Lumumba, supported by other African leaders but locked in his house. Awkwardly straddling the divide was the UN. Over the course of the fall, Dayal had little success bringing Kasavubu and Lumumba together, nor did he make any progress on reopening parliament. All he could do was refuse to formally recognize the authority of Mobutu and his commissioners, dealing with them on a strictly as-needed basis. Dayal perfected what he and Hammarskjöld called the "cold blanket" treatment or "operation deflation." In one meeting, for example, he remained seated when Mobutu entered the room. If the UN pretended Mobutu didn't exist, perhaps he wouldn't.

Hammarskjöld might have sensed that by helping remove Lumumba from power, he had overstepped his bounds and created the conditions in which Mobutu ended up seizing it. Over the course of October, the UN backpedaled in the Congo, a task made easier by the presence in Leopoldville of Dayal, who was more inclined than his predecessors to uphold the organization's neutrality.

The UN's new approach frustrated the United States. In its view, Lumumba deserved to be arrested and isolated, not protected and led back to power. Mobutu deserved to be engaged, not sidelined. As Timberlake summarized his country's position, "Mobutu is the key for the present, even though I could wish he were more able and less impulsive." For the first time, the United States could no longer rely on the UN as its ally in the Congo—partly a direct result of the influx of newly independent African and Asian states into the organization. (Eisenhower, sensing that the UN was slipping from America's grasp, thought that the organization should never have admitted these countries.) On the question of which mattered more—a government's anti-Communist credentials or its constitutionality—Washington and the UN now diverged.

Of particular dispute was the issue of Lumumba's whereabouts inside Leopoldville. Because the UN refused to let Mobutu's government arrest Lumumba, the United States proposed a compromise. State Department officials felt strongly that "the removal of Lumumba from the Prime Minister's residence would have substantial political and psychological value," and thought that the UN force could relocate him to a house in the Leopoldville suburbs, where he would no longer "hold a symbol of authority to which he is not entitled." Once again, Hammarskjöld objected. The prime minister's residence was merely one house in a government district where few Congolese ever traveled, he said. Besides, he still considered Lumumba the legal prime minister—a stunning admission for a man who just weeks earlier had compared Lumumba to Hitler and spoken of his wish to "break" him. Even veiled U.S. threats to defund the UN mission and a tense two-hour clash with U.S. officials did not lead the secretary-general to budge.

The question of military training was another point of contention.

Moroccan officers were advising the ANC as part of the UN mission, but the recent UN General Assembly resolution forbade any direct bilateral military assistance. Dayal enforced the ban by preventing a group of handpicked ANC officers from going to the U.K. for training—drawing an angry rebuke from Mobutu, who declared that the Congo was "not a colony of the United Nations"—but he could do nothing when the same officers later flew out of Leopoldville in civilian clothes for a program in Belgium. Nor could Dayal do anything when the U.S. government hosted eleven Congolese officers at the Pentagon and Fort Dix in New Jersey. The cold blanket treatment could only go so far when the United States and Belgium were rolling out the red carpet. And lingering beneath the surface, of course, was the UN's suspicion that the CIA was bankrolling Mobutu. (After State Department officials' two-hour confrontation with Hammarskjöld, Herter nervously called them to find out whether the secretary-general had asked who was paying Mobutu.)

Unwilling to publicly break with Hammarskjöld, the United States focused its animus on Dayal. Devlin considered him haughty and anti-American. Timberlake, who knew Dayal from when both were posted in Bombay in the late 1940s, complained to Washington that the UN diplomat was "violently anti-Mobutu" and that by protecting Lumumba and trying to reopen parliament, he was "reacting as a Hindu and seeking a solution which might be viable in a civilized environment but not in the Congo." He thought that Dayal's appointment—along with the arrival of Hammarskjöld's military adviser, Indar Jit Rikhye—represented the "Indianization" of the UN mission in the Congo. The notion spread that Dayal had a high-caste disdain for Africans.

Congolese supporters of Mobutu and Kasavubu, meanwhile, tried to have Dayal removed from his post. An anonymous letter sent to him by "the population" complained that he was interfering in national affairs by opposing "the arrest of the fascist Lumumba" and demanded he leave the country. Death threats came by telephone. But Hammarskjöld backed his representative, both in private and in public.

In fact, the secretary-general invited him to reply to his critics. Giving Dayal just three days, he asked for a detailed report from the Congo. Dayal and his staff answered with a sixteen-thousand-word document. To coincide with its release, Dayal flew to New York. He felt "like a deep-sea diver surfacing after two months in the depths."

In blunt language atypical of a UN document, especially one presented as a "progress report," Dayal poured out his frustrations with Mobutu and the soldiers he supposedly led. "The eruption of the army into the political scene constituted a new menace to peace and security," he wrote. "Far from the ANC providing any measure of security or stability, it became the principal fomenter of lawlessness." In less direct terms, he also singled out Belgium. The proliferating Belgian advisers in Leopoldville were interfering with the UN's work in the ministries, and Belgian officers in Katanga were responsible for "brutal and oppressive acts of violence." Dayal ended by calling for a political reconciliation involving Kasavubu and parliament—which implied the possibility of Lumumba's return to power.

The reaction was swift. Everyone expected the Belgians to declare their outrage—and indeed, Pierre Wigny, the foreign minister, threatened to withdraw his country from the UN—but more surprising was the Americans' reaction. The State Department declared itself "unable to accept the implication" that the Belgians had acted with anything but "good faith." The split between the United States and the UN had become painfully public.

Lumumba was ecstatic. Breaking a four-week silence, he issued a statement from house arrest in support of Dayal's report. Just as the West had feared, Lumumba now saw a chance to return to power. "Don't worry, my dear friends," he told supporters. "Your government, the legal government, will soon be reinstalled. My vacation is over."

Less than a week after the publication of Dayal's report, the world waited with bated breath as the results of the 1960 U.S. presidential election came in. Eisenhower, who had recently turned seventy and was not particularly enthusiastic about Richard Nixon, decided not to stay up the night of November 8. But in Hyannis Port, Massachusetts, John F. Kennedy was in his brother Bobby's cottage, keeping a vigil well past midnight. He paced back and forth in front of a television, pausing to nibble on a sandwich or answer the telephone. An ocean away, huddled around campfires in the desert, anti-French

Algerian rebels tuned their transistor radios to the election news. They remembered the senator's early pro-independence stance, and when a new round of returns put Kennedy ahead, the camp erupted in cheers. In Leopoldville, the U.S. embassy had set up a teleprinter in the lobby, with ticker tape spewing the latest tallies straight from Washington. There was only one open supporter of Nixon among the relatively young embassy staff. So when news came in that Kennedy had won—in the closest race in eighty years—the Americans rejoiced.

On the other side of town, Lumumba likely did the same. Through a Moroccan UN guard, the once and perhaps future prime minister smuggled out a congratulatory telegram in which he appealed to the president-elect's progressive values and beseeched him to throw his support behind a political compromise in the Congo. Having written off the Republicans, Lumumba and his supporters put their hopes in Kennedy.

Dayal, who remained in New York, also sensed that the page would turn. He called up his old friend Chester Bowles, a Kennedy adviser who had served as U.S. ambassador to India under President Harry Truman and was expected to take a high-ranking post in the new administration. Dayal and Bowles were natural allies: Bowles had a reputation as a backer of the UN and a reliable booster of African independence, and he shared his dislike of Clare Timberlake, having overlapped and clashed with him during his time in India. Bowles promised that the incoming administration would take Dayal's views on the Congo more seriously. The UN's efforts—including, presumably, its endeavors to bring about a constitutional government—were to be supported, not shunned.

Dayal picked up other promising signals from Kennedy's inner circle. Conversations with Dean Rusk, a leading candidate for secretary of state, and even Averell Harriman, who had previously registered his dislike of Lumumba, left him feeling assured he could henceforth expect more U.S. support. In the interim, the UN mission in the Congo simply needed to "sustain a holding operation" until Kennedy took office. Dayal left New York glowing with confidence.

Thomas Kanza was in high spirits, too. Kennedy never replied to Lumumba's congratulatory telegram, but Eleanor Roosevelt, who had introduced Kanza to Kennedy in Boston, passed the president-elect a plea from Kanza. She reported back to Kanza that Kennedy was receptive to the idea of reopening the Congo's parliament. Shortly after Kennedy's inauguration, Kanza predicted, Lumumba would walk the hundred yards from the prime minister's residence to the Palace of the Nation, present himself to a vote by a reopened parliament, and emerge once again as rightful prime minister of the Congo. All Lumumba had to do was stay in his house until January 20, 1961.

Chapter 40

Vote of Confidence

Larry Devlin's efforts to penetrate Lumumba's sanctum had gone nowhere. Both he and headquarters agreed that to get the operation moving, he needed additional manpower. So in late October, near the end of the workday, Richard Bissell, the CIA's deputy director for plans, called into his office a seasoned agency man. His name was Justin O'Donnell, and he had served as station chief in Bolivia, the Netherlands, and Thailand. Bissell's request: that O'Donnell get on the next flight to Europe that very evening, to travel to the Congo and kill Lumumba.

O'Donnell refused. He had both legal and moral concerns. He told Bissell that it was a federal crime to conspire in Washington, D.C., to commit homicide—a concern Bissell waved away—and felt further that as a Catholic he could have no hand in a murder. Yet O'Donnell was flexible, and he quickly found a way of satisfying his own conscience and his superiors' wishes: he explained that he was willing to abduct Lumumba and turn him over to Mobutu's government for a trial, even though he knew full well that this would likely mean Lumumba's execution. He was not opposed to capital punishment, after all. Bissell agreed.

O'Donnell traveled to Leopoldville via Frankfurt, West Germany, where he was to enlist the "third-country national" Devlin had asked for. The Leopoldville station needed someone who couldn't be traced back to the United States, someone who had little regard for personal safety, someone who would do as he was told without asking questions, and, above all, someone who had no moral scruples.

The CIA had just the man. It had recruited André Mankel years earlier, after the Luxembourg native and former member of the French Resistance was caught illegally exporting nickel past the Iron Curtain. The CIA station in Luxembourg valued Mankel's connections to the criminal underworld and hired him, assigning him the code name Q JWIN. Now, with O'Donnell in need of a French-speaking asset with few ethical hang-ups, the Luxembourg station agreed to lend him out. Mankel was told he would be heading to Dakar, Senegal, and was sent to Frankfurt to learn more.

Mankel—tall, thin, and jug-eared—knew to show up in the lobby of the Hotel Carlton, in downtown Frankfurt, at 2:00 p.m. on November 2. He had been instructed to look for a fat, red-faced man smoking a cigar and wearing tortoise-shell glasses. It was O'Donnell. Both parties knew the script in advance.

"Are you the salesman from Luxembourg?" O'Donnell asked.

"Yes, I am the ARBED representative," Mankel replied, naming a Luxembourg steel producer.

Their identities confirmed, O'Donnell revealed to Mankel that his true destination would be not Dakar but Leopoldville. The details of the mission were kept vague, but Mankel was informed that it would involve a high degree of personal risk and pay $1,000 a month. He agreed. He stayed behind in Frankfurt to get his immunizations and travel documents in order, while O'Donnell flew to Africa.

In Leopoldville, O'Donnell met with Devlin, who told him there was a "virus" in his office safe. (Devlin didn't spell out the pathogen's purpose, but O'Donnell thought, "I knew it wasn't for somebody to get his polio shot up to date.") Freeing Devlin from the additional workload, O'Donnell began work on a plan to lure Lumumba out of the prime minister's residence. He looked into renting an "observation post" near the house and befriended one of the UN guards. But after ten days, Mankel had yet to arrive, and the station cabled Washington asking for the "immediate expedition of Q JWIN's travel to Leopoldville."

In the meantime, Devlin continued trying, and failing, to infiltrate the prime minister's house. It was still guarded day and night by an inner circle of UN troops and an outer circle of Congolese troops. "Concentric rings of defense make the establishment of an observation post impossible," Devlin wrote. Lumumba had not left the residence in weeks, and he had reduced the number of servants in the house, making it harder to use one of them to gain entry.

Belgian efforts were equally unsuccessful. Like the American poison plot, the Belgian intelligence agency's plan to drug Lumumba, Operation L., was stymied by a lack of access to the prime minister's residence. Mobutu's Belgian military adviser gave weapons and 200,000 francs to a Greek hit man who promised to kill Lumumba, but the man took the money and promptly disappeared. Belgian intelligence was also aware of, and likely involved in, a plot in the works by a man who traveled to Leopoldville under a fake name and in the guise of a journalist to "put Lumumba definitively out of the game." But nothing came of his endeavors, either.

The CIA hoped QJWIN might fare differently. After finally alighting in Leopoldville, Mankel—a salesman for a German vending-machine company to anyone who asked—quickly developed local contacts. Soon, a plan for kidnapping Lumumba materialized. Mankel had somehow managed to get his hands on four UN vehicles and six Congolese soldiers. Wearing stolen armbands and berets, the soldiers would pose as UN soldiers and Mankel as their officer. He would enter the prime minister's residence, employ some excuse for luring Lumumba out, and escort him away—into, presumably, the hands of Mobutu's men. The goal, O'Donnell explained, was to "trick him out, if I could, and then turn him over . . . to the legal authorities and let him stand trial."

Dayal's UN report and Kennedy's election had buoyed Lumumba. So had the announcement of a UN "conciliation commission," a group of representatives from fifteen troop-contributing African and Asian countries that was charged with traveling to the Congo to find a political solution to the crisis. The group was set to arrive in late November and had let it be known that its goal was to reopen parliament. Belgian hotel managers at the Memling, the Stanley, and the Regina denied the envoys lodging, dubiously claiming to be fully booked, but the UN found them suitable accommodations at an equestrian center. To everyone's surprise, Mobutu, whose tacks and jibes were becoming hard to track, told Indar Jit Rikhye, who temporarily led the UN operation during Dayal's visit to New York, that he would not stand in the way of the conciliation commission. Mobutu forswore any future political ambitions beyond his hope that history would remember him as "the colonel who had made sacrifices to make the ANC into what it would be—good, efficient, and a disciplined army."

Just at the moment when Lumumba's return to power seemed a real possibility, he was struck by personal tragedy. Lumumba's pregnant wife, Pauline, had been denied regular access to her doctor. Surrounded by hostile troops and perhaps aware of her husband's desire to leave her, she suffered a nervous breakdown and gave birth prematurely. Thanks to the intervention of the Red Cross, the baby, a daughter named Marie-Christine, was flown to Switzerland for treatment, but the doctors there could not save her. When her undersized body was returned to Leopoldville and delivered to Lumumba's residence, ANC soldiers, whether out of suspicion or cruelty, took the liberty of opening the tiny coffin for inspection. Lumumba decided his daughter could not be buried in Leopoldville and asked if he could take her remains to Stanleyville aboard a UN airplane so that she could be buried in Onalua. The request was denied on the grounds that sending Lumumba to his stronghold in the east would amount to an act of political interference on the part of the UN. When Pauline tried to accompany the coffin instead, soldiers at the airport arrested her. The coffin flew onward as air freight. It ended up lost in transit.

Lumumba's political comeback, meanwhile, still faced obstacles. The first was down the street at the Ghanaian embassy. Instructed by Kwame Nkrumah to ignore Mobutu and treat Lumumba as the legitimate prime minister, Ghanaian diplomats had served as Lumumba's main link to the outside world. When the ANC caught one of them carrying a thick file folder to Lumumba's house, allegedly including compromising documents such as plans for a new, pro-Lumumba secessionist state in northern Katanga, Mobutu announced he was severing relations with Ghana. Acting on advice from Devlin, he demanded the expulsion of the country's chargé d'affaires. But the diplomat, following orders from Nkrumah to ignore the whims of an illegal government, refused to leave. A hundred Congolese soldiers went to the Ghanaian embassy to carry out the expulsion, leading to a standoff with the 215 Tunisian UN troops guarding the building.

As dusk fell and tensions grew, a skirmish broke out, with sporadic bursts of gunfire and grenade explosions lasting until dawn. Devlin's daughter, Maureen, happened to be next door at the Timberlakes' residence and hid in the upstairs bathroom. One Tunisian, the platoon commander, was killed, as were several Congolese, including a popular colonel. The Ghanaian diplomat whose insistence on staying had caused the incident was ushered onto a plane and returned to Accra, and the embassy was emptied. Lumumba was now without his most ardent foreign advocates in Leopoldville.

Lumumba's second political problem was in New York. Although it deplored Dayal's report, the U.S. government did see in it one toehold for furthering American interests: Dayal's insistence that Kasavubu was still the legitimate president of the Congo. Although Washington did not share Dayal's opposition to Mobutu, it agreed that Kasavubu lent a badly needed aura of constitutionality to what was in essence a military regime. With this reasoning in mind, the CIA had successfully persuaded Mobutu not to remove Kasavubu, urging the colonel to remain the power behind the throne and not claim it for himself. At the same time, two rival Congolese delegations in New York had been vying for the Congo's UN seat: one representing Lumumba and the other Kasavubu and Mobutu. In the wake of the Dayal report, the United States saw a chance to formalize Kasavubu's position on the international level by sending him to New York, where he could make a case for the seating of his delegation. Thomas Kanza made plans to follow suit and argue Lumumba's side before the UN, but he was denied a U.S. visa.

In New York, Kasavubu went up the Empire State Building, took a private tour of Macy's, gave an interview to CBS, and received visitors in his hotel suite overlooking Central Park. (Detached as ever, he left a Western playing on the television while one businessman met with him. "I have a question for you," he said as the visitor left. "Why does the cowboy always win?") The centerpiece of his visit was a speech before the General Assembly, delivered in his characteristically meek voice, urging members to seat his delegation and not Lumumba's. But among the ninety-eight voting members of that body, most either considered Lumumba's delegation the legitimate one or thought the question was too unsettled to be decided now. The United States needed a way to tip the scales. It found one a few blocks from the UN building, at the offices of Overseas Regional Surveys Associates.

Run out of a leased suite at 333 East Forty-Sixth Street, Overseas Regional Surveys Associates billed itself as a consulting and public-relations firm for African businesses and governments. It was headed by a pair of thirtysomething New Yorkers, both with extensive experience abroad. Howard Imbrey had served as a radio operator in British India during World War II. His junior partner, Thomas Goodman, had spent two years living in the jungles of Thailand on an expedition for the American Museum of Natural History. Scrappy and fleet-footed, their company claimed to be uniquely positioned to take advantage of new opportunities on the African continent. "By the time a major American company gets through making surveys, calling in consultants who have never heard of Africa, negotiating bank loans, analyzing their 'market potential' and I don't know what else, we'll have been there and gone," Imbrey boasted to *Fortune*.

In fact, the business was a front for the CIA, and its two employees were agency officers. Imbrey had joined the CIA's predecessor, the Office of Strategic Services, back in 1944 and had served as best man at Clare Timberlake's wedding. The true purpose of Overseas Regional Surveys Associates was to develop sources among Africans at the UN. The Congo was a particular focus: in the spring of 1960, the CIA had sent Imbrey to Leopoldville to help build out the station there—"a two-month assignment undertaken for a client of my firm," as he cheekily described it.

Now, at Timberlake's request, Imbrey would ensure that Kasavubu's trip was a success. In Imbrey's words, his shop worked to "nobble"—that is, bribe—UN members into supporting the seating of Kasavubu's delegation, or at least into abstaining from the vote. So extensive was the vote-buying operation that Africans would occasionally get confused as to whether they were meeting with State Department diplomats or CIA satchel carriers. The bribery, combined with an intense U.S. lobbying push, worked. Over the course of three successive votes—a particularity of UN protocol—the number of pro-Kasavubu votes ticked upward from thirty to fifty-one to fifty-three, while the number on the opposite side of the issue dropped from forty-eight to thirty-six to twenty-four. Kasavubu's delegation won the Congo's UN seat, and the Congo's president the imprimatur of the world's legislature. The United States, a shocked Rajeshwar Dayal observed, had pulled off "perhaps one of the most glaring examples of the massive and organized application of threats and pressures—along with inducements—to member states to change their votes."

News of the defeat at the General Assembly left Lumumba devastated. By now, he had been a former prime minister longer than he had ever been in office, and his enemies had just scored another victory. Now that the UN appeared beholden to them, would it continue to protect him in Leopoldville? Troubling rumors circulated that the UN guards would withdraw from his residence, freeing the ANC to make its long-awaited arrest.

On November 27, Kasavubu returned triumphantly to Leopoldville. He emerged from his chartered Sabena jet in a new white uniform, with a gold braid and epaulets. Mobutu, now firmly allied with the president, was there to greet him, along with his commissioners and a crowd of ten thousand. That evening, Kasavubu held a lavish, champagne-drenched banquet for two hundred dignitaries to celebrate his victory at the UN. Mobutu and the commissioners were again in attendance, seated at the high table, as were members of Leopoldville's diplomatic corps, including Dayal, who had returned from New York and sat silently through speeches that included subtle digs at his report.

Outside Lumumba's residence, one of the Moroccan officers standing guard felt something was amiss. The house seemed strangely quiet. The hallway lights had been turned off. He asked a secretary where Lumumba was, and was told that the former prime minister had gone to bed early because of a headache. By daybreak, the house, normally a hive of activity, remained oddly still. A Canadian UN officer let himself inside. The place was empty. Even the ashtrays were gone. Lumumba was nowhere to be found.

PART V

MARTYR

Chapter 41

The Big Rabbit Has Escaped

STANLEYVILLE HAD BEEN beckoning for weeks. Regrouping there had always been plan B for Lumumba's camp. In Leopoldville, he and his supporters faced arrest or worse; in Stanleyville, he was the native son, popular among politicians, soldiers, and residents alike. There, the MNC newspaper *Uhuru* published freely; there, the police were Lumumba partisans. In the previous two months, a growing number of his ministers, advisers, and friendly army officers had fled to the city. Victor Lundula, a high-ranking ANC general and supporter of Lumumba's, dressed in women's clothing, hid in the cargo hold of a boat, and steamed upriver. Antoine Gizenga, Lumumba's deputy prime minister, disguised himself as a Guinean UN soldier and drove to the city. The newcomers linked up with the provincial government, which was controlled by Lumumba's MNC and whose ministers included his twenty-nine-year-old brother, Louis. By late November, his supporters had vanquished the pro-Mobutu elements of the army in Stanleyville, rounded up the anti-Lumumba politicians, and effectively established a national government-in-waiting. If Lumumba somehow got himself to the city, he could use it as a springboard to retake power nationally.

But there was also good reason to wait. The UN conciliation commission was arriving imminently in Leopoldville, holding the promise of a reopened parliament and, with it, the prospect of a more straightforward return to power. The disappointing General Assembly vote in New York, however, settled the issue for Lumumba: instead of placing his faith in the UN, he would go to Stanleyville. And because flying out of Leopoldville unnoticed would be impossible—Ndjili was too well guarded, and flights too easily monitored—escaping by road was the only reasonable option. If he reached a village far enough outside the capital, perhaps he could be picked up by a plane at an airstrip. So on November 23, Lumumba sent a loyal ministerial aide to scout the route from Leopoldville. It was clear, the aide reported back, with working ferries and open roads.

When friends learned of his intentions, they grew worried. Thomas Kanza called him from his refuge at the Royal and tried, over the course of a two-hour conversation, to persuade him not to leave. "Things won't stay like this forever," he said. "Even if you have to stay in your house for years, I am convinced that sooner or later you will emerge victorious." Kanza passed the receiver around, but none of Lumumba's allies could talk him out of the plan.

"My dear Thomas, I shall probably be arrested, tortured and killed," Lumumba said near the end of the call. "One of us must sacrifice himself if the Congolese people are to understand and accept the ideal we are fighting for."

To another minister, Anicet Kashamura, Lumumba was equally fatalistic. "If I die, too bad," he said. "The Congo needs martyrs."

On the evening of November 27, as Kasavubu, Mobutu, and the Leopoldville elite clinked champagne glasses at the president's house, the skies broke open. A torrential rainstorm washed out roads and kept residents inside their homes. At Lumumba's house, the usual guard—both Mobutu's soldiers and the UN peacekeepers—had been reduced, with most huddling in a hut to avoid the downpour. At least one Congolese sentry had fallen into a deep sleep. At 9:30 p.m., a Moroccan officer witnessed two servants loading suitcases into a gray Chevrolet station wagon parked outside the entrance to the house. Half an hour later, Lumumba emerged. He got into the car and curled up in the backseat, hiding beneath the legs of the servants. The driver headed toward the exit.

There was no trouble from the UN guards, because it wasn't their job to monitor outgoing traffic. When the station wagon reached the outer ring of Congolese soldiers, they prepared to search it. But the coolheaded chauffeur brushed them off. *We're just getting some cigarettes,* he said. *We'll be right back.* The car crept down the dark, wet street, before speeding away into the night, headlights off.

Outside a small hotel on the east side of Leopoldville, Lumumba switched cars, entering a Guinean embassy vehicle. He sent the Chevrolet station wagon to retrieve his wife, Pauline, and their two-year-old son, Roland, both of whom were staying at a cousin's house. Thirty miles outside Leopoldville, Pauline and Roland caught up. A two-car convoy formed. Lumumba, his family, and his chauffeur were in the station wagon. The loyal ministerial aide, armed with a .22-caliber rifle, followed in a blue Peugeot borrowed from Cléophas Kamitatu, the pro-Lumumba president of the Leopoldville provincial government. Like others, Kamitatu had tried in vain to talk Lumumba out of the trip, but recognizing that the former prime minister had made up his mind, he agreed to do what he could to reduce the odds of capture. In addition to handing over his car keys, he rustled up two police uniforms to be worn as disguises and instructed local branches of his party to provide Lumumba with money if he passed through their village.

The two cars were slowed by mud and a flat tire, but at 4:00 a.m. they reached a ferry crossing, where a third car—a Fiat containing two more aides—was waiting. Although Kamitatu had ordered all ferries in the province to dock on the west banks so that Lumumba could be picked up without delay, the directive had apparently not reached this deep into the interior. Lumumba's aide had to canoe across the water and persuade the ferry operators on the other side to provide an early-morning crossing; Lumumba gave them 5,000 francs and one day's vacation.

The next crossing proved even more complicated. The Peugeot and the Fiat drove ahead to test the loyalty of the soldiers operating the ferry outside Kenge, a trading post and district capital. Lumumba, staying behind with his family, waited hours before learning that the scouts had been arrested and beaten. But he proceeded to the military camp where they were being held and managed to secure their release—along with a truck carrying barrels of gasoline and an armed escort. (Leave it to Lumumba to reverse the situation so easily.)

The convoy continued eastward. Twenty-four hours after escaping from his residence, Lumumba had traveled nearly 250 miles. He was less than a fifth of the way to Stanleyville, but a third of the way to Luluabourg, where perhaps he could catch a plane. For the first time in months, he was free.

Mobutu and Kasavubu first heard of Lumumba's flight from U.S. embassy officers. The two leaders were at a ceremony across the river in Brazzaville when they learned the news. Meanwhile, a note from the head of the security services reached the College of Commissioners: "The big rabbit has escaped."

Could it be true? At Lumumba's instruction, Thomas Kanza had tried to frustrate the search, issuing a communiqué saying that Lumumba was still in town, waiting for the UN conciliation commission to arrive. Adding to the confusion, a separate statement under Lumumba's name declared that he had in fact left for Stanleyville, but only for his daughter's funeral and only for two days. "I have never envisaged my departure from Leopoldville as that of a fugitive," it read.

The escape mystified everyone. How could the ANC, which wanted desperately to arrest Lumumba, have let him slip past? One rumor had it that a tunnel had been dug from the prime minister's residence to the Congo River, where he met up with a speedboat. A more plausible story alleged that he had simply bribed the ANC guards. Some speculated his true destination was not Stanleyville but Ghana; others guessed Guinea.

Upon his return to the capital, an irate Kasavubu summoned Dayal and accused him of complicity in the escape. Dayal pushed back: it was the ANC guards, not UN troops, who had failed to do their job. Even so, he conceded, "The responsibility for the protection of Mr. Lumumba rested with the UN as long as he was inside the house, and the responsibility of the UN ceased as soon as Mr. Lumumba left his house." In other words, Lumumba was now fair game.

The U.S. government was deeply worried about the prospect that Lumumba might reach Stanleyville, where he would control a sizable element of the Congolese army and could establish a credible rival government. If that happened, Allen Dulles told Eisenhower, civil war was a very real possibility.

Fortunately for Dulles, Larry Devlin had already sprung into action, meeting with Mobutu to pore over maps, identify ferry crossings, and muster a search party. As Devlin worked to set up roadblocks and alert troops along Lumumba's suspected escape route, Mobutu and his security officers mobilized a helicopter and a plane and summoned a pilot experienced in low-altitude reconnaissance. These eyes in the sky would scan the roads for any signs of the fugitive. A Belgian intelligence agent reported to Brussels that Devlin had promised "full assistance" to find Lumumba.

By now, Lumumba and his companions were proceeding more slowly than expected. They had been on the move for a full day, and his wife and son were growing hungry. The convoy stopped for food in Masi-Manimba, a modest village with a garage and a gas station, but in so doing lost another hour. More time slipped away when one of their vehicles broke down.

While stocking up on provisions in a nearby town the next morning, Lumumba was recognized and promptly mobbed by a crowd of excited supporters. Perhaps eager not to play the part of a lowly fugitive, he let himself be pressured into giving an impromptu public speech in the center of town. It was a foolish indiscretion. Watching in the crowd was a Portuguese employee of Unilever, the palm oil supplier, who immediately informed his bosses in Leopoldville of the sighting—the first indication of Lumumba's whereabouts since he had absconded. The employee also passed on crucial details that Lumumba had let slip in his speech: he was headed for Stanleyville, and in an effort to evade capture, he would not be taking the more direct route via the town of Kikwit. The news made its way to the Royal and quickly got through to Mobutu, possibly through a security officer sent to eavesdrop on UN staff. The information swiftly reached Belgian intelligence as well.

Unaware of these developments, Lumumba eventually managed to shake off his supporters and continued on his way, having once again lost valuable time. But as the group passed through village after village, the strange confluence of Lumumba's prominence as a national figure and his relative obscurity—in a country with no television and limited newspaper circulation, few of his supporters had a clear sense of what he looked like—kept causing problems. It seemed almost as if he only managed to get recognized when circumstances required remaining incognito, and vice versa. The party was on relatively friendly territory now, but at some roadblocks Lumumba struggled to convince local soldiers of his identity. Elsewhere he was instantly recognized and again pressed into leading impromptu rallies.

Sometimes, he didn't even require any pressing. "But what about them?" he asked, looking out from his car onto another town square packed with cheering supporters. "I must say at least a few words to them." What should have been a fast and discreet flight took on the air of a whistle-stop campaign tour. A provincial administrator insisted on hosting a lunch for him. Another village lit bonfires to herald his arrival. Along the way, other politicians fleeing Leopoldville joined the convoy, including two former ministers. Lumumba now had a total of eleven people in tow.

On the fourth day of the journey, December 1, the group finally reached the edge of Leopoldville province. They had successfully crossed river after river, all draining into the mighty Congo—the Nsele, the Kwango, the Wamba, the Kwilu. One more tributary before them, the Kasai, marked the beginning of the namesake Kasai province. They were now just one provincial border over from Orientale and its capital, Stanleyville. Better yet, Kasai was Lumumba's birthplace, and locals they encountered proved eager to help them. Residents emerged from huts with chickens, eggs, and bananas. To prevent anyone from catching up with Lumumba, they destroyed bridges, sank ferries, dug potholes, and erected roadblocks. "Wherever he passed, behind him remained only ruins," one observer noted.

Just hours after the group entered Kasai, however, the inevitable happened. Near the town of Mweka, the reconnaissance plane sent by Mobutu buzzed close to the ground. Its pilot spotted Lumumba's four-car convoy: the blue Peugeot, the Chevrolet station wagon, the Fiat, and the truck. The vehicles had pulled over for yet another ad hoc rally, and their location was relayed to the ANC. Upon finishing, Lumumba learned that unfriendly soldiers were on their way.

The obvious place for him to go was Luluabourg. As a provincial capital, the city held out the possibility of air transport, or at least of a major, direct road to Stanleyville. But to deceive the pursuing troops, the convoy turned away from the city and down a narrow forest lane, harsh terrain that soon required several more tire changes. The fugitives kept pressing on as night fell, the dark road illuminated by moonlight and their meager headlamps. At 11:00 p.m., they reached Lodi, a tiny village on the banks of the Sankuru River, where during the daytime travelers could catch a rudimentary ferry. The Sankuru was the last big obstacle before Stanleyville; on the other side lay good roads and a reliably pro-Lumumba population.

Once again, the ferry—a pair of dugout canoes lashed together with an outboard motor—was berthed on the wrong bank, so Lumumba traversed the six-hundred-yard-wide river in his own canoe, leaving behind most of the others. He roused the ferrymen and identified himself. The men had trouble believing that the sweaty, unkempt man before them was the famous former prime minister. "We know Lumumba well," one of them said. "He wears a suit and glasses. But you? You show up in a sports shirt." Only his identity cards convinced them, and they agreed to take his party across the river.

Back on the other side, however, trouble was brewing. The group that stayed behind had been waiting for hours when a car containing four or five ANC soldiers arrived. Since no one knew whether these were friendly forces—the loyalty of any given ANC soldier was the product of a complex calculation of paymaster, home region, ethnicity, and individual circumstance—the fugitives crouched down amid the trees, but the cries of Lumumba's two-year-old son, Roland, caused them to give up on hiding. At that point, finally, the ferry carrying Lumumba pulled up to shore.

The troops confronted Lumumba as he disembarked. "You don't have the right to order me around," he retorted. He issued a more desperate protest: "If this earth drinks my blood, it will mean your own destruction." But his words fell on deaf ears, and the arrival of reinforcements, another truckload of ANC soldiers, sealed his fate. The men hauled Lumumba and his companions back to Mweka.

Just outside the city, the soldiers' trucks came to a stop at a roadside UN camp. Manning the post was a platoon of Ghanaian soldiers and British officers. Lumumba sensed an opportunity. "Lieutenant, I am the prime minister!" he yelled at one of the officers from the back of an ANC truck. "I request United Nations protection."

Lumumba knew he could count on the sympathy of the Ghanaian troops—their government had remained a steadfast ally throughout the crisis. What he did not know was that their sympathy no longer made any difference. The reason could be traced back to UN headquarters in Leopoldville. From his office at the Royal, Rajeshwar Dayal had been following developments closely, and he had passed on clear instructions to blue helmets across the country: The UN would not be accused again of interfering in the Congo's internal matters. From here on out, it would stay on the sidelines. It would assist neither Lumumba nor his pursuers. The first part of the order was dutifully followed. At the post outside Mweka, the British officer stared back at Lumumba, stubbed out a cigarette, and turned away.

UN officials proved less diligent when it came to the other part of Dayal's order—not to assist Lumumba's pursuers. When an ANC detachment sent to retrieve Lumumba landed in Luluabourg, the local UN representative agreed that the Congolese soldiers would "intercept Lumumba... and take him directly to the airfield."

And so they did. At the Ghanaian outpost, as UN soldiers looked on, Lumumba's captors slapped, kicked, and rifle butted him, then drove him and the rest of his group to the airport in nearby Port Francqui. UN policy in the Congo dictated that airports could be used only for peaceful purposes, but the ANC soldiers paid no mind. The prisoners were forced into a DC-3 headed for the capital. UN troops made no attempt to prevent the plane from taking off.

Chapter 42

A Damp Cell

THE DC-3 CARRYING Lumumba and the others landed at Ndjili on the afternoon of December 2. The College of Commissioners had adjourned a meeting early in order to witness his arrival, and its members watched as he was led out of the plane like a tiger in captivity, his hands tied and a handler tugging him along. He looked somber yet dignified, his head held high, his glasses long since missing. His shirt was soiled; his cheek, bloody. "We've got him!" yelled excited soldiers. "Come and look!"

Lumumba was shoved into the bed of an army truck and driven away, trailed by a car of newsmen. The convoy sped triumphantly down Boulevard Albert. Thomas Kanza, himself avoiding arrest by keeping to the Royal, looked out in sadness as his erstwhile boss passed by below.

In Binza, on the outskirts of the capital, Mobutu was drinking champagne with his officers in celebration of the arrest. Then he strode onto his porch and watched, arms crossed, as the convoy pulled up. "Well!" he sneered at Lumumba. "You swore you'd have my skin, but now I have yours!" "I always said he would have a hard time getting to Stanleyville," he added to the gathered reporters.

Lumumba ignored him, looking away. One of the soldiers grabbed Lumumba by the hair and twisted his head upward at Mobutu, as if displaying a prized catch. Another soldier read out an old communiqué in which Lumumba declared himself the Congo's rightful prime minister. He then crumpled up the paper and tried to force it into the prisoner's mouth. This was Lumumba's rightful place: tied up and made to eat his words. Lumumba kept his lips sealed and turned his head away, blinking catatonically.

The show over, Lumumba was dragged out of view into a nearby building. The reporters could not see what went on. All they heard were screams.

That night, Lumumba was tortured further by Mobutu's men. They beat him and burned his beard. In the morning, it was time to leave. His legs freshly injured, Lumumba walked with difficulty and winced as he climbed into a truck. A large military convoy drove him eighty miles from Leopoldville to Camp Hardy in Thysville, where soldiers had stripped and humiliated their white officers during the mutiny five months earlier. Lumumba would end 1960 the way he had ended 1959: in prison.

U.S. officials did not feel sorry for him. One of the embassy's economic officers attended a party celebrating his capture. Hearing of Lumumba's maltreatment, Clare Timberlake worried more about the damage that news footage of the arrest would do to Mobutu's reputation. "While press accounts will be bad enough, movie recordings of these scenes will undoubtedly be picture of the year and will be a gift of an atomic bomb to the Soviet bloc and friends." He expressed a "dim hope that the television agencies concerned could be prevailed upon to suppress the pictures."

The images came out, and the reaction was as expected. In New York, African delegations besieged Hammarskjöld with complaints. Diplomats worried that Lumumba was about to face immediate execution. Hammarskjöld cabled Dayal: "The emotional tension here around the Lumumba case is considerable, and if things run wild or summary justice is executed, the consequences may be very bad also for the Organization and its operation. We are in the middle of an extraordinarily complicated and indeed politically dangerous situation."

Hammarskjöld also wrote an urgent note to Kasavubu, warning the president not to let any more harm come to Lumumba. Kasavubu had left Leopoldville for his home district, so Dayal had two of his officers track him down by helicopter. After some difficulty, they found him in his hometown of Tshela and delivered the letter to a secretary who met them at his residence. After fifteen minutes, the president came out into the garden. When one of the UN officers apologized for bothering him on a Sunday morning and explained the urgency of the matter, Kasavubu cut him off and huffed that he would answer the message "in due time." He stretched out his hand, indicating that the conversation was over. "Bon voyage."

Kasavubu's eventual reply to Hammarskjöld was equally cold. The president pronounced himself "somewhat surprised" by the concern for Lumumba given his ostensible crimes under the colonial-era penal code, which Kasavubu cited chapter and verse: "usurpation of public powers," "assaults on individual freedom accompanied by physical torture," "attacks against the security of the state," "organization of hostile bands for purposes of devastation, massacre and pillage," and "inciting soldiers to commit offenses." Hadn't Hammarskjöld himself accused Lumumba of perpetrating a "genocide" in Bakwanga? In any case, Kasavubu declared, this was a domestic matter.

At the UN Security Council, Hammarskjöld faced renewed flak from the Eastern bloc and from African and Asian nations, which accused his officials of having enabled Lumumba's arrest. He allowed that "mistakes have been made" but defended the UN's neutrality and hinted that the problem was that Mobutu was receiving Western financial support. He also warned that a UN withdrawal would trigger the Congo's complete collapse into civil war and ethnic strife. The outcome, he predicted, would be "a confused Spanish War situation, with fighting going on all over the prostrate body of the Congo."

His critics were unswayed. What did the UN have to show for its efforts in the Congo? Two secessionist states, two coups d'état, and the violent arrest of the leader who had invited in the organization to begin with. Within weeks of Lumumba's imprisonment, Guinea, Indonesia, Morocco, Egypt, and Yugoslavia—a group whose combined troops made up more than a quarter of the UN force—announced that they were withdrawing from the mission.

Lumumba's imprisonment ought to have upended the CIA's plans to kill him. But the bureaucratic machinery that had been set in motion in September, when he seemed on the verge of returning to power, had not ceased. On December 2, the same day Lumumba was forcibly returned to the city, Devlin welcomed one more addition to his station. His latest agent, code name WIROGUE, came with high praise from headquarters:

> He is a small, energetic individual, who has displayed shrewdness, cunning, ingenuity and inventiveness. He has a peculiar turn of mind which lends itself remarkably to nefarious and extra-legal activities. Excitement and intrigue are important factors in his life, he relishes it and as a result may be a little delicate to handle.... He is indeed aware of the precepts of right and wrong, but if he is given an assignment which may be morally wrong in the eyes of the world, but necessary because his case officer ordered him to carry it out, then it is right and he will dutifully undertake appropriate action for its execution without pangs of conscience. In a word, he can rationalize all actions.

Devlin was pleased. "WIROGUE appears to be just what the doctor ordered," he replied.

WIROGUE's real name was David Tzitzichvili, and he had packed several lifetimes of experience into his forty-one years. Born in Georgia during the country's short-lived brush with independence—after the collapse of the Russian Empire but before annexation by the Soviet Union—he moved with his family to Paris at the age of three, where he cycled through eighteen different schools and suffered the departure of his father and the suicide of his mother. During World War II, while working behind enemy lines in Germany to free imprisoned French officers, he was captured, interrogated for months at Gestapo headquarters, handed a death sentence, and sent to a concentration camp, but he lasted long enough to be rescued by the U.S. Army. After the German surrender, yearning for the derring-do of his wartime years, he robbed a bank of 1 million francs and was caught fleeing to Spain. He spent five years in prison before being released on parole. He was approached by the CIA in the French Alps in 1959.

The agency initially recruited Tzitzichvili to covertly enter the Soviet Union and set up electronic surveillance equipment. In preparation for the mission, Tzitzichvili was taught survival skills in the mountains of Alaska. At a safe house in the Virginia countryside, he learned how to write invisible messages, speak Russian, and withstand Soviet interrogation techniques. After the shootdown of a U-2 spy plane over the Soviet Union in May 1960, however, the operation was called off. Finding that his next assignment—make-work jobs in Sidney Gottlieb's Technical Services Staff—lacked excitement, Tzitzichvili asked to be reassigned. As luck would have it, the CIA's Africa division was looking for someone to help Devlin in the Congo.

The problem was that Tzitzichvili did not exactly blend in. A CIA file described him as "an unusual-looking man even by French standards," bald and bow-legged, with a wiry and diminutive frame and a prominent hook nose. The tips of his left forefinger and thumb were missing, the result of having picked up unexploded British ordnance in Germany during the war. His handlers worried that he was so distinctive in appearance that someone from his pre-CIA days might recognize him in the Congo. And so, before sending him on his way, the agency arranged for new dentures, a toupee, and a nose job. In the field, he would play the part of Georg Reiner, an Austrian with plans to open a small photography studio or repair shop. Devlin told Tzitzichvili to build up his cover and look out for potential intelligence assets, especially those with connections to Lumumba.

But WIROGUE quickly lived up to his code name. Devlin had trouble controlling him, likening him to an unguided missile— "the kind of man that could get you in trouble before you knew you were in trouble." He was a font of ideas, mostly wild schemes that included "a strong element of violence, mayhem or just plain larceny." Tzitzichvili had the unfortunate propensity to forget the names of people he had just met. His cover story didn't add up either: for an Austrian businessman, his German was suspiciously shaky, and yet he spoke French with a flawless Parisian accent. He was a spendthrift, to boot, quickly burning through his $500-a-month CIA salary and asking for an advance. When Devlin dug further, he discovered that in his first two weeks in Leopoldville, Tzitzichvili had splurged on three cars and three storefronts for his photography shop. He was spotted playing poker in his hotel, down 12,000 francs.

Worst of all, Tzitzichvili was indiscreet. He unwittingly checked into the same small hotel as QJWIN—the Astrid, a two-story, nineteen-room affair near the train station. When the two men inevitably ran into each other, their respective fake identities could not hide how much they had in common: Parisian childhoods, run-ins with the Nazis, criminal rap sheets. Ditching his cover story, which had him working in Vienna for the past five years, Tzitzichvili bragged about his time in Alaska, and when a suspicious Mankel pressed him, he admitted that he was working for the United States. Tzitzichvili offered Mankel $300 per month to join three teams of agents he was setting up in Leopoldville: a network for information gathering, a sabotage group, and an "execution squad." It was a scene from a Cold War spy comedy: one bumbling CIA agent unknowingly trying to recruit another.

Devlin cabled headquarters that he was "concerned by WIROGUE's free wheeling and lack of security." He went on: "The station has enough headaches without worrying about an agent who is not able to handle finances and who is not willing to follow instructions." Headquarters recommended Devlin put him "on probation" and threaten to fire him. Bronson Tweedy considered the incident "a typical example of an agent or asset full of piss and vinegar exceeding his brief."

By late December, the CIA's efforts to get Lumumba had all come to naught. Tzitzichvili had proved himself undeserving of the station's confidence. Justin O'Donnell, the senior case officer sent to move the assassination operation along, likewise gave Devlin the distinct impression of "not putting his whole heart and soul into the effort." He soon asked headquarters to be released, and left the country. Mankel had been eager to intercept Lumumba in Stanleyville—and received CIA permission to engage in "direct action"—but his target's capture rendered those plans moot, and he, too, departed.

The poisoning plot had fizzled out. At some point in December, Devlin took the assassination kit out from his office safe and carried it to the banks of the Congo River. He tossed the gloves and mask into some bushes. Then he knelt down, dug a small hole in the earth, dropped in the deadly vials, and covered them with dirt. The CIA no longer needed to take the lead in eliminating Lumumba. Mobutu was in charge of that project now. As Mobutu told the press, "Lumumba is completely finished." He let the ambiguity of his statement linger.

—

Camp Hardy lay on a plain below Thysville, linked to the hilltop town by a mile of sandy road. The military base was a neat rectangle, with the barracks, the weapons depots, and the canteen along the outside. Officers slept at the top of a low hill, in red-roofed houses whose sides were painted in calming pastels. The grounds even held a freshly built Protestant church, financed by American Baptists and clad in chipped stone.

At the center of the base sat the jail. Besides Lumumba, nine other political prisoners, MNC members all, languished behind bars: seven members of parliament (including two former ministers in Lumumba's government), a government clerk, and Lumumba's driver. They lived in cramped cells with cement floors and wooden benches for beds. As the highest-value prisoner, Lumumba was given special dispensation. He was housed separately, in an airy room usually reserved for the guard on duty, outfitted with a table, a chair, a mattress with sheets, a comforter, and a pillow.

"He sleeps in a soft bed," Mobutu noted at a press conference in Leopoldville, taking pains to advertise what he viewed as luxurious treatment. Lumumba had three servants at his disposal, he said. He even had a priest. The army was spending 1,000 francs a day taking care of him, which ostensibly included meals brought in from an upscale hotel restaurant in Thysville. Mobutu also displayed a certificate giving Lumumba a clean bill of health, signed by two Belgian doctors who had examined him. All Lumumba could complain of, Mobutu claimed, was a swollen ankle and inflammation around his eye. The UN had no right to protest. "Does Mr. Hammarskjöld think Lumumba would have done as much for me if I had been his prisoner?" he asked.

Clare Timberlake agreed, concluding that the real danger was that news of Lumumba's good treatment would generate resentment among the Congolese. As for Lumumba being beaten in full view of news cameras during his arrest, Timberlake warned Washington not to apply Western standards to African affairs: "In the Congo what passes as inhumane to us is customary among them. Thus the abuse of Lumumba shocks civilized countries while Congolese themselves consider that he is pampered." Camp Hardy, he wrote, "was probably the safest place to keep Lumumba locked up in the Congo."

Nonetheless, rumors circulated that Lumumba had gone on a hunger strike to protest the actual, far less comfortable conditions of his confinement. UN troops in Thysville reported that Lumumba's head and beard had been shaved, his hands were still bound, and his cell was filthy. His wife, Pauline Opango, freed after their forcible return to Leopoldville, was denied visits, as was the mother of his son François, Pauline Kie, who tried to gain access by disguising herself as a soldier. "She is doing everything she can to come here often and leave messages for me with the soldiers who are on our side," Lumumba recorded. Mobutu also refused for several weeks to let doctors from the International Red Cross examine the prisoner, and he flew into a rage when the organization publicly pressured him. Only in late December was a Swiss doctor from the group allowed into Camp Hardy.

The physician, Dr. Andreas Vischer, found Lumumba barefoot but dressed in clean clothes. On the table, someone had placed a hand of bananas, a bottle of water, and a bar of soap. Lumumba's eye injury, stemming from his violent arrest, was serious. Weeks later, he still suffered from intense pain and abnormal vision. The wounds to his ankles and wrists had healed, although scars remained visible. Lumumba also complained of constipation. He was allowed no exercise; for security reasons, walks were forbidden. He had no contact with the outside world, including his family, and no access to books—a particularly grievous loss, given how much they had sustained him during his previous stints behind bars. But he was still himself. "Lumumba took the opportunity to launch into vehement political statements," Vischer recorded, "which the delegate listened to without flinching."

Yet there was only so much Vischer could glean about Lumumba's condition. To secure access, the Red Cross had been forced to do away with its normal protocols. It had kept the visit secret and driven to the camp in a nondescript car to honor Mobutu's wish for minimal public attention. Contrary to Red Cross practices, spelled out in the Geneva Conventions, Vischer was not able to conduct his interviews in private. He was accompanied by Dr. Stéphane d'Arenberg, who, as a Belgian prince, a friend of King Baudouin's, and Mobutu's personal physician, was hardly a neutral party. Vischer was also watched over throughout by a crowd of spectators that included the camp commander, Louis Bobozo (Mobutu's former drill sergeant), the camp doctor, and a group of soldiers. Vischer himself might have understated the harshness of Lumumba's treatment. Lumumba claimed that his cell was damp, that he could not wash himself properly, and that his food consisted of dirty rice, bananas, or nothing at all for days at a time. But Vischer's report of the visit included no such information.

In another break with protocol, the Red Cross delayed releasing copies of the report to the authorities. Neither the Kasavubu-Mobutu government in Leopoldville nor the pro-Lumumba authorities in Stanleyville were deemed fit to receive even a "sanitized" copy. For one thing, explained Maurice Thudichum, a Red Cross official, doing so might give Lumumba's followers the false sense that he was still prime minister. For another thing, he argued, the Congolese were likely to misinterpret it. "We are dealing here with such primitive people, most of whom no doubt won't even understand the meaning of what they will be looking at."

Lumumba's condition remained the subject of rumors. At a National Security Council meeting at the White House, Allen Dulles cited "an unconfirmed report" that the prisoner had died in captivity. At the Royal, an anonymous source phoned and told Thomas Kanza that Kasavubu had visited the jail seeking a deal with Lumumba and had brought him a fresh shirt and pair of trousers as a peace offering. Rajeshwar Dayal, by contrast, heard that Lumumba had agreed to retire from politics and would be released imminently. Other sources claimed that the camp commander, Louis Bobozo, had invited Lumumba to a Christmas dinner in the officers' mess. It was an appealing image: the former prime minister, limping and straining to see, breaking bread with his captors in true holiday spirit.

Lumumba probably did not know it, but his allies back in Stanleyville—whom everyone now called Lumumbists—had grown stronger since his capture. More colleagues had joined their ranks, including Pierre Mulele, the former minister of education, and Rémy Mwamba, the former minister of justice. (They had been riding in the escape convoy with him but had evaded arrest at Lodi and trekked through the wilderness for days.) Lumumba's wife, Pauline, and their two-year-old son, Roland, had also made it to the city, in their case by plane.

While their leader remained behind bars, the Lumumbists felt they had amassed enough strength to openly challenge Mobutu. On December 12, eleven days after Lumumba's arrest, the former deputy prime minister Antoine Gizenga declared Stanleyville the temporary capital of the Republic of the Congo and named himself acting prime minister. Gizenga claimed to have six thousand troops under his control—three thousand in the city and three thousand more across Orientale province. He requested aid from the Soviets and East Germans, who stalled, but the Egyptians came through with a planeload of uniforms and weapons. The Stanleyville government also had valuable bargaining chips to push for Lumumba's release: it ruled over hundreds of whites, whom it threatened to decapitate, and had already imprisoned ten pro-Mobutu politicians, to whom it could easily do the same.

Gizenga also appeared to enjoy far greater popular support than the Kasavubu-Mobutu government. When Kasavubu took a good-will tour through Kasai province, he was shocked to be heckled with cries of "Where is Lumumba?" Whereas the Leopoldville regime controlled little territory beyond the capital, the one in Stanleyville controlled all of Orientale province, and it was making inroads elsewhere. On Christmas Day, a column of just sixty of its soldiers seized Bukavu, the capital of neighboring Kivu province, and kidnapped four local pro-Mobutu officials, including the governor. They then set their sights farther south, making plans to invade Katanga. Their easy success suggested that in the Congo political popularity trumped military power.

Mobutu spent Christmas in a panic, watching his limited writ over the country shrink even further. Working with Larry Devlin, whom headquarters had just authorized to provide additional financial support, he planned a military operation to retake Bukavu. Help also came from Belgium: in exchange for restoring diplomatic relations with Brussels, which technically remained severed, Mobutu was allowed to use the Belgian-administered territory of Ruanda-Urundi, which bordered Kivu province to the east, as a staging ground for his troops. Belgium's assistance breached international law, yet it turned out to be immaterial. Mobutu had predicted his soldiers would be "kissed on both cheeks" upon arrival in Bukavu, but as they crossed a bridge into the city, they took fire and immediately surrendered. The fiasco was a deep embarrassment for Mobutu. Discontent within the army ranks grew.

It was also rising in Western capitals, where more and more officials thought Mobutu and his commissioners should make way for a constitutional government, in keeping with his original pledge to step aside by December 31. They were none too pleased when he announced that the College of Commissioners would extend its mandate into the new year. Devlin impressed upon him the importance to world opinion of obtaining a "legal facade" for his regime, but he wasn't optimistic that Mobutu would agree, because the colonel felt—despite mounting evidence to the contrary—that he remained the only leader somewhat capable of controlling the ANC.

Dag Hammarskjöld had intended to visit the Congo for Christmas and buck up the long-suffering UN staff there but found he had too many commitments to attend to in New York. He was still under fire from all directions. The Americans thought he had lost his backbone. The Soviets wrote him off as an imperialist toady. And the Africans and Asians blamed him for Lumumba's current predicament. "I live in a kind of Congo-inferno, where I have not a moment for myself," he wrote to a friend, the Swedish artist Bo Beskow, on December 20. The next day, the secretary-general mailed a letter to another Bo, his brother: "Christmas will not give me any break, and the many books that are waiting to be read I will have to put in my suitcase when I fly to Africa in the first days of January. I must go for a few days to Leopoldville—a city I honestly dislike unusually much, even apart from the political difficulties.... So you see, I get a pleasant start to the New Year."

On Christmas Eve, he copied down a line from Psalms in his journal, which on most days that year had sat untouched on his desk: "I will lay me down in peace, and take my rest; for it is thou, Lord, only that makest me dwell in safety." The next morning, feeling lonely, he called his top Africa expert, Heinz Wieschhoff, who invited him to his home in Bronxville, just outside New York City. The two took a walk through the snow and then joined Wieschhoff's family for dinner.

Even on Christmas, they could scarcely have avoided discussing the Congo. There were now four governments laying claim to the country or to parts of it, each boasting its own army: Moise Tshombe's secessionist state in Katanga, Albert Kalonji's lesser version of the same in South Kasai—revived after Lumumba's ouster—and rivaling national governments in Leopoldville and Stanleyville. Civil war seemed imminent, and with it, the devastation of the Congolese people, the complete intrusion of the Cold War into the region, and, quite possibly, the collapse of the UN.

Thus ended the Year of Africa.

Chapter 43

Comeback

P RESIDENT-ELECT John F. Kennedy rang in 1961 by busying himself with the transition. He set to work on his inaugural address, dictating passages to his secretary while flying to Palm Beach and revising the speech on yellow legal pads at his father's villa there. He pondered policy, too. One major decision he had to make concerned Africa. At the beginning of December, in an early appointment intended to signal the priority he would give the continent, Kennedy had named G. Mennen Williams, Michigan's progressive governor, as the State Department's top Africa official. Chester Bowles, the former ambassador to India and friend of Dayal's, earned the number-two spot at Foggy Bottom, while another progressive, Adlai Stevenson, the two-time Democratic nominee for president, was announced as ambassador to the UN. All were willing to prioritize support for African nationalism over relations with Europe. All rejected a gradual approach to decolonization. All favored a strong UN.

Building a concrete action plan on these general principles was a different matter. Kennedy knew he wanted to side more openly with African aspirations than Eisenhower had, and he thought there should be more Black Foreign Service officers, but beyond that, many details remained unanswered. Most pressing of all was the question of how he would approach the Congo, which was now on the brink of civil war. Would he be wedded to the Eisenhower administration's policy of backing Mobutu and Kasavubu and rejecting Lumumba?

To inform his decisions, Kennedy met with Dag Hammarskjöld at the Carlyle Hotel in New York. He also asked his younger brother

Ted, then a twenty-eight-year-old recent law school graduate, to tag along with a delegation of Democratic senators on a two-week, ten-country Africa tour in December. The group was warmly welcomed, in large part because word had spread that the incoming American president had been an early supporter of Algerian independence. At stop after stop, crowds chanted, "Kennedy! Kennedy!"

In Leopoldville, the group met with Clare Timberlake, Larry Devlin, Mobutu, and several commissioners, but also with Rajeshwar Dayal, who judged the delegates somewhat receptive to his positions. They publicly pledged "full support" for the UN operation and, in a first for the U.S. government, urged the release of political prisoners in the Congo. In an interview with *The New York Times* after the trip, one of the senators, Frank Moss of Utah, promised a sharp break with Eisenhower's policies, noting that most Congolese supported Lumumba and opposed Mobutu. (Weeks later, Ted Kennedy even told the press of his impression that Kasavubu was a "tool" of the CIA.)

The outlines of Kennedy's Africa policy were taking shape. On his desk lay a small book of a report on the continent, written by a task force he had set up after his election. It began boldly: "Africa has been all but decolonized. In important respects, our African policy has not." On the Congo, the authors warned against an oversimplified "neat pro-Communist vs. anti-Communist frame." Of Lumumba, they noted that, although "unstable," he remained "a symbol of parliamentary legitimacy to many Africans both in and out of the Congo." Large numbers of Congolese admired him "as a man of courage and a thorough-going nationalist."

Many observers in the Congo certainly had the impression that Kennedy would change course. Antoine Gizenga, for example, issued a declaration expressing "a certain optimism" about the new president. "It was common knowledge that he would reverse Eisenhower's hard-line policies towards the Congo," Dayal noted. "He would not be averse to a coalition government to include Lumumba."

But what Lumumba's supporters saw as their due and the UN saw as a path to stability, the U.S. embassy and the CIA station in Leopoldville considered a disaster in the making. Devlin wrote to headquarters bemoaning rumors that "with the change in administration, our policy in the Congo will be reversed and that we will favor a return of Lumumba in some capacity." He added, "Insofar as our Congo policy is concerned, I firmly believe that a drastic change at this time would be both disastrous and ineffectual."

Lurking behind the firmly held policy arguments were surely more self-interested motives. When Timberlake learned that the new undersecretary of state would be Chester Bowles, an enemy from their shared time in India, he worried about his own career. Devlin had less cause for concern, since Kennedy had announced that Allen Dulles would continue at the helm of the CIA. But the station chief had good reason to think that his job was on the line as well. The return of Lumumba—a man he had bribed protesters and politicians in Leopoldville to oppose and been ordered by higher-ups in Washington to kill—could only have appeared as a conspicuous failure on his part. The same logic also applied to Dulles. The CIA was running the show in the Congo and had tied its fate to Mobutu's. What was good for Lumumba was bad for Mobutu and, by extension, his American patrons.

Kennedy, however, likely knew none of this. When Dulles and his deputy Richard Bissell flew to Palm Beach for a poolside post-election briefing, they discussed at length a planned operation against Cuba, in which CIA-trained Cuban exiles would invade their home country and overthrow the Castro regime. The Congo received less attention, and no mention was made of the CIA's efforts to assassinate Lumumba.

But what was obvious to anyone paying attention was that even from prison, Lumumba was once more on the rise. Even the CIA could not deny that its efforts to prop up the government in Leopoldville were failing. As Kennedy finished drafting his inaugural address, an official intelligence estimate painted a grim picture of the Congo. Kasavubu was a powerless figurehead. Mobutu could not reliably count on the support of his soldiers. Of the three main figures in the country, the report concluded, the former prime minister was the strongest:

Lumumba retains considerable influence in his home province, Orientale; probably enjoys more popular support throughout the rest of the country than any other leader; and has powerful friends among African nationalists and in the Bloc. In the eyes of the UN Secretary General as well as of many UN members he still has a legal basis to his claim for the Premiership. He may return to power.

Dag Hammarskjöld witnessed for himself the ex-premier's enduring power. On his way to talks with South Africa's apartheid government, the secretary-general stopped over in Leopoldville on January 4. The goal for his thirty-six hours in the Congo was to advance the UN's push for a political reconciliation, and the cries of "Free Lumumba!" greeting him outside the Royal could only have hardened his conviction that such a deal would need to include the imprisoned leader.

But that was easier said than done, and little went according to plan. Hammarskjöld realized he had left behind his briefcase, which was full of classified documents concerning the Congo operation, on the airplane. The city was largely shut down on account of a national holiday celebrating the two-year anniversary of the 1959 Leopoldville riots. And Hammarskjöld's meetings with Mobutu's commissioners—the colonel himself was away in Kasai—were frustratingly unproductive. When he pressed them to reopen parliament and release Lumumba from prison, or at least treat him humanely behind bars, the commissioners would not budge. Dayal, who was present, considered the unproductive session a "dialogue of the deaf."

For what it was worth, Mobutu had finally, after months of stonewalling, permitted the entry of the UN conciliation commission charged with brokering a settlement—a task that now included negotiating Lumumba's release. Its members, representatives of troop-contributing African and Asian states, had reached Leopoldville a day before Hammarskjöld.

The secretary-general stayed at Rajeshwar Dayal's. By now, the Indian diplomat had moved from an apartment in the Royal to a Victorian-style villa on the Congo River. An upgrade though it was, the house was infested with beetles and other creatures, and before Hammarskjöld's arrival, he and his wife had to spend an hour clearing bats from the place. But the residence proved a pleasant venue for a lunch that Hammarskjöld hosted to lift the spirits of the UN operation's hardworking staff. They had been separated for months from their families and labored under difficult conditions. Hammarskjöld mingled amiably with his subordinates and thanked them for their service. For a moment, one guest thought, everyone could "forget the horrors that lay just beyond the neatly manicured lawns."

But one reminder of the Congo's troubles came from right next door—from the home of Cléophas Kamitatu, the provincial official who had helped Lumumba escape Leopoldville. Kamitatu approached Hammarskjöld with a letter smuggled out of Lumumba's cell at Camp Hardy. Perhaps hoping to overcome the bad blood between them by appealing to Hammarskjöld's better angels, Lumumba wrote of the conditions in which he was being held:

> I have requested that fruit be brought for me with my own money, for the food I am given here is bad. Although the doctor gave his permission, the military authorities keeping me prisoner here have refused to allow this and tell me that they have orders to that effect from the head of state, Colonel Mobutu. The doctor here at Thysville has prescribed a short walk for me every evening so that I can get out of my cell for a little while, but the colonel and the district commissioner refuse to allow me to do so. The clothes that I have now worn for thirty-five days have never been washed, and I am not permitted to wear shoes. In a word, we are living amid absolutely impossible conditions.... I remain calm and hope that the United Nations will help extricate us from this situation.

When Hammarskjöld was approached with the letter, he turned red and refused to accept it.

Lumumba smuggled out a second letter. This one was addressed to Albert Onawelo, a relative from Onalua with whom he had lived after leaving prison for his embezzlement conviction. The prisoner again raised the conditions of his confinement—"worse than it was under the colonialists"—and complained about constipation. Then he tended to his financial affairs. He arranged for his wife to receive 30,000 francs, of which she would keep 17,000 herself for the care of little Roland. ("I don't want the child to go hungry or eat unsuitable food," he specified.) The rest was to be divided up among relatives and colleagues—6,000 francs to his alcoholic brother, Charles, "for his subsistence"; 3,000 to Pauline Kie, mother of his son François; and 2,000 each to Michel Tshungu, a devoted member of his household staff, and Onawelo himself. "I place all my hope in God to get out of here," he wrote.

And yet as Lumumba drafted what was essentially a will, events beyond the gates of Camp Hardy were continuing to turn in his favor. In addition to the promising signs from the incoming administration in Washington and the activity of the conciliation commission in Leopoldville, pan-Africanist leaders gathering in Morocco had issued a forceful call for his release, and the Lumumbist government in Stanleyville was gaining strength. To the south of Orientale province, its troops had entered northern Katanga, taken the mining center of Manono, and put a pro-Lumumba politician in charge. To the west, they were massing on the border with Équateur province. Stanleyville's authority was spreading like an ink stain on a map. Nearly half the country was in its hands.

The Lumumbists had also taken a valuable prisoner: Gilbert Pongo, a young security officer whom Mobutu had sent to the interior to hunt Lumumba and who had returned triumphantly with his prey. On account of that success, Pongo had been put in charge of the ANC's operation against Gizenga's troops in Bukavu. When it failed, Pongo was arrested and taken to Stanleyville, where he was made to record an audiotape urging Kasavubu to set Lumumba free. In case the message was not clear, a Stanleyville official—Christophe Gbenye, former interior minister under Lumumba—declared, "Gilbert Pongo's safety depends on the immediate liberation of our prime minister, Patrice Lumumba." A prisoner exchange, floated by Hammarskjöld days earlier, was now a distinct possibility.

In a way, the Congo crisis had come full circle. In January 1960, Lumumba had sat behind bars in Elisabethville, imprisoned by the colonial regime. But at the roundtable in Brussels, the authorities had realized that he held too much sway to be excluded from discussions about the Congo's political future and had sprung him from prison. A year later, with Lumumba locked up in Camp Hardy, the UN, the incoming U.S. administration, and perhaps—under duress—even Mobutu's own government recognized that they could no more rid themselves of the man than the Belgians. Another roundtable was even in the works, with speculation that Lumumba might be freed to attend. It seemed possible, even likely, that he could bide his time in jail until his popularity effected his freedom a second time.

But in an instant, it was not the attitudes of Kennedy administration appointees or UN diplomats that held the greatest promise of liberating Lumumba but those of Congolese troops. Among the ANC soldiers that remained under Mobutu's control, morale was continually sinking. Camp Leopold, the epicenter of the July mutiny, seemed on the verge of another uprising. Similar troubles were bedeviling Camp Hardy. From the moment Lumumba arrived, an intense debate had broken out among the rank and file. Like the ANC more broadly, the soldiers at Camp Hardy were divided. Some supported Lumumba. They passed him messages. They wanted him freed and restored to power. Others held no brief for him, but wanted him transferred elsewhere, since his presence at the camp was disruptive. Still others wanted to kill him.

On the night of January 12, around fifty young soldiers, motivated by some combination of disgruntlement over low pay, poor housing, and Lumumba's captivity, climbed the hill to the officers' quarters and stormed their houses, harassing them and their wives. Louis Bobozo, the camp commander, managed to put down the mutiny, but the next morning he called Mobutu to let him know that the situation was untenable. "I no longer want Lumumba here," Bobozo said. "I guaranteed security one time; I can't guarantee it a second time." If there was another riot, he warned Mobutu, Lumumba might walk free.

Larry Devlin had been keeping a wary eye on the situation inside the ANC. On the day of the mini-rebellion at Camp Hardy, he had urged CIA headquarters to green-light millions of dollars in "special combat bonuses" to appease restive troops around the country. In a follow-up cable the next day, he predicted that without such a cash infusion, the Mobutu-Kasavubu government could fall in a matter of days. "The result would almost certainly be chaos and the return of Lumumba to power," he wrote.

Mobutu decided to head to Thysville and calm down the troops himself, accompanied by Kasavubu, the head commissioner Justin

Bomboko, and Victor Nendaka, the head of the security services. They brushed off Devlin's advice not to walk into an unruly and potentially hostile military base.

"What if you are killed?" Devlin asked. "Or taken prisoner by the mutineers?"

"Larry, this is an all-or-nothing situation," Mobutu said. "Either we gain control in Thysville or the government will fall."

The four leaders flew to Thysville and drove to Camp Hardy. Most of the political prisoners made a ruckus, breaking the doors and windows of the building where they were held in a bid to get the attention of the visiting leaders. Not Lumumba. When a sympathetic soldier opened the door to his cell, he did not step past the threshold, suspecting a trap.

Outside, Mobutu assembled the camp's soldiers, told them to stay out of political matters, and promised everyone a pay raise— presumably to be funded with American money that he had yet to secure. He took off again without bothering to see Lumumba. But he and others agreed that it was best to send the man elsewhere.

Chapter 44

The Green Light

IT WASN'T A novel idea. As early as October, when the former premier was still under house arrest, one of Mobutu's Belgian advisers had proposed sending him on "vacation" to Katanga. After Lumumba's escape and subsequent arrest in December, Belgian intelligence reported that the same idea was again making the rounds in Leopoldville. Another option was to move Lumumba to Bakwanga in secessionist South Kasai, whose leader, Albert Kalonji, readily volunteered to take him. The trouble was that Bakwanga airport remained under the control of pro-Lumumba UN troops from Ghana, so sending him there would not be without risk. Wherever he ended up, it was no mystery how local authorities would receive the prisoner. Kalonji blamed Lumumba for the massacre in Bakwanga months earlier and was on the record calling him "an assassin who must be tried and executed" so that a vase could be made from his skull. A similar fate awaited in Elisabethville. "If he comes here, we will do what the Belgians couldn't do," Godefroid Munongo, Katanga's feared interior minister, told the press. "We will kill him."

The separatists' evident bloodlust was a godsend for Leopoldville. If Lumumba remained a political threat even from behind bars, liquidating him might be a better solution than setting him loose once again. But leaders in Leopoldville ultimately lacked the unity and resolve to act on this realization. If they bloodied their own hands, there was no telling how the ANC, foreign diplomats, and the population at large might react. Mobutu himself continued to be racked by doubt and indecision and even saw his doctor for help with the mental anguish. For reasons both political and psychological, some distance and deniability was needed. The dirty work had to be outsourced.

None of this had moved past the ideation stage before, but the growing risk that troops at Camp Hardy would free Lumumba brought on a renewed sense of urgency. On January 14, the day after Mobutu returned from Camp Hardy, the commissioners decided to take action. Using an agreed-upon code over a radio link, they asked the "Jew"—Moise Tshombe, in what was perhaps a nod to his biblical first name—to take custody of the prisoner, who had been assigned the less-than-inspired alias of "Satan."

The homicidal musings of his ministers notwithstanding, Moise Tshombe was not keen to be handed responsibility for Lumumba. His relationship with Mobutu remained tense because Elisabethville continued to reject the central government's authority, and although he detested Lumumba, bringing him to Katanga would only add to the ledger of his state's misdeeds in global opinion. But partly in response to intense lobbying by Harold d'Aspremont Lynden, the Belgian minister of African affairs, Tshombe reluctantly gave in.

Larry Devlin considered himself "an adviser to the commissioners' government" and was in touch constantly with the Binza Group, Mobutu's inner circle. So it was natural when, on January 14, he learned of the plan to transfer Lumumba (to Bakwanga, he was told). Normally, he would have kept his superiors in Washington informed of such a major development concerning the fate of the United States' main antagonist in the Congo. But as it happened, January 14 was also the date Devlin received disappointing news from headquarters: his request for millions of dollars to pay off Mobutu's troops and keep the threat of an ANC mutiny at bay was, for now, denied. Devlin's cables about the impending mutiny had kicked off a flurry of activity and debate in Washington. The CIA wanted to give Devlin the go-ahead to promise Mobutu more cash, since time was of the essence, but the State Department preferred to stall, and its views prevailed. The question was "one of high policy," in the CIA's disappointed conclusion, that needed to wait for the next president. A cable went back to Devlin: the U.S. government would not approve the funds, so he should not raise the matter with Mobutu.

This was the context in which Devlin got word from the commissioners that Lumumba would be transferred out of Thysville. At that point, he had a decision to make: What should he tell headquarters? Devlin's job was to keep them informed, but by now he had learned how to play the bureaucratic game. He had, for example, developed the trick of sending cables at 5:00 p.m., Washington time, that ended with the note, "Will assume concurrence if not advised by close of business." Devlin realized that it was easier to ask for forgiveness than beg for permission and that sometimes there was value in keeping Washington out of the loop.

If his superiors wanted to avoid major policy changes until Kennedy took office, as their opposition to additional cash for the ANC suggested, then they might ask him to stop, or at least delay, Lumumba's transfer. That seemed especially likely, given that the CIA's own plans to assassinate Lumumba had by now effectively been shelved. The State Department had recently told Timberlake to urge Congolese officials that the former prime minister's "physical treatment be as humane as is compatible with maximum security." (Timberlake passed on the directive halfheartedly.) Official Washington no longer needed Lumumba murdered; imprisonment, perhaps eventually a trial, seemed like the safest way to sideline him. Given that taking the former prime minister to rebel territory equated to his near-certain death, there was good reason to think that Washington would tell Devlin to put the brakes on the commissioners' plan.

And so Devlin sat on the explosive news about Lumumba's fate. Even as he kept headquarters informed of other twists and turns in the Congo, he chose to say nothing about the most important development. In light of his influence over the commissioners, who regularly took his advice and money, there was every reason to believe that he could have talked them out of their plan. That Devlin did not do. In fact, in the context of his intimate relationship with Mobutu and his retinue, his lack of protest could only have been interpreted as a green light. This silence sealed Lumumba's fate.

Before sunrise on January 17, well ahead of the 6:00 a.m. reveille that would awake Camp Hardy's soldiers, Lumumba's cell door squeaked open. Roused by his guards and told to leave the room, he resisted.

They pushed him out. Lumumba must have been crestfallen when he looked up to see Victor Nendaka, the head of the security services.

The two men had once been close. Nendaka had been the vice president of the MNC and had temporarily led the party after Lumumba's October 1959 arrest. At the roundtable in Brussels, Nendaka had threatened a boycott of the proceedings if Lumumba were not released from prison. But he had turned on Lumumba in the months that followed, denouncing him as a far-left radical. Nendaka went on to lose his bid for parliament, and he had held no government office until Mobutu brought him on after his coup d'état. Now a bitter foe of Lumumba's, Nendaka, a core member of the Binza Group, was the man who in December had led efforts to capture him. He had also taken part in the beatings after Lumumba's arrest. For a prisoner still holding out a glimmer of hope for release, the sight of Nendaka was bad news.

Nendaka collected two other inmates, Maurice Mpolo and Joseph Okito, both of whom had also been arrested while trying to flee to Stanleyville. Besides Lumumba, they were the highest-ranking of the nine political prisoners being held at the camp. Nendaka ushered the three men—Mpolo, Okito, and Lumumba, who continued resisting in vain—toward a line of jeeps. The convoy slipped through Thysville just as the first hints of dawn began to brighten the sleeping city. It passed a small camp of Moroccan UN troops and continued up a steep and twisty road cutting through the Crystal Mountains, the low range on Africa's Atlantic coast. Soon, the paved road turned into dirt.

After an hour and a half, the convoy reached a grassy airstrip. Employees of a nearby cement plant saw Lumumba, his face bloodied, pushed with the other prisoners into a 1930s-era biplane. Joining Nendaka and his three charges in the cabin were a trio of ANC soldiers—all Baluba from Kasai, so chosen to guarantee firmness toward Lumumba. They did not disappoint. After takeoff, the soldiers began roughing up the prisoners to the point that the French pilot had to yell at them to knock it off, lest they destabilize the light aircraft.

The plane touched down in Moanda, a seaside resort town on the Congo's slim Atlantic coast. Favored as a weekend getaway among Belgian settlers and, more recently, UN officials on leave, Moanda had a golf course, a lighthouse, and a beautiful beach. For Lumumba's captors, though, the town's attraction was its airfield's long runway and lack of UN guards. A large, four-engine DC-4 was waiting, along with two of Mobutu's commissioners, who, like the ANC soldiers, were Baluba from South Kasai and thus at low risk of harboring any residual sympathy for their prisoners.

The flight to Elisabethville was an ordeal. The guards wrapped the prisoners' mouths, eyes, and ears shut with tape and took turns forcing them to kneel in the aisle and take kicks and rifle blows to the back and stomach. At one point, the tape on Lumumba's ears and mouth came loose, and he recognized the voice of one of the commissioners, Jonas Mukamba, whom he knew faintly. "Jonas, my brother," he said, but it was no use. The vicious beatings paused only when the soldiers passed around a bottle of whiskey. They ripped out tufts of Lumumba's goatee, removed the tape over his mouth, and forced him to swallow the hair.

The violence disturbed the plane's crew—two Belgians, a Frenchman, and an Australian. The radio operator was so sickened that he vomited. The pilot emerged from the cockpit to tell the two commissioners that their sudden movements threatened the plane's stability. "Say, we have to hand Lumumba over alive," the co-pilot gently warned. Eventually, the crew gave up and simply locked shut the cockpit door, ignoring the screams from the cabin. Never did they attempt to save Lumumba and his co-captives—for example, by radioing the UN or landing at an airport where the organization's forces might intervene. After eleven hundred miles and five hellish hours, Lumumba was a sorry sight: his khaki pants and white shirt were tattered, his glasses had been smashed into his eyes, his face was swollen, blood was trickling from the corners of his mouth, and clumps of hair were missing from his head. But he was alive.

Upon touching down in Elisabethville, the plane taxied straight to a hangar for the Katangese Air Force. A storm was gathering; lightning flashed in the distance, and thunder echoed across the grassland. A member of the airport's security staff noted the time of the plane's arrival in a report: 4:45 p.m. In the column for "number of passengers," he wrote simply the initials "PL."

As the propellers of the DC-4 eased to a stop, the hatch door opened to reveal an armored vehicle, its cannon cocked toward the plane, and about a hundred police and soldiers arrayed in a semi-circle around the exit. The great and the good of Elisabethville had turned up as well: three Katangan ministers, including Godefroid Munongo, and several high-ranking Belgian intelligence and military officers.

Also watching were six Swedish UN troops, one of whom was just fifty yards from the plane and mere feet from the semicircle of guards. The men soon reported that they looked on helplessly as the prisoners emerged from the plane:

> They were blindfolded and their hands were tied behind their backs. One of them, the first to disembark, had a small beard. As they came down the stairs, the gendarmes ran on to them, kicked them all, beat them with their rifle butts, and threw them on to the jeep. Four gendarmes then jumped into the jeep and sat down. At that point one of the prisoners yelled loudly. The jeep then took the lead of the vehicle convoy and drove off along the runway towards the far end of the airfield, past the landing beacon, where an opening was cut in the fence to let the convoy out.

For some time, that was the last the outside world would hear of Lumumba.

Chapter 45

Patrice Akufi

Only late in the day on January 17, after Lumumba's transfer to Katanga became public knowledge, did Devlin inform head-quarters that he had been tipped off to the plan three days earlier. On the nineteenth, he received a cable from the CIA's man in Elisabeth-ville, David Doyle, that played off the squeaky-clean 1950 hit "If I Knew You Were Comin' I'd've Baked a Cake": "Thanks for Patrice. If we had known he was coming we would have baked a snake." Devlin had little doubt about what would happen next. "There was a general assumption, once we learned he had been sent to Katanga, that his goose was cooked."

In the absence of reliable news about Lumumba's condition and whereabouts, confusion and speculation abounded. William Canup, the U.S. consul in Katanga, found it "impossible to totally disregard persistent rumors that Patrice Lumumba died shortly after arrival as a result of mistreatment here." Clare Timberlake thought it unlikely that Lumumba's handlers had beaten him to death, a conclusion he based on a dubious anthropological analysis of central Africa's big-gest ethnic group. ("The Bantus...are quite capable of murdering each other in tribal warfare, but they do not capture people and kill them. They beat them up unmercifully, but they do not kill them.") At the UN, Rajeshwar Dayal assumed that Lumumba was alive and set about arranging another Red Cross visit. Since the ex-premier's arrest in December, Dayal had come to wonder whether he had been wrong to order his UN troops not to interfere, and he now told his men they should grant Lumumba at least temporary protection, should he request it.

Dag Hammarskjöld feared the prisoners' imminent execution. "I have learnt with considerable concern about the transfer of Lumumba, Okito, and Mpolo," he wrote to Dayal. "What this may lead to is only too obvious." He sent Moise Tshombe an urgent letter insisting on a proper trial for the captives. Tshombe's reply was not encouraging: "I am quite astonished at the concern on the part of the United Nations in regard to an ex–Prime Minister who, incidentally, has been recognized as guilty of genocide by the international organization." But although Tshombe's assertion that he merely wanted to cut Lumumba off from contact with the outside world strained credulity, it at least implied he was still alive. In another sign of hope, Justin Bomboko, the president of the College of Commissioners, announced that "Mr. Lumumba and his friends are and will remain in the Congo" and that "their transfer from Thysville to Elisabethville was not motivated by bad intentions."

Although it had not long ago tried to kill Lumumba itself, the Eisenhower administration, now in its final days, fretted about the geopolitical repercussions that his death in the custody of Katangan authorities might have. If the Congo's national hero were to die at the hands of a white-backed secessionist regime, the West might well lose Africa for good. Not that Washington harbored any sympathies for the man himself. Its interest in Lumumba's survival "stems from considerations of international opinion and not from tender feelings toward him," Canup, the U.S. consul in Elisabethville, explained to Godefroid Munongo, Katanga's interior minister. On January 18, two days before Eisenhower left office, a top State Department official told a Belgian diplomat that Lumumba must not be "liquidated."

On January 20, John F. Kennedy stood in the freezing cold outside the U.S. Capitol, placed his hand on a family Bible, and took the oath of office. His brief inaugural address included a vow to the Congolese and the millions of others who had recently achieved independence around the world. "To those new states whom we welcome to the ranks of the free," he said, "we pledge our word that one form of colonial control shall not have passed away merely to be replaced by a far more iron tyranny." But he now had real and urgent decisions to make. Lumumba's transfer to Katanga the previous week had precipitated the Congo's unraveling. In Stanleyville, gangs of pro-Lumumba youths were parading through town singing war songs and vowing revenge. Antoine Gizenga's troops were advancing into Équateur province. More countries were threatening to pull their contributions to the UN force, and Dag Hammarskjöld told the Security Council that the UN operation might have to wind down.

Right away, Kennedy ordered a wholesale review of U.S. policy toward the Congo. A task force of officials from the State Department, Pentagon, and CIA was set up to draft a new approach. Dean Rusk, the new secretary of state, issued a broad directive: "Take the ceiling off your imaginations." But when Ghana's president, Kwame Nkrumah, sent Kennedy a long and impassioned letter on January 23, pleading for a personal intervention to secure Lumumba's release, Kennedy took six days to reply with a short, noncommittal message that did not even mention Lumumba's name. He evidently felt he could not commit to a Congo policy before his review was complete.

That review was revealing the broader fissures in the administration. On the one side were those liberals willing to challenge Cold War orthodoxy and reset relations with the Soviet Union and newly independent states—the same officials whose appointment had given Dayal hope, such as Chester Bowles, G. Mennen Williams, and Adlai Stevenson. On the other were traditionalists, men whose minds were more concentrated on the Communist threat and who considered this no time to experiment with optimism. Their ranks included many Pentagon officials, such as Paul Nitze, as well as Dean Acheson and John McCloy, both of whom had served in the Truman administration and, though now out of government, still wielded influence.

When it came to the Congo, two questions stood out. The first was what to do about the UN operation: empower its forces and bring the disorderly ANC under UN control, or push for Dayal to be replaced with a more reliably pro-Western UN representative? The second was what to do about the government in Leopoldville: legitimize Kasavubu and Mobutu and help them build a full-fledged government composed of so-called moderates, or free imprisoned politicians and allow parliament to put a broad coalition of leaders in power? Bound up in this second question was the matter of Lumumba. Should the United States push for his freedom? Would it countenance him in any position of power? The debate between the two camps played out publicly, with both sides leaking to the press, resulting in contradictory stories about the direction of U.S. policy.

At first, the liberals seemed to be winning the battle. A State Department policy paper called for a "strengthened mandate" for the UN, including control over the ANC, and a "broadly based government including all principal political elements in the Congo." When Larry Devlin informed Mobutu—recently promoted to the rank of general—of the mood in Washington and suggested that he might have to step down, Mobutu became irate. He drew his revolver and waved it in front of Devlin's face. "If this happens," he said, "I will die."

Devlin reassured Mobutu that he himself disagreed vehemently with this new direction. And he soon found an opportunity to make his views known: When he and Clare Timberlake were called to Washington, D.C., for consultations, the two men set about on a rapid-fire lobbying mission. At a bar near the State Department, they discussed their frustration with the administration's liberal wing, in particular their alarm over what they viewed as the pro-UN bias of G. Mennen Williams, the new assistant secretary of state for Africa. Realizing they had a likely ally in Allen Dulles, they decided to call the CIA director from a pay phone in the bar. Sure enough, with Dulles's help, Timberlake and Devlin managed, in their brief trip to the snow-covered capital, to wrest control of Congo policy from the liberals. The State Department's proposal for "a broadly based government including all principal political elements in the Congo" got watered down into "a middle-of-the-road cabinet." And in the new plan, the United States would demand the release of Lumumba and other political prisoners only once that government had been formed.

Even Williams went along with the new line. "We do not feel that Lumumba should be released," he said during a joint appearance with Timberlake at a closed-door session of the Senate Foreign

Relations Committee. Timberlake could hardly have improved upon Williams's characterization of the danger posed by Lumumba:

> This fellow is a character who seems almost a mystical one. You lock him up like a Houdini, and somehow he winds up running the show, and we certainly do not want to end up in a place where Lumumba can start from the bottom and eventually work up to the top. And if we possibly can, we would like to keep him out of the picture entirely.

In early February, via Conakry, Casablanca, and Cairo, Thomas Kanza made it to New York, where he led a self-styled UN delegation representing the Stanleyville government. He reconnected with his old acquaintance Eleanor Roosevelt, whom he hoped would push Kennedy to take action to protect Lumumba and other political prisoners in the Congo. But he came across a piece of disturbing news. A Guinean diplomat told Kanza of a meeting at which he observed a pro-Kasavubu Congolese delegate pass a note to a colleague. Looking over his shoulder, the Guinean diplomat had been able to make out two words: *Patrice akufi*—Lingala for "Patrice is dead."

Lumumba, Maurice Mpolo, and Joseph Okito had not been seen in public for several weeks when Godefroid Munongo, the Katangan interior minister, held a series of press conferences. Munongo announced that the three prisoners had broken out of an isolated farmhouse where they were being held. They had hot-wired a black Ford sedan, crashed it into a ditch, and continued their escape on foot. Munongo invited a reporter to the scene to take photos of the damaged car. He offered a 300,000-franc reward for Lumumba's capture and asked tipsters to call a hotline. On February 13, he announced that the fugitives had been caught and killed. A group of hostile villagers—he would not say where—had massacred them in an act of vigilante justice. Munongo produced three death certificates, stamped with "State of Katanga" and signed by a Belgian doctor. One declared that a thirty-six-year-old male named Patrice Lumumba had died "in the bush of Katanga." The age was off by a year, and no cause of death was listed. "You'd recognize that goatee and those bulging eyes anywhere," the doctor said when asked how he identified the body.

"I'd be lying if I said that the death of Lumumba makes me sad," Munongo told the press. "You know my feelings on the subject: he is a common criminal." To those who accused the Katangan authorities of having carried out an assassination, he said, "Prove it."

Chapter 46

The Antelope Hunters

THE TRUTH—WHICH would come out in dribs and drabs over the ensuing years and decades as lips loosened—was less baroque. From the Elisabethville airport, Lumumba, Mpolo, and Okito were driven to a white bungalow and ushered into a sparsely furnished living room. Surrounded by tall grass and shrubs, the house had a corrugated-metal roof and a wide terrace. It belonged to a Belgian poultry farmer who was waiting to move in. Military police had been training nearby and knew the place to be vacant, so they requisitioned it in the little time they had to prepare for Lumumba's arrival and blocked off the roads leading to it.

Two Belgians ran the show that night: Julien Gat, a captain in the Force Publique before independence and now the head of the military police in the Katangese Gendarmerie, and Frans Verscheure, a commissioner in the colonial police before independence and now in the Katangan police. Verscheure and Lumumba, who happened to be the same age, had a history. In January 1960, when Lumumba had been sentenced to prison for inciting a riot and flown to Elisabethville, it was Verscheure who had led him down the stairs from the airplane. A press photo of the two briefly made Verscheure a minor celebrity in the city. This time around, Verscheure would make sure that his prisoner would not be released so easily. To ward off any potential interference from UN troops, a squad of soldiers and an armored vehicle stood guard outside the bungalow with orders to shoot UN forces on sight. The precautions proved unnecessary, for no UN rescue operation was in the works, or even under discussion.

It took Moise Tshombe and his inner circle just ninety minutes of whiskey-fueled discussion to make up their minds on how to proceed. Keeping Lumumba imprisoned, even in preparation for a show trial, was out of the question. Half measures would only invite international opprobrium and raise the prospect of negotiations for his freedom.

At the bungalow, Lumumba, Mpolo, and Okito endured three hours of torture. One Belgian officer beat the prisoners so hard he injured his hand. Splinters of wood were shoved under Lumumba's fingernails and toenails. After Lumumba was dragged into the bathroom, his head was banged into the bidet. "I'm thirsty," he let out at one point. A soldier fetched a bucket of water. "Here, have a drink," he said, throwing the bucket in his face.

The cruelty was not confined to the soldiers and police. Drunken ministers in the Katangan government shuffled in and out to taunt and beat the prisoners. Godefroid Munongo was at the house, as was Jean-Baptiste Kibwe, the Katangan minister of finance. "I told you in Brussels during the roundtable that if you set foot in Katanga, you would piss blood and your head would roll to my feet," Kibwe told Lumumba. Even Tshombe had a turn with the prisoners, staining his suit with blood in the process.

As the horrors went on, the prisoners grew dazed and listless. Lumumba spoke little. When told that he would be dead soon, he replied, "At the point where I am, it doesn't matter." A Belgian lieutenant noticed that even in this sorry state the former prime minister maintained his composure: "I remember being struck by his dignity."

Sometime after sunset, it was time to go. Again a convoy formed. Lumumba, Mpolo, and Okito slumped in the backseat of a car. The vehicles sped away from Elisabethville, beginning an hour-long journey into the moonless night.

Twenty-year-old Lwimba Movati Ndjibu happened to be walking through the bush with his father that night. Carrying a lantern and a homemade 12-gauge shotgun, they were returning to their village from a long day of antelope hunting when they spotted headlights moving through the darkness—an unusual sight in this remote area, especially at so late an hour. Father and son hurriedly extinguished their lantern and crouched behind a termite mound as the cars turned in to a clearing on the other side of the road. It was 9:30 p.m. From a short distance, they watched as a group of men—Black and white—emerged.

All told, there were about thirty figures, the serried cars bathing them in cones of cold light. Godefroid Munongo and Jean-Baptiste Kibwe spoke to each other in hushed tones. Another minister, Gabriel Kitenge, nervously chain-smoked cigarettes. Moise Tshombe covered his face with his hands. Frans Verscheure, the police commissioner, and Julien Gat of the gendarmerie had brought along two more Belgian officers—Lieutenant Gabriel Michels and Brigadier François Son—and around twenty Katangan soldiers and policemen. The ministers wore overcoats to keep warm in the frigid January night. Lumumba, Mpolo, and Okito stood handcuffed and barefoot, dressed only in their blood-soaked pants and undershirts.

"You're going to kill us, aren't you?" Lumumba asked quietly as Verscheure loosened the handcuffs.

"Yes," Verscheure replied.

A tangle of trees and roots bordered the clearing. At one end stood a large tree; at the other, a massive anthill, fifteen feet high. In the middle, a shallow hole, about six feet by six feet, had been dug into the loose, sandy soil. Throwing shadows against the earth, an all-Black quartet of soldiers lined up, submachine guns and automatic rifles at the ready.

First up was Joseph Okito, once vice president of the Senate, once Lumumba's traveling companion in New York, and still a father of seven. Verscheure propped him up in front of the thick tree. "If you're a believer, pray," he said.

"I request that someone take care of my wife and children in Leopoldville," Okito said. Munongo cut him off: "We're in Katanga, not Leo."

Okito put his hands together and began a short prayer. "Our Father, who art in heaven—"

Gat ordered the men to fire, and Okito slumped to the ground. His body was dragged into the pit.

Mpolo was next. Another round of gunshots rang out. His body was tossed into the same shallow grave.

It was Lumumba's turn now. The boy from Onalua, the studious bookworm, the Stanleyville postal clerk, the patient *évolué*, the colonial prisoner, Leopoldville's top beer promoter, the leader of the MNC, the hero of the Brussels roundtable, the happy parliamentary candidate from Orientale, the thirty-five-year-old prime minister of the Congo, a son, a husband, and a father—this was the man now stooping before a tree, squinting through hazy eyes into the head-lights, panting, trembling, and saying nothing. A burst of bullets, and Lumumba crumpled. It was over.

Verscheure took out his notebook and recorded the time, writing, "9:43: L. dead." "He was quiet from the beginning to the end," he said.

The next morning, the antelope hunters returned cautiously to the site. The burial had been hasty. Bullet cartridges were scattered everywhere. Six bare feet poked through the sandy red earth.

In Elisabethville, Munongo received reports that charcoal burn-ers had also stumbled across the bodies. "Make them disappear," he demanded. "How you do it doesn't interest me." The task fell to Gerard Soete, a forty-year-old police commissioner from Bel-gium. Soete was a colonist's colonist. He had worked in Katanga for a decade and a half and during that time posed for pictures punish-ing Congolese with a whip. He hated Lumumba, whom he always called a *crapule*—a "scoundrel." The day after the murders, Soete and a group of Katangan police drove to the execution site, dug up the corpses, wrapped them in blankets, and loaded them into a truck. They took them even farther into the bush, on an hours-long drive so bumpy that bullets shook loose from the bodies. After finding an appropriately remote location, the group buried the bodies—again beside an anthill, but this time deeper.

As rumors about Lumumba's fate spread, however, Munongo decided that the second burial was still unsatisfactory. The bodies had to disappear completely—"so that not a finger bone remains, not a tooth," he specified. Ten days after the murders, Soete returned to the new grave site, this time accompanied by his younger brother, Michel, and a few local helpers. Michel worked for Katanga's public works department and had brought one of its trucks. He loaded it with shovels, an empty oil drum, several cans of gasoline, a pair of butcher's knives, a hacksaw, two glass jugs full of sulfuric acid, and a generous supply of whiskey.

To allay the suspicions of any passersby, the Soete brothers set up road signs and surveying equipment, pretending that they were undertaking road repairs. Then they donned rubber gloves and overalls and poured the sulfuric acid into the barrel, dug up the rotting bodies, and began carving. To block the stench, they strapped sanitary pads across their noses but quickly found the improvised masks uncomfortable and let the whiskey numb their senses. "We did things an animal would not do," Soete said.

Sulfuric acid eats easily through flesh. "A column of gas, white and whistling, rises to the sky," Soete wrote in a fictionalized account of the episode. The acid, he said, turned Lumumba "into a mass of mucus." But bones and teeth survived. And when the acid ran out, the brothers doused the remaining body parts with gasoline and set them aflame.

The whole job took two days. When they had finished, they covered their tracks by sweeping away the char, tamping down the earth, and scattering twigs over the area. As they drove back to Elisabethville, they threw out the window what neither acid nor fire could vanish, strewing behind them an archipelago of teeth, ground-up bones, and belt buckles.

Gerard Soete returned home to his family reeking of whiskey. According to his daughter Godelieve, he brought with him a new darkness. "After January 1961, he was no longer the man he used to be," she said. Her father had also brought back at least one of Lumumba's fingers and a pair of his gold-capped molars, twisted out from his skull with pliers. Trophies, perhaps, or proof of a job well done.

Chapter 47

Get Hammarskjöld!

PAULINE OPANGO HEARD news of her husband's death on the radio. She was destitute now, living off the kindness of friends with her son Roland in a shack in the *cité*. She was still mourning the loss of her newborn daughter, and it had been three months since she had seen her other children, who were under the care of an adoptive family in Cairo and enrolled in a French school. Even before she knew she was a widow, she had been on the verge of suicide. All that remained of her husband was a letter, smuggled out from Camp Hardy shortly before his deportation to Katanga. It was a farewell directed more to his nation than to his wife:

My beloved companion,
   I write you these words not knowing whether you will receive them, when you will receive them, and whether I will still be alive when you read them. Throughout my struggle for the independence of my country, I have never doubted for a single instant that the sacred cause to which my comrades and I have dedicated our entire lives would triumph in the end. But what we wanted for our country—its right to an honorable life, to perfect dignity, to independence with no restrictions—was never wanted by Belgian colonialism and its Western allies, who found direct and indirect, intentional and unintentional support among certain high officials of the United Nations, that body in which we placed all our trust when we called on it for help.

They have corrupted some of our countrymen; they have bought others; they have done their part to distort the truth and defile our independence. What else can I say? That whether dead or alive, free or in prison by order of the colonialists, it is not my person that is important. What is important is the Congo, our poor people whose independence has been turned into a cage, with people looking at us from outside the bars, sometimes with charitable compassion, sometimes with glee and delight. But my faith will remain unshakable. I know and feel in my heart of hearts that sooner or later my people will rid themselves of all their enemies, foreign and domestic, that they will rise up as one to say no to the shame and degradation of colonialism and regain their dignity in the pure light of day.

We are not alone. Africa, Asia, and the free and liberated peoples in every corner of the globe will ever remain at the side of the millions of Congolese who will not abandon the struggle until the day when there will be no more colonizers and no more of their mercenaries in our country. I want my children, whom I leave behind and perhaps will never see again, to be told that the future of the Congo is beautiful and that their country expects them, as it expects every Congolese, to fulfill the sacred task of rebuilding our independence, our sovereignty; for without justice there is no dignity and without independence there are no free men.

Neither brutal assaults, nor cruel mistreatment, nor torture have ever led me to beg for mercy, for I prefer to die with my head held high, with unshakable faith and the greatest confidence in the destiny of my country, rather than live in slavery and contempt for sacred principles. History will one day have its say; it will not be the history taught in the United Nations, Washington, Paris, or Brussels, however, but the history taught in the countries that have rid themselves of colonialism and its puppets. Africa will write its own history and both north and south of the Sahara it will be a history full of glory and dignity.

Do not weep for me, my companion; I know that my country, now suffering so much, will be able to defend its

independence and its freedom. Long live the Congo! Long
live Africa!
    Patrice

On Valentine's Day, Pauline walked barefoot through the streets
of Leopoldville wearing nothing more than a wrap around her waist,
baring her breasts in a traditional show of mourning. Hundreds of
her husband's supporters trailed behind. When she reached the
Royal, she demanded to see the top UN official. Rajeshwar Dayal
welcomed her in. Holding back tears, Lumumba's widow asked for
help recovering her husband's body so she could give him a proper
burial. "She was a picture of sorrow and despair," Dayal thought. All
he could do was arrange for a UN plane to fly her and Roland to
Stanleyville. Even that small gesture elicited accusations of intoler-
able interference. So did his futile request to Moise Tshombe for the
transfer of Lumumba's remains. The irony of Tshombe's reply would
become apparent only later: "According to Bantu tradition, it is formally forbidden to unearth, even though only for several seconds, a
body which is covered by earth."

Belgian elites in Elisabethville and beyond did not conceal their
relief. A Brussels newspaper reflected the prevailing mood: "The very
existence of Lumumba was an abscess which had already infected the
Congo and was threatening to infect it even further.... It is very hard
for us to be sad."
    While Leopoldville remained eerily calm, in other world capitals,
violent protests erupted. Rallies in Warsaw, Prague, Belgrade, East
Berlin, and Havana attracted huge crowds of angry demonstrators.
In Moscow, thousands of students—holding English-language signs
for the benefit of American television cameras—pelted the Belgian
embassy with cobblestones, breaking nearly every window. In Peking,
100,000 people gathered in a stadium to hear Premier Zhou Enlai
blame the United States and Belgium for the "vile murder." But the
anger was not confined to the Communist world. Protests broke out
in Tel Aviv, Tehran, Damascus, Tokyo, New Delhi, Oslo, London,
Paris, Vienna, Rome, Tunis, Lagos, Khartoum, and Rabat. In Wash-

ington, a group of students at Howard University, which Lumumba had visited in July, threw eggs at the Belgian embassy. In Cairo, a mob breached the embassy gates, ripped a portrait of King Baudouin off the wall, replaced it with one of Lumumba, and then set the building aflame. The family that had taken in the Lumumba children tried to withhold news of their father's demise and took them on a sightseeing tour, but François, the eldest, heard about it in school anyway. The children were driven past the protesters in the streets so they could see what their father had meant to others. Juliana was confused: Why was everyone chanting her last name?

Perhaps the most shocking protest site was the normally hallowed ground of the Security Council chamber. A group of African American activists from Harlem, the women among them wearing veils, had managed to set themselves up in the spectators' gallery. When Kennedy's UN ambassador, Adlai Stevenson, began to speak, they disrupted proceedings with piercing screams. "Assassins!" yelled one of them, an aspiring writer named Maya Angelou. Hammarskjöld leaned back in his chair as Andrew Cordier rose and ordered security guards to eject the demonstrators. Only when they shouted, "Get Hammarskjöld!" was the secretary-general persuaded to leave the room.

Hammarskjöld pronounced the murder of Lumumba "a revolting crime" and "tragic," but he shed no tears for the death of a man whom he considered foolish and dangerous. As he predicted in a letter to a friend, the writer John Steinbeck, the prime minister would first be unjustly celebrated before being justly forgotten:

> *No* one, in the long pull, will really profit from Lumumba's death; least of all those outside the Congo who now strain to do so but should one day confront a reckoning with truth and decency. There may be immediately some propaganda exploitation of this blunder; indeed, we have been seeing it in staged bursts in many parts of the world, but to what avail, really, and even those efforts have required unbridled distortion. It is, I imagine, at its earliest that the big lie shines brightest; does one ever endure? Events in the Congo move quickly and, it seems, so far always badly or in bad directions; memories, even

of ghosts and legends and certainly of synthetic martyrs, are short, and everything soon gets swallowed up in the confusions, frustrations and sheer imbecilities of that arena.

More than ever before, Hammarskjöld's job was in jeopardy. The Soviet Union, declaring that "the blood of Patrice Lumumba is on the hands of this henchman of the colonialists," announced that it would no longer recognize him as secretary-general—the same tactic that had ultimately forced out his predecessor, Trygve Lie. More surprising was the threat of defection among the crucial African and Asian states that had generally supported Hammarskjöld. Their faith in him and the UN was shaken. "Why couldn't Hammarskjöld save Lumumba, the way the Greek grocers are protected by UN troops in Stanleyville?" one delegate asked. A correspondent for the London *Observer* captured the mood: "In small, private wakes for Patrice Lumumba, the Afro-Asia delegates at the United Nations swallow their drinks as if there were a bitter taste in their mouths. Even the wiser among them let this bitterness slur into their speech as they pronounce the name of Hammarskjöld."

Hammarskjöld's aides worried about his safety and arranged for extra security guards. They also noticed that he was becoming more irascible, especially when the subject of Lumumba's death came up. Yet it wasn't just Hammarskjöld's own well-being that was now at risk but that of the organization he led, too. "Can the U.N. Survive?" asked the cover of *Newsweek*.

It did not help that Lumumba's death had triggered a spate of political assassinations in the Congo. Albert Kalonji's secessionist government in South Kasai announced the execution of seven pro-Lumumba political prisoners. The seven, who included a former member of Lumumba's cabinet and the leader of MNC's youth wing, were decapitated with machetes in the presence of Kalonji himself. In retaliation, Antoine Gizenga's government in Stanleyville executed fifteen political prisoners in a single morning. The dead included Alphonse Songolo, Lumumba's former communications minister, who had sided with Mobutu, and Gilbert Pongo, the ANC officer who had captured Lumumba in December. Pongo had his legs cut off before being plunged into a barrel of salt.

John F. Kennedy learned of Lumumba's death while on a weekend trip to the Virginia countryside. His campaign promise to support African aspirations was being swept away in a wave of outrage and violence. Ahmed Sékou Touré of Guinea spoke for many African leaders when he telegrammed Kennedy, "This unspeakable crime destroys the hope that African nationalism had placed in your government."

The Congo was splintering. Gizenga's Lumumbist regime in Stanleyville was on the rise, with new offers of aid and diplomatic recognition pouring in from across the world. The Soviet Union quickly pledged $500,000. Mobutu barged massive reinforcements up the Congo River to his home province of Équateur in preparation for an invasion of Lumumbist Orientale province. Skirmishes had already broken out there and in the eastern province of Kivu and in northern Katanga.

A few months earlier, Allen Dulles had warned of the civil war that Lumumba's successful escape to Stanleyville would set off. Now Lumumba was gone, but the specter of an internecine conflict was not. On the contrary, the Stanleyville regime now boasted widespread popular support at home and newfound sympathy from abroad, and it might well manage to crush the weak, illegitimate, and unpopular regime that the United States was propping up in Leopoldville. The Pentagon drew up contingency plans for a military invasion involving eighty thousand U.S. troops. Five American naval ships in the Atlantic prepared to approach the Congo River. Kennedy's bright-eyed team had once imagined that by February 1961 they would be working out the details of an inclusive Congolese government. Instead, they found themselves contemplating an incipient war that might draw in the United States.

Chapter 48

Lovanium

Y ET FOR ALL the recriminations against the UN and the West, in a strange way Lumumba's death made international agreement on the Congo easier. With no more possibility of his return to power, Western delegates at the UN Security Council had fewer qualms about acceding to one of the chief demands of the Afro-Asian bloc— that the Congolese parliament convene and elect a constitutional government. And so just a week after news broke of Lumumba's death, a new Security Council resolution called for the reopening of parliament and empowered UN troops, hitherto barred from using force for any reasons beyond self-defense, to fire at Congolese troops in order to prevent civil war. The Soviets, dumbfounded that African countries still supported Hammarskjöld in the wake of Lumumba's murder, could only abstain. The new resolution was soon backed by new manpower for the UN force, which had shrunk as a result of troop withdrawals. India, which until then had provided only unarmed advisers, sent five thousand soldiers, including a thousand Gurkhas, the battle-hardened warriors from Nepal.

The Stanleyville regime turned out not to be ten feet tall, after all. Gizenga had none of Lumumba's charisma. A virtual foreigner in his self-proclaimed capital, he obsessed over assassination plots and spent most of his time holed up in a riverside villa, sometimes not emerging for months. Separated by hundreds of miles from the embassies and UN headquarters of Leopoldville, his government remained isolated from the outside world. With Moscow rebuffing its requests for greater military assistance, Gizenga instead asked a

U.S. diplomat for American aid—the "most amazing change," marveled Timberlake.

The change in Stanleyville was mirrored by a change in Washington, as liberals in the Kennedy administration slowly found their footing. On March 31, the administration endorsed the reconvening of parliament and said that any new government had to include Gizenga. As part of this policy reset, Kennedy cleaned house. Clare Timberlake's hysterical cables from Leopoldville, in particular, were increasingly out of step with official thinking in Washington. Ever the stick in the mud, the ambassador continued to rail against Gizenga, failing to grasp the administration's hope that bringing him into the fold would neutralize, rather than exacerbate, the possible Communist threat he posed. The final straw was Timberlake's decision, amid unrest in Leopoldville, to radio the commander of the five-ship U.S. naval flotilla off the Angolan coast and order him to head toward the Congo River, without asking permission from Washington. It was a stunningly presumptuous move, and Kennedy, himself a former naval officer, was irate. Timberlake had to go.

Conveniently, Kennedy was able to make the insubordinate ambassador into a sacrificial lamb in a deal with Dag Hammarskjöld: Kennedy would recall Timberlake, who had long been a thorn in the UN's side, and in return Hammarskjöld would recall Rajeshwar Dayal, who in any case had struggled to perform his duties on account of strong animosity with Kasavubu and Mobutu. Timberlake was put out to pasture in Alabama, at the Air War College at Maxwell Air Force Base—the first in a series of what he considered "pleasant but indifferent jobs with no use being made of what talent I possess."

Other U.S. officials who had been involved in the Congo drama were on the way out, too. William Burden, the U.S. ambassador in Brussels who had gone so native that he considered Lumumba's assassination "all to the good," was removed from his post despite Belgian pleas to Washington that he stay on. At the CIA, Kennedy had decided to fire the top two officials—Allen Dulles and Richard Bissell—after the disastrous Bay of Pigs invasion dealt the president his first major foreign policy failure.

Attempts at a political settlement in the Congo were making fitful progress. At a summit held in April in Coquilhatville, in Équateur province, delegates from across the country agreed to reconvene parliament to choose a government. By the middle of 1961, things were looking up in the Congo. The furor over Lumumba's death had faded, and the country appeared to have escaped civil war. Hammarskjöld recognized that there was now a chance of stability and peace in the troubled country. On June 22, just shy of the Congo's first anniversary of independence, he wrote a cautiously optimistic letter to his brother Bo: "If we can keep up the momentum, they may be brought to a point where we can readjust our presence and our work to a more normal operation. However, you never know with the Congolese, who are unsurpassed in their mastery of the absolutely irrational."

The campus of Lovanium University was empty. In July, UN officials had temporarily shut down the school, which sat on a plateau overlooking Leopoldville, and converted it into a meeting place where, it was hoped, politicians could convene free from interference and distraction and fear, at some remove from the chaos of the capital below. An eight-foot-high electric fence was strung up around the perimeter. At the one and only entrance, Indian machine gunners stood guard with orders to keep out what the organizers had deemed dangerous distractions: alcohol, money, guns, and women. Police dogs shipped in from Sweden prowled the grounds for intruders. Telephones were cut off. As the two hundred or so politicians filed into the campus, the proceedings took on the air of the first day of classes. Sleeping in dormitories and meeting in the auditorium, the members of parliament busied themselves with the task of national reconciliation.

But the hermetically sealed campus was no match for Larry Devlin. Earlier in the year, President Kennedy had approved the continued flow of Devlin's bribes to Mobutu and his soldiers—what the CIA was now calling its "silver bullets" program. Distributing cash to keep a mutiny at bay was an easy sell for the president, but Devlin's plans for Lovanium entailed even greater meddling, and even greater odds of disclosure. In the weeks leading up to the conference, Devlin drafted a plan to buy votes to ensure that Kasavubu, Mobutu, and their allies, as opposed to Gizenga and his, obtained a working majority in parliament. Devlin wanted permission to dispense "promises of foreign travel" and "outright payments of money" to the members of parliament meeting at Lovanium. The total cost: $400,000. The document worked its way to the White House for consideration by the Special Group, which was now chaired by Kennedy's national security adviser, McGeorge Bundy—who, incidentally, had recruited Devlin at Harvard more than a decade earlier. Despite this connection, Bundy was not willing to give the station chief a blank check. In a departure from the Eisenhower era, Devlin's plan was approved neither immediately nor in its original form. The State Department insisted that Gizenga's faction be allowed to take part in a Congolese government, and Bundy insisted that he needed Kennedy's approval.

Ultimately, the president approved the modified proposal, and Devlin got to work. Outside the electric fence, he met regularly with the United States' preferred candidate for prime minister: Cyrille Adoula, a labor leader who had become a frequent visitor to the U.S. embassy and a peripheral member of the Binza Group, the coterie of informal advisers around Joseph Mobutu. To keep tabs on the closed proceedings, Devlin communicated via radio with Justin Bomboko, the president of Mobutu's commissioners and a member of parliament. He also discovered a sewage tunnel through which he passed bundles of cash to the politicians. In his efforts, he was aided by the UN operation, which while publicly playing the role of neutral host was privately attempting to engineer an Adoula government. Ten days before the conference even began, UN officials had drawn up on the back of an envelope the outlines of an ideal cabinet.

Looming over everything was Mobutu, who hinted that the army could veto the politicians' choice of prime minister. One evening, in a reminder of where the real power lay, Leopoldville's elite gathered for a massive garden party to celebrate the christening of Mobutu's week-old baby boy. Mobutu astutely used the occasion to flatter the Congo's other two most powerful figures, Kasavubu and Tshombe. He announced that his son's first two names would be Joseph and Moise.

Had the members of parliament been left to their own devices, the result would likely have been a government dominated by Lumumbists, who enjoyed a slim majority, with Gizenga at the helm.

But the palm greasing, intimidation, and meddling worked. After two weeks of haggling and subornation—a "donnybrook," in Devlin's words—the reconstituted parliament approved a government led by Adoula and mostly free of Lumumba allies. As the parliamentarians emerged from campus and reunited with their families, *Newsweek* reported, they carried "armfuls of loot, wrapped in university bedsheets."

Lovanium was billed as a triumph. What more could one ask for, Hammarskjöld wrote, "than to give the Congolese a possibility to settle their own affairs in their way, but in democratic and peaceful forms"? But as an official from the American embassy bragged, "It was really a U.S. operation." It was yet another notch in the CIA's belt. Devlin boasted to headquarters that the agency could "take major credit for the fall of the Lumumba government and the success of the Mobutu coup, and considerable credit for Adoula's nomination as premier."

The mood in Washington was exuberant. A moderate leader had been installed as prime minister. Gizenga's wing was included enough to cease their claims that the true national government was in Stanleyville; indeed, Gizenga himself took up the position of vice-premier and returned to Leopoldville. Albert Kalonji's faction was given representation, too, and the secession in South Kasai was on its way out. For the first time since independence, the Congo seemed to be on the right track. "You should know that there is optimism all over town that the Congo situation is on the way toward solution," Walt Rostow, the deputy national security adviser, wrote to President Kennedy. "We could be witnessing the most encouraging development since you became President."

Chapter 49

The Final Flight

THERE REMAINED, HOWEVER, the problem of Katanga. Moise Tshombe had boycotted the Lovanium conference, and his state continued to style itself as independent. In fact, it had strengthened its eleven-thousand-man army by recruiting hundreds of foreign mercenaries, attracted by fat salaries and the promise of adventure. Known as *les affreux,* "the horribles," these right-wing Belgian, British, French, Italian, and South African soldiers of fortune roamed Elisabethville drunk, their revolvers and grenades clanking ostentatiously in the city's bars. In addition, Tshombe's military had acquired three Fougas, small French-made jets, also piloted by mercenaries.

But more forces were now aligned against Katanga than ever before. UN troops had set up garrisons across the province and now had explicit instructions from the Security Council to expel any foreign officers and advisers active in the Katangan forces. The parliament in Leopoldville—now back in session in its rightful home, the Palace of the Nation—passed a law to the same effect. Even Brussels was on board, after a snap election brought to power a new government that was less friendly to Katanga. It agreed to withdraw the 208 Belgian officers on loan to Tshombe's army.

To deal with Katanga once and for all, Dag Hammarskjöld sent a new UN representative to Elisabethville: Conor Cruise O'Brien. A member of the Irish foreign service and a budding literary critic, he had come to the secretary-general's attention for his well-received book on Catholic writers. As an Irishman, he had the rare combination of qualities needed to serve the UN in Elisabethville: anticolonial credentials, citizenship of a country that was officially neutral in the Cold War, and skin pale enough to reassure the local white population. But his lack of administrative expertise and inexperience in military affairs made him a poor fit for the job.

Upon assuming his post, O'Brien launched Operation Rumpunch, a surprise roundup of the five hundred remaining foreign officers and mercenaries in the Katangan military. Before dawn on August 28, UN troops occupied key locations across Elisabethville and raided the Katangan army headquarters, detaining any foreign soldiers they found. O'Brien's men encountered little resistance, and by day's end, O'Brien was popping the champagne at Elisabethville's UN head-quarters and reading a cable from Hammarskjöld commending his "skill and courage." But it soon became clear that countless *affreux* had slipped through the cracks, often thanks to help from European diplomats in Katanga.

Hammarskjöld decided once more to intervene himself. On September 12, some two weeks after the failed UN operation in Katanga, he left New York for the Congo to confer with the UN mission's military leadership about next steps. Perhaps he could also work his diplomatic magic and finally get Tshombe and the central government to negotiate in earnest. It would be his fourth trip to the country since the crisis had begun and his last try at solving its woes: if he did not break the logjam this time, he confided to a friend, he would resign from his post. He evidently also felt an urge to get his affairs in order. The day before leaving, he dictated a letter to his secretary concerning the disposition of his personal papers. The letter was sealed with Scotch tape and marked "to be opened only in case of death."

As the secretary-general was en route, the situation in Katanga dete-riorated. Refueling in Accra on September 13, Hammarskjöld learned of press reports claiming that the UN was now at war in Katanga. The fighting was the result of Conor Cruise O'Brien's attempt at a more forceful repeat of Operation Rumpunch. Hammarskjöld's rep-resentatives in the Congo had initiated an operation that went well beyond what he had in mind. Their do-over was called Morthor, Hindi for "smash," and its name conveyed its ambition: not only to remove foreign officers but also to roll back the secession of Katanga once and for all. In just two hours, the UN's military commander predicted, Katanga would be brought into the national fold, and the Congo would be unified.

Morthor went off the rails almost immediately. Because they followed the same playbook they had during Rumpunch, UN troops lacked the element of surprise and met heavy resistance from Katangan forces. Snipers picked off Indian UN troops at the post office. Mortar fire rumbled through the streets. "What had been expected to be a swift and bloodless take-over developed into wild hand-to-hand fighting," reported David Halberstam, *The New York Times*'s freshly arrived correspondent in the Congo. One of the Katangan Fouga jets—"the lone ranger," it was called—strafed and bombed UN positions across much of the province and hit a UN transport plane while in flight. In the mining town of Jadotville, Katangan forces laid siege to a company of 156 Irish UN troops, cutting off their supply of ammunition, food, and water and forcing them to surrender. By the time Hammarskjöld landed in Leopoldville, it was clear that the operation was a disaster, not only for UN troops on the ground, but also for the organization as a whole.

Horrified and caught off guard, Hammarskjöld faced a barrage of complaints by Western officials, who questioned why they had not been consulted about such a major action. The operation had to end, and he sent a message to Tshombe to this effect, requesting a cease-fire. They agreed to meet at a safe distance from the fighting, in Ndola, an industrial city just over the border in the white-ruled British protectorate of Northern Rhodesia.

At 4:45 p.m. on September 17, the propellers of the *Albertina,* a DC-6 on loan from a Swedish airline, began to stir. Inside, Dag Hammarskjöld was nervously bouncing his leg. Fifteen others would accompany him on the flight to Ndola: seven UN staffers (including Hammarskjöld's personal aide, Bill Ranallo, and his Africa expert, Heinz Wieschhoff), two Swedish soldiers, and six crew members. Since he planned on being away from Leopoldville for just a night, the secretary-general carried only a briefcase. Its contents were as varied as his interests: a Bible, a road map of southern New England, a cardboard dial used for calculating the difference between time zones, English and German copies of the Israeli philosopher Martin Buber's *I and Thou* (Hammarskjöld had agreed to translate the book into Swedish), a draft article about his castle-dwelling youth for the Swedish Tourist Association, and a yellow legal pad.

As a precaution to avoid interception by the roaming Fouga, Hammarskjöld's pilot filed a false flight plan that did not state his true itinerary and destination. The plane would also maintain radio silence for most of the flight and communicate only in Morse code in Swedish. The flight to Ndola was expected to take just under seven hours, longer than usual because the plane was taking an indirect route, flying east and then south in order to bypass Katanga. As the sun set over the vast forest passing below, Hammarskjöld worked on his translation of *I and Thou;* perhaps he also prepared for negotiations with Tshombe and chatted in his native language with the Swedish crew and soldiers.

Just after midnight local time, the *Albertina* began its descent and radioed Ndola ground control that the landing strip's lights were in sight. The air traffic controller asked the pilot to report back when he dropped to an altitude of six thousand feet. The report never came. Nine and a half miles west of the airport, the *Albertina*'s landing gear clipped the treetops of the forest below, hit the ground, cartwheeled, and burst into flames. Hammarskjöld was thrown from the wreckage. In an odd parallel with Patrice Lumumba's last moments, he landed not far from a large anthill. He most likely died instantly.

Hammarskjöld's body was flown to Stockholm and driven to Uppsala, where two thousand mourners filled the main cathedral for a state funeral held by the Swedish royal family. In the United States, President John F. Kennedy ordered flags across the country to be flown at half-mast in memory of "a noble servant of peace." At UN headquarters in New York, diplomats delivered eulogies as Hammarskjöld's chair on the green marble dais of the General Assembly hall sat empty. Despite the late secretary-general's aloof leadership style, his staff was devastated. People cried openly in the staircases. A month after his death, Hammarskjöld was awarded the Nobel Peace Prize.

The cause of the crash that killed him and all fifteen others aboard would never be determined. Even before the wreckage was found, Edmund Gullion, the new U.S. ambassador to the Congo, cabled Washington with his suspicions that a Belgian mercenary named Jan van Risseghem might be to blame for the death of Hammarskjöld. "There is a possibility," Gullion wrote, "he was shot down by a single pilot who has harassed UN operations and who has been identified by one usually reliable source as van Risseghem, a Belgian, who accepted a training mission with the so-called Katangan Air Force." The day before the crash, Hammarskjöld had sent a note of protest to Belgium's foreign minister about van Risseghem, whom he accused of shooting at, and killing, three Congolese civilians from the air.

In the years that followed, various investigations would be conducted—by the Rhodesian authorities, by the UN, by the Swedish government, by an intrepid British academic—each with its own insights and oversights. From these emerged confusing and contradictory pieces of evidence that kept alive suspicions that the plane had been brought down deliberately: eyewitness accounts of a second plane and a bright flash in the sky, a delayed search-and-rescue effort, an intriguing crash-site photograph showing what appeared to be a playing card tucked into Hammarskjöld's collar, missing autopsy reports, a late-in-life statement from a friend of van Risseghem's alleging a confession, and reports of U.S. radio intercepts supposedly capturing a shootdown.

A clear answer will probably never emerge. But the conspiracy theories should be approached with caution. For one thing, there has never been a satisfactory answer to the question of who might have had reason to kill Hammarskjöld at the time. The Katangan leaders, to whom Hammarskjöld was about to offer the concession of a cease-fire, had little to gain from his death, nor did Moise Tshombe's backers in Northern Rhodesia, who were hosting the negotiations. It beggars belief to imagine, as some theories posit, that Western intelligence agencies would have attacked the plane. Even if these countries might have disagreed with Operation Morthor, they officially backed the UN position on Katanga and were happy to see a cease-fire. Moreover, the dead included citizens of the United States, Canada, Sweden, and Ireland. Finally, eyewitness accounts of plane crashes are decidedly unreliable. So are barroom boasts years after the event.

Occam's razor suggests that the most likely explanation for the crash is that Hammarskjöld's plane went down for the same reason most planes did in 1961: as a result of pilot error. Hammarskjöld's plane was the sixth DC-6 to crash that year. It was not the first serious aviation disaster for the UN operation in the Congo, nor would it be the last. In all likelihood, there was no hidden meaning or sinister machinations behind Hammarskjöld's death—just the cruelty of chance.

As with Patrice Lumumba's violent end, Dag Hammarskjöld's death had the ironic effect of spurring progress in the Congo. His successor as UN secretary-general, the Burmese diplomat U Thant, managed to win the Security Council's approval for a more aggressive Katanga policy. In January 1963, after several more flashes of fighting, UN forces—now aided by ten Swedish fighter jets—administered the coup de grâce to the secessionist forces in the province. Moise Tshombe fled across the border into Angola and then to Spain.

Ralph Bunche, who had been pulled back into the UN operation in the Congo after Hammarskjöld's death, watched on with relief as UN forces occupied Tshombe's final stronghold. "Big day for the Congo operation," he wrote in his diary. "I feel that I've done something for Dag now."

With a measure of stability restored, the bulk of the UN troops would be withdrawn from the Congo over the following months. Soon, the costliest and deadliest peacekeeping operation in UN history was over. In the end, independent Katanga had to be broken by force, not coaxed back into the fold through negotiation. Lumumba had been right about that.

Chapter 50

Our Man in Leopoldville

FOR A MOMENT, a tenuous peace held. Elisabethville and Stanleyville both pledged allegiance to the central government in Leopoldville, which appeared to be hanging on with Joseph Kasavubu as president and Cyrille Adoula as prime minister—and copious CIA bribery to stave off any challenges from Lumumbist members of parliament.

On paper, the country had managed a return to parliamentary democracy, even if its true political center of gravity was neither parliament nor the cabinet but the Binza Group and, ultimately, Joseph Mobutu. For the United States, it was an ideal outcome. It had a CIA-picked prime minister in Adoula as well as a direct line to Mobutu via Larry Devlin, who by now was effectively an honorary member of the Binza Group. Washington had cemented its influence over the country, and it had a perch from which to fend off any Soviet encroachment. A state that had begun life as neutral—and sometimes seemed ready to side with the Soviet Union—was now an American ally.

On the morning of May 31, 1963, a smiling Mobutu stood shoulder to shoulder with John F. Kennedy at the White House's Rose Garden, looking commanding in his general's uniform and chatting amiably in front of reporters. A week earlier, he had lunched at the CIA's new headquarters in Langley, Virginia. It was an unusually elaborate reception for a mere army chief of staff, but it made more sense given his status as the Congo's de facto leader. (And, as a briefing paper for Kennedy explained, Mobutu "responds well to flattery—and expects recognition of the close and confidential relationship he has enjoyed with U.S. officials.")

"General, if it hadn't been for you," Kennedy said, "the whole thing would have collapsed and the Communists would have taken over."

"I do what I am able to do," Mobutu replied.

Yet neither Mobutu nor Adoula, the man nominally in charge, could do much about the continued inflation, unemployment, and corruption racking their country. Instead, Adoula steadily purged left-wing Lumumbists from his cabinet, with the encouragement of the U.S. embassy. As the central government came to represent an ever narrower slice of the country's political spectrum, however, its authority continued slipping, and it soon lost the support of parliament. Devlin fretted to CIA headquarters about the need for "constant vote-buying" to keep things afloat. Eventually, he convinced Adoula to dissolve parliament altogether, and in September 1963, legislators were sent packing and once again retreated to their home districts.

By then, Devlin's three-year stint as station chief had come to an end. He had been promoted to chief of the CIA's East Africa branch at the agency's headquarters, but even in that position he would continue to keep an eye on Congolese affairs. As he prepared to leave, Devlin burned all the cable traffic relating to the Lumumba plot and sent a final message to Washington in which he made the case for continuing to bet on Mobutu. The general, he said, was "the most sincere U.S. friend in the Congo."

Assassinated in November 1963, John F. Kennedy did not live to see the results of his Congo policy. Larry Devlin, for his part, could only watch from afar when, beginning in 1964, the fragile stability that had prevailed since the defeat of Katangan forces one year earlier started to unravel, and the Congo descended once more into rebellion. It began with unrest in the Kwilu region, not far from Leopoldville, where rebels took over village after village, armed with little more than knives and bicycle spokes fashioned into arrows. Their leader was Pierre Mulele, Lumumba's education minister. Recently returned from China, where he received training in Maoist guerrilla warfare tactics, Mulele now styled himself as a mystical bush commander, impervious to bullets and imbued with the power of flight. Next, the convulsions spread to the country's east. There, insurgents led by another former Lumumba minister, Christophe Gbenye, captured even more territory than their counterparts in Kwilu. Baptized in holy "Lumumba water" that was said to make them invincible and transform them into lions, the Simba, as they called themselves, stormed into battle with cries of "Long live Lumumba!"

The rebels confounded the frail central government, which by the middle of 1964 had lost more than half the country. Even the capital seemed in danger of falling. Alarmed by the insurgents' successes, the Binza Group pulled the plug on Cyrille Adoula, who was forced to resign. But the insurgents continued to gain ground. In August 1964, the Simba took Stanleyville and declared the city the seat of the "People's Republic of the Congo." In a gruesome tribute to Lumumba, they executed political prisoners under the glare of a statue of the late prime minister in a downtown square. The rebels massacred twenty-five hundred purported counterrevolutionaries, cutting open the bodies to remove their hearts and devour their organs. Unlike the martyred leader to whom they claimed allegiance, the Simba were explicitly antiwhite and anti-American. They took 250 Belgians and Americans hostage in Stanleyville and forced the U.S. consul and his colleagues to eat an American flag. Washington had never met an enemy like this. In a phone call with President Lyndon Johnson, Secretary of Defense Robert McNamara told of a rebel slitting open an enemy's torso, plucking out his kidney, and consuming it. "Now, I don't know how you deal with people like that," McNamara said.

The ANC was utterly incapable of filling the vacuum left behind by the departing UN forces. The U.S. government had no illusions about the Congolese soldiers, nor, as time went on and the failures piled up, about the man who led them. "While the General has many qualities and has performed effectively in the past," the State Department concluded about Mobutu, "his vanity and irresponsibility would appear to have contributed significantly to the ineffectiveness and disarray of the ANC." But Washington stuck with him.

Brutal though they were, the rebels were far from invincible. The rank and file was underfunded and ill-equipped, its lack of discipline glaring. When the Argentine revolutionary Che Guevara and a cadre of his Afro-Cuban followers arrived on the eastern border of the Congo in April 1965, lured by the opportunity to assist fellow freedom fighters, the rebels struck them as cowardly, more interested in swilling millet beer and frequenting brothels than in conducting raids on the ANC. "Obviously, a war is not won with such troops," Che wrote. As for their twenty-five-year-old leader, a man named Laurent Kabila, he considered him "too addicted to drink and women."

It was a testament to the ineptitude of Mobutu's ANC that it could not hold its own against this less-than-formidable enemy without massive outside assistance, which took the form of an enormous covert CIA operation—at the time the most expensive of its kind in U.S. history. With the approval of the Johnson administration, the CIA fielded a small air force for the Congo, including T-28 trainers and B-26 bombers that were piloted by Cuban Bay of Pigs veterans and, occasionally, American pilots under CIA command.

Eventually, American firepower prevailed. A joint U.S.-Belgian operation retook Stanleyville and rescued most of the white hostages, killing more than one thousand Congolese in the process. Over the course of 1965, the central government steadily regained control over the country. Che fled the eastern Congo in frustration.

Although Mobutu ostensibly remained in charge of the military effort, he owed his victory to the work of the CIA, whose station in Leopoldville had mushroomed into a "miniature war department," *The New York Times* revealed. The CIA's campaign was as brutal as it was effective, with pro-government forces displaying no concern for civilian welfare. During the recapture of the town of Kindu alone, ANC soldiers and mercenaries killed 3,000 Congolese of all ages. All told, the fighting between rebels and U.S.-backed forces claimed an estimated 100,000 Congolese lives.

Even from his new posting in Langley, Larry Devlin kept being pulled back into the Congo. So subtle was his understanding of the Congo's political dynamics and so unmatched his sway over Mobutu that from time to time he was dispatched to Leopoldville to assess the scene and reassure the general and the other members of the Binza

Group that the United States remained by their side. As G. McMurtrie Godley, Edmund Gullion's successor as U.S. ambassador to the Congo, put it, "Devlin is as close personally to Mobutu as any non-Congolese I know of."

It was partly this closeness that brought Devlin back for a second stint as CIA station chief in Leopoldville in June 1965. His expertise was needed: with the rebel threat dissipated, the uneasy wartime alliance between Mobutu and President Joseph Kasavubu was fraying, and the usual rivalries and infighting were flaring up again. Mobutu soon began hinting to Devlin that he was considering another coup d'état. He also asked for $260,000 to ensure the loyalty of his senior officers, and the CIA approved an initial payment.

It was hard to say no to Mobutu. As a National Security Council staffer wrote, "He is already our man."

Marie-Rose Kasavubu had grown accustomed to a cloistered and comfortable life. The president's twenty-year-old daughter enjoyed the privileges that her proximity to power afforded—her own room and bathroom in the luxurious official residence, servants to style her hair and fold her laundry—but cared little for politics and paid no heed to the men who came and went from her house to see her father. When an alarming ANC broadcast interrupted the radio's regular programming on the morning of November 25, however, Marie-Rose perked up, then set off to alert her father. She found him dressed in a gray three-piece suit, getting ready for work.

"They just made a coup d'état against you," she told him.

"It can't be true," he said.

Through the windows, they could see soldiers driving up to the presidential palace, telling the gardeners to disperse. The radio replayed the announcement.

The elder statesman of the Congo, the master of "wait and see," the survivor of five years of political intrigue, had finally lost out. As he realized that the game was over, Kasavubu stayed characteristically quiet, mustering nothing but a bemused "huh."

When Devlin woke up to the news, he was pleased. Mobutu's coup, he wrote to headquarters, was "the best possible solution." At 11:30 a.m., he stopped by Mobutu's house in the paratrooper camp to offer advice on the composition of the new government to an exhausted Mobutu, who had been awake for the past thirty-six hours. Before going to sleep, Mobutu gathered his officers and feted the successful coup with champagne, fish, and fried plantain served by his wife. The thirty-five-year-old general had much to celebrate. The rebellions to the east had been quelled. The political standoff in Leopoldville had been settled, with him coming out on top. The Congo crisis was over.

He was now fully in charge, on the throne rather than behind it. "The race for the top is finished," he told the press. "This is not a military coup d'état," he added, just as he had five years earlier during his first coup. Instead of the five-month deadline he had given himself after the first coup, he announced that he would remain president for five years.

He ended up staying for thirty-two.

On June 2, 1966, a jeep drove four men to an open field in Leopoldville's *cité* where some 100,000 people—the largest crowd in Congolese history—had gathered. Mobutu had declared an impromptu national holiday and invited all of Leopoldville to attend. At the edge of the field, vendors hawked ice cream to the crowd baking in the sun.

The jeep's occupants were former ministers. Three days earlier, a military tribunal had found them guilty, in an hour-and-a-half-long show trial, of plotting to overthrow the general. In all likelihood, they had been entrapped by ANC officers posing as defectors from the regime looking for new leadership. The ministers had been lured into a secret meeting, only to find themselves under arrest. Now, wearing nothing but soccer shorts, the men were led out of the car and toward a brawny executioner clad in all black. Each climbed the makeshift gallows, a hood tied over his head. A blast of bugles, the swoosh of the trapdoor, the crack of broken vertebrae, and it was on to the next. The crowd stood largely silent but for the intermittent screams of terrified children and the victims' families.

Publicly, the U.S. government had made a plea for clemency. Privately, Larry Devlin had tipped Mobutu off to the conspiracy after one of the alleged plotters approached the U.S. embassy for support. The public hanging sent a clear message: defy Mobutu, and death awaited. He had come a long way from his days as a quivering colonel racked with guilt and indecision, losing sleep over whether to betray an old friend. The execution set a badly needed "spectacular example," he now explained. "When a chief decides, he decides—period."

The rest of the world seemed to decide something, too: in the Congo, occasional barbarity was the price of stability. At least it seemed so from the relative silence and lack of protest following both Mobutu's coup and this latest barbaric spectacle. Everyone had been tired of chaos in the Congo, and Mobutu's coup seemed better than nothing. Parliament had voted to approve it the very day it was announced. The United States had formally recognized the new regime within two weeks. It expressed no resistance as Mobutu banned political parties and neutered parliament, nor could it air a peep of dissent now as a man still receiving a CIA stipend summarily executed four men, all of them likely innocent, in full view of the public.

Over the months and years to come, Mobutu would purge his remaining rivals one by one. Joseph Kasavubu was forced out of politics and confined to his home region of the lower Congo, where he died penniless, unable to pay for medical treatment despite having been promised financial security by Mobutu. Antoine Gizenga and Christophe Gbenye fled into exile. Pierre Mulele was tortured to death by soldiers who gouged out his eyes and tore off his genitals.

Even as he severed ties with his old allies and had some of them murdered, Mobutu took pains to rehabilitate his first victim: Patrice Lumumba. On June 30, 1966, six years after the first Congolese prime minister had delivered his daring independence day speech, Mobutu declared him a national hero. Now plumper in his heavily medaled general's uniform and white gloves, Mobutu asked the cheering crowd for a moment of silence, declaring "glory and honor to that illustrious Congolese, that great African, the first martyr of our economic independence." The man he had sent to his death, Mobutu elaborated, "fell victim to colonial machinations." In Katanga, the chicken farmer's house where Lumumba had spent his painful final hours was turned into a place of pilgrimage. His widow, Pauline, was invited back to the Congo from Cairo.

A mortal enemy had been resurrected in service of the new regime's legitimacy. The story of Mobutu and Lumumba, which had begun as a friendship between two young nationalists, matured into an alliance between a politician and his army chief, and ended as a fatal altercation between captive and captor, had come full circle.

Larry Devlin left the Congo a year later, in June 1967. A country consumed by crisis and power struggles both internal and geopolitical was now firmly in the hands of a man who owed his very survival, again and again, to the United States—and to Devlin, who had supported Mobutu every step of the way. A more prominent posting awaited Devlin in Laos, where the CIA was fighting at a covert front of the Vietnam War.

As Devlin packed his belongings, Mobutu pulled up to his house in a white Chevrolet convertible to say his goodbyes. His parting gift was an oversized photograph of himself, looking on sternly in his general's uniform, with a personal inscription: "To my old and excellent friend, L. Devlin, to whom the Congo and its chief owe so much."

The Arrogance of Power

O NE BY ONE, the messages landed, unexploded ordnance from an earlier phase of the Cold War. The letter summoning Sidney Gottlieb, the CIA scientist who had procured the poison targeting Lumumba, caught up with him in Istanbul, midway through a world trip. The call for Richard Bissell, the CIA official who had given Gottlieb his orders, reached him in Connecticut, where he was trying his hand at management consulting. Larry Devlin's letter found him in the Congo, where to his own surprise he had recently returned after retiring from the CIA at age fifty-two. The message the agency veterans received was the same: they would have to testify before a new Senate committee in Washington.

It was the summer of 1975. Details from the CIA's internal records on questionable covert activities—the "Family Jewels"—had leaked to the press. In the age of Vietnam and Watergate, the American public was less willing to give the executive branch a free pass, and the Senate had voted to create a special committee to investigate the intelligence community's excesses. It wasn't long before that committee, chaired by Senator Frank Church of Idaho, came across the Lumumba plot. Naturally, investigators wanted to talk to Devlin and his colleagues.

By then, the Congo was no longer the Congo; it was Zaire. As part of an "authenticity" campaign aimed at ridding his country of European influence, Mobutu had renamed it (never mind that "Zaire" was itself a Portuguese corruption of an African word). Trading his general's cap for a leopard-skin hat and his baton for a carved cane, he presented himself as a village chief on a national level (never mind that the hat was the work of a Parisian couturier). Gone were all Christian names; Joseph Mobutu himself became Mobutu Sese Seko. Leopoldville was now Kinshasa.

On the world stage, Mobutu presented Zaire as a bastion of Black pride and pan-African culture. Kinshasa had just hosted the "Rumble in the Jungle," a televised boxing match between George Foreman and Muhammad Ali that set new global viewership records. More important, at least for the United States, was that Mobutu was reliably anti-Communist. Although CIA payments to Mobutu had ceased, the United States lavished his regime with military and economic aid. At home, his consolidation of power was complete, culminating in a relentless cult of personality. Newspapers carried his photo on the front page almost daily. A new constitution officially enshrined the governing principles of "Mobutism." Mobutu no longer needed to bask in Patrice Lumumba's glow. The shrine at the farmhouse where Lumumba was tortured before his death fell into disrepair; in 1974, for the first time, the anniversary of Lumumba's murder went uncommemorated.

Despite his anti-Communist credentials, Mobutu's economic policies were decidedly statist. He nationalized—"Zairianized," in his words—countless businesses (the very thing the West had feared Lumumba would do), with much of the proceeds going into his own pocket. Evidence of graft could be seen in his flourishing real estate portfolio, which placed precious little emphasis on African authenticity: a townhouse on Avenue Foch in Paris, a villa in Switzerland, multiple properties in Belgium. American diplomats declined to confront him about the theft, worrying that to do so "would be to incur instant wrath." But after copper prices crashed in 1974, Mobutu's corruption machine became unsustainable, and the country fell into an economic crisis.

This was the country to which Devlin returned. His earlier work there had made his career, but after taking over Bronson Tweedy's former position as chief of the CIA's Africa division, he saw no way further up inside the agency and left. Separated from his wife, Colette, and in need of money to care for his ailing parents, he took a job in Zaire managing the interests of Maurice Tempelsman, a Belgian-American diamond merchant. He met often with Mobutu—

the dictator's rebranding notwithstanding, they were still "Joseph" and "Larry" to each other—so much so that U.S. diplomats griped that Devlin had better access to the president than they did. Devlin lived in the Binza neighborhood of Leopoldville, although by now, the eponymous group of backroom leaders was no more. Even Justin Bomboko and Victor Nendaka—longtime allies of Mobutu's and stalwarts of the Binza Group—had been ousted from their positions.

Summoned by the Church Committee, Devlin came back to Washington prepared to lie through his teeth. Assuming that evidence of the CIA's efforts to assassinate Lumumba remained only in the memories of men who knew how to keep secrets, he would deny everything about the affair to the committee's investigators. But before testifying, he conferred with an old agency colleague. "Larry, they got all the cable traffic," the friend told him. "They know everything. Don't perjure yourself."

And so when Devlin sat down for his interview in Room 608 of the Carroll Arms, an old hotel on Capitol Hill, he talked. Testifying under the pseudonym "Victor S. Hedgeman" (a precaution to protect himself from pro-Lumumba zealots, he explained), he abandoned his customary discretion. He told the three staffers across from him about the mysterious cable heralding the visit of Sidney Gottlieb. He told them about the meeting with Gottlieb—the gloves, the mask, the syringe, the vials of poison, the plan to adulterate Lumumba's toothpaste. And when asked where Gottlieb had said the order had come from, Devlin was unequivocal: "the president of the United States."

One of the young lawyers interviewing Devlin could hardly believe his ears. Devlin had just unlocked one of the central mysteries of the investigation, a question whose answer had never been committed to paper: how high in the U.S. government did responsibility go? Now they knew it went all the way to the White House.

The lawyer scribbled on a scrap of yellow legal paper and passed it to his colleague: "Bingo!"

The Church Committee investigated all manner of illegal overreach, including the FBI's surveillance of left-wing groups within the United States, the CIA's decades-long mail-interception program, and Gottlieb's dangerous mind-control experiments. But the committee's first report covered only the CIA's assassination efforts, which Senator Church believed would best capture the public's imagination. On the morning of November 20, 1975, copies of the 349-page document, *Alleged Assassination Plots Involving Foreign Leaders*, landed on the desks of all U.S. senators. After a last-minute attempt by Republicans to block its release to the public—a futile effort, since many of the findings had already appeared in newspapers over the previous months—the report was pressed into the grasping hands of journalists that afternoon.

The revelations were explosive. Though the CIA had been unsuccessful in getting to Lumumba itself, its efforts in the Congo had turned into something of a blueprint for subsequent covert interventions in which assassinating political targets was no longer beyond the pale. From 1960 to 1965, the report detailed, the U.S. government had considered various James Bond–style schemes to kill Fidel Castro, planning not only to send Mafia hit men after him but also to use "poison cigars, exploding seashells, and a contaminated diving suit." The CIA had backed the dissidents who shot and killed Rafael Trujillo, the Dominican Republic's dictator, in 1961 and may even have furnished the guns used in the murder. The Kennedy administration supported the 1963 coup that killed South Vietnamese President Ngo Dinh Diem and his brother Nhu. Seven years later, the Nixon administration backed and armed the plotters of a failed coup attempt in Chile, who nonetheless succeeded in assassinating the head of the country's army. But the details about the Lumumba plot were in many ways the most damning. Of the five cases studied, this was the only one in which the investigators could more or less prove that the initiative had come not from the CIA or local partners in the field but from the White House.

And yet when it came to Lumumba's ultimate death at the hands of the Katangans, the Church Committee let the CIA off the hook, finding no evidence of U.S. involvement in the murder. In the little time they had, the committee's staffers took an overly legalistic, prosecutorial approach to their investigation, focusing on the poisoning plot and other failed schemes to kill Lumumba rather than on the key American link in the chain of events that led to his death: the green light Larry Devlin gave to Congolese leaders for Lumumba's transfer to Katanga. In a puzzling omission, they made little note of the fact that Devlin had misled them about this crucial detail. The former station chief had implied he had learned about Lumumba's relocation after the fact, even though a contemporaneous cable, quoted in the committee's report, proved otherwise.

Contrary to the committee's conclusion, the United States did have blood on its hands in this instance. It had played a role in every event leading up to Lumumba's downfall and death. As early as the beginning of August 1960, five weeks into Lumumba's tenure as prime minister, the CIA urged President Kasavubu to remove him from power, and CIA-funded protests and propaganda made it easier for Kasavubu to do just that in September. The agency encouraged Mobutu to take power that same month, financed him and other members of his illegal regime, recommended that he arrange for Lumumba's "permanent disposal," and prevented a compromise in the making that would have seen the deposed prime minister return to power. Although the CIA had failed to penetrate Lumumba's entourage while he was under house arrest, it helped Mobutu search for and eventually capture him following his escape and then did nothing to ensure that his captors treated him humanely. When Devlin learned that Lumumba was about to be sent to his death, he offered no dissent to the Congolese power brokers who regularly sought—and followed—his advice. Instead, he actively kept officials in Washington out of the loop to prevent them from acting to save Lumumba.

The findings of the Church Committee led to an executive order that, at least on paper, banned the U.S. government from partaking in political assassination, but it caused no broader rethinking of U.S. foreign policy. Nothing would stop the CIA and the presidents who oversaw it from supporting unsavory actors whose sole virtue was that they opposed the United States' enemies. In the remaining decade and a half of Cold War politics, the U.S. government succored a rogues' gallery of pro-American dictators in Argentina, Chad, Haiti, Iran, and the Philippines. It backed questionable militants in Afghanistan, Angola, and Nicaragua.

That the U.S. government would act this way was hardly surprising, given the lessons it drew from its involvement in the Congo. At the CIA, Devlin's work as Leopoldville station chief earned him promotions and at least one award. Even the Church Committee concluded that, out of five different CIA paramilitary operations, the one in the Congo was the only to have "achieved its objectives." A seemingly pro-Soviet leader had been eliminated and replaced with a seemingly pro-American one. In Washington's estimation, the Congo was a success.

But only by the narrowest Cold War logic was this true. By discarding Lumumba and embracing Mobutu, the United States tilted the Congo off its natural political axis, creating an artificial gap between what the country's politics should have been and what they actually were. And because Mobutu's regime was an American creation, U.S. policy makers were invested in maintaining that gap. Propped up by the United States, Mobutu could stay in power without having to worry about securing the support of the population. He grew so complacent that he hardly even worried about staying in Washington's good graces—for example, expelling two U.S. ambassadors for displaying insufficient respect, receiving hundreds of military advisers from Communist North Korea, and, in the height of irony, accusing the CIA of plotting to overthrow him.

Why did the United States care at all about who led the Congo? Finding a clear answer to that question is harder than one might think. The Congo held vast natural resources, but the most valuable among them—its minerals—could all be found in greater quantities in North America. U.S. imports of Congolese uranium, at one point substantial, had ceased by the time of independence from Belgium. Geographically, the Congo was a backwater, far from both the United States and the Soviet Union. It wielded no global economic or political influence to speak of. And yet, as an unreleased Church Committee report concluded, "The U.S. became deeply involved through covert action in a country which represented no strategic threat to the U.S.; which housed no significant U.S. commercial interests; in which few American citizens resided; and which was contiguous to no U.S. territory."

The explanation lies partly in what the U.S. Senator William Fulbright would call "the arrogance of power," the idea that America's might gave it the right to remake foreign societies and governments in its own image. But the extensive U.S. involvement in the Congo is also explained by a Cold War shibboleth: the domino theory. If a single country fell to the Communists, then one by one, so would neighboring ones. The lack of evidence for this theory—never before had a Communist takeover actually set off such a chain reaction—did not keep it from becoming an article of faith among U.S. policy makers and the American public. Employing a different metaphor, John McCone, Allen Dulles's successor as CIA director, demonstrated the theory's grip at a Special Group meeting in 1964, when he worried that a Communist Congo would be a "cancerous growth which would soon spread."

Having convinced itself of the Congo's importance, the United States assumed that the Soviets must have considered it just as vital. They did not. At no point did Soviet activity in the Congo exceed that of Western countries. The documents uncovered with the eventual opening of the Soviet archives suggest that Moscow considered the Congo crisis a peripheral concern and Lumumba an uncertain ally. No less a cold warrior than Allen Dulles admitted as much, telling an interviewer in 1962, "I think we overrated the Soviet danger, let's say, in the Congo."

Similar distortions caused the United States to fundamentally misjudge Lumumba. He was, admittedly, tricky to pin down. He modulated his message to the recipient, and he pivoted quickly. He was reactive rather than proactive. But any politician who managed to win the contest to become Congolese prime minister was likely to demonstrate such traits and to play both sides of the Cold War.

In fact, Lumumba was naturally inclined toward the United States. After all, he had called on it to send troops to his country. Although he also was willing to ask for Soviet help—and to use the threat of such requests as political leverage—the evidence suggests that he saw such overtures as a practical measure in dire times, certainly not as indicative of an immutable allegiance. The idea that he would simply ditch his ardent anticolonialism and let his country fall under Soviet domination struck him as preposterous, and so it should have struck everyone else. But U.S. officials, eager to categorize Congolese politicians as either "moderate" or "radical," were predisposed to place any outspoken critic of Belgium, a European ally of theirs, in the latter category, no matter what he thought about America.

"For the Congo there are no blocs," Lumumba declared at one point. Through the prism of Cold War politics, however, the Americans, as well as many UN officials, saw not a nationalist tactician but a global player, a knowing combatant in a conflict that extended far beyond his own country's borders. It speaks to the flimsy basis of America's engagement in the Congo crisis that fifteen years on, when Richard Helms, Richard Bissell's deputy at the CIA, testified before the Church Committee, he could not recall which camp Lumumba belonged to. "I am relatively certain that he represented something that the United States government didn't like, but I can't remember anymore what it was," he said. He asked his interrogators for help. "Was he a rightist or leftist? . . . What was wrong with Lumumba? Why didn't we like him?"

Speaking also in the summer of 1975, Thomas Kanza, Lumumba's ambassador to the UN and ever-frustrated friend, put his finger on the error the United States had made in 1960. "The Americans believed that Lumumba was a Communist because the Belgians said he was," he told the press. "The Americans did not even know Lumumba."

American ignorance often went hand in hand with racist attitudes toward the Congolese people and their leaders. U.S. and UN cable traffic during the Congo crisis is rife with paternalism and exasperation with the "children" running the newly independent country, including the "little boy" Lumumba. What the Congolese needed, they seemed to suggest, was supervision and control. When one academic asked U.S. policy makers why they found it necessary to guide Congolese politics so closely in the early 1960s, he was told, among other explanations, that "bribery is the basis of Bantu politics," that Antoine Gizenga was "an illiterate moron," and that the Congolese were susceptible to Communist influence because they had "a short span of attention."

Even more pernicious, American officials wrote off the Congo as an uncivilized land, allowing them to permit—and be party to—violence. In this harsh, unforgiving place, niceties like sovereignty, democratic norms, and constitutional rules were no match for the Darwinian law of the jungle. To argue otherwise was to misunderstand the Congolese way of problem-solving. Explaining why he saw no need for direct U.S. involvement in Lumumba's assassination, Devlin said, "I assumed that the locals would take care of it."

Lumumba's death itself was the culmination of a long process of dehumanization. From suggestive jokes—Belgian talk of silencing him by means of an "effective injection," President Eisenhower's wish that Lumumba would suffer death by crocodile—to repeated physical abuse—in Belgian custody, at the hands of a mob of irate white evacuees—the prime minister had been turned into a disposable body long before his murder in the Katangan countryside.

It's tempting to imagine what could have been. Had Eisenhower shown a little more sympathy toward Lumumba—had he rearranged his schedule so as to meet him face-to-face at the White House—perhaps he wouldn't have ordered his assassination. Had Hammarskjöld shown the courage to defy U.S. entreaties and allowed UN peacekeepers to protect Lumumba, perhaps he could have saved the deposed prime minister's life. Had the United States and the UN shown more patience and worked with Lumumba rather than undermined him, perhaps the Congo could have pulled back from the brink and the crisis could have abated.

Lumumba was allergic to foreign domination. Had he been given a chance to stay in office, he probably would have presided over not a Soviet client state but a neutral, if left-leaning, country. ("He would have been a social democrat," his son François surmised.) Because so many of its problems were structural weaknesses inherited from its colonial history, the country was probably never destined to become a Jeffersonian democracy in the heart of Africa. But absent U.S. meddling, it could well have followed the trajectory of many postcolonial states in the region: poor and politically chaotic, but at least functional and free of mass violence.

We will never know. All we know is the fate that the country endured under Mobutu, more than thirty years of corruption, poverty, and repression. By the 1990s, Zaire had entered a death spiral. With the Soviet Union no more, the United States at last curtailed its support for Mobutu, slashing aid to his regime, nudging him to undertake modest political reforms, and denying him a visa to visit Washington. "I am the latest victim of the Cold War, no longer needed by the U.S.," he complained, with unusual self-awareness, to a reporter in 1993. Zaire's economy could no longer support Mobutu's extravagant system of graft and patronage. In 1994, the annual inflation rate hit an estimated 90,000 percent, a crisis that eased only when the government could not come up with the money to pay the company printing its currency. Refugees from the Rwandan genocide were flooding the border. Mobutu himself was dying of prostate cancer, his country reduced, in the words of *The Economist,* to "just a Zaire-shaped hole in the middle of Africa."

By May 1997, Mobutu's rickety regime was on the brink of total collapse. Impotent and incontinent from prostate surgery and ignored by his generals, Mobutu watched helplessly as rebels marched westward across Zaire. He left Kinshasa to hole up at his ornate palace in Gbadolite—"Versailles in the jungle"—but was no safer there and fled with his family for the airport. Before, he had taken shopping trips to Paris on the Concorde, having extended the runway to accommodate the supersonic jet. Now, he escaped the country in a Russian cargo plane as his own disgruntled presidential guards took potshots at the fuselage.

Mobutu lived only a few months longer, but long enough to witness the swearing in of his replacement as head of the country he had led for so long. It was the leader of the rebel invasion, Laurent Kabila, a man who had gotten his start as a commander in the Simba rebellion, the mid-1960s movement that had promised to carry on the legacy of Lumumba.

For years, Lumumba's tooth sat in a safe the size of a mini-fridge in the Belgian federal prosecutor's office in central Brussels. It had been an unexpected find: Gerard Soete, the Belgian police commissioner who had disposed of Lumumba's body in Katanga and held on to teeth and finger bones, claimed that he'd tossed the keepsakes into the North Sea. But sixteen years after Soete's death, his daughter Godelieve volunteered to a reporter that at least one tooth remained, a disclosure that prompted investigators to visit her house in Mélin and seize the molar, along with the bullets that had also been kept.

The items were taken as evidence in a slow-moving criminal

investigation into twelve Belgians whom Lumumba's son François alleged were complicit in his father's murder. But the evidence held limited forensic value, and when scientists considered analyzing the decaying tooth for DNA, they concluded that the extraction process would destroy the only part of his body that possibly remained. At this point, what good was it to know whether this was really Lumumba's tooth?

Already, prosecutors seemed to be slow-rolling the investigation. Many thought the government was waiting for the last of the twelve accused to die so it could close the case and move on. As with its colonial past, Belgium's reckoning with its role in Lumumba's death was sluggish. After the 1999 publication of an explosive book on the assassination, written by the Belgian sociologist Ludo De Witte, the Belgian parliament opened an investigation into the episode. Its final report concluded that "certain members of the Belgian government and other Belgian actors have a moral responsibility in the circumstances that led to Lumumba's death." Shortly after the report's publication, Belgium's foreign minister issued an official apology expressing "sincere regrets" for the affair. But the investigation skirted the United States' culpability altogether, and its goal was to repair relations with Belgium's former colony, not generate indictments.

Lumumba's daughter, Juliana, thought it strange that around the world, governments were still hunting aging Nazis, yet no one seemed moved to prosecute those responsible for her father's death. Adding insult to injury, the sole remaining relic of her father was moldering away in Brussels. On June 30, 2020, the sixtieth anniversary of Congolese independence, as Black Lives Matter protests spread to Belgium and Belgian mayors belatedly removed statues of Leopold II, she sent an open letter to Belgium's king demanding the return of her father's remains to the country he once led. "We simply want to bid him adieu," she wrote.

Officials in Brussels, in search of a more dignified container than a plastic evidence bag, commissioned a local jeweler to build a custom case for Lumumba's tooth. In a ceremony at a government palace in Brussels, Belgium's federal prosecutor handed over a bright blue box the size of a Bible to Juliana Lumumba and her brothers François and Roland. Then the box was placed into a coffin carved from a dark

African wood and flown to the country now known as the Democratic Republic of the Congo.

The past twenty-five years had not been kind to the nation. The collapse of Mobutu's Zaire had sparked a war so bloody and confused that estimates of its death toll range from two million to five million. In 2001, Mobutu's successor, Laurent Kabila, was assassinated and succeeded by his son Joseph, who stayed in power for seventeen years and did little to free the Congolese from the poverty, conflict, and repression they had come to know all too well. When Kabila fils finally held long-delayed elections, in 2018, the candidate who was declared the winner had not in fact won the most votes. By the time Lumumba's tooth was repatriated, in June 2022, the country still had never in history experienced a peaceful and democratic transfer of power. Then, as before, UN peacekeepers struggled to maintain order, and the central government barely functioned.

Lumumba's coffin toured Congo by plane, retracing in nine days the journey Lumumba had made over the course of thirty-five years. It went to Onalua, the town of his birth, then to Kisangani—Stanleyville, in pre-Mobutu days—and then to the clearing in the woods in Katanga where he met his end. The tooth came to rest in Kinshasa, where flags across the city had been lowered to half-mast. At a memorial service held on June 30, Independence Day, the Lumumba family watched as pallbearers wheeled his coffin down a red carpet toward a new, specially built tomb.

In spite of the solemn atmosphere, there was an artificial quality to the whole affair. The clawlike mausoleum, built by a Chinese construction company on a roundabout on the road to Ndjili airport, looked like something from a science-fiction movie set. The bronze statue atop it, cast two decades earlier by a North Korean construction firm, failed to capture Lumumba's likeness. The face was jowly; the body, hulking rather than lithe. As giant photographs of Lumumba looked on from easels, competing Lumumba impersonators mugged for the camera, each street performer having mastered the crisp part in their idol's hair and found modern equivalents to his brow-line glasses but hardly passing for the real man.

It would have to do. Dressed in black, Juliana Lumumba, the spitting image of her father, told a television reporter that she had been in mourning for sixty-one years. Now, she said, "Daddy is home."

Acknowledgments

Foreign Affairs has been my professional home for the last fifteen years, and the only one I have ever known. The institution allowed me to write this book not only in a fundamental sense, by sharpening my thinking and writing, but also in a more practical sense, by giving me the time and flexibility needed to start and finish it. I could not have asked for a better place to work, largely because of the extraordinarily smart and kind people who have walked through its doors. Three deserve special mention. Gideon Rose, the rabbi I never had, has taught me so much over the years that to enumerate it would require a separate acknowledgments section. His successor as editor of *Foreign Affairs,* Daniel Kurtz-Phelan, has also supported me immensely, from the moment I first joined the magazine and continuing through my journey through book-writing land. Justin Vogt, my coconspirator and confidant, is always game to bounce around ideas and deliver assured advice as we pick away at our salads. All three of these editors and friends didn't blink an eye when, after years of helping me, I asked them to read a draft of the book, which their comments vastly improved.

My agent, Gail Ross, was enthusiastic about my proposal from the get-go and somehow managed to drum up interest among American publishers about a book dealing with a forgotten crisis in midcentury Africa. I'm still not sure how she did it. Gail's biggest coup was to pair me with Erroll McDonald, my wise and patient editor. Erroll always believed in this book. He gave me extra time when I needed it—and a stern deadline when I needed that, too. Two other editors who were in the room the day I first met Erroll, Sonny Mehta and Dan Frank, did not live to see the finished product. But their vote of confidence kept me going as I wrote it. At Knopf, I have benefited from the talents not only of Erroll but also of the imperturbable Michael Tizzano, and their production and design colleagues Edward Allen, Michael Collica, and Ariel Harari. Ingrid Sterner gave the manuscript a meticulous copyedit. Emily Reardon and Morgan Fenton expertly handled publicity and marketing, respectively. I'm thankful for Reagan Arthur's support, too.

I was fortunate to be able to interview many people who witnessed the events described in this book. Their names are listed in the bibliography, and I am grateful to each of them and regret that some were not able to see what became of their memories. I am also grateful to Margaret Liu McConnell, who kindly shared with me letters written by her father, F. T. Liu, and Mvemba Dizolele, who did the same with the tapes of his interviews with Larry Devlin.

This book is based on a great deal of research, and I couldn't have wrangled all of it on my own. A generous grant from the International Strategy Forum at Schmidt Futures defrayed the cost of badly needed research assistance. At various times, I was helped by Evan Carr, Alexandra Gers, Anne Johnakin, Praachi Khera, Cece King, Akshat Mehta, Zamira Racher, Charlotte Staudt, Michelle Sun, and Julie Tomiche. Three research assistants took on especially important roles: Arthur Kaufman joined me at the very beginning, helping me wrap my head around the vast literature about Lumumba and the Congo crisis, locating obscure sources, and chasing historical leads. Later on, Lukas Baake painstakingly sifted through reams and reams of archival documents I had amassed, separating the wheat from the chaff and visiting more repositories himself. And as my (new) deadline loomed, Annie Crabill effortlessly tamed thousands of pages of my haphazardly organized notes so that I could spend as much time as possible writing. It has been heartening to see all three move on to bigger and better things. Also helping with research were three resourceful Congolese journalists, who arranged interviews during my trips to Congo: Papy Bambu in Kisangani, José Mukendi in Lubumbashi, and Pascal Mulegwa in Kinshasa. In Belgium, Tanja Milevska ably uncovered key information about Lumumba's tooth.

This book would have been much longer and more boring had it not been for the brilliant editing of Victor Brechenmacher. He saved me from countless infelicities and slipups, and his fingerprints are on every page. And after he had smoothed the entire book, he turned around and helped fact-check it. In that, Victor was joined by the indefatigable Katia Zoritch, whose eagle eyes went over the bulk of the book and also saved me from embarrassment. The photos in this book were curated—in record time—by the unflappable Yana Paskova. David Lindroth drew the elegant map.

Ben Alter, Andrew Han, Sam Kleiner, Rebecca Lissner, Elizabeth Ralph, and Joshua Yaffa helped me greatly in various ways during the book-writing process. When I finished a draft, I foisted it on other friends, who graciously agreed to read it and improved it with their feedback: Paul Bousquet, Rebekah Diamond, John Fine, David Herbert, Alex Palmer, David Rothenberg, David Schmidt, Thomas Sheridan, and Zach Swiss. I did the same with a number of scholars, who instead of viewing me as a PhD-less intruder on their turf, welcomed me as a fellow traveler: Pedro Monaville, Kal Raustiala, Herbert Weiss, Stephen Weissman, and Stephen Wertheim. Weiss, the dean of Congo studies, did me the favor of connecting me with Juliana Lumumba, who admitted that she met me only because of his endorsement. Weissman was especially generous, guiding me through the history ever since he wrote a 2014 *Foreign Affairs* article about the Lumumba affair.

I am lucky to be surrounded by such a loving family. This book is dedicated to my parents, Carol and Andrew Reid, who instilled in me from an early age the importance of education and hard work, values that have served me well. They also read the entire book and gave me predictably helpful comments. So did my in-laws, Heather Lawson and John Cushman, who, like my parents, pitched in enormously when it came to offering a place to write and complimentary child care. My children, Harriet and Rufus, helped me more than they know: Harriet by giving me a sense of perspective, and Rufus by issuing a firm deadline from the womb.

But the one person who deserves the most gratitude is my wife, Claire Cushman. That she was my first reader was the least of her contributions. Claire, you endured so much with me. How could I do anything without you?

A Note on Sources

This book is based on a variety of sources, especially documents produced at the time by the CIA, the State Department, the White House, the United Nations, and the Belgian government. As a result of the swift collapse of Lumumba's government and the decades of dysfunction that followed, there are far fewer Congolese documents for historians to review. I have endeavored to compensate for this unfortunate deficit as much as possible by making ample use of memoirs, contemporaneous interviews, and oral histories from the Congolese side. Beginning in 2014, I visited Congo four times—including stops in Kinshasa, Goma, Bukavu, Lubumbashi, and Kisangani—which allowed me to describe the sights and sounds recounted in this book, as well as interview witnesses to the events of 1960 and 1961.

For the reader's sake, I have corrected typos and standardized spellings. (For example, "Kasavubu" was also spelled "Kasa-Vubu.") When quoting cables, I have translated them from "cablese" into English; that is, I've inserted implied punctuation, changed capitalization, filled in missing words, and replaced acronyms and cryptonyms. Thus, Devlin's August 18, 1960, cable, which arrived in Washington as "EMBASSY AND STATION BELIEVE CONGO EXPERIENCING CLASSIC COMMUNIST EFFORT TAKEOVER GOVERNMENT," becomes the following: "The embassy and station believe the Congo is experiencing a classic Communist effort to take over the government." If a source is in French, the translation is my own unless otherwise indicated.

As with all histories, much is contested, and memories differ. The ghostwriter who helped Larry Devlin complete his memoir, for example, would routinely fact-check Devlin's recollections and dutifully present his findings to the aging spy, who was then suffering from emphysema and hooked up to an oxygen tank. "That's not the way I remember it," Devlin would reply, and that would be that. Accordingly, when encountering conflicts between accounts, I prioritized primary sources over secondary ones and contemporaneous tellings over retrospective ones. I also made my own judgment of basic plausibility. I have noted significant discrepancies in my endnotes.

Some of the most valuable documents for this book were formerly top secret cables and memos from the CIA and the State Department. Many of them, however, were striped with redactions. At times, this censorship was inconsistently applied: a name blacked out in one version of a document might be visible in another. Other redactions seemed to be motivated not by any sense of national security but by a desire to avoid institutional embarrassment: for example, when Ambassador Clare Timberlake's conclusion that it was a "fiction that we are dealing with a civilized people or a responsible government" was presented to readers of a State Department volume on Africa published in 1992, the phrase "a civilized people" was replaced with "[*less than 1 line of source text not declassified*]." (As it happened, the passage had already appeared unredacted elsewhere ten years earlier.)

Researchers looking into America's Cold War foreign policy face other needless hurdles. Declassification requests routinely take more than a decade to receive a final decision. In 2018, an investigative reporter filed a Freedom of Information Act request for the CIA's internal history of its operations against Lumumba. As of this writing, in 2023, the request is still pending. The United States spends a pittance on declassification: about $100 million a year, a fourth of the Pentagon's budget for military bands. The U.S. intelligence community has resisted efforts to replace costly manual reviews with ones conducted by the magic of artificial intelligence. And bafflingly, there is no rule that any document older than a certain number of years must be automatically declassified. Democracies are defined by openness, accountability, and free inquiry. More than six decades after Patrice Lumumba's murder, what could possibly be worth hiding, and from whom?

Notes

Abbreviations

AAP: Alleged Assassination Plots Involving Foreign Leaders: An Interim Report of the Select Committee to Study Governmental Operations with Respect to Intelligence Activities, United States Senate

ADST: Association for Diplomatic Studies and Training

AP: Associated Press

APP: Alison Palmer Papers

AWCP: Andrew W. Cordier Papers

BUC: Brian Urquhart Collection of Material About Ralph Bunche

CRISP: Centre de Recherche et d'Information Socio-politiques

CDF: Central Decimal File

CTP: Clare Timberlake Papers

DDEL: Dwight D. Eisenhower Presidential Library

DHC: Dag Hammarskjöld Collection

EP: Enquête parlementaire visant à déterminer les circonstances exactes de l'assassinat de Patrice Lumumba et l'implication éventuelle des responsables politiques belges dans celui-ci

FBV: Fonds Benoît Verhaegen

FRUS: Foreign Relations of the United States

HWP: Herbert Weiss Papers

ICRCA: International Committee of the Red Cross Archives

JFKAR: John F. Kennedy Assassination Records

JFKL: John F. Kennedy Presidential Library

NACP: National Archives at College Park, Maryland

NYT: The New York Times

OH: Oral history

RG: Record Group

RJBP: Ralph J. Bunche Papers

UNA: United Nations Archives

UPI: United Press International
WWIISCC: World War II Servicemen's Correspondence Collection

Epigraphs

vii "I have never": Lumumba, *Lumumba Speaks,* 421.
vii "I am relatively": Testimony of Richard Helms, June 13, 1975, 153–54, 157-10014-10075, JFKAR.

Prologue: The Loose Tooth

3 Nothing much happens: Information on Mélin is from "Parcours au travers des patrimoines: Dans les Plus Beaux Villages de Wallonie," Maison des Plus Beaux Villages de Wallonie, beauxvillages.be; "Gobertange Stone," Most Beautiful Villages of Wallonia A.S.B.L., beauxvillages.be; "En route vers les Plus Beaux Villages de Wallonie," VisitWallonia.be, walloniebelgique tourisme.be; "Mélin, un des plus beaux villages de Wallonie," Qualité Village Mélin, www.villagemelin.be; Patrice Biarent, "Bienvenue Chez Vous, St. Remy Melin," YouTube, Nov. 30, 2010, www.youtube.com; Marché de Mélin, Facebook, www.facebook.com; "Mélin," City Population, www.citypopulation.de.

3 "upscale villa in a rural village": The details of the raid and Soete's house come from legal documents I obtained; Maarten Goethals, "De tand des tijds van Patrice Lumumba," *De Standaard,* Jan. 24, 2016; Godelieve Soete, "De Moord op Lumumba de Dochter van de Lijkruimer Spreekt," interview by Jan Antonissen and Hanne Van Tendeloo, *HUMO,* Jan. 16, 2016; "Winter 2016 Weather History at Beauvechain Air Base," Weather Spark, weatherspark .com; Godelieve Soete, Facebook. Soete did not respond to my requests for an interview.

4 "He passed by like": Juliana Lumumba, interview.

6 And it was in the Congo: The closest the CIA would come to nearing its level of culpability in Lumumba's assassination was in the murder of South Vietnamese President Ngo Dinh Diem, but the agency did not desire or intend to cause his death—although it could have foreseen it. See *AAP,* 220–23 and Howard Jones, *Death of a Generation: How the Assassinations of Diem and JFK Prolonged the Vietnam War* (New York: Oxford University Press, 2004), 426.

6 The French philosopher: Lumumba, *Lumumba Speaks.*

1. The Boy from Onalua

11 It was said that: Omasombo and Verhaegen, *Jeunesse,* 78–84.

11 Lumumba attended: Finding aid for the Alexander and Hazel Reid Collection, Asbury University; Reid, *Congo Drumbeat,* 141; author correspondence with Bill Lovell, whose parents were missionaries in Wembo Nyama.

12 The mission was just: Omasombo and Verhaegen, *Jeunesse,* 95n10.

12 He learned to write: Reid, *Congo Drumbeat,* 30; Reeve, *In Wembo-Nyama's Land,* 143–45.

12 "The black pupil": Lumumba, *Congo, My Country,* 109.

12 "drinking alcohol": Omasombo and Verhaegen, *Jeunesse,* 96, 98.

13 Patrice's grandfather: McKown, *Lumumba,* 15; Michel, *Uhuru Lumumba,* 168.

13 As recently as the 1880s: Omasombo and Verhaegen, *Jeunesse,* 19; Hochschild, *King Leopold's Ghost,* 28.

13 The invaders made: Omasombo and Verhaegen, *Jeunesse,* 32–33.

13 Men and women were: Hochschild, *King Leopold's Ghost,* 41; Van Reybrouck, *Congo,* 31.

13 "Small country, small people": Hochschild, *King Leopold's Ghost,* 36.

13 "Dr. Livingstone": In all likelihood, Stanley never uttered these words. See Jeal, *Stanley,* 117.

13 In 1878, Leopold: Hochschild, *King Leopold's Ghost,* 63, 71. There is a dispute about how many treaties were signed and what they entailed. See Jeal, *Stanley,* 10, 286.

14 "to secure for ourselves": Hochschild, *King Leopold's Ghost,* 58.

14 "unpeopled country": Ibid., 31.

14 "gave us peace": Omasombo and Verhaegen, *Jeunesse,* 174.

14 For every twenty-five: Van Reybrouck, *Congo,* 81.

14 Occasionally they shot: Hochschild, *King Leopold's Ghost,* 111.

14 One person who: Jasanoff, *Dawn Watch,* 186–214.

14 "a little": Conrad, *Youth,* xi.

14 "To tear treasure": Conrad, *Heart of Darkness,* in ibid., 87.

15 Leopold sought to grow: Van Reybrouck, *Congo,* 81.

15 To tap enough rubber: Omasombo and Verhaegen, *Jeunesse,* 39–40, 62.

15 They knew what: Hochschild, *King Leopold's Ghost,* 161–63; Wrong, *Footsteps of Mr. Kurtz,* 46.

15 As proof to their superiors: Jasanoff, *Dawn Watch,* 209–10.

15 Owing partly to: Hochschild, *King Leopold's Ghost,* 233; Legum, *Congo Disaster,* 35.

16 Under Belgian government rule: Hochschild, *King Leopold's Ghost,* 271.

16 Father Achille de Munster: "Marcel Demunster," Profile, Geneanet, gw.geneanet .org; Omasombo and Verhaegen, *Jeunesse,* 75.

16 Bishop Walter Lambuth: "Guide to the Walter Russell Lambuth Papers," General Commission on Archives and History, United Methodist Church, catalog. gcah.org.

16 As a teenager: Omasombo and Verhaegen, *Jeunesse,* 99–101. According to some accounts, Lumumba left the school voluntarily.

16 Lumumba left Onalua: On the journey from Onalua to Kindu to Kalima, see Ibid., 103–105; McKown, *Lumumba,* 20–21. Lumumba's passport listed his height as 1.85 meters, or 6'1". See VII-BV/RDC/Lumumba N°005/02, FBV.

2. Promising Docility

18 "still living as their": Devlin to Post, Jan. 3, 1944 (incorrectly dated as 1943), WWIISCC.

18 "they love to argue": Devlin to Post, July 18, 1943, WWIISCC.

18 The only child of: Reimuller, interview; 1940 census, San Diego, Calif., Enumeration District 62-82.

18 Student life was: Devlin to Post, Feb. 22, 1943, WWIISCC.

18 Larry was a joiner: *Del Sudoeste Yearbook*, San Diego: Associated Students, San Diego State University, 1940–42, digital.sdsu.edu.

19 "I don't know which": Larry Devlin, "St. James and the Cocoa Tree," *Aztec*, Nov. 1, 1940.

19 "sort of a Stanley": "'King Congo' Opens Tuesday If OK-ed," *Aztec*, Nov. 18, 1941; Mabel Grant Hazard, "Alum-luminaries," *Aztec Alumni News*, Aug. 1, 1946; *Del Sudoeste Yearbook*, San Diego: Associated Students, San Diego State University, 1942, library.sdsu.edu; *Aztec Alumni News*, Jan. 1, 1946.

19 Barred from the air force: Reimuller, interview; Enlistment records (Electronic Army Serial Number Merged File, ca. 1938–46 [Enlistment Records]), NACP.

19 The next year: *Aztec News Letter*, Jan. 1, 1946, www-rohan.sdsu.edu.

19 "I have really been sweating": Devlin to Post, July 18, 1943, WWIISCC.

19 While everyone was camped: Reimuller, interview.

19 Colette, who accompanied: Ibid.

19 never managed to master: Mary Martin Devlin, interview.

20 To accommodate the overflow: Ferguson, *Kissinger*, 222; "Housing Tight Again in Fall," *Harvard Crimson*, Aug. 15, 1947.

20 One Sunday afternoon: Devlin, *Chief of Station*, 10; Hersh, *Dark Side*, 191. The meeting apparently did not make much of an impression on McGeorge Bundy, as Hersh recounts: "Years later, Devlin said, during a policy argument at the White House in the Johnson administration, Bundy plaintively asked Devlin, 'How did you get recruited in the agency?' His reply, Devlin said, made the national security adviser laugh: 'You recruited me.'"

20 A political theorist: Ferguson, *Kissinger*, 234–35; Gerardo L. Munck and Richard Snyder, *Passion, Craft, and Method in Comparative Politics* (Baltimore: Johns Hopkins University Press, 2007), 213.

20 The agency needed: Ferguson, *Kissinger*, 260; Winks, *Cloak and Gown*, 54–55; Weiner, *Legacy of Ashes*, 33.

20 As Bundy pitched: Devlin, *Chief of Station*, 1–2; Hersh, *Dark Side*, 191.

20 third-largest city: Young, *Politics in the Congo*, 207.

20 To remind Stanleyville's: Pons, *Stanleyville*, 24; "Liste des Rues," Stanleyville Kisangani, hier et aujourd'hui, www.stanleyville.be.

21 Lumumba lodged: Omasombo and Verhaegen, *Jeunesse*, 115.

21 So he grasped: Lumumba, *Congo, My Country*, 3; Omasombo and Verhaegen, *Jeunesse*, 121, 122, 113n9; Young, *Politics in the Congo*, 235; McKown, *Lumumba*, 28; Scott, *Tumbled House*, 5.

21 He graduated near: Omasombo and Verhaegen, *Jeunesse*, 122.

21 Restaurants, bars, and cafés: Monheim, "Léopoldville en juin 1959," cited in Young, *Politics in the Congo*, 105; Munger, *African Field Report*, 179; Houser, *Stop the Rain*, 40.

22 "Monkey!": Omasombo and Verhaegen, *Jeunesse*, 190.

22 One Sunday, he: Clément, "Patrice Lumumba," 67.

22 White and Black residents: Lemarchand, *Political Awakening*, 159; Munger, *African Field Report*, 172.

22 He earned: Omasombo and Verhaegen, *Jeunesse*, 125; Lumumba, *Congo, My Country*, 15. Descriptions of Stanleyville (including the post office and Lumumba's house) come from my visit to Kisangani.

22 Lumumba got a bank loan: Omasombo and Verhaegen, *Jeunesse*, 129–30.

23 But in 1951: Ibid., 138.

23 "undignified conduct": Ibid., 139.

23 He awoke at: Kashamura, *De Lumumba*, 6; Omasombo and Verhaegen, *Jeunesse*, 136; De Vos, *Vie et mort*, 17.

23 Eventually, he became: Lumumba, *Congo, My Country*, 91.

23 "penetrated with European civilization": Young, *Politics in the Congo*, 78, 81, 85.

23 "The territorial authority": Lumumba, *Congo, My Country*, 53.

24 Overtly political activity: Young, *Politics in the Congo*, 279.

24 At one point: Clément, "Patrice Lumumba," 73; Omasombo and Verhaegen, *Jeunesse*, 155, 163.

24 For *The Cross of the Congo*: Mutamba Makombo, *Patrice Lumumba*, 78.

24 "Our women must": Omasombo and Verhaegen, *Jeunesse*, 172.

24 "an incomparable collaborator": Clément, "Patrice Lumumba," 58.

25 "The fascination of becoming": "Congo: Boom in the Jungle," *Time*, May 16, 1955.

25 No wonder so many: Young, *Politics in the Congo*, 198–200.

25 "turn the heads": Lemarchand, *Political Awakening*, 136.

25 "Today, even the Europeans": Omasombo and Verhaegen, *Jeunesse*, 123.

26 "Negroes have the souls": Young, *Politics in the Congo*, 61.

26 The government prohibited: Ibid., 66; Van Reybrouck, *Congo*, 170.

26 "While thanking the Government": Mutamba Makombo, *Patrice Lumumba*, 151.

26 He also proposed: Omasombo and Verhaegen, *Jeunesse*, 164; Mutamba Makombo, *Patrice Lumumba*, 194–95.

26 "We promise docility": Omasombo and Verhaegen, *Jeunesse*, 154.

27 "undoubtedly the most": Ibid., 226n73.

27 "low-level staff": Ibid., 220, 227.

3. The Most Impossible Job on Earth

28 No one objected: Details on Hammarskjöld's appointment come from Urquhart, *Hammarskjold*, 12–13; Kelen, *Hammarskjöld*, 25–26.

29 "What has just": Kelen, *Hammarskjöld*, 28.

29 He spoke extemporaneously: Urquhart, *Hammarskjold*, 31–32.

29 A colleague who dined: Lipsey, *Hammarskjöld*, 119. The dinner guest may have been exaggerating; Hammarskjöld had, for instance, chaired the Swedish delegation to the UN General Assembly in 1952–53.

29 "as if he had hidden": Kelen, *Hammarskjöld*, 50.

29 "Well, I pronounce": British Movietone, "Dag Hammarskjold UN Secretary-General—1953," YouTube, 0:48, April 7, 2017, www.youtube.com.

29 "in my new official": Lipsey, *Hammarskjöld*, 121.

29 "generations of soldiers": Dag Hammarskjöld, "Old Creeds in a New World," Nov. 1953, This I Believe, thisibelieve.org.

30 His was a noble: Lash, *Dag Hammarskjöld*, 18.

30 Nonetheless, because his: Stolpe, *Dag Hammarskjöld*, 26.

30 That might have been: AP, "Sten Hammarskjöld," *Hartford Courant*, April 19, 1953.

30 "A box on the ear": Hammarskjöld, *Markings*, 180.

30 "Dag is the only one": Lipsey, *Hammarskjöld*, 27.

30 "awfully dry life": Ibid., 37; Stolpe, *Dag Hammarskjöld*, 32.

30 "I don't think we can": Urquhart, *Hammarskjold*, 368.

30 He moved to Stockholm: Lipsey, *Hammarskjöld*, 43–45.

31 "Do you speak at home": Lash, *Dag Hammarskjöld*, 29.

31 At age thirty: Details on Hammarksjöld's prewar life come from ibid., 31, 35, 42; Lipsey, *Hammarskjöld*, 47; Kelen, *Hammarskjöld*, 40; Simon, *Dag Hammarskjöld*, 47.

31 "real governor": Lipsey, *Hammarskjöld*, 48.

31 Still, Hammarskjöld viewed: Urquhart, *Hammarskjold*, 22; Lash, *Dag Hammarskjöld*, 40–41.

31 signs that a softer approach: Taubman, *Khrushchev*, 247.

32 "a sort of white paper": Hammarskjöld, *Markings*, unpaginated front matter. I have translated the Swedish *vitbok* as "white paper" in lieu of "white book."

32 "For all that has been": Ibid., 89.

4. To Brussels and Back

33 A childhood marked by: "Belgium's Quiet King," *NYT,* May 12, 1959; Gerard and Kuklick, *Death in the Congo*, 20.

33 On a visit to the Congo: Vanthemsche, "Belgian Royals," 182–83; MJM Productions, "Bwana Kitoko, 'Handsome Man' (1955—Part 2/2)," YouTube, 10:57, July 18, 2010, www.youtube.com; Van Reybrouck, *Congo*, 224–25; *Belgisch Congo Belge*, directed by Gérard de Boe, André Cauvin, and Ernest Genval (CINEMATEK, 2013).

34 But Lumumba buttonholed: Omasombo and Verhaegen, *Jeunesse*, 224n66, 223–24.

34 "the continuing existence": Merriam, *Congo*, 68.

34 "had a long interview": Omasombo and Verhaegen, *Jeunesse*, 181.

35 Belgium had so successfully: Young, *Politics in the Congo*, 274.

35   the Belgian Communist Party: Vanthemsche, *Belgium and the Congo,* 48.

35   "The jungle will": *Life,* Aug. 1, 1960.

35   "It is our fault": Van Bilsen, *Un plan de trente ans,* 1. Another reason for the thirty-year timeline was that Van Bilsen wanted to prevent fellow Belgians from being able to accuse him of, as he put it, "demagoguery." See Lemarchand, *Political Awakening,* 154.

35   Belgium's political class: Young, *Politics in the Congo,* 144.

35   "How can you encourage": Merriam, *Congo,* 70.

36   Van Bilsen's circumspect: Scott, *Tumbled House,* 24; Académie Royale des Sciences d'Outre-Mer, "Van Bilsen (Anton Arnold Jozef)," *Biographie Belge d'Outre-Mer* 9 (2015): 379–83, www.kaowarsom.be.

36   "highly sensitive to": Clément, "Patrice Lumumba," 63.

36   Lumumba felt acutely: Lumumba, *Congo, My Country,* 155.

36   His white bosses: Monheim, "Leopoldville en juin 1959," 36.

36   "We'll see if one": Omasombo and Verhaegen, *Jeunesse,* 236.

36   He had been invited: Ibid., 236–37; Etambala, "Lumumba en Belgique," 199.

36   Within twenty-four hours: Omasombo and Verhaegen, *Acteur,* 21; Omasombo and Verhaegen, *Jeunesse,* 236.

37   Having left Harvard: Devine, interview; Reimuller, interview.

37   The guides' eponymous creator: Seymour M. Hersh, "Hunt Tells of Early Work for a C.I.A. Domestic Unit," *NYT,* Dec. 31, 1974; Lawrence Van Gelder, "Fodor Denies Being Agent but Says He Helped C.I.A.," *NYT,* Jan. 9, 1975.

37   "real writers, not": Roy Bongartz, "Where Tourists Go, Fodor's Been," *NYT,* June 15, 1975.

37   Devlin was credited: Hayes, *Queen of Spies,* 302n10; WorldCat, worldcat.org; AbeBooks, abebooks.com.

37   He plagiarized: Mary Martin Devlin, interview. It was a habit he would carry over to his memoir. See Gerard and Kuklick, *Death in the Congo,* 261.

37   That opportunity came: Division of Publishing Services, Department of State, *Foreign Service List, 1958,* Jan. 1958, babel.hathitrust.org; Reimuller, interview.

37   His main responsibility: Interview and meeting summary, "Victor Hedgeman," Aug. 22, 1975, 157-10014-10185, JFKAR.

38   When Lumumba stepped: Etambala, "Lumumba en Belgique," 192, 201; April 25, 1956, weather history at Brussels Airport, Weather Spark, weatherspark.com.

38   The trip was wasted: Lumumba, *Congo, My Country,* 41.

38   His sole complaint: Etambala, "Lumumba en Belgique," 220.

38   It was Lumumba's first: The passport was issued April 11, 1956, and, remarkably, expired July 10, 1956. See VII-BV/RDC/Lumumba N°005/02, FBV.

38   "It is shabby": Etambala, "Lumumba en Belgique," 212, 207, 210.

38   "The colonial who today": Lumumba, *Congo, My Country,* 132.

38   "the rock where": Etambala, "Lumumba en Belgique," 203.

39   By all appearances: Hochschild, *King Leopold's Ghost,* 176; Daniel Boffery, "Belgium Comes to Terms with 'Human Zoos' of Its Colonial Past," *Guardian,* April 16, 2018.

39 "Certainly, mistakes were": Etambala, "Lumumba en Belgique," 216, 218.

39 "Since we are in": Ibid., 224.

39 Now he was addressing: Omasombo and Verhaegen, *Jeunesse*, 237, 188.

5. Not a Slave

40 "As I told my bosses": Omasombo and Verhaegen, *Acteur*, 27.

40 In eighty-five separate: Ibid., 81.

41 News of the high-flying: See, for example, "Un des évolués qui vinrent en Belgique, en mai dernier, avait détourné 100,000 fr.!," *Le Soir*, July 10, 1956, 4; "Un notable congolais qui encensa le colonialisme, en mai en Belgique, est arrêté pour détournements à Stanleyville," *Le Drapeau Rouge*, July 11, 1956.

41 He was the most: Omasombo and Verhaegen, *Acteur*, 95.

41 "How can a man": Lumumba, *Congo, My Country*, 19, 16.

41 The Stanleyville Central Prison: Details about the prison and Lumumba's stay there come from personal communication with Bérengère Piret; Piret, *Les cent mille briques*, 110; Bérengère Piret, "Être mis à l'ombre au Congo: Introduction au système pénitentiaire colonial belge" (PowerPoint), www.academia.edu; Omasombo and Verhaegen, *Acteur*, 35, 50, 63, 65; Mountmorres, *Congo Independent State*, 54; Lumumba, *Congo, My Country*, 76–79; André Cauvin, "Photos prises dans le cadre du tournage du film 'Le voyageur solitaire,' 1957–1958," photography, pallas.cegesoma.be; McKown, *Lumumba*, 48.

41 "a European would never serve": Monaville, *Students of the World*, 38. This quotation comes from an article in *L'Afrique et le Monde* that was published under the byline of a friend, Boniface Lupaka, but was likely written by Lumumba. See Omasombo and Verhaegen, *Acteur*, 65.

41 "To console themselves": Lumumba, *Congo, My Country*, 76–77.

42 "To send them into": Omasombo and Verhaegen, *Acteur*, 40.

42 "the mysteries of the": Lumumba, *Congo, My Country*, 7.

42 Addressed to the Belgian: Monaville, *Students of the World*, 39.

43 "total emancipation": Merriam, *Congo*, 321, 324, 333.

43 "It is easy enough": Lumumba, *Congo, My Country*, 146, 183–84, 33, 32.

43 "We are not chickens": Ibid., 85, 65, 20.

43 "I have always been": Ibid., 3–5.

44 "a mix of cunning": Omasombo and Verhaegen, *Acteur*, 66. Eventually, in 1961, the book was published—much to the annoyance of Lumumba's allies, who thought it unfair to expose his juvenilia.

44 "Hounded by almost": Ibid., 81.

44 That effort spilled: Young, *Politics in the Congo*, 143. Lumumba himself considered his arrest the result of his antagonizing the Catholic Church. As his friend Albert Onawelo recounted, when he visited Lumumba in prison in 1957, Lumumba spent an hour and a half explaining how "the Catholic Church and the authorities in Stan had plotted against him." Testimony of Albert Onawelo, VII-BV/RDC/Lumumba N°001/02, FBV.

44 Lumumba had joined: Omasombo and Verhaegen, *Jeunesse*, 226; Omasombo and Verhaegen, *Acteur*, 20. "The Catholic Missionaries are not happy with me because I cannot be influenced," he wrote to one of Buisseret's staffers. "They tried to make me sign letters of protest to attack the policy of Minister Buisseret, but I refused each time." Lumumba to Maurice, Jan. 17, 1956, box 2, folder 37, HWP.

44 Other Congolese caught: Nzongola-Ntalaja, *Patrice Lumumba*, 55; Omasombo and Verhaegen, *Acteur*, 80; McKown, *Lumumba*, 48; Munger, *African Field Report*, 164.

45 Even after he confessed: Omasombo and Verhaegen, *Acteur*, 55.

45 "We are dealing with": Ibid., 92.

45 "is still not that far": Ibid., 86.

45 "This is not about": Ibid., 93.

45 "Without our presence": Ibid., 94.

45 His hidden savior: Ibid., 20n4. Lumumba's mild-mannered manuscript might have helped secure his release. See Benoît Verhaegen, "Patrice Lumumba, martyr d'une Afrique nouvelle," *Jeune Afrique*, Feb. 1978, 85. By the time of his release, Lumumba was already in Leopoldville, where he was being held in prison for the appeal.

46 At that point: Scott, *Tumbled House*, 10. Officially, eighteen hundred Africans perished building the 227-mile railway. La Fontaine, *City Politics*, 10.

46 It was then and there: See Nuno R. Faria et al., "The Early Spread and Epidemic Ignition of HIV-1 in Human Populations," *Science* 346, no. 6205 (Oct. 3, 2014), 56–61.

46 Fourteen-story buildings: Mboka, "Leopoldville 1950s—Tropical Modernism Sets the Tone," *Kinshasa Then and Now* (blog), Aug. 15, 2011.

46 "Europe in Leo": Greene, *In Search of a Character*, 65.

46 To combat malaria: Inforcongo, *Thirteen Million Congolese*, 66; Greene, *In Search of a Character*, 16.

46 Instead of filling: Gunther, *Inside Africa*, 652.

47 just 100,000 Europeans: Vanthemsche, Belgium and the Congo, 280. The number crossed the 100,000 mark in 1956–57. The Congolese population figure for the period comes from United Nations, *Demographic Yearbook 1955* (New York: Statistical Office of the United Nations Department of Economic and Social Affairs, 1955), 117.

47 The main European quarter: La Fontaine, *City Politics*, 19; Tourist Bureau for the Belgian Congo and Ruanda-Urundi, map of Leopoldville, 1952.

47 Children splashed: "Le Congo Belge 1958 en image," Canal Congo News, YouTube, 25:22, Nov. 17, 2018, www.youtube.com.

47 Black residents weren't: Gunther, *Inside Africa*, 652; Stewart, *Rumba on the River*, 74; "Jean Depara—Photo," *Revue Noire*, www.revuenoire.com; "Le Congo Belge 1958 en image."

47 "Breweries consider this": van Beemen, *Heineken in Africa*, 13.

47 It wasn't until 1955: Young, *Politics in the Congo*, 66.

47 When Lumumba left: Details on Lumumba and the beer wars come from "Patrice Lumumba et la guerre des bières: Un Témoignage," in *Patrice Lumumba entre Dieu et diable*, eds. Halen and Riesz, 92–94; Stewart, *Rumba on the River*, 74–75; Omasombo and Verhaegen, *Acteur*, 111–14; McKown, *Lumumba*, 55; Kanza, *Rise and Fall*, 32; Brassinne, "Enquête," 32.

48 "cancer of alcoholism": Lumumba, *Congo, My Country*, 91.

48 It was Abako that: Covington-Ward, "Kasa-Vubu, ABAKO, and Performances," 77.

49 "the Bakongo Buddha": Munger, *African Field Report*, 160. See also Liu OH, 7. Kasavubu's daughter Marie-Rose denied this in an interview with me, claiming that the rumor was designed to delegitimize her father. According to Crawford Young, "It seems on the face of it unlikely, as the part of Mayombe where Kasavubu was born was virtually unpenetrated at the time of railroad construction." Young, *Politics in the Congo*, 391n.

49 "Pesa ngai Lumumba": Omasombo and Verhaegen, *Acteur*, 116.

49 Within months of his: Kanza, *Rise and Fall*, 31.

49 "Patrice Lumumba, Commercial Director": Monheim, *Mobutu*, 39.

49 Now earning five times: Omasombo and Verhaegen, *Acteur*, 113.

49 As he had in Stanleyville: Ibid., 128, 141.

49 "make the Congo": Monaville, *Students of the World*, 244.

6. Awakenings

50 The centerpiece of the: "The Atomium in Figures" and "The Atomium's Shape," Atomium, atomium.be; G. H. Davis, "A New Landmark for Brussels," *Popular Mechanics*, Jan. 1958.

50 "thrust into a corner": Stanard, *Selling the Congo*, 272.

50 Sitting on the dirt: Lucas Vanclooster, "60 jaar Expo 58: Hoe stelden wij toen Congo voor?," *VRT NWS*, April 17, 2018; Pluvinage, *Expo 58*, 111; Stanard, *Selling the Congo*, 267, 273, 284. One Congolese priest present at Expo 58 said of Europeans, "The African seems to be envisaged by them as if he were some kind of strange animal." Slade, *Belgian Congo*, 14.

50 Among them was: Mobutu and Remilleux, *Dignité pour l'Afrique*, 29. Throughout, I have relied on a mix of my own translations and those used in the English version of the book, *Dignity for Africa*.

50 During the exposition: *Le Soir*, July 1, 1958, 7.

51 "The public fluctuates": AfricaShows: 1ère chaîne de divertissement en Afrique, "MOBUTU KING OF ZAÏRE—CONGO—VOST EN—Belgique," YouTube, 5:30 of 2:09:17, May 1, 2019, www.youtube.com.

51 In fact, about a hundred: Kanza, *Rise and Fall*, 39.

51 For the first time: Young, *Politics in the Congo*, 277.

51 They could wander: "United Nations at Brussels 1958 Exhibition," UN Audiovisual Library, Jan. 1, 1958, 8:35 and 15:42 of 18:21, www.unmultimedia.org.

51 "that man is the same": Kanza, *Tôt ou tard*, 35.

51 He would come back: Monheim, *Mobutu*, 41.

52 "In a way": Mobutu and Remilleux, *Dignité pour l'Afrique*, 19. Other details on Mobutu's early life come from ibid., 19–27; Monheim, *Mobutu*, 25–27; Young and Turner, *Rise and Decline*, 173–74; Wrong, *Footsteps of Mr. Kurtz*, 72–75.

52 "to-ing and fro-ing": Mobutu and Remilleux, *Dignité pour l'Afrique*, 21.

52 Soon, he began: Mobutu's pseudonym was "De Banzy," an allusion to his father's hometown, Banzyville.

52 "Oh, Mr. Lumumba": Testimony of Albert Onawelo, VII-BV/RDC/ Lumumba N°001/02, FBV. See also Omasombo and Verhaegen, *Acteur*, 108. Monheim dates the meeting to 1956, when Lumumba had just returned from his trip to Brussels.

52 The government had: Omasombo and Verhaegen, *Acteur*, 145.

53 "Whoever wants independence": "Le discours du général de Gaulle à Braz- zaville le 24 août 1958," *Le Figaro*, Aug. 23, 2018.

53 *Why don't the Belgians:* Merriam, *Congo*, 82.

53 "anachronistic political regime": CRISP, *Congo 1959*, 26–27; Lemarchand, *Polit- ical Awakening*, 161.

53 "the Belgian Congo's": Van Reyn, *Le Congo politique*, 38.

53 The two men: Mobutu and Remilleux, *Dignité pour l'Afrique*, 41.

53 "You have to come": Monheim, *Mobutu*, 42.

53 Hours later, Lumumba: Omasombo and Verhaegen, *Acteur*, 150, 163. The description of Dendale comes from Mboka, "Leopoldville 1959—Martyrs for Independence," *Kinshasa Then and Now* (blog), Jan. 13, 2019.

54 "within a reasonable": Omasombo and Verhaegen, *Acteur*, 150.

54 "forcefully fight any": Ibid.

55 "veritable geological scandal": Nzongola-Ntalaja, *Leopold to Kabila*, 28.

55 "authentic Katangese": Young, *Politics in the Congo*, 482, 490.

55 "At 11:30 o'clock": Green to State, Dec. 9, 1958 (102), file 310 Intl. Conferences 1956–58, Security-Segregated Records, U.S. Embassy Leopoldville, RG 84, NACP. It is possible but unlikely that Lumumba had earlier official contact. Prior to the MNC's founding, in October, he would probably not have been on the Americans' radar screen.

56 The new three-story: Lambelet, interview.

56 Belgian authorities had: Lavallee to State, Dec. 9, 1958 (174), file 310 Intl. Con- ferences 1956–58, Security-Segregated Records, U.S. Embassy Leopoldville, RG 84, NACP.

56 They managed to secure: Thompson, *Ghana's Foreign Policy*, 119, claims that the Israeli ambassador in Ghana financed the trip.

56 "in a personal capacity": Omasombo and Verhaegen, *Acteur*, 171.

56 The conference brought: "All-African People's Conferences," 429; Macey, *Frantz Fanon*, 363; Homer A. Jack, "Ideological Conflicts," *Africa Today* 6, no. 1 (Jan.–Feb. 1959), 15.

56   The CIA was: Monaville, *Students of the World*, 55; Tolliver, "Fragmented Heart of Darkness," 40–41; Gaines, *American Africans in Ghana*, 95.

56   Lumumba's allies suspected: Kanza, *Rise and Fall*, 50.

56   But the most lasting: At one point, Nkrumah asked a passing American attendee to take a photograph of the two of them. Houser, *Stop the Rain*, 70.

57   Accra marked: Simons, Boghossian, and Verhaegen, *Stanleyville 1959*, 20; Lumumba, *Lumumba Speaks*, 58.

57   "scram from Africa": "'Scram!,'" *Time*, Dec. 22, 1958, 23.

57   "Address of Mr. Lumumba": Omasombo and Verhaegen, *Acteur*, 173.

57   When several thousand: Mboka, "Leopoldville 1959—Martyrs for Independence"; Omasombo and Verhaegen, *Acteur*, 173.

57   "free itself from": Lumumba, *Lumumba Speaks*, 67.

57   "wipe out the colonialist": Ibid., 62.

58   "Africa," he said: Ibid., 67.

58   He had the rare: Young, *Politics in the Congo*, 388.

58   Mobutu formally joined: Monheim, *Mobutu*, 43.

58   the Polar marketing budget: "La guerre des bières," 92–94.

58   Lumumba came often: Monheim, *Mobutu*, 36; Mboka, "Leopoldville 1952—Office des Cités Africains," *Kinshasa Then and Now* (blog), Sept. 30, 2011; Mboka, "Leopoldville 1956—the Tourist Circuit (Cité)," *Kinshasa Then and Now* (blog), Feb. 6, 2011.

58   While Mobutu's wife: My description of Mobutu and Lumumba's travels this day comes from Monheim, *Mobutu*, 44–46; Van Reybrouck, *Congo*, 247; Omasombo and Verhaegen, *Acteur*, 177; Demany, *S.O.S. Congo*, 21; "Exclusif: Des images du fameux match V.Club-Mikado (1-3), à l'origine des émeutes du 4 janvier 1959 à Léopoldville," *Mbokamosika* (blog), Oct. 21, 2017, www.mbokamosika.com; François Lumumba, interview.

59   "a human tide": Commission parlementaire chargée de faire une enquête sur les événements qui se sont produits à Léopoldville en janvier 1959, *Rapport à la Chambre*, March 27, 1959, 49, www.dekamer.be.

59   One man was seen: Janssens, *J'étais le général Janssens*, 63.

59   An enterprising member: Commission parlementaire, *Rapport à la Chambre*, 49, 46.

59   Whites who showed up: Merriam, *Congo*, 86–87.

60   "a solemn appeal": Demany, *S.O.S. Congo*, 22.

60   The roll of thunder: Roberts and Roberts, "Letters from the Congo," 103.

60   The next morning: Ibid., 105.

60   It took four days: Ibid., 107.

60   Soldiers of the Force Publique: Donald Grant, "Rioting Erupts in Leopoldville, Shops Looted, Troops in Action; Belgian Congo Growing Restive," *St. Louis Post-Dispatch*, Jan. 5, 1959.

60   not a single white person had died: Commission parlementaire, *Rapport à la Chambre*, 90–91.

60 One tract circulating: Lemarchand, *Political Awakening*, 47.

60 Force Publique officers: Omasombo and Verhaegen, *Acteur*, 177.

61 "Who are these for?": François Lumumba, interview.

61 Despite the attention: Monheim, *Mobutu*, 46.

61 Some Belgian officials proposed: Commission parlementaire, *Rapport à la Chambre*, 65.

61 "exciting Africans to violence": "Joseph Kasavubu Dies in Congo; Was His Nation's First President," *NYT*, March 25, 1969; Merriam, *Congo*, 88.

61 Thousands of jobless men: Young, *Politics in the Congo*, 152–53; Omasombo and Verhaegen, *Acteur*, 179; Lemarchand, *Political Awakening*, 47; Gondola, *Tropical Cowboys*, 161.

61 "The Congolese demand": British Pathé, "Scenes After Leopoldville Riots— Members of the Senate—Belgian Government Meet (1959)," YouTube, 1:54, April 13, 2014, www.youtube.com.

61 On January 13: Inforcongo, *Political Future*, 5.

61 "The object of our presence": Legum, *Congo Disaster*, 59.

62 There, at long last: Merriam, *Congo*, 89.

62 "The picture that had been built": Donald Grant, "Congo Riots Quickly Transform Seemingly Amiable Relationship into a Complete Estrangement," *St. Louis Post-Dispatch*, Jan. 7, 1959.

7. The Year of Africa

63 "No one knew a damn": Woodrow Wilson International Center OH, 14.

63 It was 1959 and: Devlin, *Chief of Station*, xiii; Testimony of Victor Hedgeman, Aug. 21, 1975, 8, 157-10014-10080, JFKAR.

63 It was a testament: Reimuller, interview.

63 The incumbent station chief: Bevill, interview. For Springer's pre-CIA career, see Bevill, *Blackboards and Bomb Shelters*.

63 "You'll be on the golf course": Devlin, *Chief of Station*, xiii. According to Paul Springer's son-in-law James Bevill, these words were Springer's. Bevill, interview.

63 When the department set: Schlesinger, *Thousand Days*, 551.

63 At the State Department's: Woodrow Wilson International Center OH, 13.

64 The U.S. consulate in Elisabethville: Tienken OH, 15.

64 At any given time: Division of Publishing Services, Department of State, *Foreign Service List, 1960*, Jan. 1960, 4, babel.hathitrust.org; Freeman to Timberlake, April 11, 1960, box 1, folder 9, CTP.

64 The State Department worried: Weissman, *American Foreign Policy*, 44.

64 "All in all": Roberts and Roberts, "Letters from the Congo," 21.

64 Cables from the consulate: Roberts OH, 14.

64 One political officer: Woodrow Wilson International Center OH, 22; Roberts OH, 15; Roberts and Roberts, "Letters from the Congo," 18, 171.

64 "would like to be on": *FRUS, 1958–1960,* vol. 14, doc. 6.

65 The U.S. consulate housed: Omasombo and Verhaegen, *Acteur,* 170; State to Brussels, Feb. 19, 1958 (907), box 4, Brussels Fair, Randall Series, U.S. Council of Foreign Economic Policy, Office of the Chairman, 1954–61, DDEL.

65 "We must make up": Memorandum to Council on Foreign Economic Policy, box 7, Africa, Randall Series, Journals, 1953–61, DDEL.

66 They even unscrewed: Meredith, *Fate of Africa,* 68–69.

66 Guinea's president: Notes of April 27, 1959, conversation between Savinov and de Coninck, May 9, 1959, in Namikas and Mazov, "CWIHP Conference Reader."

66 So Lumumba's interest: Muehlenbeck, *Czechoslovakia in Africa,* 55.

66 When they met: Notes of April 18, 1959, conversation between Gerasimov and Lumumba, April 28, 1959, in Namikas and Mazov, "CWIHP Conference Reader."

66 "succumbed to the provocation": Namikas, *Battleground Africa,* 40.

67 "Lumumba holds a": Notes of April 27, 1959, conversation between Savinov and de Coninck, May 9, 1959.

67 Taking a page from: Omasombo and Verhaegen, *Acteur,* 232, 190.

67 "He does...have": Tomlinson to State, April 1, 1959 (310), file 350 Congo Jan.–June 1959 Classified, Security-Segregated Records, U.S. Embassy, RG 84, NACP.

67 "The whites will": Omasombo and Verhaegen, *Acteur,* 239.

67 In Kasavubu's stronghold: Legum, *Congo Disaster,* 69.

67 "No more Colonial Ministers": Merriam, *Congo,* 146.

67 White settlers splattered: Young, *Politics in the Congo,* 158; Reuters, "M. Van Hemelrijck, Helped Free Congo," *NYT,* Oct. 11, 1964.

67 "Down with colonialism!": Omasombo and Verhaegen, *Acteur,* 224.

67 fifty-eight thousand: Ibid., 186.

68 Yet there was discord: For more on the split, see ibid., 226–31; Lemarchand, *Political Awakening,* 204–5.

68 "New political parties": "Free-for-All Ahead in Congo Elections," *York Dispatch,* June 10, 1959.

68 "Not a week goes": Lemarchand, *Political Awakening,* 196

68 "not to compete": Ibid., 213.

68 In a matter of weeks: Young, *Politics in the Congo,* 278.

68 "a madman will soon": Omasombo and Verhaegen, *Acteur,* 241, 256, 240.

68 "More than sixty chieftains": Lumumba, *Lumumba Speaks,* 109.

68 "The shores of the great river": Ibid., 115.

69 "Long live the king": Leroy, "Journal de la Province Orientale," 310.

69 "Lumumba's mission is": Kashamura, *De Lumumba,* 13.

69 At 7:00 p.m.: CRISP, *Congo 1959,* 229; AP, "Riots Quelled in Africa After 20 Die in Fighting," *Cincinnati Enquirer,* Nov. 2, 1959; Omasombo and Verhaegen, *Acteur,* 288.

69 "a simulacrum of democracy": Lumumba, *Lumumba Speaks,* 130.

69 "training for democracy": Inforcongo, *Thirteen Million Congolese,* 61.

69 The executive branch: Young, *Politics in the Congo,* 158–59; Merriam, *Congo,* 94.

69 "Independence has never": Simons, Boghossian, and Verhaegen, *Stanleyville 1959,* 109.

69 "We will walk with": Ibid., 122, 125.

70 What they didn't: Lumumba, *Lumumba Speaks,* 147.

70 "Lumumba has declared": Leroy, "Journal de la Province Orientale," 310.

70 The next morning: CRISP, *Congo 1959,* 230; Merriam, *Congo,* 153–54, 196; UPI, "24 Reported Dead as Police Clash with Rioting Natives," *Bend Bulletin,* Oct. 31, 1959.

70 As before, the dead: Young, *Politics in the Congo,* 290.

70 "lessons in revolutionary technique": Leroy, "Journal de la Province Orientale," 311–12.

70 He evaded arrest: Ibid., 314.

70 Lumumba was so hated: Merriam, *Congo,* 197.

71 "If I send you": Omasombo and Verhaegen, *Acteur,* 291.

71 "I have committed": Lumumba, *Lumumba Speaks,* 146.

71 He spent a month: De Vos, *Vie et mort,* 157; Kashamura, *De Lumumba,* 16.

71 When he stepped: AP, "Independence Cries Dog Steps of Belgian King," *Victoria Advocate,* Jan. 4, 1960; Merriam, *Congo,* 199–200; Lumumba, *Lumumba Speaks,* 145.

71 Only after it was: Leroy, "Journal de la Province Orientale," 315–16.

71 His stopover in Stanleyville: UN, "Itinerary of Secretary-General's Visit to Countries and Territories in Africa," press release, Dec. 5, 1959, box 77, DHC; Cordier and Foote, *Public Papers,* 4:508. Hammarskjöld visited Dakar, Monrovia, Conakry, Accra, Lomé, Lagos, Yaoundé, Tiko, Kaduna, Brazzaville, Leopoldville, Stanleyville, Usumbura, Dar es Salaam, Zanzibar, Mombasa, Nairobi, Entebbe, Mogadishu, Addis Ababa, Khartoum, Cairo, Tunis, Rabat, and Tangier.

71 "Year of Africa": Cordier and Foote, *Public Papers,* 4:514.

71 Yet on New Year's Day: Most estimates of when the Congo would become independent put the wait at a few years. See "The World: Cameroon and Congo," *NYT,* Jan. 3, 1960; Milton Bracker, "A Gazetteer of Emerging Africa: March to Independence Is Swift," *NYT,* Jan. 4, 1960; and Scott, *Tumbled House,* 1.

72 The Belgians had discouraged: Details on Hammarskjöld's trip to Africa come from Tomlinson to State, Jan. 14, 1960 (216), file 312, UNOC July–Aug. Classified, Security-Segregated Records, U.S. Embassy Leopoldville, RG 84, NACP; Rolf Edin, "Serving Hammarskjöld," in Hanley and Melber, *Dag Hammarskjöld Remembered,* 89–90.

72 Those who worked: Urquhart, *Hammarskjold,* 35.

72 The staffers accompanying: Wachtmeister to Lind, Jan. 16, 1960, box 77, DHC.

72 "The image I take back": Cordier and Foote, *Public Papers,* 4:516, 519.

73 After a short: Lumumba, *Lumumba Speaks,* 150.

73 "like a chimpanzee": Kashamura, *De Lumumba*, 16–17.

73 "Dirty monkey!": De Vos, *Vie et mort*, 163.

73 "I accept this expression": Young, *Politics in the Congo*, 160.

8. The Rounded Table

74 He had moved: Monheim, *Mobutu*, 48, 51.

74 To get around: Alvarez, *Lumumba; ou, L'Afrique frustrée*, 63.

74 When Lumumba visited: Kanza, *Rise and Fall*, 112–13.

74 After Lumumba was arrested: Lumumba, *Lumumba Speaks*, 146.

74 As scores of Congolese: Belga Vox, "Arrivée à Bruxelles leaders congolais pour la Table Ronde," YouTube, 0:31, Sept. 29, 2019, www.youtube.com.

75 "Are you a student": Kamitatu, *La grande mystification*, 33, 37. See also Kamitatu's comments in Woodrow Wilson International Center OH, 42–43.

75 According to the head: Kelly, *America's Tyrant*, 10–11. See also Van Bilsen, *Congo, 1945–1965*, 186; as well as Mahoney, *JFK*, 46, esp. 259n68: a CIA source told Mahoney that the Brussels CIA station was told of Mobutu's relationship in early 1960.

75 There was also the curious: Monheim, *Mobutu*, 47; Memorandum of conversation with M. C. C. De Backer and Robert McKinnon, Feb. 20, 1960, file 755A.00, CDF, 1960–63, RG 59, NACP.

76 Lumumba claimed he knew: Young and Turner, *Rise and Decline*, 438n20.

76 By one estimate: Woodrow Wilson International Center OH, 43.

76 On the morning of January 20: Legum, *Congo Disaster*, 74; Dumont, *La Table ronde belgo-congolaise*, 23. For a list of participants, see ibid., 218.

76 "the Party of Paid Negroes": Lemarchand, *Political Awakening*, 263.

76 "From the bottom": Legum, *Congo Disaster*, 73.

77 Lumumba's allies naturally: Hoskyns, *Congo Since Independence*, 38; Kamitatu, *La grande mystification*, 34; CRISP, *Congo 1960*, 1:29.

77 The room broke out: Dumont, *La Table ronde belgo-congolaise*, 39–40.

77 At 8:00 the next: Memorandum of conversation with A. A. J. Van Bilsen and Stanley Cleveland, Feb. 4, 1960 (870), file 755A.00, CDF, 1960–63, RG 59, NACP.

77 "LONG LIVE LUMUMBA!": Alvarez, *Lumumba; ou, L'Afrique frustrée*, 63–65.

77 Lumumba posed in front: *Guardian*, Jan. 27, 1960, 11. Lumumba would later claim that he would have "preferred to hide" the wounds. See Lumumba, *Lumumba Speaks*, 338.

77 Lumumba's new home: Legum, *Congo Disaster*, 76; De Vos, *Vie et mort*, 169.

77 He enlisted Mobutu: Omasombo and Verhaegen, *Acteur*, 341.

78 Glancing up from: "Bedlam in Brussels," *Time*, Feb. 22, 1960, 32.

78 "There," she said: Legum, *Congo Disaster*, 75–76.

78 "In less than": Mobutu and Remilleux, *Dignité pour l'Afrique*, 44.

78 Lumumba's opening shot: The date had been suggested earlier by the common front.

78 "Not a centime": François Ryckmans, "Congo 1960–2020, épisode 3: Le 20 février 1960, la fin de la table ronde—le pari congolais des Belges, pari perdu," RTBF, Feb. 20, 2020.

78 "We are all feeling": Hoskyns, *Congo Since Independence*, 40.

78 Suspecting that these: Stewart, *Rumba on the River*, 84.

78 The band debuted: "Indépendance Cha Cha," Joseph "Grand Kallé" Kabasele, Fonior, 1960. The lyrics can be found in Tshonga Onyumbe. "Kalle Jeef ou Joseph Kabasele Tshamala, Biographie et Oeuvre d'un Chanteur Congolais," *Annales Aequatoria* 20 (1999): 344–45.

79 The unity crumbled: Dumont, *La Table ronde belgo-congolaise*, 58, 109, 127; Young, *Politics in the Congo*, 325; "Rich, Free—but Ready?," *Newsweek*, Feb. 8, 1960, 48.

79 "If federalism were": Dumont, *La Table ronde belgo-congolaise*, 66.

80 He was not a self-made: Merriam, *Congo*, 136; "Enigmatic Congolese Moise Kapenda Tshombe," *NYT*, June 27, 1964.

80 The stakes were massive: Gunther, *Inside Africa*, 661.

80 Tshombe vehemently disagreed: The adviser was Jean Humble of Ucol. See Othen, *Katanga, 1960–1963*, 47; Lemarchand, *Political Awakening*, 89.

80 Cries and slaps: Dumont, *La Table ronde belgo-congolaise*, 102; Freeman to Herter, Feb. 13, 1960 (9588), file 755A.00 CDF, 1960–63, RG 59, NACP.

80 "Independence will not": Dumont, *La Table ronde belgo-congolaise*, 271.

81 Right before the roundtable: Cleveland to Burden, Jan. 18, 1960 (748), file 755A.00, CDF, 1960–63, RG 59, NACP.

81 "the thesis that words": Memorandum of conversation with William Ugeux and Stanley Cleveland, Jan. 14, 1960 (748), file 755A.00, CDF, 1960–63, RG 59, NACP.

81 It envisioned a: Memorandum of conversation with Van den Bosch, March 22, 1960, file 755A.001, CDF, 1960–63, RG 59, NACP; List of members of first Congolese government, Feb. 2, 1960 (824), file 755A.00, CDF, 1960–63, RG 59, NACP.

82 "He would presumably": Memorandum of conversation with Raymond Scheyven, Feb. 10, 1960, file 755A.00, CDF, 1960–63, RG 59, NACP.

82 "Belgium does not know": Dumont, *La Table ronde belgo-congolaise*, 109.

82 "racial segregation": Ibid., 152–53.

82 But without debate: Young, *Politics in the Congo*, 177–78.

82 "On July 1": *La Table ronde belgo-congolaise*, 136.

83 With or without Baudouin: Lemarchand, *Political Awakening*, 215.

83 "a mad mélange": "Bedlam in Brussels," *Time*, Feb. 22, 1960, 32.

83 "We are now going": Lumumba, *Lumumba Speaks*, 187.

83 Plainclothes policemen stalked: Legum, *Congo Disaster*, 77.

83 For both the Americans: Westad, *Global Cold War*, 4–6.

84 On February 19: Details on and quotations from the meeting come from notes of Feb. 19, 1960, conversation between Savinov and Terfve, Feb. 26, 1960, in Namikas and Mazov, "CWIHP Conference Reader." Information on Terfve

comes from Brassinne, *Les conseillers à la Table ronde belgo-congolaise*; De Vos, *La décolonisation*, 64.

84 "certain delegates to": Lumumba, *Lumumba Speaks*, 175. Anicet Kashamura, a left-leaning Congolese delegate who had gone to Prague, downplayed the trip upon his return to Brussels, saying, "I was only there for a few hours, and it was so cold that I never left my room." See Artigue, *Qui sont les leaders*, 140.

84 Other Congolese delegates: Namikas, *Battleground Africa*, 49.

84 Just three days before: Omasombo and Verhaegen, *Acteur*, 152; Memo of Feb. 16, 1960, conversation between Savinov and Nguvulu, Feb. 26, 1960, in Namikas and Mazov, "CWIHP Conference Reader."

85 "made it very clear": *FRUS, 1958–1960*, vol. 14, doc. 97.

85 Jean Van Lierde: *EP*, 684.

85 "shifty" eyes: Freund to Herter, June 15, 1960, file 755.5-MSP, CDF, 1960–63, RG 59, NACP.

85 "He has again demonstrated": These quotations come from Burden to Herter, Jan. 28, 1960 (822), file 755A.00, CDF, 1960–63, RG 59, NACP; Tomlinson to State, Feb. 3, 1960 (240), file 755A.00, CDF, 1960–63, RG 59, NACP; Burden to Herter, Feb. 10, 1960 (G87), file 755A.00, CDF, 1960–63, RG 59, NACP; Freeman to Herter, Feb. 13, 1960 (906), file 755A.00, CDF, 1960–63, RG 59, NACP; Memorandum of conversation with Gabriel Kitenge, Antoine Rubens, Robert McKinnon, and William Kinsey, Feb. 15, 1960 (894), file 755A.00, CDF, 1960–63, RG 59, NACP.

86 An employee of Inforcongo: Memorandum of conversation with M. C. C. De Backer and Robert McKinnon, Feb. 20, 1960.

86 Another contact told the CIA: Freeman to Herter, Feb. 13, 1960 (906).

86 Larry Devlin was good: Devlin, *Chief of Station*, 29; Mary Martin Devlin, interview.

86 "Well, I see him": Woodrow Wilson International Center OH, 39–40.

86 "a small bird-like Congolese": Cleveland to State, Feb. 3, 1960 (823), file 755A.001, CDF, 1960–63, RG 59, NACP.

87 "extremely vague": Memorandum of conversation with Victor Nendaka, Robert McKinnon, and Lawrence Devlin, March 25, 1960 (1081), file 755A.00, CDF, 1960–63, RG 59, NACP.

87 "One name kept": Wrong, *Footsteps of Mr. Kurtz*, 67.

9. *Uhuru!*

88 "What is independence?": Merriam, *Congo*, 179.

88 On street corners: Ibid., 202.

88 As June 30 neared: CRISP, *Congo 1960*, 1:328–30.

88 "Everyone will have": Merriam, *Congo*, 178.

89 Meanwhile, some three hundred: Young, *Politics in the Congo*, 313; "Belgium Training Congolese," *NYT*, May 4, 1960; Hoskyns, *Congo Since Independence*, 58; "Feeble Fledgling," *Newsweek*, May 2, 1960, 38.

89 Again, Congolese representatives: Among the top leaders, only Tshombe, the most financially attuned, showed up.

89 "I need you": Mobutu and Remilleux, *Dignité pour l'Afrique*, 44.

89 "I felt like the cowboy": Ibid., 45.

89 Most of the companies: Van Reybrouck, *Congo*, 261–62; Nzongola-Ntalaja, *Leopold to Kabila*, 88.

89 "We got rolled": Mobutu and Remilleux, *Dignité pour l'Afrique*, 45.

89 In some cases, the Belgians: See Nzongola-Ntalaja, *Leopold to Kabila*, 103–104.

89 "the Jews of the Congo": Young, *Politics in the Congo*, 261.

89 In May, militants: Homer Bigart, "Congo Tribal War Spreading Chaos," *NYT*, May 8, 1960; "7 Killed in Congo Attack," *NYT*, April 22, 1960; Scott, *Tumbled House*, 29.

90 "I have nothing left": Young, *Politics in the Congo*, 181.

90 the 113,000 whites: Vanthemsche, *Belgium and the Congo*, 280.

90 To many, the idea: Hoskyns, *Congo Since Independence*, 54; Scott, *Tumbled House*, 26.

90 They signed chits: Scott, *Tumbled House*, 25.

90 They circulated blacklists: Young, *Politics in the Congo*, 311; "Belgian Congo Threats Spur Europeans' Exodus," *NYT*, June 2, 1960.

90 Boards spiked with: Merriam, *Congo*, 200–201.

90 "you see pantomimes": Scott, *Tumbled House*, 10.

90 "Until now, it was African": "The Frightened Whites," *Newsweek*, June 6, 1960, 51.

91 "massacre of the Belgians": Young, *Politics in the Congo*, 311.

91 Anxious white families: Merriam, *Congo*, 202; Caroline Alexander, "Vital Powers," *New Yorker*, Jan. 22, 1989, 64; Merriam, *Congo*, 200–201.

91 Others simply left: Merriam, *Congo*, 203, 106, 259; Scott, *Tumbled House*, 25; Van Reybrouck, *Congo*, 259.

91 So much money: "Congo Has Financial Difficulties; Mining, Trade in Strong Position," *Foreign Commerce Weekly*, June 6, 1960, 12.

91 "They are afraid": Homer Bigart, "Europeans Quit Congo Province," *NYT*, May 4, 1960.

92 "hold out the hand": Hughes, "Fighting for White Rule," 598–99.

92 "efficiently and sympathetically": For the original editorial, see "Terror in the Congo," *Honolulu Star-Bulletin*, June 4, 1960; for Obama's letter, see *Honolulu Star-Bulletin*, June 8, 1960.

92 Candidates pledged that: Young, *Politics in the Congo*, 306, 312.

92 "If you must travel": Lemarchand, *Political Awakening*, 219.

93 Joseph Kasavubu toured: Spooner, *Canada*, 22; "Freedom in the Congo—the Great Gamble for Black Government," *Newsweek*, July 4, 1960, 40.

93 Lumumba was nearly alone: Lemarchand, *Political Awakening*, 220–21.

93 "Congo United": Merriam, *Congo*, 116.

93 People were drawn: Van Reybrouck, *Congo*, 245.

93 "Lumumba, slender, with": Homer Bigart, "'In-de-pen-DANCE' Comes to the Congo," *NYT,* June 26, 1960.

93 When he passed: Homer Bigart, "Lumumba Rising as a Congo Ruler," *NYT,* May 18, 1960.

93 "Our country is beautiful": Kashamura, *De Lumumba,* 31.

93 Touring the dirt: Homer Bigart, "Congo Electing First Government to Take Over in Independence," *NYT,* May 16, 1960.

94 During his imprisonment: Young, *Politics in the Congo,* 300–301.

94 Almost every decision: Lemarchand, *Political Awakening,* 259–60.

94 In addition to holding: CRISP, *Congo 1960,* 1:74.

94 A typical twenty-four: Scott, *Tumbled House,* 21–22.

94 To spread his message: Memorandum of conversation with Victor Nendaka, Robert McKinnon, and Lawrence Devlin, March 25, 1960 (1081), file 755A.00, CDF, 1960–63, RG 59, NACP; Soviet Embassy in Belgium, memo of conversation among Ustinov, Uranov, Philippe Kanza, and Thomas Kanza, May 12, 1960, in Namikas and Mazov, "CWIHP Conference Reader"; Moko Atilaoto, interview.

94 Still, all this campaigning: Namikas, *Battleground Africa,* 58.

94 The MNC funded itself: Hoskyns, *Congo Since Independence,* 68; Young, *Politics in the Congo,* 434; Merriam, *Congo,* 188.

94 But at 60 francs: Bartlett, *Communist Penetration and Subversion,* 26. The cost of eggs comes from Department of State, Leopoldville post report, May 23, 1955, courtesy of Helen Solitario.

95 One Belgian journalist: Houart, *La pénétration communiste,* 11–12. See also Bartlett, *Communist Penetration and Subversion,* 27.

95 Albert Kalonji, a onetime: Homer Bigart, "Coalition Urged in Belgian Congo," *NYT,* May 29, 1960.

95 *Moscou nous conseille:* Lemarchand, *Political Awakening,* 220.

95 Moise Tshombe's party: Mimeographed tract attributed to the MNC-Lumumba, n.d. (99), file 755A.00, CDF, 1960–63, RG 59, NACP.

95 In Brussels, a high-ranking: Burden to Herter, April 5, 1960 (1158), file 755A.00, CDF, 1960–63, RG 59, NACP.

95 Given its interest: Namikas, *Battleground Africa,* 58.

95 "Believe me, Lumumba": Monheim, *Mobutu,* 58.

95 He explicitly rejected: Lumumba, *Lumumba Speaks,* 172.

95 His vision of national: Bigart, "Lumumba Rising as a Congo Ruler."

96 "positive neutralism": "Patrice Lumumba, the assassinated first Prime Minister of the Congo," D'Lynn Waldron, dlwaldron.com.

96 "one eye": *FRUS, 1955–1957,* vol. 18, doc. 108. See also Namikas, *Battleground Africa,* 25; Woodrow Wilson International Center OH, 34.

96 "expressed regret that": Soviet Embassy in Belgium, memo of conversation among Ustinov, Uranov, Philippe Kanza, and Thomas Kanza, May 12, 1960.

96 On a steamy: Details of this encounter come from "Lumumba as a Congo 'King,'" *Guardian,* May 18, 1960; Bigart, "Lumumba Rising as a Congo Ruler";

"Uncrowned King of Belgian Congo," *Age* (Melbourne, Australia), May 19, 1960; "The Belgian Congo: Words Stilled the Guns," *Newsweek*, May 30, 1960, 45.

97 "delighted with the Belgian": Legum, *Congo Disaster*, 88.

97 "puppet government": CRISP, *Congo 1960*, 1:82. Lumumba claimed he resigned from the interim government but that his resignation was not accepted. See Lumumba, *Lumumba Speaks*, 190.

97 Although he recognized: Hoskyns, *Congo Since Independence*, 60.

97 "We are not, just because": CRISP, *Congo 1960*, 1:350.

98 "The time to push": Ibid.

98 "Napoleonic-style": Memorandum of conversation with Janssens and Cleveland, April 14, 1960 (1157), file 755A.03, CDF, 1960–63, RG 59, NACP.

98 "Let me do it": Janssens, *J'étais le général Janssens*, 179.

10. The King's Sword

99 "The climate in Leopoldville": Department of State, Leopoldville post report, May 23, 1955, courtesy of Helen Solitario.

99 "houseboys are clumsy": Provencher to Heavey, March 11, 1960, box 1, folder 8, CTP.

99 Clean, sunny, and spacious: Palmer to parents, June 12, 1960, series 6, box 1, folder 4, APP.

99 "like a Hollywood conception": Palmer to parents, July 5, 1960, series 2, box 2, folder 16, APP.

99 Nearly everything the U.S. government: Carlucci OH, 8.

100 But the new material: Lambelet, interview.

100 "fertile ground open": *FRUS, 1958–1960*, vol. 14, doc. 99.

100 In the spring: Harry Gilroy, "Congolese Found Friendly to U.S.," *NYT*, April 5, 1960; Woodrow Wilson International Center OH, 14–15.

100 "The general economic": *FRUS, 1958–1960*, vol. 14, doc. 98.

100 The State Department's answer: "Clare Timberlake; Longtime U.S. Envoy," *NYT*, Feb. 26, 1982.

101 "striped-pants boys": Harry S. Truman, "The Truman Memoirs," *Life*, Sept. 26, 1955, 110.

101 Timberlake arranged for: Timberlake to Wellborn, March 31, 1960, box 1, folder 9, CTP; Timberlake to Tomlinson, June 11, 1960, box 1, folder 8, CTP.

101 He also spent: "Briefing Schedule for Mr. Clare Timberlake," April 1960, box 3, folder 3, CTP.

101 "left on the outside": *FRUS, 1964–1968*, vol. 23, doc. 2.

101 "money and influence": Ibid., doc. 3.

101 In a joint message: Ibid., doc. 4.

102 "in the realm of intelligence": "Covert Military Operations in the Congo, 1964–1967."

102 "In most cases": *FRUS, 1964–1968*, vol. 23, doc. 5.

102　At a meeting of: Ibid., doc. 101.

102　A footdragger on: Weissman, *American Foreign Policy*, 46.

102　When Dulles pointed out: *FRUS, 1958–1960*, vol. 14, doc. 101.

102　In fact, the Congo's literacy rate: Gailey, *History of Africa*, 109; Moraes, *Importance of Being Black*, 179.

102　"many Africans still belonged": *FRUS, 1958–1960*, vol. 14, doc. 21.

103　When ground broke: "Growth in United Nations membership," United Nations, www.un.org. The four African countries were Egypt, Ethiopia, Liberia, and South Africa.

103　The architects of: Raustiala, *Absolutely Indispensable Man*, 153.

103　A plan to decorate: "U.N. Shelves Plan to Adorn Its Hall," *NYT*, Jan. 11, 1955; "Assembly Has 'Dress Rehearsal' While 'Stars' Are Still En Route," *NYT*, Sept. 18, 1960.

103　"I have a feeling": Transcript of questions and answers following the secretary-general's address to the Economic Club of New York, March 8, 1960, S-0928-0001-08, UNA.

103　Hammarskjöld estimated that: Kathleen Teltsch, "U.N. Chief Seeks Rise in Africa Aid," *NYT*, June 7, 1960.

103　A barber's son: Details on Bunche's life come from Urquhart, *Ralph Bunche*, 25, 29, 41, 65.

104　"Dr. Bunche has": Affidavit to Support Claim for Occupational Deferment, June 12, 1942, OSS file on Ralph Bunche, entry 224, OSS Personnel Files, box 92, RG 226, NACP.

104　After Hammarskjöld became: Liu OH, 1–2; Urquhart, *Ralph Bunche*, 257.

104　Afterwards, however, Bunche: Bunche, *Ralph J. Bunche*, 192.

104　"I foresee great trouble": Lipsey, *Hammarskjöld*, 391.

104　Voting, restricted to: CRISP, *Congo 1960*, 1:264; Bigart, "Congo Electing First Government to Take Over in Independence."

104　There were hitches: "Congo Area Gets Emergency Rule," *NYT*, May 26, 1960; CRISP, *Congo 1960*, 1:260; Hoskyns, *Congo Since Independence*, 68; "Frauds Charged as Vote Ends for Belgian Congo Legislature," *NYT*, May 23, 1960; Merriam, *Congo*, 185–86.

105　In Orientale province: For the Chamber of Representatives election results, see CRISP, *Congo 1960*, 1:262–63.

105　Meanwhile, in the Senate: Ibid., 1:266.

105　Along the way: On ethnicity and the Belgian role in it, see Young, *Politics in the Congo*, 238, 259, 266. Of course, many Congolese identified both as members of a particular ethnic group and as Congolese.

105　"largely an ethnic census": Ibid., 271.

106　He also tried: Hoskyns, *Congo Since Independence*, 72.

106　The U.S. consulate: Ganshof van der Meersch, *Fin de la souveraineté Belge au Congo*, 250.

106　After several weeks: Harry Gilroy, "Coalition Cabinet Formed in Congo," *NYT*, June 24, 1960.

106 "I know Joseph Kasavubu": Kanza, *Rise and Fall*, 127–29.

107 Despite the many weeks: Hoskyns, *Congo Since Independence*, 79.

107 It had twenty-three: Young, *Politics in the Congo*, 410.

107 The government included: See CRISP, *Congo 1960*, 1:308–309; Lemarchand, *Political Awakening*, 231.

107 They had worked: Young, *Politics in the Congo*, 198.

107 Many had paid: UN Security Council, 877th Meeting, S/PV.877 (July 20/21, 1960), 25.

108 Mobutu, who thought: Monheim, *Mobutu*, 62–63.

108 Although his party: CRISP, *Congo 1960*, 1:262–63, 266; Hoskyns, *Congo Since Independence*, 71–72.

108 The Belgians had banned: Young, *Politics in the Congo*, 198–99.

108 There were fewer than twenty: George, *Educational Developments*, 62. Pedro Monaville has put the number closer to thirty-five.

108 Among the rest: Lemarchand, *Political Awakening*, 133.

108 In part to appease: See Ken Opalo, *Legislative Development in Africa: Politics and Postcolonial Legacies* (Cambridge: Cambridge University Press, 2019), 37.

108 Congo's new parliament included: The lawyer's name was Victor Promontorio. Samuel Malonga, "Victor Promontorio, First Congolese University Graduate in Belgium," *Mbokamosika* (blog), Feb. 7, 2016, www.mbokamosika .com.

108 It also counted: Lemarchand, *Political Awakening*, 227–28.

109 In less than a week: Young, *Politics in the Congo*, 441; Hoskyns, *Congo Since Independence*, 12.

109 They haggled over: Kanza, *Rise and Fall*, 120.

109 Given the subdividing: Hoskyns, *Congo Since Independence*, 59, 80–81.

109 In some offices: Kashamura, *De Lumumba*, 66; see also Lumumba, *Lumumba Speaks*, 256.

109 This was a liquidation: The words come from Ganshof van der Meersch, who described the time before independence as "a period of transition which seemed to most like a period of liquidation." Hoskyns, *Congo Since Independence*, 55.

109 "I have an uneasy feeling": "Belgian Congo: A Blight at Birth," *Time*, June 27, 1960, 26.

109 On the morning: Palmer to parents, July 5, 1960.

109 The son of a distinguished Chinese painter: Paul Lewis, "F. T. Liu, 82; U.N. Official in Peace Roles," *NYT*, Feb. 23, 2001; Scott McConnell, "A UN Hero," *New York Press*, March 2001.

109 All they had been told: F. T. Liu to Joan Liu, June 26, 1960, Liu Letters; Ralph J. Bunche Diary, June 25, 1960, box 15, folder 2, Congo 1960, BUC.

110 Bunche and Liu were: Ralph J. Bunche to Ruth Bunche, June 27, 1960, box 480, folder 10, RJBP.

110 One of the biggest: Liu OH, 3–4.

110 "everybody was smiling": F. T. Liu to Joan Liu, June 26, 1960, Liu Letters.

110 "Everyone agrees that Lumumba": Bunche to Hammarskjöld, June 27, 1960, box 15, folder 2, Congo (1960), BUC.

110 He could not raise: CRISP, *Congo 1960,* 1:328–30.

111 "Thus the last act": Ibid., 330.

111 He stepped out: Reuters, "Belgian King Hears Attack on His Nation," *Spokesman-Review* (Spokane), July 1, 1960; Olivier Matthys, "King Philippe of Belgium and Queen Mathilde of Belgium Attend the Summer Exhibitions at the Royal Palace in Brussels," July 18, 2019.

111 They had in fact competed: Kanza, *Rise and Fall,* 150.

111 Mobutu bowed generously: British Pathé, "King Baudouin Declares Congo Independent (1960)," YouTube, 2:23, April 13, 2014, www.youtube.com.

111 The Western press: The quotations come from "Marred," *Guardian,* July 1, 1960; AP, "African Grabs King's Sword," *Philadelphia Inquirer,* June 30, 1960; UPI, "Congo Gains Its Freedom from Belgium," *Delphos (Ohio) Courant,* July 1, 1960. Other details come from Van Reybrouck, *Congo,* 270. See also Dries Engel et Bart Van Peel, "Ambroise Boimbo: le voleur de l'épée du Roi," Dailymotion, www.dailymotion.com.

112 At dinner that evening: "Lumumba Assails Colonialism as Congo Is Freed," *NYT,* July 1, 1960; Gerard and Kuklick, *Death in the Congo,* 25.

112 Lumumba inquired with: Bunche Diary, June 30, 1960, 11, box 15, folder 2, Congo 1960, BUC; see also Bunche to Hammarskjöld, July 4, 1960, box 132, DHC.

112 The work had just begun: Kanza, *Rise and Fall,* 148.

11. The Newest Country

115 On June 30: Janssens, *J'étais le general Janssens,* 207.

115 The Belgian government: Tomlinson to State, May 10, 1960, Belgian Congo Independence Ceremonies, Files of Visits by Heads of Government, Dignitaries, and Delegations, 1928–77, Office of Secretary/Office of the Chief of Protocol, box 8, RG 59, NACP. For education figures (19 million francs per year), see U.S. Army, *U.S. Army Area Handbook for the Republic of the Congo (Leopoldville),* 217.

115 Lumumba spent the morning: Mboka, "Kinshasa 2019—Where Does a New President Lay His Head?," *Kinshasa Then and Now* (blog), Jan. 28, 2019.

115 The Congo's new: Kanza, *Rise and Fall,* 152.

115 "Sit down and read": Ibid., 153.

116 But Lumumba had gotten: CRISP, *Congo 1960,* 1:328.

116 "I quite understand": Kanza, *Rise and Fall,* 153.

116 But it was time to go: Zeilig, *Lumumba,* 95.

117 Its cupola, clad: Lagae, "Troublesome Construction," 19.

117 "Looked at closely": AP, "African Grabs King's Sword," *Philadelphia Inquirer,* June 30, 1960.

117 The Belgians had sent: Tomlinson to State, May 10, 1960.

117 The Ethiopian empire: Van Reybrouck, *Congo,* 270; Scott, *Tumbled House,* 43–44; "Close Africa Ties a Key Bonn Policy," *NYT,* July 4, 1960; Lawrence Fellows, "Israeli Envoy to Protest," *NYT,* April 16, 1960.

117 Portuguese Angola, South Africa: Palmer to Herter, June 30, 1960, Belgian Congo Independence Ceremonies, Files of Visits by Heads of Government, Dignitaries, and Delegations, 1928–77, Office of Secretary/Office of the Chief of Protocol, RG 59, NACP.

117 "dealt another telling blow": AP, "Belgian King Frees Congo, Warns Against Foreign Greed," *St. Louis Post-Dispatch,* June 30, 1960, 2. Some observers considered the delegation "low-level." See Stevens, *Soviet Union,* 12.

118 No one from Communist China: "Peiping Assails U.S.," *NYT,* July 4, 1960; AP, "Belgian King Gives Congo to Africans, Gets Harsh Reply," *Des Moines Tribune,* June 30, 1960.

118 "There will be in the coming": Hammarskjöld to Lumumba, June 30, 1960, box 15, folder 2, Congo (1960), BUC.

118 The United States' five-man delegation: Earlier in the year, a Belgian official, playing the unlikely role of adviser on race relations, offered specific advice concerning which U.S. diplomats should attend: find one as dark as possible, since the two African Americans sent to the independence ceremonies in Cameroon had been too light-skinned to attract much notice. The State Department, after rejecting the singer Marian Anderson, settled on John Morrow, the U.S. ambassador to Guinea. See Tomlinson to Herter, March 19, 1960, Belgian Congo Independence Ceremonies, Files of Visits by Heads of Government, Dignitaries, and Delegations, 1928–77, Office of Secretary/ Office of the Chief of Protocol, RG 59, NACP.

118 "who himself had some": Fitzhugh Green, "Diffident Program of US Wins Congolese Plaudits," *Daily Princetonian,* Jan. 4, 1961.

118 "primitive people": Weissman, *American Foreign Policy,* 47. See also Murphy, *Diplomat Among Warriors,* 377.

118 Timberlake viewed them: Timberlake to Herter, Oct. 11, 1960 (949), file 312, UNOC Sept.–Oct. 1960 Classified, Security-Segregated Records, U.S. Embassy Leopoldville, RG 84, NACP.

118 Paley, for his part: Jeremy Gerard, "William S. Paley, Builder of CBS, Dies at 89," *NYT,* Oct. 27, 1990.

118 Originally, Ike was: Herter to Leopoldville, June 28, 1960, Belgian Congo Independence Ceremonies, Files of Visits by Heads of Government, Dignitaries, and Delegations, 1928–77, Office of Secretary/Office of the Chief of Protocol, RG 59, NACP; Parsons to Herter, June 25, 1960, Belgian Congo Independence Ceremonies, Files of Visits by Heads of Government, Dignitaries, and Delegations, 1928–77, Office of Secretary/Office of the Chief of Protocol, RG 59, NACP.

118 "The independence of the Congo": CRISP, *Congo 1960,* 1:318–320.

119 "like a jack-in-the-box": Janssens, *J'étais le général Janssens,* 208–209.

119 "Men and women of": *Congo 1960,* 1:323–25. Lumumba never said, as has been often repeated, "We are no longer your monkeys."

121 Cries of "Uhuru!": Recollections about the audience's reaction come from Janssens, *J'étais le general Janssens;* Gizenga, *Ma vie et mes luttes;* Kashamura, *De Lumumba;* 73–83; Scott, *Tumbled House;* Murphy, *Diplomat Among Warriors.*

121 Farther out, in: Merriam, *Congo,* 174–75; Van Reybrouck, *Congo,* 271.

121 Those who missed: Bunche Diary, June 30, 1960, box 15, folder 2, Congo 1960, BUC.

121 "shocked and pale": "Congo: Freedom at Last," *Time,* July 11, 1960; Murphy, *Diplomat Among Warriors,* 372.

122 Outside, a delirious: Reuters, "Belgian King Hears Attack on His Nation."

122 Mobutu took it upon: Monheim, *Mobutu,* 65; Close, *Beyond the Storm,* 57.

122 "Lumumba might have": AP, "New Congo Premier Lashes Belgians," *Quad-City Times* (Davenport, Iowa), July 1, 1960.

122 After much wrangling: Van Reybrouck, *Congo,* 274.

122 "The entire government": Scott, *Tumbled House,* 46. See photo 10 in Vanderstraeten, *De la Force publique,* 292.

122 "seemed to think he was not": CRISP, *Congo 1960,* 1:326.

123 "We certainly knew that": Ibid., 327.

123 "once again showed": Kalb, *Congo Cables,* 4.

123 "Lumumba seems to have": Bunche Diary, June 30, 1960, box 15, folder 2, Congo 1960, BUC.

123 With no national anthem: "Uhuru Comes to the Congo," *Africa Today,* Sept. 1960, 6–7.

123 "This is not going": Lukens OH, 9.

123 King Baudouin headed: F. T. Liu to Joan Liu, July 2, 1960, Liu Letters; "Marred," *Guardian,* July 1, 1960.

123 In honor of: Reuters, "Belgian King Hears Attack on His Nation"; Freund to Herter, June 16, 1960 (1486); Scott, *Tumbled House,* 47, 53; Young, *Politics in the Congo,* 311–12; Zeilig, *Lumumba,* 100–101.

124 Transport workers, denied: Harry Gilroy, "Congolese Police Kill 10 in Clash," *NYT,* July 5, 1960.

124 In some of the outlying: UPI, "Two Tribes Battle in Capital of Congo," *NYT,* July 3, 1960.

124 "There will be no Belgian": "Uhuru Comes to the Congo."

124 He swung through: Kashamura, *De Lumumba,* 86.

124 Mobutu came along: Monheim, *Mobutu,* 66–67.

124 As the prime minister settled: Kanza, *Rise and Fall,* 184.

124 But in the early days: F. T. Liu to Joan Liu, July 8, 1960, Liu Letters.

124 Questions about official motorcades: Kanza, *Rise and Fall,* 119; Urquhart, *Ralph Bunche,* 307.

124 "Kasavubu and Lumumba studiously": Bunche to Hammarskjöld, July 4, 1960, box 132, DHC.

125 The government in Leopoldville: Kanza, *Rise and Fall*, 184–85.

125 "useful for the": *FRUS, 1958–1960*, vol. 14, doc. 107; Murphy, *Diplomat Among Warriors*, 373.

125 "Lumumba's quick switch": *FRUS, 1958–1960*, vol. 14, doc. 107.

125 "Independence has come": Palmer to parents, July 5, 1960, series 2, box 2, folder 16, APP.

126 Three hundred guests: Ralph J. Bunche to Ruth Bunche, July 4, 1960, box 480, folder 10, RJBP; Nelson, *Congo Crisis*, 68.

126 Embassy officers and: Steigman, interview; Lambelet, interview.

126 "The Force Publique?": Barber, "Return to the Congo," 92.

12. A Nonexistent Army

127 Although they now raised: Janssens, *J'étais le général Janssens*, 159–60.

127 "independence was eluding": CRISP, *Congo 1960*, 1:388.

127 "The soldier has a": Janssens, *J'étais le général Janssens*, 213.

127 "before independence": Hoskyns, *Congo Since Independence*, 88.

128 They roughed up: Vanderstraeten, *De la Force publique*, 145.

128 "the miracle of the Congo": Young, *Politics in the Congo*, 438.

128 "I knew something": Vanderstraeten, *De la Force publique*, 148.

128 "ruthless repression of": Janssens, *J'étais le général Janssens*, 215.

128 "In the Force Publique": Ibid., 23.

128 "No way are we punishing": Vanderstraeten, *De la Force publique*, 148.

128 Instead, the prime minister: Janssens, *J'étais le general Janssens*, 215.

128 One group of soldiers cornered: CRISP, *Congo 1960*, 1:386–87, 455.

128 Another forced three civilians: Vanderstraeten, *De la Force publique*, 194.

128 "I have a piece": Ibid., 158.

128 "All privates and noncommissioned": Lumumba, *Lumumba Speaks*, 229.

129 "the most sweeping army promotion in history": "Congo: The Monstrous Hangover," *Time*, July 18, 1960, 17.

129 when President Eisenhower heard: *FRUS, 1958–1960*, vol. 14, doc. 156.

129 "remove all traces": Lumumba, *Lumumba Speaks*, 230.

129 "crazy and demagogic": Janssens, *J'étais le général Janssens*, 215.

129 Until that point: Memorandum of conversation with Hammarskjöld and Kanza, July 20, 1960, box 16, folder 3, Congo (1960), BUC; Monheim, *Mobutu*, 79–80.

129 "Lies!" they yelled: Janssens, *J'étais le general Janssens*, 216.

129 Seeking to extract: Vanderstraeten, *De la Force publique*, 160.

129 Others hurled stones: CRISP, *Congo 1960*, 1:381; "Savagery in the Congo," *Newsweek*, July 18, 1960, 17.

129 After seeing the broken: Vanderstraeten, *De la Force publique*, 165. Kasavubu did, however, join Lumumba that night in going to Thysville.

129 They extracted from him: CRISP, *Congo 1960*, 1:375; Vanderstraeten, *De la Force publique*, 160.

129 While huddling in: Vanderstraeten, *De la Force publique,* 162.

130 He decided to dismiss: Ibid., 165.

130 After briefly considering: Janssens, *J'étais le général Janssens,* 227.

130 "Your Majesty": "Congo: Jungle Shipwreck," *Time,* July 25, 1960, 23.

130 When a tank squadron: CRISP, *Congo 1960,* 1:390, 386–87, 376.

131 "There's only one": Monheim, *Mobutu,* 83.

131 "Let's talk calmly": Ibid., 84.

131 Lumumba arrived later: Vanderstraeten, *De la Force publique,* 173.

131 The bedraggled refugees: Ibid., 195.

131 Soldiers were alleged: "Congo: The Monstrous Hangover."

132 On the 6th of July: "A Preliminary Report on the Atrocities Committed by the Congolese Army Against the White Population of the Republic of the Congo Before the Intervention of the Belgian Forces," Belgian Government Information Center, 1960, 5–6.

132 They were also less widespread: Hoskyns, "Violence in the Congo," 48.

132 One estimate put: Vanderstraeten, *De la Force publique,* 449; Munger, *African Field Report,* 187–201.

132 For months, whites: "Frightened Whites."

132 And so in the white: CRISP, *Congo 1960,* 1:400–401.

132 "The word rape": Kitchen, *Footnotes to the Congo Story,* 21–22.

132 Families fled their houses: Clare Timberlake book proposal, 7, box 1, folder 10, CTP.

133 Others went to the: "Savagery in the Congo," 50; CRISP, *Congo 1960,* 1:403.

133 Soldiers mounted their: Vanderstraeten, *De la Force publique,* 196–97, 529n42; "Savagery in the Congo," 49; Scott, *Tumbled House,* 54. They did in fact find a Russian plane, but it was the one that had flown the Soviet delegation to the independence ceremonies, now sitting peacefully on the tarmac, waiting to take delegates on a tour of the country.

133 At midnight, the Belgian: The ambassador's account, including dialogue, comes from CRISP, *Congo 1960,* 1:393–99.

134 Mobutu, who had: On Mobutu becoming a go-to person for sorting out matters, see Urquhart, *Ralph Bunche,* 318.

134 By the morning: Burden to Herter, July 9, 1960 (58), box 16, Congo, Cabinet Series, Papers as President of the United States, 1953–61 (Ann Whitman File), DDEL.

134 "Leopoldville has become": CRISP, *Congo 1960,* 1:404.

134 The city's white: Carlucci OH, 13; Lambelet, interview; Scott, *Tumbled House,* 50.

134 Against this eerie: Ralph J. Bunche, "Tight Spots and Close Calls," box 16, folder 4, BUC; "Congo: The Monstrous Hangover"; F. T. Liu to Joan Liu, July 8, 1960, Liu Letters; Lisagor and Higgins, *Overtime in Heaven,* 245.

134 Their helmets were: "Note Regarding Events at Lovanium During Force Publique Mutiny in July 1960," box 9, folder 16, HWP; Devlin, *Chief of Station,* 15.

134 Fearing a repeat: Scott, *Tumbled House,* 65.

134 Then he dashed inside: Lukens, interview.

134 "All recognized authority": Houghton to Herter, July 8, 1960, box 16, Congo, Cabinet Series, Papers as President of the United States, 1953–61 (Whitman File), DDEL.

134 Inside the embassy: *FRUS, 1958–1960*, vol. 14, doc. 108; Palmer to parents, July 8, 1960, series 2, box 2, folder 16, APP; Devlin, *Chief of Station*, 15.

135 Some were collected: Steigman, interview.

135 But even so: Lambelet, interview.

135 "not eminently suited": Lisagor and Higgins, *Overtime in Heaven*, 248, 247.

135 "You cannot come": Eleanor Lansing Dulles, "The Congo—Necessary Steps, 1960," box 52, Drafts: Belgian Congo, Eleanor Lansing Dulles Papers, 1880–1973, DDEL; Lisagor and Higgins, *Overtime in Heaven*, 249–51. Eleanor Lansing Dulles claimed it was Robinson McIlvaine who opened the door.

135 "Over there!": Ralph J. Bunche to Ruth Bunche, July 9, 1960, box 480, RJBP. Other details on Bunche's scare come from Bunche Diary, box 15, folder 2, Congo 1960, BUC; Allan Morrison, "Ralph Bunche Tells About His Toughest Assignment," *Ebony*, Nov. 1960; Ralph J. Bunche to Ralph J. Bunche Jr., July 8, 1960, box 208, folder 3, RJBP; Bunche, "Tight Spots and Close Calls."

136 "Powder keg here": Bunche to Hammarskjöld, July 9, 1960 (25), box 155, DHC.

136 Second, Lumumba picked: CRISP, *Congo 1960*, 1:405–6; Kanza, *Rise and Fall*, 191.

136 "Go outside and try": Woodrow Wilson International Center OH, 71. According to Monheim, Mobutu was not present at the meeting and learned about his promotion hours later (Monheim, *Mobutu*, 97). Lumumba preferred that Mobutu be made commander of the ANC, but the job went to the older and more experienced Victor Lundula instead. Lumumba insisted that Mobutu be appointed chief of staff. See Vanderstraeten, *De la Force publique*, 241.

136 Lumumba valued his: Kanza, *Rise and Fall*, 192.

136 "really dirty job": Mobutu and Remilleux, *Dignité pour l'Afrique*, 50.

137 "Wouldn't it be ironic": Ralph J. Bunche to Ralph J. Bunche Jr., July 8, 1960.

137 A kitchenette downstairs: Devlin, *Chief of Station*, 18; Palmer to parents, July 18, 1960; Steigman, interview; Devlin, *Chief of Station*, 10; Lambelet, interview.

137 "a loose (and weak)": Bunche, *Selected Speeches and Writings*, 197.

138 "I came specially": Kanza, *Rise and Fall*, 196.

13. A Body Without a Head

139 On the frequencies that: Vanderstraeten, *De la Force publique*, 69, 370. For a discussion of the role of the radio in the mutiny, see ibid., 461.

139 General Janssens was: On the name change of the Force Publique, see CRISP, *Congo 1960*, 1:408.

139 In Kongolo: Vanderstraeten, *De la Force publique*, 217–23, 593.

140 "The Congo is falling": "Belgium's Forces Fight Congolese to Quell Risings," *NYT*, July 11, 1960.

140 "We're the masters now": CRISP, *Congo 1960,* 1:455. On the hotel, see "Hotel Metropole," *Grand Hotel Kinshasa* (blog), April 24, 2011, grandehotelkinshasa. blogspot.com.

140 Lumumba and Kasavubu freed: Vanderstraeten, *De la Force publique,* 330.

140 "We will help those": CRISP, *Congo 1960,* 1:457–58.

140 "Because I was one of them": Mobutu and Remilleux, *Dignité pour l'Afrique,* 51.

140 When he saw: Monheim, *Mobutu,* 100; George Clay, "Cheers for the U.N. Troops," *Observer* (London), July 17, 1960.

141 At the garrison in Ikela: The account of the trip to Ikela comes from Monheim, *Mobutu,* 99–100.

141 "slight twinges": Eyskens, *Mémoires,* 720.

141 "How far will the": De Vos, *Vie et mort,* 210–11.

141 In preparation for: Vanderstraeten, *De la Force publique,* 337–38.

142 "It would be madness": "Congo: The Monstrous Hangover"; Hoskyns, *Congo Since Independence,* 95.

142 Early in the morning: Vanderstraeten, *De la Force publique,* 345–46; CRISP, *Congo 1960,* 1:420, 422.

142 At 1:00 p.m.: Memorandum of conversation with Lumumba, July 10, 1960, file 350, Congo April–June 1960 Classified, Security-Segregated Records, U.S. Embassy, RG 84, NACP; Timberlake book proposal, 9, box 1, folder 10, CTP; *FRUS, 1958–1960,* vol. 14, doc. 112; "Congo—Necessary Steps, 1960."

143 "primitive way of life": Memorandum of conversation with Lumumba, July 10, 1960.

143 "convert modern Congo": *FRUS, 1958–1960,* vol. 14, doc. 111.

143 Just before independence: Bunche to Hammarskjöld, June 27, 1960, box 15, folder 2, Congo (1960), BUC.

144 "This should keep": *FRUS, 1958–1960,* vol. 14, doc. 111.

144 Indeed, Bunche was sending: For evidence that the embassy was reading Bunche's cables, see Cook to Herter, July 9, 1960 (34), file 755A.00, CDF, 1960–63, RG 59, NACP; and *FRUS, 1958–1960,* vol. 14, doc. 111n2. For Bunche's emergency plans, see Bunche to Hammarskjöld, July 9, 1960 (28), box 155, DHC. For Bunche's office, see Alison Palmer interview with Nancy McGlen and Meredith Reid Sarkees, 8, series 6, box 2, folder 21, APP; Henry Tanner, "Belgian Commandos Rout Congo Troops at Airport," *NYT,* July 14, 1960.

144 He found the idea: Bunche to Hammarskjöld, July 10, 1960 (34), box 155, DHC.

144 Small groups of unarmed: "United Nations Military Observer," 22; Mezerik, *United Nations Emergency Force,* 5; "Mandate," United Nations Military Observer Group in India and Pakistan, unmogip.unmissions.org; "Our History," United Nations Peacekeeping, peacekeeping.un.org.

144 To distinguish UN: Urquhart, *Life in Peace and War,* 134.

145 Kasavubu's hillside house: Mboka, "Kinshasa 2019—Where Does a New President Lay His Head?"

145 They were joined by: "Analytical Chronology of the Congo Crisis," 5.

145 "Belgium bears a grave": Lumumba, *Lumumba Speaks,* 236; CRISP, *Congo 1960,*

1:411. *Lumumba Speaks* dates this speech to July 11, but it in fact happened "Sunday evening," July 10. CRISP, *Congo 1960,* 1:410.

145 In Luluabourg, the capital: Vanderstraeten, *De la Force publique,* 271, 350, 567n168; Legum, *Congo Disaster,* 114; CRISP, *Congo 1960,* 1:441; Harry Gilroy, "Belgians' Exodus Led to Violence," *NYT,* July 21, 1960.

145 Even so, Bunche steered: Bunche to Hammarskjöld, July 10, 1960 (37), box 155, DHC.

145 After four hours: "Analytical Chronology of the Congo Crisis," 5. Hammarskjöld recalled Bunche telling him that the meeting lasted two and a half hours. Summary of diary on Congo Operation, July 19, 1960, box 141, DHC.

145 A deft UN switchboard: Summary of diary on Congo Operation, July 19, 1960, box 141, DHC; Urquhart, *Hammarskjold,* 394.

146 "Thus, they appeal": Bunche to Hammarskjöld, July 10, 1960 (36), box 155, DHC.

146 Larry Devlin was on vacation: Devlin, *Chief of Station,* 2; Wilson Center OH, 61.

146 "Daddy, don't go": Devlin, *Chief of Station,* 2.

146 The airline's entire: Shepard, *Forgive Us,* 216.

146 He spent the night: Devlin, *Chief of Station,* 3.

147 From the deck: Ibid., 4–5.

147 "From as far as one could": Greene, *In Search of a Character,* 8.

147 It looked calm: Devlin, *Chief of Station,* 5.

14. Magic Men from the Sky

148 On the morning: Details on the Matadi attack come from Vanderstraeten, *De la Force publique,* 352–63; "I Beat UN Troops to Siege City," *Daily Mail,* July 20, 1960; "The Madness of Matadi," *Daily Mail,* July 21, 1960; "La mutinerie de Thysville," *Le Soir,* July 20, 1960; CRISP, *Congo 1960,* 1:459; Young, *Politics in the Congo,* 317. The death toll would reach nineteen after a soldier succumbed to his injuries more than a week after the battle.

149 "There will be as many": "La mutinerie de Thysville."

149 As fighting was: In fact, even on July 12, Lumumba might not have known about the events in Matadi. See CRISP, *Congo 1960,* 1:448n2. Vanderstraeten, *De la Force publique,* 399, contends that the Matadi affair was not a factor in Lumumba's break with Belgium.

149 Rows of abandoned: Vanderstraeten, *De la Force publique,* 298, photos 29, 30, and 31.

149 In Katanga, some: "Savagery in the Congo," 51.

149 Of the Congo's 175: UN Secretariat, "Report No. 10 on United Nations Civilian Operations in the Congo: First Year of Operations, July 1960 to June 1961," ST/ONUC/PR.10 (1961), 12, 26. A few engineers later returned.

149 The national radio: "Congo: Jungle Shipwreck," *Time,* July 25, 1960, 24.

149 At the Ministry: Munger, *African Field Report,* 159.

149 This was white flight: Young, *Politics in the Congo*, 321.

149 "Foreigners who wish": "M. Lumumba a invité les Belges à rester...," *La Libre Belgique,* July 13, 1960.

150 Lumumba agreed, and: CRISP, *Congo 1960,* 1:410–11.

150 A few minutes before 8:00: Nicolaï, *Ici Radio Katanga,* 19; "Province Secedes from Congo, Premier Says, amid Gunfire," *Cincinnati Enquirer,* July 12, 1960.

150 "the arbitrary will": Gérard-Libois, *Katanga Secession,* 328–29.

150 Members of Conakat: Canup to Herter, June 23, 1960, file 755A.001, CDF, 1960–63, RG 59, NACP.

150 "be interpreted as": *FRUS, 1958–1960,* vol. 14, doc. 104.

150 "might very well result": Ibid., doc. 103.

151 "there is absolutely": Ibid., doc. 114.

151 Before the ongoing: Colvin, *Moise Tshombe,* 12.

151 Instead, they got: Hoskyns, *Congo Since Independence,* 144, 150; Gérard-Libois, *Katanga Secession,* 114.

152 "The secession of Katanga": "Synopsis of State and Intelligence Material Reported to the President," July 13, 1960, box 14, Intelligence Briefing Notes, Subject Series, Alphabetical Subseries, Office of the White House Staff Secretary, DDEL.

152 A minister suggested: Ganshof van der Meersch, *Fin de la souveraineté Belge au Congo,* 429. It was Justin Bomboko who suggested Israeli forces.

152 Timberlake agreed to: Kalb, *Congo Cables,* 8.

152 "We kindly ask": CRISP, *Congo 1960,* 2:542–43. In the version of the request that Timberlake passed on to the State Department, the number of troops was 2,000. See *FRUS, 1958–1960,* vol. 14, doc. 116n5.

152 "advisability of sending": Ibid., doc. 119.

152 Both agreed that: Weissman, *American Foreign Policy,* 59–60; Felix Belair Jr., "President Favors U.N. Role Rather Than Unilateral Action—Carrier Departs to Help Evacuate Americans," *NYT,* July 13, 1960.

152 "Maybe after this": *FRUS, 1958–1960,* vol. 14, doc. 117. In Newport, Eisenhower also swatted away embarrassing reports—accurate, of course—that Timberlake had endorsed sending troops to the faraway country. "This is not true," he said. "Mr. Timberlake just referred to the Department of State the request for troops which came from the Congo cabinet." See Belair, "President Favors U.N. Role Rather Than Unilateral Action."

153 Two companies of: Kalb, *Congo Cables,* 9.

153 The USS *Wasp:* "UN Help for the Congo," *Guardian,* July 13, 1960; Memorandum of telephone conversation with Hammarskjöld and Herter, July 12, 1960, box 13, CAH Telephone Calls, Herter Papers, DDEL; Kalb, *Congo Cables,* 9; Weissman, *American Foreign Policy,* 61.

153 "If I ordered you": Vanderstraeten, *De la Force publique,* 396–97.

153 In the days immediately: Ibid., 157.

153 "Since June 30, Belgium": Memorandum of conversation with Hammarskjöld and Kanza, July 20, 1960, box 16, folder 3, Congo (1960), BUC.

153 "magic men from": Munger, *African Field Reports,* 165.

154 "In the dark": "Congo: Jungle Shipwreck," 23. The incident was also relayed in Henry Tanner, "Bunche Expects Troops by Tomorrow—U.S. Missionaries Abused," *NYT,* July 15, 1960.

154 "The Congolese people": "Press Conference of N. S. Khrushchev," *Pravda,* July 13, 1960. For the Cold War context, see Herter to Gates, July 20, 1960, box 4, State Department (June–July 1960), Subject Series, Office of the White House Staff Secretary, DDEL.

154 "Do we really have": "Congo: Jungle Shipwreck," 23.

154 Over lunch, the: CRISP, *Congo 1960,* 1:448. On the lunch spot, see Inforcongo, *Congo Belge et Ruanda-Burundi,* 161.

154 "so that the truth": Lumumba, *Lumumba Speaks,* 242.

155 "It might mean": Ibid., 244.

155 They touched down: Ibid., 245; "Lubumbashi, Congo Dem. Rep.—Sunrise, Sunset, and Daylength," Time and Date, www.timeanddate.com.

155 "When the head": Lumumba, *Lumumba Speaks,* 246.

155 The first was a: Ibid., 246–47.

155 "to Lumumba personally": Vanderstraeten, *De la Force publique,* 582n69.

155 Lumumba was surprised: Lumumba, *Lumumba Speaks,* 247; Gilis, *Kasavubu au coeur,* 257.

155 Their aircraft reached: Vanderstraeten, *De la Force publique,* 582n71; Hoskyns, *Congo Since Independence,* 100.

155 "Go away": "UN Help for the Congo."

156 "We strongly stress": Urquhart, *Ralph Bunche,* 311; Lumumba, *Lumumba Speaks,* 256; Cordier and Foote, *Public Papers,* 5:18.

15. A Political Miracle

157 Did'st Thou give: These quotations come from Hammarskjöld, *Markings,* 8, 38, 120, 166.

157 "a fairy": Kelen, *Hammarskjöld,* 153.

157 Those close to him: Urquhart, *Hammarskjold,* 26; Brian Urquhart, "Character Sketches: Dag Hammarskjöld by Brian Urquhart," UN News, news.un.org. Sture Linnér told Roger Lipsey that Hammarskjöld denied that he was gay, and in fact that he had once been in love with a woman. See Lipsey, *Hammarskjöld,* 109–10.

157 "He was not afraid": Stolpe, *Dag Hammarskjöld,* 48.

157 The photographs he took: Photos taken and arranged by Hammarskjöld, boxes 237–45, DHC. For a report of the trip, see UPI, "Dag Hammarskjöld Off on Vacation," *Williams (Ariz.) Daily News,* Jan. 20, 1959.

158 "Because it never": Lipsey, *Hammarskjöld,* 104. A slightly different translation can be found in Hammarskjöld, *Markings,* 193.

158 On one of his: Urquhart, *Hammarskjold,* 27n; Lipsey, *Hammarskjöld,* 104.

158 The unicorn stable was: Details on Hammarskjöld's apartment come from

Rolf Edin, "Serving Hammarskjöld," in Hanley and Melber, *Dag Hammarsk-jöld Remembered,* 90–93; Lipsey, *Hammarskjöld,* 575; Betty Pepis, "Scandinavian Import," *NYT Magazine,* Aug. 1, 1954; photos of Hammarskjöld's rooms, box 123, AWCP; Kelen, *Hammarskjöld,* 57; "United Nations: Arms & the Man," *Time,* Nov. 26, 1956, 27.

158 "the world's sweetest": Lipsey, *Hammarskjöld,* 163.

158 "Is it monastic": Kelen, *Hammarskjöld,* 56–57.

158 Hammarskjöld rejected nearly: Edin, "Serving Hammarskjöld," 93; Joseph P. Lash, "The Man on the 38th Floor," *Harper's,* Oct. 1959.

158 Hammarskjöld counted among: Lash, "Man on the 38th Floor," 52.

158 Even Greta Garbo: Lipsey, *Hammarskjöld,* 184.

158 Amid the worldly curios: UN, "Itinerary of the Secretary General's Visit to Countries and Territories in Africa," press release, Dec. 5, 1959, box 77, DHC.

158 He named him: Bunche, *Ralph J. Bunche,* 191; Somaiya, *Golden Thread,* 26.

158 "Dag is crazy": Bunche's notes on farewell dinner, June 2, 1960, box 15, folder 2, Congo (1960), BUC.

159 "I must do": Kelen, *Hammarskjöld,* 186.

159 The desperate cable: Bunche to Hammarskjöld, July 13, 1960 (1340), box 155, DHC.

159 "a United Nations force": Hammarskjöld, "Summary Diary of Congo Opera-tion," July 19, 1960, box 141, DHC; Cordier and Foote, *Public Papers,* 5:19.

159 Bunche, who had earlier: Bunche to Hammarskjöld, July 13, 1960 (63), box 155, DHC.

159 "Nothing short of": Hammarskjöld, "Summary Diary of Congo Operation."

159 "bring to the attention": UN Charter, Chapter XV.

159 "to try all he can": Cordier and Foote, *Public Papers,* 2:678–79; Urquhart, *Hammarskjold,* 396.

159 "I had a tough": Hammarskjöld to Fawzi, July 26, 1960, box 2a3, DHC.

160 "Given the inability": *FRUS, 1958–1960,* vol. 14, doc. 122.

160 He told Herter: Ibid., doc. 121.

160 "In these circumstances": UN Security Council, 873rd Meeting, S/PV.873 (July 13/14, 1960), 4–5.

161 The ensuing debate: Thomas J. Hamilton, "Peace Unit Voted; U.S. and Soviet Clash in Debate—Belgians Asked to Pull Out," *NYT,* July 14, 1960; Kelen, *Hammarskjöld,* 187. Smoking was common in Security Council meetings; see United Nations, "The Security Council Discusses Congo at the 877th Meeting," filmed July 20, 1960, at United Nations Security Council, video, 11:00, www .unmultimedia.org. China (Formosa) also abstained.

161 The text, just 144: UN Security Council Resolution 143, S/4387 (July 14, 1960).

161 "The text is intentionally": UN Security Council, 873rd Meeting, S/PV.873 (July 13/14, 1960), 39.

161 "Leave it to Dag": "Mr. Hammarskjöld, We Presume," *Economist,* Jan. 2, 1960; O'Brien, *To Katanga and Back,* 47.

161 Henry Cabot Lodge Jr.: UN Security Council, 873rd Meeting, S/PV.873 (July 13/14, 1960), 43. Allen Dulles quickly recognized the ambiguity about the bases. See *FRUS, 1958–1960*, vol. 14, doc. 126.

162 "political miracle": Hammarskjöld to de Seynes, July 19, 1960, box 155, DHC.

162 Across America, in: See, for example, the late city edition of *NYT,* July 14, 1960. News of the meeting competed for attention with the convention on television, too. Urquhart, *Hammarskjold,* 397.

162 Ghana pledged to: "Congo: On Scene," *Newsweek,* Aug. 1, 1960, 37; Report by General Alexander, "Situation in the Congo," July 12, 1960, box 137, DHC; Urquhart, *Hammarskjold,* 401.

162 A name was chosen: Ibid., 399. The name was later changed to Opération des Nations Unies au Congo.

163 The prime minister was worn: Lumumba, *Lumumba Speaks,* 259.

163 The two leaders had just: Lynn Heinzerling, "Refugees Caught in Congo Battle," *NYT,* July 14, 1960; "Africa's Congo: Hot—and Cold—War," *Newsweek,* July 25, 1960, 44.

163 Communications were still: Lumumba, *Lumumba Speaks,* 265.

163 Radio reports were: CRISP, *Congo 1960,* 2:494; Tanner, "Belgian Commandos Rout Congo Troops at Airport."

163 "breaking off all diplomatic": CRISP, *Congo 1960,* 2:554.

163 "the Katanga experiment": Gérard-Libois, *Katanga Secession,* 101.

163 "a source of trouble": *FRUS, 1958–1960,* vol. 14, doc. 128n1.

163 Local officials and residents: Lumumba, *Lumumba Speaks,* 249.

164 When pressed, the pilot: Kashamura, *De Lumumba,* 114.

164 "We are independent": Lumumba, *Lumumba Speaks,* 249.

164 Their bewilderment only: On this incident, see Timberlake to State, July 14, 1960 (86), file 320, Belgium—Congo Classified, Security-Segregated Records, U.S. Embassy Leopoldville, RG 84, NACP; Timberlake to State, July 14, 1960 (88), file 320, Belgium—Congo Classified, Security-Segregated Records, U.S. Embassy Leopoldville, RG 84, NACP; von Horn, *Soldiering for Peace,* 149; Lumumba, *Lumumba Speaks,* 249–51; *Sydney Morning Herald,* July 16, 1960; "Congo: Jungle Shipwreck," 22.

164 "We have no intention": CRISP, *Congo 1960,* 2:492.

165 The pilot, implausibly: Ibid., 493.

165 In walked Larry: Devlin, *Chief of Station,* 43; *FRUS, 1958–1960,* vol. 14, doc. 127.

16. An Experiment in Peace

166 "Kiss my foot": Devlin, *Chief of Station,* xv.

166 He bought a: Ibid., 14.

167 Ambassador Timberlake soon took: *FRUS, 1958–1960,* vol. 14, doc. 127.

167 "I cannot discuss": Devlin, *Chief of Station,* 43.

167 "The reception was": *FRUS, 1958–1960,* vol. 14, doc. 127.

167 Hoping to get Lumumba: Devlin, *Chief of Station*, 43–44. Devlin recalls that it was a sedan, but all contemporaneous reports speak of a van. Details on this incident are drawn from *The Sydney Morning Herald*, July 16, 1960; "Africa's Congo: Hot—and Cold—War," 44; CRISP, *Congo 1960*, 2:493; *FRUS, 1958–1960*, vol. 14, doc. 127.

167 "Turn it over!": "Africa's Congo: Hot—and Cold—War," 44.

167 "Africa's woman of": Blouin, *My Country, Africa*, 257; "Words of the Week," *Jet*, Dec. 7, 1961, 30.

167 "reads like a chapter": Weiss, *Political Protest*, 178.

167 Blouin was born: Her life story comes from Blouin, *My Country, Africa*.

168 "The death of": Ibid., 153.

168 "We will have them": Ibid., 257.

168 "the Congolese national": CRISP, *Congo 1960*, 2:555.

168 When Hammarskjöld read: Hammarskjöld to Bunche, July 14, 1960, box 155, DHC.

169 Even though the cable: Fursenko and Naftali, *Khrushchev's Cold War*, 308.

169 "imperialist aggression": "Texts of Congolese Leaders' Appeal to Premier Khrushchev and His Reply," *NYT*, July 16, 1960; also CRISP, *Congo 1960*, 2:555–56.

169 "playing into Soviet": Devlin, *Chief of Station*, 38.

169 "should not be suppressed": *FRUS, 1958–1960*, vol. 14, doc. 128.

169 "Should other states": Ibid., doc. 129.

169 "anti-Western": Planning Board Notes, July 15, 1960, box 4, Planning Board Notes (NSC) 1960, NSC Series, Office of the White House Staff Secretary, DDEL. Other notes of the meeting offer the opposite interpretation: "Herter felt that it was understating the matter to say that Lumumba was anti-West." *FRUS, 1958–1960*, vol. 14, doc. 126. I have privileged the contemporaneous handwritten notes over the ones drafted three days later; "understating" was likely meant to be "overstating."

169 "the attitude of": Kalb, *Congo Cables*, 26–27.

169 "the whole trouble": Memorandum of conversation with Hammarskjöld and Berard, July 14, 1960, box 141, DHC.

170 Navigators, relying on: Bernard C. Nalty, *The Air Force Role in Five Crises, 1958–1965*, USAF Historical Division Liaison Office, June 1968, 32–33, nsarchive2.gwu.edu.

170 In its first three: Hoskyns, *Congo Since Independence*, 132; Memorandum for the Joint Chiefs of Staff, July 18, 1960, Situation Report for the Joint Chiefs of Staff, July 17, 1960, and Joint Chiefs of Staff Situation Report, July 22, 1960, box 3, Congo Situation Reports, International Series, Office of the Staff Secretary: Records, 1952–61, DDEL.

170 When Leopoldville seemed: Paarlberg to Higginbottom, July 28, 1960, box 804, Republic of the Congo, Central Files, General File, DDEL.

170 In little over: Joint Chiefs of Staff Situation Report, July 25, 1960, box 3, Congo

Situation Reports, International Series, Office of the Staff Secretary: Records, 1952–61, DDEL.

170 The Guineans walked: Steigman, interview; Sharp, interview.

170 In hours and tonnage: Haulman, "Crisis in the Congo," 32. The operation was eventually renamed Operation New Tape.

170 Many of the arriving: "Congo: On Scene."

170 "The UN—which tribe": Urquhart, *Hammarskjold*, 400.

170 The few among them: "Notes on recent political events in the Congo," box 9, folder 14, HWP.

170 "The men understood": Bunche to Hammarskjöld, July 13, 1960 (63), box 155, DHC.

171 "I would like to ask": Kanza, *Rise and Fall*, 367.

171 But his plane was: Von Horn, *Soldiering for Peace*, 146–47; Telephone calls of the Secretary of State, July 16, 1960, box 13, CAH Telephone Calls, Herter Papers, DDEL.

171 Donning a blue military: Urquhart, *Ralph Bunche*, 316–17; Urquhart, *Life in Peace and War*, 148–49.

171 Within hours, they: Steigman, interview; Cordier and Foote, *Public Papers*, 5:36; "Congolese Cheer U.N. Troops Taking Up Posts in Leopoldville," *NYT*, July 19, 1960; "Congo: Back from the Precipice," *Time*, Aug. 1, 1960, 21.

171 "desired psychological effect": Hammarskjöld to von Horn, July 19, 1960, box 142, DHC.

171 The Irish were sent: Urquhart, *Hammarskjold*, 402; Kennedy and Magennis, *Ireland*, 23; Behr, *Anyone Here*, 138; Urquhart, *Hammarskjold*, 402; Dorothy Jenks, "The United Nations in the Congo," *Congo News Letter* 52, no. 4 (Dec. 1960): 30–32 ; Adams, "The Monster at Gila Bend," 66.

171 The peacekeepers made: Urquhart, *Life in Peace and War*, 149; Urquhart OH, Oct. 19, 1984, 8–9; Hoskyns, *Congo Since Independence*, 135.

172 "Then go get": "Congo: Back from the Precipice," 21.

172 One minister came: Andrew Cordier, "Challenge in the Congo," box 16, folder 3, BUC.

172 When another official: Urquhart, *Life in Peace and War*, 152.

172 The UN rushed: "Report No. 10 on United Nations Civilian Operations in the Congo," 12.

172 To prevent a: Urquhart OH, Oct. 19, 1984, 9–10; Urquhart, *Hammarskjold*, 401.

172 "Every other person": Nelson, *Congo Crisis*, 22.

172 At one point: Scott, *Tumbled House*, ix.

172 At the end of a: Robinson McIlvaine OH, 14; Carlucci OH, 13.

172 "half-naked black": Farmer, *Freedom—When?*, 132. Quoted in Van Hove, *Congoism*, 248n2.

173 "New Congo Mumbo-Jumbo," *Great Bend (Kans.) Tribune*, Oct. 10, 1960; Bigart, "'In-de-pen-DANCE' Comes to the Congo."

173 "With a primeval": "Congo: The Monstrous Hangover."

173 "Anyone here been": Behr, *Anyone Here,* 136.
173 "This U.N. enterprise": Walter Lippmann, "Today and Tomorrow: The Congo and the U.N.," *Washington Post,* July 21, 1960.

17. Powerless

174 "He was a fluent": Henry, *Ralph Bunche,* 190.
174 Timberlake liked to: O'Brien, *To Katanga and Back,* 94.
174 "My dear honorable": Lumumba, *Lumumba Speaks,* 261.
175 "Lumumba's mastery of": Kanza, *Rise and Fall,* 212.
175 While the Congo burned: Lumumba, *Lumumba Speaks,* 262; Liu OH, 5–6.
175 At least one meeting: Scott, *Tumbled House,* 64; von Horn, *Soldiering for Peace,* 167–68.
175 Their conversations were: Urquhart, *Ralph Bunche,* 318.
175 "Who's there?": Liu OH, 4–5.
175 "had the annoying": Blouin, *My Country, Africa,* 262.
175 "We were ministers": Kanza, *Rise and Fall,* 119.
175 "merely two men": *FRUS, 1958–1960,* vol. 14, doc. 134.
176 Ministers had their own: Young, *Politics in the Congo,* 408.
176 "being vote-catching demagogues": Kanza, *Rise and Fall,* 104.
176 When a minister: Alexander, "Situation in the Congo."
176 "It was the king": CRISP, *Congo 1960,* 2:568.
176 The minister of public health: Kanza, *Rise and Fall,* 109. The minister was Grégoire Kamanga.
176 Mobutu had known: Alphonse Songolo was one exception; he knew Lumumba from his Stanleyville days. See Omasombo and Verhaegen, *Jeunesse,* 212–13.
176 Lumumba had named: Monheim, *Mobutu,* 103–105; Hoskyns, *Congo Since Independence,* 136; Kanza, *Rise and Fall,* 210.
176 "It's a question": Monheim, *Mobutu,* 104–105.
177 Lumumba had originally: Kashamura, *De Lumumba,* 120.
177 When that became: Timberlake to State, July 18, 1960 (139), file 320, Belgium—U.S. Classified, Security-Segregated Records, U.S. Embassy Leopoldville, RG 84, NACP; Lumumba, *Lumumba Speaks,* 260.
177 During his tour: Timberlake to State, n.d., file 350, Congo July–Aug. 1960 Classified, Security-Segregated Records, U.S. Embassy, RG 84, NACP.
177 Bunche, however, could: Bunche to Hammarskjöld, July 16, 1960 (80), box 155, DHC.
177 What he missed: Vanderstraeten, *De la Force publique,* 461.
178 "this American Negro": Urquhart, *Ralph Bunche,* 313n.
178 "fluent but utterly": Bunche to Hammarskjöld, July 16, 1960 (80).
178 Intent on preventing: Carlucci OH, 9.
178 A day after reaching: Andrew Borowiec, AP, "Congo Threatens to Ask Soviet Troops to Intervene," *Alton (Ill.) Evening Telegraph,* July 18, 1960; Vanderstraeten, *De la Force publique,* 419.

178 In a letter: Bunche to Hammarskjöld, July 18, 1960 (104), box 155, DHC. General H. T. Alexander thought Kasavubu signed the July 18 ultimatum under pressure, as he told Timberlake. Timberlake, "First Year of Independence in the Congo," 96.

178 "we may be obliged": Timberlake to State, Brussels, and Paris, July 18, 1960, file 320, Belgium–U.S. Classified, Security-Segregated Records, U.S. Embassy Leopoldville, RG 84, NACP.

178 But he did appreciate: "Texts of Congolese Leaders' Appeal to Premier Khrushchev and His Reply"; also CRISP, *Congo 1960*, 2:555–56.

178 "We need the fastest": "Soviet Appeal Weighed," *NYT,* July 20, 1960.

179 "We will call on": Lumumba, *Lumumba Speaks*, 262.

179 Even if Soviet: *FRUS, 1958–1960*, vol. 14, docs. 128, 145.

179 When the Associated Press: AP, "Soviets Charge U.S. Lands Troops in Congo," *Meriden (Conn.) Record-Journal*, July 20, 1960; Osgood Caruthers, "Moscow Demands G.I.'s Leave Congo," *NYT,* July 20, 1960.

179 "The meeting ended": Hammarskjöld, "Summary Diary of Congo Operation."

18. A Humiliating Defeat

180 At 7:00 p.m.: Bunche to Hammarskjöld, July 19, 1960 (126), box 155, DHC; Bunche to Hammarskjöld, July 20, 1960 (ONUC 19), box 155, DHC; Kalb, *Congo Cables,* 25.

180 There were now: Timberlake to Herter, July 19, 1960 (168), file 320, Belgium/Congo/UN Classified 1960, Security-Segregated Records, U.S. Embassy Leopoldville, RG 84, NACP.

181 Bunche found himself: Bunche to Hammarskjöld, July 20, 1960, box 132, DHC; Timberlake to Herter, July 21, 1960 (188), file 312, UNOC July/Aug. 1960 Classified, Security-Segregated Records, U.S. Embassy Leopoldville, RG 84, NACP.

181 "I have made no": Henry Tanner, "Lumumba Backed; Cabinet Votes Appeal for Forces to End 'All Aggression,'" *NYT,* July 21, 1960.

181 "impressive": Tanner, "Lumumba Backed"; Bunche to Hammarskjöld, July 20, 1960 (ONUC 35), box 132, DHC.

181 "The request": Urquhart, *Ralph Bunche,* 28; Bunche to Hammarskjöld, July 20, 1960 (ONUC 48), box 155, DHC.

181 "If the U.N. forces": Bunche to Hammarskjöld, July 24, 1960 (B190), box 155, DHC.

181 "They simply could": Bunche to Hammarskjöld, July 22, 1960 (B169), box 155, DHC. Even the U.S. embassy was fed up with the Belgians. When Belgian troops strung up barbed wire along Leopoldville's Boulevard Albert, reinforcing the perception that they were occupiers, Timberlake considered it merely the latest of "repeated examples of such stupidity." Timberlake to State, July 18, 1960 (134), file 320, Belgium–U.S. Classified, Security-Segregated Records, U.S. Embassy Leopoldville, RG 84, NACP.

182 On July 18: AP, "U.N. Security Council to Get Congo Report," *Virginian-Pilot* (Norfolk, Va.), July 18, 1960.

182 Anticipating Soviet remonstrations: Telephone calls of the Secretary of State, July 18, 1960, box 13, CAH Telephone Calls, Herter Papers, DDEL. See also *FRUS, 1958–1960,* vol. 14, doc. 138; Herter to USUN, Brussels, and Leopoldville, July 20, 1960 (193), file 320, Belgium–U.S. Classified, Security-Segregated Records, U.S. Embassy Leopoldville, RG 84, NACP; Kalb, *Congo Cables,* 25. At the July 20 Security Council meeting, Wigny said merely that he would begin withdrawing on Wednesday. See UN Security Council, 877th Meeting, S/PV.877 (July 20/21, 1960), 22.

182 From his hotel: Kanza, *Rise and Fall,* 218.

182 Now, on this hot: "July 20 1960 Weather History at La Guardia Airport," Weather Spark, weatherspark.com; Olver to UN NY, July 18, 1960, box 132, DHC; Kanza, *Rise and Fall,* 218.

182 From Bunche's cables: *FRUS, 1958–1960,* vol. 14, doc. 131; Hammarskjöld, "Diary," July 23, 1960, box 141, DHC.

182 The two agreed: Kanza, *Rise and Fall,* 167, 219; Urquhart, *Hammarskjold,* 406.

182 "very reasonable": Hammarskjöld, "Diary," July 21, 1960.

182 "soft-spoken, mild-mannered": *FRUS, 1958–1960,* vol. 14, doc. 139.

182 "fundamentally the Soviet Union": Kanza, *Rise and Fall,* 221.

183 "The Congo behaved": United Nations, "877th Meeting of Security Council," filmed July 20, 1960, at UN Security Council, New York, video, www.unmultimedia.org; UN Security Council, 877th Meeting, S/PV.877 (July 20/21, 1960), 7, 12, 27.

183 "What do you wish": United Nations, "877th Meeting of Security Council—Part 1," video; UN Security Council, 877th Meeting, S/PV.877 (July 20/21, 1960), 17, with my own translation.

183 "Where Congolese unity": UN Security Council, 879th Meeting, S/PV.879 (July 21/22, 1960), 29.

183 "He owes it to": Omasombo and Verhaegen, *Acteur,* 94.

183 "speedily" withdraw: UN Security Council Resolution 145, S/4405 (July 22, 1960); "U.N. Council Vote Asks Belgium to Pull Out of Congo Speedily," *NYT,* July 22, 1960.

184 "Go and have": Kanza, *Rise and Fall,* 235.

184 "This morning, I": Lumumba, *Lumumba Speaks,* 279–81.

19. Hail Lumumba!

185 Larry Devlin was at: Devlin, *Chief of Station,* 44; Woodrow Wilson International Center OH, 50; Lowell Denny, "Cuba: An African Odyssey [Parts I and II]," YouTube, 1:57:34, Nov. 5, 2019, www.youtube.com; Carlucci OH, 11. On July 21, Lumumba requested twenty passports from the Sûreté. Lumumba to Administrateur Général de la Sûreté, July 21, 1960, VII-BV/RDC/Administration Publique N°001/07/02, FBV.

185 "Christian democracy": Reid to Eisenhower, July 4, 1960, box 834, Congo, Central Files, General File, DDEL.

185 Their White House liaison: Reid, *Congo Drumbeat*, 132, 141.

185 He had tried: Tomlinson to Leopoldville, April 14, 1960 (331), file 350, Congo April–June 1960 Classified, Security-Segregated Records, U.S. Embassy, RG 84, NACP.

185 Now seemed like: Bunche to Hammarskjöld, July 21, 1960, box 155, DHC.

186 "bandits and criminals": Reuters press report, July 22, 1960, box 132, DHC; Lumumba, *Lumumba Speaks*, 279–80.

186 In Washington, he: Bunche to Hammarskjöld, July 21, 1960 (158), box 155, DHC.

186 "I reacted violently": Hammarskjöld, "Diary," July 21, 1960, box 141, DHC.

186 "was wasted breath": Bunche to Hammarskjöld, July 21, 1960 (158).

186 He scrawled "Lumumba": Hammarskjöld, appointment book, July 24, 1960, box 175, DHC.

186 "Having been informed": Hammarskjöld to Bunche, July 21, 1960, box 155, DHC.

186 "Q.S. transmitted the": Hammarskjöld, "Diary," July 21, 1960. On Quaison-Sackey, see "Debonair Diplomat Alex Quaison-Sackey," *NYT,* Dec. 1, 1964.

187 "he would be insufferable": Bunche to Hammarskjöld, July 21, 1960 (B152), box 155, DHC.

187 "destroy the Lumumba": *FRUS, 1958–1960,* vol. 14, doc. 136.

187 That summer: Memorandum of the 452nd Meeting of the National Security Council, July 21, 1960, box 12, 452nd Meeting of NSC, NSC Series, Papers as President, 1953–61 (Whitman File), DDEL.

187 "incredibly naive about": *FRUS, 1958–1960,* vol. 6, docs. 287, 551, 545.

188 "harrowing": Ibid., vol. 14, doc. 140.

188 He mentioned the: On the visit, see Lemarchand, *Political Awakening,* 202.

188 "It is safe to go": *FRUS, 1958–1960,* vol. 14, doc. 140.

188 "We have no evidence": Ibid., doc. 149.

189 Just hours after: Ibid., doc. 142.

189 On July 22: Reuters press report, July 22, 1960, box 132, DHC. Kanza, *Rise and Fall,* 236, puts the size of the entourage at sixteen.

189 "You!" he shouted: Van Reybrouck, *Congo,* 300–301.

189 At Herter's direction: Herter to Leopoldville, July 18, 1960 (139), file 312, UNOC July–Aug. 1960 Classified, Security-Segregated Records, U.S. Embassy Leopoldville, RG 84, NACP.

189 "extremely gratified": Henry Tanner, "Congo Signs Pact with U.S. Concern to Tap Resources," *NYT,* July 23, 1960.

189 "There is no further": Reuters press report, July 22, 1960.

190 "His temperament is": "Congo: Back from the Precipice," 22.

190 Reporters also explained: Tanner, "Congo Signs Pact with U.S. Concern to Tap Resources."

190 At the height: Unless otherwise noted, information on Detwiler comes from

Steigman, interview; North American Newspaper Alliance, "Mystery Man of Congo Is Wall Street Promoter," *Hays (Kans.) Daily News,* Aug. 2, 1960; "Man with a £700m. Mission," *Observer,* July 24, 1960; "Charges 'Misrepresentation' by City Centre Promoter," *Edmonton Journal,* Aug. 17, 1950; "The Big Dreamer," *Time,* Aug. 1, 1960, 62; "Canterbury as 'Rome of Protestants,'" *Observer,* March 31, 1957.

190 He presented Lumumba: *FRUS, 1958–1960,* vol. 14, doc. 151; Memorandum of telephone conversation between Herter and Lodge, July 26, 1960, box 13, CAH Telephone Calls, Herter Papers, DDEL.

190 "a quick-moving bundle": AP, "Fast-Talker Gets Congo Agreement," *Corsicana (Tex.) Daily Sun,* July 23, 1960.

190 But some around: Woodrow Wilson International Center OH, 50–52.

190 "ripe to be taken": *FRUS, 1964–1968,* vol. 23, doc. 7; Steigman, interview.

190 A young MIT: Woodrow Wilson International Center OH, 50. The researcher was Herbert Weiss.

191 "This shows we": Tanner, "Congo Signs Pact with U.S. Concern to Tap Resources."

191 "that Patrice was": Rouch, *En cage avec Lumumba,* 47. See also Woodrow Wilson International Center OH, 50–53. Lumumba later made this very point to Timberlake. According to notes of their August 18 meeting, Lumumba said that "everyone could see he was not Communist since he had first called upon an American businessman to help exploit riches of country." *FRUS, 1958–1960,* vol. 14, doc. 182.

191 The sun had just: James Feron, "Lumumba, Here, Hopeful After Hammarskjöld Talk," *NYT,* July 25, 1960.

191 At a refueling: McKown, *Lumumba,* 137.

191 During a second: Walter H. Waggoner, "Lumumba on Way Here After London Stop-Over," *NYT,* July 24, 1960.

191 "From speaking to": *FRUS, 1958–1960,* vol. 14, doc. 147.

192 At one point: Kanza, *Rise and Fall,* 238.

192 "ignorant, very suspicious": Foreign Affairs and International Trade Canada, *Documents on Canadian External Relations,* vol. 27, doc. 15, DEA/6386-D-40, 1960, epe.lac-bac.gc.ca.

192 "Whole tribes led": Hoskyns, *Congo Since Independence,* 158, 141.

192 "impossible": Hammarskjöld to Bunche, July 24, 1960, box 155, DHC.

193 Hammarskjöld often identified: Woodrow Wilson International Center OH, 93–94; Kanza, *Sans rancune,* 19.

193 "extremely demanding and": Kanza, *Rise and Fall,* 238.

193 "Now no one": Kalb, *Congo Cables,* 34.

193 But it might have: Materials for luncheon with Security Council members, July 13, 1960, box 53, DHC. The white wine was Pouilly-Fuissé; the red was Château la Mission Haut-Brion.

193 Seated behind a: AP, "Hammarskjöld Flying to Belgium, Congo Tonight,"

Boston Globe, July 26, 1960; "Africa and the World: The Pull and Tug," *Newsweek,* Aug. 8, 1960, 35.

193 "There was nothing": Kathleen Teltsch, "Asians and Africans Join to End Protocol Crisis over Lumumba," *NYT,* July 26, 1960.

193 "an agreement in": Lumumba, *Lumumba Speaks,* 299–301.

193 "If the Belgian troops": Ibid., 295, 304.

194 "a nation like any": Ibid., 305, 297.

194 This was a generous: Racial discrimination in New York housing posed a diplomatic problem in light of the influx of Black UN representatives from newly independent African states, who, the State Department feared, would have trouble finding housing near UN headquarters. To protect the African diplomats from real estate racism, the U.S. mission to the UN quietly arranged housing on their behalf. See Herter to State, July 16, 1960 (15), file 312, UNOC July–Aug. 1960 Classified, Security-Segregated Records, U.S. Embassy Leopoldville, RG 84, NACP.

194 Leaving unmentioned the: Lumumba, *Lumumba Speaks,* 290.

194 Even in the smallest: *FRUS, 1958–1960,* vol. 14, doc. 152.

194 Still, he saw: Lumumba, *Lumumba Speaks,* 306.

194 "They're all Africans": "Africa and the World: The Pull and Tug." See also Woodrow Wilson International Center OH, 179.

194 "a second Marcus Garvey": Kanza, *Rise and Fall,* 242.

194 "Hail Lumumba!": R. Waldo Williams, "The Awakening Call," *Black Challenge,* www.freedomarchives.org. The issue is undated, but an editorial on the situation in the Congo makes it clear that it was written after the secession of Katanga but before the Belgian withdrawal, dating it to around the time of Lumumba's visit to New York.

195 Alex Quaison-Sackey: *FRUS, 1958–1960,* vol. 14, doc. 147.

195 The businessman had: Anonymous, interview.

195 Some diplomats were: Kalb, *Congo Cables,* 35.

195 "adolescent pathos": Kelen, *Hammarskjöld,* 190.

195 "nothing the least sensational": Kanza, *Rise and Fall,* 237.

195 "discussed issues related": "Restoring Peace and Tranquility in the Congo," *Pravda,* July 27, 1960.

195 "If I should": Simon Malley, "Lumumba: Clerk Who Runs a Nation," *Boston Globe,* July 25, 1960.

195 "Let us not": Woodrow Wilson International Center OH, 56.

196 The prime minister stayed: "Africa and the World: The Pull and Tug"; *National Review,* Aug. 20, 1960, box 804, Republic of the Congo, Central Files, General File, DDEL; Memorandum of telephone conversation between Herter and Lodge, July 26, 1960, box 13, CAH Telephone Calls, Herter Papers, DDEL.

196 "He nonchalantly scooped": Roberts OH, 29.

196 "The meetings ended": Kelen, *Hammarskjöld,* 189.

20. The Lamp and the Statue

197 Lumumba brought with: *FRUS, 1958–1960,* vol. 14, doc. 147.

197 "thank him for": Lumumba, *Lumumba Speaks,* 298.

197 "highest levels in": For details on Lodge's conversation with Lumumba, see *FRUS, 1958–1960,* vol. 14, doc. 151; Memorandum of telephone conversation between Herter and Lodge, July 26, 1960, box 13, CAH Telephone Calls, Herter Papers, DDEL.

197 But the Congolese: Kanza, *Rise and Fall,* 237. It became an article of faith that Eisenhower snubbed Lumumba. See, for example, Woodrow Wilson International Center OH, 49; Namikas, *Battleground Africa,* 82; and Muehlenbeck, *Czechoslovakia in Africa,* 67. But the historical record shows this to be false. The earliest reference I found to Lumumba's trip to the United States came in July 21 (Memorandum of telephone conversation, Herter and Merchant, July 21, 1960, box 13, CAH Telephone Calls, Herter Papers, DDEL; also Lodge to Herter, July 22, 1960 [177], Visit of Prime Minister Lumumba, Files of Visits by Heads of Government, Dignitaries, and Delegations, 1928–77, Office of Secretary/Office of the Chief of Protocol, RG 59, NACP). And only on July 25 did Lumumba's party agree to come to Washington (Lodge to Herter, July 25, 1960 [225], Visit of Prime Minister Lumumba, Files of Visits by Heads of Government, Dignitaries, and Delegations, 1928–77, Office of Secretary/ Office of the Chief of Protocol, RG 59, NACP). But by then, Eisenhower's schedule was already set (AP, "Eisenhower Plans Denver Visit," *Missoulian,* July 17, 1960, 9). Also, Herter at the airport on July 27 was instructed to tell Lumumba that Eisenhower "will regretfully be unable to see him due to previous commitments in Chicago and Denver" (Instructions for Meeting with Lumumba, Visit of Prime Minister Lumumba, Files of Visits by Heads of Government, Dignitaries, and Delegations, 1928–77, Office of Secretary/ Office of the Chief of Protocol, RG 59, NACP).

198 "with no social functions": Telephone calls of the Secretary of State, July 23, 1960, box 13, CAH Telephone Calls, Herter Papers, DDEL.

198 And so the U.S.: Burden to State, July 28, 1960 (156), file 320, Belgium–U.S. Classified, Security-Segregated Records, U.S. Embassy Leopoldville, RG 84, NACP; Burden to State, July 27, 1960 (155), file 320, Belgium–U.S. Classified, Security-Segregated Records, U.S. Embassy Leopoldville, RG 84, NACP.

198 When Lumumba stepped: Dana Adams Schmidt, "Lumumba Urges U.S. to Aid Congo," *NYT,* July 28, 1960, photo; Buchanan to Hastings, Aug. 16, 1960, Visit of Prime Minister Lumumba, Files of Visits by Heads of Government, Dignitaries, and Delegations, 1928–77, Office of Secretary/Office of the Chief of Protocol, RG 59, NACP; "Program for the Visit to the United States of America of His Excellency Patrice Lumumba," July 27, 1960, Visit of Prime Minister Lumumba, Files of Visits by Heads of Government, Dignitaries, and Delegations, 1928–77, Office of Secretary/Office of the Chief of Protocol, RG 59, NACP; Freeman to Herter, July 30, 1960 (370), file 320, Belgium–U.S. Classi-

fied, Security-Segregated Records, U.S. Embassy Leopoldville, RG 84, NACP; "Congo: Where's the War?," *Time*, Aug. 8, 1960, 29. Herter had been instructed to offer Lumumba an additional three-week tour of the United States, complete with a stop in Puerto Rico, but this was not the friendly gesture it seemed: the idea had been Eisenhower's, and it was designed to keep Lumumba busy abroad while his political relevance in the Congo suffered. (The invitation was declined.) "Suggested Statement of Greeting by the Secretary to Prime Minister Patrice Lumumba on His Arrival in Washington," July 27, 1960, Visit of Prime Minister Lumumba, Files of Visits by Heads of Government, Dignitaries, and Delegations, 1928–77, Office of Secretary/Office of the Chief of Protocol, RG 59, NACP; *FRUS, 1958–1960,* vol. 14, doc. 148.

198 "a dignified welcome": Lumumba, *Lumumba Speaks,* 316.

198 "a magnificent house": "Congo: Tribal Warfare," *Newsweek,* Aug. 22, 1960, 40.

198 "A cordial handshake": "La presse belge se déchaîne," *Le Monde,* July 31, 1960.

199 "catastrophic" optics: Memorandum of telephone conversation, Herter and Ambassador Burden, July 27, 1960, box 13, CAH Telephone Calls, Herter Papers, DDEL. The hurt would linger for months. In September, Clarence Randall, one of Eisenhower's economic advisers, traveled to Belgium and relayed the comments of a close friend, Pierre Van der Rest, the head of Belgium's Iron and Steel Federation, who spoke of "widespread animosity against the United States" stemming in part from "the reception given to Lumumba in Washington, including his being entertained at Blair House." Notes on Pierre Van der Rest, box 5, European Trip 1960 Notes and Reports, Randall Series, U.S. Council on Foreign Economic Policy, Office of the Chairman: Records, 1954–61, DDEL.

199 Soon, Belgium's foreign: Burden to State, July 28, 1960 (156).

199 At a meeting of: Paris to Leopoldville, July 28, 1960, file 320 Belgium–U.S. Classified, Security-Segregated Records, U.S. Embassy Leopoldville, RG 84, NACP.

199 "inherited him along": *FRUS, 1958–1960,* vol. 14, doc. 153.

199 "the balance of the visit": Burden to State, July 27, 1960 (155).

199 Lumumba would rightly: Lumumba, *Lumumba Speaks,* 316–17.

199 On the contrary: Dana Adams Schmidt, "World War Peril Seen by Lumumba," *NYT,* July 29, 1960.

199 "All those who": "Congo: Where's the War?," 30.

199 From there, his: "Program for the Visit to the United States of America of His Excellency Patrice Lumumba," July 27, 1960; Schmidt, "World War Peril Seen by Lumumba."

199 "He tested doors": "Congo: Where's the War?," 30.

200 "What was the attitude": Bernard Gwertzman, "Lumumba Goes on Tour of Washington's Home," *Evening Star* (Washington, D.C.), July 27, 1960.

200 On the campus: "Information on Lumumba's Visit to Howard University," Visit of Prime Minister Lumumba, Files of Visits by Heads of Government, Dignitaries, and Delegations, 1928–77, Office of Secretary/Office of the Chief

of Protocol, RG 59, NACP; Gwertzman, "Lumumba Goes on Tour of Washington's Home," 3.

200 "work on the land": De Vos, *Vie et mort,* 224–25. See also Schmidt, "Lumumba Urges U.S. to Aid Congo."

200 At the Mayflower: Reid, *Congo Drumbeat,* 142.

200 In the ballroom: Claude A. Barnett to Timberlake, Sept. 8, 1960, box 3, folder 1, CTP.

200 Yvonne Reed: This passage is based on Seon (née Reed), interview; "April 25—Seon—from Washington to the Congo: How I Met Lumumba," CongoLive!, www.congolive.org; Yvonne Seon (HistoryMakers A2003.154), interviewed by Larry Crowe, July 14, 2003, HistoryMakers Digital Archive, www.thehistorymakers.org. Seon ended up going to the Congo, after Lumumba's death, to work on the High Commission for the Inga Dam. She went on to have a long career in American academia and, I can't help but note, is the mother of the comedian Dave Chappelle.

201 A man from the Soviet: This was probably the Soviet chargé d'affaires Mikhail Smirnovsky. See "Congo: Where's the War?," 30; Kalb, *Congo Cables,* 37–38.

201 "He was a strong": Seon, interview.

201 While Lumumba was: Devlin, *Chief of Station,* 45–48.

201 "the Congo may": *FRUS, 1958–1960,* vol. 14, doc. 130.

201 Soon, he would: Ibid., doc. 156; List of participants, 454th Meeting of the National Security Council, Aug. 1, 1960, box 3, NSC Agenda and Minutes 1960, NSC Series, Office of the Special Assistant for National Security Affairs: Records, 1952–61, DDEL.

201 "use the Congo": Devlin, *Chief of Station,* 48.

202 "felt it was getting": *FRUS, 1958–1960,* vol. 14, doc. 148.

202 Between courses of: Cassilly, interview.

202 They were constantly: Gwertzman, "Lumumba Goes on Tour of Washington's Home."

202 "You just don't do": "Congo: Where's the War?," 30.

202 One incident would: Details on Lumumba's alleged tryst with a prostitute come from Cassilly, interview; Cassilly, "Lumumba Conundrum," 152; Mahoney, *JFK,* 39. The oft-told story has a "too good to check" quality. But I did check, with Thomas Cassilly, the State Department escort officer at the time, who claimed it did indeed happen as described. "During our protocol training for the Foreign Service we were instructed on which fork to use, but not on how to act as a pimp for our country," he would write. Cassilly, "Lumumba Conundrum," 152. Robert Hennemeyer, who worked in the State Department's protocol office, has also repeated the story. See Hennemeyer OH, 5–6. Although the tale certainly fits into a racist narrative of Black men as uncontrollable sex fiends who constantly desired white women, it is plausible. Owen Roberts, Lumumba's State Department escort officer in New York, also spoke of providing the Congolese delegation with women. See Roberts OH, 19. The same allegation was made about Lumumba in Ottawa. See Spooner,

Canada, 59, 231n92. Moreover, Lumumba did not have a puritanical view of sex or relationships. See Omasombo and Verhaegen, *Jeunesse*, 135–50.

202 "the wife is not like": Lumumba, *Congo, My Country*, 126.

203 Coming on the heels: Mahoney, *JFK*, 39; Grose, *Gentleman Spy*, 107.

203 "Erratic, but a": "Congo: Where's the War?," 30.

203 The meeting began: "Program for the Visit to the United States of America of His Excellency Patrice Lumumba," July 27, 1960; Henry N. Taylor, "Christian Herter Shows U.S. State Department Not a One Man Operation," *El Paso Herald Post*, Nov. 30, 1959, 23.

203 "The people of ": For notes on the meeting, see *FRUS, 1958–1960*, vol. 14, doc. 152; Memorandum of conversation between Herter and Lumumba, July 28, 1960, folder 5.2, box 3, Records Relating to the Congo and the Congo Working Group, 1960–64, RG 59, NACP. A plane was a matter of practicality, not some indulgence. As Lumumba explained on July 15, "The planes we have been traveling on are piloted by Belgian officers who fly us around wherever they please, as if we were prisoners." Lumumba, *Lumumba Speaks*, 261.

203 Herter was sixty-five: NYT News Service, "Herter, N.Y. Urban Chief, Ex-Brahmin," *Baltimore Evening Sun*, Oct. 11, 1967; National Archives and Records Administration, "Longines Chronoscope with Rep. Christian A. Herter," filmed Dec. 19, 1951, video, 14:10, archive.org/details/gov.archives.arc.95720; "Mary Caroline Pratt Weds Christian Archibald Herter," *Brooklyn Life*, Sept. 1, 1917.

204 Officials had steeled: Schmidt, "Lumumba Urges U.S. to Aid Congo."

204 "Washington officials, who": "Congo: Where's the War?," 30.

204 "made a favorable": "Lumumba Visits U.S. Officialdom," *Christian Science Monitor*, July 28, 1960.

204 "no evidence": Kalb, *Congo Cables*, 37; *FRUS, 1958–1960*, vol. 14, doc. 152.

204 "brilliance" and "articulateness": Weissman, *American Foreign Policy*, 66. Decades later, Richard Bissell of the CIA would call Lumumba's meeting with Herter "somewhat successful." Bissell, *Reflections of a Cold Warrior*, 143.

204 Lumumba also reassured: Memorandum of telephone conversation, Herter and Black, July 28, 1960, box 13, CAH Telephone Calls, Herter Papers, DDEL.

204 When told that Detwiler: *FRUS, 1958–1960*, vol. 14, doc. 152.

204 Even Lumumba's solicitation: Cordier to Hammarskjöld and Bunche, July 29, 1960, box 155, DHC. The Americans even proposed providing Lumumba with an American C-47, to be painted with the Congolese flag. But Hammarskjöld opposed the idea. See Cordier to Hammarskjöld, Aug. 3, 1960 (644), box 155, DHC; Hammarskjöld to Cordier, Aug. 4, 1960 (B345), box 155, DHC.

204 "psychotic" and "impossible": Testimony of C. Douglas Dillon, Sept. 2, 1975, 24, 157-10014-10178, JFKAR.

205 Back in Leopoldville: *FRUS, 1958–1960*, vol. 14, doc. 155. The rival was Joseph Iléo, the president of the Senate.

205 His visit to Washington: Thomas Kanza said Lumumba was "acutely disappointed" by the cool reception. See Mahoney, *JFK*, 38.

205 "Our talks with": "Lumumba Here: Belgians Said Behind Riots," *Montreal Gazette,* July 30, 1960.

205 Over the course: Lumumba, *Lumumba Speaks,* 304; Spooner, *Canada,* 57; Archives de la Ville de Montréal, "Patrice Lumumba à l'hôtel de ville de Montréal, 29 juillet 1960 en présence du maire Sarto Fournier," July 29, 1960, photograph, www.flickr.com; "Lumumba in City on Way to Congo," *NYT,* July 31, 1960.

205 "warm welcome": Lumumba to Herter, July 29, 1960, file 755A.00/6 -160, CDF 1960–63, General Records of the Department of State, RG 59, NACP.

206 His hosts in: Spooner, *Canada,* 56.

206 The Congolese prime minister's: Foreign Affairs and International Trade Canada, *Documents on Canadian External Relations,* vol. 27, doc. 17, J.G.D./ VI/846/749.21, 1960, epe.lac-bac.gc.ca. Spooner, *Canada,* 58; "Soviet Envoy Pays Visit," *NYT,* July 31, 1960; UPI, "Congo Leader Hedges About Seeing Soviet," *Boston Globe,* July 31, 1960. Lumumba was cagey about the visit later. In New York, when asked whether he had a breakfast meeting with the Soviet ambassador to Canada, he said that he had had neither breakfast nor lunch with any Russian. "Lumumba in City on Way to Congo."

206 Lumumba did himself: Foreign Affairs and International Trade Canada, *Documents on Canadian External Relations,* vol. 27, doc. 17, J.G.D./VI/846/749.21, 1960, epe.lac-bac.gc.ca.

206 "Mr. Lumumba was": Foreign Affairs and International Trade Canada, *Documents on Canadian External Relations,* vol. 27, doc. 16, DEA/6386-D-40, 1960, epe .lac-bac.gc.ca.

206 "although honest, Canada": Spooner, *Canada,* 59.

206 "Mr. Lumumba left": Foreign Affairs and International Trade Canada, *Documents on Canadian External Relations,* vol. 27, doc. 17, J.G.D./VI/846/749.21, 1960, epe .lac-bac.gc.ca.

206 Back in Manhattan: "Congo: Where's the War?," 30.

206 He signed an agreement: "Analytical Chronology of the Congo Crisis," 17.

206 He met again with: Cordier to Hammarskjöld, July 31, 1960 (564), box 155, DHC; Cordier to Hammarskjöld, July 31, 1960, box 155, DHC; Kalb, *Congo Cables,* 41.

206 "hostile and frustrated": Cordier and Foote, *Public Papers,* 5:56.

206 "I am rather pressed": Lumumba, *Lumumba Speaks,* 301.

21. The Katanga Question

211 "In the West": Hammarskjöld to Cordier, Aug. 2, 1960 (B304), box 155, DHC.

211 "Let him play": Kanza, *Rise and Fall,* 243. This was Kanza's approximation of Hammarskjöld's sentiment.

211 To that end: UN press release, July 25, 1960, box 22, SG Trip July 26–Aug. 6, 1960, AWCP.

211 The secretary-general was: Hammarskjöld to Cordier, July 29, 1960 (B242), box 155, DHC.

211 "I hope that your": Baudouin to Hammarskjöld, July 28, 1960, box 141, DHC. Tshombe, meanwhile, was issuing curiously identical threats. In a July 26 cable to Hammarskjöld, he promised that the arrival of UN forces in Katanga would cause technicians in the public and private sectors to flee, paralyzing all economic activity. "I don't think this is the United Nations' goal," he added snarkily. See Tshombe to Hammarskjöld, July 26, 1960, box 160, AWCP.

212 Determined to avoid: Henry Tanner, "Key Issues in Congo Awaiting U.N. Chief," *NYT,* July 28, 1960; Urquhart, *Hammarskjold,* 409n.

212 In a fitting: John A. Olver, "Under Fire with Dag Hammarskjöld," in Hanley and Melber, *Dag Hammarskjöld Remembered,* 42; Urquhart, *Hammarskjold,* 410; Urquhart, *Life in Peace and War,* 158; Henry Tanner, "U.N. Chief Hailed by Congo Crowd in Leopoldville," *NYT,* July 29, 1960.

212 Gone was the relative: Joint Chiefs of Staff Situation Report, July 23, 1960, box 3, Congo Situation Reports, International Series, Office of the Staff Secretary: Records, 1952–61, DDEL.

212 "Total retreat of": Tanner, "U.N. Chief Hailed by Congo Crowd in Leopoldville."

212 Congolese women clutching: Von Horn, *Soldiering for Peace,* 179.

212 Mosquitoes buzzed about: UN Security Council, 877th Meeting, S/PV.877 (July 20/21, 1960), 3.

212 Finally, Hammarskjöld was: F. T. Liu to Joan Liu, Sept. 22, 1960, Liu Letters.

212 Its telephone system: On the Royal, see Von Horn, *Soldiering for Peace,* 178; Urquhart, *Hammarskjold,* 410; Urquhart, *Life in Peace and War,* 155–56; Urquhart, *Ralph Bunche,* 317; Rikhye, *Military Adviser,* 23; Rikhye, *Trumpets and Tumults,* 138; Dayal, *Life of Our Times,* 406; Olver, "Under Fire with Dag Hammarskjöld," 43; Morrison, "Ralph Bunche Tells About His Toughest Assignment," 31.

213 Hammarskjöld, pale and: Hammarskjöld to Cordier, July 29, 1960 (B242); von Horn, *Soldiering for Peace,* 180.

213 As he caught up: Urquhart, *Life in Peace and War,* 159.

213 "My God!": Von Horn, *Soldiering for Peace,* 180.

213 "be marked by": Cordier to Hammarskjöld, Bunche, and Wieschhoff, box 122, SG Trip July 26 to Aug. 6, 1960, United Nations and Related Files, AWCP.

213 Aside from a hastily: Olver, "Under Fire with Dag Hammarskjöld," 50.

213 Lumumba was still: Kalb, *Congo Cables,* 58.

213 Moise Tshombe had sent: "On-Scene in 'Rebel' Katanga," *Newsweek,* Aug. 8, 1960, 36–37.

213 Most important: Kennes and Larmer, *Katangese Gendarmes,* 467; Gérard-Libois, *Katanga Secession,* 114.

214 Meanwhile, the region: "The Secessionists," *Newsweek,* Aug. 1, 1960, 38–39.

214 "This is not the Congo": "On-Scene in 'Rebel' Katanga," 36–37.

214 But he pleaded: Report on meeting between Hammarskjöld and Congolese Government, Aug. 5, 1960, box 160, AWCP; Kanza, *Rise and Fall,* 246.

214 "We must act with": AP, "Congo Leaders Demand Swift Action Against Katanga by U.N.," *St. Louis Post-Dispatch,* July 30, 1960.

214 "men of real integrity": Bunche to Hammarskjöld, draft report, Aug. 6, 1960, box 141, DHC.

214 "I must confess": Hammarskjöld to Wigny, July 29, 1960, box 141, DHC.

214 At a dinner: Urquhart, *Hammarskjold,* 411; Mboka, "Kinshasa 2019—Where Does a New President Lay His Head?"; von Horn, *Soldiering for Peace,* 181–82; "On-Scene in 'Rebel' Katanga," 36.

215 Another evening, it: Urquhart, *Hammarskjold,* 411–12; Mboka, "Leopoldville 1954s—Restaurant Scene Develops," *Kinshasa Then and Now* (blog), June 28, 2011; Kanza, *Rise and Fall,* 247.

215 "In this delightful": Cordier and Foote, *Public Papers,* 5:51.

215 The food was: Merriam, *Congo,* 231.

215 "Excellency, must I": CRISP, *Congo 1960,* 2:615.

215 Blouin, who had: Blouin, *My Country, Africa,* 260; "The Female Touch," *Time,* Aug. 15, 1960, 23; AP, "Congo Leader Says U.N. Has Fallen Down on Job," *Orangeburg (S.C.) Times and Democrat,* Aug. 1, 1960; Urquhart, *Hammarskjold,* 412.

216 "History can enchain": Cordier and Foote, *Public Papers,* 5:51–52. I have taken the liberty of cleaning up the puncutation and translation.

216 "Belgium considers itself": Hammarskjöld to Cordier, Aug. 2, 1960 (B304), box 155, DHC.

217 The UN had neither: Urquhart, *Hammarskjold,* 409.

217 But might it instead: Message for oral presentation addressed to Wigny, Aug. 1, 1960, box 141, DHC.

217 "Only about two weeks": Statement by Hammarskjöld to Commission of the Council of Ministers, Aug. 2, 1960, box 160, AWCP.

218 "delighted": Bunche to Hammarskjöld, Aug. 5, 1960, box 132, DHC.

218 "general uprising in": J. van den Bosch to Hammarskjöld, Aug. 3, 1960, box 160, AWCP; AP, "U.N. Troops Will Have to Fight Their Way In, Tshombe Declares," *Hanover (Pa.) Evening Sun,* Aug. 3, 1960.

218 The Belgians, despite: Harry Gilroy, "Belgium Cautions U.N. to Stay Out of Congo Politics," *NYT,* Aug. 4, 1960. See also *FRUS, 1958–1960,* vol. 14, doc. 163.

218 Lumumba would be: Hammarskjöld to Cordier, Aug. 3, 1960 (B317), box 155, DHC.

218 "The bad appendix": Hammarskjöld to Cordier, Aug. 4, 1960 (341, 342), box 141, DHC.

22. Simba

219 "So much, and": Ralph J. Bunche to Ruth Bunche, Aug. 1, 1960, box 480, folder 11, RJBP.

219 Bunche was days away: Dayal, *Mission,* 13. Bunche was born in 1903, not 1904, even though he himself came to use 1904. The confusion stemmed from the inscription in a family Bible. See Urquhart, *Ralph Bunche,* 25n.

219 His sojourn in: F. T. Liu to Joan Liu, Aug. 1, 1960, Liu Letters. Liu wrote, "I think Ralph wants to leave as soon as possible."

219 A blood clot: Urquhart, *Ralph Bunche,* 38; Ralph J. Bunche to Ruth Bunche, Aug. 8, 1960, box 480, folder 11, RJBP.

219 More troubling was: Urquhart, *Ralph Bunche,* 290.

219 Bunche found that fresh: Urquhart, *Life in Peace and War,* 148.

219 "There has been": Ralph J. Bunche to Ruth Bunche, Aug. 1, 1960.

219 "modalities for the": Hammarskjöld to Bunche, Aug. 3, 1960, box 141, DHC.

220 "Will report soonest": Urquhart, *Ralph Bunche,* 322.

220 Bunche and eight: Bunche to Hammarskjöld, n.d., box 1a2, DHC; Ralph J. Bunche to Ruth Bunche, Aug. 4, 1960, box 480, folder 11, RJBP; Ralph J. Bunche's notes, Aug. 4, 1960, box 15, folder 11, BUC.

220 "This is being": Ralph J. Bunche to Ruth Bunche, Aug. 4, 1960.

220 "Thank heaven, *no*": Bunche to Hammarskjöld, Aug. 4, 1960, box 1a2, DHC.

220 Should the UN: AP, "Bunche Gets Katanga Snub," *Capital Times* (Madison, Wis.), Aug. 4, 1960. My account of Bunche's meeting with the diplomats comes from Bunche to Hammarskjöld, Aug. 4, 1960, box 141, DHC. They were driven to the Sabena Guest House, according to Bunche's summary. For information on the hotel, see Tourist Bureau for the Belgian Congo & Ruanda-Urundi, *Traveller's Guide,* 324.

221 Tshombe, who preferred: "On-Scene in 'Rebel' Katanga," 36–37; "Katanga v. the World," *Time,* Aug. 15, 1960, 21.

221 "An instrument of": Bunche, addendum to report, Aug. 5, 1960, box 141, DHC.

221 Tshombe mimed the: Bunche to Hammarskjöld, Aug. 4, 1960, box 141, DHC.

221 Tshombe's interior minister: Artigue, *Qui sont les leaders,* 237. For more on Munongo, see Debruyn, "The Strong Man of Katanga."

221 "riddle your soldiers": Davister, *Katanga,* 120.

221 To that end: "Katanga v. the World."

221 Munongo, for one: Urquhart, *Hammarskjold,* 418–19.

221 "There were egotism": Ian Berendsen, "Bunche's Mission to Elisabethville," draft of "History of the UN in the Congo," box 15, folder 4, BUC.

221 Tshombe falsely announced: AP, "Premier Talks with Bunche," *Boston Globe,* Aug. 4, 1960, 1.

222 But this caused: Urquhart, *Hammarskjold,* 418–19.

222 "I am still not": Report from Elisabethville, Bunche to Hammarskjöld, Aug. 4, 1960, box 141, DHC.

222 The next morning: My description of the airport incident comes from Bunche to Cordier, Aug. 6, 1960 (B377), box 132, DHC; Ralph J. Bunche, "Tight Spots and Close Calls," box 16, folder 4, BUC; Davister, *Katanga,* 151–53.

222 These were the: AP, "Katanga Doubts U.N. to Use Troops," *Titusville (Pa.) Herald,* Aug. 5, 1960, 1.

222 "wild with excitement": Bunche to Cordier, Aug. 6, 1960 (B377).

223 "We're going to": "Warriors—and Lions," *Newsweek,* Aug. 15, 1960, 32–33.

223 But Munongo insisted: Fortunately, Munongo did not find the blue helmets,

rifles, and submachine guns that were in fact on board. "Some fool in Leopoldville had permitted arms to be stored on the plane," Bunche recalled. Bunche addendum to report, Aug. 4, 1960, box 141, DHC; Bunche, "Tight Spots and Close Calls."

223 "Tell your boss": "Warriors—and Lions."

223 "Reporting fully": Bunche to Hammarskjöld, n.d., box 1a2, DHC.

223 "I think it": Bunche's report from Elisabethville, Aug. 4, 1960, box 141, DHC.

223 "Katanga had no": Bunche, *Ralph J. Bunche,* 198.

223 The Katangan army: Kennes and Larmer, *Katangese Gendarmes,* 46.

223 Tshombe's sway over: Gérard-Libois, *Katanga Secession,* 67. For one critical analysis of Bunche's decision, see Nzongola-Ntalaja, "Ralph Bunche, Patrice Lumumba," 153–54.

223 "One little breath": "On-Scene in 'Rebel' Katanga," 36–37.

224 "in very deep": Urquhart, *Hammarskjold,* 420.

224 From Ghana, Kwame Nkrumah: Cordier and Foote, *Public Papers,* 5:67, 69.

224 "The difficulties of": Fursenko and Naftali, *Khrushchev's Cold War,* 310.

224 In reaction to: "Quiet Man in a Hot Spot," *Time,* Aug. 22, 1960, 19.

224 In a sign: "'We Will Fight to Keep Them Out,'" *Newsweek,* Aug. 15, 1960, 31. The meeting ended up being postponed to Monday, August 8, so that Congolese representatives could participate.

224 "The Congo problem": UN Security Council, 884th Meeting, S/PV.884 (Aug. 8, 1960), 4.

224 By the end: UN Security Council, 886th Meeting, S/PV.886 (Aug. 8/9, 1960), 55; Thomas J. Hamilton, "Belgium Pressed; Resolution Calls for Immediate Pull-Out—Province Assured," *NYT,* Aug. 9, 1960.

225 "make the present": *FRUS, 1958–1960,* vol. 14, doc. 169.

225 It would be: Kalb, *Congo Cables,* 45.

23. The Long Way Home

226 "try a bit of": *EP,* 113.

226 From London, it: "Lumumba Stops in Tunisia," *NYT,* Aug. 4, 1960; Kanza, *Rise and Fall,* 98.

226 "Africa is not opposed": AP, "Lumumba Opens Visit in Tunis," *Corpus Christi Times,* Aug. 3, 1960.

226 At a champagne reception: Thomas F. Brady, "Aid Outside U.N. Is Goal," *NYT,* Aug. 7, 1960; Kanza, *Rise and Fall,* 249–50.

227 Then it was off to: AP, "Lumumba Ouster Demanded," *Detroit Free Press,* Aug. 8, 1960.

227 In Togo, Sylvanus Olympio: Eisenhower, *Waging Peace,* 582–83.

227 The two leaders approved: "Nkrumah Agrees to Aid Lumumba," *NYT,* Aug. 9, 1960; Thompson, *Ghana's Foreign Policy,* 125.

227 "My voyage across": Bunche to Hammarskjöld, Aug. 6, 1960 (B372), box 155, DHC. Bunche had received a copy of this cable and passed it to Hammarsk-

jöld. He got Olongo's name wrong, calling him Obongo Medar. See Omasombo and Verhaegen, *Acteur,* 125–26.

227 His wife, Pauline Opango: The child of Lumumba and Alphonsine Masuba, Guy-Patrice Lumumba, was born April 7, 1961, according to an interview he gave to *La Conscience* in 2004: Guy-Patrice Lumumba, "Guy Lumumba," interview by Dr. Tumba Tutu-De-Mukose, *La Conscience,* Nov. 5, 2004. (I was alerted to this interview by Bouwer, *Gender and Decolonization.*) If one assumes a normal-length gestation, Guy-Patrice would have been conceived around the time of independence. The relationship between Lumumba and Alphonsine Masuba started at the beginning of 1960. See Omasombo and Verhaegen, *Jeunesse,* 141. Alphonsine Masuba was also known as Alphonsine Batamba.

228 As a little girl: Juliana Lumumba, interview.

228 "Premier Patrice Lumumba": Harry Gilroy, "Belgium Weighs Its Future Role in the Congo," *NYT,* Aug. 7, 1960.

228 Rebuking Lumumba's absenteeism: McKown, *Lumumba,* 142.

228 In Leopoldville, shops: "Congo: Where's the War?," 30; Rouch, *En cage,* 81.

228 The mining royalties: Gérard-Libois, *Katanga Secession,* 115.

228 "Well, there is": Hellström, *Instant Air Force,* 4.

228 "Lumumba's Congo was": "Congo: Where's the War?," 30.

229 Members of his own: Joint Chiefs of Staff Situation Report, July 28, 1960, box 3, Congo Situation Reports, International Series, Office of the Staff Secretary: Records, 1952–61, DDEL; "Mr. Detwiler's Contract Repudiated," *Guardian,* July 27, 1960; *EP,* 104.

229 Lumumba had put: Kanza, *Rise and Fall,* 255.

229 "I'm not kept": CRISP, *Congo 1960,* 2:655. Kasavubu made the same complaint to Andrew Cordier. See Cordier OH, 509.

229 Despite his years: Young, *Politics in the Congo,* 325, 386.

229 Bunche, who was: Bunche to Hammarskjöld, Aug. 7, 1960 (317), box 155, DHC.

229 One rock beaned: "Lumumba Fought," *NYT,* Aug. 9, 1960; AP, "Quell Congo Riots," *Rutland Daily Herald,* Aug. 11, 1960; Thomas F. Brady, "Lumumba Reported Hurt by Angry African Crowd," *NYT,* Aug. 11, 1960; "Troops Out in Leopoldville After Riots," *Birmingham Post,* Aug. 11, 1960.

229 "become a martyr": Memorandum of telephone conversation, Herter and Gordon Gray, July 22, 1960, box 13, CAH Telephone Calls, Herter Papers, DDEL.

229 Worried about the: Olver to Fieldservice, Aug. 11, 1960 (359), box 155, DHC; Fieldservice to Omnipress London, Aug. 11, 1960, box 155, DHC.

229 "We are victorious!": Davister, *Katanga,* 117.

229 In Leopoldville province: AP, "Second Congo Unit Splits Off," *Springfield Leader and Press,* Aug. 8, 1960.

230 "incompetence in the": CRISP, *Congo 1960,* 2:801. The quoted comments were said on August 9 in Elisabethville. On August 8, however, the secession had been decided, and a statement had been written for the *Courrier d'Afrique* (which appeared on August 9).

230 The region exported: "The Many Lands of Congo," *Time,* Aug. 22, 1960, 21.

230 "The army will": Lumumba, *Lumumba Speaks,* 322; Reuters, "Turnabout by Rebel Premier; Congo in State of Emergency," *Saskatoon Star-Phoenix,* Aug. 9, 1960.

230 Attending the meeting: Lumumba, *Lumumba Speaks,* 339–40.

230 Not long after: "Lumumba Takes a Pummelling," *Guardian,* Aug. 11, 1960.

230 The editor of: Thomas F. Brady, "Congo Press a Target," *NYT,* Aug. 12, 1960.

230 "You do not win": Lumumba, *Lumumba Speaks,* 81.

231 "Lumumba is going": Ibid., 337.

231 The second late-night: Kanza, *Rise and Fall,* 258.

231 "In the entire": Lumumba, *Lumumba Speaks,* 310.

231 "I see that the": CRISP, *Congo 1960,* 2:607–608.

231 Earlier that day: Bunche to Cordier, Aug. 9, 1960, box 132, DHC; Mboka, "Leopoldville 1950s—Tropical Modernism Sets the Tone"; "Envoy Is Thrown Out," *Kansas City Times,* Aug. 10, 1960.

24. Operation L. Suggestions

232 The prime minister's office: The description of Lumumba's office and press conferences comes from Michel, *Uhuru Lumumba,* 59, 100–101, 112–18; Urquhart, *Life in Peace and War,* 154; Scott, *Tumbled House,* 78; Blouin, *My Country, Africa,* 264; Carlucci OH, 8; Thomas F. Hardy, "Lumumba Accuses West," *NYT,* Aug. 12, 1960; François Lumumba, interview.

233 He saw personally: Rupp, *Serge Michel,* 60.

233 At one point that: Michel, *Uhuru Lumumba,* 199–200.

233 "The Congo made me": Hoskyns, *Congo Since Independence,* 188.

233 Some who met: For more on the rumors of Lumumba's drug use, see De Vos, *Vie et mort,* 221; Scott, *Tumbled House,* 78; Hoskyns, *Congo Since Independence,* 188; Urquhart, *Hammarskjold,* 439; Legum's introduction in Lumumba, *Congo, My Country,* xv; Mahoney, *JFK,* 39; Linnér OH, 10–11; *FRUS, 1958–1960,* vol. 14, doc. 180; Cordier to Schwalm, Aug. 18, 1960, box 47, AWCP. Mobutu would come to make this allegation, too. See Paul Hofmann, "Lumumba Bounces Back," *NYT,* Oct. 16, 1960.

233 the president so opposed: Stanley Meisler, "Federal Narcotics Czar," *The Nation,* Feb. 20, 1960.

233 No one had any: Rupp, *Serge Michel,* 60.

233 Lumumba was desperately: Alvarez, *Lumumba; ou, L'Afrique frustrée,* 121.

233 "Communist advisers who": *FRUS, 1958–1960,* vol. 14, doc. 182.

233 "a growing coterie": "The Edge of Anarchy," *Time,* Aug. 29, 1960, 20.

234 "Most Western diplomats": "Red Tinge in Black Africa," *U.S. News & World Report,* Aug. 29, 1960, 29.

234 "Madame Blouin!": Margaret Anderson, "Pan-African Women's Leader Said Congo's Most Dangerous," *Asbury Park Press* (Neptune, N.J.), July 27, 1960.

234 "various high-placed": Kalb, *Congo Cables,* 50.

234 "Madame du Barry": Dayal, *Mission*, 87.

234 Blouin denied these: Blouin, *My Country, Africa*, 214.

234 And for all the: Weissman, *American Foreign Policy*, 261.

234 Despite being chief: Blouin, *My Country, Africa*, 264.

234 "Would you walk": Rouch, *En cage*, 23–24. Another group calling regularly was Ghana's diplomatic delegation in Leopoldville. Bunche complained to Hammarskjöld about the Ghanaians' access: "Almost every time I go to see him, the Ghana Ambassador, who is a fool but dangerous, is just leaving with his bizarre entourage of Ghana police with tommy guns, soldiers and fellows bare-shouldered in Kente cloth toggs." His fears were misplaced. Even though nonaligned Ghana had been warming up to the Soviet Union, its diplomats—to the extent they influenced Lumumba—were moderating, not radicalizing, his views. Bunche to Hammarskjöld, July 20, 1960 (19), box 155, DHC. See also Nkrumah, *Challenge of the Congo*, 32.

234 "Who are all": "Congo, Congo, Toil and Trouble," *Newsweek*, Aug. 29, 1960, 36.

234 Born Lucien Douchet: Information on Michel comes from Rupp, *Serge Michel*, 13, 27, 34, 62; Hoskyns, *Congo Since Independence*, 188–89; Catherine Simon, "Serge Michel," *Le Monde*, June 27, 1997; "Edge of Anarchy"; Devlin, *Chief of Station*, 53. See also Timberlake to Herter, Aug. 22, 1960, file 310, Conference of Independent African States (CIAS) Classified, Security-Segregated Records, U.S. Embassy Leopoldville, RG 94, NACP. In the same document, perhaps thanks to confusion Michel deliberately sowed, U.S. diplomats confuse Michel for Michel Rouzé, the pseudonym of Michel Kokoczynski, a Polish-born Frenchman who worked as a newspaper editor in Algeria.

235 "wanderer through": Willame, *La crise congolaise revisitée*, 229.

235 Too punctilious for: *FRUS, 1958–1960*, vol. 14, doc. 182; Willame, *La crise congolaise revisitée*, 226, 227.

235 A firebrand with: Artigue, *Qui sont les leaders*, 139.

235 "a virtual communist": Timberlake, "First Year of Independence in the Congo," 65–66.

235 in fact, Kashamura: "Analytical Chronology of the Congo Crisis," 31.

235 During the roundtable: Gizenga, *Ma vie et mes luttes*, 137–43.

235 He advocated an: Kashamura, *De Lumumba*, 66; Herter to Timberlake, July 17, 1960, file 350, Congo July–Aug. 1960 Classified, Security-Segregated Records, U.S. Embassy Leopoldville, RG 84, NACP.

235 "just as bad": Ralph J. Bunche to Ruth Bunche, Aug. 8, 1960, box 480, folder 11, RJBP.

235 Yet even Gizenga: Weissman, *American Foreign Policy*, 272; Draft text, "The Congo and United Nations," Oct. 5, 1960, box 52, Drafts: Belgian Congo, Eleanor Lansing Dulles Papers, 1880–1973, DDEL.

236 At one point: *FRUS, 1958–1960*, vol. 14, doc. 167.

236 "the easiest thing": Kanza, *Rise and Fall*, 274.

236 Mobutu was now: Monheim, *Mobutu*, 106.

236 "Hold on to": Mobutu and Remilleux, *Dignité pour l'Afrique*, 53.

236 When UN officers seized: Monheim, *Mobutu*, 107.

236 "Belgium and the": Lumumba, *Lumumba Speaks*, 329–30; CRISP, *Congo 1960*, 2:603.

236 As early as July 13: *EP*, 81, 98; Gerard and Kuklick, *Death in the Congo*, 37.

237 "Any rallying of": CRISP, *Congo 1960*, 2:740. D'Aspremont had had it in for Lumumba ever since the Congolese leader dominated the roundtable at the beginning of 1960. In March, he had told Gaston Eyskens, the Belgian prime minister, "The man to eliminate is Lumumba." Omasombo and Verhaegen, *Acteur*, 172. In August, d'Aspremont argued, "It is pointless, I would even say childish, to imagine that we could ever get anything out of a Congo dominated by Lumumba and his gang." Eyskens promised complete political cover. *EP*, 95, 100–101.

237 "overthrow and liquidation": Ibid., 104–108.

237 As laid out in: Ibid., 128–29.

237 "As you can see": Lumumba, *Lumumba Speaks*, 317–18.

25. Changing the Scenery

239 Back in Leopoldville: Testimony of Victor Hedgeman, Aug. 21, 1975, 9, 157-10014-10080, JFKAR; Devlin, *Chief of Station*, 59.

239 "The embassy and station": *FRUS, 1964–1968*, vol. 23, doc. 8.

239 "unscrupulous and untrustworthy": Timberlake, "First Year of Independence in the Congo," 184.

239 "moving steadily toward": *FRUS, 1958–1960*, vol. 14, doc. 172.

239 "Have you heard": Timberlake to Pool, Sept. 7, 1960, box 1, folder 17, CTP.

239 "a cheap embezzler": "Bulletin," *National Review*, Aug. 20, 1960, 1.

240 "We wondered whether": Summary of Douglas Dillon interview, Aug. 28, 1975, 157-10014-10178, JFKAR.

240 "a program of reinsurance": *FRUS, 1958–1960*, vol. 14, doc. 160.

240 The subject came up: *AAP*, 54.

240 Its plan began: Paul Springer to Timberlake, Aug. 9, 1960, file 350, Congo July–Aug. 1960 Classified, Security-Segregated Records, U.S. Embassy Leopoldville, RG 84, NACP.

241 But like Springer: *FRUS, 1964–1968*, vol. 23, doc. 8; Timberlake to Herter, Aug. 8, 1960, file 350, Congo July–Aug. 1960 Classified, Security-Segregated Records, U.S. Embassy Leopoldville, RG 84, NACP.

241 "Although we believe": *FRUS, 1964–1968*, vol. 23, doc. 8.

241 "might breed more": Ibid., doc. 9.

241 "more or less neutral": *FRUS, 1958–1960*, vol. 14, doc. 173.

241 "replace the Lumumba": "Covert Military Operations in the Congo, 1964–1967."

242 "a new leader": "Campaign of 1960," JFKL; "Richard Nixon for President 1960 Campaign Brochure 'Why America Needs Richard Nixon,'" www.4president .org.

242 He had developed: For Kennedy's trip to Asia and its effect on his thinking, see Logevall, *JFK*, 491–97.

242 His endorsement of: Mahoney, *JFK*, 20; "Secretary Dulles' News Conference of July 2, 1957," *Department of State Bulletin,* July 22, 1957, 143; "Foreign Relations: Burned Hands Across the Sea," *Time,* July 15, 1957.

242 "harm in our": Acheson, *Power and Diplomacy,* 126.

242 When visiting Washington: Mahoney, *JFK*, 22–23.

242 In 1958, Kennedy: Kanza, *Rise and Fall,* 214; John D. Leonard, "International Seminar," *Harvard Crimson,* July 24, 1958.

242 The next year, Kennedy: Mahoney, *JFK,* 28. When Ahmed Sékou Touré of Guinea visited California, the senator made it a priority to meet him, hiring a helicopter so he could fly from Los Angeles to Disneyland, where the two leaders exchanged views at the amusement park's replica city hall. "Kennedy 'Reluctant' to Enter State Primary," *Los Angeles Times,* Nov. 2, 1959; Robert Healy, "Sen. Kennedy Shows Savvy," *Boston Daily Globe,* Nov. 2, 1959; Morrow OH, 33.

242 "The word is out": Mahoney, *JFK,* 28; "Remarks of Senator John F. Kennedy, at a Conference of the American Society of African Culture, New York City, June 28, 1959," JFKL.

243 Nixon, for his: Russell Baker, "Nixon Leaves Today for Tour of Africa," *NYT,* Feb. 28, 1957; AP, "Nixon Returns from Africa," *Danville (Va.) Bee,* March 22, 1957; Mahoney, *JFK,* 28; *FRUS, 1955–1957,* vol. 18, doc. 129.

243 Nixon returned alarmed: Ibid., doc. 19; *Department of State Bulletin,* April 22, 1957, 635–40.

243 "animal-like charm": Gary J. Bass, "The Terrible Cost of Presidential Racism," *NYT,* Sept. 3, 2020. For the tape, see "Conversation 525-001," audio recorded June 17, 1971, at Oval Office, White House Tapes, Richard Nixon Presidential Museum & Library, www.nixonlibrary.gov.

243 "the forces of freedom": *Department of State Bulletin,* April 22, 1957, 635.

243 "more interested in": "Remarks of Senator John F. Kennedy at a Conference of the American Society of African Culture, New York City, June 28, 1959."

243 Kennedy's support for: Mahoney, *JFK,* 26; "Michigan Seems on Kennedy Side," *NYT,* June 6, 1960. For another version of Williams's endorsement, see White, *Making of the President,* 137–39.

243 An August poll: "Nixon Leading Kennedy; Opinions Fluid, Could Change," *Daily Oklahoman,* Aug. 17, 1960; White, *Making of the President,* 250.

243 White southern Democrats: White, *Making of the President,* 251.

243 Meanwhile, Kennedy's centrist: Mahoney, *JFK,* 30; Schlesinger, *Thousand Days,* 66. In the end, Kennedy managed to convince Black voters that he was more aggressive in his support for civil rights, while white voters considered his record similar to Nixon's. See Russell Middleton, "The Civil Rights Issue and Presidential Voting Among Southern Negroes and Whites," *Social Forces* 40, no. 3 (1962): 209–15.

26. Sound and Fury

244 Eventually known as: On the Congo Club, see Cordier OH, 304–305; Urquhart, *Hammarskjold,* 473; and O'Brien, *To Katanga and Back,* 50–54.

244 Dinner would be: Cable to Mr. Tooni, May 8, 1961, and cable to David Vaughan, June 9, 1961, box 58, AWCP.

244 "Late every evening": Dayal, *Mission,* 12–23.

245 "shadow government": Cordier OH, 510.

245 "The so-called ministers": Thompson, *Ghana's Foreign Policy,* 134.

245 On the military: Joint Chiefs of Staff Situation Report, Aug. 10, 1960, box 3, Congo Situation Reports, International Series, Office of the Staff Secretary: Records, 1952–61, DDEL.

245 The UN operation: Philip C. Clarke, "Strangest Army: 'They Show the Blue and White,'" *Newsweek,* Sept. 5, 1960, 35; UN General Assembly, "Budget for the Financial Year 1960," A/4353 (1960), 9.

245 The United States chipped: U.S. Congress, "United States Contributions to International Organizations. Letter from the Acting Secretary of State Transmitting the Ninth Report on the Extent and Disposition of U.S. Contributions for Fiscal Year 1960. H Doc. 222," Aug. 10, 1961, 66.

245 Joining the initial: "First Progress Report to the Secretary-General from His Special Representative in the Congo, Ambassador Rajeshwar Dayal," S/4531 (Sept. 21, 1960), annex 1, 6. I have excluded Australia from my count since it had not contributed any troops at that point.

245 Mechanics eventually had: Bowman and Fanning, "Logistics Problems of a UN Military Force," 374.

245 Each contingent was: Clarke, "Strangest Army," 35–36; Lefever, *Crisis in the Congo,* 147.

245 The Canadians insisted: Spooner, *Canada,* 73.

245 Muslim troops refused: Bowman and Fanning, "Logistics Problems of a UN Military Force," 374.

246 He was regularly: Raustiala, *Absolutely Indispensable Man,* 412; Urquhart, *Ralph Bunche,* 250.

246 To compensate for: On the incident, see Urquhart, *Ralph Bunche,* 316; Cordier OH, 113, 193. On Potrubatch, see AP, "Lumumba Asks U.N. Chief to Set Belgian Deadline," *Baltimore Sun,* July 26, 1960.

246 In the best: Berendsen OH, 6; Linnér OH, 17.

246 Some messages, sent: See, for example, Bunche to Hammarskjöld, Aug. 18, 1960 (B525), box 155, DHC.

246 That caused its: Spooner, *Canada,* 74.

246 Bunche clashed constantly: "Peace-Keeping General Carl Carlsson von Horn," *NYT,* July 18, 1960; Von Horn, *Soldiering for Peace,* 196–99; Urquhart, *Ralph Bunche,* 316.

246 "He was a": Rikhye OH, 6–7.

247 This time, Hammarskjöld: Ian Berendsen, "Arrangements for the Entry of United Nation Troops into Katanga," draft of "History of the UN in the Congo," box 15, folder 4, BUC.

247 "break the logjam": Telephone calls of the Secretary of State, Aug. 10, 1960, box 13, CAH Telephone Calls, Herter Papers, DDEL.

247 "Moises's ten commandments": Davister, *Katanga,* 154.

247 Feeling that his: Hammarskjöld to Bunche, Aug. 10, 1960 (807), box 16, folder 2, BUC.

247 "in uniform but": Cordier and Foote, *Public Papers,* 5:83.

248 "And so": Bunche to Cordier, Aug. 12, 1960, box 160, AWCP.

248 Editorial pages praised: "United Nations: Quiet Man in a Hot Spot." *Time,* Aug. 22, 1960, 18.

248 "This remarkable man": James Reston, "United Nations; A Refuge of Sanity in a Silly World," *NYT,* Aug. 10, 1960.

248 "any internal conflict": Cordier and Foote, *Public Papers,* 5:85.

248 The process took: Urquhart, *Life in Peace and War,* 160.

248 Staying behind in: Schedule for July to Sept. 1960, box 15, folder 5, BUC.

248 "verged on rage": Details of this meeting come from Bunche to Cordier, Aug. 12, 1960 (B433), box 155, DHC; Notes on conversation between Lumumba and Bunche, Aug. 12, 1960, box 141, DHC; Urquhart, *Ralph Bunche,* 327; Schedule for July to Sept. 1960.

249 "We'd have a real": Ralph J. Bunche to Ruth Bunche, Aug. 8, 1960, box 480, folder 11, RJBP.

249 As Bunche dealt with: My description of Hammarskjöld's arrival in Elisabethville draws on Davister, *Katanga,* 151–53; "Congo: Tribal Warfare," 39; Henry Tanner, "U.N. Troops Enter Katanga in Face of New Defiance," *NYT,* Aug. 13, 1960; "Dag Lands After Mixup over Troops," *Wisconsin State Journal* (Madison), Aug. 13, 1960; George Clay, "Jeers at U.N. Troops Please Belgians," *Observer,* Aug. 14, 1960; Urquhart, *Hammarskjold,* 426; "Quiet Man in a Hot Spot," 18; Cordier and Foote, *Public Papers,* 5:88–89; Hoskyns, *Congo Since Independence,* 172; Cordier OH, 505; Berendsen, "Arrangements for the Entry of United Nation Troops into Katanga"; Rikhye OH, 142–43.

250 "It seemed entirely": Urquhart, *Hammarskjold,* 427.

250 "an act out of": Rikhye, *Military Adviser,* 143.

250 "Children of Katanga": S. E. Joseph Kiwele, "La Katangaise," nationalanthems .info, recorded 1960, audio, nationalanthems.info/kat.htm. The anthem was composed by the province's minister of education, Joseph Kiwele. See Artigue, *Qui sont les leaders,* 160.

250 "There it is": Davister, *Katanga: Enjeu du monde,* 152.

250 In negotiations held: Colvin, *Moise Tshombe,* 18; "Dag Gets Hostile Reception in Katanga, Sees Tshombe," *New York Daily News,* Aug. 13, 1960.

250 Among other assurances: Hoskyns, *Congo Since Independence,* 172.

251 The Belgian government: Gérard-Libois, *Katanga Secession*, 113.

251 Soon, four thousand: Von Horn, *Soldiering for Peace*, 189.

251 The departing Belgian: Hoskyns, *Congo Since Independence*, 173.

251 Tshombe had purged: Kennes and Larmer, *Katangese Gendarmes*, 46–47; De Witte, *Assassination*, 63.

251 In fact, without: Urquhart, *Hammarskjold*, 428.

251 "preserving the de facto": De Witte, *Assassination*, 13.

251 "The president of": Davister, *Katanga: Enjeu du monde*, 157.

252 "He is recklessly": Bunche to Hammarskjöld, Aug. 13, 1960, box 16, folder 2, BUC.

252 "Belgians in disguise": Press report, "Radio Speeches on the Congolese National Radio," Aug. 13, 1960, box 132, DHC.

252 He seemed to be: Lumumba, *Lumumba Speaks*, 330–31.

252 "How can you": Michel, *Uhuru Lumumba*, 111.

252 was a "breakthrough": Hammarskjöld to Cordier, Aug. 15, 1960 (B472), box 155, DHC.

252 "Returned from Elisabethville": Hammarskjöld to Cordier, Aug. 14, 1960 (B452), box 155, DHC.

252 "We shall see": Hammarskjöld to Cordier, Aug. 15, 1960 (B466), box 155, DHC.

252 He would have preferred: Lumumba, *Lumumba Speaks*, 333; Timberlake to Herter, Aug. 8, 1960, file 350, Congo July–Aug. 1960 Classified, Security-Segregated Records, U.S. Embassy Leopoldville, RG 84, NACP.

253 "you are acting as": For the letters, see UN Secretary-General, "Second Report on the Implementation of Security Council Resolution S/4387 of 14 July 1960 and S/4405 of 22 July 1960: Addendum No. 7," S/4417 (Aug. 15, 1960).

253 "For an ex–post office": "Edge of Anarchy."

253 Some thought they: Thomas J. Hamilton, "Moscow Trips Up on Gift to Congo," *NYT,* Aug. 20, 1960. In an August 18 NSC meeting, Douglas Dillon said that Hammarskjöld believed Lumumba's letters were written by "a Belgian communist who is Lumumba's chief of cabinet." The ideological label notwithstanding, this description fits Grootaert. Jean Terfve and Albert de Coninck had not yet arrived in the Congo. See *FRUS, 1958–1960*, vol. 14, doc. 180, and Freeman to State, Aug. 20, 1960 (229), file 350, Congo July–Aug. 1960 Classified, Security-Segregated Records, U.S. Embassy Leopoldville, RG 84, NACP.

253 Another theory had: "Congo, Congo, Toil and Trouble," 35.

253 "Western sources said": Thomas J. Hamilton, "Soviet Hand Seen in Congo Protest," *NYT,* Aug. 17, 1960.

254 "illustration of political": Hammarskjöld to Cordier, Aug. 15, 1960 (B460), box 155, DHC.

254 "brought out the cold": Urquhart, *Life in Peace and War*, 161.

254 "failed to comprehend": Quaison-Sackey, *Africa Unbound*, 170.

254 Strictly speaking, the: Cordier and Foote, *Public Papers*, 5:105.

254 "that famous Monday": Lash, *Dag Hammarskjöld*, 238.

254 "could be harsh": Urquhart, *Hammarskjold*, 35.

NOTES

255 "In this game": Hammarskjöld to Cordier, Aug. 15, 1960 (B472).

255 Compared with Lumumba: "Edge of Anarchy."

255 "One or the other": Kalb, *Congo Cables,* 58, 59, 51.

27. Desperate Measures

256 He had perhaps: AP, "Soviet Envoy Pays Visit," *NYT,* July 31, 1960; Spooner, *Canada,* 58; Kanza, *Rise and Fall,* 237; "Bloc Personnel in the Congo," Sept. 9, 1960, in Namikas and Mazov, "CWIHP Conference Reader."

256 What tangible help: Joint Chiefs of Staff Situation Report, July 18, 1960, box 3, Congo Situation Reports, International Series, Office of the Staff Secretary: Records, 1952–61, DDEL; Vladimir Pardigon, "L'U.R.S.S.," in Wauters, *Le monde communiste et la crise du Congo belge,* 73; Joint Chiefs of Staff Situation Report, July 25, 1960, box 3, Congo Situation Reports, International Series, Office of the Staff Secretary: Records, 1952–61, DDEL; Bunche to Hammarskjöld, Aug. 17, 1960 (B506), box 155, DHC; Kalb, *Congo Cables,* 57–58; Mazov, *Distant Front,* 97; Iandolo, "Imbalance of Power," 41.

256 "aggression against the Congo": Kalb, *Congo Cables,* 41.

257 "friendly and unselfish": Khrushchev to Lumumba, Aug. 5, 1960, in Namikas and Mazov, "CWIHP Conference Reader."

257 "The Government of the Republic of the Congo": CRISP, *Congo 1960: Annexes et biographies,* 56. See also Houart, *La pénétration communiste,* vi.

257 "many Congolese have": Spooner, *Canada,* 73.

257 "Why? Explain to me": Namikas, *Battleground Africa,* 85.

257 "I approached the": Omasombo, *Kasaï-Oriental,* 190–91.

258 Their delegation there: Mazov, *Distant Front,* 109.

258 Alexander Shelepin, the head: Namikas, *Battleground Africa,* 86.

258 When the merchant ship *Leninogorsk*: Helmut Sonnenfeldt, "The Soviet Union and China: Where They Stood in 1960," in Kitchen, *Footnotes to the Congo Story,* 30; Snider W. Skinner, "The Agricultural Economy of the Belgian Congo and Ruanda-Urundi," Foreign Agricultural Service, U.S. Department of Agriculture, June 1960, 29.

258 The Soviet Union had no foreign: On the Soviets' limited ability to project power, see Iandolo, "Imbalance of Power," 43–44; *FRUS, 1958–1960,* vol. 14, doc. 145; Porter, *USSR in Third World Conflicts,* 43.

258 Its naval forces: The count of U.S. aircraft carriers comes from Wm. Robert Johnston, "Historical list of aircraft carriers and their fates," March 7, 2015, Johnston's Archive, www.johnstonsarchive.net.

258 The Soviet Union's meager: Kalb, *Congo Cables,* 19.

258 The hope was that this: Iandolo, "Imbalance of Power," 45.

258 But by asking for military aid: Kanza, *Rise and Fall,* 273; Houart, *La pénétration communiste,* 64.

259 "We have decided to take": Thomas F. Brady, "Lumumba Orders Rule by Military; Many Are Seized," *NYT,* Aug. 17, 1960; Kanza, *Rise and Fall,* 266.

259 That same day, Congolese: Smith to Omnipress New York, Aug. 16, 1960 (442); Smith to Cordier, Aug. 16, 1960 (443), box 132, DHC; "At the Edge of Anarchy," *Newsweek*, Sept. 5, 1960, 29.

259 "The spirit and morale": Bunche to Hammarskjöld, Aug. 16, 1960 (B491).

259 Late the next evening: Bunche to Hammarskjöld, Aug. 18, 1960 (B518), box 155, DHC; Bunche to Hammarskjöld, Aug. 18, 1960 (B520), box 155, DHC; Bunche to Hammarskjöld, Aug. 18, 1960 (B512), box 155, DHC; statement made by George Ivan, Aug. 18, 1960, box 137, DHC; Alexander, "Situation in the Congo"; *Time*, Aug. 29, 1960, 20; Urquhart, *Hammarskjold*, 432; Spooner, *Canada*, 75–76.

259 On August 18: *FRUS, 1958–1960*, vol. 14, doc. 182.

260 "We know that the U.S.": "Analytical Chronology of the Congo Crisis," 25–26.

260 At Ndjili airport, fourteen Canadian: Spooner, *Canada*, 75–79; von Horn, *Soldiering for Peace*, 194; Report from Rikhye on Aug. 18 incident, box 137, DHC; Bunche to Hammarskjöld, Aug. 19, 1960 (B527), box 155, DHC.

260 "Dear Patrice": Bunche to Hammarskjöld, Aug. 20, 1960 (B569), box 155, DHC; Nkrumah, *Challenge of the Congo*, 33; "At the Edge of Anarchy," 29.

260 "further activities may": Hammarskjöld to Security Council representatives, Aug. 18, 1960, box 137, DHC; Namikas, *Battleground Africa*, 88.

261 "The embassy and station": *FRUS, 1964–1968*, vol. 23, doc. 10.

261 After the shootdown: Thomas, *Ike's Bluff*, 385–88.

261 "I wish someone would": Ibid., 388; Memorandum, "Discussion at the 450th Meeting of the National Security Council," July 7, 1960, box 12, 452nd Meeting of NSC, NSC Series, Papers as President, 1953–61 (Whitman File), DDEL.

261 "the terrible-tempered Mr. Bang": Thomas, *Ike's Bluff*, 27, 344.

262 "destructive hurricane": Eisenhower, *Waging Peace*, 560, 572.

262 And just as he dragged: Mahoney, *JFK*, 35; Weissman, *American Foreign Policy*, 46.

262 At 9:00 a.m.: "Cabinet Room," White House Museum, www.whitehousemuseum.org; Thomas, *Ike's Bluff*, 70.

262 Each participant was given: *FRUS, 1958–1960*, vol. 14, docs. 33, 180.

262 By virtue of his big-game: "Bongo Bagger," *Ithaca (N.Y.) Journal*, Nov. 21, 1959; Peter Edson, "Budget Chief Is Bongo Hunter," *State Journal* (Lansing, Mich.), Nov. 16, 1958; Ken Ringle, "Maurice Stans, Alone," *Washington Post*, June 14, 1992. Later, as secretary of commerce during the Nixon administration, Stans would get in trouble for showing a home movie of a three-week safari in Chad. The film featured his fellow white hunters mocking a Black man who, given his first cigarette, chewed instead of smoked it. See James M. Naughton, "Controversial Commerce Chief Maurice Hubert Stans," *NYT*, Feb. 17, 1971.

263 "President Eisenhower said something": *AAP*, 55–56; testimony of Robert Johnson, June 18, 1975, 6, 157-10014-10069, JFKAR; Memorandum of conversation with Robert Johnson, June 10, 1975, 157-10014-10178, JFKAR.

263 The only written record: Gerard Smith, notes on Aug. 18, 1960, NSC meeting,

box 2, folder 2, Gerard C. Smith Series, 1957–61, John Foster Dulles Papers, 1951–1961, DDEL.

263 no "clearcut order": *AAP*, 58.

263 His son, John Eisenhower, attended: Minutes of the 456th Meeting of the National Security Council, Aug. 18, 1960, box 3, NSC Agenda and Minutes 1960, NSC Series, Office of the Special Assistant for National Security Affairs: Records, 1952–61, DDEL; Thomas, *Ike's Bluff*, 304.

264 "If Ike had": Ambrose, *Ike's Spies*, 295. Three other people at the August 18 meeting also swore that Eisenhower had never issued anything that could be interpreted as an assassination order: Gordon Gray, Andrew Goodpaster, and Marion Boggs. See *AAP*, 59, 64.

264 Having just become the first-ever: Ann Whitman's Diary, Aug. 18, 1960, box 11, ACW Diary Aug. 1960, Ann Whitman Diary Series, Papers as President of the United States, 1953–61 (Whitman File), DDEL.

28. Jungle Demagogue

265 a "showdown" with Lumumba: Hammarskjöld to Cordier, Aug. 15, 1960 (B472), box 155, DHC; F. T. Liu to Joan Liu, Aug. 19, 1960, Liu Letters; *FRUS, 1958–1960*, vol. 14, doc. 177.

265 More than one thousand: "Visitors Crowd U.N. for Session on Congo," *NYT*, Aug. 22, 1960.

265 In fact, it would take: The last troops left by September 9, according to Urquhart, *Hammarskjold*, 427.

265 "somewhat lively correspondence": Cordier and Foote, *Public Papers*, 5:105.

265 Speaking next was Antoine Gizenga: Kanza, *Rise and Fall*, 258.

266 The Soviet representative, Vasily Kuznetsov: UN Security Council, 888th Meeting, S/PV.888 (Aug. 21, 1960), 11.

266 Hammarskjöld's rebuttal was: Bunche to Hammarskjöld, Aug. 19, 1960 (B543), box 155, DHC.

266 Newspapers around the world: Bernard Dufresne, "Lumumba Apologizes for Attack on Canadians," *Kingston Whig-Standard* (Kingston, Ont.), Aug. 22, 1960; Cordier and Foote, *Public Papers*, 5:100; Thomas F. Brady, "Congo Soldiers Maul Canadians Attached to U.N.," *NYT*, Aug. 19, 1960.

266 The outcome amounted to: Urquhart, *Hammarskjold*, 434.

266 "the best of his whole career": Cordier to Schwalm, Aug. 18, 1960, box 47, AWCP. These letters were first unearthed by Carole Collins. See Carole J. L. Collins, "Cold War Comes to Africa." In a delicious twist, Collins's essay won the Andrew Wellington Cordier Prize.

266 He had been in the Congo: F. T. Liu to Joan Liu, Sept. 4, 1960, Liu Letters.

266 Reluctant to complain himself: Ralph J. Bunche to Ruth Bunche, Aug. 8, 1960, box 480, folder 11, RJBP.

267 He also wanted to return: Schedule for July to Sept. 1960, box 15, folder 5, BUC.

267 "This means so much": Bunche to Cordier, Aug. 9, 1960, box 1, AWCP.

267 "like an African": Bunche to Hammarskjöld, Aug. 24, 1960 (B603), box 155, DHC. See also Bunche to Cordier, Aug. 9, 1960, box 1, AWCP.

267 In some ways: Urquhart, *Ralph Bunche,* 330–31; Ralph J. Bunche to Ruth Bunche, Aug. 22, 1960, box 480, folder 11, RJBP.

267 "I despise Gizenga": Ralph J. Bunche to Ruth Bunche, Aug. 25, 1960, box 480, folder 11, RJBP.

267 "jungle demagogue" and "Congolese ogre": Schedule for July to Sept. 1960.

267 "I don't think I have ever": AP, "Misunderstanding Noted," *NYT,* Aug. 30, 1960; "Bunche Asserts Congo Tests in U.N.," *NYT,* Aug. 30, 1960.

267 He slumped into: Schedule July to Sept. 1960, box 15, folder 5, BUC; John Olver, "An Unexpected Challenge: Ralph Bunche as Field Commander in the Congo, 1960," in Hill and Keller, *Trustee for the Human Community,* 120.

267 "one great dream": Kanza, *Rise and Fall,* 260.

267 "a major summit conference": Lumumba, *Lumumba Speaks,* 320.

268 "perplexed and frustrated": "Congo, Congo, Toil and Trouble," 35.

268 "There is a limit to how far": Ibid.

268 After Kwame Nkrumah: Pouch to State, Sept. 2, 1960, file 310, Conference of Independent African States (CIAS) Classified, Security-Segregated Records, U.S. Embassy Leopoldville, RG 84, NACP; Thompson, *Ghana's Foreign Policy,* 137–38.

268 It ended up even less: For the number of independent countries sending delegations, see Pouch to State, Sept. 2, 1960. I counted thirteen: Cameroon, Ethiopia, Ghana, Tunisia, Guinea, Togo, Congo (Brazzaville), United Arab Republic (Egypt), Mali, Sudan, Liberia, Somalia, and Morocco. *Newsweek* counted differently, claiming, "Only nine of Africa's 23 independent nations were represented" ("At the Edge of Anarchy," 28). The two foreign ministers were those from Tunisia and Togo.

268 The Congolese organizers couldn't: Pouch to State, Sept. 2, 1960; Urquhart, *Ralph Bunche,* 332; Urquhart, *Hammarskjold,* 437.

268 Even Lumumba had difficulty: Details on the speech and riot come from *Life,* Sept. 5, 1960, 36; "Congo: Contact with Reality"; "At the Edge of Anarchy," 28–29; Thomas F. Brady, "Congolese Police Clash with Foes of Lumumba Rule," *NYT,* Aug. 26, 1960; "Riots as Lumumba Speaks," *Guardian,* Aug. 26, 1960; Michel, *Uhuru Lumumba,* 133; CRISP, *Congo 1960,* 2:667.

268 "This is our year": Lumumba, *Lumumba Speaks,* 346–47.

269 "coming into personal": Ibid., 344.

269 "Those people out there": Bunche to Hammarskjöld, Aug. 26, 1960 (B652), box 155, DHC.

269 "What do you expect?": "At the Edge of Anarchy," 28–29.

269 One of the men in the crowd: Michel, *Uhuru Lumumba,* 133; CRISP, *Congo 1960,* 2:668.

269 As part of the CIA's program: Devlin, *Chief of Station,* 58.

270 "preplanned demonstration": *FRUS, 1964–1968,* vol. 23, doc. 16.

270 But at the very hour: Lumumba arrived at 4:45 p.m. local time in Leopoldville (CRISP, *Congo 1960,* 2:666–67). The Special Group meeting began thirty minutes later, at 12:15 p.m. EST (Gray's Appointment Book, Aug. 25–26, 1960, box 2, Gordon Gray's 1960 Appointment Book, Special Assistant Series, Office of the Special Assistant for National Security Affairs: Records, DDEL).

29. The Special Group

271 The CIA's predecessor: On the Morale Operations Branch, see Clayton D. Laurie, *The Propaganda Warriors: America's Crusade Against Nazi Germany* (Lawrence: University Press of Kansas, 1996), 194. On the Office of Policy Coordination, see Gregory Mitrovich, *Undermining the Kremlin: America's Strategy to Subvert the Soviet Bloc, 1947–1956* (Ithaca, New York: Cornell University Press, 2009), 20; Ambrose, *Ike's Spies,* 297.

271 Eisenhower established the Special Group: Grose, *Gentleman Spy,* 444; Ambrose, *Ike's Spies,* 240–41, 296. The name changed from the 5412 Group to the Special Group after it "began to get some visibility in the press." Gray OH, June 25, 1975, 9. For more on the limits of the Special Group, see Leary, *Central Intelligence Agency,* 63.

272 "a group which considered": Gray OH, July 19, 1967, 270.

272 "The Special Group": Bissell to Dear, Sept. 30, 1975, box 10, Reading File Jan.–Dec. 1975, Correspondence Series, Richard M. Bissell Jr. Papers, DDEL. On Bissell's attendance, see testimony of Richard Bissell, Sept. 10, 1975, 30, 157-10014-10093, JFKAR.

272 The Special Group usually met: Gray's Appointment Book, Sept. 8–9, 1960, box 2, Gordon Gray's 1960 Appointment Book, Special Assistant Series, Office of the Special Assistant for National Security Affairs: Records, DDEL.

272 For months, Cuba had dominated: Jack B. Pfeiffer, "Official History of the Bay of Pigs Operation," vol. 3, Central Intelligence Agency, Dec. 1979, 23–24, nsarchive2.gwu.edu; *AAP,* 72, 291; Overview of subjects and actions, "NSC 5412/2 Special Group 1960," box 1, NSC 5412 Special Group Minutes and Agendas 1960, U.S. National Security Council Presidential Records, Intelligence Files, 1953–61, DDEL.

272 He made it clear that: In fact, Gray had met with Eisenhower alone that very morning, after which they both attended yet another National Security Council meeting in which Lumumba's latest antics were discussed with concern. See Gray's Appointment Book, Aug. 25–26, 1960; "Discussion at the 457th Meeting of the National Security Council," Aug. 25, 1960, box 3, 457th Meeting of NSC, NSC Series, Office of the Special Assistant for National Security Affairs: Records, 1952–61, DDEL.

272 "that his associates": *FRUS, 1964–1968,* vol. 23, doc. 12.

272 He was speaking in euphemism: *AAP,* 60.

272 Such lack of follow-through: Grose, *Gentleman Spy,* 463; Thomas, *Ike's Bluff,* 303–307.

272 "Mr. Dulles replied that": *FRUS, 1964–1968*, vol. 23, doc. 12.

273 "There isn't any doubt": Bissell OH, 19.

273 Usually, instructions to station chiefs: *AAP*, 15; Grose, *Gentleman Spy*, 502–503.

273 "In high quarters here": Testimony of Bronson Tweedy, Sept. 9, 1975, 45–46, 157-10014-10067, JFKAR; *FRUS, 1964–1968*, vol. 23, doc. 14.

273 Devlin was being handed: Reimuller, interview; Office of Personnel Management, "Rates of Pay Under the General Schedule: Effective the First Pay Period Beginning on or After July 1, 1960," available via WaybackMachine, web.archive.org.

274 "how peaceful everything": "Congo: Contact with Reality," *Time*, Sept. 5, 1960, 22; UPI, "Lumumba in Stanleyville to Prove His Popularity," *Escondido (Calif.) Daily Times-Advocate*, Aug. 27, 1960.

274 Now waiting for him: Bunche to Hammarskjöld, Aug. 29, 1960, box 137, DHC; Michel, *Uhuru Lumumba*, 147.

274 While Lumumba's plane: Details on the Stanleyville airport incident come from Bunche to Hammarskjöld, Aug. 27, 1960 (CY41), box 137, DHC; Bunche to Hammarskjöld, Aug. 28, 1960 (CY26), box 137, DHC; Bunche to Hammarskjöld, Aug. 28, 1960 (CY34), box 137, DHC; Bunche to Hammarskjöld, Aug. 29, 1960 (CY15), box 137, DHC; von Horn, *Soldiering for Peace*, 203–4; "At the Edge of Anarchy," 28; Kalb, *Congo Cables*, 68; Hoskyns, *Congo Since Independence*, 191–92; Urquhart, *Hammarskjold*, 435–36; Henry Tanner, "8 in U.S. Aircrew Beaten in Raid by Congo Troops," *NYT*, Aug. 28, 1960; Chip Bertino, "Stickevers, Kenneth," Worcester County Veterans Memorial, opvets.org.

274 "I am very happy": "Congo: Contact with Reality," *Time*, Sept. 5, 1960, 22.

274 "Hope Stanleyville incident": *FRUS, 1958–1960*, vol. 14, doc. 192, with redactions filled in by Timberlake to State, Aug. 29, 1960 (545), file 350, Congo July–Aug. 1960 Classified, Security-Segregated Records, U.S. Embassy Leopoldville, RG 84, NACP.

275 He apologized to the UN: Urquhart, *Ralph Bunche*, 332; Bunche to Hammarskjöld, Aug. 27, 1960 (B666), box 155, DHC.

275 Wiping sweat from his brow: Eugène Mannoni, "Après son voyage à Stanleyville M. Lumumba parait mesurer les dangers de la xénophobie et de l'indiscipline," *Le Monde*, Aug. 31, 1960; Rouch, *En cage*, 103; Michel, *Uhuru Lumumba*, 159.

275 At 10:00 p.m., he held: Details on and quotations from Lumumba's stadium speech come from Michel, *Uhuru Lumumba*, 151–52; Rouch, *En cage*, 103; Thomas F. Brady, "Lumumba Eases Congo 'Spy Hunt,'" *NYT*, Aug. 30, 1960; UPI, "U.S. Moves to Protest Congo Acts," *Ventura County Star* (Ventura, Calif.), Aug. 29, 1960; Michel, *Uhuru Lumumba*, 160; Rouch, *En cage*, 103.

275 "The call for fraternization": "'Le danger communiste s'accroît au Congo' estiment les milieux politiques américains," *Le Monde*, Aug. 31, 1960.

275 "Tomorrow, it's back to": Michel, *Uhuru Lumumba*, 161.

276 "was a fizzle": "At the Edge of Anarchy," 28.

276 Frantz Fanon, the Martinican psychiatrist: Macey, *Frantz Fanon*, 430; Pouch to

State, Sept. 2, 1960, file 310, Conference of Independent African States (CIAS) Classified, Security-Segregated Records, U.S. Embassy Leopoldville, RG 84, NACP.

276 His agenda for the conference: Lumumba, *Lumumba Speaks,* 344.

276 The head of the Sudanese: Bunche to Hammarskjöld, Aug. 28, 1960 (B669), box 155, DHC.

276 "Lumumba's childish behavior": "Congo: Long Way to Go," *Time,* Sept. 12, 1960, 28.

276 "calm down Lumumba": Thomas F. Brady, "Africa Nations Asking Lumumba to Support U.N.," *NYT,* Aug. 31, 1960.

276 Rather than rallying: Pouch to State, Sept. 2, 1960.

276 Listening to the tributes: "Congo," *Time,* Sept. 12, 1960, 28–30.

276 "a spirit of cooperation": Lumumba, *Patrice Lumumba,* 26–33.

30. Bakwanga

278 Early in the morning: Details on Bakwanga and the attack on it come from "Congo: Contact with Reality," *Time,* Sept. 5, 1960, 21; "At the Edge of Anarchy," 29; CRISP, *Congo 1960,* 2:801–803; Hoskyns, *Congo Since Independence,* 194; Bunche to Hammarskjöld, Aug. 31, 1960 (B687), box 155, DHC; G. C. Senn, "Trip to Bakwanga Refugee Area from 12 to 18th August," Aug. 19, 1960, B AG 280 229-063.01, ICRCA. Sources vary on the number of troops; Willame, *La crise congolaise revisitée,* 190–91, puts the figure at about a thousand.

278 Much of the indigenous population: Tourist Bureau for the Belgian Congo & Ruanda-Urundi, *Traveller's Guide,* 290.

278 The province would soon: Omasombo, *Kasaï-Oriental,* 197; "Congo Kinshasa," Hubert de Vries, www.hubert-herald.nl; "South Kasai (Democratic Republic of Congo)," Flags of the World, www.signa-fahnen.de; Stanley D. Brunn, *Stamps, Nationalism, and Political Transition* (New York: Routledge, 2023), 74.

278 And just like Tshombe: Colvin, *Moise Tshombe,* 31; Young, *Politics in the Congo,* 454; CRISP, *Congo 1960,* 2:802; Rouch, *En cage,* 118.

278 Many of the ANC troops: Cordier to Hammarskjöld, Sept. 2, 1960 (B727), box 155, DHC; Bunche to Hammarskjöld, Aug. 23, 1960 (B598), box 155, DHC; Henry Tanner, "Congo Troops Fly to Kasai to Stop Secession Effort," *NYT,* Aug. 25, 1960. Serge Michel would claim that the planes were chartered, not requisitioned. Willame, *La crise congolaise revisitée,* 190.

279 Armed with mortars: Cordier to Hammarskjöld, Sept. 2, 1960 (B727).

279 The expedition to Bakwanga: Monheim, *Mobutu,* 114. Kanza, *Rise and Fall,* 274, 283, downplays Mobutu's involvement, suggesting that he could not be trusted. See also Willame, *La crise congolaise revisitée,* 189–91. Mobutu once confided in a friendly journalist that he himself had directed the operation. "Joseph, never brag about that," the journalist advised. Brassinne and Kestergat, *Qui a tué,* 55n4.

279 "national emergency": "Congo: Contact with Reality," *Time,* Sept. 5, 1960, 21.

279 Unpaid and unfed ANC soldiers: Cordier and Foote, *Public Papers,* 5:163;

Report on trip to Luluabourg and Bakwanga, Sept. 3, 1960, B AG 280 229-063.01, ICRCA; Cordier to Hammarskjöld, Aug. 31, 1960 (B711), box 138 (4), DHC; "Currie Tells How He Got to Bakwanga," *Editor & Publisher,* Sept. 10, 1960, 11–12; "Congo: Long Way to Go," *Time,* Sept. 12, 1960, 30; Gall, *Don't Worry,* 130–42; CRISP, *Congo 1960,* 2:802–806; Omasombo, *Kasaï-Oriental,* 188–92; Cordier and Foote, *Public Papers,* 5:163; "Children Machine-Gunned in a Mission Massacre," *Sunday Times,* Sept. 4, 1960.

279 Many of the ANC troops were: Mazov, *Distant Front,* 110–11.

279 When Kalonji's fighters ambushed: Rouch, *En cage,* 115, 110; "Children Die in Congo Siege Town," *Daily Express* (London), Sept. 3, 1960.

279 Harry Taylor, a thirty-one-year-old: "Henry N. Taylor Killed Filling in for D'Lynn Waldron in Congo in Luluabourg, Belgian Congo," D'Lynn Waldon, dlwaldron.com; Higbee, *Recollections,* 416–17; "Henry Taylor Killed in Congo Tribal War," *Editor & Publisher,* Sept. 10, 1960, 11; "Henry Noble Taylor," Find a Grave, Jan. 10, 2012, www.findagrave.com; Shepard, *Forgive Us,* 228–29; "Congo Bullets Riddle Yank," *Miami News,* Sept. 16, 1960; "A Brutal Bush War and a U.S. Casualty," *Life,* Sept. 1960, 52; Rouch, *En cage,* 103–23.

280 The death toll numbered: There was no consensus on the exact number of casualties. On September 19, 1960, G. C. Senn of the Red Cross called fourteen hundred a "conservative" estimate. See ICRC Delegation in the Congo, "Information on the Situation in the Territories of Bakwanga and Gandajika," Sept. 17, 1960, B AG 280 229-063.01, ICRCA. Hammarskjöld said "hundreds." See Cordier and Foote, *Public Papers,* 5:167. Legum puts the number at three thousand. See Legum, *Congo Disaster,* 124.

280 "They are bad": Cordier to Hammarskjöld, Aug. 31, 1960 (B711).

280 When reports from: Cordier and Foote, *Public Papers,* 5:167. Earlier, Hammarskjöld called it "incipient genocide." See Hammarskjöld to Cordier, Sept. 2, 1960, box 155, DHC. Others would contend that, however tragic, the killing of the Baluba did not meet the definition of "genocide." See Nzongola-Ntalaja, *Leopold to Kabila,* 106; Legum, *Congo Disaster,* 124; and Omasombo, *Kasaï-Oriental,* 189.

280 Although Lumumba denied: Omasombo, *Kasaï-Oriental,* 190.

280 Jacques Omonombe, a top official: Omonombe to Thant, May 15, 1962, S-0730-0001-0001, UNA; Willame, *La crise congolaise revisitée,* 191; ICRC report on Jacques Omonombe, Sept. 3, 1960, B AG 280 229-063.01, ICRCA. Artigue, *Qui sont les leaders,* 279, describes him as a brother-in-law of Lumumba's.

280 Jacques Lumbala, a junior minister: Kanza, *Rise and Fall,* 339.

280 "The lions are here!": Omasombo, *Kasaï-Oriental,* 188.

280 As the massacre unfolded: Rouch, *En cage,* 110, 116.

280 "If the U.N. would": ICRC Delegation in the Congo, "Information on the Situation in the Territories of Bakwanga and Gandajika." Hammarskjöld shared Senn's fear. See Hammarskjöld to Cordier, Sept. 2, 1960 (1496, 1497), box 155, DHC.

281 "There was a feeling": Colvin, *Moise Tshombe,* 34.

281 From Elisabethville, Tshombe: AP, "Congo Unit, Insurgents May Clash," *Spokesman-Review* (Spokane), Aug. 29, 1960; CRISP, *Congo 1960,* 2:805.

281 Joined by fifty women: "Congo: Long Way to Go," *Time,* Sept. 12, 1960, 30; CRISP, *Congo 1960,* 2:805; AP, "Reds Demand Bases Be Given Lumumba," *Palladium-Item* (Richmond, Ind.), Sept. 1, 1960.

281 Facing logistical difficulties: Willame, *La crise congolaise revisitée,* 193; Monheim, *Mobutu,* 115.

281 "You're just a simple": Monheim, *Mobutu,* 115.

282 In Odessa in early August: AP, "Red Aid Ship Off to the Congo," *New York Daily News,* Aug. 6, 1960; Mazov, *Distant Front,* 96, 103; Wauters, *Le monde communiste,* 73; "Arkhangelsk—IMO 5022156," Shipspotting.com, Aug. 5, 2007, www .shipspotting.com; Cordier and Foote, *Public Papers,* 5:142.

282 More significantly, in response: For information on the Soviet planes sent to the Congo, see Hammarskjöld to Bunche, Aug. 25, 1960 (1219), box 155, DHC; Cordier to Hammarskjöld, Sept. 1, 1960 (B721), box 155, DHC; "Direct Soviet Bloc Aid to Congo Government," Sept. 12, 1960, in Namikas and Mazov, "CWIHP Conference Reader"; Memo of USSR MID about deliveries of Soviet aircraft, n.d., in Namikas and Mazov, "CWIHP Conference Reader"; *FRUS, 1958–1960,* vol. 14, doc. 191; Cordier and Foote, *Public Papers,* 5:151; Fursenko and Naftali, *Khrushchev's Cold War,* 312; Mazov, *Distant Front,* 97–98; Namikas, *Battleground Africa,* 93; Kalb, *Congo Cables,* 57–67; Urquhart, *Life in Peace and War,* 168; Thomas F. Brady, "Soviet Planes Sent to Help Lumumba in Katanga Dispute," *NYT,* Sept. 3, 1960; "Nights of Butchery," *Newsweek,* Sept. 12, 1960, 40.

282 "If they and other BCP": Freeman to State, Aug. 20, 1960 (229), file 350, Congo July–Aug. 1960 Classified, Security-Segregated Records, U.S. Embassy Leopoldville, RG 84, NACP.

282 Devlin bugged an office: Devlin, *Chief of Station,* 61, 23.

283 "a Soviet tool": Eisenhower, *Waging Peace,* 574–75.

283 "extremely concerned … about": Magnuson and Committee on Commerce, *Speeches of Senator John F. Kennedy,* 121; Herter to Kennedy, n.d., box 16, Congo, Cabinet Series, Papers as President of the United States, 1953–61 (Whitman File), DDEL.

283 "sliding slowly but surely": Lynn Heinzerling, AP, "Western Diplomats Note Congo Sliding Toward Communist Bloc," *The Plain Speaker* (Hazleton, Penn.), Aug. 27, 1960.

283 "many, if not most": Devlin, *Chief of Station,* 23, 24.

283 In truth, the total number of KGB: Mazov, *Distant Front,* 108.

283 A CIA estimate: "Bloc Personnel in the Congo," Sept. 9, 1960.

283 It became an article of faith: CRISP, *Congo 1960,* 2:804; Rouch, *En cage,* 119. For examples of this allegation, see Kalb, *Congo Cables,* 69; Mazov, *Distant Front,* 110.

284 "clearly enhanced": *FRUS, 1958–1960,* vol. 14, doc. 197.

284 "Why would our government": Omasombo, *Kasaï-Oriental,* 191.

284 The fate of the one hundred: For the conventional view on the trucks, see Cordier OH, 190, 494, 518; Hoskyns, *Congo Since Independence,* 190; Mazov, *Distant Front,* 103; Cordier and Foote, *Public Papers,* 5:142; Urquhart, *Hammarskjold,* 438; Kalb, *Congo Cables,* 60; Scott, *Tumbled House,* 77. For the UN's questions about the trucks at the time, see Cordier to Labouisse, Sept. 1, 1960 (B717), box 155, DHC. For contemporary reports that the trucks were old Force Publique trucks, see Cordier to Hammarskjöld, Sept. 2, 1960 (B727). Willame, *La crise congolaise revisitée,* 191, claims that the Soviet trucks were used in the operation, but only to transport troops from Thysville to Leopoldville.

284 As for the airplanes: There was a widespread belief at the time that the Il-14s ferried troops from Stanleyville to Luluabourg and then on to Bakwanga, an allegation that would become one of the top charges against Lumumba. On September 5, Reuters reported that the planes had landed in Luluabourg with two hundred Congolese troops. That same day, Hammarskjöld mentioned the report in a note to the Soviet Union. The State Department, the CIA, and the White House also thought Soviet planes had transported Congolese troops to Luluabourg. But Willame, *La crise congolaise revisitée,* contends that there are no eyewitness accounts of Congolese troops disembarking from Il-14s in South Kasai in August and September, even though there were journalists present at the time. The confusion, he suggests, might have come from the fact that there were Il-18s in the area being used for the UN mission. Willame also obtained records of an interview with Serge Michel, who insisted that he was waiting impatiently for the planes to be sent, but they never were. One piece of evidence pointing in the other direction is an intelligence report prepared by the State Department that states, "On September 6, U.S. Air Attache Leopoldville reported personally observing six IL-14's departing Luluabourg for Bakwanga with Congolese troops." For the Reuters report, see Reuters, "Congo Bolsters Forces in Kasai," *NYT,* Sept. 6, 1960. For Hammarskjöld's note, see Cordier and Foote, *Public Papers,* 5:151. For the State Department's, CIA's, and White House's beliefs, see *FRUS, 1958–1960,* vol. 14, doc. 199, and draft press statement, Sept. 7, 1960, box 10, Press Conferences Series, Papers as President of the United States, 1953–61 (Whitman File), DDEL. For Willame's discussion of the evidence, see Willame, *La crise congolaise revisitée,* 192, 306. For the intelligence report, see "Direct Soviet Bloc Aid to the Congo Government," Sept. 8, 1960, folder 2.7, box 3, Records Relating to the Congo and the Congo Working Group, 1960–64, RG 59, NACP.

284 And although Hammarskjöld: Hammarskjöld thought the planes were military in nature and carried disassembled machine guns. See Kalb, *Congo Cables,* 67. Cordier cabled him on September 1 about suspicious boxes on the planes in Stanleyville. See Cordier to Hammarskjöld, Sept. 1, 1960 (B721).

284 The five An-12s: "Direct Soviet Bloc Aid to Congo Government," Sept. 12, 1960.

284 "There is no conclusive": "Bloc Personnel in the Congo," Sept. 9, 1960.

284 The truth was: Mazov, *Distant Front,* 110, claims that Soviet military aid "did help get the offensive off the ground" because the trucks and planes "made Lumumba's troops genuinely mobile." This might have been true in theory, but not in practice, since the trucks, as discussed above, almost certainly did not make it to Bakwanga, and the planes might never have made it there, either. In fact, the earliest allegation of Soviet planes landing in Luluabourg came September 5—the same day Lumumba was fired by Kasavubu, after which time Lumumba had no control over the ANC.

31. The Sleeping Crocodile

287 "How do you make": Linnér OH, 22–23.

287 "like a water buffalo": Dayal, *Life of Our Times,* 403.

287 The presidential residence: Mboka, "Kinshasa 2019—Where Does a New President Lay His Head?"

287 And so as August wore on: Lukens to Herter, Aug. 19, 1960, box 1, Africa (General, 3), International Series, Office of the Staff Secretary: Records, 1952–61, DDEL; Bunche to Hammarskjöld, Aug. 21, 1960 (B580), box 155, DHC.

287 "a political zero": *FRUS, 1958–1960,* vol. 14, doc. 178.

288 Whenever Timberlake met: Kalb, *Congo Cables,* 61. "I confess I have not yet learned the secret of spurring Kasavubu to action," Timberlake reported. *FRUS, 1958–1960,* vol. 14, doc. 183. See also Woodrow Wilson International Center OH, 129–30.

288 Instead, he busied: Interview and meeting summary, "Victor Hedgeman," Aug. 22, 1975, 157-10014-10185, JFKAR.

288 As part of what came to be: "Covert Military Operations in the Congo, 1964–1967"; *FRUS, 1964–1968,* vol. 23, doc. 17; "CIA Cryptonyms: WI," Mary Ferrell Foundation, www.maryferrell.org; Weissman, "What Really Happened in Congo"; Devlin, *Chief of Station,* 67–70.

288 The White House did: "Covert Military Operations in the Congo, 1964–1967." At the September 1, 1960, Special Group meeting, participants also discussed the provision of a plane for Kasavubu that would be superior to the Il-14 the Soviets had given Lumumba. See Minutes of Special Group Meeting, Sept. 1, 1960, box 1, NSC 5412 Special Group Minutes and Agendas 1960, U.S. National Security Council Presidential Records, Intelligence Files, 1953–61, DDEL.

288 "the overthrow of the government": *EP,* 118.

288 Belgian diplomats financed: Hoskyns, *Congo Since Independence,* 187; Brassinne and Kestergat, *Qui a tué,* 79; *EP,* 108–109.

288 "There is a veritable": De Witte, *Assassination,* 19.

288 "by legal or illegal": "Congo, Congo, Toil and Trouble," 35.

288 "The Head of State": "Loi fondamentale du 19 mai 1960," Digithèque, de matériaux juridiques et politiques mjp.univ-perp.fr.

289 Article 22, like: Van Bilsen, *Congo, 1945–1965,* 249.

289 It had been nearly: Hoskyns, *Congo Since Independence,* 209.

289 Back in July: *EP,* 78. The idea of using Article 22 circulated briefly at the time. On July 8, one anti-Lumumba senator raised it with Ralph Bunche, lamenting that Kasavubu was too timid to invoke it. See Bunche Diary, July 8, 1960, box 15, folder 5, BUC.

289 But the president: *EP,* 115.

289 Even Belgium's prime minister: Eyskens, *Mémoires,* 731–32; Van Bilsen, *Congo, 1945–1965,* 249; Freeman to Leopoldville, Aug. 20, 1960 (230), file 350, Congo July–Aug. 1960 Classified, Security-Segregated Records, U.S. Embassy Leopoldville, RG 84, NACP. There was a touch of irony in Eyskens's directive. King Baudouin had recently tried—and failed—to use this very same gambit to remove Eyskens from office over his allegedly poor handling of the Congo crisis. Belgium's prime minister had balked at the idea that an unelected head of state could cast out a democratically elected leader, but that was what he was suggesting should happen in the Congo. See AP, "Cabinet Ouster Try Is Laid to Belgian King," *Baltimore Evening Sun,* Aug. 18, 1960; Gerard and Kuklick, *Death in the Congo,* 45–51.

289 When Kasavubu heard: Van Bilsen, *Congo, 1945–1965,* 249–52. Van Bilsen claimed that he disagreed with Eyskens's advice and that he made that clear to Kasavubu.

289 "a wounded animal": Eyskens, *Mémoires,* 732.

289 "Impossible": Woodrow Wilson International Center OH, 127.

289 "We're working together": As early as August 26, U.S. newspapers were reporting that Lumumba was soon to lose power. See Weissman, *American Foreign Policy,* 86.

289 "Lumumba gave little": Kanza, *Rise and Fall,* 258.

290 "I keep him in": Hammarskjöld to Bunche and Cordier, Aug. 29, 1960 (1331), box 155, DHC. The phrase "I keep him in the doghouse" was crossed out and replaced with "we are on somewhat less than speaking terms."

290 "a stooge": Memorandum, Hammarskjöld, Sept. 4, 1960, box 141, DHC. He used the same term to the British. See James, *Britain,* 67.

290 Lumumba must be "broken": Synopsis of State and Intelligence material reported to the President, Aug. 30, 1960, box 14, Intelligence Briefing Notes, Subject Series, Alphabetical Subseries, Office of the Staff Secretary, DDEL.

290 It was a curious: Dayal, *Mission,* 22; Von Horn, *Soldiering for Peace,* 60.

290 He even picked up: Geary, "Death of a Stalwart," 38, 66–67.

290 "a chunky, blue-eyed": Lash, "Man on the 38th Floor," 51.

290 Since the Congo crisis began: Cordier to Schwalm, Aug. 18, 1960, box 47, AWCP.

290 "The only time": Interview with Cordier, Aug. 21, 1962, box 123, AWCP.

290 a "little Hitler": Cordier to Schwalm, Aug. 18, 1960.

290 When Cordier arrived: Unless otherwise noted, details on Cordier's actions in Leopoldville are drawn from Collins, "Cold War Comes to Africa," 5–22; Gerard and Kuklick, *Death in the Congo,* 93–99; Urquhart, *Hammarskjold,* 436–47;

Dayal, *Mission,* 28–42; Van Bilsen, *Congo, 1945–1965,* 252–60; Kalb, *Congo Cables,* 73–75; De Witte, *Assassination,* 17–20; Cordier, OH, 510–17; Memorandum of conversation with Cordier and Hammarskjöld, Sept. 3, 1960, box 132, DHC; Memorandum by Cordier, n.d., box 160, AWCP; Hammarskjöld to Cordier, Sept. 4, 1960 (1526), box 2, AWCP; Cordier to Schwalm, Sept. 15, 1960, box 47, AWCP; draft statement for Lumumba investigation commission, Sept. 24, 1968, box 161, AWCP.

292 "regard it as constitutional": Hammarskjöld to Cordier, Sept. 3, 1960 (1502, 1505, 1504).

292 "burn immediately all texts": Ibid. See also Hammarskjöld to Dayal, Sept. 10, 1960, box 2, AWCP, where a note says that two cables were destroyed in the code room.

292 The next day: Hammarskjöld to Cordier, Sept. 4, 1960 (1526).

292 As part of a "dry run": "Operations Section," Sept. 3, 1960, S-0787-0010-03, UNA.

292 "most likely successor": *FRUS, 1958–1960,* vol. 14, doc. 178.

292 For the Americans: The minutes of the June 30, 1960, meeting appear in *FRUS, 1964–1968,* vol. 23, doc. 6, but the passage on financial support to Iléo is redacted. It appears unredacted, however, in testimony of C. Douglas Dillon, Sept. 2, 1975, 36–37, 157-10014-10178, JFKAR. On Iléo's victory, see Artigue, *Qui sont les leaders,* 91.

292 On the night of September 4: *FRUS, 1958–1960,* vol. 14, doc. 198; Cordier OH, 518–19.

293 The next morning: Van Bilsen, *Congo, 1945–1965,* 255; Cordier and Foote, *Public Papers,* 5:160.

293 "an irresponsible observation": Hammarskjöld to Cordier, Sept. 5, 1960 (1562), box 155, DHC. Hammarskjöld would later claim he thought that the dismissal of Lumumba "should never have come about." Hammarskjöld to Unden, Feb. 26, 1961, box 141, DHC.

293 At 7:00 p.m. on September 5: Van Bilsen, *Congo, 1945–1965,* 256–57.

293 "coordinated with": *FRUS, 1964–1968,* vol. 23, doc. 15.

293 Shortly after 8:00: Mboka, "Leopoldville 1960—Patrice Lumumba's Residence," *Kinshasa Then and Now* (blog), Nov. 3, 2020; Michel, *Uhuru Lumumba,* 201.

293 I have some extremely": CRISP, *Congo 1960,* 2:818.

294 "It's about time": "U.S. Quiet on Kasavubu," *NYT,* Sept. 6, 1960.

294 One Leopoldville hotel: Hoskyns, *Congo Since Independence,* 206–207.

294 Cordier and other UN: Dayal, *Mission,* 33.

294 "it was impossible": von Horn, *Soldiering for Peace,* 208.

32. A Bungled Firing

295 After issuing his: Devlin, *Chief of Station,* 67; Young, *Politics in the Congo,* 392; Scott, *Tumbled House,* 79.

295 Lumumba, however, sprang: "Congo President Ousts Lumumba as Premier," *Bangor Daily News,* Sept. 6, 1960.

295 They were led by a British: Kasavubu to Cordier, Sept. 5, 1960, box 132, DHC; " 'Dismissed' Congo Leader Remains in Control," *Sydney Morning Herald,* Sept. 7, 1960.

295 Lumumba burst past: Lumumba, *Lumumba Speaks,* 380.

295 "No one, not even": For Lumumba's address, see CRISP, *Congo 1960,* 2:820–21. See also Hoskyns, *Congo Since Independence,* 201; Urquhart, *Hammarskjold,* 442; Cordier to Hammarskjöld, Sept. 5, 1960 (B794), box 155, DHC.

295 To prevent Congolese troops: Dayal, *Mission,* 34; Cordier OH, 522–23; von Horn, *Soldiering for Peace,* 209.

295 In Leopoldville, UN cars: Cordier to Hammarskjöld, Sept. 5, 1960 (B799), box 155, DHC.

296 A Moroccan detachment: von Horn, *Soldiering for Peace,* 208.

296 Mobutu did as he: Cordier to Hammarskjöld, Sept. 5, 1960 (B795), box 155, DHC; Dayal, *Mission,* 35.

296 Cordier cabled Hammarskjöld: "Congo: Lumumba Army Paid Off by U.N., OK's Cease Fire," *San Francisco Examiner,* Sept. 11, 1960; Hoskyns, *Congo Since Independence,* 213; Urquhart, *Hammarskjold,* 447; Dayal, *Mission,* 34, 65–66, 227; Cordier OH, 524; Dayal to Hammarskjöld, Sept. 12, 1960 (B913), box 155, DHC.

296 "Strange country": Cordier to Hammarskjöld, Sept. 5, 1960 (B800), box 155, DHC. Cordier later wrote, "Mobutu...had gone to [Kasavubu's] home at three o'clock on Tuesday morning but Kasavubu was asleep and could not apparently be disturbed. This was fatal." Cordier to Schwalm, Sept. 15, 1960, box 47, AWCP.

296 Sacrificing sleep for: Hoskyns, *Congo Since Independence,* 202.

296 Congolese troops stood: UPI, "Kasavubu and Premier in Battle to Seize Control," *York Daily News-Times,* Sept. 6, 1960.

296 "null and void": Lumumba, *Lumumba Speaks,* 358–61.

296 He had not expected: *FRUS, 1964–1968,* vol. 23, docs. 15, 16; *EP,* 124.

296 "Unfortunately, and for": *FRUS, 1964–1968,* vol. 23, doc. 16.

297 To Devlin's further: Devlin OH; Devlin, *Chief of Station,* 67; Interview and meeting summary, "Victor Hedgeman," Aug. 22, 1975, 157-10014-10185, JFKAR.

297 Now playing catch-up: Devlin, *Chief of Station,* 68.

297 Clare Timberlake called Cordier: Cordier to Hammarskjöld, Sept. 5, 1960 (B797), box 155, DHC; Dayal, *Mission,* 35.

297 Watching the drama: Houghton to Herter, Sept. 6, 1960 (930), Files of Visits by Heads of Government, Dignitaries, and Delegations, Office of Secretary, RG 59, NACP.

297 Shortly after noon: Mahoney, *JFK,* 47; Dayal, *Mission,* 38; von Horn, *Soldiering for Peace,* 210; Cordier OH, 522.

297 "The man whose magic": Henry Tanner, "Premier and President," *NYT,* Sept. 11, 1960.

297 Lumumba tried in vain: Dayal, *Mission*, 59; Henry Tanner, "U.N. Troops Halt Raid by Lumumba on Radio in Congo," *NYT,* Sept. 12, 1960; Michel, *Uhuru Lumumba,* 222–23; Dayal to Hammarskjöld, Sept. 11, 1960 (B911), box 155, DHC.

297 The grounding of all: Hoskyns, *Congo Since Independence,* 204.

297 Moreover, the ban: UPI, "Kasavubu and Premier in Battle to Seize Control"; Weissman, *American Foreign Policy,* 92.

297 "in a rather distraught": Cordier and Dayal to Hammarskjöld, Sept. 6, 1960 (B822), box 155, DHC; Dayal, *Mission,* 41.

298 When Lumumba tried: Cordier to Hammarskjöld, Sept. 6, 1960 (B806), box 155, DHC; Cordier to Schwalm, Sept. 15, 1960; Dayal, *Mission,* 41. "You will not and cannot see him," Hammarskjöld wrote to Cordier. See Gerard and Kuklick, *Death in the Congo,* 96.

298 "We have not": Cordier to Hammarskjöld, Sept. 6, 1960 (B809), box 155, DHC.

298 "gamesmanship," he confided: *FRUS, 1958–1960*, vol. 14, doc. 202.

298 "basically regrettable": Hammarskjöld to Cordier, Sept. 6, 1960 (1567), box 155, DHC. See also Urquhart, *Hammarskjold,* 446; Dayal, *Mission,* 172; and Liu OH, 38. Cordier would claim that the secretary-general congratulated him for his brave decision. See Cordier OH, 522–23.

298 made a point of noting: Cordier and Foote, *Public Papers,* 5:165.

298 He was relieved: Ibid., 152; Cordier's itinerary, box 78, Congo Trip, Aug.–Sept. 1960, AWCP.

298 "During the few": Kanza, *Rise and Fall,* 276.

298 It was not a position: Geary, "Death of a Stalwart," 79–84, 93, 113, 164.

298 "violent public speeches": CRISP, *Congo 1960,* 2:819; *EP,* 148.

298 "A phantom": *FRUS, 1958–1960*, vol. 14, doc. 243.

298 Lumumba's followers detained: Kanza, *Rise and Fall,* 292; Report on message from Timberlake, Sept. 7, 1960, box 132, DHC; Devlin, *Chief of Station,* 72.

298 The closest anyone: "M. Lumumba raconte lui-même sa 'folle après-midi' …," *Le Monde,* Sept. 14, 1960.

299 As Kasavubu cloistered: Dayal to Hammarskjöld, Sept. 12, 1960 (B935), box 155, DHC; Synopsis of State and Intelligence Material Reported to the President, Sept. 13, 1960, box 52, Briefings Sept. 1960, Diary Series, Papers as President of the United States, 1953–61 (Whitman File), DDEL.

299 "Fear not, your": Monheim, *Mobutu,* 122.

299 "We must follow": Lumumba, *Lumumba Speaks,* 399, 368, 402.

299 "rhetorical wizardry": "The Situation in the Congo," Sept. 14, 1960, FO 371/146630, National Archives of the U.K.

299 "To watch Premier Lumumba": Tanner, "Premier and President."

299 Lumumba had even more: Hoskyns, *Congo Since Independence,* 203, 204; Devlin, *Chief of Station,* 70. It is worth noting that all senators in Kalonji's and Tshombe's parties were absent.

299 "devastated" his opponents' points: "Analytical Chronology of the Congo Crisis," 34.

299 An avid equestrian: Biographical information on Dayal comes from Dayal,

Life of Our Times, 24, 44; "Calm U.N. Aide in Congo," *NYT,* Sept. 13, 1960; Urquhart, *Hammarskjold,* 265; UN, "Biographical Note on Rajeshwar Dayal," press release, Aug. 20, 1960, 0752-0017-01, UNA.

300 Although Hammarskjöld had: *FRUS, 1958–1960,* vol. 14, doc. 190.

300 "substitute the broadcasting": Dayal, *Mission,* 32.

300 By now, it was: "Congo: Dag's Problem Child," *Time,* Sept. 19, 1960, 28.

300 Disturbed by this apparent: Nkrumah to Lumumba, Sept. 12, 1960, S-0752-0016-10, UNA.

300 A day after his: Urquhart, *Hammarskjold,* 450; Dayal to Hammarskjöld, Sept. 13, 1960 (B941), box 155, DHC.

300 In an amateurish: F. T. Liu to Joan Liu, Sept. 15, 1960, Liu Letters. "Imagine someone losing the key to the studio when all were fighting to gain its control!" Liu wrote. "It is completely crazy and to anyone not on the spot utterly unbelievable." See also Dayal to Hammarskjöld, Sept. 14, 1960 (B958), box 155, DHC.

300 Parliament held yet another: Hoskyns, *Congo Since Independence,* 205–206. As Hoskyns notes, soldiers were present during the vote, and there were doubts about whether a quorum was reached.

300 After being carried: Blouin, *My Country, Africa,* 266.

300 Word circulated that: Hoskyns, *Congo Since Independence,* 207, 220.

300 "Lumumba in opposition": *FRUS, 1964–1968,* vol. 23, doc. 17; *AAP,* 17. The Congolese contact with whom Devlin shared this conclusion replied that he understood and suggested that he might "physically eliminate Lumumba." The draft report of *AAP* indicates that this comment was said by Devlin. See draft of Congo section of assassination report, Oct. 6, 1975, 9, 157-10014-10136, JFKAR.

300 "Lumumba's talents and": *FRUS, 1964–1968,* vol. 23, doc. 21.

301 "not easy to run a": *FRUS, 1958–1960,* vol. 14, doc. 199.

301 "the top-level feeling": *AAP,* 62.

301 The U.S. government recognized: *FRUS, 1964–1968,* vol. 23, doc. 16.

301 "Power at this point": Young, *Politics in the Congo,* 450.

33. Hamlet of the Congo

302 He had met him just: Devlin, *Chief of Station,* 72; Woodrow Wilson International Center OH, 123, 161.

302 But as Devlin now learned: Details of Devlin's meetings with Mobutu during the period of September 5, 1960, to September 14, 1960, are drawn from *FRUS, 1964–1968,* vol. 23, doc. 19; Devlin OH; Interview and meeting summary, "Victor Hedgeman," Aug. 22, 1975, 157-10014-10185, JFKAR; Devlin to director, Sept. 16. 1960, in testimony of Victor Hedgeman, Aug. 21, 1975, 157-10014-10080, JFKAR; Devlin, *Chief of Station,* 76–79; Woodrow Wilson International Center OH, 163–65. By September 13, the CIA was providing Mobutu "with financial help." See *FRUS, 1964–1968,* vol. 23, doc. 19. In 1967, Devlin told his CIA debriefers that, as *FRUS* puts it, "this was the begin-

ning of the plan for Mobutu to take over the government." In 1975, he told Church Committee investigators that Mobutu's coup, in their words, "was arranged and supported, and indeed, managed, by the Central Intelligence Agency." See summary of interview with Victor Hedgeman, Aug. 22, 1975, 3, 157-10014-10185, JFKAR. For a view that casts doubt on Devlin's influence at this time, see Gerard and Kuklick, *Death in the Congo,* 112–14.

303 In the week following: Cordier OH, 530; Urquhart, *Hammarskjold,* 450–51; Liu OH, 33–34; Dayal, *Mission,* 62.

303 He said he owed his career: Mobutu was also no doubt annoyed that the prime minister was claiming credit for the pay the UN had provided, which had been distributed at a parade under Mobutu's supervision and was intended to redound to his own credit. Kalb, *Congo Cables,* 96; Hoskyns, *Congo Since Independence,* 213.

303 "Mobutu has no influence": Herter to Leopoldville, Sept. 18, 1960 (770), file 312, UNOC Sept.–Oct. Classified, Security-Segregated Records, U.S. Embassy Leopoldville, RG 84, USNA.

303 a "frightened boy": Cordier to Schwalm, Jan. 11, 1961, box 47, AWCP.

303 "was so troubled by": Dayal, *Mission,* 62.

303 "I can't go on": CRISP, *Congo 1960,* 2:865.

303 One day, Mobutu turned: Dayal to Hammarskjöld, Sept. 12, 1960 (B913), box 155, DHC; Cordier OH, 530; Urquhart, *Hammarskjold,* 450–51.

304 Lumumba was marched: Rouch, *En cage,* 167; Henry Tanner, "Lumumba Jailed 3 Hours by Army; Status in Doubt," *NYT,* Sept. 13, 1960; Dayal to Hammarskjöld, Sept. 12, 1960 (B935), box 155, DHC; Dayal, *Mission,* 59; Dayal to Hammarskjöld, Sept. 12, 1960 (B927), box 155, DHC; Kanza, *Rise and Fall,* 303.

304 "the Hamlet of the Congo": Legum, *Congo Disaster,* 8. See also Dayal, *Mission,* 62; and Rikhye, *Military Adviser,* 104.

304 "Mobutu's heart was swinging": Kanza, *Rise and Fall,* 303.

34. This Is Not a Military Coup

305 "This is not a military coup": CRISP, *Congo 1960,* 2:869.

305 "That's me!": Urquhart, *Life in Peace and War,* 169; Urquhart OH, Oct. 19, 1984, 15; Dayal, *Mission,* 63–64, gives a slightly different version of events, but all agree that Mobutu went to the Royal that night and was forced to leave.

305 His message had been: Hoskyns, *Congo Since Independence,* 214.

305 Most listeners had no: "Congo: The U.N. Under Fire," *Time,* Sept. 26, 1960.

306 He turned up later: For the Regina and Mobutu's announcement there, see Mboka, "Leopoldville 1942—Hotel Le Regina," *Kinshasa Then and Now* (blog), March 29, 2011; Tourist Bureau for the Belgian Congo & Ruanda-Urundi, *Traveller's Guide,* 229; Devlin, *Chief of Station,* 85–86; Rouch, *En cage,* 181–85; Monheim, *Mobutu,* 134–35; Urquhart, *Life in Peace and War,* 169; "Who's In: Who's Out?—the Congo Riddle," *Evening Standard* (London), Sept. 15, 1960;

CRISP, *Congo 1960*, 2:869; Dayal to Hammarskjöld, Sept. 14, 1960 (B975), box 155, DHC; Weissman, "What Really Happened in Congo"; Devlin OH; "Report on Colonel Mobutu's Press Conference at the Regina Hotel on 14 September at 2200 Hours," Oct. 21, 1960, S-0752-0024-10, UNA.

306 Waving a pamphlet: For more on this pamphlet, see AP, "Communists Pouring into Congo Capital," *York Dispatch*, Aug. 23, 1960; "Ex–Congo Premier Reported in Hiding," *Fort Worth Star-Telegram*, Sept. 18, 1960.

306 "I see you pulled": Robinson McIlvaine OH, 18.

306 And just like that: Note that by using "sub-Saharan," I am deliberately excluding Egypt and Sudan, both of which experienced coups before the Congo did.

306 "corrupted by the imperialists": CRISP, *Congo 1960*, 2:870.

306 Then he confronted: My account of Lumumba's experience at Camp Leopold comes from Dayal to Hammarskjöld, Sept. 15, 1960 (B983), box 155, DHC; Dayal to Hammarskjöld, Sept. 15, 1960 (B977), box 155, DHC; Dayal to Hammarskjöld, Sept. 15, 1960 (ONUC 1037), box 155, DHC; Dayal to Hammarskjöld, Sept. 15, 1960 (B978), box 155, DHC; Dayal to Hammarskjöld, Sept. 15, 1960 (B986), box 155, DHC; Dayal, *Mission*, 69–74; Rikhye, *Military Adviser,* 106–8; Monheim, *Mobutu,* 140–43; "General Hides in Closet," *NYT,* Sept. 16, 1960; AP, "Two Attempts Made," *NYT,* Sept. 16, 1960; *Newsweek,* Sept. 26, 1960, 38; Raustiala, *Absolutely Indispensable Man,* 401.

307 "What power?": Mobutu and Remilleux, *Dignité pour l'Afrique,* 53.

308 Their discipline, questionable: Hoskyns, *Congo Since Independence,* 212.

308 The ten Soviet Il-14s: *FRUS, 1958–1960,* vol. 14, doc. 223; Mazov, *Distant Front,* 118; Scott, *Tumbled House,* 82.

308 Two Soviet cargo ships: *FRUS, 1964–1968,* vol. 23, doc. 21; *FRUS, 1958–1960,* vol. 14, doc. 223.

308 Left-wing advisers: Dayal to Hammarskjöld, Sept. 22, 1960 (B1060), box 155, DHC. Blouin managed to stay until November. See Blouin, *My Country, Africa,* 274.

308 "had succeeded … in neutralizing": *FRUS, 1958–1960,* vol. 14, doc. 242. Blouin also came up in an October 20, 1960, Special Group meeting, where a participant referenced "the operation in connection with Madame Blouin." Minutes of Special Group Meeting, Oct. 20, 1960, box 1, Minutes of Special Group Meetings, Intelligence Files 1953–61, U.S. National Security Council Presidential Records, DDEL.

308 In downtown Leopoldville: Dayal, *Mission,* 76; Dayal to Hammarskjöld, Sept. 16, 1960 (B995), box 155, DHC; Mazov, *Distant Front,* 117.

308 Mikhail Yakovlev, the ambassador: "In the Mad Congo," *Newsweek,* Sept. 26, 1960, 38.

308 "This new and troubled": *FRUS, 1958–1960,* vol. 14, doc. 217. The original cable says "blob," which in context is clearly a typo.

308 "completely honest" and "dedicated": Ibid., doc. 220.

308 "aside from Lumumba": Ibid., doc. 223.

308 In another decisive move: Rikhye, *Military Adviser,* 115.

308 "The College of Commissioners": CRISP, *Congo 1960,* 2:872–73; Gerard and Kuklick, *Death in the Congo,* 107. One of its members was Étienne Tshisekedi, who would go on to become a prominent opponent of Mobutu's. He was the father of Félix Tshisekedi, who became Congo's president in 2019. The College of Commissioners would grow to a total of thirty-nine members.

309 The CIA advised Mobutu: "Covert Military Operations in the Congo, 1964–1967."

309 They also cleared: Hoskyns, *Congo Since Independence,* 217, 239.

309 Having detained and promptly: "Si l'O.N.U. ne m'écoute pas je ferai appel à n'importe quelle armée ute re le colonel Mobutu," *Le Monde,* Sept. 20, 1960.

309 This indecision offered: *FRUS, 1964–1968,* vol. 23, doc. 25.

309 "actions indicate that he": *FRUS, 1958–1960,* vol. 14, docs. 216, 223. John Eisenhower would defend Dulles, saying, "I would not conjecture that the words 'disposed of' meant an assassination, if for no other reason than that if I had something as nasty as this to plot, I wouldn't do it in front of 21 people—I counted the number present before the meeting." Testimony of John Eisenhower, July 18, 1975, 9–10, 157-10014-10044, JFKAR.

309 "Lumumba would fall into": *FRUS, 1958–1960,* vol. 14, doc. 221. John Eisenhower would say the crocodile comment "was all just a big laugh." Testimony of John Eisenhower, July 18, 1975, 17, 157-10014-10044, JFKAR.

309 "come out on top": *FRUS, 1964–1968,* vol. 23, docs. 25, 22. Accordingly, Devlin urged two of his Congolese contacts to "try to work with Mobutu in an effort to eliminate Lumumba." The station also met with Joseph Iléo, the CIA-funded senator whom Kasavubu had previously designated prime minister. Iléo, a cable reported, "reluctantly agrees Lumumba must go permanently" and asked for a supply of weapons to equip a team of soldiers who would "take direct action" against him. The station agreed to consider supplying weapons for Lumumba's murder. Weissman, "An Extraordinary Rendition," 203–204; *AAP,* 17–18.

309 Mobutu, his wife, Marie-Antoinette: "Mobutu Guns Rout Rebellious Troops," *San Francisco Examiner,* Sept. 23, 1960, 14; Devlin, *Chief of Station,* 88; "Congo: The Three-Headed State," *Time,* Oct. 3, 1960, 21.

309 His office was a madhouse: *FRUS, 1958–1960,* vol. 14, doc. 220.

309 On September 18: The would-be assassin was Alphonse Pakassa, a roommate from Mobutu's time in army training. Some sources call him Vital Pakassa. Monheim, *Mobutu,* 27–28, 146–49 (this source claims that Mobutu had already learned of the plot and summoned Pakassa to confront him); Henry Tanner, "Colonel Escapes Death," *NYT,* Sept. 19, 1960; Dayal to Hammarskjöld, Sept. 18, 1960 (B1011), box 155, DHC; *FRUS, 1964–1968,* vol. 23, doc. 23; *EP,* 208. In his memoir, Devlin claimed that he jumped a gunman at Camp Leopold—"a Congolese in civilian clothes" who had known Mobutu from

military training—who was about to assassinate Mobutu, but that Mobutu later took credit himself for foiling the attempt (Devlin, *Chief of Station,* 89–90). He repeated this story to others. See Wrong, *Footsteps of Mr. Kurtz,* 63, and Devlin OH. Yet according to a cable that the Leopoldville station sent to headquarters on September 21, it was Mobutu who grappled with Pakassa. See *FRUS, 1964–1968,* vol. 23, doc. 23.

310 The next day, someone: "Try for Peace in Kasavubu, Lumumba Row," *Chicago Tribune,* Sept. 20, 1960.

310 Afterward, Devlin met with: Weissman, "Extraordinary Rendition," 204; *AAP,* 18; Devlin to director, Sept. 20, 1960 (0974), in testimony of Victor Hedgeman, Aug. 25, 1975, 157-10014-10076, JFKAR. The cable makes it clear that the meeting took place the night of September 19.

310 "arrest or other more permanent": Devlin to director, Sept. 20, 1960 (0974). The word "permanent" was becoming a common adjective applied to Lumumba's removal. On September 21, Timberlake reported that Fulbert Youlou, the president of the other Congo, "believes Lumumba must be permanently removed." Timberlake to Herter, Sept. 21, 1960 (768), Files of Visits by Heads of Government, Dignitaries, and Delegations, Office of Secretary, RG 59, NACP.

310 Even so, Mobutu: *FRUS, 1964–1968,* vol. 23, doc. 23.

310 Devlin readily provided: *EP,* 439; De Witte, *Assassination,* 28. The original figure is 20 million francs, and the adviser was Louis Marlière.

310 Soon, UN military officers: Dayal, *Mission,* 65–66, 99–100; Dayal, *Life of Our Times,* 415. The support might have come as early as September 12, before Mobutu's coup. In a cable from that day, Dayal passed on a clarification that the payment already given the ANC was not from the $1 million requested from the UN. Rather, "the ANC officers under pressure from their men decided to give an advance out of a sum which belonged to Belgians in their custody." See Dayal to Hammarskjöld, Sept. 12, 1960 (B913), box 155, DHC. But as he later wrote, he suspected this was a lie to cover up the true source of the funds. See also Rikhye, *Military Adviser,* 99.

310 "from company sources": Dayal to Hammarskjöld, Oct. 4, 1960 (B1171), box 156, DHC.

310 Dayal protested to Timberlake: Dayal to Hammarskjöld, Sept. 22, 1960 (B1060), box 155, DHC. "Mobutu seems now amply supplied with funds whose source we do not know but can guess," Dayal wrote to Hammarskjöld. Dayal to Hammarskjöld, Sept. 21, 1960 (B1051), box 155, DHC.

310 The former prime minister: Kalb, *Congo Cables,* 100; Dayal to Hammarskjöld, Sept. 16, 1960 (B998), box 155, DHC; Dayal to Hammarskjöld, Sept. 16, 1960 (B995), box 155, DHC; Wieschhoff to Herter, Sept. 21, 1960, box 16, Congo (2) [Aug.–Dec. 1960], Cabinet Series, Papers as President of the United States, 1953–61 (Whitman File), DDEL. Lumumba's doctor was an Italian Communist named Giovanni Manca. See Kashamura, *De Lumumba,* 162; Gabriele Sira-

cusano, "La lutte armée au Congo et au Cameroun. Un acteur inattendu: Le Parti communiste italien," *Monde(s)* 1, no. 21 (2022): 155.

310 On September 20: On the attempt to arrest Lumumba, see Dayal to Hammarskjöld, Sept. 21, 1960 (B1039), box 155, DHC; Dayal to Hammarskjöld, Sept. 21, 1960 (B1047), box 155, DHC; Wieschhoff to Herter, Sept. 21, 1960, box 16, Congo (2) [Aug.–Dec. 1960], Cabinet Series, Papers as President of the United States, 1953–61 (Whitman File), DDEL; Dayal, *Mission,* 86; *FRUS, 1958–1960,* vol. 14, doc. 220.

310 Devlin was not the only: Dayal to Hammarskjöld, Sept. 19, 1960 (B1021), box 155, DHC.

310 "I have no time to eat": "Congo: The Three-Headed State," *Time,* Oct. 3, 1960, 21.

311 "illusions of grandeur": Dayal to Hammarskjöld, Sept. 21, 1960 (B1051), box 155, DHC; Dayal to Hammarskjöld, Sept. 19, 1960 (B1021); Dayal to Hammarskjöld, Sept. 22, 1960 (B1060), box 155, DHC; Dayal to Hammarskjöld, Sept. 26, 1960 (B1058), box 155, DHC.

311 A group of parliamentarians: *FRUS, 1958–1960,* vol. 14, doc. 226.

311 Both men expressed: Hoskyns, *Congo Since Independence,* 221; Dayal to Hammarskjöld, Sept. 16, 1960 (B988). For the text of the agreement, see "Contre-projet," box 160, AWCP. It appears to bear Kasavubu's signature, although Kasavubu would deny having signed it. Lumumba to UNGA President, n.d., box 1a8, DHC; and Communiqué du Cabinet du Premier Ministre, Sept. 18, 1960, S-0752-0024-10, UNA. The State Department thought it "vital that Kasavubu publicly deny that such an agreement has been reached." Dillon to Leopoldville, Sept. 20, 1960 (835), file 312, UNOC Sept.–Oct. 1960 Classified, Security-Segregated Records, U.S. Embassy Leopoldville, RG 84, NACP.

311 "joint declaration that puts an end": Communiqué du Cabinet du Premier Ministre, Sept. 18, 1960.

311 On September 22: Dayal, *Mission,* 86.

311 on the "right track": Dayal to Hammarskjöld, Sept. 24, 1960 (B1076), box 155, DHC.

311 He cruised through: Henry Tanner, "Victory in Congo Seen by Lumumba," *NYT,* Sept. 26, 1960; AP, "Lumumba Ventures Out," *News Press,* Sept. 26, 1960; Dayal to Hammarskjöld, Sept. 25, 1960 (B1084), box 155, DHC.

311 He now said he wanted: "Lumumba's Talk to Journalists," Sept. 25, 1960, S-0752-0024-10, UNA. Contrary to Urquhart, *Hammarskjold,* 455, Lumumba had not issued a statement threatening on September 16 to forcibly expel the UN and invite in the Soviets. The U.S. embassy in Leopoldville considered this document a "forgery which should not be given credibility." Timberlake to Herter, Sept. 23, 1960 (804), Files of Visits by Heads of Government, Dignitaries, and Delegations, Office of Secretary, RG 59, NACP.

311 "high-ranking African diplomats": Henry Tanner, "Comeback by Lumumba Hinted; Mobutu Acts to End Congo Rift," *NYT,* Sept. 25, 1960.

35. Spitting on the UN

312 Hammarskjöld was a reader: Dayal, *Mission*, 12–13; Conor Cruise O'Brien, "My Case," *Observer*, Dec. 17, 1961; Lipsey, *Hammarskjöld*, 385.

312 "I don't believe that": Sauvage, *Voyages en Onusie*, 318; Lipsey, *Hammarskjöld*, 661n80.

312 He had produced a: Little, *The Poet and the Diplomat*, 97; Beskow, *Dag Hammarskjöld*, 170–72.

313 "You must have": Little, *The Poet and the Diplomat*, 109–10. I have removed the quotation marks around "think aloud," which the translator used to indicate that these words were written originally in English.

313 Its closure of: Rikhye, *Military Adviser*, 108; Hoskyns, *Congo Since Independence*, 235–36.

313 "The key melody here": Dayal, *Mission*, 83.

314 "not taken one single step": UN General Assembly, 858th Plenary Meeting, A/PV.858 (Sept. 17, 1960), 10. See also Lipsey, *Hammarskjöld*, 439.

314 "Their pretense of": UN General Assembly, 858th Plenary Meeting, A/PV.858 (Sept. 17, 1960), 15.

314 He believed passionately: See, for example, "The Walls of Distrust," in Cordier and Foote, *Public Papers*, 4:91.

314 His private correspondence: See, for example, Hammarskjöld to Cordier, Aug. 14, 1960 (B452), box 155, DHC; Hammarskjöld to Fawzi, Aug. 4, 1961, box 2a3, DHC. See also Dayal, *Mission*, 111.

314 Yet at heart: Lipsey, *Hammarskjöld*, xv; Mountz, "Americanizing Africanization," 17.

314 At the end of the emergency: Cordier and Foote, *Public Papers*, 5:191; Hoskyns, *Congo Since Independence*, 234–35. As Hoskyns notes, Western countries voted yes "not because they accepted the real intention of the resolution but because its adoption would mark a considerable defeat for the Soviet Union."

314 Khrushchev was en route: Taubman, *Khrushchev*, 472.

314 "That good-for-nothing Ham": Shevchenko, *Breaking with Moscow*, 102.

314 "Mr. Hammarskjöld used": UN General Assembly, 882nd Plenary Meeting, A/PV.882 (Oct. 3, 1960), 319.

315 Hammarskjöld, not usually: Urquhart, *Hammarskjöld*, 84.

315 "It is not the Soviet Union": UN General Assembly, 883rd plenary meeting, A/PV.883 (Oct. 3, 1960), with corrections made according to footage of the speech, available at "Dag Hammarskjöld: 'I Shall Remain in My Post!' (1960)," YouTube, www.youtube.com.

315 The much-mythologized shoe-banging: Taubman, *Khrushchev*, 476. See also Lipsey, *Hammarskjöld*, 444.

315 "Did I read it all right": Ralph J. Bunche's notes, Sept. 1960, box 15, folder 2, BUC; Urquhart, *Hammarskjöld*, 465.

315 "outstanding secretary-general": UN General Assembly, 868th plenary meeting, A/PV.868 (Sept. 22, 1960), 46.

36. Sid from Paris

316 The two spies found: Details about Gottlieb's arrival and meeting are drawn from *AAP,* 22–26; testimony of Bronson Tweedy, Sept. 9, 1975, 157-10014-10067, JFKAR; testimony of Bronson Tweedy, Oct. 9, 1975, 157-10014-10068, JFKAR; testimony of Bronson Tweedy, Oct. 10, 1975, 157-10014-10089, JFKAR; Tweedy to Devlin, Sept. 19, 1960, in testimony of Bronson Tweedy, Oct. 10, 1975; testimony of Victor Hedgeman, Aug. 21, 1975, 157-10014-10080, JFKAR; draft of assassination report, Oct. 16, 1975, 15, 157-10005-10297, JFKAR; Woodrow Wilson International Center OH, 132–33; Devlin, *Chief of Station,* 94–96. Accounts of Devlin and Gottlieb's first meeting vary. For example, the September 19 cable indicates that the two were to meet at the Stanley Hotel. In his 1975 Church Committee interview, Devlin said he couldn't recall where they met. At the 2004 Wilson Center oral history conference, he claimed that it was Café de la Presse, across the street from the U.S. embassy. In his 2007 memoir, he again identified the location as a café across from the U.S. embassy. In my retelling, I have given more weight to contemporaneous cables and earlier recollections.

316 Devlin had just received: For Gottlieb's accent, see "Crazy Rulers of the World—Parts 1–3," YouTube, 1:51:15 mark, www.youtube.com.

316 They arranged to meet: Information on the hotel comes from Mboka, "Kinshasa 1914—Hotel A.B.C. Opens Its Doors," *Kinshasa Then and Now,* March 27, 2011.

316 The man had traveled: *FRUS, 1964–1968,* vol. 23, doc. 24. *AAP,* 23, gives the alias as "Joseph Braun," but that appears to have been done to protect Gottlieb's identity, in keeping with the pseudonym under which he testified, Joseph Scheider. On Gottlieb's appearance, see Kinzer, *Poisoner in Chief,* 199.

316 He was well known: "Key Witness in C.I.A. Inquiry," *NYT,* Sept. 20, 1977.

316 Looking out over Leopoldville: Devlin, *Chief of Station,* 101; Reimuller, interview.

317 Inside were a gauze: Devlin, *Chief of Station,* 1. Devlin later recalled a tube of toothpaste, but he was likely misremembering. In his 1975 testimony to Church Committee investigators, he talked instead about a substance that would be administered to Lumumba's toothpaste. See ibid., 95, and see testimony of Victor Hedgeman, Aug. 21, 1975, 24, 82.

317 "We are on the same": Testimony of Bronson Tweedy, Oct. 10, 1975.

317 For the empress Xu Pingjun: Lily Xiao Hong Lee and A. D. Stefanowska, eds., *Biographical Dictionary of Chinese Women: Antiquity Through Sui, 1600 B.C.E.–618 C.E.* (Armonk, N.Y.: M. E. Sharpe, 2007), 227.

317 For the Roman emperor: Tacitus, *The Annals,* bk. 22, chaps. 66–67.

317 For Dmitry Shemyaka: Jeffrey Gedmin, "A Short History of Russian Poisoning," *American Interest,* June 4, 2015.

318 In 1953 in Iran: Weiner, *Legacy of Ashes,* 95–104. For a debate about the U.S. role in Mossadegh's removal, see Ray Takeyh, "What Really Happened in Iran,"

Foreign Affairs, July/Aug. 2014; and Christopher de Bellaigue and Ray Takeyh, "Coupdunnit: What Really Happened in Iran?," *Foreign Affairs,* Sept./Oct. 2014.

318 During Operation Success: Weiner, *Legacy of Ashes,* 107–19.

318 Over the course of the 1950s: For the Stalin plot, see Grose, *Gentleman Spy,* 328–29. For the Sukarno plot, see *AAP,* 4, and Thomas, *Very Best Men,* 213–14. For the Zhou plot, see Church Committee, Final Report, bk. 4, 133; Grose, *Gentleman Spy,* 411; and Urquhart, *Hammarskjold,* note on 121–22.

318 see Castro "sawed off": Eisenhower also included Rafael Trujillo, the president of the Dominican Republic, on this list. His comment would not be taken as an assassination order. Stephen G. Rabe, "Eisenhower and the Overthrow of Rafael Trujillo," *Journal of Conflict Studies* 6, no. 1 (1986): 39.

318 Two months later: *AAP,* 72–73; Thomas, *Very Best Men,* 209–10.

318 But the episode marked: Ibid., 209–210. During the Árbenz plot, hit lists were drawn up. Fursenko and Naftali, *Khrushchev's Cold War,* 314.

318 what it called "executive action": *AAP,* 181n1, 182.

319 Among the Waspy: Biographical information on Gottlieb is drawn from Kinzer, *Poisoner in Chief;* and Ted Gup, "The Coldest Warrior," *Washington Post Magazine,* Dec. 16, 2001.

319 Gottlieb and his men: Thomas, *Very Best Men,* 212; Tim Weiner, "Sidney Gottlieb, 80, Dies; Took LSD to C.I.A.," *NYT,* March 10, 1999.

319 At an addiction treatment: Marks, *The Search for the "Manchurian Candidate,"* 67.

319 Gottlieb even ran: Michael Ignatieff, "What Did the C.I.A. Do to His Father?," *NYT Magazine,* April 1, 2001; Gup, "Coldest Warrior." Olson's family believes he was murdered.

319 "Health Alteration Committee": *AAP,* 181n1; Thomas, *Very Best Men,* 214.

319 lace Castro's beloved cigars: "Reports on Plots to Assassinate Fidel Castro," May 23, 1967, 21, 104-10213-10101, JFKAR. The box of cigars was received by the CIA's Office of Medical Services on August 16, 1960. The name of the person in the Technical Services Division who provided the poison for the cigars is redacted, but it is probably that of Sidney Gottlieb.

319 Not long after the: *AAP,* 19–24.

320 "either kill the individual": Ibid., 21.

320 And then there was botulinum toxin: Regis, *Biology of Doom,* 183. Although *AAP* does not mention botulinum toxin, several pieces of evidence suggest it was very probably the poison used for the Lumumba plot. Botulinum toxin was used in the cigar plot against Castro around the same time. "Reports on Plots to Assassinate Fidel Castro," May 23, 1967, 21, 104-10213-10101, JFKAR. In his Church Committee testimony, Devlin said "botulism rings a bell." Testimony of Victor Hedgeman, Aug. 21, 1975, 22, 157-10014-10080, JFKAR. Devlin also said that Gottlieb provided him with multiple types of lethal agents, but the Church Committee's report, citing Gottlieb, claims that he "selected one material from the list." *AAP,* 21. In 1997, Devlin told a journalist who asked about the substance, "The only thing that I remember is that it was supposed to cause paralysis." Shoumatoff, "Mobutu's Final Days," 100.

320 In crystallized form: Cynthia Koons, "The Wonder Drug for Aging (Made from One of the Deadliest Toxins on Earth)," *Bloomberg Businessweek*, Oct. 30, 2017.

37. Homebound

321 Kasavubu and Lumumba had been prepared: Weissman, *American Foreign Policy*, 94–95; Charles P. Howard, "Katanga and the Congo Betrayal," *Freedomways* 2 (Spring 1962): 146; Gendebien, *L'intervention des Nations Unies au Congo*, 79n24. See also the letter from Andrew Djin to Nkrumah, quoted in Nkrumah, *Challenge of the Congo*, 58–61.

321 The caller's identity: *FRUS, 1958–1960*, vol. 14, doc. 223.

321 "Measures to Be Applied": For the text of the letters, see "Document 18: Documents saisis sur M. Lumumba lors de son arrestation au camp de la Force Publique à Leopoldville le 14 septembre 1960," *Chronique de Politique Étrangère* 14, no. 5/6 (1961): 652–58. For information on their release, see Situation Report 71-60, Joint Chiefs of Staff Operations Directorate, Sept. 30, 1960, box 3, Congo Situation Reports, International Series, Office of the Staff Secretary: Records, 1952–61, DDEL. For evidence that they were forgeries, see Hoskyns, *Congo Since Independence*, 216; Dayal, *Mission*, 88; Dayal, *Life of Our Times*, 425; Scott, *Tumbled House*, 81; Michel, *Uhuru Lumumba*, 241–42.

322 In the paranoid atmosphere: Officials who believed they were genuine included Carl von Horn (von Horn, *Soldiering for Peace*, 212–13) and Brian Urquhart (Urquhart, *Hammarskjold*, 455). So did Timberlake and, initially at least, Dayal (Dillon to Leopoldville, Sept. 20, 1960 [835], file 312, UNOC Sept.–Oct. 1960 Classified, Security-Segregated Records, U.S. Embassy Leopoldville, RG 84, NACP). The same went for some MNC leaders (*Bulletin de Nouvelles du Congo*, Oct. 5, 1960, S-0752-0024-10, UNA).

322 "the Soviet design": Joseph Alsop, "Khrushchev's Washpot," *New York Herald Tribune*, Sept. 26, 1960.

322 "some foreign hand": Dayal, *Mission*, 88.

322 "Lumumba's definitive elimination": De Witte, *Assassination*, xvi; Van Bilsen, *Congo, 1945–1965*, 263; *EP*, 154, 211. See also De Witte, *Assassination*, 25. *EP* suggests that given the context of the cable, the phrase "definitive elimination" implied Lumumba's political isolation rather than physical liquidation.

322 In this scheme: Days after Kasavubu had renounced reconciliation, the State Department instructed the U.S. embassy in Leopoldville to approach Kasavubu and Mobutu "to persuade them of the desirability of putting the present government structure on a more secure legal footing." Following these instructions, Ambassador Timberlake called on the president one afternoon. After telling Kasavubu that the United States strongly supported him, the ambassador suggested that the president join forces with Mobutu and encourage him to arrest Lumumba, who, he added, was "an evil influence who would be bad for the Congo." Kasavubu "seemed to be eager to

follow our recommendations," Timberlake concluded. Dillon to Leopoldville, Sept. 25, 1960 (886), Files of Visits by Heads of Government, Dignitaries, and Delegations, Office of Secretary, RG 59, NACP; *FRUS, 1958–1960*, vol. 14, doc. 229.

322 He now praised: CRISP, *Congo 1960*, 2:870; Henry Tanner, "Kasavubu Assigns Power in the Congo to Student Regime," *NYT*, Sept. 30, 1960.

322 "In the best interest": Kasavubu speech, Sept. 29, 1960, S-0752-0024-10, UNA.

323 "I never thought that": Kanza, *Rise and Fall*, 340.

323 He had survived: *FRUS, 1958–1960*, vol. 14, doc. 220.

323 "Too anxious to eat": Monheim, *Mobutu*, 148–49. "Mobutu obviously is under great pressure and is extremely nervous," Timberlake reported on September 29. "He said he has had to force himself to eat since his coup, that he drinks much more than in the past." Timberlake to Herter, Sept. 29, 1960 (863), file 770G.00, CDF, General Records of the Department of State, 1960–63, RG 59, NACP. This cable appears in *FRUS, 1958–1960*, vol. 14, doc. 233, with the comments about Mobutu's lack of appetite and increased drinking redacted.

323 "was so fed up that": *FRUS, 1964–1968*, vol. 23, doc. 29.

323 By early October: *EP*, 137.

323 He played with: Mahoney, *JFK*, 59; Mboka, "Kinshasa 2019—Where Does a New President Lay His Head?"; De Vos, *Vie et Mort*, 241–42.

324 Clinging to the idea: Reuters, "Lumumba Thwarted Again," *NYT*, Oct. 8, 1960; "Congo: The Three-Headed State," *Time*, Oct. 3, 1960, 21.

324 "psychological advantage": *FRUS, 1958–1960*, vol. 14, doc. 229.

324 He acquired a pistol: Colonel Möllerswärd to Force Commander, "Extract from Ghana BDE Files Concerning Mr. Lumumba," Sept. 6, 1961, S-0752-0007-07, UNA.

324 his "Messianic" beliefs: Dayal to Hammarskjöld, Sept. 22, 1960 (B1060), box 155, DHC.

324 He accepted dinner: Timberlake, "First Year of Independence in the Congo," 111; Rikhye, quoted in UN Security Council, "Report of the Commission of Investigation Established Under the Terms of General Assembly Resolution 1601 (XV) of 15 April 1961," S/4976 (Nov. 11, 1961), 78; Kashamura, *De Lumumba*, 156.

324 "I am still prime minister": De Vos, *Vie et Mort*, 243.

324 On October 9: Details on Lumumba's October 9 excursion come from "Lumumba Claims Congo Rule Again," *NYT*, Oct. 10, 1960; Paul Hofmann, "Lumumba Bounces Back," *NYT*, Oct. 16, 1960; "UN Protects Lumumba," *Fort Lauderdale News*, Oct. 11, 1960; "Congo: A Night on the Town," *Time*, Oct. 24, 1960; Michel, *Uhuru Lumumba*, 240; Behr, *Anyone Here*, 142–43; Kashamura, *De Lumumba*, 156–57. (Kashamura gets the date wrong.) Mobutu would later allege that Lumumba had also been smoking marijuana.

325 "not very sober": McIlvaine to State, Oct. 12, 1960, Files of Visits by Heads of Government, Dignitaries, and Delegations, Office of Secretary, RG 59, NACP.

325 The next day: Details of the events of October 10, including the dialogue, come from François Lumumba, interview; Juliana Lumumba, interview; Hammarskjöld to Cordier, Aug. 14, 1960 (B452), box 155, DHC; *EP,* 153; Reuters, "Lumumba Calls for a Duel," *NYT,* Oct. 11, 1960; "Lumumba Seeks to Duel Mobutu," *Fort Worth Star-Telegram,* Oct. 11, 1960, 2.

325 What was more: *EP,* 182–83.

38. Backup Plans

327 By one count: Mahoney, *JFK,* 30.

327 "I have seen us": Transcript of Oct. 21, 1960, presidential debate, Commission on Presidential Debates, www.debates.org.

327 "policies which refuse": Muehlenbeck, *Betting on the Africans,* 44.

327 Kennedy's choice of: In August, in a meeting in the bathroom of Johnson's Senate office, Kennedy earned the endorsement of Georgia's segregationist governor, Ernest Vandiver, by quietly promising never to send in federal troops to integrate schools in Georgia the way Eisenhower had done in Arkansas. Vandiver OH, 26–27; "Vandiver Remains Silent, Meets Kennedy Today," *Atlanta Constitution,* Aug. 19, 1960.

327 Kennedy also sent: "Harriman Warns on Communist Takeover in Congo," *Chicago Tribune,* Sept. 17, 1960.

328 The prime minister said: *FRUS, 1958–1960,* vol. 14, doc. 207. See also Dayal to Hammarskjöld, Sept. 14, 1960 (B892), box 155, DHC.

328 "reign of terror": "Harriman Calls Lumumba Defiant Rabble Rouser," *Chicago Tribune,* Sept. 13, 1960.

328 Whether Lumumba is: "Fifth Message from Harriman to Kennedy," Sept. 13, 1960, JFKPOF-114-006-p0038, Congo: General, 1959–60, JFKL. On Harriman's assessment of Lumumba, I differ from Mahoney, who writes that Harriman's "reading of Lumumba was essentially neutral" (Mahoney, *JFK,* 43). After returning from Africa, Harriman wrote up his findings in a report for Kennedy that was no more sympathetic than his initial message: "Lumumba is emotionally convinced that it is his mission to unify the Congo through a strong centralized government. He believes he is the only man who speaks for the Congolese people.... To achieve his ambition for the establishment of a centralized government, he is prepared to plunge the country into civil war." "Summary of the Report on the Congo and West Africa to Senator John F. Kennedy by W. Averell Harriman," JFKPOF-114-006-p0031, Congo: General, 1959–60, JFKL. Harriman also met with Kasavubu, whom he found disappointing. As Dayal told Hammarskjöld, the president "asked for funds and displayed little evidence of his awareness of the situation." Dayal to Hammarskjöld, Sept. 14, 1960 (B892).

328 "long way from the troubled": For the text of the speech, see speech by Senator John F. Kennedy, City Hall Square, Bowling Green, Kentucky (advance release text), Oct. 8, 1960, American Presidency Project, www.presidency.ucsb

.edu. For other details about it, see "Kennedy Heads South After Night in Louisville," *Madisonville (Ky.) Messenger,* Oct. 10, 1960, 1; "Kennedy Given Kentucky Ham," *Tennessean* (Nashville), Oct. 9, 1960, 6; Jonathan Jeffrey, "Kennedy Campaign Comes to Bowling Green in October 1960," *Kentucky Explorer* 28, no. 7 (2013): 41–44, digitalcommons.wku.edu.

329 When the passenger jet: Details on Maureen and Colette Devlin's arrival and living arrangements are from Reimuller, interview; Devlin, *Chief of Station,* 101–102.

330 There was also an army: Devlin to Tweedy, Sept. 27, 1960 (0026), in testimony of Bronson Tweedy, Oct. 10, 1975, 157-10014-10068, JFKAR. The five Baluba may be a reference to a group another source referred to around the same time as "five Bayakas." See *EP,* 198.

330 The man, referred to: The name "Schotroffe" is left unredacted in the version of the following cable released in 2022: Director to Devlin, Sept. 30, 1960, in testimony of Bronson Tweedy, Oct. 9, 1975, 157-10014-10089, JFKAR. The name can also be seen in the Sept. 22, 1960, cable quoted in draft of Congo section of assassination report, Oct. 6, 1975, 26, 157-10014-10136. It is not clear whether this is a pseudonym. A more common surname is "Schottroff." Devlin identified the person as a "non-American agent with potential access to Lumumba's kitchen and living quarters," and "a European who worked as an adviser to Mulele." Devlin, *Chief of Station,* 90, 96–97.

330 "act as inside man": *AAP,* 27.

330 "a double-talk way": Testimony of Victor Hedgeman, Aug. 21, 1975, 43, 157-10014-10080, JFKAR; *AAP,* 38.

330 "third-country national": *AAP,* 29.

330 For now, the poisoning: Devlin and Gottlieb would offer different accounts of what happened to the poison. Devlin cabled headquarters saying that Gottlieb had left "certain items of continuing usefulness," which would seem to indicate that Gottlieb left behind the poisons, and later claimed that he got rid of them only after Lumumba was imprisoned in December. Justin O'Donnell would back up this account, recalling that a month after Gottlieb's departure Devlin had told him that the station's safe contained a lethal substance. Gottlieb, however, claimed that he took the toxic materials home with him, since, he said, they were "not refrigerated and unstable." Ibid., 29–30.

330 What about forming: Tweedy to Devlin, Oct. 15, 1960 (first cable), in testimony of Bronson Tweedy, Oct. 9, 1975.

331 Ironically, Lumumba was: See *FRUS, 1958–1960,* vol. 14, doc. 243.

331 "It seems to us": Tweedy to Devlin, Oct. 15, 1960 (second cable), in testimony of Bronson Tweedy, Oct. 9, 1975.

331 Devlin would later claim: In this I differ slightly from *AAP,* 26, which concluded that "the cables portray [Devlin] as taking an affirmative, aggressive attitude toward the assignment, while he testified that his pursuit of the operation was less vigorous." Weissman shares that assessment, writing, "Whatever reservations he may have held about the assassination plot, there is no inde-

pendent evidence that Devlin actually stalled it" (Weissman, "Extraordinary Rendition," 206). Although Devlin's September 28 cable did propose seven ideas, A through G, he himself deemed many of them impractical. And after Gottlieb's departure on October 5, the only proposal Devlin made was his request for a rifle, though he pointed out that this plan, too, could not be enacted immediately. See Devlin to Tweedy, Oct. 17, 1960, in testimony of Bronson Tweedy, Oct. 9, 1975. See also Thomas, *Very Best Men,* 223, which reports that "the cable traffic makes Devlin look like a willing warrior, but his old colleagues say that he intentionally stalled."

331 In a series of: *AAP,* 27.

331 He talked to a Congolese: Draft of Congo section of assassination report, Oct. 6, 1975, 13, 157-10014-10136, JFKAR.

331 "high-powered, foreign-make": Devlin to Tweedy, Oct. 17, 1960, in testimony of Bronson Tweedy, Oct. 9, 1975; *AAP,* 32.

331 "great mental torture": "Report by Capt. N. Y. Sowani on His Talk with Mr. Lumumba at 121230," Oct. 12, 1960, S-0735-0015-03, UNA. The report about psychiatric care comes from "Entr'acte," *Time,* Oct. 17, 1960, 25.

331 A plan to cut off: Heinz and Donnay, *Lumumba,* 27.

331 His five-year-old daughter: Juliana Lumumba, interview.

332 Even so, Lumumba: Kashamura, *De Lumumba,* 159; Dayal, *Mission,* 127; Kanza, *Rise and Fall,* 311.

332 "Our difficulties are": Blouin, *My Country, Africa,* 271.

332 Yet his own advisers: Memorandum, no author listed but almost certainly drafted by Dayal, Oct. 7, 1960, box 137, DHC; Kanza, *Rise and Fall,* 311; Alvarez, *Lumumba; ou, L'Afrique frustrée,* 126; Henry Tanner, "Soldiers Calmed in Leopoldville," *NYT,* Sept. 23, 1960; draft of Congo section of assassination report, Oct. 6, 1975, 13. The Congolese helper was in fact the same person who told Devlin he was trying to kill Lumumba.

332 As the number of: Timberlake to State, Oct. 12, 1960 (962), file 361.2, Classified, Security-Segregated Records, U.S. Embassy Leopoldville, RG 84, NACP.

332 After dusk on: Details on the operation to extract the Lumumba children from the Congo come from Juliana Lumumba, interview; François Lumumba, interview; Kanza, *Rise and Fall,* 310–11; "Escape to Cairo," *Making Contact* (podcast), Kerning Cultures, July 27, 2022, www.radioproject.org.

333 Louis Armstrong was: Ricky Riccardi, "'Satchmo Charms Congo Cats': Louis Armstrong and Leopoldville, 60 Years Later," Oct. 28, 2020, Louis Armstrong House Museum Virtual Exhibits; AP, "Louis Armstrong in Congo," Dec. 1960, www.youtube.com; Maureen Reimuller, interview; Paul Hofmann, "Satchmo Plays for Congo's Cats," *NYT,* Oct. 29, 1960; "Leapin' in Leopoldville," *Tampa Bay Times,* Oct. 29, 1960; von Eschen, *Satchmo Blows Up the World,* 67–70.

333 "Many murders, assaults": Dayal to Hammarskjöld, Oct. 22, 1960 (1289), box 156, DHC.

333 It was not unusual: "U.N. in Africa—Showdown," *Newsweek,* Nov. 7, 1960, 53; *FRUS, 1958–1960,* vol. 14, doc. 249; Dayal to Hammarskjöld, Oct. 20, 1960

(B1276), box 156, DHC; UN Security Council, "Second Progress Report to the Secretary General from his Special Representative in the Congo," S/4557 (Nov. 2, 1960), 37; "Violence in Congo Results in Curfew," *Edmonton Journal,* Oct. 18, 1960; "U.N. Army Apologizes for Attack," *La Crosse (Wis.) Tribune,* Oct. 16, 1960; Dayal to Hammarskjöld, Oct. 22, 1960 (B1288), box 156, DHC; Artigue, *Qui sont les leaders congolais?,* 189. The minister was Josué Maboshi.

333 Starving Luba refugees: Dayal to Hammarskjöld, Oct. 15, 1960 (B1255), box 156, DHC; von Horn, *Soldiering for Peace,* 232; Rikhye to Hammarskjöld, Nov. 10, 1960 (B1396), box 156, DHC.

334 "full moral, economic": Paul Hofmann, "Mobutu Reports 'Full Backing' by Tshombe for His Congo Rule," *NYT,* Oct. 18, 1960.

334 "neutralize Lumumba completely": *EP,* 473. The ellipsis is in the original.

334 And yet despite: For relations between the College of Commissioners and Katanga at the time, see Gerard-Libois, *Katanga Secession,* 133–34, and Hoskyns, *Congo Since Independence,* 241.

334 He sent a lobbyist: Burden to State, Sept. 30, 1960 (738), Belgian Congo Independence Ceremonies, Files of Visits by Heads of Government, Dignitaries, and Delegations, 1928–77, Office of Secretary/Office of the Chief of Protocol, box 8, RG 59, NACP; "Envoy for Tshombe," *NYT,* Aug. 3, 1964; Dayal, *Mission,* 108.

334 Nearly three hundred: "Second Progress Report to the Secretary General from his Special Representative in the Congo," 15.

334 In the town of Kabalo: Dayal to Hammarskjöld, Oct. 22, 1960 (B1288).

334 At a bridge near: On the Niemba massacre, see Sean O'Riordan, "60 Years On: Why Nine Peacekeeping Irish Soldiers Were Murdered in the Congo," *Irish Examiner,* Nov. 11, 2020, www.irishexaminer.com; Kennedy and Magennis, *Ireland,* 33–36; von Horn, *Soldiering for Peace,* 231.

335 According to notes: Notes on Mobutu and Bomboko's meeting with the College of Commissioners, Oct. 12, 1960, S-0735-0015-03, UNA.

335 Equally inexperienced: Dayal to Hammarskjöld, Sept. 24, 1960 (B1068), box 155, DHC; Hoskyns, *Congo Since Independence,* 242.

335 Pointing to his failure: Paul Hofmann, "Congo Commission Berates Mobutu," *NYT,* Oct. 16, 1960.

335 Rumors swirled that: Dayal to Hammarskjöld, Oct. 22, 1960 (B1291), box 156, DHC; AP, "Terror Reigning in Stanleyville," *NYT,* Nov. 13, 1960; Hoskyns, *Congo Since Independence,* 243.

335 "Mobutu is encountering": Synopsis of State and Intelligence material, Oct. 18, 1960, box 14, Intelligence Briefing Notes, Subject Series, Alphabetical Subseries, Office of the Staff Secretary, DDEL.

335 "the possibility of a pro-Soviet": *FRUS, 1964–1968,* vol. 23, docs. 41, 42; "Covert Military Operations in the Congo, 1964–1967."

335 Realizing that sleeping: "New Drive Starts for Lumumba," *Fort Worth Star-Telegram,* Oct. 22, 1960; Dayal to Hammarskjöld, Nov. 2, 1960 (B1347), box 156, DHC.

336 Over the course of one: Paul Hofmann, "Mobutu Arrests 15 During Curfew," *NYT,* Oct. 20, 1960; Kashamura, *De Lumumba,* 158; Dayal, *Mission,* 127.

336 Mobutu still appeared: "U.N. in Africa—Showdown," *Newsweek,* Nov. 7, 1960, 53; "Squeezing the Colonel," *Time,* Nov. 7, 1960, 32–33; Dayal to Hammar-skjöld, Oct. 4, 1960 (B1171), box 156, DHC.

336 "a childish individual": *FRUS, 1958–1960,* vol. 14, doc. 242. For the full discussion, which shows that the president was present, see Memorandum, Discussion at the 463rd Meeting of the National Security Council, Oct. 13, 1960, box 13, 463rd Meeting of NSC, NSC Series, Papers as President, 1953–61 (Whitman File), DDEL.

336 When Devlin heard rumors: *FRUS, 1964–1968,* vol. 23, doc. 31.

336 When he got wind: *FRUS, 1958–1960,* vol. 14, doc. 247.

336 When Mobutu wanted: *FRUS, 1964–1968,* vol. 23, doc. 37; Timberlake to Herter, Oct. 23, 1960 (1029), file 312, UNOC Sept.–Oct. 1960 Classified, Security-Segregated Records, U.S. Embassy Leopoldville, RG 84, NACP. After Mobutu's trip was canceled, Dayal wrote, "There is good reason to believe that he would have been deposed had he gone"—which raises an interesting counterfactual. Dayal to Hammarskjöld, Oct. 24, 1960 (B1301), box 156, DHC.

336 If a stern talking-to: *FRUS, 1964–1968,* vol. 23, docs. 35, 37. Dayal also believed a coup was imminent. Dayal to Hammarskjöld, Oct. 21, 1960 (B1281), box 156, DHC.

336 "convince him of the advantages": *FRUS, 1964–1968,* vol. 23, docs. 37, 38.

336 The budget for this: "Covert Military Operations in the Congo: 1964–1967," 21–22. For a sense of comparison, the annual salary of Gordon Gray, a top White House official, was around $22,000. Order given by Eisenhower, July 22, 1958, box 244, OF 72-A-2 Gray, Aides to the President, John Foster Dulles, White House Central Files, Official Files, 1953–61, DDEL.

337 He began working closely: On the Binza Group, see Young, *Politics in the Congo,* 379–80; Devlin, *Chief of Station,* 98–99; Weissman, *American Foreign Policy,* 109; and Brassinne, "Enquête," testimony 36.2.

337 "la petite Maureen": Reimuller, interview.

337 He found him intelligent: Devlin OH.

39. Cold Storage

338 "basically a weak person": Dayal to Hammarskjöld, Nov. 2, 1960 (B1347), box 156, DHC; Dayal to Hammarskjöld, Oct. 22, 1960 (B1289), box 156, DHC; Dayal to Hammarskjöld, Oct. 26, 1960 (B1306), box 156, DHC.

338 He reminded the press: Dayal's zingers come from Timberlake to Herter, Oct. 24, 1960 (1036), file 312, UNOC Sept.–Oct. 1960 Classified, Security-Segregated Records, U.S. Embassy Leopoldville, RG 84, NACP; "The Faltering Colonel," *Time,* Oct. 31, 1960, 21–22.

338 "like a child": "New Drive Starts for Lumumba." See also Cordier OH, 530.

338 In this, he had: Dayal, *Mission,* 134.

338 At the core of: Kalb, *Congo Cables*, 135.

339 "A political personality": CRISP, *Congo 1960*, 2:926.

339 "no other leader of ": *AAP*, 15.

339 "in cold storage": Dayal, *Mission*, 104.

339 "way out of the": Dayal to Hammarskjöld, Oct. 27, 1960 (B1314), box 156, DHC.

339 Dayal perfected what: Dayal, *Mission*, 109; Dayal to Hammarskjöld, Oct. 5, 1960 (B1181), box 156, DHC; Dayal to Hammarskjöld, Oct. 13, 1960 (B1241), box 156, DHC; Linnér OH, 15–16.

340 "Mobutu is the key": *FRUS, 1958–1960*, vol. 14, doc. 263.

340 Eisenhower, sensing that: *FRUS, 1961–1963*, vol. 20, doc. 4.

340 State Department officials felt: Herter to US UN, Oct. 17, 1960 (1091), file 312, UNOC Sept.–Oct. 1960 Classified, Security-Segregated Records, U.S. Embassy Leopoldville, RG 84, NACP; *FRUS, 1958–1960*, vol. 14, doc. 241.

340 Besides, he still considered: *FRUS, 1958–1960*, vol. 14, docs. 243, 206.

340 Even veiled U.S. threats: Ibid., docs. 248, 249.

341 Moroccan officers were: Hammarskjöld to Mobutu, Oct. 2, 1960, box 133, DHC.

341 "not a colony of ": Mobutu to Hammarskjöld, Oct. 1, 1960, box 133, DHC; Monheim, *Mobutu*, 190–91; Dayal to Hammarskjöld, Oct. 28, 1960 (B1318), box 156, DHC.

341 Nor could Dayal do: Paul Hofmann, "11 Congo Officers Receive U.S. Visas," *NYT*, Nov. 2, 1960.

341 After State Department: Telephone Calls, Oct. 22, 1960, box 13, CAH Telephone Calls, Herter Papers, DDEL.

341 Unwilling to publicly: *FRUS, 1958–1960*, vol. 14, doc. 255.

341 Devlin considered him: Woodrow Wilson International Center OH, 88.

341 "violently anti-Mobutu": *FRUS, 1958–1960*, vol. 14, doc. 253.

341 "reacting as a Hindu": Timberlake to Herter, Oct. 11, 1960 (950), file 312, UNOC Sept.–Oct. 1960 Classified, Security-Segregated Records, U.S. Embassy Leopoldville, RG 84, NACP. For more on their overlap in India, see Dayal, *Mission*, 44; biographical information on Timberlake, box 1, folder 4, CTP *FRUS, 1958–1960*, vol. 14, doc. 253.

341 represented the "Indianization": Timberlake to Herter, Nov. 4, 1960 (1110), file 312, UNOC Nov. 1960 Classified, Security-Segregated Records, U.S. Embassy Leopoldville, RG 84, NACP.

341 The notion spread: Kalb, *Congo Cables*, 139. It seems likely that policy disagreements morphed into personal ones, and that Dayal was not in fact haughty. As Conor Cruise O'Brien would write, "Mr. Dayal's whole bearing... was extremely impressive; I found in it no trace of the 'arrogance' so persistently ascribed to him, but on the contrary an unusual degree of considerate courtesy." O'Brien, *To Katanga and Back*, 64.

341 An anonymous letter: Anonymous letter ("la population") to Dayal, Oct. 12, 1960, S-0735-0015-03, UNA; Dayal, *Mission*, 136.

341 Giving Dayal just: "Congo—The Jungle," *Newsweek*, Nov. 14, 1960, 49; Dayal, *Mission*, 110.

342 "like a deep-sea diver": Ibid., 113.

342 "The eruption of the army": "Second Progress Report to the Secretary-General from His Special Representative in the Congo," S/4557 (Nov. 2, 1960), 37, 9, 35; Hoskyns, *Congo Since Independence*, 254.

342 Everyone expected the Belgians: Urquhart, *Hammarskjold*, 476.

342 "unable to accept": "Text of U.S. Statement," *NYT*, Nov. 5, 1960. Wigny said his government would be "everlastingly grateful" for this statement. Wadsworth to Herter, Nov. 7, 1960 (1310), file 312, UNOC Nov. 1960 Classified, Security-Segregated Records, U.S. Embassy Leopoldville, RG 84, NACP.

342 Breaking a four-week silence: Paul Hofmann, "Lumumba Praises U.N. Congo Report," *NYT*, Nov. 8, 1960. The United States, Lumumba noted, was "attacking it in a twisted way." Lumumba to UNGA President, n.d., box 1a8, DHC.

342 "Don't worry, my dear": Hoskyns, *Congo Since Independence*, 255.

342 Eisenhower, who had: Thomas, *Ike's Bluff*, 389–90, 393.

342 He paced back: White, *Making of the President*, 21–22.

342 An ocean away: Mahoney, *JFK*, 33; Williams OH, 66.

343 There was only one: Palmer to parents, Nov. 10, 1960, series 5, box 2, folder 16, APP.

343 So when news came: It was the closest election in eighty years as defined by the popular vote margin. See "Presidential Election Margin of Victory," American Presidency Project, www.presidency.ucsb.edu.

343 On the other side: Woodrow Wilson International Center OH, 78, 122–23, 177; Kanza, *Rise and Fall*, 314.

343 Through a Moroccan: Kanza, *Rise and Fall*, 314; Mahoney, *JFK*, 59.

343 He called up: Dayal, *Mission*, 258; Dayal, *Life of Our Times*, 457; Joseph Alsop, "Appointments: Kennedy & the Cape Cod Clams," *Charlotte News*, Nov. 15, 1960.

343 Dayal and Bowles: Biographical information on Timberlake, box 1, folder 4, CTP; Devlin, *Chief of Station*, 125. When Bowles visited the Belgian Congo in 1955, he doubted the official line that the Belgians were there to stay and instead concluded that they would soon flee in panic. In a series of lectures the next year, published in *The Reporter*, he issued an ahead-of-its-time appeal for the United States to ally itself with African independence movements. When Bowles accurately observed that the Belgian authorities had "no intention of granting independence," one such official replied with a letter saying that the Congolese were neither interested in nor ready for independence—a reply that Lumumba quoted approvingly in his 1956 book manuscript. See Chester Bowles, "Africa: We'd Better Mean What We Say," *Reporter*, July 12, 1956, 32; Alfred Claeys Bouuaert, "Mr. Bowles and Africa," *Reporter*, Sept. 20, 1956, 6; Lumumba, *Congo, My Country*, 184.

343 The UN's efforts: Memorandum of telephone conversation between Dayal and Bowles, Nov. 16, 1960, box 141, DHC.

343 Conversations with Dean Rusk: Dayal, *Mission*, 121, 114; *FRUS, 1958–1960*, vol. 14, doc. 283.

343 "sustain a holding operation": Dayal, *Life of Our Times,* 441.

343 Kennedy never replied: Woodrow Wilson International Center OH, 121–22, 180–82; Kanza, *Rise and Fall,* 314.

40. Vote of Confidence

345 His name was Justin O'Donnell: *AAP,* 292; testimony of Richard Bissell, Sept. 10, 1975, 51–52, 157-10014-10093, JFKAR; J. Y. Smith, "J. E. O'Donnell Dies," *Washington Post,* Aug. 26, 1983, www.washingtonpost.com.

345 He was not opposed: *AAP,* 40–42.

346 It had recruited André Mankel: Biographical details on Mankel come from Olivier Tasch, "Le Luxembourgeois de la CIA," *Le Jeudi,* Sept. 5, 2013; Notes on Q_JWIN, Nov. 22, 1978, 180-10143-10212, JFKAR; Brussels to Director, Feb. 4, 1955 (728), 104-10079-10364, JFKAR; Mason Cargill to File, April 30, 1975, 157-10003-10490, JFKAR; Urgent HSCA request for file search on Mankel, April 4, 1978, 104-10079-10112, JFKAR; Summary of interview with William Harvey, n.d., 157-10004-10138, JFKAR; Description and photograph of Mankel, Oct. 7, 1960, 104-10185-10015, JFKAR; Trace request on André Mankel, Sept. 9, 1958, 104-10178-10017, JFKAR. While there has been uncertainty over the years as to whether Jose Marie André Mankel was his real name, it appears to be. In December 1960, the Leopoldville station requested that $500 be deposited in the account of his wife, Simone Mankel. Director to Leopoldville, Dec. 6, 1960, 104-10185-10007, JFKAR.

346 Mankel was told: Details on O'Donnell's meeting with Mankel and travel to Leopoldville come from Director to Luxembourg, Oct. 26, 1960, 104-10185-10079, JFKAR; Luxembourg to Director, Oct. 27, 1960, 104-10185-10078, JFKAR; Frankfurt to Director, Nov. 2, 1960, 104-10185-10011, JFKAR; Luxembourg to Director, Nov. 11, 1960, 104-10125-10399, JFKAR.

346 He looked into renting: *AAP,* 41, 43.

346 "immediate expedition of": Ibid., 43.

346 "Concentric rings of": *FRUS, 1964–1968,* vol. 23, doc. 43.

347 Mobutu's Belgian military adviser: *EP,* 202, 183–84, 777, 835–36.

347 Wearing stolen armbands: *FRUS, 1964–1968,* vol. 23, doc. 46.

347 "trick him out": *AAP,* 42.

347 The group was set: Wadsworth to State, Nov. 22, 1960 (1339), UNOC Nov. 1960 Classified, Security-Segregated Records, U.S. Embassy Leopoldville, RG 84, NACP; Lindesay Parrott, "U.N. Congo Group to Try to Revive Parliament Rule," *NYT,* Nov. 6, 1960.

347 Belgian hotel managers: Rikhye to Hammarskjöld, Nov. 14, 1960 (B1425), box 156, DHC; Rikhye to Hammarskjöld, Nov. 17, 1960 (B1454), box 156, DHC.

348 "the colonel who had": Rikhye to Hammarskjöld, Nov. 20, 1960 (B1476), box 156, DHC.

348 Lumumba's pregnant wife: Details on Lumumba's daughter's death and the

transfer of her remains come from Kashamura, *De Lumumba*, 162; UN Security Council, "Report to the Secretary-General from His Special Representative in the Congo Regarding Certain Actions Taken Against Mr. Patrice Lumumba," S/4571 (Dec. 5, 1960); Dayal to Hammarskjöld, Nov. 23, 1960 (B1502), box 156, DHC; "Hearing of Mr. Thomas Kanza and Mr. Dragoslav Protitch," May 19, 1961, box 153, DHC; "Hearing of General Rikhye," box 161, AWCP; Allan Morrison, "The Tragedy of Mrs. Lumumba," *Jet*, March 9, 1961, 14–18; Heinz and Donnay, *Lumumba*, 31–32; Dayal, *Mission*, 132; Urquhart, *Hammarskjold*, 478–79; *EP*, 219; Borsinger to Geneva, Dec. 8, 1960 (note 370), B AG 225 229-002, ICRCA; testimony of Albert Onawelo, VII-BV/RDC/Lumumba N°001/02, FBV; and ordre de mission, Nov. 24, 1960, VII-BV/RDC/Lumumba N°007/02, FBV.

348 The first was down: Details on the Ghanaian embassy incident come from Alexander, *African Tightrope*, 52–60; Dayal, *Mission*, 129–32; Nkrumah, *Challenge of the Congo*, 86–87; Rikhye, *Military Adviser*, 148–49; Rikhye, *Trumpets and Tumults*, 149; Rikhye to Martin, Nov. 16, 1960, S-0752-0003, UNA; Rikhye to Hammarskjöld, Nov. 17, 1960 (B1445); Rikhye to Hammarskjöld, Report on the situation in the Republic of the Congo, Nov. 22, 1960, box 137, DHC; Reimuller, interview; "President's Week," *Time*, Nov. 28, 1960, 24; "The Embassy Firefight," *Time*, Dec. 5, 1960, 26; "The Congo: Stormy to Clearing?," *Newsweek*, Dec. 5, 1960, 42; Paul Hofmann, "Congo Expelling Ghana Diplomats; Resists U.N. Visits," *NYT*, Nov. 19, 1960.

348 Acting on advice: Devlin, *Chief of Station*, 123.

349 Thomas Kanza made plans: Rikhye to Hammarskjöld, Nov. 8, 1960 (B1383), box 156, DHC.

349 In New York, Kasavubu: Richard F. Shepard, "Kasavubu Talks on TV Tomorrow," *NYT*, Nov. 12, 1960; Virginia Lee, "Watch Night Rites Planned," *Mansfield News-Journal*, Dec. 31, 1960.

349 "I have a question": Anonymous, interview.

349 The centerpiece of his: Hoskyns, *Congo Since Independence*, 260. Behind the scenes, the U.S. mission to the UN also worked to arrange this outcome: State Department officials ghostwrote for Kasavubu a letter to the General Assembly committee in charge of credentials, asking for his people to be deemed the legitimate representatives of the Congo, and then, when the committee met, recommended that the request be granted. *FRUS, 1958–1960*, vol. 2, docs. 241, 246. Gerard and Kuklick, *Death in the Congo*, 178.

349 But among the ninety-eight: Hoskyns, *Congo Since Independence*, 263.

350 Run out of a leased suite: 333 East Forty-Sixth Street was also home to the African Research Foundation, another CIA front. See David H. Price, *Cold War Anthropology: The CIA, the Pentagon, and the Growth of Dual Use Anthropology* (Durham, N.C.: Duke University Press, 2016). See also Don Irwin and Vincent J. Burke, "21 Foundations, Union Got Money from CIA," *Los Angeles Times*, Feb. 26, 1967.

350 It was headed: Imbrey OH, ADST, 9.

350 His junior partner: AP, "Vanishing Deadpan Tribe Found Deep in Thailand," *Leader-Post* (Regina, Saskatchewan, Canada), May 1, 1956.

350 "By the time a": "Two Young Americans Show How to Succeed in Business in Africa," *Negro Digest,* May 1962.

350 Imbrey had joined: "Obituaries," *Washington Post,* Dec. 6, 2002; Imbrey OH, ADST, 30.

350 "a two-month assignment": Imbrey to Timberlake, July 1, 1960, box 3, folder 1.

350 In Imbrey's words: Imbrey OH, ADST, 30–31; Imbrey, interview by Curtis Ostle, 12. See also Roberts OH, 30.

350 So extensive was: Roberts OH, 31.

350 The bribery, combined: *FRUS, 1958–1960,* vol. 14, doc. 264; Hoskyns, *Congo Since Independence,* 263–64.

351 "perhaps one of the": Dayal, *Mission,* 119. See also Quaison-Sackey, *Reflections of an African Statesman,* 90.

351 Troubling rumors circulated: Paul Hofmann, "U.N. Troops Put on Alert as Congo's Army Digs In," *NYT,* Nov. 24, 1960.

351 He emerged from his: Dayal, *Mission,* 142; Paul Hofmann, "Cries of 'King!' Hail Kasavubu as He Returns to Leopoldville," *NYT,* Nov. 28, 1960; "Bringing Him Back Alive," *Time,* Dec. 12, 1960, 28; Dayal to Hammarskjöld, Nov. 28, 1960 (B1529), box 156, DHC; Dayal to Hammarskjöld, Nov. 28, 1960 (B1528), box 156, DHC; Dayal to Hammarskjöld, Nov. 28, 1960 (B1527), box 156, DHC; Brassinne and Kestergat, *Qui a tué,* 69.

351 The place was empty: Dayal, *Mission,* 142; von Horn, *Soldiering for Peace,* 247; Leopoldville to State, Dec. 2, 1960 (178), file 755A.00, CDF, General Records of the Department of State, 1960–63, RG 59, NACP; "Extract from Moroccan BDE Files Concerning Mr. Lumumba," S-0752-0007-07, UNA; Carlucci to State, Dec. 2, 1960 (177), Classified General Records, 1934–63, Security-Segregated Records, U.S. Embassy Leopoldville, RG 84, NACP.

41. The Big Rabbit Has Escaped

355 There, the MNC: AP, "Gizenga Rallying Congo Force to Return Lumumba to Power," *Portland (Maine) Press Herald,* Nov. 14, 1960, 24.

355 Victor Lundula, a high-ranking: Gizenga, *Ma vie et mes luttes,* 267; Dayal to Hammarskjöld, Nov. 24, 1960 (B1504), box 156, DHC; Kanza, *Rise and Fall,* 316. Lundula nominally led the ANC before Mobutu took charge.

355 Antoine Gizenga, Lumumba's: Gizenga, *Ma vie et mes luttes,* 222.

355 The newcomers linked: Omasombo and Verhaegen, *Jeunesse,* 80; Henry Tanner, "Mobutu Reports 'Sedition' Foiled," *NYT,* Oct. 6, 1960.

355 By late November: CRISP, *Congo 1960,* 2:998; Hoskyns, *Congo Since Independence,* 243–44; AP, "Gizenga Rallying Congo Force to Return Lumumba to Power"; Timberlake to Herter, Sept. 4, 1960 (103), file 312, UNOC Sept.–Oct. 1960 Classified, Security-Segregated Records, U.S. Embassy Leopoldville, RG 84, NACP.

356 It was clear: The aide was Bernardin Diaka. Artigue, *Qui sont les leaders,* 64; Heinz and Donnay, *Lumumba,* 9.

356 "Things won't stay": Protocol of the hearing of Thomas Kanza and Dragoslav Protitch, May 19, 1961, box 153, DHC; Kanza, *Rise and Fall,* 312. See also Heinz and Donnay, *Lumumba,* 10.

356 "If I die": Kashamura, *De Lumumba,* 165.

356 At Lumumba's house: Details of Lumumba's escape are drawn from Heinz and Donnay, *Lumumba,* 3–47, except when otherwise noted.

356 At 9:30 p.m.: Omar Joussi to M. M. El Glaoui, Nov. 28, 1960, S-0752-0007-07, UNA.

357 The car crept: Paul Hofmann, "Lumumba Flees Guards in Congo," *NYT,* Nov. 29, 1960.

357 The loyal ministerial: Kamitatu, *La grande mystification,* 76.

357 Kenge, a trading post: Tourist Bureau for the Belgian Congo & Ruanda-Urundi, *Traveller's Guide,* 243.

357 He was less than: For the possibility of a plane in Luluabourg, see Gerard and Kuklick, *Death in the Congo,* 180.

358 Mobutu and Kasavubu first: Kalb, *Congo Cables,* 158.

358 "The big rabbit": Heinz and Donnay, *Lumumba,* 4, 41.

358 At Lumumba's instruction: Kanza, *Rise and Fall,* 313.

358 "I have never": Hofmann, "Lumumba Flees Guards in Congo"; Carlucci to State, Dec. 2, 1960 (177), Classified General Records, 1934–63, Security-Segregated Records, U.S. Embassy Leopoldville, RG 84, NACP; CRISP, *Congo 1960,* 2:1053.

358 A more plausible story: Carlucci to State, Dec. 2, 1960 (177); Hammarskjöld to Dayal, Nov. 30, 1960 (3828), S-0735-00015-03, UNA.

358 Dayal pushed back: Dayal, *Mission,* 143.

358 "The responsibility for": "Meeting of the Special Representative with President Kasavubu," Nov. 28, 1960, S-0752-0003-04, UNA.

358 If that happened: *FRUS, 1958–1960,* vol. 14, doc. 273. The meeting was attended by Eisenhower. See "The President's Appointments," Presidential Appointment Books, Dec. 1960, DDEL.

358 Fortunately for Dulles: Devlin, *Chief of Station,* 114–15; testimony of Victor Hedgeman, Aug. 21, 1975, 65, 157-10014-10080, JFKAR. Speaking to Church Committee investigators, Devlin later claimed he was "not a major assistance" in finding Lumumba. *AAP,* 49.

359 As Devlin worked: *AAP,* 48; Dayal to Hammarskjöld, Nov. 29, 1960 (B1545), box 156, DHC. Von Horn's Canadian military assistant, J. A. Berthiaume, would later claim that he told Mobutu to send paratroopers to arrest Lumumba in a particular village. See Spooner, *Canada,* 116.

359 These eyes in the: De Witte, *Assassination,* 54; *EP,* 224. For information on the airline involved, Air Brousse, see Brassinne, "Enquête," testimony 44.1.

359 promised "full assistance": On December 1, a cable from Brazzaville referred to support in the chase that was offered by "Raymond in the name of his

house." De Witte considers this a reference to Raymond Linard, a pilot (De Witte, *Assassination*, 54). By contrast, the Belgian Parliamentary Report claims it referred to the CIA. (*EP*, 222n23). According to Gerard and Kuklick, "Raymond" was indeed the code name Belgian security officials used for Devlin (Gerard and Kuklick, *Death in the Congo*, 163).

359 More time slipped: Kamitatu, *La grande mystification*, 78; Tourist Bureau for the Belgian Congo & Ruanda-Urundi, *Traveller's Guide*, 244.

359 The information swiftly: *EP*, 223; Kamitatu, *La grande mystification*, 78; Hearing of General Rikhye by the Commission of Investigation, June 5, 1961, box 161, AWCP.

360 "But what about": Lev Volodin, "Last Days of Freedom," in Lumumba, *Fighter for Africa's Freedom*, 108.

360 Lumumba now had: Veillet-Lavallee to Dayal, Dec. 3, 1960, S-0735-0015-03, UNA.

360 Residents emerged from: Volodin, "Last Days of Freedom," 106.

360 "Wherever he passed": Kashamura, *De Lumumba*, 167.

360 The vehicles had pulled: CRISP, *Congo 1960*, 2:1054.

360 a narrow forest lane: Tourist Bureau for the Belgian Congo & Ruanda-Urundi, *Traveller's Guide*, 278.

361 illuminated by moonlight: "Moon Phase: Dec. 01, 1960," MoonGiant, www.moongiant.com; "Moonrise and Moonset Times (Location) Calculator," ke!san Online Calculator, keisan.casio.com.

361 The Sankuru was the: De Witte, *Assassination*, 54.

361 the six-hundred-yard-wide: Tourist Bureau for the Belgian Congo & Ruanda-Urundi, *Traveller's Guide*, 278.

361 "We know Lumumba": Kashamura, *De Lumumba*, 169.

361 Back on the other: Accounts of Lumumba's capture in Lodi would become much mythologized and vary widely. On the competing versions of the story, see Kalb, *Congo Cables*, 161–62, and Heinz and Donnay, *Lumumba*, 37–39. I have relied on the account of Heinz and Donnay from "a direct witness, especially well-located to observe the events and report them objectively." See Heinz and Donnay, *Lumumba*, 39–40. There is some ambiguity in that account, however, regarding on which side of the river the confrontation with Lumumba took place.

361 "You don't have": Heinz and Donnay, *Lumumba*, 39.

361 "Lieutenant, I am": Volodin, "Last Days of Freedom," 110. On the role of the Ghanaians, see A. C. Gilpin and Catherine Hoskyns, "An Exchange on the Death of Lumumba," *New York Review of Books*, April 22, 1971. Hammarskjöld would later claim, inaccurately, that it would have been impossible for the UN to protect Lumumba. De Witte, *Assassination*, 151.

362 It would assist neither: Dayal, *Mission*, 143; Hearing of General Rikhye by the Commission of Investigation, June 5, 1961. See also von Horn to Michel, Nov. 30, 1960, S-0735-0015-03, UNA. In a cable to Hammarskjöld, Dayal reported with alarm that the Ghanaian forces in Kasai "casually mentioned their inten-

tion to provide protective custody to Lumumba in case it was requested." Dayal put an end to such thinking: "We have taken the firm position that he was under ONUC guard at his residence only and cannot be allowed ONUC cover or protection in pursuit of his aims, and ONUC must be entirely dissociated from his activities.... I believe this line is consistent with your ruling." Dayal to Hammarskjöld, Dec. 1, 1960 (B1561), box 156, DHC.

362 "intercept Lumumba": Ankrah and Veillet-Lavallee to Dayal, von Horn, and Rikhye, Dec. 2, 1960, S-0735-0015-03, UNA. See also Gerard and Kuklick, *Death in the Congo*, 180. Veillet-Lavallee, the UN representative in Luluabourg, later stated—in the words of the UN officials in Geneva who worried when the UN investigatory commission requested his testimony—"that he received a cable from Leo informing him that Lumumba had left Leo and was heading towards Lulua, and that he was informed that no protection measures had to be taken since Lumumba had of his own accord given up the protection offered to him." Telex conversation between Cordier and Palthey and Schachter, July 28, 1961, box 161, AWCP.

362 UN troops made no attempt: This was a reversal from the UN's policy that airports in the Congo could be used only for peaceful purposes, and it appears to have come about after U.S. pressure. On December 2, James Wadsworth, the U.S. ambassador to the UN, reported to the State Department a conversation he had had with Heinz Wieschhoff after having lobbied Hammarskjöld: "The new UN policy is to avoid any interference with efforts of the ANC to put down 'mutinies.' [Wieschhoff] noted that the UN had given up control of airfields and therefore could no more prevent air movements of the ANC than prevent movements by riverboats." Wadsworth to State, Dec. 3, 1960 (165), file 312, UNOC Dec. 1960 Classified, Security-Segregated Records, U.S. Embassy Leopoldville, RG 84, NACP.

42. A Damp Cell

363 "We've got him!": The description of Lumumba's arrival comes from British Movietone, "Lumumba Arrested," YouTube, 1:30, July 21, 2015, www .youtube.com; Adeyinka Makinde, "Patrice Lumumba's Arrest by Troops Loyal to Colonel Joseph Mobutu, Leopoldville, December 1960," YouTube, 0:58, Feb. 15, 2020, www.youtube.com; Heinz and Donnay, *Lumumba*, 45–47; AP, "Manacled Lumumba Returns for Trial," *Daily Oklahoman* (Oklahoma City), Dec. 3, 1960; Michael Goldsmith, AP, "Treatment of Lumumba May Backfire," *Casper (Wyo.) Star-Tribune*, Dec. 4, 1960; "Lumumba to Be Tried for Incitement," *Guardian*, Dec. 3, 1960; Paul Hofmann, "Ex-chief Jeered," *NYT*, Dec. 3, 1960; AP, "Beating of Lumumba Related," *NYT*, Dec. 4, 1960; UN Security Council, "Report of the Commission of Investigation Established Under the Terms of General Assembly Resolution 1601 (XV) of 15 April 1961," S/4976 (Nov. 11, 1961); Dayal to Hammarskjöld, Dec. 2, 1960 (B1571), box 156, DHC; Dayal to Hammarskjöld, Dec. 3, 1960 (B1575), box 156, DHC; Dayal to

Hammarskjöld, Dec. 3, 1960 (B1586), box 156, DHC; Extract from Tunisian Bde. Files Concerning Mr. Lumumba, S-0752-0007-07, UNA; Brassinne and Kestergat, *Qui a tué,* 73.

363 Thomas Kanza, himself: Protocol of the hearing of Thomas Kanza and Dragoslav Protitch, May 19, 1961, box 153, DHC.

363 "You swore you'd have": Kamitatu, *La grande mystification,* 81–82.

364 One of the embassy's: Steigman, interview.

364 "While press accounts": Timberlake to Herter, Dec. 3, 1960, Classified General Records, 1934–63, Security-Segregated Records, U.S. Embassy Leopoldville, RG 84, NACP.

364 Diplomats worried that: Wadsworth to State, Dec. 3, 1960, Classified General Records, 1934–63, Security-Segregated Records, U.S. Embassy Leopoldville, RG 84, NACP.

364 "The emotional tension": Hammarskjöld to Dayal, Dec. 2, 1960 (2898–99), box 156, DHC.

364 Hammarskjöld also wrote: UN Security Council, "Report to the Secretary-General from His Special Representative in the Congo Regarding Certain Actions Taken Against Mr. Patrice Lumumba," S/4571 (Dec. 5, 1960), annex 1.

364 Kasavubu had left: Duran to Dayal, Dec. 4, 1960, S-0735-0015-03, UNA. Hammarskjöld sent another letter on December 5, decrying the "physical violence and degrading treatment" to which Lumumba had been subjected and asking Kasavubu to grant him "a fair and public hearing by an independent and impartial tribunal." UN Security Council, "Report to the Secretary-General from His Special Representative in the Congo Regarding Certain Actions Taken Against Mr. Patrice Lumumba, S/4571 (Dec. 5, 1960), annex 2. On Tshela, see Artigue, *Qui sont les leaders,* 132.

365 "usurpation of public": UN Security Council, "Report to the Secretary-General from His Special Representative in the Congo Regarding Certain Actions Taken Against Mr. Patrice Lumumba, S/4571 (Dec. 5, 1960), annex 3.

365 "mistakes have been": Cordier and Foote, *Public Papers,* 5:243; Wadsworth to Herter, Dec. 7, 1960 (1678), file 312, United Nations Organization Classified 1960, Security-Segregated Records, U.S. Embassy Leopoldville, RG 84, NACP.

365 "a confused Spanish War": Cordier and Foote, *Public Papers,* 5:256.

365 Within weeks of Lumumba's: Hoskyns, *Congo Since Independence,* 309; "Congo: The Noisy Cockpit," *Time,* Dec. 26, 1960, 22.

366 He is a small, energetic: Tweedy to Devlin, Nov. 14, 1960 (08782), 104-10182-10069, JFKAR.

366 "WIROGUE appears to be": Leopoldville to Director, Nov. 2, 1960 (86554), 104-10182-10057, JFKAR.

366 WIROGUE's real name: Information on Tzitzichvili and his mission comes from the following documents: Report on Tzitzichvili, Sept. 13, 1961, 104-10182-10052, JFKAR; Report on interviews on Jan. 8, 9, 10, 1959, 104-10182-10057, JFKAR; Leopoldville to Director, Dec. 17, 1960, 104-10182-10057, JFKAR; List with biographical information on Tzitzichvili, 104-10182-10057, JFKAR; Evalu-

ation of Tzitzichvili's training Nov. 2–4, 1960, 104-10182-10057; Project outline "Wirogue," 104-10182-10057, JFKAR; Tweedy to Deputy Director for Security, Oct. 17, 1960 (73532), 104-10182-10057, JFKAR; Contact report, Sept. 13, 1960, 104-10182-10057, JFKAR; Characteristics of Tzitzichvili, 104-10182-10057, JFKAR; Memorandum on upper dentures for Tzitzichvili, July 5, 1960, 104-10182-10057, JFKAR; Devlin to Tweedy, Nov. 14, 1960 (08782); Information on faked documents, 104-10182-10069, JFKAR; Director to Leopoldville, Dec. 19, 1960, 104-10182-10069, JFKAR; Director to Frankfurt, Nov. 16, 1960, 104-10182-10069, JFKAR; Tweedy to Paris, Oct. 29, 1964, 104-10182-10069, JFKAR; Memorandum on Tzitzichvili, Oct. 9, 1964, 104-10182-10069; "Subject: WIROGUE," 104-10182-10194, JFKAR. Although a November 1960 cable describes his right hand as missing fingertips, a more extensive description from January 1959 says that it was in fact his left hand.

367 "the kind of man that": *AAP*, 47–48.

367 "a strong element": Devlin to Tweedy, March 16, 1961, 104-10182-10052, JFKAR.

367 the Astrid, a two-story: Mboka, "Leopoldville 1940s—a Quintet of Small Hotels," *Kinshasa Then and Now* (blog), March 30, 2011.

368 "concerned by WIROGUE's": Leopoldville to Director, Dec. 17, 1960 (18739), 104-10185-10057, JFKAR; Director to Leopoldville, Dec. 19, 1960 (8284), 104-10182-10069, JFKAR.

368 "a typical example": Testimony of Bronson Tweedy, Sept. 9, 1975, 66, 157-10014-10067, JFKAR.

368 "not putting his whole": Testimony of Victor Hedgeman, Aug. 21, 1975, 88–89, 157-10014-10080, JFKAR; "Reports on Plots to Assassinate Fidel Castro," 38, 104-10213-10101, JFKAR.

368 Mankel had been eager: *FRUS, 1964–1968*, vol. 23, doc. 46; *AAP*, 43–44.

368 At some point in December: Testimony of Victor Hedgeman, Aug. 21, 1975, 84–85. Devlin allowed that it was possible he waited until after Lumumba's death to dispose of the poisons. See also *AAP*, 29–30.

368 "Lumumba is completely": UPI, "Mobutu to Keep Congo Control on 'Indefinitely,'" *Wisconsin State Journal* (Madison, Wisc.), Dec. 4, 1960.

369 Camp Hardy lay on: The description of Camp Hardy is from "Rapport technique sur la visite aux détenus politiques du camp militaire Hardy à Thysville, Congo," Dec. 28, 1960, B AG 225 229-002, ICRCA; "The New Protestant Church at the Military Camp Hardy," *Congo Mission News*, July 1959; and Brassinne, "Enquête," 66.

369 Besides Lumumba, nine: "Rapport sur la visite aux détenus politiques du camp militaire Hardy à Thysville, Congo," B AG 225 229-002, ICRCA; "Rapport technique sur la visite aux détenus politiques du camp militaire Hardy à Thysville, Congo," Dec. 28, 1960; Lumumba, *Lumumba Speaks*, 424. On the provenance of the letter to the UN containing these details, see Brassinne and Kestergat, *Qui a tué*, 76.

369 "He sleeps in": On Mobutu's characterization of Lumumba's treatment,

see Heinz and Donnay, *Lumumba*, 54–55; ONUC Léopoldville Bulletin d'Information 74, Dec. 7, 1960, B AG 225 229-002, ICRCA; "Notes on Colonel Mobutu's Press Conference," Dec. 6, 1960, S-0752-0024-10, UNA; Paul Hofmann, "Mobutu Denies Charge by U.N.," *NYT*, Dec. 7, 1960. For information on the hotel, see Tourist Bureau for the Belgian Congo & Ruanda-Urundi, *Traveller's Guide*, 220.

369 "Does Mr. Hammarskjöld": Heinz and Donnay, *Lumumba*, 54.

369 Clare Timberlake agreed: Timberlake to Herter, Dec. 6, 1960 (1340), Classified General Records, 1934–63, Security-Segregated Records, U.S. Embassy Leopoldville, RG 84, NACP.

369 "In the Congo what passes": *FRUS, 1958–1960*, vol. 14, doc. 278. The document capitalizes "US," suggesting "the United States," but the cable would have been transmitted in capital letters, and in context "us" makes more sense.

370 "was probably the safest": Timberlake to Herter, Dec. 6, 1960 (1340).

370 Nonetheless, rumors circulated: Heinz and Donnay, *Lumumba*, 54.

370 UN troops in Thysville: Thomas J. Hamilton, "U.N. Aide Reports Congolese Army Abused Lumumba," *NYT*, Dec. 6, 1960; Heinz and Donnay, *Lumumba*, 53.

370 His wife, Pauline Opango: Bouwer, *Gender and Decolonization*, 64; "U.N. Force Is Alerted," *NYT*, Jan. 20, 1961; Omasombo and Verhaegen, *Jeunesse*, 138.

370 "She is doing everything": Verhaegen, "Patrice Lumumba, martyr d'une Afrique Nouvelle," 87.

370 Mobutu also refused: Thudichum to Geneva (note 408), Dec. 28, 1960, B AG 225 229-001, ICRCA.

370 Only in late December: Perret and Bugnion, *From Budapest to Saigon*, 258; "Remarques complémentaires au rapport technique sur la visite aux détenus politiques du Camp militaire Hardy, à Thysville," Dec. 30, 1960, B AG 225 229-001, ICRCA.

370 Weeks later, he still suffered: "Rapport technique sur la visite aux détenus politiques du camp militaire Hardy à Thysville, Congo," Dec. 28, 1960.

370 Contrary to Red Cross: Although the Geneva Conventions regulate conduct during war, "the same rules customarily apply in situations other than international armed conflicts." Alain Aeschlimann and Nicolas Roggo, "Visits to Persons Deprived of Their Freedom," ICRC, www.icrc.org.

370 He was accompanied by: "Les apports de la Belgique en Afrique centrale, dans le domaine médical, de 1885 a ce jour (2)"; Close, *Doctor's Life*, 91.

371 Vischer was also watched: "Rapport sur la visite aux détenus politiques du camp militaire Hardy à Thysville, Congo." Mobutu and Bombozo were close, with Bobozo having mentored Mobutu when the latter was a private in the Force Publique, and they came from the same ethnic group, the Ngbandi. Monheim, *Mobutu*, 28; Brassinne, "Enquête," 118; Brassinne and Kestergat, *Qui a tué*, 74.

371 Lumumba claimed: Lumumba, *Lumumba Speaks*, 424; Verhaegen, "Patrice Lumumba, martyr d'une Afrique Nouvelle," 87; De Witte, *Assassination*, 61.

371 "We are dealing here": Thudichum to Geneva (note 408), Dec. 28, 1960. In

the event, only Mobutu's side was provided with a copy. See Thudichum to Geneva (note 479), Jan. 17, 1961, B AG 225 229-007, ICRCA; Thudichum to Geneva (note 264), Jan. 10, 1961 , B AG 225 229-007, ICRCA.

371 "an unconfirmed report": *FRUS, 1958–1960*, vol. 14, doc. 288; *FRUS, 1964–1968*, vol. 23, doc. 51.

371 At the Royal: Protocol of the hearing of Thomas Kanza and Dragoslav Protitch, May 19, 1961.

371 Rajeshwar Dayal, by contrast: Barco to Herter, Dec. 28, 1960 (1848), file 312, UNOC Dec. 1960 Classified, Security-Segregated Records, U.S. Embassy Leopoldville, RG 84, NACP.

372 Other sources claimed: On the Christmas dinner and Lumumba's treatment, see Protocol of the hearing of Thomas Kanza and Dragoslav Protitch, May 19, 1961; UN Security Council, "Report of the Commission of Investigation Established Under the Terms of General Assembly Resolution 1601 (XV) of 15 April 1961," S/4976 (Nov. 11, 1961), 88; Brassinne and Kestergat, *Qui a tué*, 75; Kanza, *Rise and Fall*, 316; Paul Hofmann, "Jailers Favor Lumumba," *NYT*, Dec. 27, 1960.

372 They had been riding: Kanza, *Rise and Fall*, 316.

372 Lumumba's wife, Pauline: "Extract from Tunisian BDE Files Concerning Lumumba," S-0752-0007-07, UNA.

372 On December 12: Iyassu to Dayal, Dec. 13, 1960, S-0735-0015-03, UNA.

372 Gizenga claimed to have: "Pro-Red Lumumba Aide Claims Authority to Rule," *NYT*, Dec. 14, 1960.

372 He requested aid from: "Analytical Chronology of the Congo Crisis," 69; Scott, *Tumbled House*, 105; Namikas, *Battleground Africa*, 121–22; Kalb, *Congo Cables*, 171–72.

372 The Stanleyville government: Cable to ONUC Leopoldville, Dec. 1960, S-0735-0015-03, UNA; Brassinne and Kestergat, *Qui a tué*, 80; "The Congo: 'Off with Their Heads,'" *Newsweek*, Dec. 19, 1960, 37; "Rapport technique sur la visite aux détenus politiques de la ferme—École Lula," Dec. 22, 1960, B AG 225 229-002, ICRCA. Already, the political prisoners had been subjected to such humiliating treatment as being forced to cut grass with their teeth.

372 Gizenga also appeared: Hoskyns, *Congo Since Independence*, 292.

372 "Where is Lumumba?": Timberlake to Herter, Dec. 27, 1960 (1437), file 312, UNOC Dec. 1960 Classified, Security-Segregated Records, U.S. Embassy Leopoldville, RG 84, NACP; Hoskyns, *Congo Since Independence*, 306.

372 Whereas the Leopoldville: Dayal, *Mission*, 158.

372 On Christmas Day: "Lumumba Group Seizes 4 in Raid on Area in Congo," *NYT*, Dec. 26, 1960; "Analytical Chronology of the Congo Crisis," 57; Kalb, *Congo Cables*, 175.

372 Their easy success: "Analytical Chronology of the Congo Crisis," 69.

372 Working with Larry Devlin: Devlin, *Chief of Station*, 117; *FRUS, 1964–1968*, vol. 23, doc. 53.

372 Help also came: From Ruanda-Urundi, Belgian military trucks drove the

ANC soldiers into the Congo. Officially, Brussels claimed that its offer of ground transport was an act of expulsion. But the collusion was impossible to hide once it became known that the troops had been given a ride not to the closest border crossing, twelve miles away, but to the one at Bukavu, a ninety-mile drive. See Kalb, *Congo Cables,* 177; Dayal, *Mission,* 162; Urquhart, *Hammarskjold,* 492; "Congo: Lumumba's Loyalists," *Time,* Jan. 13, 1961, 25.

373 "kissed on both": Reuters, "Mobutu Airlifts 200 Paratroops," *NYT,* Jan. 1, 1961.

373 The fiasco was: Hoskyns, *Congo Since Independence,* 306.

373 They were none too: "Notes on Colonel Mobutu's Press Conference," Dec. 6, 1960; Michael Goldsmith, AP, "2 High-Ranking Congo Officials Under Arrest," *Tacoma News Tribune,* Dec. 26, 1960.

373 a "legal facade": *FRUS, 1964–1968,* vol. 23, doc. 48.

373 Dag Hammarskjöld had: Urquhart, *Hammarskjold,* 491; Hoskyns, *Congo Since Independence,* 273.

373 "I live in a kind": Beskow, *Dag Hammarskjöld,* 167.

373 "Christmas will not": Lipsey, *Hammarskjöld,* 466–67.

373 "I will lay me": Hammarskjöld, *Markings,* 198.

373 The next morning: Urquhart, *Hammarskjold,* 491.

374 There were now four: Young, *Politics in the Congo,* 331. Arguably, there were five, if one counted Iléo's abortive government. See "Analytical Chronology of the Congo Crisis," 49.

43. Comeback

375 He set to work: Thurston Clarke, *Ask Not: The Inauguration of John F. Kennedy and the Speech That Changed America* (New York: Henry Holt, 2004), 17, 42–43.

375 At the beginning of: Schlesinger, *Thousand Days,* 130, 555.

375 Chester Bowles, the former: AP, "Rusk Is Secretary of State; Stevenson Takes U.N. Post; Bowles Undersecretary," *Decatur Daily Review,* Dec. 12, 1960.

375 All were willing: For a summary of these officials' views, see Weissman, *American Foreign Policy,* 117–30.

375 Kennedy knew he wanted: Schlesinger, *Thousand Days,* 158–59.

375 To inform his: Thomas J. Hamilton, "Kennedy Confers with U.N.'s Chief," *NYT,* Dec. 8, 1960.

375 He also asked: Clymer, *Edward M. Kennedy: A Biography* (New York: HarperCollins, 2000), 32; AP, "Edward Kennedy on Way to Africa," *Stockton Evening and Sunday Record,* Dec. 3, 1960; UPI, "Edward Kennedy Touring Africa," *Pittsburgh Press,* Dec. 4, 1960.

376 At stop after stop: Congressional Record–Senate, Feb. 17, 1965, 2870, congress .gov.

376 In Leopoldville, the group: Reception guest list, Dec. 6, 1960, series 8.2, box 1, folder 35, Frank Church Papers, Boise State University Special Collections and Archives; Dayal to Hammarskjöld, Dec. 7, 1960 (B1628), box 156, DHC;

Note on meeting between Dayal and visiting American senators and Mr. Edward Kennedy, Dec. 7, 1960, S-0752-0003-04, UNA.

376 pledged "full support": AP, "3 Senators in Congo Voice U.N. Confidence," *Charleston Daily Mail*, Dec. 8, 1960; Kalb, *Congo Cables*, 194–95.

376 In an interview: "New U.S. Policy on Africa Seen," *NYT*, Dec. 24, 1960.

376 "tool" of the CIA: UPI, "Kennedy Says Lumumba Death 'Great Shock,'" *Republican Herald* (Pottsville, Pennsylvania), Feb. 13, 1961.

376 On his desk lay: Schlesinger, *Thousand Days*, 160.

376 "Africa has been": Africa task force report, box 1073, folder 2, pre-presidential papers, transition files, JFKL. For the passages quoted, see 8, 40, and appendixes 5-4 and 5-7. The report did not envision a government that included Lumumba nor did it think the United States should insist on his release. Dayal and Lumumba's allies did not know this, of course.

376 "a certain optimism": CRISP, *Congo 1961*, 153.

376 "It was common knowledge": Dayal, *Life of Our Times*, 446. See also Liu OH, 45.

376 But what Lumumba's: Devlin, *Chief of Station*, 125.

376 "with the change in": *FRUS, 1964–1968*, vol. 23, doc. 64.

377 When Timberlake learned: Devlin, *Chief of Station*, 125; Carlucci OH, 18.

377 Devlin had less: Srodes, *Allen Dulles*, 510.

377 When Dulles and his: *AAP*, 120; Srodes, *Allen Dulles*, 510; Grose, *Gentleman Spy*, 512.

377 "Lumumba retains considerable": *FRUS, 1961–1963*, vol. 20, doc. 2.

378 The goal for his: Paul Hofmann, "New Violence Erupts in Congo as U.N. Chief Arrives for Talks," *NYT*, Jan. 5, 1961.

378 Hammarskjöld realized he: Cordier to Hammarskjöld, Jan. 5, 1961, box 78, DHC; State to Leopoldville, Jan. 14, 1961 (1669) file 312, UN/New York, Classified, Security-Segregated Records, U.S. Embassy Leopoldville, RG 84, NACP.

378 The city was largely: Hofmann, "New Violence Erupts in Congo as U.N. Chief Arrives for Talks."

378 "dialogue of the deaf": Dayal, *Mission*, 170, 171.

378 For what it was: Thomas J. Hamilton, "U.N. Conciliators Delay Congo Trip," *NYT*, Nov. 17, 1960; "Kasavubu Warned U.N.," *NYT*, Nov. 26, 1960; *FRUS, 1958–1960*, vol. 14, docs. 267, 274; Liu OH, 43–44, 47–48.

378 By now, the Indian diplomat: Dayal, *Mission*, 26.

379 "forget the horrors": Olver, "Under Fire with Dag Hammarskjöld," 56.

379 "I have requested": Lumumba, *Lumumba Speaks*, 424–26.

379 When Hammarskjöld was: Kamitatu, *La grande mystification*, 83–84. The letter was addressed to Dayal. Dayal later wrote to Hammarskjöld that Lumumba's letter was "shown to you here on 5 January." Dayal to Hammarskjöld, Jan. 25, 1961 (D193), box 157a, DHC.

379 Lumumba smuggled out: Verhaegen, "Patrice Lumumba, martyr d'une Afrique Nouvelle," 87; De Witte, *Assassination*, 61. For the original letter, see Lumumba to Onawelo, Jan. 4, 1961, VII-BV/RDC/Lumumba N°007/02, FBV. He also wrote letters to Cléophas Kamitatu and Antoine-Roger Bolamba, who

had served as his secretary of state for information. Willame, *La crise congolaise revisitée*, 455–56. On Albert Onawelo, Charles Lumumba, and Michel Tshungu, see Omasombo and Verhaegen, *Jeunesse*, 77–78; Omasombo and Verhaegen, *Acteur*, 392

380 In addition to the promising: "Congo: Lumumba's Loyalists," *Time*, Jan. 13, 1961, 24. For the communiqué, see Legum, *Pan-Africanism*, 192.

380 To the west: Cordier to Hammarskjöld, Jan. 10, 1961 (SG-31), box 78, DHC; *EP*, 245; Hoskyns, *Congo Since Independence*, 302, 303; Artigue, *Qui sont les leaders*, 247–48.

380 On account of that success: Dayal to Abbas, Jan. 8, 1961 (D35), box 157, DHC.

380 "Gilbert Pongo's safety": Heinz and Donnay, *Lumumba*, 70.

380 A prisoner exchange: Dayal, *Mission*, 170.

380 Another roundtable was: Paul Hofmann, "Army and Tribal Ties Are Keys to Congo Power," *NYT*, Jan. 15, 1960.

381 From the moment Lumumba: *FRUS, 1958–1960*, vol. 14, doc. 290.

381 "I no longer want": Brassinne, "Enquête," 117; testimony 46.1.

381 Larry Devlin had been: Devlin might also have sent David Tzitzichvili—WIROGUE—to monitor Camp Hardy. According to an expense report later filed, he ordered Tzitzichvili to drive to Thysville sometime in January, though when exactly and for what purpose are not clear. See Williams, *White Malice*, 387; Devlin to Chief, Finance Division, July 27, 1961, WIROGUE, vol. 4, 104-10182-10052, JFKAR.

381 "The result would almost": *FRUS, 1964–1968*, vol. 23, docs. 54, 55.

381 Mobutu decided to head: Information on Mobutu's plan and Devlin's reaction comes from *EP*, 306; Heinz and Donnay, *Lumumba*, 72; Devlin, *Chief of Station*, 127; and Devlin OH.

382 Outside, Mobutu assembled: *FRUS, 1964–1968*, vol. 23, doc. 57; Brassinne, "Enquête," 119, testimony 46.1.

382 He took off: Mobutu would claim he had no role in, or knowledge of, Lumumba's transfer. See Monheim 181–82. That is implausible. Indeed, he received a copy of Nendaka's order to hand over the prisoners. See Nendaka to Bobozo, Jan. 14, 1961, VII-BV/RDC/Administration Publique N°001/07/02, FBV.

44. The Green Light

383 sending him on "vacation": *EP*, 313. The idea of Katanga as a receptacle for unwanted politicians went back even further, and there was little doubt about what a transfer would mean. In September, Gizenga and Mpolo were arrested in Leopoldville. As Dayal wrote to Hammarskjöld on September 26, "Yesterday morning UN troops rescued them at the airport from an attempt to spirit them away to Katanga where a dire fate would have befallen them." Dayal to Hammarskjöld, Sept. 26, 1960 (B1058), box 155, DHC.

383 After Lumumba's escape: *EP*, 227.

383 "an assassin who must": Heinz and Donnay, *Lumumba*, 59–61; Kamitatu, *La grande mystification*, 87. Kalonji later said Lumumba's life should be spared.

383 "If he comes here": De Witte, *Assassination*, 83.

383 Mobutu himself continued: Brassinne and Kestergat, *Qui a tué*, 109–10. Mobutu, his adviser Louis Marlière would claim, "always maintained everything happened unbeknownst to him while he was perfectly aware of what was being plotted." De Witte, *Assassination*, 72–73.

384 For reasons both: De Witte, *Assassination*, 83; Gerard and Kuklick, *Death in the Congo*, 194.

384 Using an agreed-upon: Brassinne, "Enquête," 92. There is a debate about whether and when exactly this code was used. See *EP*, 294–96.

384 The homicidal musings: In 1964, a letter was published in which Tshombe supposedly granted Bomboko permission for the transfer, but its authenticity is in doubt. See *EP*, 297–98.

384 But partly in response: It is likely that Kasavubu promised to also do something about Jason Sendwe, a bitter Tshombe opponent who was then in Leopoldville. See Gerard and Kuklick, *Death in the Congo*, 197.

384 "an adviser to": Devlin, *Chief of Station*, 125.

384 "one of high policy": *FRUS, 1964–1968*, vol. 23, docs. 59, 57.

385 "Will assume concurrence": Reimuller, interview. One time, this backfired, when he immediately received a nonconcurrence.

385 "physical treatment be": *FRUS, 1958–1960*, vol. 14, docs. 275, 278.

385 Even as he kept: For example, on January 15, Devlin reported that Camp Leopold was again on the brink of mutiny and that some troops were en route to Thysville to free Lumumba. *FRUS, 1964–1968*, vol. 23, doc. 57n4. Only on January 17 did he inform headquarters about Lumumba's transfer, while it was under way. See *AAP*, 49–50; and *FRUS, 1964–1968*, vol. 23, doc. 59. Such a three-day delay was unusual. The most thorough and convincing treatment of Devlin's decision can be found in Weissman, "Extraordinary Rendition," 214–16. As Weissman notes, Louis Marlière, Mobutu's adviser, would claim of the decision to transfer Lumumba, "What is certain is that there was a 'consensus' and that no 'adviser,' be they Belgian or U.S., thought to dissuade them!" See Brassinne, "Enquête," testimony 36.2.

385 Before sunrise on: Unless otherwise noted, details on Lumumba's departure from Camp Hardy and time at Moanda come from Heinz and Donnay, *Lumumba*, 85–92; Brassinne, "Enquête," 145–66; Brassinne and Kestergat, *Qui a tué*, 126–31; De Witte, *Assassination*, 93–96; and Gerard and Kuklick, *Death in the Congo*, 198–200.

386 For a prisoner still: Omasombo and Verhaegen, *Acteur*, 289–99; Artigue, *Qui sont les leaders congolais?*, 256; Kanza, *Rise and Fall*, 85–86; De Witte, *Assassination*, 57–58.

386 Nendaka collected two: Heinz and Donnay, *Lumumba*, 52.

386 a steep and twisty road: Tourist Bureau for the Belgian Congo & Ruanda-Urundi, *Traveller's Guide*, 219.

386 Favored as a weekend: Ibid., 209.

387 The flight to Elisabethville: Unless otherwise noted, details on the flight from Moanda and the arrival at Elisabethville come from Heinz and Donnay, *Lumumba*, 93–118; Brassinne, "Enquête," 167–258; Brassinne and Kestergat, *Qui a tué*, 132–47; De Witte, *Assassination*, 97–103; *EP*, 375–78; and Gerard and Kuklick, *Death in the Congo*, 198–201.

387 A storm was gathering: Mydans and Mydans, *Violent Peace*, 313.

388 Also watching were: Dayal to Hammarskjöld, Jan. 21, 1961 (0-157), S-0735-0015-03, UNA.

388 "They were blindfolded": "Transfer of Mr. Lumumba and His Two Colleagues to Elizabethville," Jan. 1961, box 134, DHC.

45. *Patrice Akufi*

389 Only late in the day: *FRUS, 1964–1968*, vol. 23, doc. 59.

389 On the nineteenth: Ibid., doc 62; *AAP*, 51; Devlin, *Chief of Station*, 130. Doyle later claimed that he worried the cable would get him fired but that he eventually learned that Allen Dulles had found it funny. Doyle, *Inside Espionage*, 148.

389 "There was a general": Testimony of Victor Hedgeman, Aug. 21, 1975, 78, 157-10014-10080, JFKAR.

389 "impossible to totally": Kalb, *Congo Cables*, 187.

389 "The Bantus": U.S. Senate, *Executive Sessions of the Senate Foreign Relations Committee*, vol. 13, part 1, Eighty-Seventh Congress, First Session, 1961, 103. On the other hand, some U.S. officials thought Timberlake believed Lumumba was dead. Weissman, *American Foreign Policy*, 137.

389 At the UN: Dayal to Hammarskjöld, Jan. 18, 1961 (D120), box 157, DHC.

389 Since the ex-premier's: Dayal, *Mission*, 194.

390 "I have learnt with": Hammarskjöld to Dayal, Jan. 18, 1961, box 157, DHC.

390 He sent Moise Tshombe: For Hammarksjöld's letter and Tshombe's reply, see UN Security Council, "Report of the Commission of Investigation Established Under the Terms of General Assembly Resolution 1601 (XV) of 15 April 1961," S/4976, 91–92.

390 Mr. Lumumba and his friends: Bomboko to Hammarskjöld, Jan. 21, 1961, box 134, DHC.

390 "stems from considerations": *FRUS, 1961–1963*, vol. 20, doc. 8.

390 must not be "liquidated": Vandewalle, *Mille et quatre jours*, fascicule 4, 54; Heinz and Donnay, *Lumumba*, 153.

390 "To those new": John F. Kennedy, Inaugural Address, Jan. 20, 1961, American Presidency Project, www.presidency.ucsb.edu.

391 In Stanleyville, gangs: Dayal to Hammarskjöld, Jan. 20, 1961 (D155), box 157, DHC.

391 More countries were: Kalb, *Congo Cables*, 208; "Congo: Blow to the U.N.," *Time*, Feb. 3, 1961, 25.

391 "Take the ceiling off": Mahoney, *JFK*, 63. See also *FRUS, 1961–1963*, vol. 20, doc. 10.

391 But when Ghana's president: Nkrumah to Kennedy, Jan. 23, 1961, and Kennedy to Nkrumah, n.d., box 117b, Ghana: Security, Jan. 1961, President's Office Files, Presidential Papers, JFKL. The text of the latter was cabled to Accra on January 29. Kalb, *Congo Cables*, 422n17.

391 Their ranks included: Kalb, *Congo Cables*, 200–202; Weissman, *American Foreign Policy*, 138–39.

392 The debate between: See, for example, Wallace Carroll, "U.N.'s Congo Role Is Worrying U.S.," *NYT*, Jan. 18, 1961; Dana Adams Schmidt, "President Calls for Reappraisal of Congo Policy," *NYT*, Jan. 30, 1961; AP, "New Congo Policy," *Wellsville Daily Reporter*, Feb. 4, 1961.

392 a "strengthened mandate": Kalb, *Congo Cables*, 209–10.

392 "If this happens": Interview and meeting summary, "Victor Hedgeman," Aug. 22, 1975, 157-10014-10185, JFKAR.

392 At a bar near: Devlin, *Chief of Station*, 136.

392 "a middle-of-the-road cabinet": *FRUS, 1961–1963*, vol. 20, doc. 17. As a backup option, "the United States would give its full support to the establishment of a more broadly based Congolese Government which would include Lumumba elements but not Lumumba himself as Prime Minister." As Kalb suggests, Timberlake's influence over that particular paper was likely limited, given that he arrived in Washington on January 31 and the document was sent to the White House on February 1. Kalb, *Congo Cables*, 210–11.

393 "This fellow is": U.S. Senate, *Executive Sessions of the Senate Foreign Relations Committee*, vol. 13, part 1, Eighty-Seventh Congress, First Session, 1961, 95, 116. Williams went on to say that it was unlikely the United States could sideline Lumumba.

393 Looking over his: For Kanza's entreaties to Roosevelt, see Woodrow Wilson International Center OH, 181; and Kanza, *Rise and Fall*, 322. For his memory of the moment he learned of Lumumba's death, see Kanza, *Rise and Fall*, 323. Kanza appears to have confused the timing in his memoir. He places the moment he learned of Lumumba's death on January 19, and he says that he was asking Roosevelt to lobby Kennedy before his inauguration. In fact, however, Kanza did not arrive in New York until early February, at which point he was still calling for the release of Lumumba, believing him to be alive. See UPI, "Congo Debate Delayed Till Monday," *Arizona Republic*, Feb. 10, 1961.

393 Munongo announced that: For more on the fake story, see Linnér to Wattles, Dec. 19, 1961, S-0752-0007-06, UNA.

393 He offered a: Brassinne and Kestergat, *Qui a tué*, 188; ONUC Elisabethville to ONUC Leopoldville, Feb. 10, 1961, S-0735-0015-03, UNA; Adrian Porter, AP, "Lumumba Dead? Big Question in Congo," *Ironwood Daily Globe*, Feb. 11, 1961; "The Congo: A Place at the Table," *Newsweek*, Feb. 20, 1961, 46.

393 One declared that: Heinz and Donnay, *Lumumba*, 124; Brassinne and Kestergat, *Qui a tué*, 189–92.

393 "You'd recognize that": "The Congo: Death of Lumumba—& After," *Time*, Feb. 24, 1961, 19–20.

46. The Antelope Hunters

395 From the Elisabethville airport: Unless otherwise noted, details about the time at the Brouwez house come from Heinz and Donnay, *Lumumba*, 119–24; Brassinne, "Enquête," 258–319, annex 31.1, testimony 17.2, testimony 45.1; Brassinne and Kestergat, *Qui a tué*, 148–54; De Witte, *Assassination*, 104–107, 113–19; *EP*, 333–46; and Gerard and Kuklick, *Death in the Congo*, 201–203. Although the confession attributed to Verscheure is more likely a secondhand reconstruction than a firsthand account, it can still be considered reliable. See *EP*, 352–56.

396 "I told you in Brussels": Brassinne, "Enquête," annex 31.1.

396 "I remember being struck": Ibid., testimony 17.2.

396 Carrying a lantern: Ndjibu, interview.

397 All told, there were: Unless otherwise noted, details of the execution come from Heinz and Donnay, *Lumumba*, 129–46; Brassinne, "Enquête," 321–50, testimony 38.1; and Brassinne and Kestergat, *Qui a tué*, 163–68; De Witte, *Assassination*, 119–24; *EP*, 336–69; Gerard and Kuklick, *Death in the Congo*, 5, 203–205; and my visit to the execution site. Accounts of Lumumba's final hours differ on the details, and with the exception of Verscheure's diary entry no primary source documents about it exist.

397 First up was Joseph Okito: On Okito, see *Parliamentary Debates: National Assembly Official Report* (Ghana: Government Printing Department, 1961), 85.

397 Mpolo was next: On Mpolo, see "Toute l'histoire de Maurice Mpolo," Foundation Maurice Mpolo M., fondation-mauricempolo.org.

398 "9:43: L. dead": Gerard and Kuklick, *Death in the Congo*, 213.

398 The next morning: Ndjibu, interview.

398 "Make them disappear": "Who Killed Lumumba?," *Correspondent*, BBC, Oct. 21, 2000, news.bbc.co.uk.

398 The task fell to Gerard Soete: Details on the exhumation, burial, re-exhumation, and destruction of the bodies come from Gerard and Kuklick, *Death in the Congo*, 207–208; De Witte, *Assassination*, xvi, 128, 140–43; Brassinne and Kestergat, *Qui a tué*, 178–84; Brassinne, "Enquête," 399–414; Soete, *De Arena*, 132–91; Godelieve Soete, "De Moord op Lumumba de Dochter van de Lijkruimer Spreekt."

398 "so that not a finger": Brassinne and Kestergat, *Qui a tué*, 180.

399 "We did things an animal": "Who Killed Lumumba?"

399 "A column of gas": De Witte, *Assassination*, 142. For Soete's comments that the novelization reflected reality, see Brassinne, "Enquête," 409.

399 "After January 1961": Godelieve Soete, "De Moord op Lumumba de Dochter van de Lijkruimer Spreekt."

47. Get Hammarskjöld!

400 Pauline Opango heard: Details on Pauline Opango's reaction come from "U.N. Force Is Alerted," *NYT,* Jan. 20, 1961; UPI, "Widow of Lumumba Marches in Mourning to Ask U.N. Help," *NYT,* Feb. 15, 1961; "Congo: Death of Lumumba—& After," *Time,* Feb. 24, 1961, 19; AP, "Wake Held for Lumumba," *NYT,* Feb. 15, 1961; Morrison, "Tragedy of Mrs. Lumumba."

400 Even before she knew: Poullain to Dayal, Jan. 18, 1961, S-0735-0015-03, UNA.

400 "My beloved companion": Lumumba, *Lumumba Speaks,* 421–23. I have adjusted some punctuation. The letter was published in the July 1962 edition of *Afrique Réelle* and presented as a letter to "Madame Lumumba." For the question of which Pauline the former prime minister was writing to, see De Witte, *Assassination,* 184; and Willame, *La crise congolaise revisitée,* 456.

402 "She was a picture": Dayal, *Mission,* 198; Berthoud memorandum of conversation with Kasavubu, Feb. 19, 1961, S-0735-0015-02, UNA.

402 "According to Bantu": Heinz and Donnay, *Lumumba,* 176.

402 Belgian elites in: Hoskyns, *Congo Since Independence,* 316.

402 "The very existence": De Witte, *Assassination,* 145.

402 While Leopoldville remained: Dayal to Hammarskjöld, Feb. 14, 1961 (D410), box 157a, DHC.

402 in other world capitals: Details on the protests come from "Civil Disobedience: Red China Stages Big Lumumba Rally," British Pathé, YouTube, www.youtube.com; Arthur J. Olsen, "Polish Mob Sacks Belgian Embassy," *NYT,* Feb. 16, 1961; Michel, *Uhuru Lumumba,* 266–68; De Witte, *Assassination,* 148; "Guard on Belgian Embassy," *Guardian Journal,* Feb. 16, 1961; "Bombs Exploded Near Cuban Rally," *NYT,* Feb. 16, 1961; "Negroes Hurl Eggs at Belgian Embassy," *NYT,* Feb. 16, 1961; "The Bear's Teeth," *Time,* Feb. 24, 1961, 16; Elaine Shepard, *Forgive Us,* 255.

403 The family that had taken: François Lumumba, interview; AP, "Lumumba Kin Not Told," *NYT,* Feb. 14, 1961; "Lumumba Kin 'On Picnic,'" *NYT,* Feb. 15, 1961; "Embassies Attacked in Cairo," *NYT,* Feb. 16, 1961.

403 Juliana was confused: Juliana Lumumba, interview.

403 A group of African American: On the protests at the UN, see Maya Angelou, *The Heart of a Woman* (New York: Random House, 2009), 185, 194; "Riot in Gallery Halts U.N. Debate," *NYT,* Feb. 16, 1961; *Newsweek,* Feb. 27, 1961, 19; "Anti-Belgium Demonstrations over Congo Crisis," British Pathé, YouTube, www.youtube.com; Rosa Guy, "Castro in New York," *Black Renaissance* 1, no. 1 (Oct. 1996); Dworkin, *Congo Love Song,* 227; Urquhart, *Hammarskjold,* 507. Later, after Ralph Bunche suggested that the protesters did not represent mainstream African American opinion, he himself became the target of protests. Walking outside the UN one day, he spotted a man with a sign that said, "Kill Bunche." When he asked who this Bunche character was, the man replied, "I guess he's some joker in the UN." Urquhart, *Ralph Bunche,* 339.

403 "a revolting crime": UN Security Council, 935th meeting, S/PV.935 (Feb. 15, 1961), 2; UN Security Council, 933rd meeting, S/PV.933 (Feb. 13, 1961), 1.

403 *No* one, in the: Urquhart, *Hammarskjold*, 506.

404 "the blood of Patrice Lumumba": Lindesay Parrott, "U.N. Chief Facing Old Soviet Tactic," *NYT,* Feb. 15, 1961; Lipsey, *Hammarskjöld,* 479. On Lie's resignation, see Lipsey, *Hammarskjöld,* 96.

404 "Why couldn't Hammarskjöld": Philip Deane, London Observer Service, "Talk of Lumumba Leaves Bad Taste," *State* (Columbia, S.C.), March 7, 1961.

404 They also noticed: Urquhart, *Hammarskjold,* 507; Urquhart OH, Oct. 19, 1984, 25. Andrew Cordier was so concerned about Hammarskjöld's state that he back-channeled with the secretary-general's good friend and former aide Per Lind, an official in the Swedish Foreign Ministry, asking that he come to New York to stay with Hammarskjöld and comfort him. Cordier to Lind, Feb. 20, 1961, box 44, AWCP.

404 "Can the U.N. Survive?": "Can the U.N. Survive?," *Newsweek,* Feb. 27, 1961.

404 The seven, who included: "L'État du Sud-Kasaï: De la province minière à l'État fédéré," in Omasombo, *Kasaï-Oriental,* 193; Brassinne, "Enquête," 375–77; Young, *Politics in the Congo,* 331; UN Security Council, "Report of the Special Representative of the Secretary-General Concerning Arrest and Deportation of Political Personalities," S/4727 (Feb. 18, 1961).

404 Pongo had his legs: Brassinne, "Réflexions sur le rapport de la Commission d'enquête parlementaire sur l'assassinat de Lumumba," Jan. 25, 2002, www.brassinnedelabuissiere-lumumba.be.

404 John F. Kennedy learned: UPI, "Kennedy Says Lumumba Death 'Great Shock,'" *Republican and Herald* (Pottsville, Pennsylvania), Feb. 13, 1961. A Jacques Lowe photograph of Kennedy is often said to depict the moment the president learned of the news, in the Oval Office. But contemporaneous reporting puts the moment earlier, before he left Virginia for Washington, D.C., and so the timing makes this characterization implausible. For the conventional story, see Mahoney, *JFK,* 70. For the photograph, see Jacques Lowe, "Lumumba," at www.jacqueslowe.com. For Kennedy's schedule that day, see appointment book for Feb. 13, 1961, Presidential Papers, Miscellaneous Presidential Files, President's Appointment Books, JFKL.

405 His campaign promise: Dana Adams Schmidt, "Kennedy Shocked by Congo Slaying," *NYT,* Feb. 14, 1961.

405 "This unspeakable crime": *FRUS, 1961–1963,* vol. 20, doc. 45n6.

405 Gizenga's Lumumbist regime: Heinz and Donnay, *Lumumba,* 156; "Three More Countries Shift Congo Recognition," *NYT,* Feb. 16, 1961.

405 The Soviet Union quickly: Mazov, *Distant Front,* 160.

405 Skirmishes had already: Dayal, *Mission,* 181–84, 201.

405 On the contrary: Weissman, *American Foreign Policy,* 142; Jack Raymond, "U.S. Navy Ready for Congo Role," *NYT,* Feb. 20, 1961.

48. Lovanium

406 With no more possibility: Hoskyns, *Congo Since Independence,* 336.

406 And so just a week: UN Security Council Resolution 161, S/RES/161 (Feb. 21, 1961). Hammarskjöld was not a fan of the new resolution, which he thought gave him new responsibilities but no additional means to carry them out. Urquhart, *Hammarskjold,* 509.

406 India, which until: Urquhart, *Hammarskjold,* 512; AP, "India's Congo Brigade Not Likely to Be Routed," *Arizona Daily Star,* March 16, 1961. For India's previous contributions, see "Second Progress Report to the Secretary-General from His Special Representative in the Congo," S/4557 (Nov. 2, 1960), 40–43.

406 Separated by hundreds: Young, *Politics in the Congo,* 389–90, 332.

406 With Moscow rebuffing: Transcript of talk between Kuznetsov and Mulele, March 8, 1961, in Namikas and Mazov, "CWIHP Conference Reader." "It is known that Mulele lives in Cairo in easy circumstances and is surrounded by the company of very dubious persons," a Czech diplomat warned the Soviets. "Agents of intelligence services of imperialist states may be among them." Indeed, when Mulele tried to have a messenger ferry $250,000 in Soviet funds (the second installment of the $500,000 that had been promised earlier) from Cairo to Stanleyville, the money was intercepted in Sudan by the CIA, which had been tipped off about the transfer. Mulele claimed that the money never made it because "Sudan refused to grant a visa to our trusted person." Transcript of talk between Kuznetsov and Mulele, March 8, 1961; transcript of talk between Firubin and Dvorzhak, March 9, 1961; and transcript of talk between Kuznetsov and Mulele, March 8, 1961; all in Namikas and Mazov, "CWIHP Conference Reader." See also Devlin, *Chief of Station,* 141; testimony of Richard Bissell, Sept. 10, 1975, 80, 157-10014-10093, JFKAR.

407 "most amazing change": *FRUS, 1961–1963,* vol. 20, doc. 48. See also Carlucci to State, Feb. 27, 1961 (328), Classified General Records, 1934–63, Republic of the Congo, U.S. Embassy and Consulate, Leopoldville; Classified General Records, Security-Segregated Records, RG 84, NACP.

407 On March 31: Max Frankel, "U.S. Congo Plan Due in U.N. Soon," *NYT,* April 1, 1961.

407 Ever the stick: Kalb, *Congo Cables,* 261.

407 The final straw: "Chronology of Events Leading to Change of Orders of Task Force 88," n.d., box 77, Defense, 1961: Jan.–March, President's Office Files, JFKL; Mahoney, *JFK,* 79; Kalb, *Congo Cables,* 240–41. Timberlake might also have worried about clashes between UN and Congolese troops in Matadi.

407 Conveniently, Kennedy was: Dayal, *Mission,* 260. The British ambassador, Ian Scott, was also recalled as part of the swap. For details on the deal, see Hoskyns, *Congo Since Independence,* 365; Mahoney, *JFK,* 84; Kalb, *Congo Cables,* 262; Carlucci OH, 19. Dayal himself explained his removal this way: "The convening of the Congolese parliament was imminent, but a pro-western majority could not

be ensured without the UN actively participating in suborning or intimidating the parliamentarians. The US administration was convinced—and rightly so—that I would never be a party to this." Dayal, *Life of Our Times,* 461.

407 "pleasant but indifferent jobs": Timberlake to "Peter," June 20, 1963, box 1, folder 9, CTP. See also Lisagor and Higgins, *Overtime in Heaven,* 269. Taking Timberlake's desk at the embassy in Leopoldville would be Edmund Gullion, a Foreign Service officer who had impressed Kennedy with his nuanced thinking during a 1951 visit to Indochina. Dayal would make way for Sture Linnér, the Swedish head of the UN's civilian aid program in the Congo. Mahoney, *JFK,* 108; Logevall, *JFK,* 493, 554; Dayal, *Mission,* 266.

407 "all to the good": For Burden's view on the assassination, see Burden OH, 42. For efforts to keep him on, see Herter to Burden, Jan. 4, 1961, Chronological File, Jan.–Feb. 1961 (3), box 9, Herter Papers, DDEL; Gerard and Kuklick, *Death in the Congo,* 211. Burden was a political appointee, rather than a career Foreign Service officer, so his departure was less surprising. When he left, King Baudouin awarded him the Great Ribbon of the Order of Leopold.

407 At the CIA: Kennedy decided immediately that Dulles had to go, but it would take months. Bissell, whose downfall after the Bay of Pigs fiasco was also obvious, was given a chance to take up various economic postings, but he declined the offers and retired. See Grose, *Gentleman Spy,* 529–31, 535; and Thomas, *Very Best Men,* 266, 272.

408 "If we can keep": Lipsey, *Hammarskjöld,* 510–11.

408 The campus of Lovanium: Details on the Lovanium conference come from Hoskyns, *Congo Since Independence,* 374–83; "The Congo: Empty Campus," *Time,* July 14, 1961; "Congo: The Parliament Meets," *Time,* Aug. 4, 1961; "The Congo: One More Try," *Time,* Aug. 11, 1961; UPI, "Congo Unity Hope Dim Again," *Indianapolis Star,* July 2, 1961; "Congo: New Chapter," *Newsweek,* Aug. 14, 1961; Dayal, *Mission,* 256; Devlin, *Chief of Station,* 156–59.

408 "silver bullets" program: *FRUS, 1964–1968,* vol. 23, doc. 77; *FRUS, 1961–1963,* vol. 20, doc. 41.

408 In the weeks leading: *FRUS, 1964–1968,* vol. 23, docs. 82–87; *FRUS, 1961–1963,* vol. 20, doc. 71. The plan was drafted by Devlin originally, but the document submitted to the Special Group incorporated comments from the State Department. It also stated that efforts might be scaled down in the event that Gizenga declined to attend the conference, which he did.

409 The total cost: "Covert Military Operations in the Congo: 1964–1967."

409 Ultimately, the president: On Devlin's efforts, see Devlin, *Chief of Station,* 157–58; Mahoney, *JFK,* 87; Kelly, *America's Tyrant,* 80; and Dayal, *Life of Our Times,* 467–68. The allegation about the sewage tunnel comes from Mahoney, who cites his interviews with officers from the State Department and CIA. It was also confirmed by Kelly. There is some possibility that the CIA played another hidden role in the proceedings. UN officials suspected that the CIA or another Western intelligence agency made large deposits into Mobutu's Belgian bank account in order to secure the last-minute release of Tshombe

from house arrest so he could attend the Lovanium conference. In late June, Sture Linnér obtained from Cyrille Adoula a letter to Mobutu from his military adviser, Louis Marlière, outlining the conditions under which Tshombe would be liberated. See Linnér to Hammarskjöld, June 29, 1961, and Linnér to O'Brien, June 30, 1961, both in S-0752-0030-07, UNA; and O'Brien, *To Katanga and Back*, 115–16.

409 Outside the electric: Devlin, *Chief of Station*, 99.

409 Ten days before: O'Brien, *To Katanga and Back*, 189.

409 Looming over everything: Henry Tanner, "Kasavubu Tells Lawmakers He Will Nominate Premier—Mobutu Gives Warning," *NYT*, July 28, 1961.

409 One evening, in: "Congo: New Chapter"; UPI, "Congo Rivals Plan Parleys to Help Both," *Record* (Hackensack, N.J.), July 31, 1961. See also Monheim, *Mobutu*, 227.

409 Had the members: Hoskyns, *Congo Since Independence*, 376.

410 a "donnybrook": *FRUS, 1964–1968*, vol. 23, doc. 90. Gizenga, who ultimately decided not to attend the conference, was made one of the two deputy prime ministers.

410 "armfuls of loot": "Congo: New Chapter."

410 "than to give the Congolese": Hammarskjöld to Fawzi, Aug. 4, 1961, box 2a3, DHC.

410 "It was really": Weissman, *American Foreign Policy*, 147.

410 "take major credit for": *FRUS, 1964–1968*, vol. 23, doc. 101. Immediately after Adoula's election, the Special Group also authorized a program to burnish his international reputation. History does not record whether the gesture was his own initiative or that of his American advisers, but Adoula soon flew to Stanleyville and laid a wreath at the foot of a new statue of Lumumba. "Covert Military Operations in the Congo: 1964–1967"; Weissman, "CIA Covert Action in Zaire and Angola," 270; and UPI, "Congo Head Greeted in Stanleyville," *Bangor Daily News*, Aug. 17, 1961.

410 "You should know": Mahoney, *JFK*, 88. See also *FRUS, 1961–1963*, vol. 20, doc. 93.

49. The Final Flight

411 In fact, it had strengthened: Gérard-Libois, *Katanga Secession*, 215. Although Tshombe boycotted the conference, his party, Conakat, did send parliamentarians to convene in Leopoldville.

411 Known as *les affreux*: O'Brien, *To Katanga and Back*, 198–99; Urquhart OH, Oct. 19, 1984, 28.

411 In addition, Tshombe's military: Urquhart, *Hammarskjold*, 550. Urquhart claims that only one of them ever became operational.

411 The parliament in Leopoldville: Ofosu-Amaah to Linnér, Aug. 9, 1961 (171), S-0752-0007-06, UNA.

411 Even Brussels was: Hoskyns, *Congo Since Independence*, 369.

411 It agreed to withdraw: Urquhart, *Hammarskjold*, 554.

412 But his lack of: "Good God!" said Brian Urquhart, one of Hammarskjöld's aides and O'Brien's friends, when the secretary-general told him of the appointment. "Not Conor!" Urquhart OH, Oct. 19, 1984, 31, 35. See also Urquhart, *Life in Peace and War*, 174.

412 Upon assuming his: This account of Operation Rumpunch comes from O'Brien, *To Katanga and Back*, 216–22; Urquhart, *Hammarskjold*, 556–65; Power, *Siege at Jadotville*, 102–106; Gérard-Libois, *Katanga Secession*, 218–20; AP, "U.N. Troops Take Over in Katanga," *Johnson City Press-Chronicle*, Aug. 28, 1961.

412 "skill and courage": O'Brien, *To Katanga and Back*, 219.

412 "to be opened only": Affidavit of Hannah Platz, Nov. 2, 1961, box 217, DHC; Per Lind, "An Unusual Letter," in Hanley and Melber, *Dag Hammarskjöld Remembered*, 94–97.

412 Refueling in Accra: Urquhart, *Hammarskjold*, 565; James Tomlins, Reuters, "Bitter Congo Fight," *Ottawa Citizen*, Sept. 13, 1961.

412 Their do-over was called: This account of Operation Morthor and the period through September 17 comes from Urquhart, *Hammarskjold*, 559–79; O'Brien, *To Katanga and Back*, 249–88; Lipsey, *Hammarskjöld*, 545–50; Gérard-Libois, *Katanga Secession*, 221–22; Hoskyns, *Congo Since Independence*, 414–25.

413 "What had been expected": David Halberstam, "U.N. Army Takes Katanga," *NYT*, Sept. 14, 1961.

413 "the lone ranger": Gerard-Libois, *Katanga Secession*, 221.

413 At 4:45 p.m.: Details on Hammarskjöld's last flight come from Urquhart, *Hammarskjold*, 587–89; Lipsey, *Hammarskjöld*, 553–72; Williams, *Who Killed Hammarskjöld?*, 68–70; Linnér OH; Linnér to Bunche, Sept. 17, 1961 (A2186), S-0735-0014-09, UNA; boxes 215 and 216, DHC.

414 Hammarskjöld's body was: Lipsey, *Hammarskjöld*, 575, 582–83.

414 In the United States: John F. Kennedy, "Proclamation 3430—Death of Dag Hammarskjöld," Sept. 19, 1961, American Presidency Project, www .presidency.ucsb.edu; John F. Kennedy, Address Before the General Assembly of the United Nations, Sept. 25, 1961, JFKL.

414 People cried openly: Lipsey, *Hammarskjöld*, 577–79; Hanley and Melber, *Dag Hammarskjöld Remembered*, 28.

414 The cause of the crash: It is beyond the scope of this book to evaluate the various investigations into and theories of the crash. For that, see Lipsey, *Hammarskjöld*, 559–70; Williams, *Who Killed Hammarskjöld?*; Williams, *White Malice*, 413–18. A 2022 UN report concluded, "From the totality of the information at hand, it appears plausible that an external attack or threat may have been a cause of the crash." UN General Assembly, "Investigation into the conditions and circumstances resulting in the tragic death of Dag Hammarskjöld and of the members of the party accompanying him," A/76/892 (Aug. 25, 2022).

415 "There is a possibility": Gullion to State, Sept. 17, 1961 (CN-996), 312-UN/ New York, Republic of the Congo, U.S. Embassy and Consulate, Leopoldville, Classified General Records, 1956–63 Security-Segregated Records, 1959–61,

file 310–12, box 8, RG 84, NACP. The cable misspelled his name as "Van Riesseghem."

415 The day before: Hammarskjöld to Bunche, Sept. 16, 1961 (218), box 136, DHC.

415 The Katangan leaders: Urquhart, *Life in Peace and War,* 177. O'Brien writes, "Tshombe had no more reason to murder Hammarskjöld on the way to Ndola than Hitler had to murder Chamberlain on the way to Munich." He also writes that Hammarskjöld's death was not in the interest of Roy Welensky, the prime minister of the Federation of Rhodesia and Nyasaland. O'Brien does, however, posit that Munongo "would have been capable of such an act." O'Brien, *To Katanga and Back,* 286.

415 It beggars belief: Seven Seas Airlines, an American air transport company, did fly the three Fougas to Katanga in February—much to Kennedy's embarrassment. Mahoney, *JFK,* 80–81, claims that the firm "was under contract with the CIA" as part of a plan to "build up a fall-back regime [in Katanga] if the government in Leopoldville fell to the Lumumbists." However, an undated Special Group memo from around February 1961 concluded that although Katanga had requested U.S. aid, given that the Belgians were already supplying the secessionist state with weapons, "no action on our part in this regard is considered advisable at this time." *FRUS, 1964–1968,* vol. 23, doc. 71. Moreover, when, in February 1961, news of the American company's involvement in an in-progress delivery to Katanga came out, a cable from the State Department lamented that the planes' arrival "may very well take place despite our efforts to stop it." *FRUS, 1961–1963,* vol. 20, doc. 31. The exact relationship between the CIA and the airline is not clear, nor is it clear the degree to which the agency was involved in, or even knew about, the delivery.

415 Finally, eyewitness: Dave English and Michael Kuzel, "Reliability of Eyewitness Reports to a Major Aviation Accident," *International Journal of Aviation, Aeronautics, and Aerospace* 1, no. 4 (2014).

415 So are barroom: Emma Graham-Harrison, Andreas Rocksen, and Mads Brügger, "Man Accused of Shooting Down UN Chief," *Guardian,* Jan. 12, 2019.

416 Hammarskjöld's plane was: In February 1961, a C-119 crashed after taking off from Luluabourg, killing three, and in June 1961, a UN DC-3 crash-landed in Tshikapa, in Kasai, with everyone unhurt. UPI, "Plane Crash in Congo Claims Lives of Three," *Urbana Daily Citizen,* Feb. 15, 1961; and MacEoin to Bunche, June 15, 1961, box 136, DHC. A week after Hammarskjöld's plane crashed, another UN plane overshot the runway in Kamina. AP, "Irish Aide Unhurt in Congo Accident," *Daily Press* (Newport News, Virginia), Sept. 25, 1961. For the list of other DC-6 crashes in 1961, see "Accident list: DC-6," Aviation Safety Network, aviation-safety.net.

416 In January 1963: Urquhart, *Hammarskjold,* 593; Ernest W. Lefever and Wynfred Joshua, *United Nations Peacekeeping in the Congo: 1960–1964* (Washington, D.C.: Brookings Institution, 1966), 2:367.

416 Moise Tshombe fled: Colvin, *Moise Tshombe,* 141, 146.

416 "Big day for": Urquhart, *Ralph Bunche,* 360.

50. Our Man in Leopoldville

417 Elisabethville and Stanleyville: Weissman, *American Foreign Policy,* 185.

417 On paper, the country: While Adoula was at various times considered a member of the Binza Group, as a State Department report put it at the time, "the pro-Western 'Binza' political group...advises Adoula." Memorandum on General Joseph Mobutu, May 17, 1963, Records Relating to the Congo and the Congo Working Group, 1960–64, box 4, RG 59, NACP.

417 It had a CIA-picked: Weissman, "What Really Happened in Congo."

417 A week earlier: *FRUS, 1964–1968,* vol. 23, doc. 144.

417 "responds well to flattery": Memorandum on General Joseph Mobutu, May 17, 1963.

418 "General, if it hadn't": *FRUS, 1961–1963,* vol. 20, doc. 423.

418 Yet neither Mobutu: Ibid., doc. 419.

418 As the central government: Weissman, *American Foreign Policy,* 200–201, 207–208.

418 "constant vote-buying": *FRUS, 1964–1968,* vol. 23, doc. 137.

418 Eventually, he convinced: Ibid., doc. 140. Formally speaking, it was Kasavubu who dissolved parliament.

418 He had been promoted: Reimuller, interview.

418 As he prepared: Testimony of Victor Hedgeman, Aug. 21, 1975, 89, 157-10014-10080, JFKAR.

418 "the most sincere": *FRUS, 1964–1968,* vol. 23, doc. 144.

418 It began with unrest: My description of the Kwilu and Simba rebellions comes from Renee C. Fox, Willy de Craemer, and Jean-Marie Ribeaucourt, "'The Second Independence': A Case Study of the Kwilu Rebellion in the Congo," *Comparative Studies in Society and History* 8, no. 1 (1965): 93–98; Markowitz and Weiss, "Rebellion in the Congo," 215; M. Crawford Young, "Significance of the 1964 Rebellion," in Kitchen, *Footnotes to the Congo Story;* Nzongola-Ntalaja, *Leopold to Kabila,* 126–40; Van Reybrouck, *Congo,* 320–24.

419 Even the capital: Weissman, *American Foreign Policy,* 236.

419 Alarmed by the insurgents': In a surprise move, the Binza Group replaced Adoula with a man who not long before had been a fierce enemy of the central government: Moise Tshombe. The former secessionist leader had recently been invited back to the Congo from exile in Spain and pledged to crush the rebellions. See Weissman, "What Really Happened in Congo."

419 They took 250 Belgians: "We chewed on it awhile, but it was pretty durable," the diplomat reported afterward. "Congolese Forced American Officials to Eat U.S. Flag," *NYT,* Nov. 25, 1965.

419 "Now, I don't know": *FRUS, 1964–1968,* vol. 23, doc. 330.

419 "While the General": Ibid., doc. 172.

420 "Obviously, a war": Guevara, *Congo Diary,* 26, 32, 86, 83. Anderson, *Che Guevara,* 596–636.

420 With the approval: *FRUS, 1964–1968,* vol. 23, doc. 178; "How C.I.A. Put 'Instant

Air Force' into Congo," *NYT,* April 26, 1966; Weissman, "What Really Happened in Congo"; Weissman, *American Foreign Policy,* 229, 240; Lefever, *Crisis in the Congo,* 131.

420 A joint U.S.-Belgian: Weissman, *American Foreign Policy,* 247; Nzongola-Ntalaja, *From Leopold to Kabila,* 138.

420 "miniature war department": "How C.I.A. Put 'Instant Air Force' into Congo." Johnson, increasingly tied down in Indochina, worried out loud about "another Vietnam." *FRUS, 1964–1968,* vol. 23, doc. 359.

420 The CIA's campaign: Weissman, *American Foreign Policy,* 240; Weissman, "What Really Happened in Congo."

420 So subtle was his: See, for example, *FRUS, 1964–1968,* vol. 23, docs. 191, 192, 370; Devlin, *Chief of Station,* 211.

421 "Devlin is as close": *FRUS, 1964–1968,* vol. 23, doc. 453.

421 It was partly: Testimony of Victor Hedgeman, Aug. 21, 1975, 6–7; Devlin, *Chief of Station,* 223. *FRUS, 1964–1968,* vol. 23, doc. 419.

421 Mobutu soon began: Ibid., doc. 446.

421 He also asked: Ibid., docs. 448, 450. Mobutu asked for 39 million Congolese francs. The exchange rate at the time was 150 Congolese francs to 1 U.S. dollar. "Treasury Reporting Rates of Exchange as of March 31, 1965," Treasury Department, www.govinfo.gov.

421 "He is already": *FRUS, 1964–1968,* vol. 23, doc. 449.

421 The president's twenty-year-old: Marie-Rose Kasavubu, interview.

421 "the best possible": *FRUS, 1964–1968,* vol. 23, doc. 459.

421 At 11:30 a.m.: Devlin, *Chief of Station,* 234–35; *FRUS, 1964–1968,* vol. 23, docs. 453, 454.

422 Before going to sleep: Van Reybrouck, *Congo,* 330.

422 "The race for": UPI, "Military Takes Power in Congo," *Memphis Press-Scimitar,* Nov. 25, 1965.

422 On June 2, 1966: The description of the June 2 hanging comes from Van Reybrouck, *Congo,* 336–40; Young and Turner, *Rise and Decline,* 56–57; UPI, "80,000 Congolese See Hanging of 4," *Lincoln Journal Star,* June 2, 1966; UPI, "Mobutu Follows 4 Hangings by Continuing Congo Purge," *Minneapolis Star,* June 3, 1966; "100,000 in Congo See Hanging of Ex-Premier and 3 Others," *NYT,* June 3, 1966.

422 Publicly, the U.S. government: "U.S. Makes Plea for Clemency," *NYT,* June 3, 1966.

422 Privately, Larry Devlin: *FRUS, 1964–1968,* vol. 23, docs. 470, 471. Mobutu claimed he already knew about the plot.

423 "When a chief decides": Kamitatu, *La grande mystification,* 176.

423 Parliament had voted: Young and Turner, *Rise and Decline,* 52.

423 The United States had: UPI, "U.S. Recognizes Mobutu Regime," *Valley Evening Monitor* (McAllen, Tex.), Dec. 9, 1965; Reuters, "Congo Man of Action," *Philadelphia Inquirer,* May 31, 1966; Weissman, "What Really Happened in Congo."

423 Joseph Kasavubu was forced: Marie-Rose Kasavubu, interview; Young and Turner, *Rise and Decline*, 52.

423 Antoine Gizenga and Christophe Gbenye: Gizenga, *Ma vie et mes luttes*, 385; Kisangani and Bobb, *Historical Dictionary of the Democratic Republic of the Congo*, 198.

423 Pierre Mulele was tortured: Wrong, *Footsteps of Mr. Kurtz*, 90.

423 On June 30, 1966: Los Angeles Times News Service, "Congo's Mobutu Proclaims Lumumba a National Hero," *Spokesman Review* (Spokane), July 1, 1966.

423 "glory and honor to": Mobutu, *Recueil des discours et harangues du président de la République Démocratique du Congo, août 1960—janvier 1967*, 105–6.

423 In Katanga, the chicken: De Witte, *Assassination*, 166.

423 His widow, Pauline: Juliana Lumumba, interview.

424 "To my old and excellent": Devlin, *Chief of Station*, 257–58.

Epilogue: The Arrogance of Power

425 The letter summoning Sidney Gottlieb: Gup, "Coldest Warrior"; Kinzer, *Poisoner in Chief*, 209–10. Kinzer, *Poisoner in Chief*, 222, dates the message to the spring of 1975 and places Gottlieb in India at the time.

425 The call for Richard Bissell: Bissell, *Reflections of a Cold Warrior*, 241–42; Thomas, *The Very Best Men*, 339.

425 Larry Devlin's letter: Devlin, *Chief of Station*, 261, 265.

425 Details from the CIA's internal: Johnson, *A Season of Inquiry Revisited*, 5–6.

425 "Zaire" was itself: Turner, *The Congo Wars*, 62.

426 the work of a Parisian: Wrong, *Footsteps of Mr. Kurtz*, 71.

426 Although CIA payments: Weissman, "CIA Covert Action in Zaire and Angola," 273.

426 Newspapers carried his photo: Young and Turner, *Rise and Decline*, 168–69; Constitution of Zaire, Aug. 15, 1974, preamble.

426 He nationalized: Young and Turner, *Rise and Decline*, 7, 73–74.

426 Evidence of graft: Henri Schoup, "Zaire's Mobutu," *Ottawa Citizen*, Feb. 15, 1975.

426 "would be to incur": *FRUS*, 1964–1968, vol. 23, doc. 577.

426 His earlier work: Reimuller, interview; Devlin, *Chief of Station*, 264.

426 Separated from his wife: Reimuller, interview; Mary Martin Devlin interview.

427 U.S. diplomats griped: Jeff Gerth, "Former Intelligence Aides Profiting from Old Ties," *NYT*, Dec. 6, 1981.

427 Devlin lived in the: Young and Turner, *Rise and Decline*, 60–61.

427 "Larry, they got all": Reimuller, interview.

427 "the president of the United States": Testimony of Victor Hedgeman, Aug. 21, 1975, 31, 157-10014-10080, JFKAR.

427 "Bingo!": Church Committee OH, 18; Baron, interview. The other piece of evidence, which investigators already had, was the testimony of Robert John-

son, the notetaker at the fateful National Security Council meeting where President Eisenhower issued his apparent order to kill Lumumba. But Devlin's testimony was even more damning evidence of presidential authorization, since it proved that Eisenhower's approval was communicated down the chain of command.

428 Church believed would: Baron, interview.

428 On the morning of: Johnson, *A Season of Inquiry Revisited*, 132–36.

428 its efforts in the Congo: Although the CIA had played a role in the 1953 coup in Iran and the 1954 coup in Guatemala, in both cases, the ousted leaders survived.

428 "poison cigars, exploding seashells": *AAP*, 255.

428 The CIA had backed: AAP, 5.

428 Seven years later: Ibid.

428 Of the five cases: Ibid., 267.

428 finding no evidence: Ibid., 4.

428 In the little time: On the limits of the Church Committee's Lumumba investigation, see Weissman, "An Extraordinary Rendition," 216–19.

429 The former station chief: Testimony of Victor Hedgeman, Aug. 21, 1975, 78–79. For the cable, see *FRUS, 1964–1968*, vol. 23, doc. 59. Devlin specified that he didn't know about any plan to send Lumumba to Katanga, which was technically true, since he had heard only about one involving Bakwanga. As *AAP* noted, however, Devlin "clearly had prior knowledge of the plan to transfer Lumumba to a state where it was probable that he would be killed." *AAP*, 50. As Weissman notes, the committee's staffers only discovered the smoking-gun cable after they had interviewed Devlin. Weissman, "An Extraordinary Rendition," 218.

429 The findings of the Church Committee: Johnson, *A Season of Inquiry Revisited*, 197.

429 At the CIA: Devlin, *Chief of Station*, unpaginated photo spread; Scott Shane, "Memories of a C.I.A. Officer Resonate in a New Era," *NYT*, Feb. 24, 2008.

430 "achieved its objectives": Weissman, "What Really Happened in Congo"; "Foreign and Military Intelligence, Book I, Report of the Select Committee to Study Governmental Operations with Respect to Intelligence Activities, United States Senate," 1976, 155.

430 And because Mobutu's: For a thorough treatment of the consequences of U.S. policy in the Congo, see Stephen Weissman, "What Really Happened in Congo." As he writes, "The CIA had not only fostered a regime; it had stamped it 'made in America' for future policymakers in Washington."

430 expelling two U.S. ambassadors: Kelly, *America's Tyrant*, 247–48.

430 receiving hundreds of military advisers: Jide Owoeye, "The Metamorphosis of North Korea's African Policy," *Asian Survey* 31, no. 7 (1991), 640.

430 accusing the CIA: Young and Turner, *Rise and Decline*, 372–73.

430 The Congo held vast: Kelly, *America's Tyrant*, 246; John Harriman, "Congo,

Cuba Outlook for Trade Bleak, *Boston Globe,* Aug. 30, 1960; Tom Zoellner, "In Congo, Silence Surrounds Forgotten Mine That Fueled First Atom Bombs," *Al Jazeera America,* July 23, 2015.

430 "The U.S. became": "Covert Military Operations in the Congo: 1964–1967," 4.

431 The lack of evidence: On the absurdity of the domino theory, see Logevall, *JFK,* 575–76.

431 "cancerous growth": *FRUS,* 1964–1968, vol. 23, doc. 373.

431 The documents uncovered: See the conclusions of Namikas, *Battleground Africa,* 227, and Mazov, *Distant Front,* 254.

431 "I think we overrated": Weissman, *American Foreign Policy,* 280.

432 "For the Congo": "Lumumba Visits U.S. Officialdom," *Christian Science Monitor,* July 28, 1960, p. 16

432 "I am relatively certain": Testimony of Richard Helms, June 13, 1975, 153–54, 157-10014-10075, JFKAR.

432 "The Americans believed": Don Marshall, "Angola Following Congo Down Road to Bloody Civil Strife," *Boston Globe,* Aug. 17, 1975.

432 "children": *FRUS,* 1958-1960, vol. 14, doc. 192.

432 "little boy": Hammarskjöld to Bunche, Aug. 29, 1960 (1363), box 155, DHC.

432 "bribery is the basis": Weissman, *American Foreign Policy,* 208.

433 "I assumed that": Weissman, "An Extraordinary Rendition," 212. See also Devlin, *Chief of Station,* 261.

433 "He would have": François Lumumba, interview.

434 "I am the latest victim": Adam Zagorin, "Leaving Fire in His Wake," *Time,* Feb. 22, 1993.

434 In 1994, the annual inflation: Philippe Beaugrand, "Zaire's Hyperinflation, 1990–96," International Monetary Fund Working Paper, April 1997, 2.

434 "just a Zaire-shaped hole": "A Hole in the Map of Africa," *The Economist,* July 8, 1995.

434 Impotent and incontinent: Details on Mobutu's escape and death come from Wrong, *Footsteps of Mr. Kurtz,* 273–88; Gourevitch, *We Wish to Inform You,* 321; Shoumatoff, "Mobutu's Final Days"; Bob Drogin and Mary Williams Walsh, "Rebel Chief Kabila Takes Over in Zaire," *Los Angeles Times,* May 18, 1997.

434 For years, Lumumba's tooth: Details on the journey taken by Lumumba's tooth and the complaint filed by François Lumumba come from my interview with Eric Van Duyse of the Belgian federal prosecutor's office; Andres Schipani, "The 60-Year, 4,000-Mile Journey Home of Lumumba's Tooth," *FT Magazine,* Jan. 27, 2023; Camille Gijs and Stephan Faris, "Lumumba's Tooth," *Politico,* June 2, 2022; Jennifer Rankin, "Belgium mulls charges over 1961 killing of Congo's first elected leader," *The Guardian,* July 1, 2020; "Murdered Congolese Hero Lumumba's Tooth Laid to Rest," Reuters, YouTube, www.youtube.com.

435 "certain members": *EP,* 839.

435 "sincere regrets": Agence France-Presse, "Belgium: Apology for Lumumba Killing," *NYT,* Feb. 6, 2002.

435 But the investigation skirted: De Witte, *Assassination,* 187.

435 "We simply want": Juliana Lumumba, "Lettre ouverte à Sa Majesté le Roi des Belges," June 30, 2020. Available via RTBF, www.rtbf.be.

436 The collapse of: Most of those who died in the Second Congo War did so from disease and starvation. On dueling death tolls, see "DR Congo War Deaths 'Exaggerated,'" BBC News, Jan. 20, 2010, news.bbc.co.uk; and Joe Bavier, "Congo War-Driven Crisis Kills 45,000 a Month: Study," Reuters, Jan. 22, 2008, www.reuters.com. On the war, see Stearns, *Dancing in the Glory*.

436 "Daddy is home": "Murdered Congolese Hero Lumumba's Tooth Laid to Rest," Reuters, YouTube, www.youtube.com.

A Note on Sources

444 "That's not the way": de St. Jorre, interview.

444 "fiction that we are": The redacted version appears in *FRUS, 1958–1960*, vol. 14, doc. 192. A decade before the publication of that volume, it appeared in full in Kalb, *Congo Cables*, 68. The original can be found in Timberlake to State, Aug. 29, 1960 (545), file 350, Congo July–Aug. 1960 Classified, Security-Segregated Records, U.S. Embassy Leopoldville, RG 84, NACP.

444 Declassification requests routinely: William Burr, "Trapped in the Archives," *Foreign Affairs*, Nov. 29, 2019, www.foreignaffairs.com. A 2009 executive order providing for automatic declassification has so many exceptions as to render the provision meaningless.

444 In 2018, an investigative: The journalist is Emma Best, the CIA history is titled "Fifty-Four Days to Victory in the Congo: CIA's Operation Against Lumumba in 1960," and the request can be viewed at Muckrock, www.muckrock.com.

444 The United States spends: Matthew Connelly, *The Declassification Engine* (New York: Pantheon, 2023), 389.

444 The U.S. intelligence community has: Ibid., x.

Bibliography

Sources

Archival Materials

Bunche, Ralph J. Papers. Library Special Collections, Charles E. Young Research Library, University of California, Los Angeles.

Church, Frank. Papers. Special Collections and Archives, Boise State University, Boise, Idaho.

Cordier, Andrew W. Papers. Columbia University.

Dwight D. Eisenhower Presidential Library, Abilene, Kansas.

Hammarskjöld, Dag. Collection. National Library of Sweden, Stockholm.

International Committee of the Red Cross Archives, Geneva, Switzerland.

John F. Kennedy Presidential Library, Boston.

Kennedy, John F. Assassination Records. National Archives and Records Administration.

National Archives at College Park, Maryland.

National Archives of the U.K., London.

Palmer, Alison. Papers. Burke Library at Union Theological Seminary, New York.

Reid, Alex and Hazel. Collection. Kinlaw Library, Asbury University, Wilmore, Kentucky.

Timberlake, Clare. Papers. Howard Gotlieb Archival Research Center, Boston University.

United Nations Archives, New York.

Urquhart, Brian. Collection of Material About Ralph Bunche. Library Special Collections, Charles E. Young Research Library, University of California, Los Angeles.

Verhaegen, Benoît. Fonds. Library of Independent Congo, Royal Museum for Central Africa, Tervuren, Belgium.

Weiss, Herbert. Papers. Hoover Institution Library and Archives, Stanford University.

Wieschhoff, Heinrich. Papers. New York Public Library.

World War II Servicemen's Correspondence Collection. University Library, San Diego State University.

Oral Histories

Apter, David. Interview by James Sutterlin, Feb. 27, 1991. UN Oral History Project, Dag Hammarskjöld Library.

Berendsen, Ian. Interview by Jean Krasno, May 4, 1990. UN Oral History Project, Dag Hammarskjöld Library.

Bissell, Richard. Interview by Thomas Soapes, Nov. 9, 1976. DDEL.

Burden, William. Interview by John Luter, Jan. 29, 1968. Columbia Center for Oral History, Columbia University.

Carlucci, Frank. Interview by Charles Stuart Kennedy, April 1, 1997. ADST.

Cordier, Andrew. Interviews by Donald Shaughnessy and Arthur Rovine, Aug. 21, 1962, Oct. 23, 1963, Oct. 30, 1963, Nov. 6, 1963, Nov. 13, 1963, Nov. 20, 1963, Nov. 26, 1963, Dec. 4, 1963, Dec. 13, 1963, Dec. 18, 1963, and Jan. 9, 1964. Columbia Center for Oral History, Columbia University.

Devlin, Larry. Interview by Mvemba Dizolele. Dec. 2, 2005. Unpublished.

Gray, Gordon. Interview by Maclyn Burg, June 25, 1975. DDEL.

Gray, Gordon. Interviews by Paul Hopper, Dec. 7, 1966, Jan. 23, 1967, Jan. 27, 1967, Feb. 7, 1967, March 7, 1967, May 23, 1967, July 19, 1967, Oct. 10, 1967, Nov. 30, 1967. Columbia Center for Oral History, Columbia University.

Gullion, Edmund. Interview by Jean Krasno, May 8, 1990. UN Oral History Project, Dag Hammarskjöld Library.

Hennemeyer, Robert T. Interview by Charles Stuart Kennedy, Feb. 15, 1989. ADST.

Hoffacker, Lewis. Interview by Charles Stuart Kennedy, July 17, 1998. ADST.

Imbrey, Howard. Interview by Charles Stuart Kennedy, June 21, 2001. ADST.

Imbrey, Howard. Interview by Curtis Ostle, Dec. 28, 2000. American Century Project, Dreyfuss Library, St. Andrew's Episcopal School.

Lind, Per. Interview by Jean Krasno, Nov. 7, 1990. UN Oral History Project, Dag Hammarskjöld Library.

Linnér, Sture. Interview by Jean Krasno, Nov. 8, 1990. UN Oral History Project, Dag Hammarskjöld Library.

Liu, F. T. Interview by James Sutterlin, March 23, 1990, and Sept. 22, 1990. United Nations Oral History Project, Dag Hammarskjöld Library.

McIlvaine, Robinson. Interview by Charles Stuart Kennedy, April 1, 1988. ADST.

McIlvaine, Stevenson. Interview by Charles Stuart Kennedy, Sept. 23, 2003. ADST.

Morrow, John Howard. Interview by Celestine Tutt, May 11, 1981. ADST.

Palmer, Alison. Interview by Karen Lamoree, June 14, 1988. Pembroke Center Oral History Project, Brown University.

Rikhye, Indar Jit. Interview by James Sutterlin, March 26, 1990. UN Oral History Project, Dag Hammarskjöld Library.

Roberts, Owen. Interview by Charles Stuart Kennedy, Feb. 11, 1991. ADST.

Steigman, Andrew. Interview by Charles Stuart Kennedy, April 29, 1989. ADST.

Tienken, Arthur. Interview by Charles Stuart Kennedy, June 12, 1989. ADST.

Urquhart, Brian. Interviews by Leon Gordenker, May 30, 1984, June 1, 1984, June 27, 1984, July 20, 1984, Oct. 15, 1984, Oct. 17, 1984, Oct. 19, 1984, Oct. 22, 1984. UN Oral History Project, Dag Hammarskjöld Library.

U.S. Senate Historical Office. "Select Committee to Study Governmental Operations with Respect to Intelligence Activities (Church Committee) Members and Staff: Oral History Interviews." July 24, 2013–March 10, 2015.

Williams, G. Mennen. Interview by William W. Moss, Jan. 28, 1970. JFKL.

Woodrow Wilson International Center. "The Congo Crisis, 1960–1961: A Critical Oral History Conference." Sept. 23–24, 2004.

Author Interviews

Baron, Frederick (Church Committee staffer)

Bevill, James (son-in-law of Paul Springer)

Blouin, Eve (daughter of Andrée Blouin)

Carlucci, Frank (Foreign Service officer)

Cassilly, Thomas (Foreign Service officer)

De St. Jorre, John (ghostwriter for Larry Devlin)

Devine, Jack (CIA officer)

Devlin, Mary Rountree (second wife of Larry Devlin)

Higbee, Arthur (journalist in the Congo)

Holm, Richard (CIA officer)

Kalonji, Marceline (daughter of Isaac Kalonji)

Kandolo, Leonnie (daughter of Damien Kandolo)

Kandolo, Monique (daughter of Damien Kandolo)

Kasavubu, Marie-Rose (daughter of Joseph Kasavubu)

Lambelet, Shirley Huff (CIA secretary)

Lukens, Alan (U.S. consul in Brazzaville)

Lumumba, François (son of Patrice Lumumba)

Lumumba, Juliana (daughter of Patrice Lumumba)

McIlvaine, Stevenson (son of Robinson McIlvaine)

Moko Atilaoto, Albert (resident of Kisangani)

Naegele, Beth (daughter of missionaries in the Congo)

Ndjibu, Lwimba Movati (antelope hunter)

Reimuller, Maureen Devlin (daughter of Larry Devlin)

Schwarz, Frederick A. O., Jr. (chief counsel to the Church Committee)

Seon (née Reed), Yvonne (student recruited by Lumumba)

Sharp, Steven (son of missionaries in the Congo)

Solitario, Helen (embassy secretary)

Steigman, Andrew (Foreign Service officer)

Timberlake, Charles (son of Clare Timberlake)

Waldron, D'Lynn (journalist in the Congo)
Weiss, Herbert (MIT field researcher in the Congo)
Wides, Burt (Church Committee staffer)

Unpublished Materials

"An Analytical Chronology of the Congo Crisis," Jan. 25, 1961, Presidential Papers. President's Office Files, JFKL.

Brassinne, Jacques. "Enquête sur la mort de Patrice Lumumba." PhD diss., Université Libre de Bruxelles, 1991.

"Covert Military Operations in the Congo, 1964–1967," unpublished Church Committee report.

Debruyn, Stan. "The Strong Man of Katanga: Godefroid Munongo and the Katangese Secession of 1960–1963." Master's thesis, London School of Economics, 2020.

Geary, Doreen. "Death of a Stalwart: A Profile of Andrew W. Cordier." Manchester University Archives and Brethren Historical Collection.

Higbee, Arthur. *Recollections.* Self-published, 2018.

Liu, F. T. Letters from the Congo.

Roberts, Owen W., and Janet K. Roberts. *Letters from the Congo, 1958–1960.* Self-published. Available in the Owen W. and Janet K. Roberts Papers, Mudd Manuscript Library, Princeton University.

Timberlake, Clare. "First Year of Independence in the Congo: Events and Issues." Master's thesis, George Washington University, 1963.

Vandewalle, Frédéric. *Mille et quatre jours: Contes du Zaïre et du Shaba.* Self-published, 1974–77.

Published Materials

Acheson, Dean. *Power and Diplomacy.* Cambridge, Mass.: Harvard University Press, 2013.

Adams, Lewis R. "The Monster at Gila Bend." *Military Review* 42, no. 6 (June 1962): 63–69.

Alexander, Caroline. "Vital Powers." *New Yorker,* Jan. 22, 1989.

Alexander, H. T. *African Tightrope: My Two Years as Nkrumah's Chief of Staff.* London: Pall Mall Express, 1966.

"All-African People's Conferences." *International Organization* 16, no. 2 (Spring 1962): 429–34.

Alvarez, Luis López. *Lumumba; ou, L'Afrique frustrée.* Paris: Cujas, 1964.

Ambrose, Stephen E., and Richard H. Immerman. *Ike's Spies: Eisenhower and the Espionage Establishment.* New York: Anchor Books, 2012.

Anderson, Jon Lee. *Che Guevara: A Revolutionary Life.* Rev. ed. New York: Grove Press, 2010.

Artigue, Pierre. *Qui sont les leaders congolais?* Brussels: Éditions Europe-Afrique, 1961.

Barber, Frank. "Return to the Congo." *Africa South*, no. 1 (Oct.–Dec. 1960), 89–95.

Bartlett, Robert E. *Communist Penetration and Subversion of the Belgian Congo, 1946–1960*. Berkeley, Calif.: Acarn Press, 1962.

Behr, Edward. *Anyone Here Been Raped and Speak English? A Foreign Correspondent's Life Behind the Lines*. London: New English Library, 1985.

Beskow, Bo. *Dag Hammarskjöld: Strictly Personal: A Portrait*. Garden City, N.Y.: Doubleday, 1969.

Bevill, James B. *Blackboards and Bomb Shelters: The Perilous Journey of Americans in China during World War II*. Atglen, Penn: Schiffer Publishing, 2021.

Bissell, Richard. *Reflections of a Cold Warrior: From Yalta to the Bay of Pigs*. New Haven, Conn.: Yale University Press, 1996.

Blouin, Andrée. *My Country, Africa: Autobiography of the Black Pasionaria*. With Jean Scott MacKellar. New York: Praeger, 1983.

Borstelmann, Thomas. *The Cold War and the Color Line: American Race Relations in the Global Arena*. Cambridge, Mass.: Harvard University Press, 2003.

Bouwer, Karen. *Gender and Decolonization in the Congo: The Legacy of Patrice Lumumba*. New York: Palgrave Macmillan, 2010.

Bowie, Robert R., and Richard H. Immerman. *Waging Peace: How Eisenhower Shaped an Enduring Cold War Strategy*. New York: Oxford University Press, 1998.

Bowman, Edward H., and James E. Fanning. "The Logistics Problems of a UN Military Force." *International Organization* 17, no. 2 (March 1963).

Brassinne, Jacques, and Jean Kestergat. *Qui a tué Patrice Lumumba?* Paris: Duculot, 1991.

Bunche, Ralph J. *Ralph J. Bunche: Selected Speeches and Writings*. Edited by Charles P. Henry. Ann Arbor: University of Michigan Press, 1996.

Centre de Recherche et d'Information Socio-politiques. *Congo 1959*. Brussels: Centre de Recherche et d'Information Socio-politiques, 1960.

———. *Congo 1960*. 2 vols. Edited by Benoît Verhaegen and J. Gérard-Libois. Brussels: Centre de Recherche et d'Information Socio-politiques, 1961.

———. *Congo 1960: Annexes et Biographies*. Brussels: Centre de Recherche et d'Information Socio-politiques, 1961.

———. *Congo 1961*. Brussels: Centre de Recherche et d'Information Socio-politiques, 1962.

Chambre des Représentants de Belgique. *Enquête parlementaire visant à déterminer les circonstances exactes de l'assassinat de Patrice Lumumba et l'implication éventuelle des responsables politiques belges dans celui-ci*. Nov. 16, 2001.

Clément, Pierre. "Patrice Lumumba (Stanleyville, 1952–1953)." *Présence Africaine*, Jan.–April 1962.

Close, William T. *Beyond the Storm: Treating the Powerless and the Powerful in Mobutu's Congo/Zaire*. Marbleton, Wyo.: Meadowlark Springs Productions, 2006.

———. *A Doctor's Life: Unique Stories*. Marbleton, Wyo.: Meadowlark Springs Productions, 2000.

Collins, Carole J. L. "The Cold War Comes to Africa: Cordier and the 1960 Congo Crisis." *Journal of International Affairs* 47, no. 1 (1993): 243–69.

Colvin, Ian Goodhope. *The Rise and Fall of Moise Tshombe: A Biography.* London: Frewin, 1968.

Conrad, Joseph. *Youth, and Two Other Stories.* Garden City, N.Y.: Doubleday, Page, 1924.

Cordier, Andrew W., and Wilder Foote, eds. *Public Papers of the Secretaries-General of the United Nations.* 7 vols. New York: Columbia University Press, 1969–77.

————. *The Quest for Peace: The Dag Hammarskjöld Memorial Lectures.* New York: Columbia University Press, 1967.

Covington-Ward, Yolanda. "Joseph Kasa-Vubu, ABAKO, and Performances of Kongo Nationalism in the Independence of Congo." *Journal of Black Studies* 43, no. 1 (Jan. 2012): 72–94.

Davister, P. *Katanga: Enjeu du monde.* Brussels: Editions Europe-Afrique, 1960.

Dayal, Rajeshwar. *A Life of Our Times.* New Delhi: Orient Longman, 1998.

————. *Mission for Hammarskjöld: The Congo Crisis.* London: Oxford University Press, 1976.

Demany, Fernand. *S.O.S. Congo: Chronique d'un soulèvement.* Brussels: Labor, 1959.

Devlin, Larry. *Chief of Station, Congo: Fighting the Cold War in a Hot Zone.* New York: PublicAffairs, 2007.

De Vos, Pierre. *La décolonisation: Les évènements du Congo de 1959 à 1967.* Brussels: ABC, 1975.

————. *Vie et mort de Lumumba.* Paris: Calmann-Lévy, 1961.

De Witte, Ludo. *The Assassination of Lumumba.* London: Verso, 2002.

Doyle, David W. *Inside Espionage: A Memoir of the True Men and Traitors.* London: St. Ermin's Press, 2000.

Dumont, Georges-H. *La Table ronde belgo-congolaise (janvier–février 1960).* Paris: Éditions Universitaires, 1961.

Dworkin, Ira. *Congo Love Song: African American Culture and the Crisis of the Colonial State.* Chapel Hill: University of North Carolina Press, 2017.

Eisenhower, Dwight D. *Waging Peace, 1956–1961: The White House Years.* Garden City, N.Y.: Doubleday, 1965.

Etambala, Zana Aziza. "Lumumba en Belgique, du 25 avril au 23 mai 1956: Son récit de voyage et ses impressions, document inédit." In *Figures et paradoxes de l'histoire au Burundi, au Congo et au Rwanda,* edited by Marc Quaghebeur, 191–229. Paris: L'Harmattan, 2002.

Eyskens, Gaston. *Mémoires.* Brussels: Centre de Recherche et d'Information Sociopolitiques, 2012.

Farmer, James. *Freedom—When?* New York: Random House, 1965.

Ferguson, Niall. *Kissinger, 1923–1968: The Idealist.* New York: Penguin Press, 2015.

Foreign Relations of the United States, 1958–1960. Vol. 14, *Africa.* Edited by Harriet Dashiell Schwar and Stanley Shaloff. Washington, D.C.: U.S. Government Printing Office, 1992.

Foreign Relations of the United States, 1958–1960. Vol. 18, *Africa.* Edited by Stanley Shaloff. Washington, D.C.: U.S. Government Printing Office, 1989.

Foreign Relations of the United States, 1961–1963. Vol. 20, *Congo Crisis.* Edited by

Harriet Dashiell Schwar. Washington, D.C.: U.S. Government Printing Office, 1994.

Foreign Relations of the United States, 1964–1968. Vol. 23, *Congo, 1960–1968.* Edited by Nina D. Howland, David C. Humphrey, and Harriet D. Schwar. Washington, D.C.: U.S. Government Printing Office, 2013.

Fursenko, Aleksandr, and Timothy Naftali. *Khrushchev's Cold War: The Inside Story of an American Adversary.* New York: W. W. Norton, 2007.

Gailey, Harry A. *History of Africa: From 1800 to 1945.* Malabar, Fla.: R. E. Krieger, 1989.

Gaines, Kevin K. *American Africans in Ghana: Black Expatriates and the Civil Rights Era.* Chapel Hill: University of North Carolina Press, 2006.

Gall, Sandy. *Don't Worry About the Money Now.* London: H. Hamilton, 1983.

Ganshof van der Meersch, W. J. *Fin de la souveraineté Belge au Congo.* Brussels: Institut Royal des Relations Internationales, 1963.

Gendebien, Paul-Henry. *L'intervention des Nations Unies au Congo, 1960–1964.* Paris: Mouton et Cie, 1967.

George, Betty Grace Stein. *Educational Developments in the Congo (Leopoldville).* Washington, D.C.: U.S. Government Printing Office, 1966.

Gerard, Emmanuel, and Bruce Kuklick. *Death in the Congo: Murdering Patrice Lumumba.* Cambridge, Mass.: Harvard University Press, 2015.

Gérard-Libois, Jules. *Katanga Secession.* Madison: University of Wisconsin Press, 1967.

Gibbs, David N. *The Political Economy of Third World Intervention: Mines, Money, and U.S. Policy in the Congo Crisis.* Chicago: University of Chicago Press, 1991.

Gilis, Charles-André. *Kasavubu au coeur du drame congolaise.* Brussels: Éditions Europe-Afrique, 1964.

Gizenga, Antoine. *Ma vie et mes luttes.* Paris: L'Harmattan, 2011.

Gondola, Ch. Didier. *The History of Congo.* Westport, Conn.: Greenwood Press, 2002.

———. *Tropical Cowboys: Westerns, Violence, and Masculinity in Kinshasa.* Bloomington: Indiana University Press, 2016.

Greene, Graham. *In Search of a Character: Two African Journals.* London: Penguin Books, 1981.

Grose, Peter. *Gentleman Spy: The Life of Allan Dulles.* Boston: Houghton Mifflin, 1994.

Guevara, Ernesto Che. *Congo Diary: Episodes of the Revolutionary War in the Congo.* New York: Seven Stories Press, 2021.

Gunther, John. *Inside Africa.* New York: Harper & Brothers, 1955.

———. *Meet the Congo and Its Neighbors.* New York: Harper & Brothers, 1959.

Halen, Pierre, and János Riesz, eds. *Patrice Lumumba entre Dieu et diable: Un héros africain dans ses images.* Paris: L'Harmattan, 1997.

Hammarskjöld, Dag. *Markings.* New York: Knopf, 1964.

Hanley, Mary-Lynn, and Henning Melber, ed. *Dag Hammarskjöld Remembered: A Collection of Personal Memories.* Uppsala, Sweden: X-O Graf Tryckeri, 2011.

Haulman, Daniel L. "Crisis in the Congo: Operation NEW TAPE." In *Short of War: Major USAF Contingency Operations, 1947–1997,* edited by A. Timothy Warnock, 23–32. Montgomery, Ala.: Air University Press, 2000.

Hayes, Paddy. *Queen of Spies: Daphne Park, Britain's Cold War Spy Master.* New York: Abrams Press, 2016.

Heinz, G., and H. Donnay. *Lumumba: The Last 50 Days.* New York: Grove Press, 1969.

Hellström, Leif. *The Instant Air Force: The Creation of the CIA Air Unit in the Congo, 1962.* Saarbrücken: VDM Verlag Dr. Müller, 2008.

Henry, Charles P. *Ralph Bunche: Model Negro or American Other?* New York: New York University Press, 1999.

Hersh, Seymour M. *The Dark Side of Camelot.* New York: Back Bay Books, 1998.

Hill, Robert A., and Edmond J. Keller, eds. *Trustee for the Human Community: Ralph J. Bunche, the United Nations, and the Decolonization of Africa.* Athens: Ohio University Press, 2010.

Hochschild, Adam. *King Leopold's Ghost.* Boston: Houghton Mifflin, 1998.

Hoskyns, Catherine. *The Congo Since Independence: January 1960–December 1961.* London: Oxford University Press, 1965.

———. "Violence in the Congo." *Transition,* no. 21 (1965): 47–50.

Houart, Pierre. *La pénétration communiste au Congo: Commentaires et documents sur les événements de juin–novembre 1960.* Brussels: Centre de Documentation Internationale, 1960.

Houser, George M. *No One Can Stop the Rain: Glimpses of Africa's Liberation Struggle.* Cleveland: Pilgrim Press, 1989.

Hughes, Matthew. "Fighting for White Rule in Africa: The Central African Federation, Katanga, and the Congo Crisis, 1958–1965." *International History Review* 25, no. 3 (Sept. 2003): 592–615.

Iandolo, Alessandro. "Imbalance of Power: The Soviet Union and the Congo Crisis, 1960–1961." *Journal of Cold War Studies* 16, no. 2 (2014): 32–55.

Inforcongo. *Congo Belge et Ruanda-Burundi: Guide du voyager.* Brussels: Inforcongo, 1958. www.memoiresducongo.be.

———. *The Political Future of the Belgian Congo: The Royal Message and the Government's Declaration of January 13, 1959.* Brussels: C. Van Cortenbergh, 1959.

———. *Thirteen Million Congolese.* Brussels: Inforcongo, 1959.

James, Alan. *Britain and the Congo Crisis, 1960–1963.* New York: St. Martin's Press, 1996.

Janssens, Émile. *J'étais le général Janssens.* Brussels: C. Dessart, 1961.

Jasanoff, Maya. *The Dawn Watch: Joseph Conrad in a Global World.* New York: Penguin Press, 2017.

Jeal, Tim. *Stanley: The Impossible Life of Africa's Greatest Explorer.* New Haven, Conn.: Yale University Press, 2007.

Kalb, Madeleine G. *The Congo Cables: The Cold War in Africa—from Eisenhower to Kennedy.* New York: Macmillan, 1982.

Kamitatu, Cléophas. *La grande mystification du Congo-Kinshasa: Les crimes de Mobutu.* Paris: F. Maspero, 1971.

Kanza, Thomas R. *The Rise and Fall of Patrice Lumumba: Conflict in the Congo.* Rev. ed. Boston: G. K. Hall & Co., 1979.

———. *Sans rancune.* Paris: L'Harmattan, 2006.

————. *Tôt ou tard....* Brussels: Le Livre Africain, 1959.

Kashamura, Anicet. *De Lumumba aux colonels.* Paris: Buchet-Chastel, 1966.

Kelen, Emery. *Hammarskjöld: The Political Man.* New York: Funk & Wagnalls, 1957.

Kelly, Sean. *America's Tyrant: The CIA and Mobutu of Zaire.* Lanham, Md.: American University Press, 1993.

Kennedy, Michael, and Art Magennis. *Ireland, the United Nations, and the Congo: A Military and Diplomatic History, 1960–1.* Dublin: Four Courts Press, 2014.

Kennes, Erik, and Miles Larmer. *The Katangese Gendarmes and War in Central Africa: Fighting Their Way Home.* Bloomington: Indiana University Press, 2016.

Kinzer, Stephen. *Poisoner in Chief.* New York: Henry Holt and Company, 2019.

Kisangani, Emizet François and F. Scott Bobb. *Historical Dictionary of the Democratic Republic of the Congo.* 3rd ed. Lanham, Md.: Scarecrow Press, 2010.

Kitchen, Helen, ed. *Footnotes to the Congo Story: An "Africa Report" Anthology.* New York: Walker, 1967.

Korn, Hallen. "Law or Order: The Politics of Development and Humanitarian Intervention in the Congo Crisis, 1960-61." Undergraduate thesis, Columbia University, 2014.

Kwitny, Jonathan. *Endless Enemies: The Making of an Unfriendly World.* New York: Congdon & Weed, 1984.

La Fontaine, J. S. *City Politics: A Study of Léopoldville, 1962–63.* Cambridge, U.K.: Cambridge University Press, 1970.

Lagae, Johan. "The Troublesome Construction of the 'Résidence du Gouverneur Général du Congo Belge' in Leopoldville, 1922–1960." *METU Journal of the Faculty of Architecture* 20, no. 1–2 (2000): 5–27.

Lash, Joseph P. *Dag Hammarskjöld.* London: Cassell, 1962.

Leary, William M., ed. *The Central Intelligence Agency: History and Documents.* Tuscaloosa: University of Alabama Press, 1984.

Lefever, Ernest W. *Crisis in the Congo: A United Nations Force in Action.* Washington, D.C.: Brookings Institution, 1965.

Legum, Colin. *Congo Disaster.* London: Penguin Books, 1961.

————. *Pan-Africanism: A Short Political Guide.* New York: Praeger, 1962.

Lemarchand, René. "The C.I.A. in Africa: How Central? How Intelligent?" *The Journal of Modern African Studies* 14, no. 3 (1976): 401–26.

————. *Political Awakening in the Belgian Congo.* Berkeley: University of California Press, 1964.

Lenzner, Terry. *The Investigator.* New York: Blue Rider Press, 2013.

Leroy, Pierre. "Journal de la Province Orientale, 1959–1960." In *Congo, 1955–1960: Recueil d'études,* 307–28. Brussels: Académie Royale des Sciences d'Outre-Mer, 1992.

Lipsey, Roger. *Hammarskjöld: A Life.* Ann Arbor: University of Michigan Press, 2015.

Lisagor, Peter, and Marguerite Higgins. *Overtime in Heaven: Adventures in the Foreign Service.* Garden City, N.Y.: Doubleday, 1964.

Little, Marie-Noelle ed. *The Poet and the Diplomat: The Correspondence of Dag Hammarskjöld and Alexis Leger.* New York: Syracuse University Press, 2001.

Logevall, Fredrik. *JFK: Coming of Age in the American Century, 1917–1956*. New York: Random House, 2020.

Lumumba, Patrice. *Congo, My Country*. New York: Praeger, 1962.

———. *Lumumba Speaks: The Speeches and Writings of Patrice Lumumba, 1958–1961*. Boston: Little, Brown, 1972.

———. *Patrice Lumumba: Fighter for Africa's Freedom*. Moscow: Progress Publishers, 1961.

Macey, David. *Frantz Fanon: A Biography*. London: Verso Books, 2012.

Magnuson, Warren G., and Committee on Commerce, ed. *Freedom of Communications Final Report: The Speeches of Senator John F. Kennedy, Presidential Campaign 1960*. Washington, D.C.: U.S. Government Printing Office, 1961.

Mahoney, Richard. *JFK: Ordeal in Africa*. New York: Oxford University Press, 1983.

Manya, Cécile. *Patrice Lumumba: Le Sankuru et l'Afrique*. Paris: Le Lys Bleu, 2021.

Marks, John. *The Search for the "Manchurian Candidate": The CIA and Mind Control: The Secret History of the Behavioral Sciences*. New York: W. W. Norton & Company, 1991.

Mazov, S. V. *A Distant Front in the Cold War: The USSR in West Africa and the Congo, 1956–1964*. Stanford, Calif.: Stanford University Press, 2010.

Mboka, Mwana. *Kinshasa Then and Now* (blog). kosubaawate.blogspot.com/.

McKown, Robin. *Lumumba: A Biography*. Garden City, N.Y.: Doubleday, 1969.

Meredith, Martin. *The Fate of Africa: A History of the Continent Since Independence*. New York: PublicAffairs, 2006.

Merriam, Alan P. *Congo: Background of Conflict*. Evanston, Ill.: Northwestern University Press, 1961.

Mezerik, Avrahm G. *The United Nations Emergency Force (UNEF), 1956–1967: Creation, Evolution, End of Mission*. New York: International Review Service, 1969.

Michel, Serge. *Uhuru Lumumba*. Paris: René Julliard, 1962.

Michel, Thierry. *Mobutu, roi du Zaïre*. Liège, Belgium: Les Films de la Passerelle, 1999. Filmstrip, 135 min.

Mobutu Sese Seko and Jean-Louis Remilleux. *Dignité pour l'Afrique: Entretiens avec Jean-Louis Remilleux*. Paris: Albin Michel, 1989.

———. *Dignity for Africa: Interviews with Jean-Louis Remilleux*. Paris: Albin Michel, 1989.

Monaville, Pedro. *Students of the World: Global 1968 and Decolonization in the Congo*. Durham, N.C.: Duke University Press, 2022.

Monheim, Francis. "Léopoldville en juin 1959." *Revue Generale Belgique*, no. 7 (July 1959): 29–46.

———. *Mobutu, l'homme seul*. Brussels: Actuelles, 1962.

Moraes, Frank. *The Importance of Being Black: An Asian Looks at Africa*. New York: Macmillan, 1965.

Mountmorres, William Geoffrey Bouchard de Montmorency. *The Congo Independent State: A Report on a Voyage of Enquiry*. London: Williams & Norgate, 1906.

Mountz, William. "Americanizing Africanization: The Congo Crisis, 1960–1967." PhD dissertation, University of Missouri–Columbia, 2014.

Muehlenbeck, Philip. *Betting on the Africans: John F. Kennedy's Courting of African Nationalist Leaders.* New York: Oxford University Press, 2012.

——. *Czechoslovakia in Africa, 1945–1968.* New York: Palgrave Macmillan, 2016.

——. "Kennedy & Touré: A Success in Personal Diplomacy." *Diplomacy and Statecraft* 19, no. 1 (Spring 2008): 69–95.

Munger, Edwin. *African Field Report: 1952–1961.* Cape Town: C. Struik, 1961.

Murphy, Robert. *Diplomat Among Warriors: The Unique World of a Foreign Service Expert.* Garden City, N.Y.: Doubleday, 1964.

Mutamba Makombo, Jean-Marie. *Patrice Lumumba correspondant de presse (1948–1956).* Paris: L'Harmattan, 2005.

Mydans, Carl, and Shelley Mydans. *The Violent Peace: A Report on Wars in the Postwar World.* New York: Atheneum, 1968.

Namikas, Lise. *Battleground Africa: Cold War in the Congo, 1960–1965.* Stanford, Calif.: Stanford University Press, 2015.

Namikas, Lise, and Sergey Mazov, eds. "A CWIHP Conference Reader Compiled for the International Conference 'The Congo Crisis, 1960–61.'" Washington, D.C., 2004.

Nelson, Robert Gilbert. *Congo Crisis and Christian Mission.* St. Louis: Bethany Press, 1961.

Nicolaï, Marie. *Ici Radio Katanga . . . 1960–1961.* Brussels: Jean-Marie Collet, 1987.

Nkrumah, Kwame. *Challenge of the Congo.* New York: International Publishers, 1967.

Nzongola-Ntalaja, Georges. *The Congo from Leopold to Kabila: A People's History.* London: Zed Books, 2013.

——. *Patrice Lumumba.* Athens: Ohio University Press, 2014.

——. "Ralph Bunche, Patrice Lumumba, and the First Congo Crisis." In Hill and Keller, *Trustee for the Human Community.*

O'Brien, Conor Cruise. *To Katanga and Back: A UN Case History.* New York: Grosset & Dunlap, 1966.

O'Malley, Alanna. *The Diplomacy of Decolonisation: America, Britain and the United Nations During the Congo Crisis 1960–1964.* Manchester: Manchester University Press, 2018.

Omasombo, Jean. *Le Kasaï-Oriental: Un nœud gordien dans l'espace congolais.* Tervuren: Museé Royal de l'Afrique Centrale, 2014.

Omasombo, Jean, and Benoît Verhaegen. *Patrice Lumumba: Acteur politique: De la prison aux portes du pouvoir, Juillet 1956–février 1960.* Paris: L'Harmattan, 2005.

——. *Patrice Lumumba: Jeunesse et apprentissage politique, 1925–1956.* Paris: L'Harmattan, 1998.

Othen, Christopher. *Katanga, 1960–1963: Mercenaries, Spies, and the African Nation That Waged War on the World.* Cheltenham, U.K.: History Press, 2015.

Peck, Raoul. *Lumumba, la mort d'un prophète.* Berlin: Velvet Film, 1990. Filmstrip, 69 min.

Perret, Françoise, and François Bugnion. *From Budapest to Saigon: History of the International Committee of the Red Cross, 1956–1965.* Geneva: International Committee of the Red Cross, 2018.

Piret, Bérengère. *Les cent mille briques: La prison et les détenus de Stanleyville*. Lille, France: Centre d'Histoire Judiciaire, 2014.

Pluvinage, Gonzague. *Expo 58: Between Utopia and Reality.* Brussels: Racine, 2008.

Pons, Valdo. *Stanleyville: An African Urban Community Under Belgian Administration.* London: Oxford University Press, 1969.

Porter, Bruce D. *The USSR in Third World Conflicts: Soviet Arms and Diplomacy in Local Wars, 1945–1980*. Cambridge, U.K.: Cambridge University Press, 1986.

Power, Declan. *Siege at Jadotville: The Irish Army's Forgotten Battle.* Dunboyne, Ireland: Maverick House, 2005.

Quaison-Sackey, Alex. *Reflections of an African Statesman.* New York: Praeger, 1965.

Raustiala, Kal. *The Absolutely Indispensable Man: Ralph Bunche, the United Nations, and the Fight to End Empire.* New York: Oxford University Press, 2022.

Reeve, Thomas Ellis. *In Wembo-Nyama's Land.* Nashville: Publishing House of the M.E. Church, 1922.

Regis, Ed. *The Biology of Doom: The History of America's Secret Germ Warfare Project.* New York: Henry Holt, 1999.

Reid, Alexander J. *Congo Drumbeat: History of the First Half Century in the Establishment of the Methodist Church Among the Atetela of Central Congo.* New York: World Outlook Press, 1964.

Rikhye, Indar Jit. *Military Adviser to the Secretary-General: U.N. Peacekeeping and the Congo Crisis.* New York: St. Martin's Press in association with the International Peace Academy, 1993.

———. *Trumpets and Tumults: The Memoirs of a Peacekeeper.* New Delhi: Manohar, 2002.

Rouch, Jane. *En cage avec Lumumba.* Paris: Les Éditions du Temps, 1961.

Rupp, Marie-Joëlle. *Serge Michel: Un libertaire dans la décolonisation.* Paris: Ibis, 2007.

Sauvage, Léo. *Voyages en Onusie.* Paris: B. Grasset, 1968.

Schlesinger, Arthur. *A Thousand Days: John F. Kennedy in the White House.* Boston: Houghton Mifflin, 1965.

Scott, Ian. *Tumbled House: The Congo at Independence.* London: Oxford University Press, 1969.

Shepard, Elaine. *Forgive Us Our Press Passes.* Englewood Cliffs, N.J.: Prentice-Hall, 1962.

Shevchenko, Arkady N. *Breaking with Moscow.* New York: Knopf, 1985.

Shoumatoff, Alex. "Mobutu's Final Days," *Vanity Fair,* Aug. 1997.

Simon, Charlie May. *Dag Hammarskjöld.* New York: E. P. Dutton, 1967.

Simons, Edwine, Roupen Boghossian, and Benoît Verhaegen. *Stanleyville 1959: Le procès de Patrice Lumumba et les émeutes d'octobre.* Paris: L'Harmattan, 1996.

Slade, Ruth. *The Belgian Congo.* London: Oxford University Press, 1961.

Soete, Gerard. *De Arena.* Brugge: Uitgeverij Raaklijn, 1978.

Somaiya, Ravi. *The Golden Thread: The Cold War and the Mysterious Death of Dag Hammarskjöld.* New York: Twelve Books, 2020.

Spooner, Kevin A. *Canada, the Congo Crisis, and UN Peacekeeping, 1960–64.* Vancouver: UBC Press, 2010.

Srodes, James. *Allen Dulles: Master of Spies*. Washington, D.C.: Regnery, 1999.

Stanard, Matthew G. *Selling the Congo: A History of European Pro-empire Propaganda and the Making of Belgian Imperialism*. Lincoln: University of Nebraska Press, 2012.

Stearns, Jason K. *Dancing in the Glory of Monsters: The Collapse of the Congo and the Great War of Africa*. New York: PublicAffairs, 2011.

Stevens, Christopher. *The Soviet Union and Black Africa*. New York: Holmes & Meier, 1976.

Stewart, Gary. *Rumba on the River: A History of the Popular Music of the Two Congos*. London: Verso Books, 2003.

Stolpe, Sven. *Dag Hammarskjöld: A Spiritual Portrait*. New York: Charles Scribner's Sons, 1966.

Taubman, William. *Khrushchev: The Man and His Era*. New York: W. W. Norton, 2004.

Thomas, Evan. *Ike's Bluff: President Eisenhower's Secret Battle to Save the World*. New York: Back Bay/Little, Brown, 2013.

———. *The Very Best Men: Four Who Dared: The Early Years of the CIA*. New York: Simon & Schuster, 1995.

Thompson, Willard Scott. *Ghana's Foreign Policy, 1957–1966: Diplomacy, Ideology, and the New State*. Princeton, N.J.: Princeton University Press, 1969.

Tolliver, Cedric. "The Fragmented Heart of Darkness: The Congo Crisis in African American Culture and Politics." In *Neocolonial Fictions of the Global Cold War*, edited by Steven Belletto and Joseph Keith, 38–56. Iowa City: University of Iowa Press, 2019.

Tourist Bureau for the Belgian Congo & Ruanda-Urundi. *Traveller's Guide to the Belgian Congo and the Ruanda-Urundi*. 2nd ed. Brussels: Tourist Bureau for the Belgian Congo & Ruanda-Urundi, 1956.

Tully, Andrew. *CIA: The Inside Story*. New York: William Morrow, 1962

Urquhart, Brian. *Hammarskjöld*. New York: W. W. Norton, 1994.

———. *A Life in Peace and War*. New York: W. W. Norton, 1991.

———. *Ralph Bunche: An American Odyssey*. New York: W. W. Norton, 1998.

U.S. Senate. *Alleged Assassination Plots Involving Foreign Leaders: An Interim Report of the Select Committee to Study Governmental Operations with Respect to Intelligence Activities, United States Senate*. Washington, D.C.: U.S. Government Printing Office, 1975.

van Beemen, Olivier. *Heineken in Africa: A Multinational Unleashed*. London: Hurst, 2019.

Van Bilsen, A. A. J. *Un plan de trente ans pour l'emancipation politique de l'Afrique Belge*. Courtrai: Vooruitgang, 1956.

Van Bilsen, Jef. *Congo, 1945–1965: La fin d'une colonie*. Brussels: Centre de Recherche et d'Information Socio-politiques, 1994.

Vanderstraeten, Louis-François. *De la Force publique à l'Armée nationale congolaise: Histoire d'une mutinerie, juillet 1960*. Brussels: Académie Royale de Belgique, 1993.

Van Dusen, Henry P. *Dag Hammarskjöld: A Biographical Interpretation of Markings*. London: Faber and Faber, 1967.

Van Hove, Johnny. *Congoism: Congo Discourses in the United States from 1800 to the Present*. New York: Columbia University Press, 2017.

Van Reybrouck, David. *Congo: The Epic History of a People.* New York: HarperCollins, 2014.

van Reyn, Paul. *Le Congo politique: Les partis et les élections.* Brussels: Éditions Europe-Afrique, 1960.

Vanthemsche, Guy. "Belgian Royals on Tour in the Congo, 1909–1960." In *Royals on Tour: Politics, Pageantry, and Colonialism,* edited by Robert Aldrich and Cindy McCreery. Manchester: Manchester University Press, 2018.

———. *Belgium and the Congo, 1885–1960.* Cambridge, U.K.: Cambridge University Press, 2012.

von Eschen, Penny M. *Satchmo Blows Up the World: Jazz Ambassadors Play the Cold War.* Cambridge, Mass.: Harvard University Press, 2004.

von Horn, Carl. *Soldiering for Peace.* New York: David McKay, 1967.

Wauters, Arthur, ed. *Le monde communiste et la crise du Congo Belge.* Brussels: L'Institut de Sociologie Solvay, 1961.

Weiner, Tim. *Legacy of Ashes: The History of the CIA.* New York: Anchor Books, 2008.

Weiss, Herbert. *Political Protest in the Congo: The Parti Solidaire Africain During the Independence Struggle.* Princeton, N.J.: Princeton University Press, 1967.

Weissman, Stephen R. *American Foreign Policy in the Congo, 1960–1964.* Ithaca, N.Y.: Cornell University Press, 1974.

———. "CIA Covert Action in Zaire and Angola: Patterns and Consequences." *Political Science Quarterly* 94, no. 2 (1979): 263–86.

———. "An Extraordinary Rendition," *Intelligence and National Security* 25, no. 2 (July 5, 2010): 198–222.

———. "Opening the Secret Files on Lumumba's Murder," *Washington Post,* July 21, 2002.

———."What Really Happened in the Congo: The CIA, the Murder of Lumumba, and the Rise of Mobutu," *Foreign Affairs* 93, no. 4 (2014): 14–24.

Westad, Odd Arne. *The Global Cold War: Third World Interventions and the Making of Our Times.* Cambridge, U.K.: Cambridge University Press, 2011.

White, Theodore H. *The Making of the President, 1960.* New York: Atheneum House, 1961.

Willame, Jean-Claude. *Patrice Lumumba: La crise congolaise revisitée.* Paris: Karthala, 1990.

Williams, Susan. *White Malice: The CIA and the Covert Recolonization of Africa.* New York: PublicAffairs, 2021.

———. *Who Killed Hammarskjöld?* New York: Oxford University Press, 2014.

Winks, Robin. *Cloak and Gown: Scholars in the Secret War, 1939–1961.* New Haven, Conn.: Yale University Press, 1996.

Wrong, Michela. *In the Footsteps of Mr. Kurtz: Living on the Brink of Disaster in Mobutu's Congo.* New York: HarperCollins, 2001.

Young, Crawford. *Politics in the Congo: Decolonization and Independence.* Princeton, N.J.: Princeton University Press, 1965.

Young, Crawford, and Thomas Edwin Turner. *The Rise and Decline of the Zairian State.* Madison: University of Wisconsin Press, 2013.

Zeilig, Leo. *Lumumba: Africa's Lost Leader.* London: Haus, 2015.

Index

Page numbers in *italics* refer to maps.

Abbreviations

ANC: Armée Nationale Congolaise
FP: Force Publique
MNC: Congolese National Movement
PNP: National Progress Party

Illustration Credits

Page 10 Top left: AP

Page 10 Top right: UN

Page 10 Middle: H Babout / AP / Shutterstock

Page 10 Bottom: AFP via Getty Images

Page 11 Top: Terence Spencer / Popperfoto via Getty Images

Page 11 Bottom: Terence Spencer / Popperfoto via Getty Images

Page 12 Top: TopFoto

Page 12 Bottom: © Marilyn Silverstone / Magnum Photos

Page 13 Top: IMAGO / United Archives

Page 13 Middle: Bettman via Getty Images

Page 13 Bottom: Bettman via Getty Images

Page 14 Top: Terence Spencer / The Chronicle Collection via Getty Images

Page 14 Middle: Elisabethville to Leopoldville, Jan. 19, 1961, in testimony of Victor Hedgeman, Aug. 25, 1975, 157-10014-10076, JFKAR

Page 14 Bottom: TopFoto

Page 15 Top: AP / Horst Faas

Page 15 Middle: TopFoto

Page 15 Bottom: Bettman via Getty Images

Page 16 Top: Hulton-Deutsch Collection via Getty Images

Page 16 Bottom: © Sammy Baloji / The site where Patrice Lumumba, Maurice Mpolo, and Joseph Okito were executed and first buried, 2010